Lecture Notes in Computer Science 16163

Founding Editors

Gerhard Goos
Juris Hartmanis

Editorial Board Members

Elisa Bertino, *Purdue University, West Lafayette, IN, USA*
Wen Gao, *Peking University, Beijing, China*
Bernhard Steffen, *TU Dortmund University, Dortmund, Germany*
Moti Yung, *Columbia University, New York, NY, USA*

The series Lecture Notes in Computer Science (LNCS), including its subseries Lecture Notes in Artificial Intelligence (LNAI) and Lecture Notes in Bioinformatics (LNBI), has established itself as a medium for the publication of new developments in computer science and information technology research, teaching, and education.

LNCS enjoys close cooperation with the computer science R & D community, the series counts many renowned academics among its volume editors and paper authors, and collaborates with prestigious societies. Its mission is to serve this international community by providing an invaluable service, mainly focused on the publication of conference and workshop proceedings and postproceedings. LNCS commenced publication in 1973.

Zhouchen Lin · Liang Wang · Yugang Jiang ·
Xuesong Wang · Shengcai Liao · Shiguang Shan ·
Risheng Liu · Jing Dong · Xin Yu

Editors

Image and Graphics

13th International Conference, ICIG 2025
Xuzhou, China, October 31 – November 2, 2025
Proceedings, Part III

 Springer

Editors
Zhouchen Lin
Peking University
Beijing, China

Yugang Jiang
Fudan University
Shanghai, China

Shengcai Liao
United Arab Emirates University
Abu Dhabi, United Arab Emirates

Risheng Liu
Dalian University of Technology
Dalian, China

Xin Yu
The University of Queensland
Brisbane, QLD, Australia

Liang Wang
Institute of Automation, CAS
Beijing, China

Xuesong Wang
China University of Mining and Technology
Xuzhou, China

Shiguang Shan
Institute of Computing Technology, CAS
Beijing, China

Jing Dong
Institute of Automation, CAS
Beijing, China

ISSN 0302-9743   ISSN 1611-3349 (electronic)
Lecture Notes in Computer Science
ISBN 978-981-95-3728-0   ISBN 978-981-95-3729-7 (eBook)
https://doi.org/10.1007/978-981-95-3729-7

© The Editor(s) (if applicable) and The Author(s), under exclusive license
to Springer Nature Singapore Pte Ltd. 2026

This work is subject to copyright. All rights are solely and exclusively licensed by the Publisher, whether the whole or part of the material is concerned, specifically the rights of translation, reprinting, reuse of illustrations, recitation, broadcasting, reproduction on microfilms or in any other physical way, and transmission or information storage and retrieval, electronic adaptation, computer software, or by similar or dissimilar methodology now known or hereafter developed.

The use of general descriptive names, registered names, trademarks, service marks, etc. in this publication does not imply, even in the absence of a specific statement, that such names are exempt from the relevant protective laws and regulations and therefore free for general use.

The publisher, the authors and the editors are safe to assume that the advice and information in this book are believed to be true and accurate at the date of publication. Neither the publisher nor the authors or the editors give a warranty, expressed or implied, with respect to the material contained herein or for any errors or omissions that may have been made. The publisher remains neutral with regard to jurisdictional claims in published maps and institutional affiliations.

This Springer imprint is published by the registered company Springer Nature Singapore Pte Ltd.
The registered company address is: 152 Beach Road, #21-01/04 Gateway East, Singapore 189721, Singapore

If disposing of this product, please recycle the paper.

Preface

These are the proceedings of the 13th International Conference on Image and Graphics (ICIG 2025), which was held in Xuzhou, China, on October 31 – November 2, 2025. The conference was hosted by the China Society of Image and Graphics (CSIG), organized by the China University of Mining and Technology, co-organized by Nanjing University of Science & Technology.

ICIG is a biennial conference that focuses on innovative technologies of image, video, and graphics processing and fosters innovation, entrepreneurship, and networking. It features world-class plenary speakers, exhibits, and high-quality peer-reviewed oral and poster presentations.

CSIG has hosted the ICIG conference series since 2000. Details about past conferences are as follows:

Conference	Place	Date	Submissions	Accepted
1st (ICIG 2000)	Tianjin, China	August 16–18	220	156
2nd (ICIG 2002)	Hefei, China	August 15–18	280	166
3rd (ICIG 2004)	Hong Kong, China	December 17–19	460	140
4th (ICIG 2007)	Chengdu, China	August 22–24	525	184
5th (ICIG 2009)	Xi'an, China	September 20–23	362	179
6th (ICIG 2011)	Hefei, China	August 12–15	329	183
7th (ICIG 2013)	Qingdao, China	July 26–28	346	181
8th (ICIG 2015)	Tianjin, China	August 13–16	345	170
9th (ICIG 2017)	Shanghai, China	September 13–15	370	172
10th (ICIG 2019)	Beijing, China	August 23–25	384	183
11th (ICIG 2021)	Haikou, China	December 26–28	421	198
12th (ICIG 2023)	Nanjing, China	September 22–24	409	166

For ICIG 2025, 420 submissions were received and 137 papers were accepted, corresponding to an acceptance rate of 32.62%. Each paper received three double-blind reviews, on average. To facilitate the search for a required paper in these proceedings, the accepted papers have been arranged into different sections according to their topic.

We sincerely thank all the contributors, who came from all over the world to present their advanced work at this event. We would also like to thank all the reviewers, who carefully reviewed all submissions and made their valuable comments for improving the accepted papers. The proceedings could not have been produced without the invaluable efforts of the members of the Organizing Committee, and a number of active members of CSIG.

October 2025

Zhouchen Lin
Liang Wang
Yugang Jiang
Xuesong Wang
Shengcai Liao
Shiguang Shan
Risheng Liu
Jing Dong
Xin Yu

Organization

General Chairs

Yaonan Wang	Hunan University, China
Hongwei Zhao	China University of Mining and Technology, China
Kyoung Mu Lee	Seoul National University, South Korea
Oliver Deussen	University of Konstanz, Germany

Technical Program Chairs

Zhouchen Lin	Peking University, China
Liang Wang	Institute of Automation, CAS, China
Yugang Jiang	Fudan University, China
Xuesong Wang	China University of Mining and Technology, China
Shengcai Liao	United Arab Emirates University, UAE

Organizing Committee Chairs

Huimin Ma	University of Science and Technology Beijing, China
Yuxin Peng	Peking University, China
Bingkun Bao	Nanjing University of Posts and Telecommunications, China
Jun Wang	China University of Mining and Technology, China

Publicity Chairs

Yuanlong Yu	Fuzhou University, China
Jinchang Ren	Robert Gordon University, UK
Wei Jia	Hefei University of Technology, China
Feifei Zhang	Tianjin University of Technology, China
Phoebe Chen	La Trobe University, Australia

Award Chairs

Changsheng Xu   Institute of Automation, CAS, China
Jian Yang   Nanjing University of Science and Technology,
                               China
Jingkuan Song   Tongji University, China
Han Yu   Nanyang Technological University, Singapore

Publication Chairs

Shiguang Shan   Institute of Computing Technology, CAS, China
Risheng Liu   Dalian University of Technology, China
Jing Dong   Institute of Automation, CAS, China
Xin Yu   University of Queensland, Australia

Workshop Chairs

Yao Zhao   Beijing Jiaotong University
Xi Li   Zhejiang University, China
Kun Tan   East China Normal University, China
Guosheng Lin   Nanyang Technological University, Singapore

Tutorial Chairs

Weiwei Xu   Zhejiang University, China
Weishi Zheng   Sun Yat-sen University, China
Zechao Li   Nanjing University of Science and Technology,
                               China
Yong Zhou   China University of Mining and Technology,
                               China

Exhibits Chairs

Cheng Deng   Xi'an University of Electronic Science and
                               Technology, China
Min Xia   Western University, Canada
Shengsheng Qian   Institute of Automation, CAS, China
Yisen Wang   Peking University, China

Sponsorship Chairs

Xucheng Yin	University of Science and Technology Beijing, China
Jin Tang	Anhui University, China
Junchi Yan	Shanghai Jiao Tong University, China
Shan An	Tianjin University, China

Finance Chairs

Xi Peng	Sichuan University, China
Kai Qin	China University of Mining and Technology, China
Zhi Jin	Sun Yat-sen University, China
Yi Jin	Beijing Jiaotong University, China

Website Chairs

Anan Liu	Tianjin University, China
Rushi Lan	Guilin University of Electronic Technology, China
Chenping Hou	National University of Defense Technology, China
Haoyu Wang	China University of Mining and Technology, China

Program Committee

Chenyan Bai	Ping Hu
Jie Cao	Huaibo Huang
Changsheng Chen	Junjun Jiang
Tao Chen	Taisong Jin
Runmin Cong	Rushi Lan
Qiongjie Cui	Chenglong Li
Junxian Duan	Hui Li
Bin Fan	Jia Li
Wei Feng	Tianrui Li
Changxin Gao	Jian Liang
Junyu Gao	Baodi Liu
Chen Gong	Dong Liu

Meng Liu
Qi Liu
Chunlei Peng
Jie Qin
Dongwei Ren
Nong Sang
Linlin Shen
Cong Wang
Gaoang Wang
Yuheng Wang
Jinjian Wu
Chunyan Xu
Jufeng Yang
Shiqi Yu
Xin Yu
Zhenhua Yu
Hui Yuan
Donglin Zhang
Hua Zhang
Jinglin Zhang
Bin Zhao
Liang Zhao
Bineng Zhong
Quan Zhou
Yu Zhou
Anna Zhu
Linchao Zhu
Liang Zou

Additional Reviewers

Chenyan Bai
Zhengyao Bai
Yanqi Bao
Yi Chang
Bo Chen
Cheng Chen
Gongping Chen
Hao Chen
Hui Chen
Jinyong Chen
Lu Chen
Qinghui Chen
Ruoyu Chen
Shuhuang Chen
Xiaolin Chen
Zheng Chen
Zhenyuan Chen
Ming-Ming Cheng
Chaoran Cui
Hui Cui
Jinrong Cui
Yimian Dai
Haoyou Deng
Jiajun Deng
Hui Ding
Jin Ding
Neng Dong
Huanzhang Dou
Hong Fan
Junkai Fan
Yuchun Fang
Lunke Fei
Chen Feng
Zhanxiang Feng
Congrui Fu
Sichao Fu
Zhaojin Fu
Zhenqi Fu
Guangwei Gao
Shaobing Gao
Shengxiang Gao
Zhenghao Gao
Mingrong Gong
Kuangpu Guo
Xiaoying Guo
Conghao Han
Hong Han
Pengfei Han
Changhao He
Xiangteng He
Wang Heng
Yuqing Hou
Zhi-Qiang Hou
Junlin Hu

Junxing Hu
Shizhe Hu
Yan Hu
Yongguan Hu
Bao Hua
Hongbo Huang
Kaiwen Huang
Lei Huang
Panjian Huang
Zhenyang Huang
Shuwei Huo
Fan Ji
Fanfan Ji
Naye Ji
Guoli Jia
Jieru Jia
Zhen Jia
Guang Jiang
Lianwen Jin
Mingxin Jin
Yi Jin
Jiuyao Jing
Tang Kai
Qingjie Kong
Jian-Huang Lai
Bowen Li
Changzhen Li
Chenghua Li
Huafeng Li
Hui Li
Jun Li
Qingyong Li
Ru Li
Senmao Li
Yunchen Li
Zhaojian Li
Zhenbo Li
Yuanfeng Lian
Yiyuan Liang
Guangfeng Lin
Yijie Lin
Yuji Lin
Yongguo Ling
Bin Liu
Chang Liu

Chengxin Liu
Hanye Liu
Hongmin Liu
Jin Liu
Jing Liu
Jinyuan Liu
Leyuan Liu
Qi Liu
Qingjie Liu
Shuaiqi Liu
Weifeng Liu
Xinpu Liu
Yan Liu
Yang Liu
Yang Liu
Yi Liu
Yimin Liu
Yunlong Liu
Zhiang Liu
Ruihan Lu
Wen Lu
Xiankai Lu
Yuwu Lu
Lingkun Luo
Fan Lyu
Bingpeng Ma
Shubin Ma
Wei Ma
Xinke Ma
Cai Meng
Lu Mingdong
Yifeng Niu
Yan Pang
Gensheng Pei
Chunlei Peng
Gang Peng
Jiangjun Peng
Hao Ping
Cheng Qian
Zheng Rao
Shulan Ruan
Yuanjie Shao
Jiangrong Shen
Shanxi Shen
Zhongwei Shen

Wenjun Shi
Heping Song
Lijuan Song
Honglei Su
Zhuo Su
Liyan Sun
Xiaoyang Tan
Sheng Tang
Zhangyong Tang
Nimol Thuon
Bin Wan
Chenyang Wang
Chenyang Wang
Chenye Wang
Di Wang
Elle Wang
Gaoang Wang
Jianzong Wang
Jinjia Wang
Kun Wang
Kunyu Wang
Lei Wang
Limin Wang
Runxi Wang
Shengke Wang
Shunzhou Wang
Tianshi Wang
Xianquan Wang
Yingjie Wang
Yuehuan Wang
Zhengxue Wang
Hongxi Wei
Yang Wei
Yanyan Wei
Tao Wu
Chao Xiao
Zhang Xiaolei
Weicheng Xie
Rui Xing
Qiu Xinyu
Maomao Xiong
Qi Xiong
Chunyan Xu
Yang Xu
Shuanglin Yan

Jucheng Yang
Mouxing Yang
Peng Yang
Rui Yang
Zhixiong Yang
Chao Yao
Chengtang Yao
Mao Ye
Junhui Yin
Aijing Yu
Haoran Yu
Qian Yu
Shiqi Yu
Wentao Yu
Ye Yu
Guorong Yuan
Hui Zeng
Zuo Zengyuan
Hongjian Zhan
Chao Zhang
Chen Zhang
Dongbo Zhang
Donglin Zhang
Ji Zhang
Lin Zhang
Pengyu Zhang
Qian Zhang
Xiaowei Zhang
Yonggang Zhang
Yu Zhang
Yunzhu Zhang
Zekai Zhang
Zeyang Zhang
Zhicheng Zhang
Zhongchi Zhang
Andy Zhao
Chenxi Zhao
Haifeng Zhao
Shaochuan Zhao
Dong Zhemeng
Jin Zheng
Xianwei Zheng
Yushan Zheng
Zhang Zhengxuan
Wang Zhiqiang

Dexing Zhong
Guoqiang Zhong
Daoxiang Zhou
Kangneng Zhou
Qian Zhou
Tao Zhou
Tao Zhou
Yong Zhou

Zhen Zhou
Zhou Zhou
Guoqing Zhu
Hancan Zhu
Lei Zhu
Xukun Zhu
Peixian Zhuang
Yuan Zong

Contents – Part III

Surveillance and Remote Sensing

Virtual Reality

Computer Vision and Pattern Recognition

RWD-YOLO: A Novel Approach for Small Object Detection in Aerial Drone Imagery

Wei Hong, Hongbin Yan, Weitao Wu, and Xinjian Huang[(✉)]

Nanjing University of Science and Technology, Nanjing 210094, China
`huangxinjian@njust.edu.cn`

Abstract. Recently, unmanned aerial vehicles (UAVs) for aerial target detection has gained significant attention. UAV-based target detection faces challenges like small target regions, limited feature information, complex backgrounds, and frequent occlusions by other objects. Existing detection methods often fail to preserve crucial details in small targets, reducing detection accuracy. To address these issues, we propose the RWD-YOLO model, which enhances the accuracy of small target detection in aerial imagery, while effectively improving detection performance for dense and occluded objects. Specifically, we use RepVGG blocks for downsampling to enhance small target detection by preserving low-level details. We then implement a weighted cross-layer feature fusion module for better feature integration. For the detection head, we design a tiny target detection head and introduce DynamicHead, incorporating three attention mechanisms to improve detection across scales and complex backgrounds. Extensive experiments conducted on four datasets demonstrate the superiority of the proposed UAV-based object detection method, particularly for small target detection. Codes will be released upon publication.

Keywords: Small object detection · Aerial imagery

1 Introduction

Over the past decade, the Unmanned Aerial Vehicle (UAV) industry has experienced significant growth [1], driven by its enhanced efficiency, portability, and cost-effectiveness, which have broadened its range of applications [2–4]. A crucial aspect of UAVs' ability to perceive their environment is object detection, which is essential for facilitating subsequent decision-making processes [5–7].

In recent years, the field of object detection has witnessed substantial advancements, largely due to the remarkable progress in deep convolutional networks. Feature extraction architectures, such as ResNet [8] and Darknet [9], have undergone rapid evolution, enabling the development of models like YOLO [10] and Faster R-CNN [11], which demonstrate exceptional detection performance across a range of object detection tasks. Despite their success with natural images, these models often exhibit suboptimal performance in recognizing small

© The Author(s), under exclusive license to Springer Nature Singapore Pte Ltd. 2026

Z. Lin et al. (Eds.): ICIG 2025, LNCS 16163, pp. 3–14, 2026.
https://doi.org/10.1007/978-981-95-3729-7_1

objects within UAV aerial imagery. Contemporary feature extraction networks for natural images typically increase network depth to capture more complex semantic information; however, this approach may result in the loss of small object features. Consequently, there is a critical need to design efficient network models specifically tailored for the detection of small targets.

In this study, we introduce the RWD-YOLO model, specifically tailored for aerial applications, with the objective of addressing the constraints inherent in conventional models when it comes to extracting features for densely packed small targets and differentiating these small targets from complex background elements in aerial imagery. The main contributions are summarized as follows.

1. A novel neural network method, RWD-YOLO, is proposed for multi-scale object detection in UAV imagery. The method emphasizes small-scale feature extraction and feature fusion by utilizing RepVGG blocks for feature extraction. A weighted cross-layer feature fusion structure is implemented to enhance the probability of multi-scale feature fusion, effectively mitigating the issue of false positives and false negatives of small targets in aerial images.
2. The detection head structure has been redesigned by adding an additional small object detection head. Additionally, scale awareness, spatial awareness, and task awareness have been integrated into the detection head, thereby improving the detection of small objects by concentrating on pertinent features and reducing background noise.
3. Ablation experimental results demonstrate the effectiveness and generalizability of RWD-YOLO. Compared to the baseline model, The proposed model achieves an improvement of 6.8% and 5.2% in mAP performance on the open-source datasets VisDrone and RGBT-Tiny, respectively.

2 Related Work

In recent years, object detection algorithms have achieved remarkable advancements, attaining high accuracy across numerous datasets. However, most conventional deep convolutional neural networks, primarily designed for natural scene images, fail to deliver optimal performance when directly applied to UAV-based aerial detection tasks. This limitation stems from aerial imagery's unique challenges:1information loss from downsampling operations, noisy feature interference due to background clutter, and sparse, uneven object distribution - all significantly increasing computational costs for target search.

To address the aforementioned challenges, existing small object detection methods typically build upon robust frameworks that perform well in general object detection tasks, incorporating strategies specifically designed for small object feature extraction and fusion. Zhang et al. [12] proposes an end-to-end Transformer-based object detection framework for unmanned aerial vehicle imagery, Tan et al. [13] proposed a Transformer-based model and successfully applied it to solar panel detection tasks. In the following sections, we will provide a categorized overview of these approaches.

Scale-Aware Methods: Aerial images often feature an uneven distribution of large, medium, and small objects, and these scale variations pose significant challenges for a single detector during inference. To address this challenge, inspired by the success of multi-level reasoning in other computer vision domains [14], modern aerial object detectors tend to adopt multi-branch architectures, which significantly mitigate information loss during feature extraction. For instance, Liu et al. [15] designed a lightweight multi-scale head to enhance the model's sensitivity to small-scale targets in infrared images.

Hierarchical Feature Fusion: Deep convolutional architectures generate a series of feature maps at various resolutions during feature extraction. Low-level features retain fine-grained details and spatial localization, while high-level features encapsulate richer semantic information [16]. For aerial detection tasks, high-level features often struggle to effectively respond to small objects, while low-level feature maps are more susceptible to variations such as illumination, deformation, and target posture, thereby increasing the difficulty of classification tasks. T. Lin et al. first introduced the Feature Pyramid Network [17], a method that concatenates high- and low-level features to effectively combine the detailed information of shallow layers.

Attention-Based Methods: Visual attention mechanisms mimic human behavior in observing a complete scene. Inspired by attention mechanisms, KB-RANN [18] employs a neural network model that incorporates long- and short-term attention modules, enhancing focus on small object instances in images. Hu et al. [19] propose MAFDet—a multi-attention fusion-based object detection network for UAV aerial imagery, which effectively addresses the critical challenge of dense small object detection.

3   Method Introduction

3.1   RWD-YOLO Network

The overall architecture of the RWD-YOLO network model is shown in Fig. 1. This model represents an enhancement of the YOLOv8n framework. Firstly, the RepVGG block is employed as the down-sampling module. During the training phase, this module simultaneously trains on both 3×3 and 1×1 convolutional kernels. In the inference stage, these convolutions are consolidated into a single 3×3 convolution. This approach facilitates enhanced feature extraction without compromising inference speed. Secondly, considering that the baseline model uses a unidirectional feature fusion method, which can lead to the loss of low-dimensional feature information and consequently result in reduced accuracy in small object detection and missed detections. We introduce an improved bidirectional feature pyramid network structure with an integrated weighting mechanism. This mechanism utilizes learnable weights to perform weighted fusion of various feature maps, enabling the model to autonomously adjust the contribution of each feature layer. Finally, given that the original YOLOv8 small detection head employs an eightfold down-sampling process, resulting in tiny objects occupying a minimal proportion of pixels on the feature map, we propose an additional detection head specifically for tiny objects. Furthermore, we incorporate three distinct attention mechanisms into the detection head to create a Dynamic head. This approach effectively captures contextual information from the image, thereby enhancing the global dependencies associated with small objects.

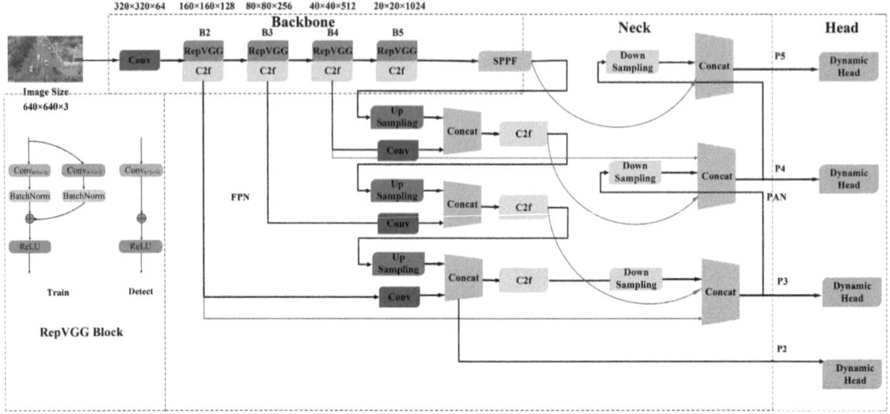

Fig. 1. Improved YOLOv8 network structure diagram.

3.2   RepVGG Block

As illustrated in the Fig. 1, we utilize the RepVGG module as the down-sampling structure. This module represents an enhanced single-path network derived from VGG [20], primarily utilizing the concept of structural reparameterization. The network exclusively uses a 3×3 convolution operator paired with a ReLU activation function. The 3×3 convolution has been continuously optimized in machine learning hardware acceleration libraries such as cuDNN [21], making 3×3 convolutions computationally denser than that of 1×1 and 5×5 convolutions. The essence of the RepVGG module involves employing a multi-branch architecture during the training phase to enhance performance. During model deployment and inference, however, the multi-branch model is equivalently transformed into a single-path model. This approach allows the model to leverage the high performance afforded by the multi-branch architecture during training, while achieving faster inference speed and reduced memory usage through the single-path model during deployment.

3.3   Weighted Cross-Layer Feature Fusion Module

During the feature extraction process, deep feature maps are characterized by rich semantic information but exhibit reduced localization precision. To enhance complementary fusion between deep and shallow features, the proposed weighted cross-layer feature fusion module employs a bidirectional sampling strategy, as illustrated in Fig. 2. The proposed method: (1) removes single-input nodes from the PAN network that offer minimal feature extraction advantages while contributing to increased model parameters and computational costs, and (2) establishes cross-layer connections (highlighted in red) with learnable weighting coefficients to dynamically balance feature-level contributions. This weighted cross-layer feature fusion module can adaptively assign greater weights to low-level feature maps, which are rich in information about small aerial targets, thereby preserving the detailed information of small objects more effectively. Concurrently, through bidirectional fusion, it successfully integrates low-level detail features with high-level semantic information, enhancing the model's capability to recognize small objects. Following feature fusion, the fused feature maps are subsequently input into the detection head for final object detection.

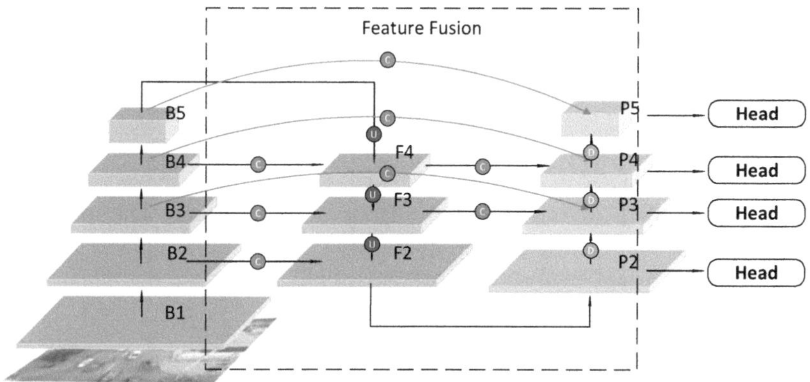

Fig. 2. The weighted cross-layer feature fusion module. (Color figure online)

3.4   Dynamic Head Mechanism

To address the challenges posed by complex background information and partial occlusion of targets, we propose the dynamic head module, as shown in Fig. 3. This approach integrates three different attention mechanisms into the detection head: the spatial-aware attention for feature layers, the spatial-aware attention for spatial locations, and the task-aware attention for the final output task type. This model can efficiently capture contextual information from the image, enhancing the global dependencies for single-object detection. These contextual global features play a critical role in aerial remote sensing images, significantly reducing the impact of target occlusion.

The input to the detection head has three dimensions, which can be represented as *level* × *space* × *channel*. Our method performs attention map calculations on each input dimension individually, and then multiplies the attention maps obtained from each of the three dimensions to generate the final attention map.

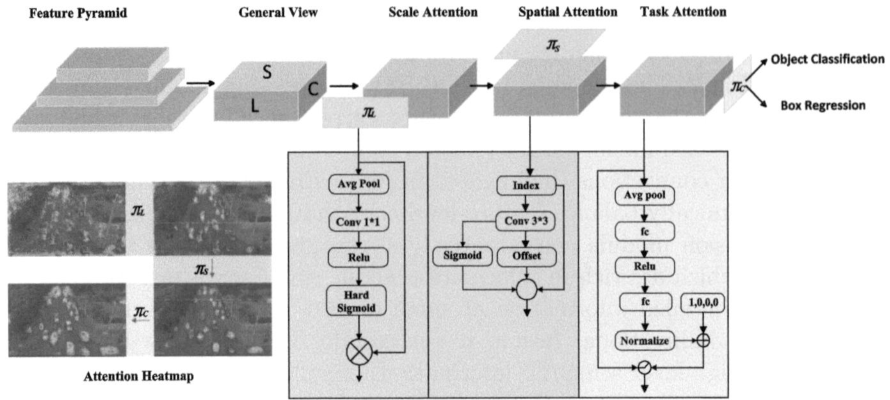

Fig. 3. Dynamic head mechanism.

4　Experimental Results

4.1　Datasets

To demonstrate the effectiveness of RWD-YOLO, we directly test it on four datasets: the VisDrone2019 DET dataset [22], the RGBT-Tiny dataset [23], the UAVDT dataset [24], and the Spanish Roundabouts Traffic Dataset (SRTD) [25], which share the common characteristic of being aerial-view datasets and containing a large number of small targets. Table 1 presents a comparison of the four datasets.

Table 1. Comparison of benchmark datasets for object detection.

Dataset	Images	Annotations	Classes	year	Key Features
UAVDT	42,860	1.2M	3	2018	Traffic tracking
VisDrone	8,629	343K	10	2019	Crowded urban scenes
RGBT-Tiny	3,034	48K	9	2021	RGB-Thermal pairs
SRTD	15,474	245K	4	2022	Aerial roundabouts

4.2　Experimental Settings

This section describes the experimental setup and training parameter configurations. The hardware used includes a 24 GB NVIDIA GeForce RTX 4090 GPU, with PyTorch 2.2.2 as the deep learning framework, Python 3.10.14, CUDA 12.1, and Ubuntu 22.04 as the operating system. The dataset was divided into training, validation, and test sets in a 7 : 1 : 2 ratio. The training process consisted of 300 epochs with a batch size of 16, where the first three epochs were used for warm-up training. The learning rate adjustment followed the SGD optimization strategy with an initial rate of 0.01, and the input image size was normalized.

To ensure fairness in the experiments, no pre-trained weights were used in either the ablation or comparison experiments. All training processes shared consistent hyperparameter settings.

The evaluation metrics used include precision (P), recall (R), mean average precision (mAP), mean average precision at 50% IOU (mAP_{50}), and AP for small objects (AP_{small})[1].

4.3 Comparison Experiments

We compared our experimental results with those of methods, including Yolov5n [10], Yolov6n [26], Yolov9t [27], Yolov10n [28], Yolov8s [29], Retinanet [30], FasterRCNN [11], and DroneYOLO [31].

During the training phase of these models, we maintained uniformity in hyperparameter configurations between the comparison models and our proposed model. Specifically, training images were resized to a resolution of 640×640 prior to being input into the network. Upon completion of training, performance validation and comparative analyses were conducted using the test datasets. The evaluation metrics employed for model comparison included mAP_{50}, mAP_{95}, and AP_{small}. The results of these validations are detailed in Table 2.

Table 2. Experimental results on multiple datasets.

Method	VisDrone			RGBT-Tiny			UAVDT			SRTD		
	AP_{50}	AP_{50-95}	AP_{small}	AP_{50}	AP_{50-95}	AP_{small}	AP_{50}	AP_{50-95}	AP_{small}	AP_{50}	AP_{50-95}	AP_{small}
Yolov5n	0.352	0.205	0.106	0.847	0.502	0.316	<u>0.985</u>	0.749	0.627	0.956	0.764	0.688
Yolov6n	0.340	0.198	0.094	0.823	0.482	0.286	0.979	0.748	0.619	0.979	0.762	0.632
Yolov9t	0.369	0.216	0.107	0.844	0.502	0.322	0.984	0.756	0.632	0.946	0.735	0.664
Yolov10n	0.360	0.205	0.107	0.864	0.524	0.328	0.983	0.749	0.621	0.952	0.746	0.684
Yolov8s	<u>0.402</u>	<u>0.237</u>	0.128	0.888	**0.552**	0.346	<u>0.985</u>	<u>0.758</u>	0.628	0.963	0.754	0.685
Retinanet	0.277	0.164	0.060	0.713	0.440	**0.427**	0.980	0.718	0.598	0.891	0.710	0.638
FasterRCNN	0.327	0.193	0.095	0.548	0.394	0.385	0.980	0.726	0.644	0.828	0.686	0.626
DroneYOLO	0.389	0.225	<u>0.132</u>	<u>0.892</u>	0.532	0.305	<u>0.985</u>	<u>0.758</u>	<u>0.654</u>	<u>0.985</u>	<u>0.798</u>	<u>0.753</u>
Ours	**0.427**	**0.251**	**0.146**	**0.906**	<u>0.551</u>	0.352	**0.988**	**0.771**	**0.670**	**0.990**	**0.813**	**0.785**

The experimental results demonstrate that, compared to other methods, our proposed RWD-YOLO achieves significant accuracy improvements across all four datasets. Notably, our improved model demonstrates outstanding performance in small-object categories, validating its high accuracy and effectiveness.

4.4 Ablation Experiment

To evaluate the contribution of each component to the model's performance, ablation experiments were performed. YOLOv8n was chosen as the (1) baseline framework and several modifications were introduced: (2) using RepVGG

---

[1] Small objects are defined as targets in an image whose bounding box area less than 16×16 pixels.

blocks as downsampling units in the backbone, (3) the redesign of the neck using the weighted cross-layer feature fusion network, (4) adding an additional detection head P2, and (5) utilizing the dynamic detection head. A comprehensive summary of the experimental results is presented in Table 3.

Table 3. Ablation study results under different configurations and datasets.

Dataset	1	2	3	4	5	P	R	mAP_{50}	mAP_{50-95}	AP_{small}
VisDrone	✓					0.473	0.372	0.359	0.209	0.104
	✓	✓				0.483	0.385	0.375	0.221	0.117
	✓	✓	✓			0.494	<u>0.401</u>	0.387	0.227	0.128
	✓	✓	✓	✓		<u>0.505</u>	0.400	<u>0.398</u>	<u>0.234</u>	<u>0.132</u>
	✓	✓	✓	✓	✓	**0.517**	**0.429**	**0.427**	**0.251**	**0.146**
RGB-Tiny	✓					0.875	0.812	0.854	0.512	0.304
	✓	✓				0.903	0.840	0.891	0.539	0.310
	✓	✓	✓			<u>0.913</u>	<u>0.847</u>	<u>0.897</u>	0.542	0.305
	✓	✓	✓	✓		**0.915**	0.844	0.894	<u>0.543</u>	<u>0.319</u>
	✓	✓	✓	✓	✓	<u>0.913</u>	**0.856**	**0.906**	**0.551**	**0.323**
UAVDT	✓					0.933	0.886	0.954	0.687	0.632
	✓	✓				0.954	0.898	0.972	0.703	0.645
	✓	✓	✓			<u>0.963</u>	**0.902**	0.963	<u>0.704</u>	0.646
	✓	✓	✓	✓		0.962	<u>0.901</u>	<u>0.976</u>	0.701	<u>0.648</u>
	✓	✓	✓	✓	✓	**0.968**	0.892	**0.988**	**0.711**	**0.670**
SRTD	✓					0.979	0.953	0.978	0.801	0.604
	✓	✓				0.982	0.976	0.982	0.804	0.632
	✓	✓	✓			**0.992**	<u>0.983</u>	<u>0.989</u>	0.806	<u>0.664</u>
	✓	✓	✓	✓		0.987	**0.985**	0.987	<u>0.808</u>	0.657
	✓	✓	✓	✓	✓	<u>0.990</u>	<u>0.983</u>	**0.990**	**0.813**	**0.687**

As detailed in Table 3, as the configuration incrementally progresses from 1 to 5, the performance metrics exhibit a consistently increasing trend. This suggests that each successive configuration positively contributes to the model's performance. The results demonstrate that the implementation of the downsampling method, the weighted cross-layer feature fusion mechanism, and the dynamic detection head significantly enhance the efficacy of UAV small target detection.

4.5 Visualization Results

Evaluation metrics have demonstrated the superior performance of our approach, particularly in the detection of small objects and occluded targets. To provide a more intuitive illustration of RWD-YOLO's inference capabilities, we selected images containing dense small objects and occluded targets from four datasets for comparative analysis'. The inference results of both the baseline model and RWD-YOLO were evaluated against ground truth bounding boxes. The results across the four datasets are presented in Fig. 4. For instance, in Fig. 4 (a1), our model successfully detected small targets such as motorcycles and accurately identified cars that were partially occluded by trees.

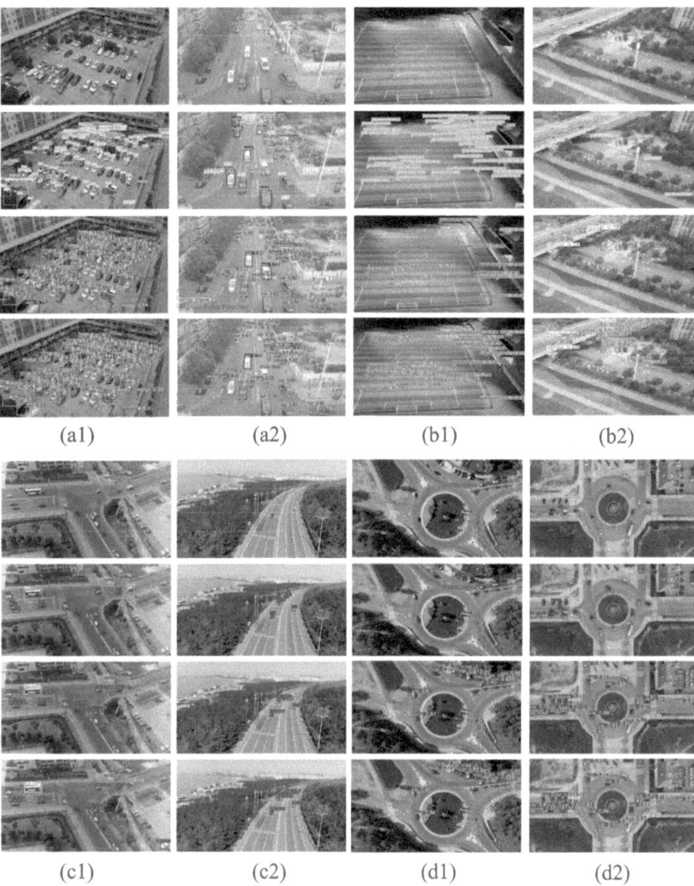

Fig. 4. Comparison of detection results across multiple datasets. Rows from top to bottom: (1) Original images, (2) Ground truth annotations, (3) YOLOv8n predictions (4) RWD-YOLO predictions. Sample pairs are selected from: a1–a2 (VisionDrone), b1–b2 (RGBT-Tiny), c1–c2 (UAVDT), and d1–d2 (SRTD).

To elucidate the impact of the dynamic attention mechanism within the detection head on mitigating background noise and enhancing sensitivity to densely packed and small objects, we employed feature heatmap visualizations employing the Gradient-weighted Class Activation Mapping Method (Grad-CAM). This method calculates gradients via backpropagation to generate heatmaps that highlight the regions the model focuses on when making decisions. As shown in Fig. 5, areas of high attention are indicated in deep red, while areas of low attention are shown in deep blue. These visualizations identify the specific regions of the image that RWD-YOLO prioritizes during classification and localization processes. The baseline model demonstrated reduced attention to distant small objects and a lack of sensitivity to dense targets. In contrast, RWD-YOLO effectively suppressed background noise, concentrated more on small and dense

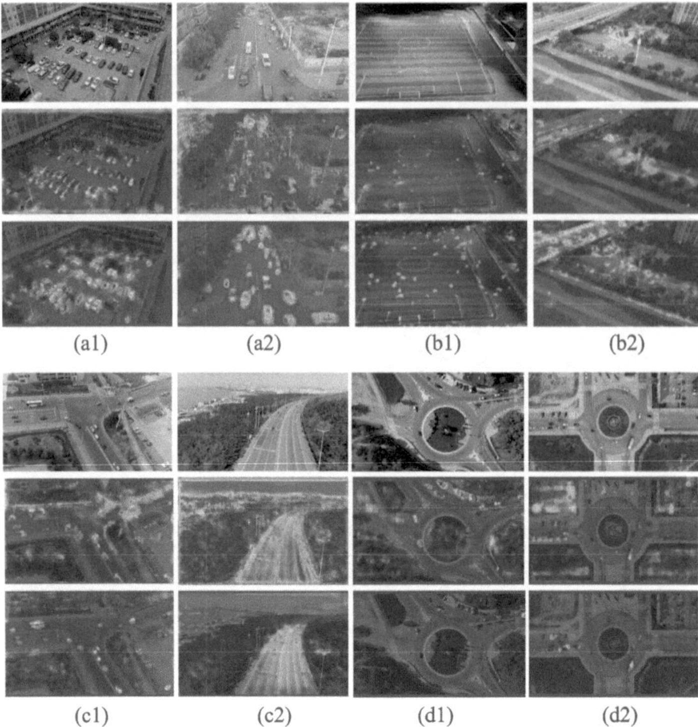

(a1)   (a2)   (b1)   (b2)

(c1)   (c2)   (d1)   (d2)

Fig. 5. Feature visualization heatmaps across multiple datasets. Rows from top to bottom: (1) Original input images, (2) Activation heatmaps from YOLOv8n, and (3) Heatmaps generated by RWD-YOLO. Sample pairs are drawn from: a1–a2 (Vision-Drone), b1–b2 (RGBT-Tiny), c1–c2 (UAVDT), and d1–d2 (SRTD). The heatmaps highlight region-specific feature importance for detection tasks.

objects, and predicted bounding boxes with greater accuracy. This enhancement significantly improves overall detection performance.

5   Conclution

For UAV object detection, we propose the RWD-YOLO method, an improved model based on YOLOv8. First, we incorporate RepVGG as the downsampling layer in the feature extraction component. This integration augments the network's capacity to extract multi-scale features and optimizes the preservation of low-level features, which are essential for detecting small objects. Second, in the feature fusion phase, we develop a weighted cross-layer feature fusion network to restructure the model's neck architecture. This enables efficient fusion of low-level detailed location information and high-level semantic information. Finally, we introduce a specialized detection head tailored for tiny object detection and augment the original detection head by employing the DynamicHead with multiple attention mechanisms, thereby significantly enhancing detection accuracy.

Comparative and ablation experiments conducted across various datasets validate the modelnn's efficacy and robustness, particularly in enhancing the detection performance of small objects.

However, visual inference results reveal persistent challenges, such as the misdetection of small objects and category misclassification. Our future work will focus on further optimizing the model to enhance its feature extraction and fusion capabilities for small UAV targets, while also improving its lightweight metrics to facilitate deployment on real devices.

Acknowledgements. This work was supported by the National Key Research and Development Program of China (Grant No. 2021YFC3100705), the National Natural Science Foundation of China (Grant No. 62501284) and the Fundamental Research Funds for the Central Universities (No. 30925010533).

References

1. Ma, S., Zhang, Y., Peng, L., Sun, C., Ding, B., Zhu, Y.: OWRT-DETR: a novel real-time transformer network for small-object detection in open-water search and rescue from UAV aerial imagery. IEEE Trans. Geosci. Remote Sens. **63** (2025)
2. Li, C., Zhao, R., Wang, Z., Xu, H., Zhu, X.: RemDet: rethinking efficient model design for UAV object detection. In: Proceedings of the AAAI Conference on Artificial Intelligence, vol. 39, pp. 4643–4651 (2025)
3. Zeng, S., Yang, W., Jiao, Y., Geng, L., Chen, X.: SCA-YOLO: a new small object detection model for UAV images. Vis. Comput. **40**, 1787–1803
4. Chen, L., Liu, C., Li, W., Xu, Q., Deng, H.: DTSSNet: dynamic training sample selection network for UAV object detection. IEEE Trans. Geosci. Remote Sens. (2024)
5. Jiang, L., Yuan, B., Du, J., Chen, B., Xie, H., Tian, J.: MFFSODNet: multiscale feature fusion small object detection network for UAV aerial images. IEEE Trans. Instrum. Meas. **73** (2024)
6. Li, J., Zhang, J., Shao, Y., Liu, F.: SRE-YOLOv8: an improved UAV object detection model utilizing swin transformer and RE-FPN. Sensors **24**(12), 3918 (2024)
7. Li, Q., Zhang, Y., Fang, L., Kang, Y., Li, S., Zhu, X.X.: DREB-Net: dual-stream restoration embedding blur-feature fusion network for high-mobility UAV object detection. IEEE Trans. Geosci. Remote Sens. **63** (2025)
8. He, K., Zhang, X., Ren, S., Sun, J.: Deep residual learning for image recognition. In: Proceedings of the IEEE/CVF Conference on Computer Vision and Pattern Recognition, pp. 770–778 (2016)
9. Redmon, J.: YOLOv3: an incremental improvement. arXiv preprint arXiv:1804.02767 (2018)
10. Redmon, J., Divvala, S., Girshick, R., Farhadi, A.: You only look once: unified, real-time object detection. In: Proceedings of the IEEE/CVF Conference on Computer Vision and Pattern Recognition (2016)
11. Ren, S., He, K., Ross, G., Sun, J.: Faster R-CNN: towards real-time object detection with region proposal networks. In: Advances in Neural Information Processing Systems, vol. 28 (2015)

12. Zhang, H., Liu, K., Gan, Z., Zhu, G.N.: UAV-DETR: efficient end-to-end object detection for unmanned aerial vehicle imagery. arXiv preprint arXiv:2501.01855 (2025)
13. Tan, L., Liu, Z., Liu, H., Li, D., Zhang, C.: A real-time unmanned aerial vehicle (UAV) aerial image object detection model. In: International Joint Conference on Neural Networks, pp. 1–7 (2024)
14. Hariharan, B., Arbelaez, P., Girshick, R., Malik, J.: Object instance segmentation and fine-grained localization using hypercolumns. IEEE Trans. Pattern Anal. Mach. Intell. **39**(4), 627–639 (2016)
15. Liu, Q., Liu, R., Zheng, B., Wang, H., Fu, Y.: Infrared small target detection with scale and location sensitivity. In: IEEE/CVF Conference on Computer Vision and Pattern Recognition, pp. 17490–17499 (2024)
16. Liu, L., et al.: Deep learning for generic object detection: a survey. Int. J. Comput. Vision **128**, 261–318 (2020)
17. Lin, T.Y., Dollár, P., Girshick, R., He, K., Hariharan, B., Belongie, S.: Feature pyramid networks for object detection. In: Proceedings of the IEEE/CVF Conference on Computer Vision and Pattern Recognition, pp. 2117–2125 (2017)
18. Yi, K., Jian, Z., Chen, S., Zheng, N.: Feature selective small object detection via knowledge-based recurrent attentive neural network. arXiv preprint arXiv:1803.05263 (2018)
19. Hu, J., Pang, T., Peng, B., Shi, Y., Li, T.: A small object detection model for drone images based on multi-attention fusion network. Image Vis. Comput. **155**, 105436 (2025)
20. Simonyan, K., Zisserman, A.: Very deep convolutional networks for large-scale image recognition. arXiv preprint arXiv:1409.1556 (2014)
21. Chetlur, S., et al.: cuDNN: efficient primitives for deep learning. Nature **1410** (2014)
22. Zhu, P., et al.: Detection and tracking meet drones challenge. IEEE Trans. Pattern Anal. Mach. Intell. **44**(11), 7380–7399 (2021)
23. Ying, X., et al.: Visible-thermal tiny object detection: a benchmark dataset and baselines. IEEE Trans. Pattern Anal. Mach. Intell. (2025)
24. Du, D., et al.: The unmanned aerial vehicle benchmark: object detection and tracking. In: Ferrari, V., Hebert, M., Sminchisescu, C., Weiss, Y. (eds.) ECCV 2018. LNCS, vol. 11214, pp. 375–391. Springer, Cham (2018). https://doi.org/10.1007/978-3-030-01249-6_23
25. Puertas, E., De-Las-Heras, G., Fernández-Andrés, J., Sánchez-Soriano, J.: Dataset: roundabout aerial images for vehicle detection. Data **7**(4), 47 (2022)
26. Li, C., et al.: YOLOv6: a single-stage object detection framework for industrial applications. arXiv preprint arXiv:2209.02976 (2022)
27. Wang, C.Y., Yeh, I.H., Liao, H.Y.M.: YOLOv9: learning what you want to learn using programmable gradient information (2024). https://arxiv.org/abs/2402.13616
28. Wang, A., et al.: YOLOv10: real-time end-to-end object detection (2024). https://arxiv.org/abs/2405.14458
29. Varghese, R., Sambath, M.: YOLOv8: a novel object detection algorithm with enhanced performance and robustness. In: International Conference on Advances in Data Engineering and Intelligent Computing Systems
30. Lin, T.Y., Goyal, P., Girshick, R., He, K., Dollár, P.: Focal loss for dense object detection. IEEE Trans. Pattern Anal. Mach. Intell. **PP**(99), 2999–3007 (2017)
31. Zhang, Z.: Drone-YOLO: an efficient neural network method for target detection in drone images. Drones **7**(8) (2023)

CDHQA: A Quality Assessment Database for Conversational Digital Human

Yingjie Zhou[1], Jing Wan[2], Sitong Liu[2], Yinghan Xia[2], Zhixiang Lu[2], Farong Wen[1], Zicheng Zhang[1], Yu Wang[1], Yu Zhou[2], Xiaohong Liu[1], Xiongkuo Min[1], Jiezhang Cao[3], and Guangtao Zhai[1(✉)]

[1] Shanghai Jiao Tong University, Shanghai, China
zhaiguangtao@sjtu.edu.cn
[2] China University of Mining and Technology, Xuzhou, China
[3] Harvard Medical School, Cambridge, USA

Abstract. Conversational Digital Humans (CDHs) are increasingly deployed across domains such as healthcare, education, and entertainment, owing to their realistic visual appearance, lifelike motion, and smooth interactive capabilities. However, inconsistencies between a CDH's visual appearance, vocal timbre, body movements, and interactive textual content can significantly impair the user's audio-visual experience. To systematically evaluate such multimodal inconsistencies, we introduce the first CDH Quality Assessment (CDHQA) Dataset, comprising 254 videos of eight diverse 3D digital humans. The dataset includes 134 high-quality videos and 120 samples exhibiting three types of quality degradations: mismatches between timbre and appearance, mismatches between actions and interactive text, and combined mismatches. Subjective experiments are conducted to assess the perceptual impact of these issues, revealing their substantial effect on user experience. In addition, we benchmark classical objective quality assessment methods on the dataset, which expose the limitations of existing methods in handling CDH-specific quality issues. These findings underscore the urgent need for more robust and multimodal-aware assessment techniques tailored to CDHs.

Keywords: Quality assessment database · Digital human · Human-computer interaction · Streaming media

1 Introduction

Virtual digital humans represent an emerging frontier in digital media technology, gaining increasing attention due to their capabilities in visual characterization, realistic movement, and voice generation. Beyond traditional applications in animation and gaming [43], Conversational Digital Humans (CDHs) are now widely

This work was supported in part by the Major Key Project of PCL (PCL2023A10-2) and National Natural Science Foundation of China (623B2073, 62101326, 62225112).

© The Author(s), under exclusive license to Springer Nature Singapore Pte Ltd. 2026
Z. Lin et al. (Eds.): ICIG 2025, LNCS 16163, pp. 15–26, 2026.
https://doi.org/10.1007/978-981-95-3729-7_2

employed across industries to deliver immersive and interactive user experiences [6,32]. The design of CDHs is inherently complex, requiring the integration and synchronization of multiple modalities, including visual appearance, vocal timbre, body motion, and interactive text content, to achieve a high level of realism and naturalness. Currently, the coordination of these multimodal components heavily relies on the designer's expertise and manual effort, making the process time-consuming and prone to inconsistencies. Recent advances in Artificial Intelligence (AI), particularly in speech synthesis [7,13], large language models (LLMs) [5,20], and action generation [8,27,35], have introduced new tools to automate and simplify CDH development. However, the reduced human oversight inherent in AI-driven workflows has also introduced new challenges, most notably modality mismatches, which can severely compromise the user's audiovisual and interactive experience. This underscores the urgent need for reliable methods to detect and evaluate the degree of multimodal alignment in CDHs.

To address this issue, we conduct a systematic quality assessment research on CDHs. We construct CDHQA, the first dedicated quality assessment dataset for CDHs, comprising a total of 254 video samples. This includes 134 high-quality CDHs designed with well-coordinated visual, auditory, and textual elements using eight distinct 3D digital character models. Additionally, we simulate three types of common multimodal degradation: mismatch between voice and visual appearance, mismatch between action and interaction text, and combined mismatches, resulting in 120 degraded CDHs. To evaluate the perceptual impact of these degradations, we conduct subjective quality assessment experiments involving human participants. The results reveal significant differences in perceived quality across the different degradation types, reaffirming the importance of multimodal consistency in CDH experiences. Furthermore, we benchmark the dataset using classical objective quality assessment models, which highlight substantial limitations in existing algorithms when applied to CDHs. These findings emphasize the need for the development of specialized quality assessment techniques tailored to the unique challenges of CDH design.

2   Related Work

2.1   Digital Human

Digital humans, virtual avatars designed with human-like appearances, are widely regarded as a key gateway to the metaverse [48]. Based on their data formats, digital humans can generally be classified into two categories: 2D digital humans and 3D digital humans. Despite variations in their production pipelines and visual presentation, the development of digital human systems typically follows a three-stage process: visual image design, motion actuation, and interactive behavior modeling. The image design stage is foundational and involves either 2D character illustration or 3D character modeling. Traditionally, this process has relied on manual artistic creation or sensor-based image acquisition techniques. However, recent advances in generative models, such as text-to-image

Table 1. Existing digital human quality assessment datasets and their details.

Database	Content Form	Scale	Distortion Types	Description
DHH-QA [40]	3D Mesh	1,540	Computer Simulation	Scanned Real Human Heads
DDH-QA [39]	Mesh Sequence	800	Computer Simulation	Dynamic 3D Digital Humans
SJTU-H3D [37]	3D Mesh	1,120	Computer Simulation	Static 3D Digital Humans
6G-DHQA [42]	Mesh Sequence	400	Computer Simulation	Digital Twins
THQA [46]	2D Video	800	AI Generation	Speech-driven Talking Heads
THQA-3D [47]	Mesh Sequence	1,000	Computer Simulation	Scanned Real Talking Heads
ReLI-QA [50]	2D Image	840	AI Generation	Relighted Human Heads
MEMO-Bench [44]	2D Image	7,145	AI Generation	Emotional Human Heads
AHQA [45]	2D Video	1,200	AI Generation	Animated Human
CDHQA (Proposed)	**2D Video**	**254**	**Computer Simulation**	**Conversational Digital Human**

synthesis [15, 21, 22] and 3D reconstruction [9, 16, 49], have introduced more efficient and scalable solutions for digital human appearance design. The actuation stage, which governs the motion and animation of digital humans, is critical to achieving realistic and expressive behaviors. While conventional methods such as keyframe animation and motion capture remain prevalent, they often entail significant cost and labor. In contrast, AI-driven approaches, such as voice-driven facial animation [23, 30, 34] and motion retargeting [8, 27, 35], offer more automated and cost-effective alternatives for generating lifelike movement. Finally, the integration of LLMs [5, 20] has significantly enhanced the interactivity of digital humans, enabling natural language-based interactions and providing users with more immersive and context-aware experiences. These developments collectively advance the design and deployment of intelligent, responsive digital avatars in both virtual and augmented environments.

2.2   Digital Human Quality Assessment

With the continued advancement and increasing adoption of digital human technologies across various domains, the issue of quality assessment has garnered growing attention. To address the need for systematic evaluation, several pioneering efforts have been made to establish representative datasets focused on various dimensions of digital human quality assessment (see Table 1). These datasets provide multidimensional evaluations encompassing aspects such as visual fidelity, speech quality, motion naturalness, lighting conditions, communicative effectiveness, and emotional expressiveness. An analysis of Table 1 reveals that although existing datasets offer valuable insights into specific facets of digital human quality, they predominantly focus on isolated modalities. Consequently, they often overlook the holistic audiovisual presentation of digital humans during real-time interactions. This limitation is particularly critical in the context of CDHs, where the interplay between appearance, voice, motion, and interactive content is essential for user experience.

Building on these datasets, a number of effective digital human quality assessment methods [2, 36, 38, 41] have been proposed. For example, Zhang *et al.* [40] implement a full-reference (FR) assessment of static digital human heads using

Fig. 1. Overview of chosen digital human. Each image is assigned a Human ID (HID).

a siamese network based on Swin Transformer [14]. They also develop a no-reference (NR) method leveraging geometric descriptors [41], such as Gaussian curvature and dihedral angle distributions. Similarly, Zhou *et al.* propose specialized quality assessment algorithms for talking heads [47] and animated avatars [45], employing metrics such as phoneme-lip synchronization [3] and XT-slice analysis [25], respectively. Despite these advances, current methodologies fall short in evaluating multimodal consistency within CDHs, particularly the alignment between visual, auditory, and textual modalities. This oversight highlights the need for more targeted and integrative quality assessment frameworks capable of capturing the full complexity of multimodal interactions in AI-driven digital humans.

3   Database Construction

3.1   Image of Digital Human

To more accurately simulate real-world interactions between CDHs and users, we select eight digital human avatars from the IFLYTEK Virtual Human Platform[1], as illustrated in Fig. 1. Consistent with trends observed in the service industry, where female digital humans are generally perceived as more approachable and empathetic, the selected avatars predominantly feature female appearances. One male avatar is retained to preserve a degree of gender diversity. Regarding stylistic representation, digital humans can be broadly categorized into hyper-realistic and cartoon-stylized forms, each serving distinct application contexts. To ensure the diversity and generalizability of our dataset, we include two cartoon-style avatars among the eight selected digital humans.

---

[1] https://virtual-man.xfyun.cn/.

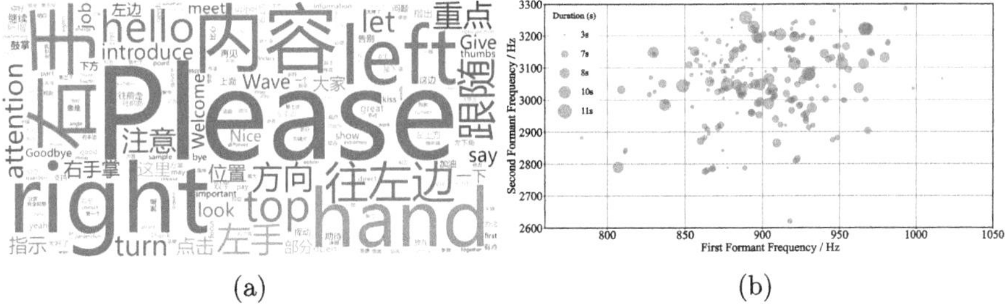

(a)   (b)

Fig. 2. The content of the script used with the sound source characterization. (a) Word cloud composed of script content. (b) Phonological features of the synthesized speech, where the first formant peak frequency is related to the degree of mouth opening and closing, while the second formant peak frequency is related to the position of the tongue during articulation.

3.2   Interactive Scripts and Sound Sources

To enable digital humans to engage in naturalistic dialogue with users, we develop a set of interaction scripts grounded in real-world application scenarios. To enhance the linguistic and contextual diversity of the dataset, the scripts are composed in both English and Chinese. The primary keywords are visualized in Fig. 2(a), confirming that the scripted content aligns well with typical conversational topics encountered in practical settings.

To synthesize spoken dialogue for the digital humans, we employ 12 distinct voice sources from the IFLYTEK Virtual Human Platform to perform text-to-speech (TTS) conversion of the interaction scripts. To evaluate the diversity of the selected voice profiles, we conduct an acoustic analysis using the cepstral to extract formant peaks from the synthesized speeches. As illustrated in Fig. 2(b), the first formant peaks are primarily distributed within the 750–1025 Hz, while the second formant peaks fall within the 2600–3300 Hz. These distributions not only demonstrate the phonetic richness and variability of the selected voice sources but also indicate that the designed dialogue scripts encompass a broad range of phonemic features, contributing to the overall realism and expressiveness of the conversational interactions.

3.3   Digital Human Movements

Non-verbal behaviors play a critical role in conversational interactions involving digital humans. These actions not only serve as complements to verbal communication but also act as primary channels for conveying emotion, facilitating social engagement, and enhancing information comprehension, thereby contributing significantly to users' sense of immersion and realism. To enhance the naturalness and expressiveness of the digital human characters in our study, we incorporate a diverse set of actions for each avatar. Representative samples of these actions are illustrated in Fig. 3, which highlights the breadth of physical expressiveness,

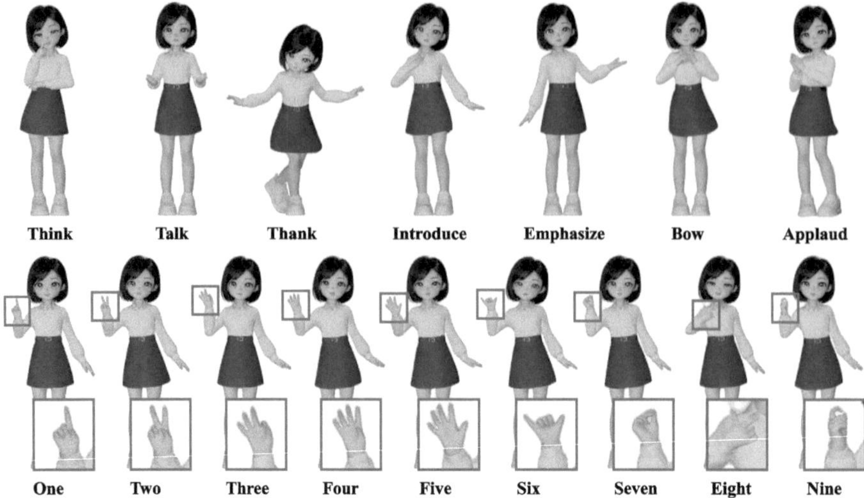

Fig. 3. Some of the actions of the digital human, including actions and gestures that are common during conversation.

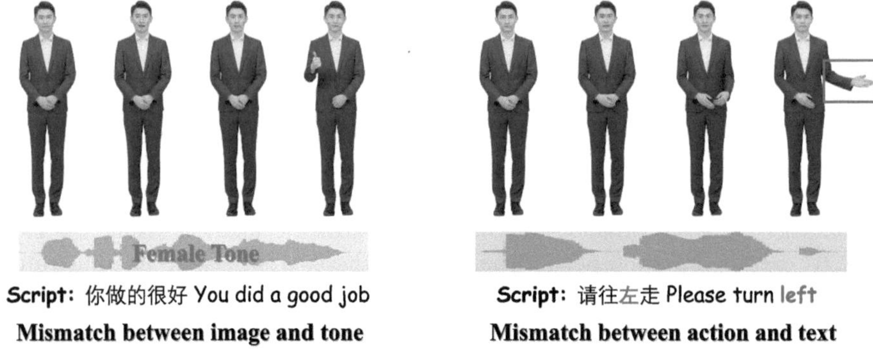

Fig. 4. Two classic cases of possible degradation of digital human in conversation.

spanning bodily gestures, hand movements, and facial expressions, exhibited by the digital humans during conversations. These multimodal behaviors contribute to a more authentic and engaging user experience. During the construction of the CDHQA dataset, we carefully align each action with a corresponding interaction script, ensuring semantic coherence between verbal and non-verbal modalities. The associated speech is synthesized using voice profiles matched to the visual characteristics of the respective digital humans. As a result, we curate a total of 134 high-quality CDH video samples, each featuring rich and coordinated verbal and non-verbal communication.

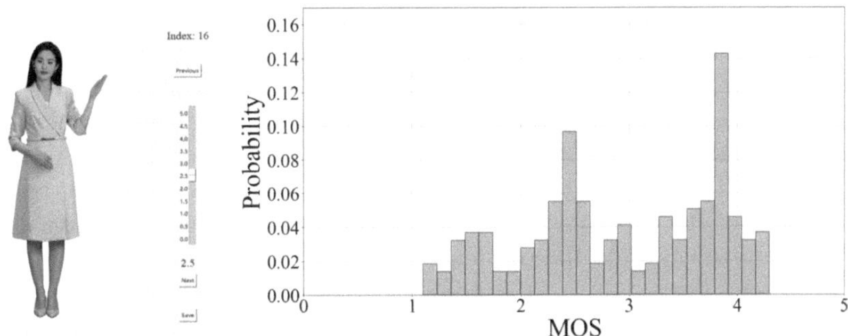

Fig. 5. Subjective experimental interface and distribution of MOS.

3.4 Distortion Simulation

To simulate quality degradation that may arise in real-world applications of CDHs, we deliberately model two primary categories of distortion and their combination, as illustrated in Fig. 4. Specifically, for each digital human avatar, we introduce three distinct types of degradation, resulting in five video samples per distortion type, each featuring different actions. The first degradation type involves a mismatch between the visual representation and the voice, wherein a speech tone is assigned that does not align with the perceived gender or age of the digital human. This intentional mismatch creates a clear image-audio incongruity, negatively impacting the realism of the interaction. The second degradation type addresses the mismatch between text and action, where non-corresponding gestures or movements are paired with spoken content, thereby disrupting the semantic coherence of the interaction. A third, combined degradation type is created by concurrently applying both the voice-image mismatch and the action-text incongruity. Through this controlled simulation of quality impairments, we construct a total of $120 = 8 \times 5 \times 3$ CDH video samples exhibiting quality issues. These degraded samples serve as a critical resource for evaluating the robustness of CDH quality assessment models.

3.5 Database Details and Subjective Experiment

The CDHQA dataset comprises a total of 254 CDHs, including 134 high-quality and 120 degraded instances. All videos are encoded at a resolution of 720×1080 pixels and a frame rate of 25 frames per second (FPS). The video durations range from 3 to 11 s, allowing for the evaluation of CDH performance across varying temporal lengths.

To obtain accurate and reliable measures of user-perceived audiovisual quality, a subjective quality assessment is conducted in accordance with the ITU-R BT.500-13 [1]. A total of 33 participants (17 male, 16 female) are recruited to evaluate the quality of each CDH. The experiment is carried out in a controlled laboratory environment, with all CDH displayed individually in randomized order on a high-resolution iMac display, as illustrated in Fig. 5. The subjective evaluation follows the Absolute Category Rating (ACR) protocol. To mitigate potential visual fatigue or discomfort from prolonged viewing, the experiment is divided into five sessions, with each session containing no more than 60 CDHs. Participants are required to take a 15-min break after completing each session, and no individual is allowed to complete more than three sessions per day. Prior to the formal assessment, participants complete a 15-min training session to ensure familiarity with the evaluation procedure. This session introduces the objectives of the experiment, explains the scoring interface, and provides example stimuli to calibrate the participants' quality judgment criteria.

3.6 Subjective Data Processing

Following the completion of the subjective experiment, a total of $8{,}382 = 254 \times 33$ subjective ratings are collected. In accordance with standard procedures for constructing quality assessment datasets, a z-score is calculated for each CDH:

$$z_{jk} = \frac{s_{jk} - \mu_j}{\sigma_j}, \tag{1}$$

where $\mu_j = \frac{1}{N_i} \sum_{k=1}^{N_i} s_{jk}$, $\sigma_j = \sqrt{\frac{1}{N_i-1} \sum_{k=1}^{N_i} (s_{jk} - \mu_j)}$, and N_i represents the total number of CDHs evaluated by subject k. To ensure the integrity of the dataset, ratings from unreliable subjects, identified through the subject rejection procedure outlined in [1], are excluded. The remaining z-scores are linearly rescaled to the interval $[0, 5]$. The mean opinion scores (MOSs) for the j-th CDH are computed by averaging these rescaled z-scores.

3.7 Subjective Data Analysis

To facilitate the interpretation of the subjective experiment results, a bar chart of the MOS for all CDHs is generated, as shown in Fig. 5. Several key observations can be drawn from the analysis of this figure: 1) The majority of CDHs receive MOS values clustered around 4.0, suggesting that the selected digital human images, designed interaction scripts, and assigned voice sources generally meet the audiovisual expectations of participants. This outcome highlights the practical effectiveness and representative quality of the constructed CDHQA dataset; 2) The distribution of MOS values reveals three distinct peaks approximately centered at 1.5, 2.5, and 4.0. A closer inspection indicates that these peaks correspond to the three quality categories represented in the dataset: CDHs with both types of degradation (image-tone mismatch and action-text mismatch), CDHs with only one type of degradation, and high-quality CDHs with no degradation, respectively. These findings reaffirm the significant impact that mismatches in multimodal content can have on users' perceived audiovisual experience and underscore the necessity of effective quality assessment for conversational digital humans.

4 Benchmark Experiment

4.1 Competitors

Given the absence of dedicated quality assessment methods for CDHs, we employ existing quality assessment algorithms as baseline benchmarks to establish a reference for future CDH-specific evaluation methods. Specifically, we select 13

Table 2. Benchmark performance on the CDHQA database. Best in **BOLD.**

Type	Method	SRCC↑	PLCC↑	KRCC↑	RMSE↓
IQA	BRISQUE [17]	0.2721	0.4289	0.1807	0.7945
	NIQE [19]	0.1397	0.1927	0.0935	0.8630
	IL-NIQE [33]	**0.3853**	0.4468	**0.2572**	0.7868
	CPBD [4]	0.1300	0.2603	0.0969	0.8491
VQA	VIIDEO [18]	0.2920	0.3368	0.2016	0.8281
	V-BLIINDS [24]	0.3246	**0.5043**	0.2180	**0.3164**
	TLVQM [10]	0.1563	0.3855	0.1097	0.3471
	VIDEVAL [28]	0.2776	0.3601	0.1465	0.3362
	VSFA [12]	0.1441	0.1206	0.1006	0.9501
	RAPIQUE [29]	0.1536	0.3269	0.0964	0.3566
	SimpVQA [26]	0.2418	0.3057	0.1758	0.7827
	FAST-VQA [31]	0.3455	0.3857	0.2480	0.9112
	BVQA [11]	0.1679	0.2424	0.1375	0.9381

representative quality assessment algorithms, which are broadly categorized into two groups: four image quality assessment (IQA) methods and nine video quality assessment (VQA) methods. Among these, V-BLIINDS [24], VSFA [12], RAPIQUE [29], SimpVQA [26], FAST-VQA [31], and BVQA [11] are deep learning-based models that require additional training. The remaining methods are based on hand-crafted feature extraction and operate in a zero-shot manner. All selected algorithms are implemented using the official source code provided by the respective authors, with default parameters retained to ensure fairness and reproducibility in the benchmarking experiments.

4.2   Experimental Setup

To ensure the robustness of the experimental results, the CDHQA dataset is partitioned into five folds, with each fold containing no fewer than 50 CDHs. A five-fold cross-validation strategy is employed, wherein the average performance across all five folds is recorded. For quantitative evaluation, we adopt 4 widely-used metrics: Spearman Rank Order Correlation Coefficient (SRCC), Pearson Linear Correlation Coefficient (PLCC), Kendall Rank Order Correlation Coefficient (KRCC) and Root Mean Square Error (RMSE).

4.3   Performance and Analysis

The benchmark experiment results are presented in Table 2, where several insights can be drawn from: 1) The overall suboptimal performance of existing IQA and VQA methods on CDHQA dataset highlights their limitation in evaluating CDHs; 2) The performance deficiency can be attributed to the fact that the quality degradations in CDHs primarily involve mismatches across multiple modalities, rather than solely visual distortions. Consequently, methods that focus exclusively on visual features are inherently inadequate for perceiving the degradation of CDHs; 3) These findings collectively underscore two important implications: the urgent need to develop more sophisticated and targeted quality assessment algorithms specifically designed for CDHs, and the critical importance of incorporating multimodal information fusion in future quality assessment frameworks to accurately model user experience in CDH interactions.

5 Conclusion

With the rapid advancement of digital human and their growing deployment across diverse application domains, there is an increasing demand for enhanced quality in digital human systems. While prior studies have addressed specific aspects of digital human performance, less attention has been paid to the overall multimodal coherence. In this work, we focus on Conversational Digital Humans (CDHs), a widely adopted type of digital humans, and present a systematic study on their quality assessment. Specifically, we construct CDHQA, the first quality assessment dataset specifically tailored for CDHs, comprising 134 high-quality and 120 artificially degraded CDH video samples. To maximize the diversity and generalizability of the CDHQA dataset, we carefully curate content using eight distinct character images, twelve different voice profiles, and a variety of interaction scripts and actions. Each CDH is manually synthesized to ensure representative variations in audiovisual and behavioral features. A comprehensive subjective evaluation is conducted with human participants to gather Mean Opinion Scores (MOS) reflecting perceived audiovisual quality and user experience. Finally, we conduct benchmark experiments using a suite of representative quality assessment algorithms on the CDHQA dataset. The experimental outcomes reveal the inadequacy of existing methods in handling CDH-specific multimodal degradations and underscore the importance of multimodal feature fusion for developing reliable and effective CDH quality assessment frameworks.

References

1. BT, R.I.R.: Methodology for the subjective assessment of the quality of television pictures. Int. Telecommun. Union (2002)
2. Chen, S., Zhang, Z., Zhou, Y., Sun, W., Min, X.: A no-reference quality assessment metric for dynamic 3D digital human. Displays **80**, 102540 (2023)
3. Chung, J.S., Zisserman, A.: Out of time: automated lip sync in the wild. In: Chen, C.-S., Lu, J., Ma, K.-K. (eds.) ACCV 2016. LNCS, vol. 10117, pp. 251–263. Springer, Cham (2017). https://doi.org/10.1007/978-3-319-54427-4_19
4. Guan, J., Zhang, W., Gu, J., Ren, H.: No-reference blur assessment based on edge modeling. JVCIR **29**, 1–7 (2015)
5. Guo, D., et al.: DeepSeek-R1: incentivizing reasoning capability in LLMs via reinforcement learning. arXiv preprint arXiv:2501.12948 (2025)

6. Guo, S., Guo, J., Wang, H., Wang, H., Huang, X., Zhang, L.: An efficient ophthalmic disease QA system integrated with knowledge graphs and digital humans. In: 2024 ICICSP, pp. 1094–1098. IEEE (2024)
7. Hao, H., et al.: Boosting large language model for speech synthesis: an empirical study. In: ICASSP, pp. 1–5. IEEE (2025)
8. Hu, L.: Animate anyone: consistent and controllable image-to-video synthesis for character animation. In: CVPR, pp. 8153–8163 (2024)
9. Kerbl, B., Kopanas, G., Leimkühler, T., Drettakis, G.: 3D Gaussian splatting for real-time radiance field rendering. ACM Trans. Graph. **42**(4), 1–139 (2023)
10. Korhonen, J.: Two-level approach for no-reference consumer video quality assessment. IEEE Trans. Image Process. **28**(12), 5923–5938 (2019)
11. Li, B., Zhang, W., Tian, M., Zhai, G., Wang, X.: Blindly assess quality of in-the-wild videos via quality-aware pre-training and motion perception. IEEE TCSVT **32**(9), 5944–5958 (2022)
12. Li, D., Jiang, T., Jiang, M.: Quality assessment of in-the-wild videos. In: ACM MM, pp. 2351–2359 (2019)
13. Li, Y.A., Han, C., Mesgarani, N.: StyleTTS: a style-based generative model for natural and diverse text-to-speech synthesis. IEEE JSTSP (2025)
14. Liu, Z., et al.: Swin transformer: hierarchical vision transformer using shifted windows. In: CVPR, pp. 10012–10022 (2021)
15. Midjourney (2023). https://www.midjourney.com/home
16. Mildenhall, B., Srinivasan, P.P., Tancik, M., Barron, J.T., Ramamoorthi, R., Ng, R.: NeRF: representing scenes as neural radiance fields for view synthesis. Commun. ACM **65**(1), 99–106 (2021)
17. Mittal, A., Moorthy, A.K., Bovik, A.C.: No-reference image quality assessment in the spatial domain. IEEE TIP **21**(12), 4695–4708 (2012)
18. Mittal, A., Saad, M.A., Bovik, A.C.: A completely blind video integrity oracle. IEEE Trans. Image Process. **25**(1), 289–300 (2015)
19. Mittal, A., Soundararajan, R., Bovik, A.C.: Making a "completely blind" image quality analyzer. IEEE SPL **20**(3), 209–212 (2012)
20. OpenAI (2024). https://openai.com/index/hello-gpt-4o/
21. OpenDalleV1.1 (2023). https://huggingface.co/dataautogpt3/OpenDalleV1.1
22. Podell, D., et al.: SDXL: improving latent diffusion models for high-resolution image synthesis. arXiv preprint arXiv:2307.01952 (2023)
23. Prajwal, K., Mukhopadhyay, R., Namboodiri, V.P., Jawahar, C.: A lip sync expert is all you need for speech to lip generation in the wild. In: ACM MM, pp. 484–492 (2020)
24. Saad, M.A., Bovik, A.C., Charrier, C.: Blind prediction of natural video quality. IEEE TIP (2014)
25. Shan, Y., Wang, S., Zhang, Z., Huang, K.: An XT slice based method for action recognition. In: 2011 ICCV Workshops, pp. 1897–1903. IEEE (2011)
26. Sun, W., Min, X., Lu, W., Zhai, G.: A deep learning based no-reference quality assessment model for UGC videos. In: ACM MM, pp. 856–865 (2022)
27. Tong, Z., Li, C., Chen, Z., Wu, B., Zhou, W.: MusePose: a pose-driven image-to-video framework for virtual human generation. arxiv (2024)
28. Tu, Z., Wang, Y., Birkbeck, N., Adsumilli, B., Bovik, A.C.: UGC-VQA: benchmarking blind video quality assessment for user generated content. IEEE TIP **30**, 4449–4464 (2021)
29. Tu, Z., Yu, X., Wang, Y., Birkbeck, N., Adsumilli, B., Bovik, A.C.: RAPIQUE: rapid and accurate video quality prediction of user generated content. IEEE OJSP **2**, 425–440 (2021)

30. Wang, S., Li, L., Ding, Y., Fan, C., Yu, X.: Audio2head: audio-driven one-shot talking-head generation with natural head motion. arXiv preprint arXiv:2107.09293 (2021)
31. Wu, H., et al.: Fast-VQA: efficient end-to-end video quality assessment with fragment sampling. In: European Conference on Computer Vision, pp. 538–554 (2022)
32. Yang, J., Abdel-Malek, K., Farrell, K., Nebel, K.: The IOWA interactive digital-human virtual environment. In: ASME International Mechanical Engineering Congress and Exposition, vol. 47136, pp. 1059–1067 (2004)
33. Zhang, L., Zhang, L., Bovik, A.C.: A feature-enriched completely blind image quality evaluator. IEEE TIP **24**(8), 2579–2591 (2015)
34. Zhang, W., et al.: SadTalker: learning realistic 3d motion coefficients for stylized audio-driven single image talking face animation. In: CVPR, pp. 8652–8661 (2023)
35. Zhang, Y., et al.: MimicMotion: high-quality human motion video generation with confidence-aware pose guidance. arXiv preprint arXiv:2406.19680 (2024)
36. Zhang, Z., et al.: GMS-3DQA: projection-based grid mini-patch sampling for 3D model quality assessment. ACM TOMM **20**(6), 1–19 (2024)
37. Zhang, Z., et al.: Advancing zero-shot digital human quality assessment through text-prompted evaluation. arXiv preprint arXiv:2307.02808 (2023)
38. Zhang, Z., et al.: A reduced-reference quality assessment metric for textured mesh digital humans. In: ICASSP, pp. 2965–2969. IEEE (2024)
39. Zhang, Z., et al.: DDH-QA: a dynamic digital humans quality assessment database. In: ICME, pp. 2519–2524. IEEE (2023)
40. Zhang, Z., Zhou, Y., Sun, W., Min, X., Wu, Y., Zhai, G.: Perceptual quality assessment for digital human heads. In: ICASSP, pp. 1–5. IEEE (2023)
41. Zhang, Z., Zhou, Y., Sun, W., Min, X., Zhai, G.: Geometry-aware video quality assessment for dynamic digital human. In: ICIP, pp. 1365–1369. IEEE (2023)
42. Zhang, Z., et al.: Quality-of-experience evaluation for digital twins in 6g network environments. IEEE Trans. Broadcast. (2024)
43. Zhou, Y., Chen, Y., Bi, K., Xiong, L., Liu, H.: An implementation of multimodal fusion system for intelligent digital human generation. arXiv preprint arXiv:2310.20251 (2023)
44. Zhou, Y., et al.: Memo-bench: a multiple benchmark for text-to-image and multimodal large language models on human emotion analysis. arXiv preprint arXiv:2411.11235 (2024)
45. Zhou, Y., et al.: Who is a better imitator: subjective and objective quality assessment of animated humans. TCSVT (2025)
46. Zhou, Y., et al.: THQA: a perceptual quality assessment database for talking heads. arXiv preprint arXiv:2404.09003 (2024)
47. Zhou, Y., Zhang, Z., Sun, W., Liu, X., Min, X., Zhai, G.: Subjective and objective quality-of-experience assessment for 3D talking heads. In: ACM MM 2024 (2024)
48. Zhou, Y., Zhang, Z., Sun, W., Min, X., Ma, X., Zhai, G.: A no-reference quality assessment method for digital human head. In: ICIP, pp. 36–40. IEEE (2023)
49. Zhou, Y., et al.: 3DGCQA: a quality assessment database for 3D AI-generated contents. arXiv preprint arXiv:2409.07236 (2024)
50. Zhou, Y., et al.: ReLI-QA: a multidimensional quality assessment dataset for relighted human heads. In: VCIP (2024)

Dual-Chain Reasoning: Enhancing Multimodal Document VQA Through Positive and Negative Reasoning Paths

Yiyuan Zhang[1,3,4], Hanxiao Wu[2,3,4], Zhaopeng Gu[1,3,4], Dong Yi[1], Guibo Zhu[1,3,4(✉)], and Jinqiao Wang[1,3,4]

[1] School of Artificial Intelligence, University of Chinese Academy of Sciences, Beijing, China
gbzhu@nlpr.ia.ac.cn
[2] School of Computer Science and Artificial Intelligence, Wuhan University of Technology, Wuhan, China
[3] Institute of Automation, Chinese Academy of Sciences, Beijing, China
[4] Wuhan AI Research, Wuhan, China

Abstract. While Multimodal Large Language Models excel at many reasoning tasks, they face limitations in complex scenarios due to reasoning path divergence and cognitive overload. Current approaches predominantly focus on strengthening correct reasoning pathways while overlooking the critical need to identify and rectify erroneous ones. We introduce the Dual-Chain Reasoning (DCR) framework, a metacognition-inspired approach that addresses these fundamental challenges through two synergistic reasoning chains. The positive chain performs hierarchical task decomposition, systematically breaking down complex problems into manageable components. Simultaneously, the negative chain actively identifies error patterns and corrects logical fallacies, creating a comprehensive verification system. This bidirectional architecture enables iterative optimization through continuous cognitive verification, allowing the model to refine its reasoning process dynamically. Experimental results on ScienceQA and DocVQA benchmarks demonstrate DCR's effectiveness, achieving accuracy improvements of 2.42% and 1.28% respectively over baseline models.

Keywords: Supervised Fine-tuning · Chain-of-Thought · Dual-Chain Reasoning · Neuroplasticity

1 Introduction

Multimodal Visual Question Answering (VQA) has emerged as a cornerstone challenge in Artificial Intelligence, demanding seamless integration of visual and textual information as well as robust multimodal reasoning. This challenge is particularly prominent in advanced reasoning-capable Large Language Models (LLMs) such as Deepseek-R1 [7], OpenAI GPT-4o [1], and Gemini [20], which

© The Author(s), under exclusive license to Springer Nature Singapore Pte Ltd. 2026

Z. Lin et al. (Eds.): ICIG 2025, LNCS 16163, pp. 27–39, 2026.
https://doi.org/10.1007/978-981-95-3729-7_3

are designed to tackle with complex problems involving mathematics, logic, and visual understanding through step-by-step reasoning. Despite impressive progress, state-of-the-art systems [1,7,20] continue to face persistent challenges, including visual hallucinations, path-dependent biases, and cognitive overload in complex reasoning workflows that critically hinder interpretability and overall task performance.

Although reasoning-centric LLMs [7] have made rapid progress in unimodal tasks, extending their capabilities to multimodal VQA remains highly challenging. Existing Visual Language Models (VLMs) [12,21] often exhibit insufficient performance on multimodal logical reasoning tasks, particularly in chart-based VQA, where the model must accurately interpret complex tables, charts, and accompanying textual descriptions to draw correct inferences. A major limitation lies in their difficulty understanding intricate visual structures, such as nested tables and multidimensional plots, which significantly impairs their ability to perform precise reasoning in such tasks.

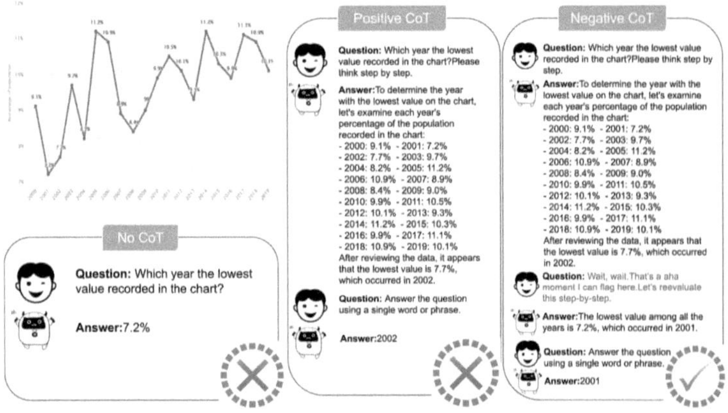

Fig. 1. Introduction to Positive Chain and Negative Chain.

In the context of complex chart understanding tasks, models often encounter three core challenges that significantly hinder accurate reasoning: visual hallucinations, path dependence, and cognitive overload. Visual hallucinations arise when a model generates responses that are not grounded in the actual visual input. Path dependence refers to the model's tendency to overly rely on initial reasoning steps, which can propagate early mistakes and derail subsequent inference. Cognitive overload occurs when models are overwhelmed by dense or multidimensional visual data, impairing their ability to extract and prioritize task-relevant information. Recent methodologies such as Chain-of-Thought (CoT) prompting and contrastive learning have introduced structured reasoning processes and discriminative representation learning, offering partial relief. While effective in reinforcing coherent reasoning paths, these methods largely focus on amplifying correct inference trajectories, often neglecting the detection and correction of erroneous ones. This critical limitation leaves models vulnerable to subtle reasoning fallacies, where outputs may appear superficially plausible yet remain logically unsound, ultimately compromising their reliability in real-world applications.

Inspired by cognitive science principles, we propose the Dual-Chain Reasoning (DCR) framework to address these document VQA challenges. DCR explicitly integrates both success-driven and failure-aware learning paradigms, encouraging models to dynamically contrast correct and flawed reasoning trajectories. As show in Fig. 1, in the positive chain the model provides incorrect reasoning paths and results, but in the negative chain, the model not only corrects the incorrect paths but also obtains the correct results. By doing so, the framework fosters metacognitive capabilities that enable autonomous evaluation, critique, and refinement of intermediate inference steps. Additionally, DCR incorporates adaptive cognitive load balancing and self-corrective feedback loops to emulate human-like error resilience while enhancing multimodal reasoning accuracy. Empirical evaluations demonstrate the effectiveness of DCR, which achieves performance gains of 2.42% on ScienceQA and 1.28% on DocVQA, highlighting its strength in complex, knowledge-intensive multimodal reasoning tasks. To better understand the contributions of individual components within the DCR framework, we also conduct extensive ablation studies across various document-based VQA benchmarks. Our contributions are listed as follows:

1) We introduce both positive and negative CoT prompting in document VQA tasks to form a bidirectional reasoning process that enhances robustness and accuracy.
2) DCR demonstrates the neural plasticity effect in LLMs, where reinforcing erroneous reasoning paths leads to measurable performance degradation, underscoring the importance of failure-aware mechanisms.
3) By extending evaluations from document-based QA to broader domains such as scientific QA and geometric reasoning, we observe that increased dataset diversity significantly enhances the model's generalization and adaptability.

2   Related Work

2.1   Document VQA and Multimodal Reasoning

Document Visual Question Answering (VQA), a more complex subset of VQA tasks requires models to jointly reason over textual content, layout, and visual cues in document images. This has made it a prominent research area in multimodal reasoning. State-of-the-art multimodal large language models (MLLMs) typically consist of a visual encoder, a large language model (LLM), and a visual-language projector. These models have demonstrated strong performance across a variety of vision-language tasks, including image segmentation, anomaly detection, and VQA. Several influential architectures have emerged. For example, BLIP [11] introduces a unified vision-language pretraining framework using a multimodal encoder-decoder structure, along with synthetic caption generation and filtering for learning from noisy web-scale image-text pairs. LLaVA [12] combines a visual encoder with the Vicuna LLM to form a general-purpose vision-language assistant, capable of complex multimodal reasoning and achieving state-of-the-art performance on tasks such as science-related VQA.

These approaches reflect the diversity of strategies in multimodal understanding, requiring both general-purpose vision-language pretraining and domain-specific adaptations for documents. Recently, researchers have incorporated Chain-of-Thought (CoT) prompting [5] into vision-language models to enhance multi-step reasoning.

Despite these advances, significant challenges remain. Traditional CoT approaches typically produce a single reasoning path, neglecting the diversity of human-like cognitive processes and limiting the exploration of alternative reasoning strategies. Moreover, current multimodal CoT systems often lack flexibility, generalizability, and interpretability. In addition, the absence of mechanisms to guide and evaluate incorrect reasoning chains increases the risk of reinforcing biases and faulty inferences. Furthermore, recent work on grounded CoT in multimodal LLMs [23] has identified the issue of visual hallucination, where generated answers deviate from the actual visual content, underscoring ongoing challenges in cross-modal alignment and stable reasoning.

To address these issues, we propose a novel collaborative reasoning framework incorporating both positive and negative chains for document VQA tasks. We design a Dual-Chain model, in which the positive chain performs conventional reasoning while the negative chain conducts counterexample-based analysis.

2.2 Reflection and Self-correction in LLMs

Chain-of-Thought (CoT) is a step-by-step reasoning strategy that significantly enhances the problem-solving capabilities of large language models (LLMs) by introducing intermediate reasoning steps prior to answer generation. For instance, Self-Consistency [22] proposes a self-consistency decoding strategy, in which multiple reasoning paths are sampled to select the most consistent final answer. Empirical studies [17] have further demonstrated that when LLMs are prompted to reflect on incorrect answers and suggest improvements, their performance on multiple-choice questions improves significantly. Iterative feedback and self-critique mechanisms have also been shown to enhance the accuracy of model outputs. These findings suggest that LLMs exhibit a degree of self-correction ability, as they can recognize and amend logical or computational flaws in their own reasoning processes, thereby reducing the likelihood of severe errors.

However, most prior work on CoT and self-correction strategies has been primarily focused on purely textual tasks. More recently, researchers have begun to explore the adaptation of CoT reasoning and self-correction mechanisms to multimodal reasoning scenarios. Structured CoT methods have been introduced into VQA.

Previous studies highlight the potential of CoT and self-correction strategies in large multimodal models, where diversified reasoning paths and internal review mechanisms not only improve transparency but also enhance the robustness and accuracy of multimodal reasoning.

2.3 Neuroplasticity and Path Dependence

Path-dependence theory further elucidates how early-formed cognitive pathways exert long-term influence over decision-making. As specific reasoning routes are repeatedly utilized, their activation thresholds are lowered, making the brain increasingly reliant on these familiar pathways when encountering similar problems. This feedback loop can lead to mental rigidity and resistance to novel approaches.

Analogous phenomena have been observed in artificial neural networks. Inspired by biological synaptic plasticity, [2] proposes a dynamic memory pathway reinforcement mechanism, allowing LLMs to incrementally strengthen memory traces relevant to the current context during both training and inference. However, this mechanism introduces a potential risk: if erroneous reasoning paths are reinforced repeatedly, it may result in a form of plasticity loss. Recent research has shown that conventional deep neural networks are vulnerable to such degradation, particularly in continual learning settings.

Integrating insights from neuroscience, particularly theories of memory consolidation and pathway reinforcement, can deepen our understanding of the reasoning dynamics in large-scale models. Research in reinforcement learning and human cognition emphasizes the role of pathway reinforcement in memory retention, while plasticity loss theory underscores the dangers of overcommitting to a single solution pathway. In this context, we analogize the reasoning process of LLMs to that of biological neural systems and propose the introduction of negative CoT reasoning as a hedging strategy against the over-reinforcement of erroneous cognitive routes.

3 Method

3.1 Dual-Chain Collaborative Reasoning Framework

In multimodal image-text question answering tasks, models must exhibit strong reasoning capabilities to comprehend and respond to complex questions effectively. However, current visual language models often struggle with document and chart-based reasoning tasks due to their limited ability to accurately interpret complex visual structures.

To address these challenges and enhance both reasoning performance and generalization capabilities, we propose a novel Dual-Chain Collaborative Reasoning Framework. This framework introduces a synergistic mechanism of positive and negative reasoning chains, enabling the model to evaluate answers through bidirectional, contrastive inference pathways.

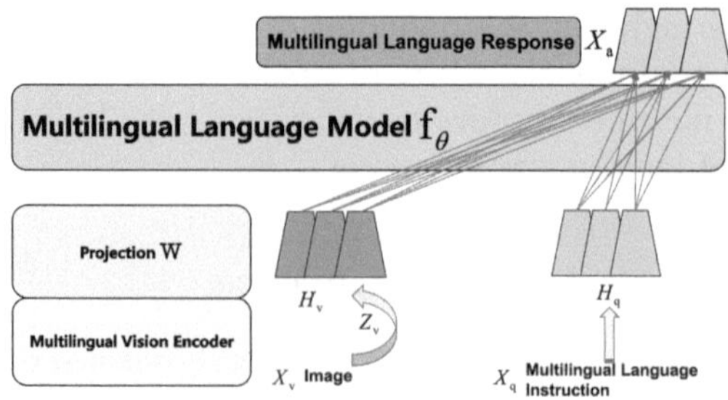

Fig. 2. Dual-Chain Architecture adapted from LLaVA.

As show in Fig. 2, our approach builds upon the LLaVA 1.5 architecture. Specifically, for each input image X_v, a visual encoder is employed to extract visual features Z_v, which are subsequently linearly projected into the language embedding space via a learnable transformation matrix W, yielding multimodal representations. These embeddings are then integrated into the language model for downstream reasoning and answer generation.

3.2   Design of Positive and Negative Chains

In the Dual-Chain Collaborative Reasoning Framework, the positive and negative chains serve complementary functions. The positive chain is responsible for generating coherent reasoning trajectories and plausible answers, while the negative chain is designed to identify and correct flawed reasoning paths. By integrating these two components in a unified framework on the dataset shown in Table 1, our approach substantially enhances the model's reasoning capacity and generalization performance, enabling more robust and interpretable multimodal inference.

Table 1. Instruction-following Data Mixture.

Task	Dataset
General VQA	VQAv2 [6], GQA [8]
Document	DocVQA [16]
OCR	InfoVQA [15], TextVQA [19]
Math	GeoQA+ [3], CLEVER-Math [9]
Chart	ChartQA [14]
ScienceQA	AI2D [10], ScienceQA [18], M3CoT [4]

Positive Chain. The positive chain takes an input image and its corresponding natural language question and sequentially generates a step-by-step reasoning trajectory. In document VQA tasks, the model is required to progressively infer relevant information and appropriate processing strategies based on the question context. Through this incremental reasoning process, a series of intermediate conclusions are produced, ultimately leading to the final answer.

Negative Chain. To construct the negative chain, we adopt a dual strategy depending on the availability of explicit ground-truth answers. For samples with explicitly annotated correct answers, we employ a correctness-based sampling pipeline: multiple candidate reasoning paths are generated, and those aligned with the ground-truth answer are retained as positive samples, while those that diverge are treated as negative samples.

To simulate a cognitive "correction" moment, we append a predefined re-evaluation prompt: *Wait, wait. That is an aha moment I can flag here. Let us reevaluate this step-by-step.* at the end of negative samples. This interrupts the faulty reasoning and cues the model to generate a corrected, positive reasoning chain. This strategy encourages the model to identify, reflect on, and amend its own reasoning errors, enhancing its self-correction abilities and improving overall prediction accuracy.

The positive and negative chains play complementary roles in the Dual-Chain Collaborative Reasoning Framework. While the positive chain focuses on generating coherent and accurate reasoning processes, the negative chain emphasizes the detection and correction of faulty reasoning. By organically integrating both chains, our framework significantly strengthens the model's reasoning capabilities and generalization performance, particularly in complex VQA tasks.

4   Experiment

4.1   Experimental Setup

To evaluate the effectiveness and generalization ability of the proposed Dual-Chain Reasoning Framework, we conducted experiments on a variety of document and science question answering datasets. Specifically, we used DocVQA and InfographicVQA, both of which contain thousands of document and infographic images annotated with natural language questions and corresponding answers, as well as the ScienceQA dataset, which includes approximately 21,000 multimodal, cross-disciplinary science questions, each accompanied by detailed explanations and answer choices. As a strong baseline, we adopted the LLaVA model, which combines a CLIP-based vision encoder with the Vicuna language model and achieves a benchmark accuracy of 66.8% on ScienceQA. To ensure consistency and fair comparison, we unified the model architecture across all experiments by using CLIP-ViT-L/14 as the visual encoder and Vicuna-7B as the language model, and applied end-to-end fine-tuning under the same set of hyperparameters across all datasets. This standardized experimental setting shown in Table 2 enables a rigorous and reliable assessment of the performance gains introduced by our Dual-Chain framework.

Table 2. Hyperparameters are the same as the original LLaVA

Hyperparameter	Pretrain	Finetune
batch size	256	128
weight decay	0	0
epoch	1	1
learning rate	1e−3	2e−5
lr schedule	cosine decay	cosine decay
lr warmup ratio	0.03	0.03
Optimizer	AdamW	AdamW
DeepSpeed stage	2	3

4.2   Main Results

In the control experiments, we compared the proposed Dual-Chain model against several benchmarks, including the standard LLaVA 1.5-7B model (which utilizes only a positive reasoning chain) and variants augmented with different proportions of negative chain instances. For document-related question answering tasks, we adopted the Average Normalized Levenshtein Similarity (ANLS) metric, which is designed to evaluate string-level prediction accuracy based on tree-structured matching.

Formally, the ANLS* metric between a ground-truth string g and a predicted string p is computed by normalizing a Levenshtein-based similarity score. Let $s(g,p)$ denote the raw similarity, defined as the difference between the maximum possible edit distance score and the actual Levenshtein distance, and let $l(g,p) = \max(|g|, |p|)$ denote the length of the longer string. The normalized score is given by:

$$\text{ANLS}^*(g,p) = \frac{s(g,p)}{l(g,p)}, \tag{1}$$

which yields a length-invariant similarity score in the range $[0,1]$. A value of 1 indicates an exact match, while scores closer to 0 reflect increasingly dissimilar or error-prone predictions. This normalization not only facilitates fair comparisons across answers of varying lengths but also introduces a smooth penalty mechanism that is tolerant to minor transcription or OCR errors, making it particularly well-suited for document question answering tasks.

For science question answering tasks such as ScienceQA, answer accuracy is adopted as the primary evaluation metric. The Accuracy (ACC) metric measures the overall correctness of the model's predictions by comparing the number of correct predictions to the total number of instances. Specifically, let TP and TN represent the counts of true positives and true negatives, respectively, while FP and FN denote the counts of false positives and false negatives. The accuracy is then computed as:

$$\text{ACC} = \frac{TP + TN}{TP + TN + FP + FN} \tag{2}$$

This score yields a value in the range $[0, 1]$, where 1 denotes perfect prediction alignment with the ground truth (i.e., all answers are correct), and 0 indicates that none of the model's predictions are correct. Accuracy is a straightforward and interpretable metric, making it particularly suitable for evaluating multiple-choice science questions where answers are discrete and unambiguous.

Table 3. Fine-tuning the LLaVA model using Dual-Chain.

Model	DocVQA	InfoVQA	ChartQA	TextVQA
Dinov2	8.20	19.70	12.00	15.10
SigLIP	16.90	20.70	14.40	44.10
BLIP2-OPT-6.7B	3.20	11.30	3.40	23.50
InstructBLIP	4.50	16.40	5.30	29.10
LLaVA 1.5-7B LoRA	19.14	18.18	17.56	**54.69**
LLaVA 1.5-7B LoRA + Positive Chain	18.51	18.54	15.80	52.50
LLaVA 1.5-7B LoRA + Negative Chain	**19.16**	**18.79**	**17.64**	52.98

As show in Table 3, the LLaVA 1.5-7B LoRA model exhibits excellent performance in all tasks after adding positive or negative chains, especially in DocVQA and TextVQA, highlighting the effectiveness of its multimodal inference method. Although BLIP2-OPT-6B performs relatively weakly in tasks such as DocVQA, it may still demonstrate its value in other areas such as ChartQA. The negative chain configuration brings the most significant performance improvement, which may be due to its focus on error correction and optimization of the inference process, making it a robust solution for complex inference tasks.

4.3   Ablation Experiments

To investigate the individual contributions of the positive and negative reasoning chains, we designed the following ablation studies: (1) retaining only the positive reasoning chain; (2) retaining only the negative reasoning chain; and (3) retaining the complete Dual-Chain structure. Experimental results demonstrate that the Dual-Chain model consistently outperforms either single-chain variant across all evaluated tasks. Specifically, the positive chain ensures the generation of accurate answers, while the negative chain plays a crucial role in identifying and correcting potential biases, thereby preventing the model from becoming trapped in erroneous reasoning paths. The complementary interaction between the positive and negative chains enables the model to achieve a more robust understanding and improved question answering performance.

The correctness indicator function used to evaluate prediction accuracy is defined as follows:

$$\text{Correct}(y, \hat{y}) = \begin{cases} 1, & \text{if } \left| \dfrac{y - \hat{y}}{y} \right| \leq \delta, \\ 0, & \text{otherwise.} \end{cases} \tag{3}$$

where y denotes the ground-truth value, $\hat{y}$ is the predicted value, and δ is a predefined tolerance threshold.

To accommodate minor discrepancies in numerical predictions, we adopt the Quantitative Accuracy (QA) metric in Table 4 following TextMonkey [13], a relaxed accuracy measure that considers a prediction correct if it lies within a specified relative tolerance of the ground-truth value. This metric is widely used in visual question answering tasks involving numeric reasoning, such as ChartQA and DocVQA, effectively mitigating the impact of floating-point errors or rounding inconsistencies.

Table 4. Fine-tuning the LLaVA model using Dual-Chain.

Model	DocVQA	InfoVQA	ChartQA	TextVQA
BLIP2-OPT-6.7B	3.2	11.3	3.4	23.5
InstructBLIP	4.5	16.4	5.3	29.1
LLaVAR	12.3	16.5	12.2	41.8
BLIVA	5.8	23.6	5.3	8.7
UniDoc	7.7	14.7	10.9	46.2
mPLUG-Owl	7.4	20.0	7.9	34.0
TGDoc	9.0	12.8	12.7	46.2
LLaVA 1.5-7B LoRA	6.8	12.4	6.8	34.0
LLaVA 1.5-7B LoRA with Positive Chain	7.6	12.9	6.6	36.9
LLaVA 1.5-7B LoRA with Negative Chain	8.1	**14.9**	**8.4**	**37.7**

Additionally, as show in Table 5, we performed a simulation experiment on negative reasoning chain reinforcement by repeatedly training the model on samples containing incorrect answers. The results revealed that as the frequency of reinforcement on the negative reasoning chain increased, the model's performance on correctly answered tasks gradually deteriorated. This observation aligns with the phenomenon of plasticity loss in deep learning, supporting the hypothesis that excessive reinforcement of erroneous reasoning pathways can lead to performance degradation.

The underlying learning mechanism of the brain is grounded in neuroplasticity, which describes the strengthening of neural connections through repeated behaviors or thought processes. Analogously, if erroneous behaviors are repeatedly reinforced, the brain may consolidate these error-prone patterns rather

Table 5. Fine-tune the LLaVA model using different proportions of Dual-Chain.

Model	DocVQA	InfoVQA	ChartQA	TextVQA
LLaVA 1.5-7B LoRA	6.8	12.4	6.8	34.0
LoRA with 1 Positive and 1 Negative Chain	9.8	15.3	8.9	**37.6**
LoRA with 1 Positive and 2 Negative Chain	**10.4**	**16.9**	**9.2**	37.2
LoRA with 1 Positive and 3 Negative Chain	9.1	15.6	8.5	36.8

than the correct ones. This phenomenon closely corresponds to path dependence observed in model training. Our experiments further indicate that when the volume of erroneous examples surpasses the model's cognitive load threshold, the model, which is much like humans, struggles to effectively extract key discriminative features. These findings underscore the necessity of balancing the quantity of positive and negative reasoning chains during training to avoid cognitive overload and the consequent decline in reasoning capability.

5   Conclusion and Future Outlooks

The Dual-Chain collaborative reasoning framework proposed in this paper effectively mitigates reasoning biases in complex document visual question answering tasks by simultaneously incorporating positive and negative reasoning chains. This parallel architecture significantly enhances the model's generalization capability. Empirical results demonstrate that the Dual-Chain structure consistently outperforms single-chain models across multiple datasets, with observed performance gains underscoring the value of diverse reasoning pathways in improving model robustness. Notably, our study provides the first empirical validation of the "neuroplasticity degradation" phenomenon in large-scale models: repeated reinforcement of erroneous reasoning paths leads to a marked decline in performance. This observation corroborates existing theories of neuroplasticity loss in both neuroscience and deep learning, thereby offering novel insights into the intersection of cognitive processes and computational modeling.

Acknowledgement. This work was supported in part by the National Key R&D Program of China (No. 2022AD0160601), in part by Guangdong Provincial Key Laboratory of Intellectual Property and Big Data under Grant 2018B030322016, and National Natural Science Foundation of China (No. 62276260, 6207625, 62176254, 62472423).

References

1. Achiam, J., et al.: GPT-4 technical report. arXiv preprint arXiv:2303.08774 (2023)
2. Applegarth, G., Weatherstone, C., Hollingsworth, M., Middlebrook, H., Irvin, M.: Exploring synaptic resonance in large language models: a novel approach to contextual memory integration. arXiv preprint arXiv:2502.10699 (2025)

3. Cao, J., Xiao, J.: An augmented benchmark dataset for geometric question answering through dual parallel text encoding. In: Proceedings of the 29th International Conference on Computational Linguistics, pp. 1511–1520 (2022)
4. Chen, Q., Qin, L., Zhang, J., Chen, Z., Xu, X., Che, W.: M^{3}cot: a novel benchmark for multi-domain multi-step multi-modal chain-of-thought. arXiv preprint arXiv:2405.16473 (2024)
5. Ge, J., Luo, H., Qian, S., Gan, Y., Fu, J., Zhang, S.: Chain of thought prompt tuning in vision language models. arXiv preprint arXiv:2304.07919 (2023)
6. Goyal, Y., Khot, T., Summers-Stay, D., Batra, D., Parikh, D.: Making the V in VQA matter: elevating the role of image understanding in visual question answering. In: Proceedings of the IEEE Conference on Computer Vision and Pattern Recognition, pp. 6904–6913 (2017)
7. Guo, D., et al.: DeepSeek-R1: incentivizing reasoning capability in LLMs via reinforcement learning. arXiv preprint arXiv:2501.12948 (2025)
8. Hudson, D.A., Manning, C.D.: GQA: a new dataset for real-world visual reasoning and compositional question answering. In: Proceedings of the IEEE/CVF Conference on Computer Vision and Pattern Recognition, pp. 6700–6709 (2019)
9. Johnson, J., Hariharan, B., Van Der Maaten, L., Fei-Fei, L., Lawrence Zitnick, C., Girshick, R.: CLEVR: a diagnostic dataset for compositional language and elementary visual reasoning. In: Proceedings of the IEEE Conference on Computer Vision and Pattern Recognition, pp. 2901–2910 (2017)
10. Kembhavi, A., Salvato, M., Kolve, E., Seo, M., Hajishirzi, H., Farhadi, A.: A diagram is worth a dozen images. In: Leibe, B., Matas, J., Sebe, N., Welling, M. (eds.) ECCV 2016, Part IV. LNCS, vol. 9908, pp. 235–251. Springer, Cham (2016). https://doi.org/10.1007/978-3-319-46493-0_15
11. Li, J., Li, D., Xiong, C., Hoi, S.: BLIP: bootstrapping language-image pre-training for unified vision-language understanding and generation. In: International Conference on Machine Learning, pp. 12888–12900. PMLR (2022)
12. Liu, H., Li, C., Wu, Q., Lee, Y.J.: Visual instruction tuning. Adv. Neural. Inf. Process. Syst. **36**, 34892–34916 (2023)
13. Liu, Y., et al.: TextMonkey: an OCR-free large multimodal model for understanding document. arXiv preprint arXiv:2403.04473 (2024)
14. Masry, A., Long, D.X., Tan, J.Q., Joty, S., Hoque, E.: ChartQA: a benchmark for question answering about charts with visual and logical reasoning. arXiv preprint arXiv:2203.10244 (2022)
15. Mathew, M., Bagal, V., Tito, R., Karatzas, D., Valveny, E., Jawahar, C.: InfographicVQA. In: Proceedings of the IEEE/CVF Winter Conference on Applications of Computer Vision, pp. 1697–1706 (2022)
16. Mathew, M., Karatzas, D., Jawahar, C.: DocVQA: a dataset for VQA on document images. In: Proceedings of the IEEE/CVF Winter Conference on Applications of Computer Vision, pp. 2200–2209 (2021)
17. Renze, M., Guven, E.: Self-reflection in LLM agents: effects on problem-solving performance. arXiv preprint arXiv:2405.06682 (2024)
18. Saikh, T., Ghosal, T., Mittal, A., Ekbal, A., Bhattacharyya, P.: ScienceQA: a novel resource for question answering on scholarly articles. Int. J. Digit. Libr. **23**(3), 289–301 (2022)
19. Singh, A., et al.: Towards VQA models that can read. In: Proceedings of the IEEE/CVF Conference on Computer Vision and Pattern Recognition, pp. 8317–8326 (2019)
20. Team, G., et al.: Gemini: a family of highly capable multimodal models. arXiv preprint arXiv:2312.11805 (2023)

21. Wang, W., et al.: VisionLLM: large language model is also an open-ended decoder
    for vision-centric tasks. Adv. Neural. Inf. Process. Syst. **36**, 61501–61513 (2023)
22. Wang, X., et al.: Self-consistency improves chain of thought reasoning in language
    models. arXiv preprint arXiv:2203.11171 (2022)
23. Wu, Q., et al.: Grounded chain-of-thought for multimodal large language models.
    arXiv preprint arXiv:2503.12799 (2025)

Enhanced Multi-scale Hierarchical Network for Micro-expression Recognition

Yee Hwai Yip[1] and Junlin Hu[1,2(✉)]

[1] School of Software, Beihang University, Beijing, China
`{riveryip,hujunlin}@buaa.edu.cn`
[2] Engineering Research Center of Integration and Application of Digital Learning Technology, Ministry of Education, Beijing, China

Abstract. Facial expressions are a complex form of biological motion involving dynamic configurations of facial muscle movements that encode affective states, cognitive processes, and social intentions. Micro-expressions as a subset of facial expressions are particularly valuable for emotion analysis due to their involuntary nature, brief duration, and high truthfulness. This paper proposes an Enhanced Multi-scale Hierarchical Network (EMHNet) for micro-expression recognition. Our architecture introduces a Hierarchical Mixture of Experts (HMoE) system employing specialized transformers for four critical facial regions coupled with a global transformer for holistic integration and an adaptive multi-scale framework featuring dynamic block partitioning and cross-scale attention gates for optimized feature extraction. Experimental evaluation is performed on SMIC, CASME II and SAMM benchmarks and a composite dataset of the three datasets. Experimental results show that our proposed EMHNet achieves competitive performance compared to existing state-of-the-art methods, demonstrating its effectiveness.

Keywords: micro expressions · hierarchical Transformer · multi-scale feature · mixture of experts

1 Introduction

Micro-expressions [3] are brief and subtle facial expressions, typically lasting between 1/25 to 1/5 of a second. Unlike macro-expressions, micro-expressions often reveal a person's genuine emotions and intentions more accurately. This makes them highly valuable for practical applications including clinical therapy, human-computer interaction, consumer behaviour analysis and national security. In recent years, significant studies have focused on computer vision-based methods for micro-expression analysis. To date, micro-expression research has reached a milestone where existing approaches have achieved near-saturated performance on the existing benchmark datasets. However, micro-expression recognition remains challenging due to the inherently low-intensity and short-duration nature of micro expression, making it difficult to learn discriminative and generalizable features from limited annotated datasets.

© The Author(s), under exclusive license to Springer Nature Singapore Pte Ltd. 2026
Z. Lin et al. (Eds.): ICIG 2025, LNCS 16163, pp. 40–51, 2026.
https://doi.org/10.1007/978-981-95-3729-7_4

Early research in micro-expression recognition mainly relies on handcrafted feature extraction methods. Local binary patterns [20] were widely adopted for their computational efficiency and discriminative texture-based features. On the other hand, optical flow (OF) [7] methods, such as bi-weighted oriented optical flow [16], main directional mean optical flow [17] and fuzzy histogram of optical flow orientations [9] leveraged inter-frame brightness variations to model subtle facial motions. However, these approaches faced inherent limitations as handcrafted feature design may lead to suboptimal performance if the selected features fail to capture discriminative micro-expression characteristics. To overcome this limitation, recent studies have introduced end-to-end deep learning methods [14] as a powerful alternative to traditional approaches, achieving promising results in micro-expression recognition. For instance, Kim et al. [11] developed a micro-expression recognition framework that combines convolutional neural networks for spatial feature extraction with long short-term memory networks for temporal modeling. Xie et al. [25] introduced an AU-assisted graph attention convolutional network (GACN) which utilizes facial action units (AUs) as prior knowledge to guide graph attention learning for micro-expression recognition. While GACN improved localization accuracy, its reliance on expensive AU annotations and rigid graph structures limited its generalizability. Fan et al. [5] introduced a vision Transformer (ViT) framework to address the small-data challenge of micro-expression recognition via transferable multi-scale attention features. However, vanilla transformers remain computationally intensive and fail to specialize attention for critical facial regions. Wang et al. [24] proposed a hierarchical transformer network (HTNet) that addresses micro-expression recognition by dividing the face into four muscle-specific regions for localizing self-attention and aggregating local-to-global semantic features. However, HTNet shares a single transformer across all regions, which cannot effectively model region-specific characteristics, leading to suboptimal feature discrimination. In addition, HTNet relies solely on hierarchical aggregation for multi-scale fusion, resulting in inefficient cross-scale feature enhancement.

In this paper, we present an enhanced multi-scale hierarchical network (EMH-Net) that significantly advances micro-expression recognition. Our contributions can be summarized as: 1) we propose a Hierarchical Mixture of Experts (HMoE) system that deploys specialized expert transformers for four anatomical regions (left eyes, right eyes, left lips and right lips) at fine scales and maintains a shared global transformer at the base level for holistic integration, enabling precise modeling of region-dependent micro-movements; 2) we introduce an enhanced multi-scale feature learning framework that implements dynamic block partitioning and introduces explicit cross-scale attention gates; and 3) extensive experiments on public benchmark datasets demonstrate that our proposed EMHNet method consistently outperforms previous state-of-the-art approaches, which proves that our method is effective for micro-expression recognition task.

2   Related Work

2.1   Traditional Methods for Micro-expression Recognition

Early micro-expression recognition methods primarily utilize traditional hand-crafted features. For the appearance-based method, Zhao et al. [29] proposed the local binary pattern (LBP) from three orthogonal planes algorithm to capture spatiotemporal texture features from video sequences, establishing a foundation for subsequent research. This work inspired more compact and efficient descriptors such as LBP with six intersection points [23] for improving feature discrimination and spatio-temporal completed local quantization patterns [10] for enhancing dynamic texture representation. While these methods effectively extracted spatiotemporal texture changes of micro-expressions, their recognition performances were limited due to inherent sensitivity to illumination variations and inability to capture subtle muscle dynamics.

For the geometric-based method, optical flow techniques emerged as the dominant approach by modeling facing motion through pixel-intensity changes. Liong et al. [16] introduced a bi-weighted oriented optical-flow (BI-WOOF) feature descriptor, which improved recognition accuracy through dual magnitude-orientation weighting. Liu et al. [17] proposed main directional mean optical flow feature for micro-expression recognition by encoding dominant motion patterns through directional averaging. The optical flow map describes facial motion information and improves recognition accuracy. However, these optical flow approaches face critical limitations including high sensitivity to lighting conditions and non-expression motions such as eye blinks and head rotations, along with significant computational demands that hindered real-time applications. These fundamental constraints of both appearance and geometric methods ultimately motivated the field's shift toward deep learning-based approaches for more robust and automated micro-expression recognition.

2.2   Deep Learning Methods for Micro-expression Recognition

Deep learning approaches have achieved remarkable success across various computer vision tasks. Recent studies have shown their great potential for micro-expression recognition through automated learning of discriminative spatiotemporal features from facial expression data. Nevertheless, the scarcity of micro-expression training datasets remains a critical bottleneck in developing robust deep learning-based recognition systems. To address these challenges, Patel et al. [19] introduced an evolutionary algorithm to optimize deep convolutional neural network (CNN) features and enhance feature discriminability. Ayyalasomaya-jula et al. [1] proposed a hybrid framework combining CNN with Eulerian video magnification framework to amplify and analyze subtle facial dynamics characteristic of micro-expressions. Fan et al. [6] introduced self-supervised motion learning for micro-expression recognition that eliminates dependency on traditional optical-flow preprocessing by directly extracting facial motion features through self-supervised learning.

2.3 Transformer Methods for Micro-expression Recognition

Although CNNs have been the cornerstone of computer vision applications such as facial expression detection and classification, the advent of self-attention mechanisms, particularly transformer architectures, has fundamentally transformed the field's methodological landscape. Zhai et al. [27] proposed a feature representation learning framework with adaptive displacement generation and transformer fusion (FRL-DGT), which captures dynamic features through a convolutional displacement generation module (DGM) and further enhances recognition performance via self-supervised learning. Lei et al. [12] proposed an action-unit graph convolutional network (AU-GCN) that combines facial graph representation learning with action unit information to improve understanding of complex facial expressions. Wang et al. [24] designed a hierarchical transformer network (HTNet) for micro-expression recognition, which addresses the limitations of conventional methods in characterizing subtle muscle movements by hierarchically integrating local and global facial features to capture dynamic micro-expression details. However, existing models cannot model region-specific characteristics as they share a single transformer across all regions. In addition, existing models rely solely on hierarchical aggregation for multi-scale fusion and have inefficient cross-scale feature enhancement.

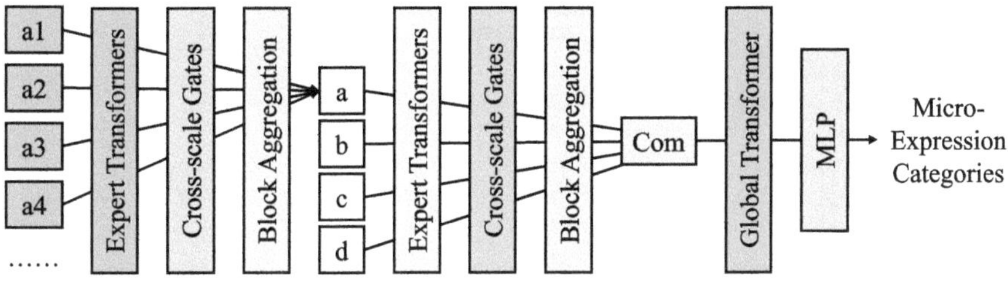

Fig. 1. The overall architecture of our proposed EMHNet method. The expert transformers focus on local features of their corresponding anatomical region. The cross-scale attention gates establish connections between information at different scale. The aggregation blocks is employed to integrate same-level block features. At the beginning of the model, the facial optical flow map is divided into 16 local blocks (marked as a1, a2, a3, a4, b1, ..., b4, c1, ..., c4, d1, ..., d4), and then merged into four anatomical regions (marked as a, b, c, d) which corresponding to four facial areas. "Com" is the combination of the four facial areas.

3 Proposed Method

This section presents our enhanced multi-scale hierarchical network (EMHNet) for micro-expression recognition, which consists of optical flow map extraction, expert transformers, multi-scale gates, and block aggregation at every level of hierarchical structure. Figure 1 shows the overall architecture of our EMHNet. Our EMHNet uses the backbone of HTNet [24] that also serves as the baseline.

3.1   Optical Flow Map Extraction

The optical flow method estimates object motion between consecutive video frames by computing a displacement field that encodes the movement of each pixel. Unlike grayscale images, optical flow maps inherently suppress facial identity features while preserving motion dynamics. This property makes them particularly effective for characterizing subtle facial deformations and transient motion patterns in micro-expressions as they focus exclusively on spatiotemporal changes rather than static appearance. To extract facial-region optical flow features from the full optical flow map, we use multi-task cascaded convolutional networks to detect facial landmarks in the apex frame. Based on these landmarks, we crop four distinct facial optical flow feature maps from the full optical flow map. Each cropped feature map has size of $\frac{W}{2} \times \frac{H}{2} \times 3$, where W and H are the weight and height of the frame respectively, corresponding to half the spatial resolution of the original optical flow image. After extraction, we concatenate these four feature maps and input the combined representation into EMHNet for micro-expression recognition. Figure 2 shows the optical flow feature extraction process of our EMHNet method.

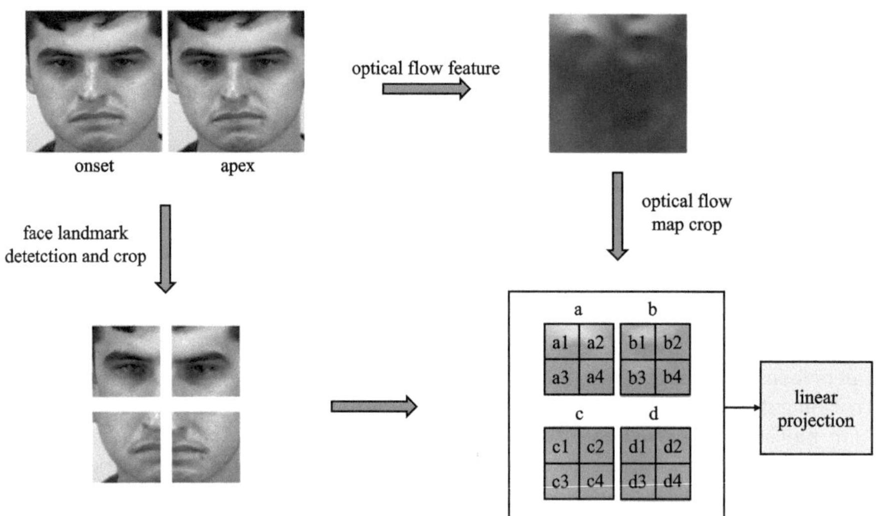

Fig. 2. Optical flow feature extraction process. The input facial optical flow map is divided into 4 primary anatomical regions, where a is the left eye region (blocks a1, a2, a3, a4), b is the right eye region (blocks b1, b2, b3, b4), c is the left lip region (blocks c1, c2, c3, c4) and d is the right lip region (blocks d1, d2, d3, d4).

3.2   Hierarchical Mixture of Experts

Our EMHNet works on the backbone of HTNet [24]. HTNet introduces a hierarchical transformer design that captures both local fine-grained features through low-level self-attention and global coarse-grained features via high-level self-attention. This dual-scale approach is critical for micro-expressions, which requires modeling subtle muscle movements while maintaining contextual relationships. Instead of processing the entire facial image, HTNet targets four key facial regions to reduce noise from irrelevant regions and improve computational efficiency. This spatial partitioning aligns with the physiological basis of micro-expressions. In addition, HTNet introduces a block aggregation mechanism that merges local features hierarchically, enabling interactions between regions while preserving locality. This outperforms global self-attention methods that lose fine-grained details. However, HTNet applies identical transformer layers to all facial regions, ignoring the region-specific characteristics. For example, eye and lip movements may require different feature extraction strategies due to varying muscle dynamics and texture properties. Besides that, HTNet processes all facial regions uniformly, even when some areas like forehead contribute little to micro-expressions. This leads to redundant computations and limits scalability.

To address these weaknesses, we introduce a Hierarchical Mixture of Experts (HMoE) system that deploys specialized expert transformers for four anatomical regions, including left eyes, right eyes, left lips, and right lips at fine scales (i.e., regions a, b, c, and d of level $= 1$ in Fig. 1 and Fig. 2) and maintains a shared global transformer at the base level (level $= 0$) for holistic integration. This design enables us to precisely model the region-dependent micro-movements. At the fine scale level, each expert transformer focuses on the local features of its corresponding anatomical region and can capture the subtle changes in muscle movements within that region. For example, the expert transformer for the left eye region can specifically learn the unique movement patterns of the muscles around the left eye, such as blinking and eye rotation. At the base level, the shared global transformer is responsible for integrating the information from each region to grasp the overall facial expression features.

3.3   Enhanced Multi-scale Feature Learning

HTNet [24] achieves multi-scale feature extraction through hierarchical aggregation. This hierarchical structure enables the model to capture feature information at different scales, thus providing a more comprehensive understanding of the data. For instance, when dealing with image data, it can focus on both the global and local features of the image simultaneously. While the hierarchical aggregation can capture multi-scale features effectively, it exhibits several limitations when handling complex real-world micro-expressions. First, the fixed block size approach of HTNet fails to adapt to varying expression intensities. For example, when analyzing a suppressed smile where only the right lip corner twitches slightly, the uniform blocks dilute this subtle signal by averaging it with surrounding static facial regions. In cases of rapid eye blinking during attempted neutral expressions, the temporal aspect of micro-expressions gets lost as the model processes all frames with identical spatial granularity. Second, the hierarchical structure also lacks explicit mechanisms to share information across scales, and this may cause the important relationships between local muscle movements and global expression context to be missed. This becomes particularly problematic when analyzing compound expressions like disgust, which combines nose wrinkling and lip curling, as the model struggles to correlate these spatially separated but semantically connected features.

Thus, we design a dynamic block partitioning that allows the model to automatically adjust the block size and partitioning method according to the characteristics of the input data, hence it can better adapt to different facial expressions and muscle movements. For example, for some subtle micro-expressions, the model can partition the blocks smaller to capture more detailed features. For some more obvious expressions, larger blocks can be used to improve computational efficiency. On the other hand, the explicit cross-scale attention gates are used to establish connections between features at different scales. This enables the model to focus on important information at different scales. In this way, the model can comprehensively utilize features at different scales to improve the feature representation ability.

3.4   Loss Function

We employ a cross-entropy loss function to train our EMHNet as

$$L = -\frac{1}{N} \sum_{n=1}^{N} \sum_{c=1}^{C} y_{n,c} \log(p_{n,c}), \tag{1}$$

in which N and C are numbers of samples and categories, $y_{n,c}$ and $p_{n,c}$ are the ground truth label and the predicted probability for sample of index n belonging to category c, $n = 1, 2, \cdots, N$, and $c = 1, 2, \cdots, C$.

4   Experiments

4.1   Datasets

We evaluate our EMHNet method on three widely used micro-expression datasets: Spontaneous Micro-expression Database (SMIC) [13], Chinese Academy of Sciences Micro-Expression II Database (CASME II) [26] and SAMM [4]. To ensure consistent evaluation metrics and enable fair comparison with existing methods, a composite dataset (Full) is created by merging these three datasets using unified emotion categories. While many researches commonly classify human emotions into six fundamental categories, which are anger, disgust, fear, happiness, sadness, and surprise, we adopt a three-category classification scheme consisting of positive (happiness), negative (anger, disgust, fear and sadness) and surprise (surprise) classes.

The SMIC [13] dataset consists of 164 micro-expression video clips elicited from 16 participants. The dataset provides video samples in three acquisition modalities: visible light camera (VIS, 100fps), high-speed camera (HS, 100fps) and near-infrared camera (NIR, 25fps), with the HS modality being most commonly used for micro-expression analysis. All recordings maintain a resolution of 640×480 pixels, with the facial region processed at a cropped resolution of 150×130 pixels for detailed analysis. Each micro-expression clip is annotated with one of the three emotion categories: positive, negative or surprise.

The CASME II [26] dataset is a widely-used benchmark in micro-expression research. It consists of 255 micro-expression samples collected from 26 participants under controlled laboratory conditions. All video samples were captured using high-speed cameras operating at 200 frames per second to ensure precise temporal resolution for subtle facial movement analysis. The facial region of interest in each sample maintains a resolution of 280×340 pixels. The ground-truth information provided by the dataset includes the emotion state, the action unit, the onset, apex and offset frame indices.

The SAMM [4] dataset is a high-resolution dataset designed to advance research in micro-expression analysis by addressing key limitations in existing datasets such as low participant diversity and insufficient resolution. It contains 159 spontaneous micro-movements captured from 32 participants with a wide demographic range aged from 19 to 57. This ensures representation across ethnicities and age groups. The dataset was collected under controlled laboratory conditions using a high-speed Basler Ace camera recording at 200fps with a resolution of 2040×1088 pixels. The facial region was cropped to 400×400 pixels for detailed analysis, and LED lighting with diffusers ensured consistent illumination without flickering.

4.2 Performance Metrics

We use the unweighted F1-score (UF1) to evaluate overall recognition performance and use the unweighted average recall (UAR) as our evaluation metric for emotion classification to account for class imbalance.

UF1 is the unweighted mean of F1-scores computed independently for each class. It ensures equitable evaluation across all classes, making it particularly valuable for unbalanced datasets where certain classes may have significantly fewer samples than others. To compute UF1, one must first obtain all the True Positives (TP), False Positives (FP), and False Negatives (FN) for each class across all folds of the evaluation process, such as in Leave-One-Subject-Out (LOSO) cross-validation. The final UF1 score is obtained by averaging the per-class F1-scores, providing a balanced measure of overall performance that is not skewed by class distribution. This metric is especially useful in tasks like emotion recognition or medical diagnosis, where minority classes are critical and avoiding bias toward dominant classes is essential. By equally weighting all classes, UF1 offers a fair assessment of a model's ability to generalize across the entire dataset, complementing other metrics like UAR for a comprehensive evaluation. If there are C classes, for a given class c, based on LOSO strategy, we will test each k ($k = 68$) and get false negative samples (FN_c), true positive samples (TP_c) and false positive samples (FP_c). Then, UF1 can be calculated as:

$$UF1 = \frac{1}{C} \sum_{c=1}^{C} UF1_c, \quad UF1_c = \frac{2TP_c}{2TP_c + FP_c + FN_c}. \tag{2}$$

UAR serves as a more equitable alternative to standard accuracy metrics, which often exhibit bias toward classifiers that perform well on majority classes while neglecting minority ones. UAR ensures that each class contributes equally to the final evaluation. To compute UAR, the per-class accuracy score Acc_c is first calculated before averaging the number of classes. This approach is particularly critical in unbalanced classification tasks where a fair assessment of minority class performance is essential. By mitigating bias toward dominant classes, the UAR provides a clearer measure of a model's ability to generalize across the entire label space, making it indispensable for robust and fairness-aware evaluation. UAR can be calculated as

$$UAR = \frac{1}{C} \sum_{c=1}^{C} Acc_c, \qquad Acc_c = \frac{TP_c}{N_c}, \tag{3}$$

where N_c is the number of samples in the c class.

4.3   Experiment Results

Table 1 presents a comprehensive comparison of our EMHNet against state-of-the-art methods across three benchmark datasets and their composite dataset (Full). Our EMHNet establishes new benchmarks on the composite dataset with scores of 0.8684 (UF1) and 0.8584 (UAR), which outperforms the baseline HTNet [24] by 1.76% (UF1) and 1.09% (UAR). This significant margin is especially notable against traditional CNNs like AlexNet [28] (UF1 of 0.6933) and GoogleNet [2] (UF1 of 0.5573), demonstrating the limitations of conventional architectures for this task. While HTNet shows competitive performance with a result of 0.8508 (UF1), our EMHNet achieves a consistent advantage and this proves its superior ability to learn transferable features from diverse data sources, surpassing previous approaches such as FeatRef [30] and EMR [18].

Experimental results on SMIC reveal greater challenges, with all methods showing lower absolute performance compared to other datasets. Our EMHNet obtains the best performance with scores of 0.8164 (UF1) and 0.8065 (UAR), which outperforms HTNet by 1.90% (UF1) and 1.60% (UAR). This substantial gap highlights the effectiveness of our EMHNet in handling real-world variability compared to conventional architectures. Experimental results on CASME II show an interesting exception, where HTNet achieves exceptional performance with scores of 0.9532 (UF1) and 0.9516 (UAR). This suggests that the architecture of HTNet may be uniquely suited to this lab-controlled dataset. However, our EMHNet remains highly competitive with scores of 0.9509 (UF1) and 0.9487 (UAR). This shows that EMHNet has a consistent excellence across different data characteristics. Experimental results on high-resolution SAMM dataset prove most challenging for many approaches, with traditional CNNs like VGG16 scoring only 0.4870 (UF1) and 0.4793 (UAR). EMHNet achieves the best performance among these methods, with scores of 0.8419 (UF1) and 0.8381 (UAR), which outperforms HTNet by 2.86% (UF1) and 2.57% (UAR). These results underscore the importance of specialized architectures for handling SAMM's

Table 1. Comparisons of EMHNet against state-of-the-art methods across CASME II, SAMM, SMIC, and their composite dataset (Full).

Method	Full		SMIC [13]		CASME II [26]		SAMM [4]	
	UF1	UAR	UF1	UAR	UF1	UAR	UF1	UAR
AlexNet [28]	0.6933	0.7154	0.6201	0.6373	0.7994	0.8312	0.6104	0.6642
GoogLeNet [2]	0.5573	0.6049	0.5123	0.5511	0.5989	0.6414	0.5124	0.5992
VGG16 [21]	0.6425	0.6516	0.5800	0.5964	0.8166	0.8202	0.4870	0.4793
OFF-ApexNet [8]	0.7196	0.7096	0.6817	0.6695	0.8764	0.8681	0.5409	0.5392
STSTNet [15]	0.7353	0.7805	0.6801	0.7013	0.8382	0.8686	0.6588	0.6810
CapsuleNet [22]	0.6520	0.6506	0.5820	0.5877	0.7068	0.7018	0.6209	0.5989
Dual-Inception [31]	0.7322	0.7278	0.6645	0.6726	0.8621	0.8560	0.5868	0.5663
EMR [18]	0.7885	0.7824	0.7461	0.7530	0.8293	0.8209	0.7754	0.7152
FeatRef [30]	0.7838	0.7832	0.7011	0.7083	0.8915	0.8873	0.7372	0.7155
HTNet [24]	0.8508	0.8475	0.7974	0.7905	**0.9532**	**0.9516**	0.8131	0.8124
EMHNet (Ours)	**0.8684**	**0.8584**	**0.8164**	**0.8065**	0.9509	0.9487	**0.8419**	**0.8381**

unique characteristics, including its temporal dynamics and subtle expression features.

5 Conclusions

In this paper, we proposed an enhanced multi-scale hierarchical network that significantly advances micro-expression recognition. First, we introduced a Hierarchical Mixture of Experts (HMoE) system for four key anatomical regions (left eyes, right eyes, left lips, and right lips) at fine scales while maintaining a shared global transformer for holistic integration. This novel architecture enables unprecedented precision in modeling region-specific micro-movements, addressing a critical limitation of previous methods that treated facial regions uniformly. Second, we proposed an enhanced multi-scale feature learning framework. We designed a dynamic block partitioning that adapts to expression intensity variations and explicit cross-scale attention gates that optimize information flow between different resolution levels. These mechanisms work synergistically to capture both subtle local details and broader expression contexts. Lastly, we evaluated our method across three benchmark datasets (SMIC, CASME II and SAMM) and a composite dataset of these datasets, demonstrating consistent superiority over existing methods.

Acknowledgments. This work was supported by the Engineering Research Center of Integration and Application of Digital Learning Technology, Ministry of Education (1311019), and the National Natural Science Foundation of China under Grant 62476020.

References

1. Ayyalasomayajula, S.C., Ionescu, B., Ionescu, D.: A CNN approach to micro-expressions detection. In: IEEE 15th International Symposium on Applied Computational Intelligence and Informatics, pp. 345–350 (2021)
2. Ballester, P., Araujo, R.: On the performance of GoogleNet and AlexNet applied to sketches. In: AAAI Conference on Artificial Intelligence, pp. 1124–1128 (2016)
3. Ben, X., et al.: Video-based facial micro-expression analysis: a survey of datasets, features and algorithms. IEEE Trans. Pattern Anal. Mach. Intell. **44**(9), 5826–5846 (2021)
4. Davison, A.K., Lansley, C., Costen, N., Tan, K., Yap, M.H.: SAMM: a spontaneous micro-facial movement dataset. IEEE Trans. Affect. Comput. **9**(1), 116–129 (2016)
5. Fan, H., et al.: Multiscale vision transformers. In: IEEE/CVF International Conference on Computer Vision, pp. 6824–6835 (2021)
6. Fan, X., Chen, X., Jiang, M., Shahid, A.R., Yan, H.: SelfME: self-supervised motion learning for micro-expression recognition. In: IEEE/CVF Conference on Computer Vision and Pattern Recognition, pp. 13834–13843 (2023)
7. Fortun, D., Bouthemy, P., Kervrann, C.: Optical flow modeling and computation: a survey. Comput. Vis. Image Underst. **134**, 1–21 (2015)
8. Gan, Y.S., Liong, S.T., Yau, W.C., Huang, Y.C., Tan, L.K.: Off-ApexNet on micro-expression recognition system. Signal Process. Image Commun. **74**, 129–139 (2019)
9. Happy, S., Routray, A.: Fuzzy histogram of optical flow orientations for micro-expression recognition. IEEE Trans. Affect. Comput. **10**(3), 394–406 (2017)
10. Huang, X., Zhao, G., Hong, X., Zheng, W., Pietikäinen, M.: Spontaneous facial micro-expression analysis using spatiotemporal completed local quantized patterns. Neurocomputing **175**, 564–578 (2016)
11. Kim, D.H., Baddar, W.J., Ro, Y.M.: Micro-expression recognition with expression-state constrained spatio-temporal feature representations. In: ACM International Conference on Multimedia, pp. 382–386 (2016)
12. Lei, L., Chen, T., Li, S., Li, J.: Micro-expression recognition based on facial graph representation learning and facial action unit fusion. In: IEEE/CVF Conference on Computer Vision and Pattern Recognition, pp. 1571–1580 (2021)
13. Li, X., Pfister, T., Huang, X., Zhao, G., Pietikäinen, M.: A spontaneous micro-expression database: inducement, collection and baseline. In: IEEE International Conference and Workshops on Automatic Face and Gesture Recognition, pp. 1–6 (2013)
14. Li, Y., Wei, J., Liu, Y., Kauttonen, J., Zhao, G.: Deep learning for micro-expression recognition: a survey. IEEE Trans. Affect. Comput. **13**(4), 2028–2046 (2022)
15. Liong, S.T., Gan, Y.S., See, J., Khor, H.Q., Huang, Y.C.: Shallow triple stream three-dimensional CNN (STSTNet) for micro-expression recognition. In: IEEE International Conference on Automatic Face & Gesture Recognition, pp. 1–5 (2019)
16. Liong, S.T., See, J., Wong, K., Phan, R.C.W.: Less is more: micro-expression recognition from video using apex frame. Signal Process. Image Commun. **62**, 82–92 (2018)
17. Liu, Y.J., Zhang, J.K., Yan, W.J., Wang, S.J., Zhao, G., Fu, X.: A main directional mean optical flow feature for spontaneous micro-expression recognition. IEEE Trans. Affect. Comput. **7**(4), 299–310 (2015)
18. Liu, Y., Du, H., Zheng, L., Gedeon, T.: A neural micro-expression recognizer. In: IEEE International Conference on Automatic Face & Gesture Recognition, pp. 1–4 (2019)

19. Patel, D., Hong, X., Zhao, G.: Selective deep features for micro-expression recognition. In: International Conference on Pattern Recognition, pp. 2258–2263 (2016)
20. Pietikäinen, M.: Local binary patterns. Scholarpedia **5**(3), 9775 (2010)
21. Sengupta, A., Ye, Y., Wang, R., Liu, C., Roy, K.: Going deeper in spiking neural networks: VGG and residual architectures. Front. Neurosci. **13**, 95 (2019)
22. Van Quang, N., Chun, J., Tokuyama, T.: CapsuleNet for micro-expression recognition. In: IEEE International Conference on Automatic Face & Gesture Recognition, pp. 1–7 (2019)
23. Wang, Y., See, J., Phan, R.C.W., Oh, Y.H.: LBP with six intersection points: reducing redundant information in LBP-top for micro-expression recognition. In: Asian Conference on Computer Vision, pp. 525–537 (2014)
24. Wang, Z., Zhang, K., Luo, W., Sankaranarayana, R.: HTNet for micro-expression recognition. Neurocomputing **602**, 128196 (2024)
25. Xie, H.X., Lo, L., Shuai, H.H., Cheng, W.H.: AU-assisted graph attention convolutional network for micro-expression recognition. In: ACM International Conference on Multimedia, pp. 2871–2880 (2020)
26. Yan, W.J., et al.: CASME II: an improved spontaneous micro-expression database and the baseline evaluation. PLoS ONE **9**(1), e86041 (2014)
27. Zhai, Z., Zhao, J., Long, C., Xu, W., He, S., Zhao, H.: Feature representation learning with adaptive displacement generation and transformer fusion for micro-expression recognition. In: IEEE/CVF Conference on Computer Vision and Pattern Recognition, pp. 22086–22095 (2023)
28. Zhang, H., Zhang, H.: A review of micro-expression recognition based on deep learning. In: International Joint Conference on Neural Networks, pp. 01–08 (2022)
29. Zhao, G., Pietikainen, M.: Dynamic texture recognition using local binary patterns with an application to facial expressions. IEEE Trans. Pattern Anal. Mach. Intell. **29**(6), 915–928 (2007)
30. Zhou, L., Mao, Q., Huang, X., Zhang, F., Zhang, Z.: Feature refinement: an expression-specific feature learning and fusion method for micro-expression recognition. Pattern Recogn. **122**, 108275 (2022)
31. Zhou, L., Mao, Q., Xue, L.: Dual-inception network for cross-database micro-expression recognition. In: IEEE International Conference on Automatic Face & Gesture Recognition, pp. 1–5 (2019)

AIGC Video Detection Based on Missing Motion Details

Yongpeng Cao[1,2], Yi Tian[1,2(✉)], Likun Huang[1,2], Yajiao Bao[1,2], and Qiang Li[1,2]

[1] Wuhan Institute of Technology, Wuhan 430205, China
[2] Huazhong University of Science and Technology, Wuhan 430073, China
`04004069@wit.edu.cn`

Abstract. The rapid development of AIGC makes it very important to study efficient AIGC video detection methods. Compared with the detection methods that detect low-level artifacts and frequency-domain features, the detection methods that utilize high-level semantic features have better detection and generalization effects. This study finds that in some AIGC videos, the situation of missing motion details occurs. Therefore, this study proposes a method for AIGC video detection using the absence of motion details. This method extracts the motion features of animals and humans through 3D keypoint detection, and determines whether there is the absence of motion details by calculating the cosine similarity of the relative position vectors of adjacent positions in two adjacent frames. In the experiments, an AIGC video dataset of missing motion details is constructed, based on which the proposed method outperforms the state-of-the-arts.

Keywords: AIGC video detection · Lack of movement details · Cosine similarity

1 Introduction

With the development of generative artificial intelligence, the quality of images and videos generated through AIGC is getting higher and higher, and many have even reached the point of being indistinguishable from the real thing, which has brought a great impact on Internet information security and social stability. Therefore, the research value of AIGC image and video detection is also increasing day by day. Some early studies utilized Convolutional Neural Networks (CNN) to learn forged features on large-scale face forgery datasets. Some subsequent studies such as [1] utilized the low-level artifact features in the images, using features such as the unnatural distortion of facial muscles and abnormal changes in skin color as the basis for judgment. There are also some methods [2,3] that utilize frequency-domain information and believe that editing images will cause changes in the frequency-domain. In addition, there are some multimodal methods [4,5] that take into account factors such as audio, emotion analysis, consecutive frames, and blink frequency.

© The Author(s), under exclusive license to Springer Nature Singapore Pte Ltd. 2026
Z. Lin et al. (Eds.): ICIG 2025, LNCS 16163, pp. 52–63, 2026.
https://doi.org/10.1007/978-981-95-3729-7_5

At present, some achievements have been made in the detection of AIGC images and videos. The research methods mainly include detection methods based on low-level features and detection methods based on high-level semantic features. The former has poor generalization for new generative models and datasets, while the latter has higher generalization. With the development of AIGC models, detection methods based on advanced semantic features are becoming increasingly valuable for research. However, the current detection methods based on advanced semantic features mainly focus on the face and head, and there is still a lack of discussion on methods that utilize human motion features. There is still a lot of research space in the field of AIGC video detection.

To solve these problems, this study proposes a detection method for determining AIGC videos using the absence of motion details. The similarity degree of authenticity of adjacent frames is determined by calculating the cosine similarity of the relative position vectors of adjacent positions in two adjacent frames, and a frame-level discrimination mechanism is proposed to determine the authenticity degree of each frame. The main contributions of this study are summarized as follows:

1. We propose a motion detail missing detection strategy based on cosine similarity, which determines whether there are traces of motion detail missing in the video by calculating the cosine similarity of adjacent frames in the video.
2. We propose a video frame sequence authenticity discrimination strategy based on a frame-level discrimination mechanism to determine the authenticity degree of each frame in the video.
3. We have constructed an AIGC video detection dataset on the absence of motion details, mainly targeting the absence of motion details in animals or humans.

The innovation of this study lies in the fact that we have adopted a new perspective for AIGC video detection, that is, by detecting whether there are missing movement details in animals or humans and whether they conform to objective physiological and physical laws to detect whether the video is likely to be generated by AI, thus opening up new research ideas for AIGC video detection.

2   Related Work

To deal with increasingly realistic AIGC images and videos, researchers have adopted a variety of methods to detect the features within them. We reviewed the main research methods and classifications of current AIGC image and video detection, especially the detection methods based on advanced semantic features.

2.1   Based on Low-Level Features

The detection method based on low-level features mainly detects pixel-level artifacts introduced during the synthesis process and distinguishes the generated image from the real image according to the inherent traces in the generation process. The advantage of this detection method based on low-level features lies in its ability to automatically extract artifacts and the differences between the synthesized content and the real content. The disadvantage is that it is relatively sensitive to the adjustment of the generative model and the generalization of new datasets, so the generalization of the detection effect is poor.

The detection methods based on low-level features mainly include detection methods based on artifacts, detection methods based on spectrum, detection methods based on color information, and detection methods based on texture features, etc. [6,7] identify the images generated by GAN by detecting the artifacts produced by the generative model. The research of [8] found that the artifacts in the images generated by GAN are manifested as the replication of the spectrum in the frequency domain, and proposed a classifier model based on spectrum input rather than pixel input. Through qualitative and quantitative research [9], it is proposed that color can be used as a key transferable forensic feature in the universal detector of AIGC images. By taking advantage of the contrast of the inter-pixel correlation between the rich texture regions and the poor texture regions in the image, and comparing the characteristics of the inter-pixel correlation differences [10], it is used for artificial intelligence-generated image detection across different generation models. A dual-stream network composed of residual flow and content flow was developed [11]. It can not only precisely extract various texture information from the image by using the Spatial Richness Model (SRM), but also capture the forged traces in the low frequency, thereby comprehensively capturing the inherent anomalies generated during the AIGC image generation process.

2.2 Based on Advanced Semantic Features

Detection methods based on advanced features mainly detect more semantically meaningful features in synthetic images and videos. At present, the research on this type of detection method is mainly based on facial and head movements. On this basis, studies based on identity features, physiological signal features, movements and postures are carried out. Compared with the detection methods based on low-level features, the detection methods based on high-level semantic features have the advantage that they are more flexible in adjusting the generative model and generalizing to new datasets. Therefore, this detection method has stronger generalization.

Identity-based methods represent each individual by extracting some specific biological characteristics, which are difficult to be replicated by generators. The work of Agarwal et al. [12] models facial expressions and movements that represent an individual's speaking patterns, and it is the first method to utilize the unique patterns of an individual's facial and head movements to detect AIGC videos. In the study of [13], the inconsistency between mouth shape dynamics and spoken phonemes was utilized. The research of [14] is based on biometrics, combining static biometrics based on facial recognition with temporal behavior biometrics based on facial expressions and head movements, and using CNN with

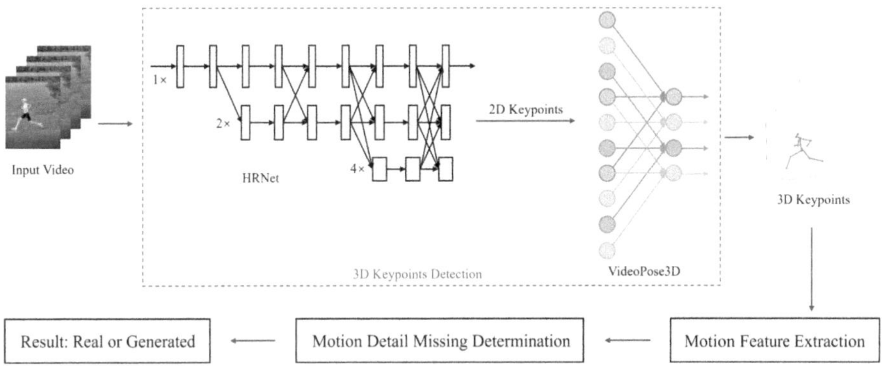

Fig. 1. AIGC Video Detection Based on Missing Motion Details.

metric learning objective functions to learn behavior embeddings. The research of [15] proposed a new method for learning temporal facial features, ID-Reveal, to detect the generated facial videos based on the identity of the test subject, especially the facial movements specific to a certain person. The research of [16] proposed a face forgery detection technology Identity Consistency Transformer (ICT) based on advanced semantics. The key idea is to detect the identity consistency in the face images suspected to be AIGC, that is, whether the internal face and the external face belong to the same person.

The method based on the characteristics of physiological signals focuses on generating specific artifacts in the video, which are often related to physiological signals. In the study of [17], the detection based on blinking in videos was proposed. Blinking is a physiological signal that is not well presented in synthetic fake videos. Methods based on physiological signal characteristics can often be combined with features based on motion and posture. For example, in the study of [18], the inconsistency detection of 3D head posture was used to generate videos, and in the study of [19], the artifacts of face distortion generated during the process of generating face videos were used as significant features to distinguish between real and generated images and videos. Some other studies have used heartbeats [20,21] and other biological signals hidden in portrait videos [22] to discover inconsistencies in the spatial and temporal directions in the generated videos.

3   Methods

The overall structure of this study is shown in Fig. 1. Firstly, the two-dimensional keypoints in the video are detected through the HRNet network. Then, the two-dimensional keypoints are transformed into three-dimensional keypoints through the VideoPose3D model to obtain the three-dimensional motion trajectories of each part. The motion features of the three-dimensional motion trajectory are extracted, and the extracted features are sent to the part for determining the missing motion details.

3.1 Motion Feature Extraction

This study refers to the MMPose method [23]. The VideoPose3D [24] model based on High-Resolution Network (HRNet) [25] and semi-supervised trained Temporal Convolutional Networks (TCN) [26] is used. Keypoint detection is carried out on the animals and human bodies in the input video to obtain the three-dimensional coordinates of the joint parts. The coordinates of each keypoint will change over time in different video frames, thus forming time series data for analyzing the changes in motion.

In this study, the MMPose keypoint detection model is utilized to extract the motion data of moving objects in the video, and an AIGC video detection feature matrix is proposed. For a video that detects m keypoints of the moving object per frame and a total of n frames, an $m \times n$ feature matrix $\boldsymbol{A}$ can be obtained:

$$A = \begin{bmatrix} a_{11} & a_{12} & \cdots & a_{1n} \\ a_{21} & a_{22} & \cdots & a_{2n} \\ \vdots & \vdots & \ddots & \vdots \\ a_{m1} & a_{m2} & \cdots & a_{mn} \end{bmatrix} \tag{1}$$

Among the above feature matrices, each element a_{ij} in the matrix represents the coordinate $a_{ij} = (x_{ij}, y_{ij}, z_{ij})$ of the i-th keypoint in the j-th frame. The row vector $[a_{i1}, a_{i2}, \cdots, a_{in}]$ represents the motion sequence of the i-th keypoint in n frames of video. The column vector $[a_{1j}, a_{2j}, \cdots, a_{mj}]^T$ represents all the keypoint positions of the j-th frame video.

3.2 Motion Detail Missing Determination

In AI-generated videos, it is often the case that some movement details are missing. For instance, the limbs of a human body or the legs of an animal may be missing parts in certain frames of the video. Therefore, this study proposes a motion detail missing determination module, which determines whether the video is likely to be generated by AI by judging whether the motion details are missing. The absence of motion details is determined by the absence of human keypoints during motion. Firstly, the relative position vectors between keypoints are calculated, and then cosine similarity detection is used. Specifically as follows:

Let the keypoint vector of the j-th frame video be denoted as:

$$\boldsymbol{\xi}_j = [a_{1j}, a_{2j}, \cdots, a_{mj}]^T, (1 \leq j \leq n) \tag{2}$$

Each element a_{ij} in the vector $\boldsymbol{\xi}_j$ represents the absolute position of this keypoint in this frame of image. In this study, the coordinate points a_{ij} and $a_{i+1,j}$ at two adjacent positions were subtracted to obtain the relative position vectors $\boldsymbol{q}_i$ of these two adjacent keypoints. Among the m keypoints, a total of

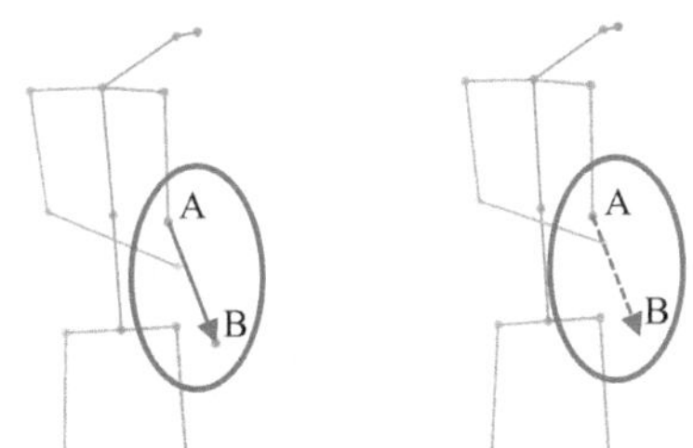

(a) Real Video Skeleton (b) Generated Video Skeleton

Fig. 2. The situation where motion details are missing in the generated video is mainly manifested in the absence of keypoints.

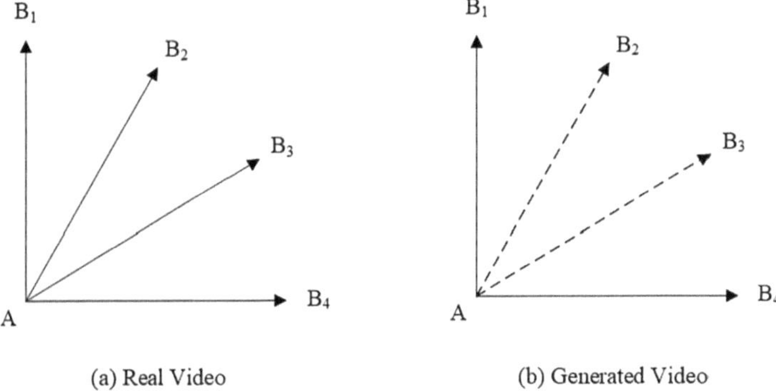

(a) Real Video   (b) Generated Video

Fig. 3. The basic principle of detecting missing motion details by using cosine similarity.

$m - 1$ relative position vectors can be obtained:

$$
\begin{aligned}
\boldsymbol{q}_i &= a_{ij} - a_{i+1,j} \\
&= (x_{ij}, y_{ij}, z_{ij}) - (x_{i+1,j}, y_{i+1,j}, z_{i+1,j}) \\
&= (x_{ij} - x_{i+1,j}, y_{ij} - y_{i+1,j}, z_{ij} - z_{i+1,j}), (1 \leq i \leq m - 1)
\end{aligned}
\tag{3}
$$

The effect of missing motion details in the real video and the generated video is shown in Fig. 2. Let point A be the elbow keypoint and point B be the wrist keypoint. Figure 2-(a) is the real video skeleton, and Fig. 2-(b) is the generated video skeleton with the missing human body part represented by point B.

Taking the keypoint A on the elbow as the reference frame, the difference in the relative position vector $\boldsymbol{q}_i = \boldsymbol{AB}_i$ of the keypoint B on the wrist relative to point A is shown in Fig. 3. Taking the relative position vectors of the two keypoints, elbow and wrist, as examples for comparison, B_1 to B_4 respectively represent the position changes of the keypoints on the wrist from the first frame to the fourth frame. Figure 3-(a) shows the relative position vectors in the real video $\boldsymbol{AB_1}$, $\boldsymbol{AB_2}$, $\boldsymbol{AB_3}$, $\boldsymbol{AB_4}$. In two adjacent frames, the relative position vectors $\boldsymbol{AB_i}$ and $\boldsymbol{AB_{i+1}}$ of the wrist relative to the elbow have a certain degree of similarity and the same direction. In this case, the cosine similarity between vectors $\boldsymbol{AB_i}$ and $\boldsymbol{AB_{i+1}}$ should be relatively high and positive. If the movement details of the wrist are missing in the AIGC video, the specific situation of its relative position vectors is shown in Fig. 3-(b). Points B_1 and B_4 are displayed normally, while points B_2 and B_3 are missing. Therefore, the modulus values of vectors $\boldsymbol{AB_2}$, $\boldsymbol{AB_3}$ are 0. This means that the cosine similarity between the relative position vectors $\boldsymbol{AB_i}$ and $\boldsymbol{AB_{i+1}}$ of adjacent frames will suddenly drop to 0, indicating that the adjacent vectors are completely unrelated in the direction of motion, and it can be considered that there is a loss of motion details. The cosine similarity of $\boldsymbol{AB_i}$ and $\boldsymbol{AB_{i+1}}$ is calculated by the following formula:

$$cos\theta = \frac{\boldsymbol{AB_i} \cdot \boldsymbol{AB_{i+1}}}{|\boldsymbol{AB_i}| \times |\boldsymbol{AB_{i+1}}|} \tag{4}$$

Among them, $\boldsymbol{AB_i} \cdot \boldsymbol{AB_{i+1}}$ is the dot product of vectors $\boldsymbol{AB_i}$ and $\boldsymbol{AB_{i+1}}$, and $|\boldsymbol{AB_i}|$ and $|\boldsymbol{AB_{i+1}}|$ are the modules of vectors $\boldsymbol{AB_i}$ and $\boldsymbol{AB_{i+1}}$ respectively.

For the problem of missing motion details in the generated video, what is presented in the feature matrix is that some keypoint data are missing in certain frames. These frames with missing keypoint data exhibit obvious forgery features. Therefore, we propose a frame-level discrimination mechanism to determine the authenticity degree of each frame. The implementation process of the frame-level discrimination mechanism is shown in Fig. 4. For the relative position vector q_j of the j-th frame video, in this study, the data q_1 of the first frame is assumed to be true by default, and then the cosine similarity between the relative position vector q_j of the j-th frame and the relative position vector q_{j+1} of the $(j+1)$-th frame is calculated successively. Let the cosine similarity between the j-th frame and the $(j+1)$-th frame be $cos\theta_j$, and the threshold δ for motion detail loss determination is used, where the threshold δ is obtained by the model training using the training dataset. The determination process is as follows:

When $cos\theta_j > \delta$, the degree of authenticity of the video at the j-th frame is determined to be the same as that at the $(j+1)$-th frame. When $cos\theta_j \leq \delta$, the degree of authenticity of the video at the j-th frame is determined to be opposite to that at the $(j+1)$-th frame.

4   Experiments and Results

First, we introduce the dataset and experimental Settings in detail. Then, we study the influence of model parameters on performance. Finally, we compare our method with the state-of-the-arts to demonstrate its advancement.

Fig. 4. Frame-level Discrimination Mechanism.

4.1   Experimental Setup

Dataset. To test the AIGC video detection method proposed in this study, we designed an AIGC video detection dataset for the absence of motion details. This dataset consists of two parts: real motion videos and generated motion videos. The real motion videos are downloaded from various video websites and undergo preliminary screening and processing. Generated videos mainly include two types: text-generated videos and text-guided image-generated videos. Among them, there are 133 real videos, 100 of which are training datasets, and 33 are test datasets. A total of 141 videos were generated, among which 100 were the training dataset and 41 were the test dataset. Each video lasts for 5 to 20 s and is all in mp4 format. We utilize some current AI video generation models (such as GAN, Diffusion Model, etc.) and download full-body images of animals or humans from the Internet as materials for text-guided image generation of videos. Through these methods, we obtain the generated video datasets required for this research.

In this study, the above detection model was utilized to detect the real video dataset and the generated video dataset respectively. The accuracy rate of detecting the videos in the real video dataset as real videos by using model checking, and the accuracy rate of detecting the videos in the generated video dataset as generated videos by using model checking.

Experimental Details and Evaluation Indicators. In this study, Accuracy Rate (ACC), Precision Rate (Precision), Recall Rate (TPR), False Positive Rate (FPR), True Negative Rate (TNR) and False Negative Rate (FNR) were selected as evaluation indicators.

Accuracy (ACC) is an indicator used to evaluate classification models, referring to the proportion of correctly predicted results by the model:

$$ACC = \frac{Number\ of\ correct\ predictions}{Total\ number\ of\ predictions} = \frac{TP + TN}{TP + TN + FP + FN} \tag{5}$$

Precision: It refers to the proportion of samples identified as positive categories that are indeed positive. In this study, it refers to the proportion of samples identified as real videos that are indeed real videos.

$$Precision = \frac{TP}{TP + FP} \tag{6}$$

Recall Rate (True Positive Rate, TPR): It refers to the proportion of all positive classes predicted as positive classes (positive class predictions are correct), that is, the recall rate. In this study, it refers to the proportion of all real video samples determined as true by the model.

$$TPR = \frac{TP}{TP + FN} \tag{7}$$

False Positive Rate (FPR): It refers to the proportion of all negative classes predicted as positive classes (positive classes predict wrongly). In this study, it refers to the proportion of all generated video samples determined as true by the model.

$$FPR = \frac{FP}{FP + TN} \tag{8}$$

True Negative Rate (TNR): It refers to the proportion of all negative classes predicted as negative classes (the prediction of negative classes is correct). In this study, it refers to the proportion of all generated video samples determined by the model as generated.

$$TNR = \frac{TN}{FP + TN} \tag{9}$$

False Negative Rate (FNR): It refers to the proportion of all positive classes predicted as negative classes (negative classes predict wrongly). In this study, it refers to the proportion of all real video samples judged as generated by the model.

$$FNR = \frac{FN}{TP + FN} \tag{10}$$

The specific meanings of all the symbols in the above formula are as follows:

TP (True Positive): It refers to the positive class samples predicted correctly. In this study, it refers to the real video samples that are determined as true by the model.

TN (True Negative): It refers to the negative class samples predicted correctly. In this study, it refers to the generated video samples that are determined as generated by the model.

FP (False Positive): It refers to the negative class samples that are wrongly judged as positive. In this study, it refers to the generated video samples that are determined to be true by the model.

FN (False Negative): It refers to the positive class samples that are wrongly judged as negative. In this study, it refers to the real video samples that are determined to be generated by the model.

4.2 The Influence of Model Parameters on Performance

We utilized the AIGC video detection method based on the absence of motion details proposed in this study to detect the videos in the dataset. Firstly, the model is trained for 100 rounds using the training dataset. Then, the videos in the test dataset are randomly selected 50 times, with 20 videos selected each time. The average values of TP, TN, FP and FN in the 50 experiments are calculated to be used for the subsequent calculation of the model's ACC, Precision, TPR, FPR, TNR and FNR.

This study uses the threshold δ for determining the loss of motion details for determination. To prove the accuracy and validity of the threshold selection, we made δ adjustments and calculated the ACC, Precision, TPR, FPR, TNR and FNR of the model under different motion detail loss determination thresholds. We observed the impact of the threshold adjustment on the overall performance of the model. The specific results are shown in Table 1.

Table 1. Experimental results under different thresholds for determining missing motion details

Experimental Indicators	$\delta = 0.01$	$\delta = 0.05$	$\delta = 0.1$
ACC	66.6%	65.4%	65.1%
Precision	64.59%	64.98%	66.39%
TPR	73.4%	66.8%	61.2%
FPR	40.2%	36%	31%
TNR	59.8%	64%	69%
FNR	26.6%	33.2%	38.8%

According to the experimental results, we can see that as the threshold δ for missing motion details increases, the detection accuracy of the model will gradually improve, the false positive rate (FPR) will gradually decrease, and the false negative rate (FNR) will gradually increase. This is because as δ increases, more videos that were originally real will be determined to be generated, that is, FN will gradually increase, while TP will gradually decrease.

4.3 Comparison with the State-of-the-Arts

We compared the method proposed in this study with the state-of-the-arts on the dataset we created. In this study, ID-Reveal [15], the facial and head motion inconsistency detection method [14], and the method in this study were selected for comparison. The results of the specific evaluation indicators are shown in Table 2.

Table 2. Comparison with the State-of-the-Arts

Method	ACC	Precision
ID-Reveal	47.9%	46.4%
The Facial and Head Movements are Inconsistent	60.1%	59.4%
The Methods in This Study	71.2%	70.3%

By comparing with other methods, we can clearly see that on the dataset of human movement, the model of this study has higher accuracy and precision. This is because other methods focus on detecting the inconsistency of facial or head movements, ignoring the feature of missing movement details. However, this study conducts AIGC video detection from this new perspective, opening up new research ideas for this field.

5   Conclusion

In this study, we propose a method for detecting AIGC videos using motion detail loss. This method detects whether there is a problem of local detail loss caused by AIGC by calculating the cosine similarity of adjacent video frames, providing a new method and research idea for AIGC video detection. The evaluation results on the dataset of this study indicate that the method in this study performs well in the intra-dataset evaluation.

References

1. Xu, Y., et al.: Visual-semantic transformer for face forgery detection. In: 2021 IEEE International Joint Conference on Biometrics (IJCB), pp. 1–7 (2021)
2. Le, B.M., Woo, S.S.: ADD: frequency attention and multi-view based knowledge distillation to detect low-quality compressed DeepFake images. In: AAAI Conference on Artificial Intelligence (2021)
3. Jeong, Y., et al.: FrePGAN: robust DeepFake detection using frequency-level perturbations. In: AAAI Conference on Artificial Intelligence (2022)
4. Haliassos, A., et al.: Lips don't lie: a generalisable and robust approach to face forgery detection. In: 2021 IEEE/CVF Conference on Computer Vision and Pattern Recognition (CVPR), pp. 5037–5047 (2020)
5. Zhou, Y., Lim, S.-N.: Joint audio-visual DeepFake detection. In: 2021 IEEE/CVF International Conference on Computer Vision (ICCV), pp. 14780–14789 (2021)
6. Nataraj, L., et al.: Detecting GAN generated fake images using co-occurrence matrices. arXiv:abs/1903.06836 (2019). n. pag
7. Tan, C., et al.: Learning on gradients: generalized artifacts representation for GAN-generated images detection. In: 2023 IEEE/CVF Conference on Computer Vision and Pattern Recognition (CVPR), pp. 12105–12114 (2023)
8. Zhang, X., et al.: Detecting and simulating artifacts in GAN fake images. In: 2019 IEEE International Workshop on Information Forensics and Security (WIFS), pp. 1–6 (2019)

9. Chandrasegaran, K., et al.: Discovering transferable forensic features for CNN-generated images detection. In: Avidan, S., Brostow, G., Cissé, M., Farinella, G.M., Hassner, T. (eds.) ECCV 2022. LNCS, vol. 13675, pp. 671–689. Springer, Cham (2022). https://doi.org/10.1007/978-3-031-19784-0_39
10. Zhong, N., et al.: Rich and poor texture contrast: a simple yet effective approach for AI-generated image detection. arXiv:abs/2311.12397 (2023). n. pag
11. Xi, Z., et al.: AI-generated image detection using a cross-attention enhanced dual-stream network. In: 2023 Asia Pacific Signal and Information Processing Association Annual Summit and Conference (APSIPA ASC), pp. 1463–1470 (2023)
12. Agarwal, S., et al.: Protecting world leaders against deep fakes. In: CVPR Workshops (2019)
13. Agarwal, S., et al.: Detecting deep-fake videos from phoneme-viseme mismatches. In: 2020 IEEE/CVF Conference on Computer Vision and Pattern Recognition Workshops (CVPRW), pp. 2814–2822 (2020)
14. Agarwal, S., et al.: Detecting deep-fake videos from appearance and behavior. In: 2020 IEEE International Workshop on Information Forensics and Security (WIFS), pp. 1–6 (2020)
15. Cozzolino, D., et al.: ID-reveal: identity-aware DeepFake video detection. In: 2021 IEEE/CVF International Conference on Computer Vision (ICCV), 15088–15097 (2020)
16. Dong, X., et al.: Protecting celebrities from DeepFake with identity consistency transformer. In: 2022 IEEE/CVF Conference on Computer Vision and Pattern Recognition (CVPR), pp. 9458–9468 (2022)
17. Li, Y., et al.: In ICTU oculi: exposing AI generated fake face videos by detecting eye blinking. arXiv:abs/1806.02877 (2018). n. pag
18. Yang, X., et al.: Exposing deep fakes using inconsistent head poses. In: ICASSP 2019 - 2019 IEEE International Conference on Acoustics, Speech and Signal Processing (ICASSP), pp. 8261–8265 (2018)
19. Li, Y., Lyu, S.: Exposing DeepFake videos by detecting face warping artifacts. In: CVPR Workshops (2018)
20. Fernandes, S.L. et al.: Predicting heart rate variations of Deepfake videos using neural ODE. In: 2019 IEEE/CVF International Conference on Computer Vision Workshop (ICCVW), pp. 1721-1729 (2019)
21. Qi, H., et al.: DeepRhythm: exposing DeepFakes with attentional visual heartbeat rhythms. In: Proceedings of the 28th ACM International Conference on Multimedia (2020). n. pag
22. Ciftci, U.A., Demir, I.: FakeCatcher: detection of synthetic portrait videos using biological signals. IEEE Trans. Pattern Anal. Mach. Intell. **PP** (2019). n. pag
23. Jiang, T., et al.: RTMPose: real-time multi-person pose estimation based on MMPose. arXiv:abs/2303.07399 (2023). n. pag
24. Pavllo, D., et al.: 3D human pose estimation in video with temporal convolutions and semi-supervised training. In: 2019 IEEE/CVF Conference on Computer Vision and Pattern Recognition (CVPR), pp. 7745–7754 (2018)
25. Sun, K., et al.: Deep high-resolution representation learning for human pose estimation. In: 2019 IEEE/CVF Conference on Computer Vision and Pattern Recognition (CVPR), pp. 5686–5696 (2019)
26. Lea, C.S., et al.: Temporal convolutional networks for action segmentation and detection. In: 2017 IEEE Conference on Computer Vision and Pattern Recognition (CVPR), pp. 1003–1012 (2016)

CLEST-IQA: Contrastive Learning-Enhanced Swin Transformer for Image Quality Assessment

Jiacheng Zhang[1], Yongqian Li[1], Dixiao Tao[1], Yong Luo[1(✉)], Xin Zhou[2(✉)], Dehua Cao[3], Cheng Li[3], and Yi Zhang[4]

[1] School of Cyber Science and Engineering, Wuhan University, Wuhan, China
`{jiachengzhang,yongqianli,taodixiao,luoyong}@whu.edu.cn`
[2] Jiangxi Science and Technology Normal University, Nanchang, China
`zhouxin@jxstnu.edu.cn`
[3] Langding Artificial Intelligence Industry Research Institute, Wuhan, China
`{caodehua,licheng}@landing-med.com`
[4] Department of Electronics and Information Engineering, Wenhua College Wuhan, Wuhan, China

Abstract. Image Quality Assessment (IQA), especially No-Reference Image Quality Assessment (NR-IQA), is a crucial yet challenging task in image processing. Although deep learning-based methods have achieved remarkable progress, they often struggle with the domain gap between synthetic and authentic distortions, which limits their generalization capability. Moreover, effectively capturing multi-scale distortion features, particularly high-frequency details and global structural information, remains a persistent challenge. To tackle these issues, we propose CLEST-IQA, a novel NR-IQA model based on contrastive learning and the Swin Transformer. Our approach employs a cross-domain contrastive learning framework, where synthetic data is used in an auxiliary task to learn distortion-specific features, while authentic data enhances generalization ability in real-world distorted scenes through an instance discrimination task. Additionally, we utilize the hierarchical structure of the Swin Transformer to extract multi-scale features, which are dynamically fused with contrastive learning representations via a hierarchical attention fusion module. This module adaptively balances global structural information and local details, ensuring robust performance across diverse distortion types. Extensive experiments on seven widely-used datasets have demonstrated that CLEST-IQA surpasses state-of-the-art methods, particularly in cross-domain scenarios.

Keywords: No-Reference Image Quality Assessment · Swin Transformer · Contrastive Learning

1 Introduction

Image Quality Assessment (IQA) is a fundamental task in computer vision that aims to automatically evaluate image quality [27]. It plays a crucial role in various applications, including mobile photography, video streaming, and medical

© The Author(s), under exclusive license to Springer Nature Singapore Pte Ltd. 2026
Z. Lin et al. (Eds.): ICIG 2025, LNCS 16163, pp. 64–75, 2026.
https://doi.org/10.1007/978-981-95-3729-7_6

imaging. With the rapid growth of social media and online content platforms, the ability to automatically assess image and video quality has become increasingly important. Based on the availability of reference images, IQA methods are generally categorized into Full-Reference (FR) IQA, Reduced-Reference (RR) IQA, and No-Reference (NR) IQA [27]. Among these, NR-IQA is the most challenging, as it must predict image quality without any reference information [21].

Early NR-IQA methods [17,21] primarily relied on Natural Scene Statistics (NSS) to assess quality, but their effectiveness was limited. With the rapid advancement of deep learning, IQA has seen significant improvements. Deep neural networks, with their powerful feature extraction capabilities [2], can automatically learn rich representations from image data, achieving superior accuracy compared to traditional methods. Recent IQA models [1,6,25,32] based on Convolutional Neural Networks (CNNs) and Transformers have demonstrated remarkable performance across various datasets. However, further enhancing the generalization ability of deep learning-based methods remains an ongoing research challenge.

Recent studies [15,24] have explored contrastive learning to help models distinguish different distortion types and severity levels, improving IQA performance. For example, Shi et al. [24] applies contrastive learning to synthetic datasets, enabling the model to learn rich semantic features for synthetic distortions. However, a significant domain gap exists between synthetic distortions (e.g., artificial noise, blur) and authentic distortions (e.g., real-world low-light conditions, compression artifacts), limiting the model's generalization to real-world scenarios. Moreover, training on authentic distortion images is difficult because they often lack explicit distortion labels for auxiliary tasks.

Multi-scale feature fusion is essential in IQA for capturing both low- and high-frequency distortions [25]. Swin Transformers [14] offer a promising architecture due to their multi-stage design. However, Swin Transformer is originally designed for high-level tasks like classification and is not inherently optimized for IQA. Using only its final-stage features may lead to a loss of sensitivity to local distortions, while naive feature aggregation risks introducing noise and reducing effectiveness.

To address these challenges, we propose CLEST-IQA, a Contrastive Learning-Enhanced Swin Transformer model for NR-IQA. First, a contrastive learning framework extracts cross-domain robust features as semantic priors. This framework applies unsupervised contrastive learning on authentic distorted data without distortion labels and supervised learning on synthetic data with explicit distortion labels. Second, a cross-attention module dynamically aligns these features with Swin Transformer's multi-stage outputs, generating adaptive fusion weights. Finally, the multi-stage features are aggregated for quality prediction. This approach adaptively adjusts feature contributions based on distortion types, enhancing sensitivity to high-frequency noise while preserving structural distortion awareness.

The main contributions of this paper are as follows:

- We introduce a cross-domain contrastive learning strategy to extract robust semantic priors, enabling the model to focus on universal distortion-related features and bridge the gap between synthetic and authentic data.
- We propose a hierarchical attention fusion mechanism within a multi-stage Swin Transformer backbone, which dynamically aligns contrastive features with multi-scale outputs to generate content-adaptive fusion weights.
- Extensive experiments on multiple synthetic and authentic distortion datasets validate the effectiveness and generalization of the proposed method.

2   Related Work

2.1   CNN-Based NR-IQA

CNN-based No-Reference Image Quality Assessment (NR-IQA) methods, such as WaDIQaM [1], DB-CNN [32], MetaIQA [33], and HyperIQA [25], have gained prominence due to their strong feature representation capabilities. Notable works include Zhang et al.'s Deep Bilinear CNN (DB-CNN) [32], which uses a dual-branch structure to model synthetic and authentic distortions, and Zhu et al.'s MetaIQA [33], which employs meta-learning to extract shared quality priors for rapid adaptation to new distortions. Su et al.'s HyperIQA [25] further enhances performance on authentic datasets by dynamically generating content-aware quality prediction rules.

However, CNN-based methods face limitations. Their reliance on local convolutional kernels restricts their ability to model long-range distortions. For example, they struggle to capture non-local distortions like block artifact propagation due to their limited receptive fields, leading to incomplete quality assessments.

2.2   Transformer in NR-IQA

Transformer-based No-Reference Image Quality Assessment (NR-IQA) methods leverage self-attention mechanisms to overcome the local receptive field limitations of traditional CNNs, enabling joint modeling of global distortion features and image semantics. These methods can be categorized into pure Transformer architectures (e.g., MUSIQ [8], MANIQA [29], DEIQT [20]) and hybrid architectures (e.g., TRes [6]). Pure Transformer methods process image patches directly, capturing global information but often producing abstract features that are difficult to align with human subjective quality scores. Hybrid methods combine CNNs for local feature extraction and Transformers for long-range dependency modeling. For instance, TRes [6] integrates CNNs and Transformers with relative ranking and self-consistency to enhance robustness. However, these hybrid approaches often fail to explicitly distinguish degradation patterns of different distortion types and face challenges in feature alignment.

Recently, Swin Transformer [14], a hierarchical vision Transformer, has also been applied to NR-IQA tasks. For instance, MSTRIQ [26] achieves multi-scale feature fusion by concatenating features from different stages. However, this fusion strategy is relatively simplistic, and more efficient approaches could theoretically be employed.

2.3 Contrastive Learning in NR-IQA

Contrastive learning enhances discriminative feature representation by minimizing feature distances between similar samples and maximizing those between dissimilar ones. Recently, it has been applied to IQA to improve distortion feature modeling. Some methods [3] focus on instance discrimination, where multiple augmented versions of a sample are treated as distinct classes. Other works [13,15,24] leverage auxiliary tasks with labeled datasets for richer feature learning. Liu et al. [13] employed image ranking as an auxiliary task, achieving competitive results on datasets with synthetic artifacts, while CONTRIQA [15] and SaTQA [24] used distortion type and level classification to pretrain a local distortion feature extractor.

We observe that auxiliary task-based contrastive learning (e.g., distortion type/level) works well for synthetic datasets with annotations, while authentic distortions, lacking prior labels, rely more on instance discrimination. However, domain differences between synthetic and real distortions often lead to feature transfer bias. To address this, we propose a cross-domain contrastive learning framework that jointly optimizes auxiliary classification and instance discrimination tasks, ensuring robust distortion-aware feature extraction across domains.

3 Method

3.1 Overall Architecture

For NR-IQA tasks, to enhance the cross-domain generalization capability of contrastive learning while focusing on multi-scale feature representation, we propose a method, namely Contrastive Learning-Enhanced Swin Transformer for Image Quality Assessment(CLEST-IQA), and Fig. 1 shows the architecture of our proposed model. The core pipeline consists of two stages: pretraining the contrastive learning network and quality score inference. During pretraining, we employ auxiliary tasks for distortion type and level prediction on synthetic data and instance discrimination tasks on authentic data, extracting contrastive features with robust cross-domain generalization. In the quality score inference stage, we use a Swin Transformer backbone to extract multi-scale features. These features are dynamically fused with contrastive learning features through the Swin-Contrast Fusion Module (SCFM). Subsequently, the Dynamic Weighted Fusion Module (DWFM) adaptively aggregates multi-scale features to generate the final feature representation, which is then fed into a regression head to predict the image quality score.

3.2 Cross-Domain Contrastive Learning

To enhance the cross-domain capability of CNN-based contrastive models for both authentic and synthetic distortion data, we propose a cross-domain contrastive learning strategy. This strategy jointly optimizes an auxiliary task on synthetic data and an instance discrimination task on authentic data, enabling the learning of cross-domain quality-aware features.

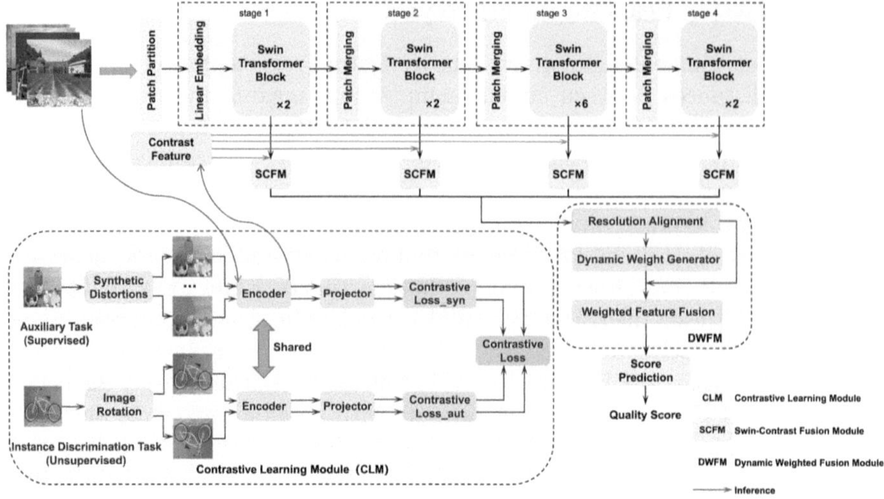

Fig. 1. The overall architecture of the proposed CLEST-IQA framework including Swin Transformer Backbone, Contrastive Learning Module(CLM), Swin-Contrast Fusion Module(SCFM), and Dynamic Weighted Fusion Module (DWFM).

Auxiliary Task. We adopt distortion type and level classification as auxiliary tasks to improve distortion feature learning. Given D distortion types, each with L levels, the task becomes a $(D \times L + 1)$-way classification (including the original image). For the i-th sample in a batch, samples with the same distortion type and level form its positive set $P\{i\}$. Following [3], we use a ResNet-based encoder $f(\cdot)$ and an MLP projector $g(\cdot)$ to extract and project features, where the projected feature representation for the input image $\mathbf{x}_i$ is denoted as $\mathbf{z}_i = g(f(\mathbf{x}_i))$. The contrastive loss employs the NT-Xent loss:

$$\mathcal{L}_{syn} = -\frac{1}{|P(i)|} \sum_{j \in P(i)} \log \frac{\exp(\phi(z_i, z_j)/\tau)}{\sum_{k \neq i} \exp(\phi(z_i, z_k)/\tau)}, \tag{1}$$

where $\phi(z_i, z_j) = \frac{z_i^T z_j}{\|z_i\|_2 \|z_j\|_2}$ is the cosine similarity, and τ is the temperature hyperparameter controlling the similarity distribution sharpness.

Instance Discrimination Task. For authentic distortion data, distortion types and levels are often too complex to generate auxiliary task labels. Thus, we employ an instance discrimination task, treating each image as a unique class. For a given real image, we generate its rotation version, which does not affect image quality, forming a positive pair (x_i, x_i^+). Any other image in the dataset forms a negative pair with them. The instance contrastive loss is defined as:

$$\mathcal{L}_{aut} = -\log \frac{\exp(\phi(z_i, z_i^+)/\tau)}{\sum_{k \neq i} \exp(\phi(z_i, z_k)/\tau)}. \tag{2}$$

Unified Contrastive Loss Function. To enable our contrastive training network to handle both synthetic and authentic images simultaneously, we employ a unified loss function for training the contrastive learning model. The loss function is defined as follows:

$$\mathcal{L} = \frac{1}{N} \sum_{i=1}^{N} \left[\mathbb{I}_{(x_i \notin \mathcal{D}_{authentic})} \mathcal{L}_{syn} + \mathbb{I}_{(x_i \in \mathcal{D}_{authentic})} \mathcal{L}_{aut} \right], \tag{3}$$

where N is the batch size, $\mathbb{I}$ are indicator functions for real and synthetic datasets, respectively. It is worth noting that balancing the number of real and synthetic images in each batch during training helps reduce bias.

3.3 Swin-Transformer Backbone

For an input image $I \in \mathbb{R}^{H \times W \times 3}$, we first perform patch embedding using a 4×4 convolution, transforming the pixel space into vector embeddings. This generates the initial feature map $F_{swin}^0 \in \mathbb{R}^{\frac{H}{4} \times \frac{W}{4} \times C_1}$, where $C_1 = 96$. In the hierarchical processing stage, each stage contains $[2, 2, 4, 6]$ Swin Transformer Blocks. The output dimension of the i-th stage is given by:

$$F_{swin}^i \in \mathbb{R}^{\frac{H}{2^{i+1}} \times \frac{W}{2^{i+1}} \times 2^i C}, \quad i = 1, 2, 3, 4. \tag{4}$$

3.4 Swin-Contrast Fusion Module (SCFM)

This module takes the i-th stage feature F_{swin}^i from Swin Transformer and the feature $F_{contrast}$ from the contrastive learning network as inputs. While F_{swin}^i captures local-to-global structural information, $F_{contrast}$ encodes cross-domain robustness and distortion semantics through synthetic-real data pre-training. SCFM aims to fuse these features efficiently via cross-attention, generating enhanced fused features F_{fused}^i.

Since $F_{contrast}$ and F_{swin}^i initially have different channel dimensions, we use a MLP to project $F_{contrast}$ to match F_{swin}^i's dimensions. In the cross-attention mechanism, F_{swin}^i serves as the query Q, capturing contextual information, while $F_{contrast}$ provides the key-value pair (K, V) for cross-domain semantics. The cross-attention is computed as:

$$F_{fused}^i = CrossAttn(F_{swin}^i, F_{contrast}), \tag{5}$$

where $CrossAttn$ is formulated as:

$$CrossAttn(Q, K, V) = Softmax\left(\frac{QK^T}{\sqrt{d_k}}\right) V. \tag{6}$$

This fusion mechanism enables SCFM to dynamically align the most relevant parts of the contrastive features with the Swin stage features. The output F_{fused}^i combines Swin's multi-scale properties and contrastive learning's semantic discriminability.

3.5   Dynamic Weighted Fusion Module (DWFM)

DWFM integrates multi-scale features $\{F^1_{fused}, F^2_{fused}, F^3_{fused}, F^4_{fused}\}$ from SCFM. It aligns features to the highest resolution (56×56) and generates dynamic weights:

$$w = Softmax(FC([z_1, z_2, z_3, z_4])) \in \mathbb{R}^4, \tag{7}$$

where $z_i = GAP(F^i_{fused})$. The final feature F_{final} is computed as:

$$F_{final} = \sum_{i=1}^{4} w_i \cdot F^i_{fused}, \tag{8}$$

serving as the unified representation for quality score prediction. DWFM enhances the model's ability to assess complex distortions.

3.6   IQA Regression

The dynamically weighted fused features are fed into a single-layer regression head to obtain the quality score. We employ the Mean Absolute Error (MAE) as the loss function, which is robust to outliers and enhances the model's prediction robustness. The loss function is defined as follows:

$$\mathcal{L}_{quality} = \frac{1}{N} \sum_{i=1}^{N} |\hat{q}_i - q_i|, \tag{9}$$

where N is the batch size, $\hat{q}_i$ is the predicted score for the i-th image, and q_i is its ground-truth score.

4   Experiments

4.1   Datasets

For the cross-domain contrastive learning network, we pretrain on both synthetic and authentic distortion datasets. The synthetic dataset, Kadis-700k [11], contains 140,000 reference and 700,000 distorted images, covering 25 distortion types and 5 levels, resulting in 126 synthetic classes. For instance discrimination task, we utilize datasets such as AVA [18], COCO [12], CERTH-Blur [16], and VOC [4], which contain a rich variety of authentic distortion types. We evaluate the proposed CLEST-IQA on seven widely-used IQA datasets. Synthetic datasets include LIVE [23] (799 images, 5 distortion types), CSIQ [9] (866 images, 6 distortion types), TID2013 [19] (3,000 images, 24 distortion types), and KADID-10k [10] (10,125 images, 25 distortion types). Authentic datasets include LIVEC [5] (1,162 images), KonIQ [7] (10,073 images), and LIVE-FB [30] (39,810 images, the largest authentic dataset).

Quality scores are represented by Mean Opinion Score (MOS) and Difference Mean Opinion Score (DMOS). Higher MOS and lower DMOS values indicate better quality.

4.2   Evaluation Metrics

In IQA tasks, the Spearman Rank Order Correlation Coefficient (SRCC) and the Pearson Linear Correlation Coefficient (PLCC) are commonly used as evaluation metrics. SRCC measures the monotonicity of predictions, while PLCC quantifies prediction accuracy. Both SRCC and PLCC are scaled between 0 and 1, with performance quality increasing as the values approach 1.

4.3   Implementation Details

We employ a ResNet-50 encoder and a two-layer MLP projector for the pre-trained cross-domain contrastive learning network. Each training batch contains an equal number of synthetic and real-world distorted images. The backbone network uses a pre-trained Swin Transformer encoder with stage depths $[2, 2, 6, 2]$. For each dataset, 80% of the data is used for training and 20% for testing. We conduct 10 independent experimental trials with varying random seeds to minimize random fluctuations.

4.4   Performance Comparison

We compare our proposed method, CLEST-IQA, with 11 state-of-the-art or competitive NR-IQA methods, including ILNIQE [31], WaDIQaM [1], DBCNN [32], MetaIQA [33], P2P-BM [30], HyperIQA [25], TRes [6], MSTRIQ [26], DEIQT [20], Re-IQA [22], and LoDa [28]. Table 1 presents the performance comparison on four synthetic distortion datasets, and Table 2 shows the results on three authentic distortion datasets.

The experimental results demonstrate that our CLEST-IQA achieves the most competitive performance on synthetic distortion datasets, with strong SRCC and PLCC scores, indicating the effectiveness of the auxiliary task-based contrastive learning strategy in learning distortion features. Furthermore, our model also performs well on authentic distortion datasets. Compared with well performed methods such as DEIQT and LoDa, our model not only performs well on synthetic distortion datasets, but also achieves the most competitive results on authentic distortion datasets, which reflects the recognition ability of our method for real scenarios.

4.5   Visual Analysis

Saliency maps, effective for visual saliency representation, intuitively highlight images' most visually attractive regions. For IQA tasks, ideal saliency maps should accurately emphasize distortions. To verify performance, after training on KADID-10k, four test images with authentic distortions were randomly selected for visual analysis (original images and saliency maps in Fig. 2). Results show generated saliency maps precisely localize distortions. The model identifies motion blur in the first image, detects large-scale blurring in the second, and captures exposure anomalies in the latter two. These confirm the CLEST-IQA model effectively captures image distortions in authentic scenarios.

Table 1. Performance comparison on four synthetic distortion datasets, with top two results in bold.

Method	LIVE		CSIQ		TID2013		KADID-10K	
	SRCC	PLCC	SRCC	PLCC	SRCC	PLCC	SRCC	PLCC
ILNIQE [31]	0.902	0.906	0.822	0.865	0.521	0.648	0.528	0.558
WaDIQaM [1]	0.960	0.955	–	–	0.835	0.855	0.739	0.752
DB-CNN [32]	0.968	0.971	0.946	0.959	0.816	0.865	0.851	0.856
MetaIQA [33]	0.960	0.959	0.899	0.908	0.856	0.868	0.762	0.775
P2P-BM [30]	0.959	0.958	0.899	0.902	0.862	0.856	0.840	0.849
HyperIQA [25]	0.962	0.966	0.923	0.942	0.840	0.858	0.852	0.845
TRes [6]	0.969	0.968	0.922	0.942	0.863	0.883	0.858	0.859
MSTRIQ [26]	–	–	–	–	0.882	0.895	–	–
DEIQT [20]	**0.980**	0.982	0.946	**0.963**	0.892	0.908	0.889	0.887
Re-IQA [22]	0.970	0.971	0.947	0.960	0.804	0.861	0.872	0.885
LoDa [28]	0.975	0.979	–	–	0.869	0.901	**0.931**	**0.936**
CLEST-IQA	0.979	**0.983**	**0.953**	0.962	**0.902**	**0.914**	0.922	0.927

Table 2. Performance comparison on three authentic distortion datasets, with top two results in bold.

Method	LIVEC		KonIQ-10k		FLIVE	
	SRCC	PLCC	SRCC	PLCC	SRCC	PLCC
ILNIQE [31]	0.508	0.508	0.523	0.537	0.294	0.332
WaDIQaM [1]	0.682	0.671	0.804	0.807	0.455	0.467
DBCNN [32]	0.869	0.869	0.875	0.884	0.545	0.551
MetaIQA [33]	0.835	0.802	0.887	0.856	0.540	0.507
P2P-BM [30]	0.844	0.842	0.872	0.885	0.526	0.598
HyperIQA [25]	0.859	0.882	0.906	0.917	0.544	0.602
TRes [6]	0.846	0.877	0.915	0.928	0.544	0.625
MSTRIQ [26]	–	–	**0.946**	**0.954**	–	–
DEIQT [20]	0.875	0.894	0.921	0.934	0.571	0.663
Re-IQA [22]	0.840	0.854	0.914	0.923	–	–
LoDa [28]	0.876	0.899	0.932	0.944	0.578	**0.679**
CLEST-IQA	**0.883**	**0.906**	0.934	0.943	**0.580**	0.669

4.6   Ablation Study

Effect of Training Data in Contrastive Learning. We perform an ablation study to analyze the effect of synthetic and authentic data in the contrastive learning network. Table 3 shows pretraining only on synthetic distortion images improves synthetic dataset performance more, while authentic distortion images benefit authentic datasets more. However, mixed pretraining yields better generalization with balanced performance across both dataset types.

Ablation for Components. To assess the contribution of each module, we performed full ablation experiments focusing on the contrastive learning module (CLM), Swin-Contrast feature fusion module (SCFM), and dynamic weighted fusion module (DWFM) using the LIVE and CSIQ datasets. Table 4 clearly demonstrates the importance of each component. The CLM enhances

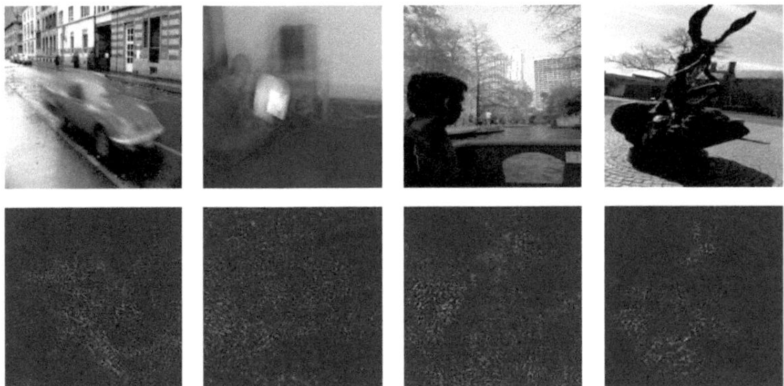

Fig. 2. Saliency maps of some images with authentic distortions.

Table 3. Ablation study on the impact of training data for the contrastive learning network on two datasets, with top results in bold.

Training Data	LIVEC		CSIQ	
	SRCC	PLCC	SRCC	PLCC
Synthetic	0.867	0.881	0.950	**0.964**
Authentic	0.879	0.904	0.937	0.951
Both(Ours)	**0.883**	**0.906**	**0.953**	0.962

Table 4. Results of the ablation for components on the LIVE and CSIQ datasets, with top results in bold.

Method	LIVEC		CSIQ	
	SRCC	PLCC	SRCC	PLCC
CLEST-IQA	**0.883**	**0.906**	**0.953**	**0.962**
w/o CLM	0.863	0.878	0.932	0.945
w/o SCFM	0.875	0.898	0.947	0.956
w/o DWFM	0.882	0.896	0.951	0.960

cross-domain generalization, the SCFM enables effective feature fusion, and the DWFM ensures adaptive feature aggregation. Together, these components contribute to the superior performance of our method in no-reference image quality assessment.

5 Conclusion

In this paper, we proposed a novel method for no-reference image quality assessment (NR-IQA) that addresses the challenges of cross-domain generalization and multi-scale distortion sensitivity. Our method integrates a Swin-Contrast feature fusion module (SCFM) to dynamically align multi-scale Swin Transformer features with contrastive learning-based semantic priors, and a dynamic weighted fusion module (DWFM) to adaptively aggregate these features based on their relevance to the input distortion. Experimental results on both synthetic and authentic distortion datasets demonstrate that our approach significantly outperforms existing methods in terms of accuracy and robustness.

Acknowledgments. This work was supported by the National Natural Science Foundation of China (No. 62262026) and the Jiangxi Natural Science Foundation (No. 20232BAB202020).

References

1. Bosse, S., Maniry, D., Müller, K.R., Wiegand, T., Samek, W.: Deep neural networks for no-reference and full-reference image quality assessment. IEEE Trans. Image Process. **27**(1), 206–219 (2017)
2. Cai, H., et al.: Learning deep discriminative embeddings via joint rescaled features and log-probability centers. Pattern Recogn. **114**, 107852 (2021)
3. Chen, T., Kornblith, S., Norouzi, M., Hinton, G.: A simple framework for contrastive learning of visual representations. In: International Conference on Machine Learning, pp. 1597–1607. PmLR (2020)
4. Everingham, M., Van Gool, L., Williams, C.K., Winn, J., Zisserman, A.: The pascal visual object classes (VOC) challenge. Int. J. Comput. Vision **88**, 303–338 (2010)
5. Ghadiyaram, D., Bovik, A.C.: Massive online crowdsourced study of subjective and objective picture quality. IEEE Trans. Image Process. **25**(1), 372–387 (2015)
6. Golestaneh, S.A., Dadsetan, S., Kitani, K.M.: No-reference image quality assessment via transformers, relative ranking, and self-consistency. In: Proceedings of the IEEE/CVF Winter Conference on Applications of Computer Vision, pp. 1220–1230 (2022)
7. Hosu, V., Lin, H., Sziranyi, T., Saupe, D.: Koniq-10k: an ecologically valid database for deep learning of blind image quality assessment. IEEE Trans. Image Process. **29**, 4041–4056 (2020)
8. Ke, J., Wang, Q., Wang, Y., Milanfar, P., Yang, F.: MuSiq: multi-scale image quality transformer. In: Proceedings of the IEEE/CVF International Conference on Computer Vision, pp. 5148–5157 (2021)
9. Larson, E.C., Chandler, D.M.: Most apparent distortion: full-reference image quality assessment and the role of strategy. J. Electron. Imaging **19**(1), 011006–011006 (2010)
10. Lin, H., Hosu, V., Saupe, D.: Kadid-10k: A large-scale artificially distorted IQA database. In: 2019 Eleventh International Conference on Quality of Multimedia Experience (QoMEX), pp. 1–3. IEEE (2019)
11. Lin, H., Hosu, V., Saupe, D.: Deepfl-IQA: weak supervision for deep IQA feature learning. arXiv preprint arXiv:2001.08113 (2020)
12. Lin, T.-Y., et al.: Microsoft COCO: common objects in context. In: Fleet, D., Pajdla, T., Schiele, B., Tuytelaars, T. (eds.) ECCV 2014. LNCS, vol. 8693, pp. 740–755. Springer, Cham (2014). https://doi.org/10.1007/978-3-319-10602-1_48
13. Liu, X., Van De Weijer, J., Bagdanov, A.D.: Exploiting unlabeled data in CNNs by self-supervised learning to rank. IEEE Trans. Pattern Anal. Mach. Intell. **41**(8), 1862–1878 (2019)
14. Liu, Z., et al.: Swin transformer: hierarchical vision transformer using shifted windows. In: Proceedings of the IEEE/CVF International Conference on Computer Vision, pp. 10012–10022 (2021)
15. Madhusudana, P.C., Birkbeck, N., Wang, Y., Adsumilli, B., Bovik, A.C.: Image quality assessment using contrastive learning. IEEE Trans. Image Process. **31**, 4149–4161 (2022)
16. Mavridaki, E., Mezaris, V.: No-reference blur assessment in natural images using Fourier transform and spatial pyramids. In: 2014 IEEE International Conference on Image Processing (ICIP), pp. 566–570 (2014). https://doi.org/10.1109/ICIP.2014.7025113
17. Moorthy, A.K., Bovik, A.C.: Blind image quality assessment: from natural scene statistics to perceptual quality. IEEE Trans. Image Process. **20**(12), 3350–3364 (2011)

18. Murray, N., Marchesotti, L., Perronnin, F.: Ava: a large-scale database for aesthetic visual analysis. In: 2012 IEEE Conference on Computer Vision and Pattern Recognition, pp. 2408–2415 (2012). https://doi.org/10.1109/CVPR.2012.6247954

19. Ponomarenko, N., et al.: Image database tid2013: peculiarities, results and perspectives. Signal Process. Image Commun. **30**, 57–77 (2015)

20. Qin, G., et al.: Data-efficient image quality assessment with attention-panel decoder. In: Proceedings of the AAAI Conference on Artificial Intelligence, vol. 37, pp. 2091–2100 (2023)

21. Saad, M.A., Bovik, A.C., Charrier, C.: Blind image quality assessment: a natural scene statistics approach in the DCT domain. IEEE Trans. Image Process. **21**(8), 3339–3352 (2012)

22. Saha, A., Mishra, S., Bovik, A.C.: Re-IQA: unsupervised learning for image quality assessment in the wild. In: Proceedings of the IEEE/CVF Conference on Computer Vision and Pattern Recognition, pp. 5846–5855 (2023)

23. Sheikh, H.R., Sabir, M.F., Bovik, A.C.: A statistical evaluation of recent full reference image quality assessment algorithms. IEEE Trans. Image Process. **15**(11), 3440–3451 (2006)

24. Shi, J., Gao, P., Qin, J.: Transformer-based no-reference image quality assessment via supervised contrastive learning. In: Proceedings of the AAAI Conference on Artificial Intelligence, vol. 38, pp. 4829–4837 (2024)

25. Su, S., et al.: Blindly assess image quality in the wild guided by a self-adaptive hyper network. In: Proceedings of the IEEE/CVF Conference on Computer Vision and Pattern Recognition, pp. 3667–3676 (2020)

26. Wang, J., et al.: MSTRIQ: no reference image quality assessment based on Swin transformer with multi-stage fusion. In: Proceedings of the IEEE/CVF Conference on Computer Vision and Pattern Recognition, pp. 1269–1278 (2022)

27. Wang, Z., Bovik, A.C.: Modern image quality assessment. Ph.D. thesis, Springer (2006)

28. Xu, K., et al.: Boosting image quality assessment through efficient transformer adaptation with local feature enhancement. In: Proceedings of the IEEE/CVF Conference on Computer Vision and Pattern Recognition, pp. 2662–2672 (2024)

29. Yang, S., : ManIQA: multi-dimension attention network for no-reference image quality assessment. In: Proceedings of the IEEE/CVF Conference on Computer Vision and Pattern Recognition, pp. 1191–1200 (2022)

30. Ying, Z., Niu, H., Gupta, P., Mahajan, D., Ghadiyaram, D., Bovik, A.: From patches to pictures (PAQ-2-PIQ): mapping the perceptual space of picture quality. In: Proceedings of the IEEE/CVF Conference on Computer Vision and Pattern Recognition, pp. 3575–3585 (2020)

31. Zhang, L., Zhang, L., Bovik, A.C.: A feature-enriched completely blind image quality evaluator. IEEE Trans. Image Process. **24**(8), 2579–2591 (2015)

32. Zhang, W., Ma, K., Yan, J., Deng, D., Wang, Z.: Blind image quality assessment using a deep bilinear convolutional neural network. IEEE Trans. Circuits Syst. Video Technol. **30**(1), 36–47 (2019)

33. Zhu, H., Li, L., Wu, J., Dong, W., Shi, G.: MetaIQA: deep meta-learning for no-reference image quality assessment. In: Proceedings of the IEEE/CVF Conference on Computer Vision and Pattern Recognition, pp. 14143–14152 (2020)

An Industrial Inspection Model Compression Framework Combining Group Slimming and Channel-Wise Distillation

Xinyu Zhang and Bei Wang[✉]

School of Information Science and Engineering, East China University of Science and Technology, No. 130 Meilong Road, Shanghai 200237, China
beiwang@ecust.edu.cn

Abstract. With the widespread application of deep learning in industrial surface defect detection, YOLO-series object detection models have become mainstream due to their compact structure and high inference efficiency. However, deployment on embedded devices is limited by computational resources. Therefore, effective model compression is required for lightweight deployment. In this study, a joint compression strategy combining channel pruning and feature distillation is proposed for the YOLOv7-Tiny model. Specifically, the Group_slim method is first applied to perform channel-level structural compression, which removes redundant channels and reduces model complexity. Then, the original uncompressed model is used as the teacher network. The student network is guided using the Channel-Wise Distillation (CWD) method to learn key feature representations after pruning. Extensive experiments on the MVTecAD-Screw industrial defect dataset show that the proposed strategy reduces model parameters and computational cost while maintaining high accuracy. A good balance between inference speed and precision is achieved. Compared with other single pruning or knowledge distillation methods, the Group_slim + CWD scheme demonstrates superior overall performance across multiple evaluation metrics.

Keywords: Pruning · Knowledge Distillation · Model Compression · Defect Detection · Lightweight Deployment

1 Introduction

With the development of deep learning in the field of industrial inspection, convolutional neural network (CNN)-based object detection models have shown strong performance in surface defect recognition of mechanical components. YOLO (You Only Look Once) models have been widely adopted in industrial vision systems due to their compact structure and fast detection speed. However, embedded devices commonly used in production environments often suffer from limited computing power and storage capacity, which prevents the direct deployment of original models. Therefore, it is important to compress the model size while keeping the detection accuracy.

© The Author(s), under exclusive license to Springer Nature Singapore Pte Ltd. 2026
Z. Lin et al. (Eds.): ICIG 2025, LNCS 16163, pp. 76–89, 2026.
https://doi.org/10.1007/978-981-95-3729-7_7

In recent years, model compression methods have attracted increasing attention. Pruning techniques reduce model complexity by removing redundant weights or structures [13]. Knowledge distillation introduces a teacher-student framework to improve the representation ability of lightweight models. Although both approaches have achieved success in various tasks, most existing studies focus on single compression strategies. A systematic analysis of combining pruning and distillation is still lacking. Moreover, a mature compression solution for practical task-specific deployment has not yet been established.

To address the above issue, a compression evaluation framework combining pruning and distillation is proposed for industrial defect detection. The Group_slim pruning method, based on BatchNorm scaling factors, is integrated with the Channel-Wise Distillation (CWD) mechanism. The proposed strategy enables model size reduction without significant loss of accuracy. It also meets practical needs for both accuracy and efficiency, making it suitable for deployment on resource-constrained embedded platforms.

The main contributions of this work are as follows: (1) A pruning-distillation collaborative compression framework is proposed and its performance is evaluated. (2) Multiple pruning methods based on structural sparsity and higher-order information are introduced. The advantages of the Group_slim + CWD scheme are demonstrated. (3) Empirical studies are conducted on a typical industrial defect dataset. The results show that the proposed scheme significantly improves inference efficiency while maintaining accuracy.

2 Related Work

In recent years, channel pruning has played a key role in improving the deployment efficiency of deep neural networks. This technique removes redundant structures that have little effect on the output, based on importance scores of channels or filters. As a result, computation is reduced and inference is accelerated [1].

Filter pruning with minimal accuracy loss was first explored by Li H. et al. [2] in 2017, Liu Z et al. put forward a novel CNN learning scheme. By enforcing channel-level sparsity within the network, this scheme achieved simultaneous reductions in model size, runtime memory footprint, and the number of computational operations. Not only did this method simplify the model, but it also improved its operational efficiency [3]. To improve pruning accuracy across layers, Lee J. et al. introduced a layer-adaptive magnitude-based importance score. This scoring mechanism enabled more precise identification of redundant filters, enhancing the pruning process [4]. Fang G. et al. further broadened the scope of pruning by introducing "any-structure pruning", a strategy designed to generalize across CNNs, RNNs, GNNs, and Transformers, thus extending the applicability of structured pruning [5]. In practical applications, in 2025, Ge Shaojuan et al. applied a performance-aware pruning strategy to pig pose detection under multi-object occlusion scenarios, validating the practical value of channel pruning [6].

Knowledge distillation has become a widely adopted method for model compression. Its core idea is to transfer knowledge from a large teacher model to a compact student model, thereby maintaining accuracy with reduced model size [7]. Hinton et al. established the standard framework for distillation by aligning the output distributions of the teacher and student using the Kullback–Leibler divergence [8]. In 2019, Park et al. put forward the relational knowledge distillation method, which focuses on inter-layer relationships between teacher and student models rather than solely on the output layer [9]. Also in 2019, Cho et al. explored the integration of multi-task learning and knowledge distillation in their research. By conducting classification tasks and distillation tasks simultaneously, they enhanced the performance of student models [10]. Phuong et al. introduced a method that maximized mutual information between teacher and student feature representations, facilitating more effective knowledge transfer [11]. In recent research, pruning and distillation are often integrated. Xu Z. et al. developed the CAP-YOLO model, combining channel attention-guided pruning with distillation mechanisms. The model achieved both structural compression and high detection performance, and demonstrated effectiveness in real-time coal mine monitoring applications [12].

3 Method

3.1 Model Architecture

To address the dual constraints of model size and inference speed imposed by embedded devices in industrial scenarios, this paper proposes and constructs a detection model design scheme oriented toward structural compression based on the YOLOv7 detection framework. YOLOv7 was used as the detection backbone. Structural pruning and knowledge distillation were introduced. Feature extraction and fusion modules were designed to support lightweight deployment and enable efficient detection of multi-scale defect targets.

As shown in Fig. 1, the original YOLOv7 network consists of three parts: the backbone, the neck, and the detection head. The backbone is constructed by stacking multiple ELAN and ELAN-H modules. These modules are used to extract shallow and deep semantic features, respectively. The ELAN module improves feature reuse through a multi-path residual fusion mechanism. The ELAN-H module increases channel interactions, which enhances the perception of small targets and complex textures.

To enhance the compressibility and pruning controllability of the YOLOv7 backbone, in the network design phase, this paper explicitly constructs the CBS module with BatchNorm-Conv-SiLU as the basic unit. This thereby makes channel importance evaluation and sparse structure constraints more unified and easier to quantify. Meanwhile, in the Neck structure, the SPPCSPC pyramid pooling module and multi-branch fusion structure are introduced to achieve information fusion between features of different scales, providing rich contextual support for subsequent multi-layer output detection.

Based on the above network, a unified pruning-distillation compression framework was further constructed. The Group-Slim pruning method was applied. Group sparsity regularization was imposed on BatchNorm scaling factors to enable pruning in the backbone. For accuracy preservation, the full pre-compression model was used as the teacher network. Channel-Wise Distillation (CWD) was applied to guide the student network. The pruning-distillation framework provides a joint optimization mechanism for both accuracy and efficiency.

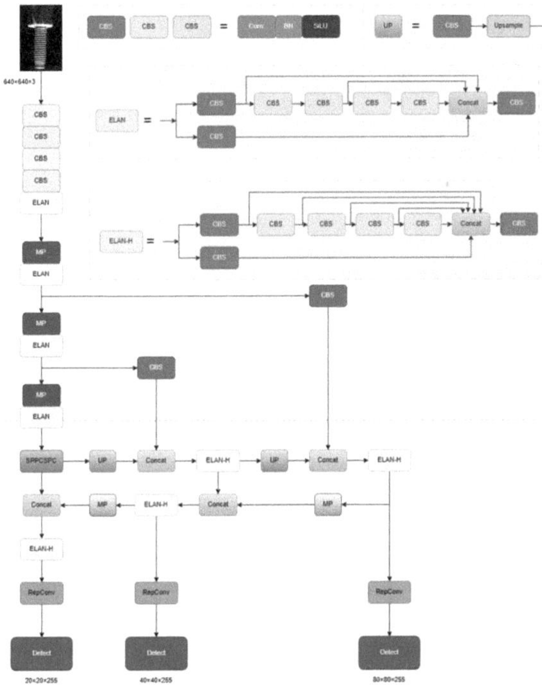

Fig. 1. Schematic diagram of the proposed network architecture. The network includes a feature extraction backbone (ELAN, ELAN-H), a feature fusion module (SPPCSPC and multi-level concatenation), and the detection head (RepConv and Detect).

3.2 Group-Slim Pruning Module

To achieve a balance between structural compression and computational complexity in the "pruning + distillation" collaborative compression framework, a channel pruning strategy based on group sparsity regularization, called Group-Slim, was introduced. The Group-Slim module is designed to identify redundant channel structures in convolutional neural networks and compress them in a structure-friendly manner. The overall pruning process consists of two stages: channel importance evaluation and structural reconstruction. The pruning structure is illustrated in Fig. 2.

The Group-Slim pruning module consists of two main stages: channel importance evaluation and progressive pruning. In the evaluation stage, a pruning strategy based on BatchNorm scaling factors is employed. The absolute values of the scaling parameters (γ) in the BatchNorm layers are ranked. Channels with lower values are marked as pruning candidates [14]. The approach is structure-independent and easy to implement. It can be applied to different convolutional network architectures.

Let the output feature tensor of a convolutional layer be denoted as $\mathbf{X} \in \mathbb{R}^{C \times H \times W}$, where C is the number of channels, and H and W represent the height and width of the feature map, respectively. The BatchNorm layer applies a scaling parameter γ_c to each channel. The importance of channel c is defined as:

$$I_c = |\gamma_c|, c = 1, 2, \ldots, C \tag{1}$$

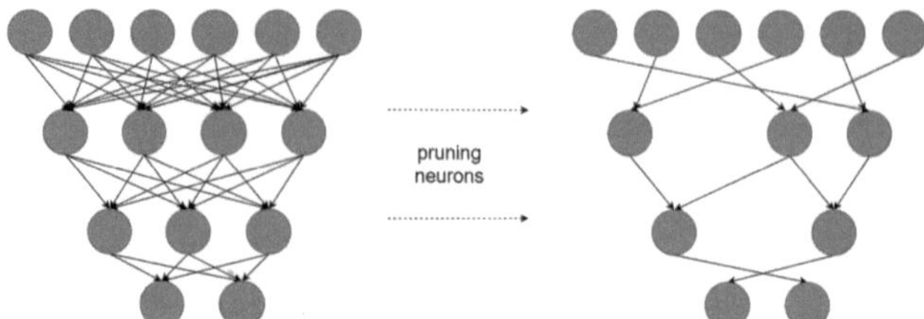

Fig. 2. Schematic of the Group-Slim pruning module. The diagram shows the structural changes in network connections before and after pruning, highlighting the removal of redundant channels and links.

when pruning is embedded into network training as a sparse regularization term, an L_1 regularization term can be added to the loss function to enhance sparsity [5]:

$$L_{total} = L_{det} + \lambda \sum_{c=1}^{C} |\gamma_c| \tag{2}$$

where $\boldsymbol{L_{det}}$ represents the detection loss, which includes both classification and regression losses. λ is the regularization coefficient used to balance detection accuracy and sparsity. After training, channel importance scores are sorted to generate a set of retained channel indices $\mathcal{S} \subset \{1, 2, \ldots, C\}$. Based on the pruning ratio $\boldsymbol{p}$, the top $(1 - \boldsymbol{p}) \times \boldsymbol{C}$ channels are selected to reconstruct the model structure.

Once pruning is completed, the network structure must be adjusted. The original convolution kernels and the associated BatchNorm parameters need to be remapped. To prevent significant performance degradation, fine-tuning is required after pruning to restore detection performance.

The number of channels in each convolutional layer of YOLOv7-tiny before and after pruning is illustrated in Fig. 3. The Group-Slim strategy was applied to reduce redundant channels. A noticeable reduction in channel count can be seen in many intermediate and output layers. The strong compression ability of the proposed method is confirmed by these results. The original number of channels is shown in orange, while the retained channels after pruning are shown in red. Model complexity is effectively reduced through this structured pruning approach.

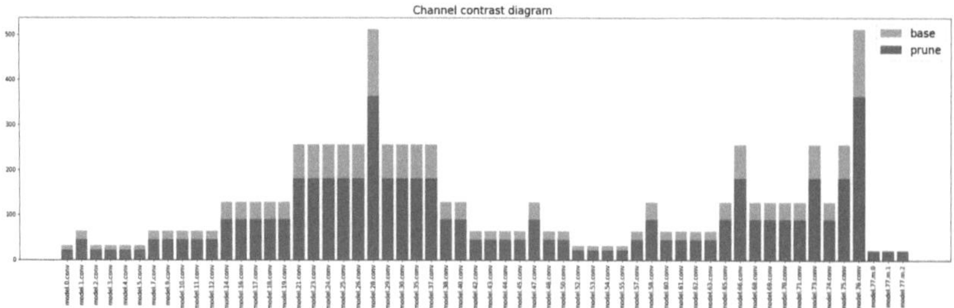

Fig. 3. Comparison of the number of channels in each convolutional layer of YOLOv7-tiny before and after pruning.

3.3 Channel-Wise Distillation

To enhance the expressive capability of the pruned model and mitigate performance degradation caused by structural compression, this paper introduces a knowledge distillation mechanism during the training phase, constructing a teacher-student model architecture. Guided by the high-performance teacher model on intermediate layer features or output probability distributions, the performance of the lightweight student model is thereby improved. As illustrated in Fig. 4, the knowledge distillation process comprises two main components: the teacher model extracts effective knowledge, and the student model performs knowledge alignment learning through loss functions.

Depending on different distillation targets, knowledge distillation can be categorized into two types: logits distillation based on output layer probability distributions, and feature distillation based on intermediate layer feature representations. Compared with logits distillation, feature distillation is more suitable for object detection tasks with complex structures and clearly stratified receptive fields. It can maintain detection accuracy while enhancing the sensitivity of the student model to local and semantic details of images.

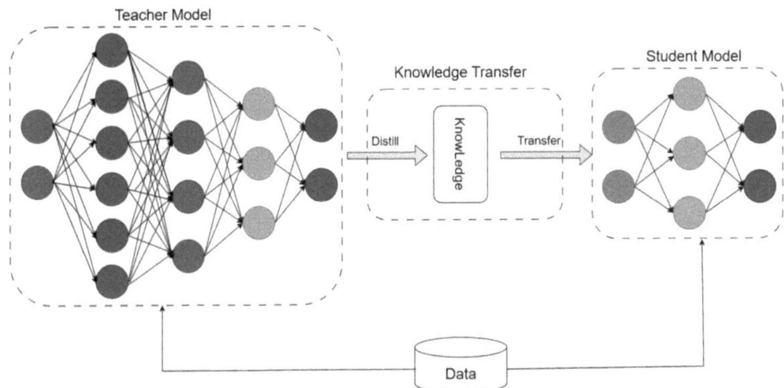

Fig. 4. Schematic diagram of Channel-Wise Distillation (CWD). Knowledge is transferred from the teacher model to the student model through both logical outputs and feature representations. The student model is guided to recover performance under structural compression.

In this study, the Channel-Wise Distillation (CWD) method was adopted. CWD minimizes the difference between feature maps of the teacher and student models at each channel. The above process guides the student model to align its feature representations channel by channel with those of the teacher. Let $\mathbf{f}_t^{(i)}$ and $\mathbf{f}_s^{(i)}$ denote the outputs of the teacher and student models at the i-th channel, respectively. The basic CWD loss function can be expressed as:

$$\mathcal{L}_{cwd} = \sum_{i=1}^{C} \left\| \mathbf{f}_t^{(i)} - \mathbf{f}_s^{(i)} \right\|_2^2 \tag{3}$$

To improve training stability and enhance feature alignment across different scales, the CWD method is often combined with channel-wise normalization. Let $\mu_t^{(i)}$ and $\sigma_t^{(i)}$ denote the mean and standard deviation of the feature map from the teacher model at the i-th channel. The normalized feature can then be expressed as:

$$\tilde{f}_t^{(i)} = \frac{f_t^{(i)} - \mu_t^{(i)}}{\sigma_t^{(i)} + \epsilon}, \tilde{f}_s^{(i)} = \frac{f_s^{(i)} - \mu_s^{(i)}}{\sigma_s^{(i)} + \epsilon} \tag{4}$$

the channel-aligned distillation loss after normalization can be written as:

$$\mathcal{L}_{cwd-norm} = \sum_{i=1}^{C} \left\| \tilde{f}_t^{(i)} - \tilde{f}_s^{(i)} \right\|_2^2 \tag{5}$$

In addition, to further enhance inter-channel collaborative representation, CWD can also incorporate a weighted channel response mechanism. The importance of each channel is learned through weighting. Let α_i denote the weight of the i-th channel. The final distillation loss can be defined as:

$$\mathcal{L}_{cwd-w} = \sum_{i=1}^{C} \alpha_i \cdot \left\| \tilde{f}_t^{(i)} - \tilde{f}_s^{(i)} \right\|_2^2, \ \alpha_i = \frac{\left\| f_t^{(i)} \right\|_2}{\sum_{i=1}^{C} \left\| f_t^{(j)} \right\|_2} \tag{6}$$

weighting strategy emphasizes the distillation guidance from high-response channels in the teacher model. It further strengthens the student model's ability to model important semantic regions. In this study, the proposed CWD framework was applied on top of the channel-pruned YOLOv7-tiny model. Feature transfer learning was performed to effectively improve the student model's performance on multiple defect detection sub-tasks.

3.4 Model Compression Framework

To achieve a balance between model compression and accuracy preservation, a lightweight optimization framework was constructed. The pruning-distillation framework is based on pruning and centered on knowledge distillation. The overall process is shown in Fig. 5. The method consists of two main stages: channel pruning and knowledge distillation.

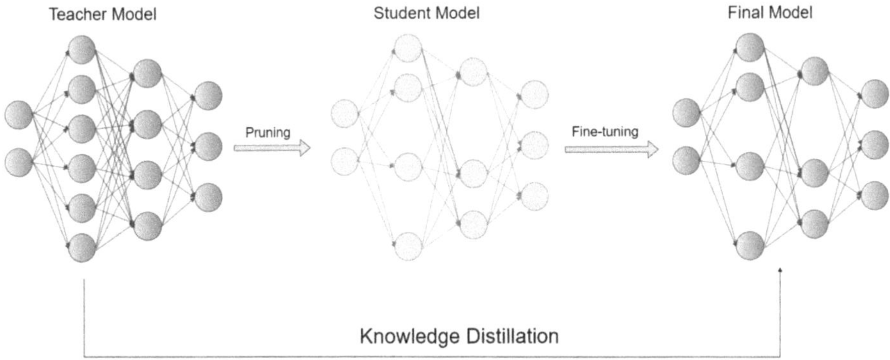

Fig. 5. Overall framework of the proposed model compression method. The YOLOv7-tiny model is first pruned using Group-Slim, followed by channel-wise distillation guided by the original model.

First, a trained YOLOv7 model with a complete structure is used. The Group-Slim strategy is applied to perform channel pruning. This strategy imposes group sparsity regularization on the scaling factors in BatchNorm layers. As a result, unimportant channels gradually approach zero during training. Efficient and structurally stable compression is achieved during pruning. After pruning, a student model with significantly reduced parameters and a simplified structure is obtained.

Next, the original full model is used as the teacher model. Intermediate features from the teacher are used as the knowledge source. Knowledge distillation is applied to guide the student model in feature alignment. To adapt to structural changes caused by pruning, the Channel-Wise Distillation method is selected. This method aligns the feature distributions of the student and teacher models channel by channel. It ensures that the student model maintains effective discriminative capability after compression. The final lightweight model meets deployment requirements. The proposed method reduces both model size and computational cost. It also suppresses performance degradation caused by compression. A good trade-off between efficiency and accuracy is achieved.

4   Experimental Results and Analysis

4.1   Experimental Settings

To comprehensively evaluate the performance of the proposed pruning and distillation-based compression strategy on defect detection tasks, experiments were conducted on the Screw subset of the MVTecAD dataset released by MVTec. MVTecAD-Screw Dataset contains a total of 433 images, including 361 non-defective images and 72 defective images. The defective images are categorized into three types: head scratch (24 images), neck scratch (25 images), and thread scratch (23 images).

Table 1. Category Description and Sample Distribution of the MVTecAD-Screw Dataset.

Category	Example	Quantity (images)
Good		361
Scratch_head		24
Scratch_neck		25
Thread_top		23

For evaluation, five quantitative metrics were used to assess model performance: number of parameters, computational cost, model size, detection accuracy (mAP50), and inference time. Here, mAP50 refers to the mean average precision when the IoU threshold is set to 0.5.

All models were evaluated under the same hardware platform and training configuration. The experiments were conducted on an NVIDIA RTX 3060 GPU. The Adam optimizer was used during training. The initial learning rate was set to 0.001, and the batch size was set to 32. Model accuracy and inference latency were measured on the test set independently to ensure the objectivity and reproducibility of the results.

4.2 Experimental Results

To verify the overall performance of the proposed compression strategy in terms of accuracy and efficiency, the original YOLOv7-Tiny model was used as the baseline. Based on this baseline, two compressed models were constructed: one using Group-Slim pruning alone, and the other combining Group-Slim pruning with Channel-Wise Distillation (CWD) after pruning. The three models were compared across five metrics: number of parameters, computational complexity, model size, detection accuracy, and inference time. The effectiveness of the proposed strategy was evaluated from multiple perspectives. The experimental results are shown in Table 2 and Fig. 6.

Table 2. Performance Comparison of Three Models on the MVTecAD-Screw Dataset. Key metrics are quantitatively compared under the same computing platform and configuration.

model	Parameters	mAP50	Inference Time
screw-tiny	6,015,306	0.790	1.97 ms
screw_tiny_group_slim	4,006,354	0.773	1.84 ms
screw_tiny_group_slim_cwd	4,006,354	0.795	1.82 ms

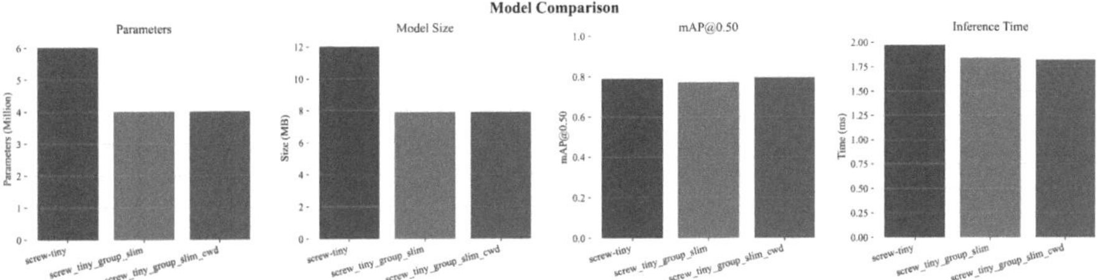

Fig. 6. Comparison of four performance metrics among the screw-tiny baseline, Group-Slim pruned model, and Group-Slim + CWD compressed-distilled model. The metrics include the number of parameters, model size, mAP50 accuracy, and inference time.

For comparisons of model parameters and size, both the pruned model (Group-Slim) and the compressed-distilled model (Group-Slim + CWD) reduced the number of parameters from 6.02M to 4.01M. The model size was decreased from 12MB to 7.9MB, resulting in a compression rate of approximately 33%.For inference latency, the pruned and compressed-distilled models achieved inference times of 1.84ms and 1.82ms, respectively. Compared with the original model's 1.97ms, both compressed models achieved faster execution. These results indicate that pruning significantly improves model efficiency.

For detection accuracy, the original model achieved an mAP50 of 0.790. The Group-Slim model achieved 0.773, showing a slight decrease (-0.017) but still maintaining a high level of accuracy. After applying CWD on top of pruning, the mAP50 increased to 0.795, which surpassed the original model (+0.005). The above method shows that feature distillation effectively compensates for the information loss caused by pruning and enhances the feature representation capability of the student model.

Based on the above analysis, the proposed Group-Slim pruning + CWD feature distillation strategy significantly reduces model parameters and computational complexity while maintaining or even improving detection accuracy. The above method achieves a good balance between inference latency, model compactness, and performance. It provides a practical solution for deploying defect detection models on edge devices or in resource-constrained environments.

4.3 Ablation Studies

To further analyze the impact of different pruning algorithms on model performance, experiments were conducted on the YOLOv7-Tiny model using the MVTecAD-Screw dataset. A pruning ratio of 33% was applied to evaluate the compression effect and performance retention of various pruning methods in object detection tasks. The original model (Baseline) was used as the control group. Several mainstream structured pruning methods were compared, including Random pruning, L1 pruning, LAMP, GroupNorm-based pruning, Slim, and Group-Slim. The comparison was designed to investigate the influence of compression strength on model performance.

Table 3. Comparison of compression and detection performance across different channel pruning methods on the YOLOv7-Tiny model.

model	Parameters	GFLOPs	mAP50	Inference Time
BaseLine	6,015,306	13.148	0.790	1.97 ms
Slim	4,006,155	8.761	0.772	1.84 ms
Group_slim	4,006,354	8.760	0.773	1.84ms
LAMP	4,006,872	8.761	0.766	1.86 ms
GroupNorm	4,006,244	8.761	0.740	1.92 ms
Random	4,006,106	8.761	0.742	1.86 ms
L1	4,006,194	8.760	0.720	1.90 ms

Several channel pruning methods were evaluated on the MVTecAD-Screw dataset. The results are presented in Table 3. All methods achieved model compression under a similar compression ratio (approximately 4 million parameters and 8.76 GFLOPs), but differences were observed in detection accuracy and inference time.

In terms of mAP50, the Group_slim method achieved the best result (0.773). This indicates that critical channels were preserved more effectively. The Slim method reached a comparable accuracy (0.772). In contrast, unstructured pruning methods such as Random and L1 showed a clear performance drop, with mAP50 reduced to 0.742 and 0.720, respectively.

In terms of inference time, all pruned models ran faster than the baseline (1.97 ms). The fastest inference (1.84 ms) was obtained by both Group_slim and Slim. LAMP and Random methods recorded 1.86 ms, while GroupNorm and L1 reached 1.92 ms and 1.90 ms, respectively. These values were close to the unpruned model, indicating limited structural simplification. Overall, the Group_slim method provided the best balance between accuracy and efficiency.

To verify the effectiveness of different knowledge distillation methods in improving the performance of lightweight models, distillation experiments were conducted using YOLOv7-Tiny as the student model and YOLOv7-X as the teacher model on the entire MVTecAD dataset. All models were set to the same computational complexity of 13.1 GFLOPs to eliminate the influence of network scale and ensure fair comparisons. The mAP50 metric was used for evaluation. The results are shown in Table 4.

From the overall results, the baseline YOLOv7-Tiny model without distillation achieved an mAP50 of 0.762, while the teacher model YOLOv7-X reached 0.827, indicating a significant performance gap. After applying different distillation strategies, the student models achieved various levels of accuracy improvement in most cases.

Among them, the CWD method showed the most stable performance. All four experiments using CWD achieved improvements ranging from + 0.004 to + 0.017. The CWD-exp2 experiment obtained the highest mAP50 of 0.779, indicating that the channel-aligned distillation mechanism effectively guided the student model to learn key discriminative features. The L2 distillation method also achieved good results. The best mAP50 reached 0.770 in one of the experiments, slightly lower than CWD-exp2, but still showed good generalization ability. The Mimic method provided noticeable improvements in some experiments, but its performance showed larger variance, making it less stable than CWD and L2. The MGD method demonstrated some instability. A slight improvement was observed in exp1, while exp2 showed a drop below the baseline, suggesting sensitivity to the choice of feature layers.

Table 4. Detection performance comparison of different knowledge distillation methods on the YOLOv7-Tiny model.

model	GFLOPs	mAP50
YOLOv7-tiny	13.1	0.762
YOLOv7-X	17.8	0.827
YOLOv7-tiny cwd exp1	13.1	0.763(+0.010)
YOLOv7-tiny cwd exp2	13.1	0.779(+0.017)
YOLOv7-tiny cwd exp3	13.1	0.767(+0.005)
YOLOv7-tiny cwd exp4	13.1	0.766(+0.004)
YOLOv7-tiny mgd exp1	13.1	0.763(+0.010)
YOLOv7-tiny mgd exp2	13.1	0.757(-0.005)
YOLOv7-tiny mimic exp1	13.1	0.769(+0.007)
YOLOv7-tiny mimic exp2	13.1	0.763(+0.001)
YOLOv7-tiny l2 exp1	13.1	0.769(+0.007)
YOLOv7-tiny l2 exp2	13.1	0.770(+0.008)
YOLOv7-tiny l2 exp3	13.1	0.767(+0.005)

5 Conclusion

A lightweight model compression framework combining Group-Slim channel pruning and CWD feature distillation was proposed for industrial defect detection tasks. The pruning-distillation framework addresses the deployment limitations of the YOLOv7 model in embedded environments. The model size and computational cost were significantly reduced while maintaining detection accuracy, achieving a balance between performance and efficiency.

In the pruning stage, the Group-Slim method based on BatchNorm scaling factors was adopted. Group sparsity regularization was applied to suppress redundant channels during training. This approach enabled efficient and structurally stable pruning. Compared to the original model, the above method achieved over 33% parameter reduction and decreased inference latency by approximately 7%, with negligible accuracy loss. These results verified the effectiveness of the pruning strategy.

To mitigate the performance degradation caused by pruning, a channel-aligned feature distillation strategy (CWD) was further applied to the pruned model. The student model was guided to align feature representations with the teacher model at the channel level. This process enhanced the student model's semantic modeling ability. Experimental results showed that the proposed joint compression strategy not only compensated for the information loss from pruning but also improved the mAP50 beyond that of the original model, demonstrating strong accuracy recovery and enhancement. Ablation experiments further validated the effectiveness of each component in the proposed framework.

References

1. Huang, T., Li, Y., Wang, L., Liu, A.: Defect detection method for substations with multi-class classification based on improved YOLOv7-tiny. Control Eng. (2025)
2. Li, H., Kadav, A., Durdanovic, I., et al.: Pruning filters for efficient convnets. arXiv preprint arXiv:1608.08710 (2016)
3. Liu, Z., Li, J., Shen, Z., et al.: Learning efficient convolutional networks through network slimming. In: Proceedings of the IEEE International Conference on Computer Vision, pp. 2736–2744 (2017)
4. Lee, J., Park, S., Mo, S., et al.: Layer-adaptive sparsity for the magnitude-based pruning. arXiv preprint arXiv:2010.07611 (2020)
5. Fang, G., Ma, X., Song, M., et al.: DepGraph: towards any structural pruning. In: Proceedings of the IEEE/CVF Conference on Computer Vision and Pattern Recognition, pp. 16091–16101 (2023)
6. Ge, S., Ji, H., Zhan, Y., Li, X., Zheng, W., Wang, T.: Lightweight pig posture recognition method after improving YOLOv5s. J. China Agricultural Univ. (2025)
7. Zhu, Y., Hao, S., Zheng, W., Jin, C., Yin, X., Zhou, P.: Multi-teacher cotton field weed detection model based on knowledge distillation. Trans. Chin. Soc. Agric. Eng. (2025)
8. Hinton, G., Vinyals, O., Dean, J.: Distilling the knowledge in a neural network. arXiv preprint arXiv:1503.02531 (2015)
9. Park, W., Kim, D., Lu, Y., et al.: Relational knowledge distillation. In: Proceedings of the IEEE/CVF Conference on Computer Vision and Pattern Recognition, pp. 3967–3976 (2019)
10. Cho, J.H., Hariharan, B.: On the efficacy of knowledge distillation. In: Proceedings of the IEEE/CVF International Conference on Computer Vision, pp. 4794–4802 (2019)
11. Phuong, M., Lampert, C.: Towards understanding knowledge distillation. In: International Conference on Machine Learning. PMLR, pp. 5142–5151 (2019)
12. Xu, Z., Li, J., Meng, Y., et al.: CAP-YOLO: channel attention based pruning YOLO for coal mine real-time intelligent monitoring. Sensors 22(12), 4331 (2022)

13. Xu, F., Zhang, L., Yu, T., Zhang, R.: Network pruning method combining channel classification contribution and feature scaling factor. Comput. Eng. Appl. (2025)

14. Huang, Q., Jin, G., Xiong, X., Wang, L., Li, J.: Lightweight SAR target detection based on channel pruning and knowledge distillation. Acta Geodaetica et Cartographica Sinica **53**(04), 712–723 (20244)

15. Dong, X., Chen, S., Pan, S.: Learning to prune deep neural networks via layer-wise optimal brain surgeon. Adv. Neural Inf. Process. Syst., 103–128 (2017)

16. Bai, L., Tabia, H., Santos-Rodríguez, R.: Beyond pruning criteria: the dominant role of fine-tuning and adaptive ratios in neural network robustness. arXiv preprint arXiv:2410.15176 (2024)

GLDNN: A Group-Level Dynamic Neural Network via Knowledge Distillation for Image Recognition

Yuhang Xiao, Qi Zhao(✉), Ahmed Oluwatoyin, Shuchang Lyu, and Alhassan Kamara

Beihang University, Beijing 100191, China
`zhaoqi@buaa.edu.cn`

Abstract. In recent years, Dynamic Neural Networks (DNNs) have attracted significant attention as they can adapt to limited-resource platforms such as mobile devices and self-driving cars. DNNs can dynamically adjust their parameters and architectures through adaptive inference, reducing computational complexity and balancing accuracy and efficiency. This study presents the Group-Level Dynamic Neural Network (GLDNN), aiming to address the deployment challenges of DNNs in real-world scenarios. During training, this model constructs multiple subnets, each optimized for a different accuracy-efficiency trade-off. At deployment, the most suitable subnets can be selected according to the requirements of the target device, enabling efficient resource utilization and excellent performance. The experimental results on the FMNIST dataset are remarkable. Subnets A and B of the proposed model outperform the existing models by 50% and 70% respectively. Moreover, knowledge distillation training is employed to mitigate the accuracy decline caused by a high pruning rate, strongly demonstrating the effectiveness of the model.

Keywords: Knowledge distillation · Network pruning · Dynamic neural network · Image recognition

1 Introduction

The rising prevalence of mobile devices, autonomous vehicles, robotics, and drones highlights the need for efficient machine learning models on resource-constrained platforms [1–3]. Traditional static CNNs [4–6], while successful in many domains, struggle in resource-limited environments due to inflexibility. Their fixed parameters and computational graphs hinder effective handling of diverse inputs with varying processing needs.

Dynamic Neural Networks (DNNs) have garnered significant attention in recent years due to their inherent adaptive capabilities [2,7,8]. Unlike static CNNs, DNNs can dynamically adjust their parameters and architectures for each input, a feature referred to as Adaptive Inference. This adaptability substantially

© The Author(s), under exclusive license to Springer Nature Singapore Pte Ltd. 2026

Z. Lin et al. (Eds.): ICIG 2025, LNCS 16163, pp. 90–101, 2026.
https://doi.org/10.1007/978-981-95-3729-7_8

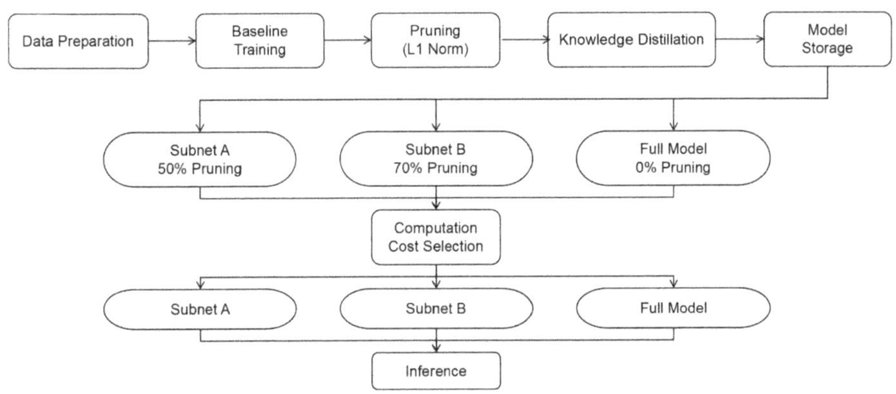

Fig. 1. The architecture diagram of GLDNN.

reduces computational complexity, leading to expedited inference times while maintaining an optimal balance between accuracy and efficiency.

This study debuts a Group-Level Dynamic Neural Network (GLDNN), tackling DNN deployment hurdles in real-world contexts. GLDNN crafts multiple sub-networks in training, each optimizing a distinct accuracy-efficiency balance. This flexibility allows adaptive performance adjustment to computational limits. At deployment, GLDNN picks the ideal sub-network for the device's specs, securing efficient resource use and top-tier performance. This adjustable strategy outshines static CNNs, excelling in speed-critical, resource-sensitive scenarios. The architecture diagram of GLDNN is shown in Fig. 1.

This paper comprehensively analyzes these findings, bolstered by detailed tables, charts, and result discussions. By harnessing dynamic neural network architectures, the study aims to enable efficient, practical deployment of machine learning models in resource-constrained settings—advancing adaptive inference methodologies.

Notable Contributions:

- **Novel Training Framework:** We propose GLDNN, which utilizes group-level pruning to construct multiple subnets within a full-net. Then, via knowledge distillation training, the subnets with high pruning rates can achieve encouraging performance.
- **Comparative Experiment Advantage:** Compared with multiple models on the same datasets, the method shows excellent performance and competitiveness.
- **Cost-Accuracy Balance:** Proved that higher pruning rates lead to lower accuracy but reduced cost. Our method can mitigate accuracy loss, and in some cases, high pruning rates result in higher accuracy, offering practical cost-accuracy balance options.

2 Related Works

2.1 Effective Network Structures

The goal of efficient network architectures is to maintain or even improve performance while reducing memory and computational costs. To fulfill these objectives, several notable architectures have been created.

MobileNet [9,10] uses depthwise separable convolutions to reduce parameters for mobile vision. DenseNet [11] employs all-layer connections for feature reuse. ShuffleNet [12] uses channel shuffle and group convolutions for efficiency. EfficientNet [13] balances depth/width/resolution via compound scaling for minimal FLOPs.

2.2 Effective Techniques for Compression/Slimming

The goal of effective compression and slimming techniques is to minimize the size and complexity of neural networks without materially sacrificing their functionality.

Lower-rank matrices [14] use SVD to approximate weight matrices, boosting inference and training efficiency without major performance loss. Quantization reduces weight/activation precision [15] to shrink models and speed inference, via quantization-aware training or post-training methods. Pruning removes unneeded weights/neurons for sparser models, with fine-tuning preserving performance [3,16,17]. Knowledge distillation [18,19] trains a small "student" to mimic a "teacher," enabling deployment in resource-constrained settings.

2.3 Dynamic Neural Networks (DNN)

Research on dynamic neural networks is gaining traction in deep learning. Sample-wise dynamic networks modify model structure/parameters by assigning input-adaptive computations [20–22].

Spatial-wise dynamic networks operate under the premise that all input feature spots equally impact CNN predictions [23–25]. They boost efficiency by performing operations only on essential spatial locations (pixels, regions, resolution), ignoring insignificant areas.

There have been several researches that focus on temporal dynamic networks. Adaptive computation is employed to process sequential data, such as texts and films, by focusing on relevant temporal areas and minimizing computation for unnecessary ones, resulting in efficient networks [26–28].

3 Methodology

3.1 Normal Training

Training a deep learning model involves fundamental procedures, summarized below with relevant equations. The initial step is dataset preparation, typically dividing data into training, validation, and test sets: the training set fits the model, the validation set tunes hyperparameters and monitors performance [29, 30], and the test set evaluates final performance.

For instance, in regression projects, it is customary to employ the mean squared error (MSE) as the loss function, whereas in classification tasks, the categorical cross-entropy is usually utilized. The loss function is commonly represented as:

$$\mathbf{L}(\mathbf{y}, \hat{\mathbf{y}}) \tag{3.1}$$

where $\mathbf{y}$ represents the true label and $\hat{\mathbf{y}}$ represents the anticipated label. Select an optimization algorithm to minimize the loss and adjust model weights. Gradient descent is a prevalent deep learning approach, with the fundamental updating rule:

$$\mathbf{w}_{t+1} = \mathbf{w}_t - \alpha \cdot \nabla \mathbf{L}(\mathbf{w}_t) \tag{3.2}$$

The current weight is denoted as $(\mathbf{w}_t)$, the learning rate is represented by α, and the gradient of the loss function as it relates to the weights is symbolized as $\nabla \mathbf{L}(\mathbf{w}_t)$. The training method involves iterating over the training dataset (epochs) and updating model weights using loss-derived gradients.

During training, tune hyperparameters (learning rate, batch size, epochs) to optimize validation performance. Post-training, test set evaluation gauges model efficacy on unseen data via metrics like accuracy and F1 score. Forward propagation transforms input data through network layers—using weights and activation functions to generate predictions, calculated as:

$$\hat{\mathbf{y}} = \mathbf{f}(\mathbf{x}; \boldsymbol{\theta}) \tag{3.3}$$

The function $\mathbf{f}$ denotes a neural network with parameters $\boldsymbol{\theta}$ (weights and biases), while the loss function measures the discrepancy between the predicted output $\hat{\mathbf{y}}$ and true target $\mathbf{y}$—serving as the optimization target during training. The backward pass computes loss gradients with respect to $\boldsymbol{\theta}$ via the chain rule, using these gradients to update parameters and minimize loss. The derivative of the loss with respect to a parameter $\boldsymbol{\theta}$ is $\frac{\partial l}{\partial \theta}$.

Gradient descent is a prevalent optimization approach used to update the parameters of a neural network according on the calculated gradients. The fundamental update rule for a parameter $\boldsymbol{\theta}$ utilizing gradient descent is:

$$\boldsymbol{\theta}_{t+1} = \boldsymbol{\theta}_t - \alpha \cdot \frac{\partial l}{\partial \boldsymbol{\theta}} \tag{3.4}$$

The learning rate α is a hyperparameter governing the gradient descent step size, crucial for optimizing training convergence speed and stability. A too-high α may overshoot the optimal solution, while a too-low α slows convergence.

3.2 Knowledge Distillation Training

Knowledge distillation involves: preparing a dataset, training/importing a high-performing teacher model, and designing a smaller student model. During training, the teacher provides soft target probabilities—richer than hard labels—to guide the student. The student learns via a dual loss function: Cross-Entropy for prediction accuracy and Distillation Loss (KL divergence between student predictions p_s and teacher soft targets p_t) to align with the teacher's outputs.

$$\mathrm{KL}(p_t, p_s) = \sum_i p_{t,i} \log \frac{p_{t,i}}{p_{s,i}} \tag{3.5}$$

The total loss is the sum of the cross-entropy loss and the distillation loss, with weights determined by hyperparameters:

$$L_{\text{total}} = (1 - \alpha) \cdot \mathrm{CE}(p_s, y) + \alpha \cdot \mathrm{KL}(p_t, p_s) \tag{3.6}$$

The cross-entropy loss CE and hyperparameter α balance the two loss components. Train the student model using combined loss L_{total} and optimizers like SGD/Adam, with dataset and teacher-generated soft targets. Tune hyperparameters (learning rate, batch size, epochs, softmax temperature) crucial for performance, validate, adjust training, and evaluate generalization on a test set.

3.3 Proposed Training Process

- We train baseline model and get $ft(\cdot; \mathbf{wt})$; where $\mathbf{wt}$ represent teachers weights
    - We then apply our pruning technique and get $ft(\cdot; \mathbf{wp})$, where $\mathbf{wp}$ represents teachers weights after pruning. From $\mathbf{wt} \rightarrow \mathbf{wp}$, we prune all weights according to their **L1** norm, a mask is then applied on the weight selected for pruning
    - We generate two pruned version of baseline model; $\mathbf{wp}'$ and $\mathbf{wp}''$
    - We then distill $ft(\cdot; \mathbf{wt})$ to the two students $fs(\cdot; \mathbf{wt}')$, $fs(\cdot; \mathbf{wp}'')$
    - Illustration of the proposed method can be seen in Fig. 2 (a) and (b)

4 Experiments

4.1 Experiment Outline

We conducted experiments to demonstrate model compression via pruning and knowledge distillation. A CNN model was trained on a dataset, from which several sub-models (2 in this paper) were created using unstructured pruning at specified ratios (50% and 70% in this paper). After experiments and ablation studies, results and observations are recorded.

Experiments used four networks: ResNet18, ResNet34, ResNet50, GoogleNet, and DenseNet121, with CIFAR10, CIFAR100, and FMNIST datasets. The SGD optimizer (momentum 0.09, weight decay 0.0005, initial lr 0.01) used a multi-step

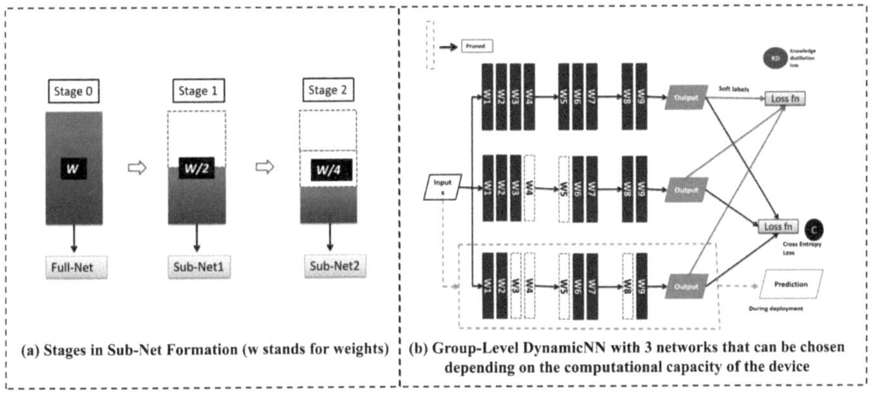

Fig. 2. Paradigm & Overview of proposed training framework, GLDNN.

scheduler (factor 0.1 at 30/70 epochs). Unstructured pruning created sub-models (50%/70% ratios), and standard knowledge distillation (KL loss, alpha 0.9) was applied. Each model trained for 200 epochs: 100 for the full model, then pruning to generate sub-models, which were trained as students with the full model as teacher for another 100 epochs, with observations recorded.

5   Results and Analysis

5.1   CIFAR10

Table 1 presents CIFAR-10 results for ResNet, GoogleNet, and DenseNet with pruning ratios (0%, 50%, 70%). ResNet accuracy generally declines with higher pruning, with ResNet50 most affected; ResNet34 outperforms others at all levels, indicating robustness. ResNet18 excels at lower ratios, showing efficient parameter use. GoogleNet mirrors this trend but is more pruning-sensitive. DenseNet121 varies: 50% pruning slightly improves accuracy over 0%/70%. Findings highlight ResNet34 and 50%-pruned DenseNet121 as more resilient to pruning.

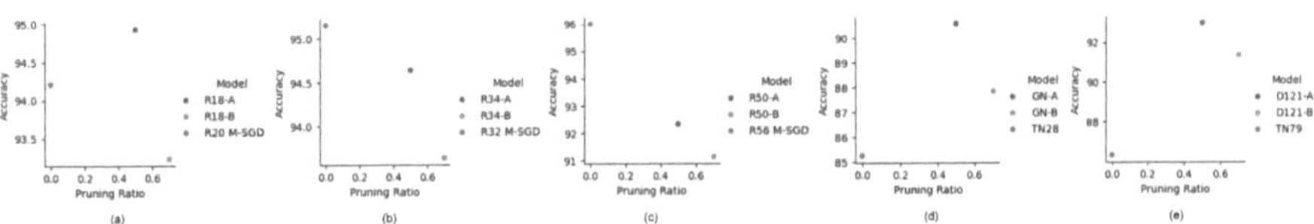

Fig. 3. Plot comparing the subnets (A, B) to existing models on the CIFAR10 dataset.

Figure 3 compares ResNet18/34/50 variants (A/B) with R20/32/56 M-SGD [31] and GN-A/B/D121-A/B with TN28/TN79 [32] on CIFAR10 across pruning ratios. ResNet and GoogleNet variants maintain stable accuracy,

Table 1. Showing CIFAR10 Results

Model	Pruning Ratio	Accuracy (%)
ResNet18	0%	95.97
ResNet18-A	**50%**	**94.93**
ResNet18-B	**70%**	93.23
ResNet34	0%	95.96
ResNet34-A	**50%**	94.64
ResNet34-B	**70%**	93.64
ResNet50	0%	95.82
ResNet50-A	**50%**	92.33
ResNet50-B	**70%**	91.14
GoogleNet	0%	95.96
GoogleNet-A	**50%**	**90.59**
GoogleNet-B	**70%**	87.85
DenseNet121	0%	91.73
DenseNet121-A	**50%**	**92.98**
DenseNet121-B	**70%**	91.36

with A models leading and controlled declines, outperforming baseline models (R20/R32/R56/TN28) at specific ratios. DenseNet121-A/B similarly stay stable, with A ahead and mild drops, outperforming TN79 under heavy pruning. All variants demonstrate resilience and effectiveness.

5.2   CIFAR100

Table 2 shows CIFAR100 results for deep learning models at different pruning levels. The "Pruning Ratio" column denotes parameter removal percentage (0% = no pruning), while "Accuracy" shows post-pruning performance. The table highlights pruning impacts to identify models resilient enough for resource-constrained environments.

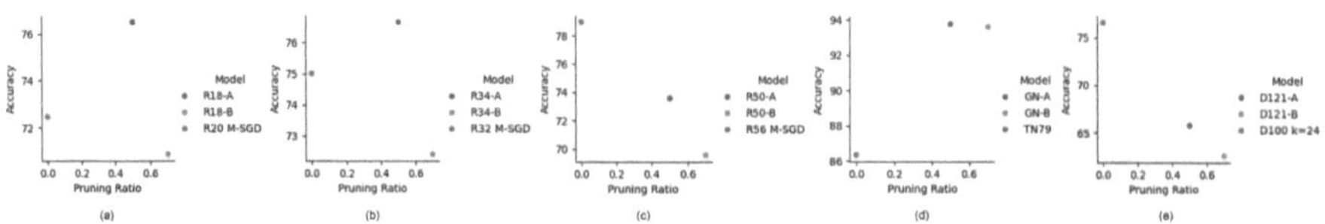

Fig. 4. Plot comparing the subnets (A, B) to existing models on the CIFAR100 dataset.

Table 2. Showing CIFAR100 Results

Model	Pruning Ratio	Accuracy (%)
ResNet18	0%	81.17
ResNet18-A	**50%**	**76.50**
ResNet18-B	**70%**	70.87
ResNet34	0%	81.92
ResNet34-A	**50%**	**76.67**
ResNet34-B	**70%**	72.42
ResNet50	0%	81.15
ResNet50-A	**50%**	73.59
ResNet50-B	**70%**	69.59
GoogleNet	0%	93.42
GoogleNet-A	**50%**	**93.77**
GoogleNet-B	**70%**	93.62
DenseNet121	0%	68.88
DenseNet121-A	**50%**	65.76
DenseNet121-B	**70%**	62.61

Figure 4 compares ResNet18/34/50 variants (A/B), GN-A/B, and D121-A/B with baseline models on CIFAR100 under pruning. ResNet variants maintain stable accuracy: R18-A outperforms R20 at specific ratios, R34-A surpasses R32, and R50-A stays close to R56. GN-A/B outperform TN79, especially GN-B at 70% pruning, while D121-A/B show moderate drops and commendable resilience despite slight underperformance against D100 $k = 24$. The proposed method mitigates pruning impacts, verifying model resilience and effectiveness.

5.3 FMNIST

Table 3 summarizes FMNIST pruning tests, showing expected accuracy drops with higher pruning. ResNet18 stands out, maintaining high accuracy at 50% and 70% pruning, ideal for size-restricted use. ResNet34 shows gradual decline, while ResNet50 mirrors the trend despite higher initial scores. GoogleNet sustains high accuracy through significant pruning, similar to ResNet18 but slightly lower at 0%. DenseNet121's stability across ratios indicates strong resistance to parameter reduction, highlighting its robustness.

Figure 5 compares models on FMNIST across pruning ratios. ResNet18/34/50 variants (A/B) maintain stable accuracy: R18-A/B outperform Swin-T [33] at specific ratios, R34-A/B surpass R34 orig, and R50-A/B outperform GECCO [34], demonstrating pruning resilience. GoogleNet and DenseNet121 variants also stay stable: GN-A/B exceed Fast VIT [35] (notably GN-B at 70%

Table 3. Showing FMNIST Results

Model	Pruning Ratio	Accuracy (%)
ResNet18	0%	94.89
ResNet18-A	**50%**	**93.88**
ResNet18-B	**70%**	93.60
ResNet34	0%	94.00
ResNet34-A	**50%**	92.81
ResNet34-B	**70%**	**92.97**
ResNet50	0%	94.19
ResNet50-A	**50%**	92.89
ResNet50-B	**70%**	**93.35**
GoogleNet	0%	95.66
GoogleNet-A	**50%**	**94.78**
GoogleNet-B	**70%**	94.40
DenseNet121	0%	94.74
DenseNet121-A	**50%**	**94.77**
DenseNet121-B	**70%**	94.26

pruning), while D121-A/B outperform VGG16-orig, highlighting their effectiveness and accuracy retention under pruning.

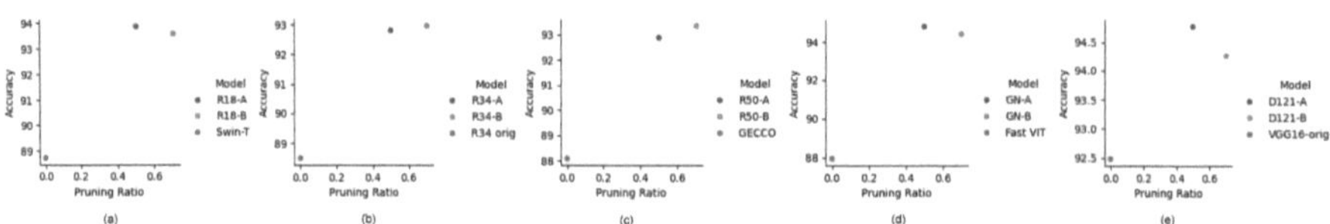

Fig. 5. Plot comparing the subnets (A, B) to existing models on the FMNIST dataset.

5.4   Pruning-Accuracy Trade-Off

Balancing pruning levels and performance loss is vital to retain model accuracy, as shown in Table 4. While pruned models typically trade accuracy for sparsity, knowledge distillation mitigates this. Notably, some datasets showed higher pruning ratios improving performance, an anomaly analyzed in this section.

Table 4. Pruning ratio effect on computation cost

Model	Pruning Ratio	Computation Cost (flops)
ResNet18	0%	1.8billions
ResNet18-A	**50%**	0.9billions
ResNet18-B	**70%**	0.5billions
ResNet34	0%	3.6billions
ResNet34-A	**50%**	1.9billions
ResNet34-B	**70%**	1.3billions
ResNet50	0%	4.0billions
ResNet50-A	**50%**	2.1billions
ResNet50-B	**70%**	1.2billions
GoogleNet	0%	3.2billions
GoogleNet-A	**50%**	1.7billions
GoogleNet-B	**70%**	1.1billions
DenseNet121	0%	1.5billions
DenseNet121-A	**50%**	0.75billions
DenseNet121-B	**70%**	0.45billions

6   Conclusion

The Group-Level Dynamic Neural Network Model (GLDNN) advances Dynamic Neural Networks (DNNs) by enabling efficient deployment in resource-constrained environments. By leveraging DNN flexibility and group-based learning, GLDNN trains multiple subnetworks optimized for different accuracy-efficiency trade-offs, allowing adaptive performance without sacrificing functionality.

We compared our method with state-of-the-art techniques, and Tables 1, 2, 3 and 4 show our model's superiority. On CIFAR10 and FMNIST, our model excelled—e.g., DenseNet121-A achieved 94.77% accuracy at 50% pruning, outperforming the 94.74% teacher model. Submodels consistently outperformed benchmarks, with A/B variants differing by 1.65% accuracy (e.g., ResNet34 on FMNIST).

In conclusion, our technique demonstrates superiority across multiple metrics, underscoring its strength and efficiency. The method offers scalable, adaptable models that balance high accuracy with minimal complexity, making it highly valuable for real-time processing and energy-efficient applications.

References

1. Chen, Y.-H., Krishna, T., Emer, J.S., Sze, V.: Eyeriss: an energy-efficient reconfigurable accelerator for deep convolutional neural networks. IEEE J. Solid-State Circuits **52**(1), 127–138 (2016)

2. Yang, T.-J., et al.: NetAdapt: platform-aware neural network adaptation for mobile applications. In: Ferrari, V., Hebert, M., Sminchisescu, C., Weiss, Y. (eds.) ECCV 2018. LNCS, vol. 11214, pp. 289–304. Springer, Cham (2018). https://doi.org/10.1007/978-3-030-01249-6_18

3. Han, S., Pool, J., Tran, J., Dally, W.: Learning both weights and connections for efficient neural network. In: Advances in Neural Information Processing Systems, vol. 28 (2015)

4. Szegedy, C., et al.: Going deeper with convolutions. In: Proceedings of the IEEE Conference on Computer Vision and Pattern Recognition, pp. 1–9 (2015)

5. LeCun, Y., Bottou, L., Bengio, Y., Haffner, P.: Gradient-based learning applied to document recognition. Proc. IEEE **86**(11), 2278–2324 (1998)

6. Simonyan, K.: Very deep convolutional networks for large-scale image recognition. arXiv preprint arXiv:1409.1556 (2014)

7. Yu, J., Huang, T.S.: Universally slimmable networks and improved training techniques. In: Proceedings of the IEEE/CVF International Conference on Computer Vision, pp. 1803–1811 (2019)

8. Lin, J., Rao, Y., Lu, J., Zhou, J.: Runtime neural pruning. In: Advances in Neural Information Processing Systems, vol. 30 (2017)

9. Howard, A.G.: MobileNets: efficient convolutional neural networks for mobile vision applications. arXiv preprint arXiv:1704.04861 (2017)

10. Sandler, M., Howard, A., Zhu, M., Zhmoginov, A., Chen, L.-C.: Mobilenetv2: inverted residuals and linear bottlenecks. In: Proceedings of the IEEE Conference on Computer Vision and Pattern Recognition, pp. 4510–4520 (2018)

11. Huang, G., Liu, Z., Van Der Maaten, L., Weinberger, K.Q.: Densely connected convolutional networks. In: Proceedings of the IEEE Conference on Computer Vision and Pattern Recognition, pp. 4700–4708 (2017)

12. Zhang, X., Zhou, X., Lin, M., Sun, J.: Shufflenet: an extremely efficient convolutional neural network for mobile devices. In: Proceedings of the IEEE Conference on Computer Vision and Pattern Recognition, pp. 6848–6856 (2018)

13. Tan, M., Le, Q.E.: Rethinking model scaling for convolutional neural networks. arxiv 2019. arXiv preprint arXiv:1905.11946 (1905)

14. Tai, C., Xiao, T., Zhang, Y., Wang, X., et al.: Convolutional neural networks with low-rank regularization. arXiv preprint arXiv:1511.06067 (2015)

15. Zhou, A., Yao, A., Guo, Y., Xu, L., Chen, Y.: Incremental network quantization: towards lossless CNNs with low-precision weights. arXiv preprint arXiv:1702.03044 (2017)

16. Molchanov, P., Tyree, S., Karras, T., Aila, T., Kautz, J.: Pruning convolutional neural networks for resource efficient inference. arXiv preprint arXiv:1611.06440 (2016)

17. Zhu, M., Gupta, S.: To prune, or not to prune: exploring the efficacy of pruning for model compression. arXiv preprint arXiv:1710.01878 (2017)

18. Furlanello, T., Lipton, Z., Tschannen, M., Itti, L., Anandkumar, A.: Born again neural networks. In: International Conference on Machine Learning. PMLR, pp. 1607–1616 (2018)

19. Heo, B., Lee, M., Yun, S., Choi, J.Y.: Knowledge transfer via distillation of activation boundaries formed by hidden neurons. In: Proceedings of the AAAI Conference on Artificial Intelligence, vol. 33, no. 01, pp. 3779–3787 (2019)

20. Teerapittayanon, S., McDanel, B., Kung, H.-T.: Branchynet: fast inference via early exiting from deep neural networks. In: 23rd International Conference on Pattern Recognition (ICPR). IEEE 2016, pp. 2464–2469 (2016)

21. Bengio, Y., Léonard, N., Courville, A.: Estimating or propagating gradients through stochastic neurons for conditional computation. arXiv preprint arXiv:1308.3432 (2013)
22. Bejnordi, B.E., Blankevoort, T., Welling, M.: Batch-shaping for learning conditional channel gated networks. arXiv preprint arXiv:1907.06627 (2019)
23. Cao, S., et al.: Seernet: predicting convolutional neural network feature-map sparsity through low-bit quantization. In: Proceedings of the IEEE/CVF Conference on Computer Vision and Pattern Recognition, pp. 11 216–11 225 (2019)
24. Wu, J., Li, D., Yang, Yu., Bajaj, C., Ji, X.: Dynamic filtering with large sampling field for ConvNets. In: Ferrari, V., Hebert, M., Sminchisescu, C., Weiss, Y. (eds.) ECCV 2018. LNCS, vol. 11214, pp. 188–203. Springer, Cham (2018). https://doi. org/10.1007/978-3-030-01249-6_12
25. Gao, H., Zhu, X., Lin, S., Dai, J.: Deformable kernels: adapting effective receptive fields for object deformation. arXiv preprint arXiv:1910.02940 (2019)
26. Shen, Y., Huang, P.-S., Gao, J., Chen, W.: Reasonet: learning to stop reading in machine comprehension. In: Proceedings of the 23rd ACM SIGKDD International Conference on Knowledge Discovery and Data Mining, pp. 1047–1055 (2017)
27. Yu, A.W., Lee, H., Le, Q.V.: Learning to skim text. arXiv preprint arXiv:1704.06877 (2017)
28. Ghodrati, A., Bejnordi, B.E., Habibian, A.: Frameexit: conditional early exiting for efficient video recognition. In: Proceedings of the IEEE/CVF Conference on Computer Vision and Pattern Recognition, pp. 15 608–15 618 (2021)
29. Wong, S.C., Gatt, A., Stamatescu, V., McDonnell, M.D.: Understanding data augmentation for classification: when to warp? In: International Conference on Digital Image Computing: Techniques and Applications (DICTA). IEEE 2016, pp. 1–6 (2016)
30. Padigela, J., Balla, S.S., Akula, P., Sravani, K.: Comparison of data augmentation techniques for training CNNs to detect pneumonia from chest x-ray images. In: 2023 International Conference on Computational Intelligence for Information, Security and Communication Applications (CIISCA), pp. 35–39. IEEE (2023)
31. He, K., Zhang, X., Ren, S., Sun, J.: Deep residual learning for image recognition. In: Proceedings of the IEEE Conference on Computer Vision and Pattern Recognition, pp. 770–778 (2016)
32. Ju, R.-Y., Lin, T.-Y., Jian, J.-H., Chiang, J.-S., Yang, W.-B.: Threshnet: an efficient densenet using threshold mechanism to reduce connections. IEEE Access 10, 82 834–82 843 (2022)
33. Liu, Z., et al.: Swin transformer: hierarchical vision transformer using shifted windows. In: Proceedings of the IEEE/CVF International Conference on Computer Vision, pp. 10 012–10 022 (2021)
34. Fein-Ashley, J., Wickramasinghe, S., Zhang, B., Kannan, R., Prasanna, V.: A single graph convolution is all you need: efficient grayscale image classification. In: 2024 IEEE International Conference on Image Processing (ICIP), pp. 849–855. IEEE (2024)
35. Vasu, P.K.A., Gabriel, J., Zhu, J., Tuzel, O., Ranjan, A.: FastVIT: a fast hybrid vision transformer using structural reparameterization. In: Proceedings of the IEEE/CVF International Conference on Computer Vision, pp. 5785–5795 (2023)

Selective Kernel and Offset Prediction Network for Video Super-Resolution

Tengjie Hu[1,2], Jiheng Hong[1,2], Jiahao Li[1,2], Chaoyi Huang[1,2],
and Rushi Lan[1,2(✉)]

[1] Guangxi Key Laboratory of Image and Graphic Intelligent Processing, Guilin
University of Electronic Technology, Guilin 541004, Guangxi, China
[2] International Joint Research Laboratory of Spatio-temporal Information and
Intelligent Location Services, Guilin University of Electronic Technology,
Guilin 541004, Guangxi, China
rslan2016@163.com

Abstract. In the field of Video Super-Resolution (VSR), accurately modeling inter-frame propagation and feature alignment are key to improving reconstruction quality. Although existing methods have achieved certain success, they still face challenges such as the accumulation of alignment errors, insufficient alignment for complex motions in dynamic scenes, and inadequate multi-frame feature fusion. This paper proposes a novel video super-resolution network called Selective Kernel and Offset Prediction Network (SK-OPNet). We designed two modules: the Multi-Input Selective Kernel Attention (M-SKA) module and the Multi-Scale Offset Prediction (MSOP) module. The M-SKA module dynamically fuses multi-frame features, enhancing information interaction across temporal scales and improving the stability and representational capacity of feature propagation. The MSOP module leverages multi-scale features for offset prediction, effectively increasing alignment accuracy in low-texture and large-motion regions. Experimental results show that SK-OPNet achieves excellent propagation stability and alignment performance, improving video super-resolution performance.

Keywords: Video Super-Resolution · Inter-Frame Propagation ·
Feature Alignment · Selective Kernel · Offset Prediction

1 Introduction

Video Super-Resolution (VSR) aims to reconstruct high-resolution (HR) video sequences from low-resolution (LR) inputs by leveraging temporal information, with applications in film restoration, surveillance, and video enhancement [1–3]. However, complex motions pose challenges in modeling inter-frame relationships.

Early flow-based methods [4] relied on optical flow for motion estimation but suffered from error accumulation. Subsequent works [5] improved feature fusion but still faced alignment inaccuracies. Recent approaches [6] employed multi-scale deformable convolutions for better alignment but lacked global motion perception. To address the above issues, we designed SK-OPNet, which integrates

© The Author(s), under exclusive license to Springer Nature Singapore Pte Ltd. 2026
Z. Lin et al. (Eds.): ICIG 2025, LNCS 16163, pp. 102–113, 2026.
https://doi.org/10.1007/978-981-95-3729-7_9

dynamic fusion of temporal features and multi-scale offset prediction within a grid propagation framework to enhance propagation stability and alignment accuracy in VSR tasks. Specifically, it includes two key improved modules: the Multi-Input Selective Kernel Attention (M-SKA) module and the Multi-Scale Offset Prediction (MSOP) module. M-SKA dynamically adjusts the contributions of features from the previous frame, the frame before that, and the current node, enhancing information interaction and selective modeling across temporal scales, thereby mitigating the accumulation of alignment errors. MSOP leverages feature fusion at different receptive field scales to improve offset estimation accuracy in complex motion and low-texture regions, strengthening the effect of second-order deformable alignment.

Our main contributions are as follows:

1) We propose a method for dynamically adjusting multi-frame features, which enhances information interaction and selective modeling across temporal scales, effectively alleviating the accumulation of alignment errors along the propagation chain, thereby improving propagation stability and feature representation capability.
2) We introduce a method that calculates offsets by combining features at different receptive field scales, significantly improving alignment accuracy in complex motion and low-texture areas, and reinforcing second-order deformable convolution-based alignment.
3) We conduct systematic evaluations on multiple mainstream video super-resolution datasets. Experimental results demonstrate that our method achieves a good balance between reconstruction quality and computational efficiency while improving inter-frame propagation stability and feature alignment accuracy, outperforming existing state-of-the-art methods.

2   Related Work

VSR as a vital research direction in the field of computer vision. It is widely applied in areas such as film production, intelligent surveillance, and augmented reality. Early VSR methods primarily relied on motion estimation based on optical flow techniques to achieve inter-frame alignment and feature fusion. For example, TOFlow [4] proposed a dynamic frame fusion strategy based on optical flow, which effectively captures video motion information and significantly improves video reconstruction quality. However, the optical flow estimation process suffers from uncertainty and error propagation issues, especially in regions with rapid motion or occlusion. The accumulation of errors degrades alignment quality and limits overall performance improvement.

To overcome the limitations of optical flow methods, deformable convolution based on deep learning has been widely applied in VSR tasks to enhance adaptability to complex motion and non-rigid deformations. EDVR [6] introduced a multi-scale deformable convolution alignment module combined with multiple attention mechanisms to achieve efficient feature alignment and fusion, improving super-resolution results in dynamic scenes. Subsequently, BasicVSR [7] proposed network architectures based on recursive propagation, utilizing bidirectional propagation strategies and second-order deformable convolutions to further strengthen feature propagation stability and large motion modeling capability, achieving better performance. However, these methods still face challenges such as accumulation of alignment errors and insufficient compression of redundant information during multi-frame feature fusion.

Regarding feature fusion mechanisms, researchers have explored attention mechanisms and multi-scale fusion strategies to enhance model expressiveness. PFNL [5] optimized the utilization efficiency of temporal features by multi-stage fusion of neighboring frame information, effectively enhancing detail restoration capability. Other works like TDAN [8] introduced dynamic convolution kernel adjustment mechanisms to dynamically adapt to motion compensation. Multi-scale attention methods, such as Non-Local Attention and channel attention mechanisms, have also been applied in video feature extraction to improve the model's perception of multi-level information.

Despite these advances, existing methods still face significant bottlenecks. On one hand, alignment errors tend to amplify during recursive propagation, especially in complex dynamic environments, adversely affecting the modeling of long-term dependencies. On the other hand, multi-scale dynamic selection strategies remain underexplored, making it difficult to maintain accurate alignment of large-range motions while preserving local details. Moreover, channel redundancy and dynamic fusion of multi-frame information still have considerable room for optimization, directly impacting the balance between computational efficiency and model performance.

3   Methodology

3.1   Selective Kernel Attention and Offset Prediction Network

The network architecture of SK-OPNet is illustrated in Fig. 1. At the i-th node of the grid propagation, given the features at three scales f_{i-1}^{j}, f_{i-2}^{j}, f_i^{j-1} ($(i-1)$-th frame, $(i-2)$-th frame, and the previous propagation branch) (where i represents the time step, and j denotes the propagation branch), the multi-input selective kernel attention produces the aligned results k_1, k_2, k_3:

$$k_1, k_2, k_3 = SKA(f_{i-1}^{j}, f_{i-2}^{j}, f_i^{j-1}). \tag{1}$$

where $g_i = f_i^0$ represents the features extracted from the low-resolution frame using multiple residual blocks, f_i^j denotes the features computed at the i-th time step in the j-th propagation branch. SKA stands for multi-input selectable kernel attention module, which will be mentioned in Sect. 3.1 later. Then, a flow-guided deformable convolution enhanced with Multi-Scale Offset Prediction (MSOP) is used to align features k_1 and k_2, resulting in the output feature $\widehat{f}_i^{j}$ at this node:

$$\widehat{f}_i^{j} = A_{OP}(g_i, k_1, k_2, s_{i \to i-1}, s_{i \to i-2}). \tag{2}$$

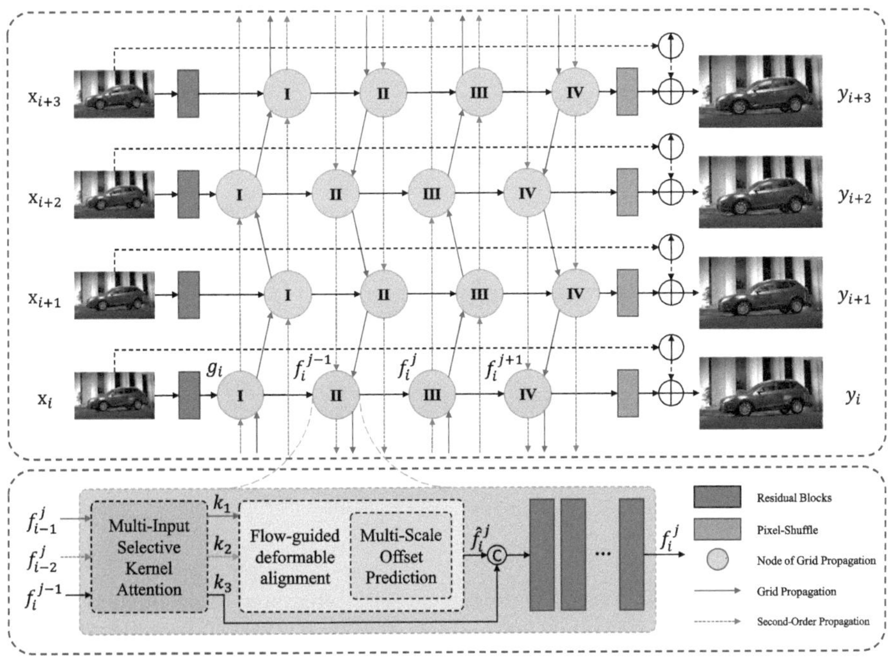

Fig. 1. Overall architecture of SK-OPNet.

where A_{OP} denotes the flow-guided deformable alignment (FGDA) integrated with Multi-Scale Offset Prediction (MSOP). The features k_1 and k_2 correspond to f_{i-1}^j and f_{i-2}^j after being processed by the Multi-Input Selective Kernel Attention (M-SKA) module. The optical flows si→i-1 and si→i-2 represent the motion from the i-th frame to the $(i-1)$-th and $(i-2)$-th frames, respectively. These aligned features are then concatenated and passed through a stack of residual blocks.

$$f_i^j = \widehat{f}_i^j + R(c(k_3, \widehat{f}_i^j)). \tag{3}$$

To leverage the diversity of offsets while mitigating instability, optical flow is used to guide deformable alignment, and multi-scale offset prediction is introduced. This process is illustrated in Fig. 2. Taking the forward propagation alignment as an example, at the i-th time step, given the feature g_i (where $g_i = f_i^0$) extracted from the i-th image frame, along with the features k_1 and k_2 from the previous two time steps extracted via M-SKA, and the optical flows $s_{i→i-1}$ and $s_{i→i-2}$ to the previous two frames. First, f_{i-1} and f_{i-2} are warped using the corresponding optical flows $s_{i→i-1}$ and $s_{i→i-2}$ (where the propagation branch index j is omitted for brevity):

$$\overline{f}_{i-p} = W(k_p, s_{i→i-p}). \tag{4}$$

where W denotes the spatial warping operation ($p = 1, 2$). Then, we use the Multi-Scale Offset Prediction (MSOP) module to pre-align features and compute

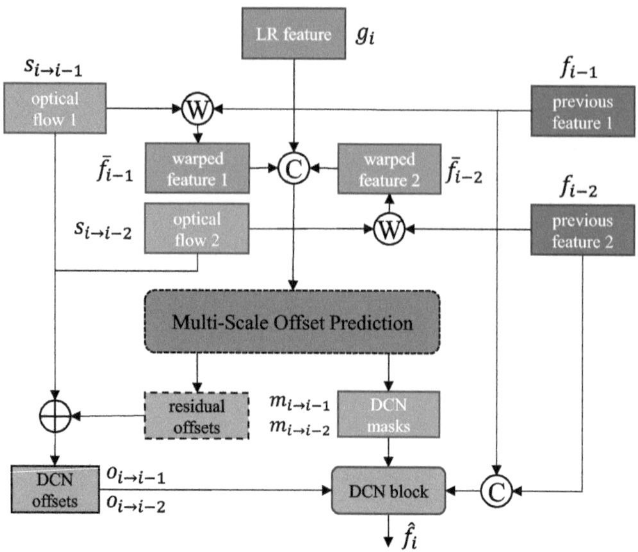

Fig. 2. Flow-guided deformable alignment with integrated offset prediction.

the DCN offsets $o_{i \to i-p}$ and modulation masks $m_{i \to i-p}$ ($p = 1, 2$). The flow guidance is reflected in the fact that the DCN offset includes the residual between the learned offset and the optical flow:

$$o_{i \to i-p} = s_{i \to i-2} + OP(c(g_i, \overline{f}_{i-1}, \overline{f}_{i-2})). \tag{5}$$

$$m_{i \to i-p} = \sigma(OP(c(g_i, \overline{f}_{i-1}, \overline{f}_{i-2}))). \tag{6}$$

where OP represents the Multi-Scale Offset Prediction module, and σ denotes the sigmoid function. Finally, the DCN is applied to the original, unwarped features k_1 and k_2:

$$\widehat{f}_i = D(c(k_1, k_2); c(o_{i \to i-1}, o_{i \to i-2}); c(m_{i \to i-1}, m_{i \to i-2})). \tag{7}$$

where D denotes the deformable convolution [9].

3.2   Multi-Input Selective Kernel Attention (M-SKA)

In VSR tasks, the temporal dimension plays a critical role. Traditional methods [11,12] typically rely on features from the previous and current frames. However, in complex scene variations—such as rapid motion or occlusion—excessive temporal information can lead to adverse effects. We propose the Multi-Input Selective Kernel Attention (M-SKA) module to dynamically adjust the contributions of features across time steps to enhance super-resolution performance. To address this issue. Network architecture is illustrated in Fig. 3.

During the propagation process at each time step, the input features to the current node come from three directions: the previous frame feature f_{i-1}^j, the feature from two frames before f^j_{i-2}, and the feature from the previous propagation branch f^{j-1}_i. These input features are weighted in the M-SKA module to dynamically adjust their influence, thereby generating more accurate feature. Our model adopts the Selective Kernel (SK) [10] mechanism, which automatically selects appropriate convolution kernels based on the characteristics of the input features and performs weighted fusion of multi-scale information.

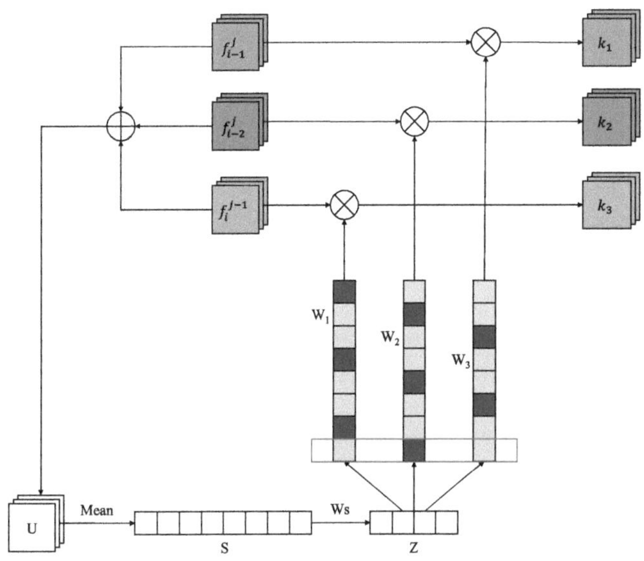

Fig. 3. Architecture of the M-SKA module.

In the M-SKA module, we first extract features through convolution operations at multiple scales. For the three input features f^j_{i-1}, f^j_{i-2}, and f^{j-1}_i, we process each of them using a set of convolution kernels with different scales $c1, c2, c3$. For each scale cn ($n = 1, 2, 3$), the result of the convolution operation is as follows:

$$\begin{cases} f_1^{conv} = Conv_{c_1}(f^j_{i-1}), \\ f_2^{conv} = Conv_{c_1}(f^j_{i-2}), \\ f_3^{conv} = Conv_{c_1}(f^{j-1}_i). \end{cases} \tag{8}$$

where f_n^{conv} denotes the convolution result obtained using the kernel at scale c_n. Next, the three convolution results are fused through a weighted combination. The weights are computed via a global pooling operation as follows:

$$S = Mean(c(f_1^{conv}, f_2^{conv}, f_3^{conv})). \tag{9}$$

where $Mean(\cdot)$ denotes mean pooling over the spatial dimensions. Then, the pooled feature S is projected into a lower-dimensional space through a fully connected layer W_s:

$$Z = W_S(S). \tag{10}$$

Based on the obtained global descriptor Z, another fully connected layer is used to compute the weights $\sigma(W_n Z)$ for each scale. Finally, the features f_n^{conv} from the three scales are adjusted by their respective weights $\sigma(W_n Z)$ and then fused to obtain the final output features k_n $(n = 1, 2, 3)$:

$$k_n = \sigma(W_n Z) \cdot f_n^{conv}. \tag{11}$$

This mechanism enables the M-SKA module to adaptively adjust the contribution of information at each scale and dynamically select the most appropriate scale for feature fusion. In this way, we can fully exploit multi-frame temporal information while avoiding interference from excessive temporal steps in complex scenes.

3.3 Multi-Scale Offset Prediction (MSOP)

In VSR tasks, traditional model [7,13,14] employs a single-scale offset estimation approach, which performs well in some scenarios but struggles to handle both small displacements (local details) and large displacements (global transformations) simultaneously. In complex scenes, single-scale offset estimation often fails to effectively align large-range motions, leading to insufficient alignment accuracy in low-texture and large-motion areas, ultimately degrading the super-resolution performance.

To address this issue, we propose the Multi-Scale Offset Prediction (MSOP) module. Its network architecture is illustrated in Fig. 4. Specifically, the MSOP module combines features at different scales, allowing it to adapt to various magnitudes of motion. This enables more accurate alignment, particularly in cases involving large-scale motions. The Multi-Scale Offset Prediction (MSOP) module consists of two main components: a coarse offset branch and a fine offset branch. The structure of the module is designed as follows:

Coarse Offset Branch: This branch performs average pooling on the input features, followed by offset estimation through convolutional layers, mainly used for handling global transformations; **Fine Offset Branch**: This branch progressively extracts features and estimates offsets through two layers of convolution, mainly used for estimating small-range offsets, suitable for aligning local details; **Fusion**: The output features of the two offset branches are concatenated and fused through convolution operations to generate the final offset prediction result.

By fusing multi-scale features, the MSOP module leverages high-resolution features to better handle small displacements with rich details, while relying on low-resolution features to manage large displacements. This design enables more accurate alignment of large-motion regions and significantly enhances the overall super-resolution performance.

The input feature required by the MSOP module described in Sec. 3.1 is defined as $feat = c(\overline{f}_{i-1}, g_i, \overline{f}_{i-2})$. After being processed by the two offset branches, two offset estimations at different scales are obtained. First, the coarse offset branch processes the input feature to generate the coarse offset:

$$offset_{corase} = Branch_{corase}(feat). \tag{12}$$

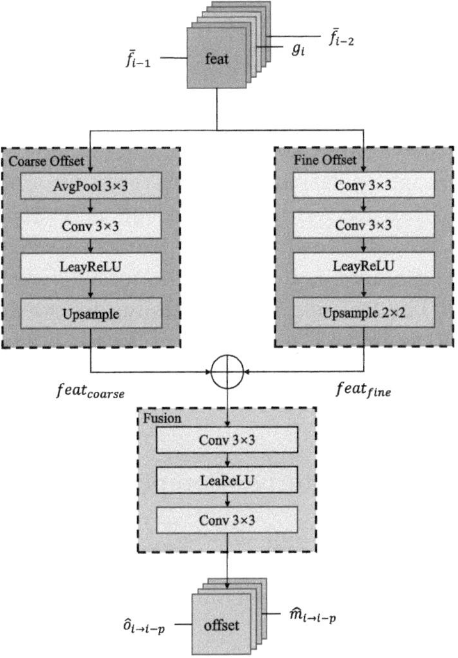

Fig. 4. Architecture of the MSOP module.

Next, the fine offset branch downsamples and processes the input feature to obtain fine offset, which is then upsampled via bilinear interpolation to match the resolution of corase offset.

$$offset_{fine} = UpSample(Branch_{fine}(feat)). \tag{13}$$

Then, the two offset features are concatenated and processed through a fusion convolution layer to obtain the final offset prediction:

$$offset = Fuse(c(offset_{corase}, offset_{fine})). \tag{14}$$

where c denotes the concatenation of the two offset features along the channel dimension, and $Fuse$ refers to the convolution layer that fuses the concatenated features to generate the final offset output.

In this way, the MSOP module is better equipped to handle complex motions, especially in cases involving large-range movement and low-texture regions. By performing multi-scale offset prediction, it significantly improves feature alignment accuracy and enhances the overall super-resolution performance.

4   Experiment

4.1   Settings

We use the mainstream dataset Vimeo90K [4] to train our model and test the model's performance using Vimeo90K-T. For the degradation method of video frames, we use bicubic interpolation (BI) with a downsampling factor of 4.

Both training and testing were conducted on a NVIDIA V100 GPU. The optical flow estimation module utilized a pre-trained SpyNet [15]. During training, we used the Charbonnier loss [17] as the loss function, and adopted the Adam optimizer [18]. The learning rate scheduling followed the Cosine Annealing strategy [19], with an initial learning rate of 2×10^{-4}. The model was trained for a total of 300,000 iterations. Each batch contained 8 samples, and the low-resolution input frames were cropped into 64×64 patches.

4.2   Quantitative and Qualitative Comparison

We compared our proposed method (SK-OPNet) with several mainstream or recent VSR methods. Table 1 presents the quantitative comparison results. Compared to existing methods, our approach offers the best balance between accuracy and efficiency.

Table 1. Quantitative evaluation (PSNR/SSIM) on the Y-channel (RGB-channel for REDS4). Red/blue denote top two performances. Missing entries indicate unavailable results.

Models	Params(M)	Viemo90K-BI PSNR	SSIM
Bicubic [20]	-	31.32	0.8684
TOFlow [4]	-	33.08	0.9054
RBPN [21]	12.2	37.07	0.9435
EDVR-M [6]	3.3	37.09	0.9446
EDVR [6]	20.6	37.61	0.9489
PFNL [5]	3.0	36.14	0.9363
MuCAN [22]	-	37.32	0.9465
BasicVSR [7]	6.3	37.18	0.9450
IconVSR [7]	8.7	37.47	0.9476
ESAFN [23]	8.2	37.42	0.9467
SK-OPNet(ours)	9.9	37.60	0.9484

Figure 5, Fig. 6 present the qualitative comparison results. We compare the proposed method, SK-OPNet, with various VSR methods on the Vimeo90K-T and Vid4 datasets. The results show that our method produces visual effects that are closer to the ground truth (GT) images.

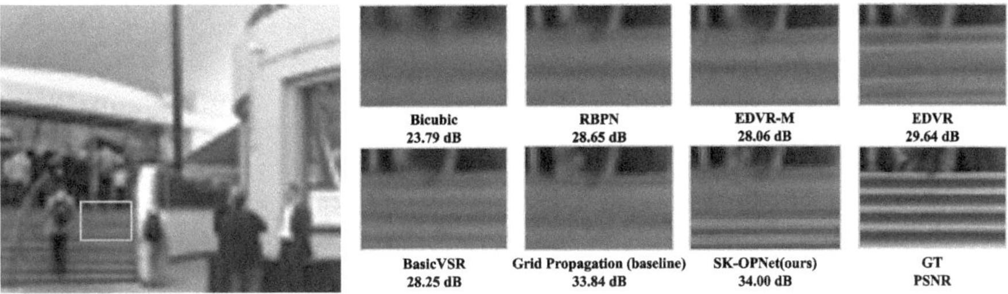

Fig. 5. Qualitative comparison of our method with other methods in Vimeo90-T.

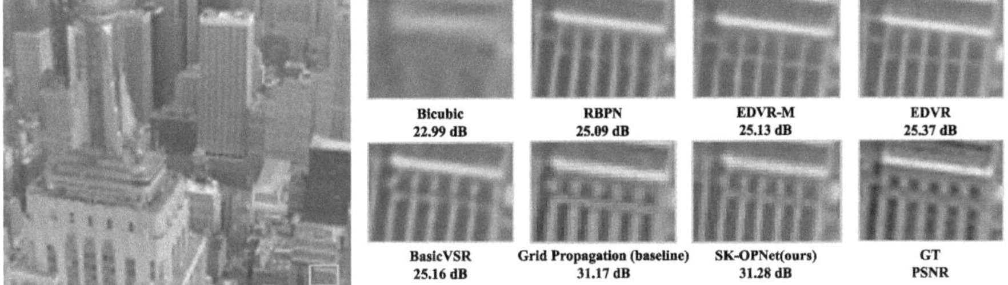

Fig. 6. Qualitative comparison of our method with other methods in Vid4.

4.3 Ablation Studies

To evaluate the contribution of the modules proposed in SK-OPNet, Table 2 presents the results of the ablation studies. Our baseline model includes only the grid propagation structure (excluding the M-SKA and MSOP modules). The ablation results show that integrating the MSOP module is integrated into the baseline model, it effectively fuses local and global details, leading to a 0.22dB improvement in PSNR with an increase of 2.5 M parameters. Integrating M-SKA module seems to be counterproductive (0.08dB reduction in PSNR), but when both the M-SKA and MSOP modules are integrated into the baseline model (i.e., forming SK-OPNet), a further improvement of 0.03dB is achieved compared to the model with only the MSOP module. This is because the combined model

Table 2. Ablation studies of our proposed module. The PSNR/SSIM is computed on Vimeo90K-T. Red indicate the best results.

Models	PSNR/SSIM	Params(M)
Baseline	37.49/0.9476	7.3
Baseline+M-SKA	37.41/0.9472	7.5
Baseline+MSOP	37.57/0.9485	9.8
Baseline+M-SKA+MSOP(SK-OPNet)	37.60/0.9484	9.9

can not only adjust the information contribution of input features at different scales but also perform more refined offset prediction.

5   Conclusion

In this study, we propose a novel video super-resolution network architecture, SK-OPNet, designed to enhance reconstruction accuracy while maintaining computational efficiency. The network consists of two key modules: the Multi-Input Selective Kernel Attention (MISKA) module, which adaptively selects convolution kernels of different scales based on the input features and performs weighted fusion of multi-scale information, thereby enhancing the network's ability to model spatial structures; and the Multi-Scale Offset Prediction (MSOP) module, which fuses high- and low-resolution features for offset prediction, effectively improving the modeling of large-range motion scenarios and enhancing inter-frame alignment accuracy.

Acknowledgments. This research was supported in part by Guangxi Natural Science Foundation, China (Nos. AB25069496 and 2024GXNSFFA010014); the National Natural Science Foundation of China (Nos. 62172120, 82360356, 82272075 and 62362014).

References

1. Wan, Z., Zhang, B., Chen, D., et al.: Bringing old films back to life. In: Proceedings of the IEEE/CVF Conference on Computer Vision and Pattern Recognition, pp. 17694–17703 (2022)
2. Srinivas, R., Sumathi, R., Mokshith, N., et al.: Intelligent surveillance with real time object detection coupled with distance estimation and voice alerts. In: 2024 8th International Conference on Electronics, Communication and Aerospace Technology (ICECA), pp. 1609–1614. IEEE (2024)
3. Li, C., Guo, C., Han, L., et al.: Low-light image and video enhancement using deep learning: a survey. IEEE Trans. Pattern Anal. Mach. Intell. **44**(12), 9396–9416 (2021)
4. Xue, T., Chen, B., Wu, J., et al.: Video enhancement with task-oriented flow. Int. J. Comput. Vision **127**, 1106–1125 (2019)
5. Yi, P., Wang, Z., Jiang, K., et al.: Progressive fusion video super-resolution network via exploiting non-local spatio-temporal correlations. In: Proceedings of the IEEE/CVF International Conference on Computer Vision, pp. 3106–3115 (2019)
6. Wang, X., Chan, K.C.K., Yu, K., et al.: EDVR: video restoration with enhanced deformable convolutional networks. In: Proceedings of the IEEE/CVF Conference on Computer Vision and Pattern Recognition Workshops (2019)
7. Chan, K.C.K., Wang, X., Yu, K., et al.: BasicVSR: the search for essential components in video super-resolution and beyond. In: Proceedings of the IEEE/CVF Conference on Computer Vision and Pattern Recognition, pp. 4947–4956 (2021)
8. Tian, Y., Zhang, Y., Fu, Y., et al.: TDAN: temporally-deformable alignment network for video super-resolution. In: Proceedings of the IEEE/CVF Conference on Computer Vision and Pattern Recognition, pp. 3360–3369 (2020)

9. Dai, J., Qi, H., Xiong, Y., et al.: Deformable convolutional networks. In: Proceedings of the IEEE International Conference on Computer Vision, pp. 764–773 (2017)
10. Li, X., Wang, W., Hu, X., et al.: Selective kernel networks. In: Proceedings of the IEEE/CVF Conference on Computer Vision and Pattern Recognition, pp. 510–519 (2019)
11. Caballero, J., Ledig, C., Aitken, A., et al.: Real-time video super-resolution with spatio-temporal networks and motion compensation. In: Proceedings of the IEEE Conference on Computer Vision and Pattern Recognition, pp. 4778–4787 (2017)
12. Jo, Y., Oh, S.W., Kang, J., et al.: Deep video super-resolution network using dynamic upsampling filters without explicit motion compensation. In: Proceedings of the IEEE Conference on Computer Vision and Pattern Recognition, pp. 3224–3232 (2018)
13. Ying, X., Wang, L., Wang, Y., et al.: Deformable 3D convolution for video super-resolution. IEEE Signal Process. Lett. **27**, 1500–1504 (2020)
14. Sajjadi, M.S.M., Vemulapalli, R., Brown, M.: Frame-recurrent video super-resolution. In: Proceedings of the IEEE Conference on Computer Vision and Pattern Recognition, pp. 6626–6634 (2018)
15. Ranjan, A., Black, M.J.: Optical flow estimation using a spatial pyramid network. In: Proceedings of the IEEE Conference on Computer Vision and Pattern Recognition, pp. 4161–4170 (2017)
16. Liu, C., Sun, D.: On Bayesian adaptive video super resolution. IEEE Trans. Pattern Anal. Mach. Intell. **36**(2), 346–360 (2013)
17. Charbonnier, P., Blanc-Feraud, L., Aubert, G., et al.: Two deterministic half-quadratic regularization algorithms for computed imaging. In: Proceedings of 1st International Conference on Image Processing, vol. 2, pp. 168–172. IEEE (1994)
18. Kingma, D.P., Ba, J.: Adam: a method for stochastic optimization. In: International Conference on Learning Representations (2015)
19. Loshchilov, I., Hutter, F.: SGDR: stochastic gradient descent with warm restarts. arXiv preprint arXiv:1608.03983 (2016)
20. Keys, R.: Cubic convolution interpolation for digital image processing. IEEE Trans. Acoust. Speech Signal Process. **29**(6), 1153–1160 (1981)
21. Haris, M., Shakhnarovich, G., Ukita, N.: Recurrent back-projection network for video super-resolution. In: Proceedings of the IEEE/CVF Conference on Computer Vision and Pattern Recognition, pp. 3897–3906 (2019)
22. Li, W., Tao, X., Guo, T., Qi, L., Lu, J., Jia, J.: MuCAN: multi-correspondence aggregation network for video super-resolution. In: Vedaldi, A., Bischof, H., Brox, T., Frahm, J.-M. (eds.) ECCV 2020. LNCS, vol. 12355, pp. 335–351. Springer, Cham (2020). https://doi.org/10.1007/978-3-030-58607-2_20
23. Li, B., Zhao, X., Yuan, S., et al.: Enhanced spatial adaptive fusion network for video super-resolution. In: Chinese Conference on Pattern Recognition and Computer Vision (PRCV), pp. 491–505. Springer, Singapore (2024)

Unified Token Representation and Accurate Attribute Prediction for Generalized Zero-Shot Learning

Rui Ren[1,2] and Huihui Bai[1,2(✉)]

[1] Institute of Information Science, Beijing Jiaotong University, Beijing, China
[2] Beijing Key Laboratory of Advanced Information Science and Network Technology, Beijing, China
{23120304,hhbai}@bjtu.edu.cn

Abstract. Generalized zero-shot enables the recognition of unseen classes by transferring semantic knowledge from seen classes, which is achieved by learning the latent relationship between visual features and attribute features. Previous works simply align the feature of an image with its associated attribute descriptions. However, direct alignment of image and text modalities often results in spurious visual-semantic correlations, owing to the inherent differences in semantic levels and granularity between the features extracted from image samples and text representations. To solve this situation, we introduce a Finite Discrete Token Module (FDTM) across the two modalities, using unified token representations to encode images and texts, achieving consistency between image and text embeddings at both the granularity and semantic levels. In addition, we propose a Semantic Correlation Intervention Module (SCIM) analyzes the relationships between different attribute response values in the attention mechanism, making the predictions closer to the ground truth and improving attribute prediction accuracy. The proposed method is evaluated on three ZSL benchmarks, and the results demonstrate the feasibility of our proposed method.

Keywords: Image Classification · Generalized zero-shot learning · Visual-semantic Correlation

1 Introduction

Deep learning has achieved remarkable success, relying on large-scale labeled datasets. However, in real scenarios, some categories may have only a few samples, or even no samples. In contrast, humans can recognize unseen objects by leveraging prior knowledge. Thus, inspired by human recognition process [1], zero-shot learning (ZSL) has been proposed to recognize novel objects by using auxiliary semantic information (e.g., category attributes [2], word embeddings [3], or textual descriptions [4]). Based on different learning paradigms, GZSL methods can be divided into generative-based approaches and embedding-based approaches.

Generative-based methods [5,6] synthesize artificial visual features for unseen classes. These synthetic features augment the training data, converting the GZSL task

© The Author(s), under exclusive license to Springer Nature Singapore Pte Ltd. 2026
Z. Lin et al. (Eds.): ICIG 2025, LNCS 16163, pp. 114–125, 2026.
https://doi.org/10.1007/978-981-95-3729-7_10

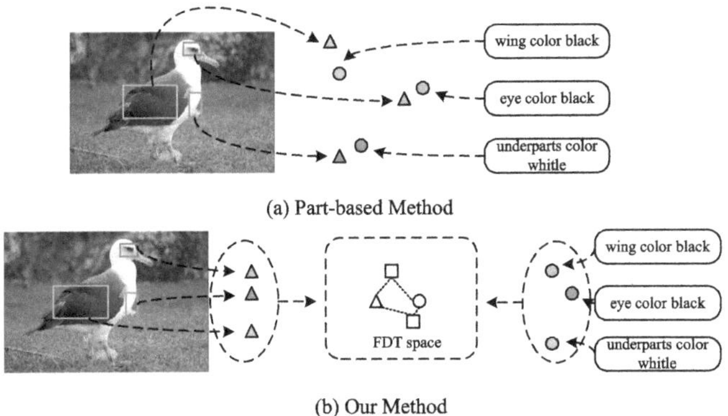

Fig. 1. Comparison of different feature representation learning methods. (a) feature alignment in most part-based methods. (b) our feature alignment using Finite Discrete Tokens.

into a fully supervised learning problem. In contrast, embedding-based methods provide a more direct solution by learning a shared latent space where both visual features and semantic descriptions are projected. Early embedding-based methods [7–9] learn projections between images and class-level attributes. However, these approaches use global visual features, and fail to focus local regions, which are associated with discriminative attributes that benefit classification. To address this limitation, subsequent works introduced attention mechanisms into the ZSL [10, 11] to better localize and emphasize these informative local regions, as shown in Fig. 1(a).

Recent embedding-based ZSL methods directly align visual and textual features, overlooking a crucial fact: the inherent semantic granularity difference between images and text. For example, textual attributes often describe abstract concepts like a "pointy tail", while visual features inherently contain more information, including both shapes and other details like color or texture. So aligning all visual information with abstract textual attributes will lead to spurious visual-semantic correlation, limiting semantic knowledge transfer. To address this, we argue that bridging the gap between the rich visual hierarchy and abstract textual descriptions to establish substantial correlation between visual and semantic representations.

In this work, we introduce a novel representation framework based on Finite Discrete Token Module (FDTM). FDTM consists of a set of modal-shared tokens that capture cross-modal semantic concepts at different granularity levels. All visual and textual features are represented using shared tokens, unifying the granularity of the information (see Fig. 1(b)). The core of modal-shared tokens is to enforce the aligned visual and semantic concepts to activate the same subsets of tokens. For instance, both the visual patches containing a bird's tail and the textual attribute "pointy tail" should activate the same tokens representing tail-related concepts. In addition, we introduce a Semantic Correlation Intervention Module (SCIM) to evaluate the accuracy of semantic prediction. Compared to conventional methods where visual features and attribute vectors contain different semantic levels, our method ensures feature alignment at the same granularity level, leading to more accurate localization of attribute-relevant image regions, this substantially enhances the visual-semantic correspondence. The experiments demonstrate the feasibility of our proposed method on public benchmark datasets.

In summary, the main contributions of this work are as follows. (1) We introduce a Finite Discrete Token Module to represent image and attribute embeddings using shared tokens, visual-semantic relationships are established by unifying the levels of granularity and semantic. (2) We propose a Semantic Correlation Intervention Module that improves attribute prediction accuracy by modeling the relationships between attribute responses in the attention mechanism. (3) Extensive experimental results on public benchmark datasets demonstrate that our method enhances the performance of GZSL.

2 Related Work

2.1 Zero-Shot Learning

Zero-Shot Learning addresses data dependency issue by directly recognizing unseen class samples through the knowledge transferred from seen classes [12–15]. Inspired by human recognition mechanisms, semantic information has emerged as a crucial bridge connecting the seen and unseen domains. Establishing the relationship between raw visual features and original semantic labels becomes a challenge in zero-shot learning. Due to the absence of unseen class samples in the training phase, generative-based approaches synthesize visual features for unseen classes. Them typically rely on Generative Adversarial Networks [5], Variational Auto-Encoders [16], or a combination of both [17] to generate corresponding visual features based on semantic information. Although such methods mitigate the issue of missing unseen class samples, they also tend to transform the generalized zero-shot learning task into a fully supervised problem, weakening its applicability in real-world scenarios.

Recently, embedding-based methods [18–20] have become the most prevalent approach in GZSL. Early works directly projected global visual features and semantic information into a shared embedding space. However, global visual features are often inadequate to capture subtle yet crucial local regions that distinguish between fine-grained categories. This limitation weakens the discrimination of the visual representations. To address this issue, part-based methods have emerged to enhance feature discriminability. By attending to these distinctive regions, the intra-class variation is reduced, while the inter-class differences among visual features are amplified. However, these methods overlook the fact that the semantic information conveyed by visual features and textual features is inherently different. To address this problem, we refined the representation of visual and attribute features for desirable visual-semantic alignment.

2.2 Attention Mechanism

Early part-based research on local representation primarily relied on part detection methods [21, 22]. However, these approaches face limitations due to the dependency on expensive part-level annotations for detector training. So attention mechanism was initially introduced in ZSL because its outstanding capability and low computational cost in extracting discriminative local features. [23] employed an attention module to filter

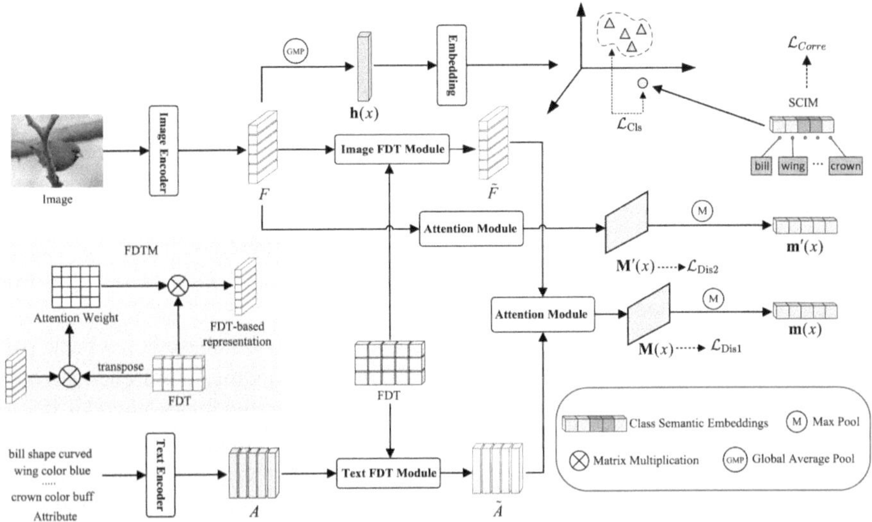

Fig. 2. The overall architecture of our proposed model, which includes two encoders, attention module, a Finite Discrete Tokens Module (FDTM), and a Semantic Correlation Intervention Module (SCIM).

out background noise and focus on semantically rich areas, improving visual-semantic alignment. Subsequently, attribute-guided attention emerged as a dominant approach, with models like [10,24] leveraging class-level attributes to direct the attention module toward informative regions. This was followed by the development of multi-head and cross-modal attention strategies. [25] activated attention regions based on class semantics to better perceive unseen categories, while [26] modeled the spatial distribution of various attributes through multiple attention heads. More recently, with the rise of large-scale vision-language pretraining models like CLIP, attention mechanisms have become integral to cross-modal alignment. [18] further integrated human gaze data as an additional attention signal, emulating real-world visual perception for enhanced recognition accuracy.

3   Methods

In this section, we first define the GZSL setting, notations and present the details of each module in our methods.

3.1   Problem Formalization

ZSL aims to recognize novel samples from unseen domains. Formally, the training set consists of N_s seen class samples $\mathcal{S} = \{(x_i^s, y_i^s)\}_{i=1}^{N_s}$, where $x_i^s \in \mathcal{X}^s$ denotes the seen images, $y_i^s \in \mathcal{Y}^s$ represents seen classes labels. Similarly, the test set contains N_u unseen class samples $\mathcal{U} = \{(x_i^u, y_i^u)\}_{i=1}^{N_u}$, where $\mathcal{Y}^s \cap \mathcal{Y}^u = \emptyset$. To address the domain shift problem arising from the disjoint label spaces between training and testing, ZSL use semantic vector of class c, denoted as $\mathbf{S}_c = \begin{bmatrix} s_c^1 & s_c^2 & \cdots & s_c^k \end{bmatrix}^\top$, where s_c^k denotes the value of the k-th attribute for class c. These class semantic vectors are available for both seen and unseen classes throughout the entire learning process. In conventional zero-shot learning, the objective is to classify images exclusively from unseen classes, formally expressed as: $f_{\text{CZSL}} : \mathcal{X}^U \to \mathcal{Y}^U$, where $\mathcal{X}^U$ represents the feature space of unseen classes and $\mathcal{Y}^U$ denotes the corresponding label space. The more challenging generalized zero-shot learning setting extends this formulation to include both seen and unseen classes: $f_{\text{GZSL}} : \mathcal{X} \to \mathcal{Y}^U \cup \mathcal{Y}^S$. Here, $\mathcal{X} = \mathcal{X}^S \cup \mathcal{X}^U$ indicates images from the seen and unseen domains.

Figure 2 illustrates our approach. Specifically, our method is based on a basic part-based ZSL backbone which consists of image encoder module, word encoder module, attention module and attribute localization module. Firstly, image encoder is used to extract visual features from images, and word encoder is used to extract attribute embeddings from texts. Next, FDTM transforms visual features and attribute embeddings into FDT-based visual features and attribute representations. Then, SCIM are employed to identify part features with localized discriminative attribute, enabling a comparative analysis of their responses. Finally, the joint global and local feature and the class semantic embedding are used to learn a cosine metric space.

3.2 FDT-Based Representation

As shown in Fig. 2, the key to part-based ZSL is accurately locating discriminative image regions. Due to differences in semantic granularity and abstraction levels between vision and text, prior methods struggled with cross-modal alignment, limiting attribute representation. To tackle this, we propose FDT-based feature representations and describe how to obtain them next.

In the image modality, we employ an image encoder to extract visual features $f(x) \in \mathbb{R}^{H \times W \times C}$ for seen classes images, where H and W represent height and width of the feature map, C denotes the dimension of visual features. Then we apply global average pooling over $H \times W$ to obtain global discriminative representation $\mathbf{h}(x) \in \mathbb{R}^C$. Finally, We use $\mathbf{h}(x)$ to compute cosine similarity.

In classification stage, We project $\mathbf{h}(x)$ to semantic space via a linear transformation $\mathbf{V} \in \mathbb{R}^{C \times K}$. The classification probability is computed using scaled cosine similarity:

$$p(y|x) = \frac{\exp(\sigma \cdot \cos(\mathbf{h}(x)^\top \mathbf{V}, \mathbf{S}_c))}{\sum_{\hat{y} \in \mathcal{Y}^s} \exp(\sigma \cdot \cos(\mathbf{h}(x)^\top \mathbf{V}, \mathbf{S}_k))} \tag{1}$$

where σ is the temperature scaling factor. The corresponding classification loss is:

$$\mathcal{L}_{\text{CLS}} = -\log p(y|x) \tag{2}$$

In the text modality, we first employ a word encoder to extract attribute word vectors $\{\mathbf{a}_k\}_{k=1}^K \in \mathbb{R}^{K \times D}$, where $\mathbf{a}_k$ denotes the average GloVe embeddings of the k-th attribute word, K denotes the number of attributes, D is the dimension of word embeddings. Attribute word vectors are then projected into visual feature space to ensure the visual attribute features $\mathbf{A}$ have the same dimensions with visual features.

After obtaining $\mathbf{F}$ and $\mathbf{A}$, we use learnable tokens to unify the cross-modal information granularity of two modalities. For images, the Finite Discrete Tokens Module learns FDT-based visual features grounded on modal-shared tokens $\mathbf{R}$. Specifically, given a image feature $\mathbf{F}$, it serves as the query to select relevant modal-shared tokens and generates the output:

$$\tilde{\mathbf{F}} = \mathrm{softmax}(\mathbf{Q}_F \mathbf{K}_R^\top)\mathbf{V}_R \tag{3}$$

where $\mathbf{Q}_S$, $\mathbf{K}_R$, and $\mathbf{V}_R$ are linear transformations of the query (attribute text), key (modal-shared tokens), and value (modal-shared tokens) respectively.

Similarly, we perform a similar operation on the text modality. We obtain FDT-based attribute embeddings according to the following formula:

$$\tilde{\mathbf{A}} = \mathrm{softmax}(\mathbf{Q}_A \mathbf{K}_R^\top)\mathbf{V}_R \tag{4}$$

Through this framework, visual and textual modalities are represented as linear combinations of the modal-shared tokens. This representation induces an explicit cross-modal alignment.

3.3 Discriminative Part Feature Learning

Since discriminative visual features contribute to classification, after aligning the semantic levels of visual and attribute features, we employ attention mechanisms to extract local image features. This guides the model to focus on regions most relevant to specific attributes, thereby enhancing the interaction between the visual and semantic spaces.

In this process, we designate $\tilde{\mathbf{A}}$ as the query and $\tilde{\mathbf{F}}$ as the key. By computing their correlation matrix followed by softmax normalization, we obtain attribute attention map $\mathbf{M}(x) \in \mathbb{R}^{H \times W \times K}$, which captures the spatial distribution of attribute-related features across the image. Each attention map $\mathbf{M}^k(x) \in \mathbb{R}^{H \times W}$ contains the k-th localized attribute information and we constrain each attribute information is concentrated to a single peak region, rather than dispersed distributions. This is achieved through a spatial concentration loss:

$$\mathcal{L}_{\mathrm{Dis1}} = \sum_{k=1}^{K}\sum_{i=1}^{H}\sum_{j=1}^{W}\mathbf{M}_{i,j}^k(x) \cdot (\|i - \tilde{i}^k\|_2^2 + \|j - \tilde{j}^k\|_2^2) \tag{5}$$

where $(\tilde{i}^k, \tilde{j}^k) = \arg\max_{i,j}\mathbf{M}_{i,j}^k(x)$ denotes the peak coordinates. The attribute response map $\mathbf{M}(x)$ is reduced to attribute response value $\mathbf{m}(x)$ through max pooling. This vector is optimized using Mean Squared Error loss against ground truth attribute annotations:

$$\mathcal{L}_{\mathrm{MSE}} = \|\mathbf{m}(x) - \mathbf{S}_c\|_2^2 \tag{6}$$

This loss function achieves alignment between visual features and semantic attributes while promoting the learning of discriminative features.

3.4 Semantic Correlation Intervention

In Sect. 3.2, we build visual-semantic correlation using shared tokens. In Sect. 3.3, we predict attribute scores via attention maps to focus on part features. To enhance the impact of attribute prediction on classification, we introduce a Semantic Correlation Intervention Module.

We define I as the input comprising image and attribute information, S as the semantic prediction, and Y as the label prediction. Our model first predicts S from I, denoted as $I \rightarrow S$, and then uses S to predict Y, denoted as $S \rightarrow Y$.

As shown in Sect. 3.3, S is obtained by computing the similarity between FDT-based visual features and FDT-based attribute embeddings. To reinforce the unification capability of the FDTM and to obtain more accurate S, we argue that the semantic prediction S, derived from $\tilde{\mathbf{F}}$ and $\tilde{\mathbf{A}}$, is more reliable than S', which is obtained from visual features $\mathbf{F}$ directly extracted from the visual feature extractor. Therefore, maximize the difference between S and S' can in turn promote the consistency in granularity representation and semantic level alignment. The formula is defined as follows:

$$\mathcal{L}_{\text{Corre}} = S(I = (\tilde{\mathbf{F}}, \tilde{\mathbf{A}})) - S'(I = (\mathbf{F}, \tilde{\mathbf{A}})) \tag{7}$$

In addition, we also constrain the attention map $\mathbf{M}'(x)$, obtained from $\mathbf{F}$, to encourage a more focused distribution of its predicted values.

$$\mathcal{L}_{\text{Dis2}} = \sum_{k=1}^{K} \sum_{i=1}^{H} \sum_{j=1}^{W} \mathbf{M}'^{k}_{i,j}(x) \cdot (\|i - \tilde{i}^k\|_2^2 + \|j - \tilde{j}^k\|_2^2) \tag{8}$$

3.5 Optimization and Zero-Shot Prediction

To optimize our model, we need to minimize the overall objective function, which can be represented as:

$$\mathcal{L} = \mathcal{L}_{\text{Cls}} + \lambda_1 \mathcal{L}_{Corre} + \lambda_2 (\mathcal{L}_{\text{Dis1}} + \mathcal{L}_{\text{Dis1}}) \tag{9}$$

where λ_1 and λ_2 are the weight to control the semantic correlation loss, spatial concentration loss.

Upon completion of model training, zero-shot recognition is conducted within the learned cosine similarity space. The test image x is first projected into this space through the visual-semantic embedding layer. Subsequently, classification is performed by identifying the class embedding that exhibits the highest compatibility score with the embedded image representation via the following:

$$\hat{u} = \arg\max_{u \in \mathcal{Y}^U} \cos(h(x)^T \mathbf{V}, \mathbf{S}) \tag{10}$$

Because the training process involves only seen classes, the resulting predictions often exhibit a strong bias toward them. To address this issue, we adopt the calibrated stacking technique (CS), which adjusts the prediction scores by subtracting a calibration factor γ from the scores of seen classes. Consequently, the GZSL classifier is formulated as:

$$\hat{y} = \arg\max_{\tilde{y} \in \mathcal{Y}}(\sigma \cos(h(x)^T \mathbf{V}, \mathbf{S}) - \gamma \mathbb{I}[\tilde{y} \in \mathcal{Y}^S]) \tag{11}$$

where $\mathbb{I}[\cdot]$ is the indicator function (1 for seen classes, 0 otherwise), γ denotes the calibration factor for seen class scores.

4 Experiments

4.1 Experiments Settings

Datasets. We evaluate our framework on three standard zero-shot learning benchmark datasets, including CUB-200-2011 (CUB) [27], SUN Attribute (SUN) [28], and Animals with Attributes 2 (AWA2) [15]. Each dataset includes pre-defined attributes that serve as semantic descriptors. To split the datasets into seen and unseen classes, we followed the Proposed Split (PS) protocol outlined in [15].

Evaluation Metrics. For standard ZSL evaluation, we report the average per-class Top-1 accuracy. In the GZSL setting, we separately measure the Top-1 accuracy on seen classes (denoted as S) and unseen classes (denoted as U). The overall GZSL performance is assessed using the harmonic mean H, computed as H = (2 × S × U) / (S + U), which balances recognition performance across both seen and unseen domains.

Implementation Details. We apply ResNet101 [29] pretrained on ImageNet [30] as the visual feature encoder. Model training utilizes the SGD optimizer with a momentum of 0.9 and a weight decay of 1×10^{-5}. The learning rate is fixed at 1×10^{-3} for CUB and SUN datasets, and 3×10^{-4} for AWA2 datasets. The loss balancing hyperparameters are set as $\lambda_2 = 0.2$, $\lambda_1 = 0.5$ for SUN and AWA2, 2.0 for CUB. The calibration factor γ is assigned a value of 3.5 for AWA2, and 0.7 for both CUB and SUN datasets.

4.2 Comparison with State-of-the-Art

Table 1 reports the comparison between our method and recent state-of-the-art approaches on three datasets. We evaluate both ZSL and GZSL settings.

We found that on CUB dataset, our method achieves **new state-of-the-art** performance in all metrics (ZSL-T1: 79.1%, GZSL-H: 71.1%), outperforming the previous best (SCE) by 0.5% and 3.5% respectively. For AWA2, we obtain **72.2%** harmonic mean, which is 1.9% higher than the second-best method (SCE with 70.3%). The results on the SUN dataset are competitive but not outstanding. This may be due to its large number of classes, abstract attributes, and difficulty in precise semantic alignment, which challenge our model's fine-grained alignment and intervention design. Notably, our approach maintains balanced performance between seen and unseen classes, as evidenced by the H scores.

Table 1. Comparison with state-of-the-art methods on CUB, SUN, and AWA2 datasets under the ZSL and GZSL settings. T1: Top-1 accuracy for ZSL. U/S: Top-1 accuracy on unseen/seen classes in GZSL. H: Harmonic mean.

Methods	CUB				SUN				AWA2			
	ZSL	GZSL			ZSL	GZSL			ZSL	GZSL		
	T1	U	S	H	T1	U	S	H	T1	U	S	H
f-CLSWGAN [14]	57.3	43.7	57.7	49.7	60.8	42.6	36.6	39.4	-	-	-	-
SGMA [24]	71.0	36.7	71.3	48.5	-	-	-	-	68.8	37.6	87.1	52.5
AREN [10]	71.8	38.9	**78.7**	52.1	60.6	19.0	38.8	25.5	67.9	15.6	**92.9**	26.7
DAZLE [25]	65.9	56.7	59.6	58.1	-	52.3	24.3	33.2	-	60.3	75.7	67.1
APN [26]	72.0	65.3	69.3	67.2	61.6	41.9	34.0	37.6	68.4	56.5	78.0	65.5
AGZSL [31]	57.2	41.4	49.7	54.2	-	29.9	40.2	34.3	-	65.1	78.9	71.3
FREE [17]	-	55.7	59.8	57.7	-	47.4	37.2	41.7	-	60.4	75.4	67.1
HSVA [16]	62.8	52.7	58.3	55.3	63.8	**48.6**	39.0	43.3	-	56.7	79.8	66.3
SCE [32]	**78.6**	66.5	68.6	67.6	62.5	45.9	**41.7**	43.7	69.4	**64.3**	77.5	70.3
TDCSS [33]	-	44.2	62.8	51.9	-	-	-	-	-	59.2	74.9	66.1
CMC-GAN [34]	61.4	52.6	65.1	58.2	**63.7**	48.2	40.8	**44.2**	-	-	-	-
ISAE-GZSL [35]	-	52.5	57.1	54.4	-	48.1	37.1	42.2	-	-	-	-
Ours	79.1	**67.1**	75.6	**71.1**	60.8	37.2	35.1	36.2	**71.4**	63.8	83.2	**72.2**

4.3 Ablation Study

To validate the effectiveness of our proposed FDTM and SCIM, we conduct comprehensive ablation studies on three datasets. The performance is shown in Table 2.

We begin by training a baseline model comprising an Image Encoder optimized with cross-entropy loss. The class logits are computed using the cosine distance between the projected visual features and each class embedding. We can see FDTM improves the T1 of ZSL over the baseline consistently by 2.0%(CUB), 1.3%(SUN), 5.4%(AWA2), and the H of GZSL over the baseline by 1.6% (CUB), 1.5% (SUN), 3.2% (AWA2) respectively. Also, SCIM boosts the H over the baseline with FDT module by 1.1% (CUB), 0.6% (SUN), 0.8% (AWA2) respectively. The results confirm that both FDTM and SCIM contribute synergistically to our model's performance.

4.4 Visualization of Attribute Attention Map

Figure 3 shows the visualization results of attribute attention maps. Compare the baseline method and ours on attributes "furry" and "black", The baseline model tends to generate scattered attention, often influenced by irrelevant background regions. In contrast, our method focuses more precisely on the regions associated with the target attributes. For instance, for the attribute "furry", our model accurately highlights the lion's mane area, and for "black", it concentrates on the panda's black torso and limbs. These results demonstrate that our approach achieves more accurate semantic alignment and improves both attribute recognition.

Table 2. Ablation study on the effect of FDTM and SCIM

FDTM	SCIM	CUB				SUN				AWA2			
		ZSL	GZSL			ZSL	GZSL			ZSL	GZSL		
		T1	U	S	H	T1	U	S	H	T1	U	S	H
		77.3	62.1	76.1	68.4	60.3	36.9	31.6	34.1	65.3	62.5	76.2	68.7
✓		79.3	62.5	79.6	70.0	61.3	37.8	33.6	35.6	70.7	63.7	82.4	71.9
✓	✓	79.1	67.1	75.6	71.1	60.8	37.2	34.1	36.2	71.4	63.8	83.2	72.2

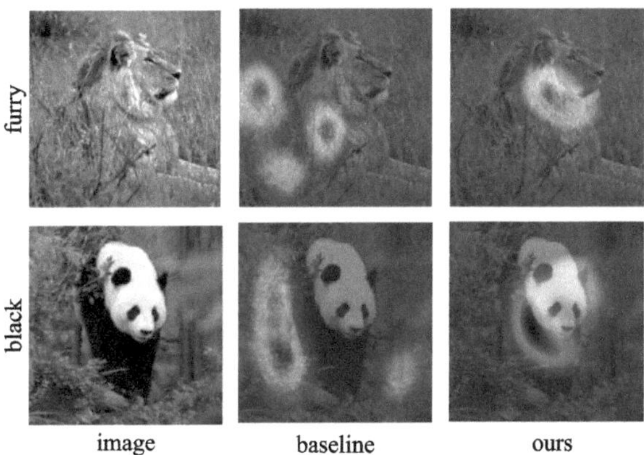

Fig. 3. Visualization of attribute attention maps learned by baseline and ours on AWA2.

5 Conclusion

This paper proposes a token-aligned semantic harmonization for generalized zero-shot learning. The proposed Finite Discrete Tokens Module (FDTM) effectively aligns the feature representations, and the Semantic Correlation Intervention Module (SCIM) improves semantic predictions. Our method consistently outperforms other approaches on three benchmarks, demonstrating its effectiveness in generalized zero-shot learning.

References

1. Lampert, C.H., Nickisch, H., Harmeling, S.: Learning to detect unseen object classes by between-class attribute transfer. In: 2009 IEEE Conference on Computer Vision and Pattern Recognition, pp. 951–958. IEEE (2009)
2. Farhadi, A., Endres, I., Hoiem, D., Forsyth, D.: Describing objects by their attributes. In: 2009 IEEE Conference on Computer Vision and Pattern Recognition, pp. 1778–1785. IEEE (2009)
3. Li, Y., Wang, D., Hu, H., Lin, Y., Zhuang, Y.: Zero-shot recognition using dual visual-semantic mapping paths. In: Proceedings of the IEEE Conference on Computer Vision and Pattern Recognition, pp. 3279–3287 (2017)

4. Lei Ba, J., Swersky, K., Fidler, S., et al.: Predicting deep zero-shot convolutional neural networks using textual descriptions. In: Proceedings of the IEEE International Conference on Computer Vision, pp. 4247–4255 (2015)
5. Han, Z., Fu, Z., Chen, S., Yang, J.: Contrastive embedding for generalized zero-shot learning. In: Proceedings of the IEEE/CVF Conference on Computer Vision and Pattern Recognition, pp. 2371–2381 (2021)
6. Hou, W., et al.: Visual-augmented dynamic semantic prototype for generative zero-shot learning. In: Proceedings of the IEEE/CVF Conference on Computer Vision and Pattern Recognition, pp. 23627–23637 (2024)
7. Romera-Paredes, B., Torr, P.: An embarrassingly simple approach to zero-shot learning. In: International Conference on Machine Learning, pp. 2152–2161. PMLR (2015)
8. Xian, Y., Akata, Z., Sharma, G., Nguyen, Q., Hein, M., Schiele, B.: Latent embeddings for zero-shot classification. In: Proceedings of the IEEE Conference on Computer Vision and Pattern Recognition, pp. 69–77 (2016)
9. Zhang, L., Xiang, T., Gong, S.: Learning a deep embedding model for zero-shot learning. In: Proceedings of the IEEE Conference on Computer Vision and Pattern Recognition, pp. 2021–2030 (2017)
10. Xie, G.S., et al.: Attentive region embedding network for zero-shot learning. In: Proceedings of the IEEE/CVF Conference on Computer Vision and Pattern Recognition, pp. 9384–9393 (2019)
11. Zhu, P., Wang, H., Saligrama, V.: Generalized zero-shot recognition based on visually semantic embedding. In: Proceedings of the IEEE/CVF Conference on Computer Vision and Pattern Recognition, pp. 2995–3003 (2019)
12. Palatucci, M., Pomerleau, D., Hinton, G.E., Mitchell, T.M.: Zero-shot learning with semantic output codes. Advances in neural information processing systems **22** (2009)
13. Verma, V.K., Arora, G., Mishra, A., Rai, P.: Generalized zero-shot learning via synthesized examples. In: Proceedings of the IEEE Conference on Computer Vision and Pattern Recognition, pp. 4281–4289 (2018)
14. Xian, Y., Lorenz, T., Schiele, B., Akata, Z.: Feature generating networks for zero-shot learning. In: Proceedings of the IEEE Conference on Computer Vision and Pattern Recognition, pp. 5542–5551 (2018)
15. Xian, Y., Lampert, C.H., Schiele, B., Akata, Z.: Zero-shot learning–a comprehensive evaluation of the good, the bad and the ugly. IEEE Trans. Pattern Anal. Mach. Intell. **41**(9), 2251–2265 (2018)
16. Chen, S., et al.: Hsva: hierarchical semantic-visual adaptation for zero-shot learning. Adv. Neural. Inf. Process. Syst. **34**, 16622–16634 (2021)
17. Chen, S., et al.: Free: feature refinement for generalized zero-shot learning. In: Proceedings of the IEEE/CVF International Conference on Computer Vision, pp. 122–131 (2021)
18. Liu, Y., et al.: Goal-oriented gaze estimation for zero-shot learning. In: Proceedings of the IEEE/CVF Conference on Computer Vision and Pattern Recognition, pp. 3794–3803 (2021)
19. Liu, M., Zhang, C., Bai, H., Zhao, Y.: Part-object progressive refinement network for zero-shot learning. IEEE Trans. Image Process. (2024)
20. Liu, M., Li, F., Zhang, C., Wei, Y., Bai, H., Zhao, Y.: Progressive semantic-visual mutual adaption for generalized zero-shot learning. In: Proceedings of the IEEE/CVF Conference on Computer Vision and Pattern Recognition, pp. 15337–15346 (2023)
21. Elhoseiny, M., Zhu, Y., Zhang, H., Elgammal, A.: Link the head to the "beak": zero shot learning from noisy text description at part precision. In: Proceedings of the IEEE Conference on Computer Vision and Pattern Recognition, pp. 5640–5649 (2017)
22. Yang, S., Wang, K., Herranz, L., van de Weijer, J.: On implicit attribute localization for generalized zero-shot learning. IEEE Signal Process. Lett. **28**, 872–876 (2021)

23. Chen, L., Zhang, H., Xiao, J., Liu, W., Chang, S.F.: Zero-shot visual recognition using semantics-preserving adversarial embedding networks. In: Proceedings of the IEEE Conference on Computer Vision and Pattern Recognition, pp. 1043–1052 (2018)
24. Zhu, Y., Xie, J., Tang, Z., Peng, X., Elgammal, A.: Semantic-guided multi-attention localization for zero-shot learning. Advances in Neural Information Processing Systems **32** (2019)
25. Huynh, D., Elhamifar, E.: Fine-grained generalized zero-shot learning via dense attribute-based attention. In: Proceedings of the IEEE/CVF Conference on Computer Vision and Pattern Recognition, pp. 4483–4493 (2020)
26. Xu, W., Xian, Y., Wang, J., Schiele, B., Akata, Z.: Attribute prototype network for zero-shot learning. Adv. Neural. Inf. Process. Syst. **33**, 21969–21980 (2020)
27. Welinder, P., et al.: Caltech-ucsd birds 200 (2010)
28. Patterson, G., Hays, J.: Sun attribute database: Discovering, annotating, and recognizing scene attributes. In: 2012 IEEE Conference on Computer Vision and Pattern Recognition, pp. 2751–2758. IEEE (2012)
29. He, K., Zhang, X., Ren, S., Sun, J.: Deep residual learning for image recognition. In: Proceedings of the IEEE Conference on Computer Vision and Pattern Recognition, pp. 770–778 (2016)
30. Deng, J., Dong, W., Socher, R., Li, L.J., Li, K., Fei-Fei, L.: Imagenet: a large-scale hierarchical image database. In: 2009 IEEE Conference on Computer Vision and Pattern Recognition, pp. 248–255. IEEE (2009)
31. Chou, Y.Y., Lin, H.T., Liu, T.L.: Adaptive and generative zero-shot learning. In: International Conference on Learning Representations (2020)
32. Han, Z., Fu, Z., Chen, S., Yang, J.: Semantic contrastive embedding for generalized zero-shot learning. Int. J. Comput. Vision **130**(11), 2606–2622 (2022)
33. Feng, Y., Huang, X., Yang, P., Yu, J., Sang, J.: Non-generative generalized zero-shot learning via task-correlated disentanglement and controllable samples synthesis. In: Proceedings of the IEEE/CVF Conference on Computer Vision and Pattern Recognition, pp. 9346–9355 (2022)
34. Yang, F.E., Lee, Y.H., Lin, C.C., Wang, Y.C.F.: Semantics-guided intra-category knowledge transfer for generalized zero-shot learning. Int. J. Comput. Vision **131**(6), 1331–1345 (2023)
35. Zhang, X., Zheng, Z.: Isae-gzsl: interpolated incomplete semantic attribute enhancement for generalized zero-shot learning. In: International Symposium on Computational Intelligence and Industrial Applications, pp. 371–386. Springer (2024)

Greenhouse Tomato Seedling Detection Algorithm Based on OMB-YOLO

Boyang Li and Daming Liu[✉]

Ningxia University, Yinchuan 75001, China
nxldm@126.com

Abstract. To address the challenges of complex background interference and insufficient multi-scale morphological adaptability in tomato seedling detection under greenhouse conditions, an improved OMB-YOLO model is proposed based on the YOLOv11 framework. The model reconstructs the backbone network with full-dimensional dynamic convolution (ODConv) to enhance the feature representation of stem and leaf textures. A feature enhancement module based on Multi-Scale Dilated Attention (MSDA) is introduced to suppress glare noise interference, while a Bi-directional Weighted Feature Pyramid Network (Bi-FPN)-based neck structure optimizes dense object localization, achieving synergistic improvements in detection performance. Experimental results show that the improved model achieves an mAP of 98.0% on a custom dataset, a 1.6% improvement over the original model. With a computational cost of 6.8 GFLOPs, the model improves mAP by 1.9–4.8% compared to the YOLOv5–10 series, with Precision and Recall reaching 94.8% and 93.4%, respectively. Through dynamic architecture optimization, this model provides an efficient solution for greenhouse tomato seedling detection.

Keywords: Tomato Seedlings · Target Detection · YOLOv11 · ODConv

1 Introduction

Accurate detection of crop seedlings is a key technology for intelligent management in protected agriculture systems [1]. However, in greenhouse environments, complex environmental parameters and morphological variations of plants often lead to feature confusion and localization errors in general detection models. As a major eco-nomic crop grown in protected cultivation, tomato seedlings exhibit dynamic morphological changes during early developmental stages, posing unique challenges for detection algorithms. Existing methods often struggle to capture seedling features under low-light conditions and in the presence of texture interference, resulting in missed detections and false positives [2]. Therefore, there is an urgent need to devel-op a high-precision detection model optimized for the morphological characteristics of seedlings.

Recent advances in computer vision, especially deep learning-based object detection algorithms, have shown remarkable potential for agricultural applications [3]. Among them, single-stage object detectors represented by the YOLO (You Only Look Once)

© The Author(s), under exclusive license to Springer Nature Singapore Pte Ltd. 2026

Z. Lin et al. (Eds.): ICIG 2025, LNCS 16163, pp. 126–137, 2026.
https://doi.org/10.1007/978-981-95-3729-7_11

series have emerged as key technologies for seedling recognition, due to their favorable balance between real-time performance and detection accuracy. YOLOv1, proposed by Redmon et al. [4], was the first to achieve end-to-end real-time detection; however, its limited capability in detecting small objects renders it less effective in agricultural scenarios characterized by low contrast between seed-lings and background. To address these limitations, Zhang et al. [5] introduced the YOLO-VOLO-LS model, which combines the high-level feature abstraction capabilities of the VOLO architecture with the YOLO detection framework, resulting in an 11.6% improvement in small-object detection accuracy for lettuce variety recognition. Liu et al. [6] enhanced YOLOv4-tiny by integrating attention mechanisms and a Dense Spatial Pyramid Pooling (Dense SPP) module, achieving 86.69% mAP in corn weed detection under complex weather conditions, while maintaining a lightweight model size of only 34.08 MB. Tang et al. [7] developed the CGS-YOLO algorithm, which preserves spatial details in multispectral imagery through the CARAFE up-sampling operator and boosts seedling feature responses using the GAM attention module, enabling corn seedling detection accuracy of 89.2% even under 75% weed coverage. Shi et al. [8] proposed the YOLO11-CGB model, which incorporates attention modules for enhanced trait differentiation, and combines a bidirectional feature pyramid with lightweight strategies to achieve 94.7% detection accuracy for cabbage seedlings.

However, current research faces significant limitations. First, most of the main-stream improved models are designed for open-field environments, lacking adaptability to the complex backgrounds and high-density planting conditions typical of greenhouses [9]. Second, existing cross-scale feature fusion methods struggle to effectively capture the dynamic morphological changes of tomato seedlings through-out their development—from the cotyledon stage to the mature seedling stage [10]. To address these gaps, this study proposes an improved detection model, OMB-YOLO, based on the conventional YOLOv11 framework. The specific enhancements are as follows:

First, full-dimensional dynamic convolution (ODConv) is incorporated into the backbone network. This mechanism enhances the feature representation of seedling stem and leaf textures through a multi-dimensional dynamic adjustment based on kernel space, channel dimensions, and the number of convolution kernels. Next, in the feature fusion stage, a Multi-Scale Dilated Attention (MSDA) module is de-signed. Through a divide-and-conquer sliding window and a dynamic dilation rate selection strategy, a composite attention mechanism is constructed to capture both local details and global semantic relations, effectively suppressing illumination interference and branch/leaf occlusion noise. Finally, a Bidirectional Weighted Feature Pyramid Network (Bi-FPN) is used to reconstruct the neck network. By leveraging cross-layer bidirectional connections and a learnable weight fusion mechanism, this model addresses the multi-scale feature degradation problem in dense seedling distribution scenarios. This model forms an adaptive seedling detection framework for complex greenhouse environments, optimized through dynamic feature adaptation, noise robustness enhancement, and cross-layer information fusion.

2 Omb-Yolo

YOLOv11 [11] is the latest single-stage object detection algorithm in the YOLO series. The algorithm builds upon the classic three-stage architecture and achieves a good balance between accuracy, speed, and generalization ability by optimizing feature extraction, multi-scale fusion, and prediction mechanisms. It achieves an mAP of 46.9% on the COCO dataset and offers multiple parameterized versions, with the lightweight YOLOv11n being particularly suitable for the dense small-object detection requirements in agricultural scenarios. A structural diagram is shown in Fig. 1.

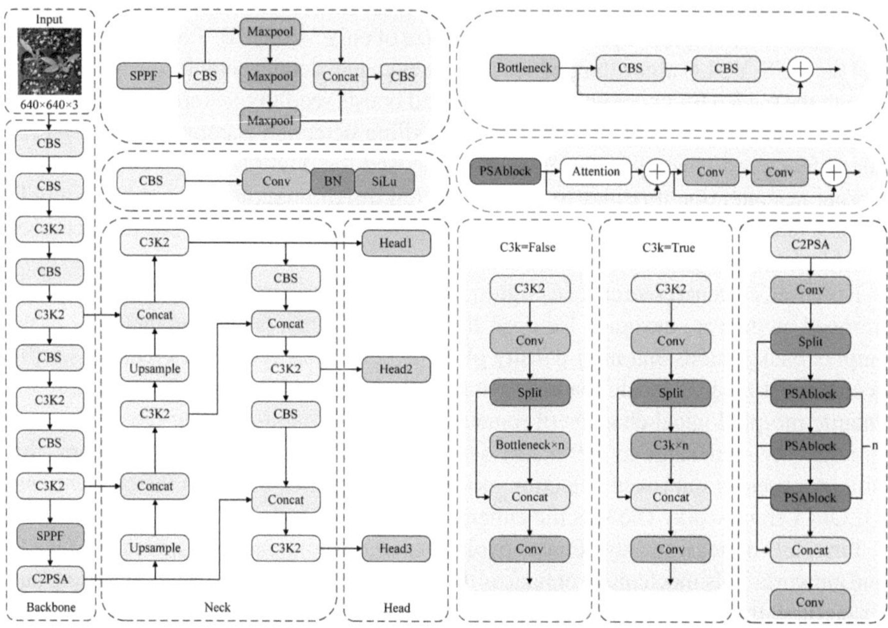

Fig. 1. Structure of YOLOv11n

Due to the stringent real-time requirements and the small scale of targets in greenhouse tomato seedling detection tasks, the original YOLOv11 model exhibits limitations in detecting small objects with sufficient accuracy. Therefore, this study selects YOLOv11n as the baseline model for improvement and designs the OMB-YOLO model to enhance the recognition accuracy of tomato seedlings across multiple growth stages. The model structure is shown in Fig. 2.

2.1 ODConv

Seedling plants are relatively small, and the imaging size varies significantly due to the varying distances from the camera. Additionally, the dense leaves of the seed-lings may cause occlusions, leading to insufficient feature extraction capabilities in the YOLOv11 model and limiting recognition accuracy. Traditional convolution operations use static

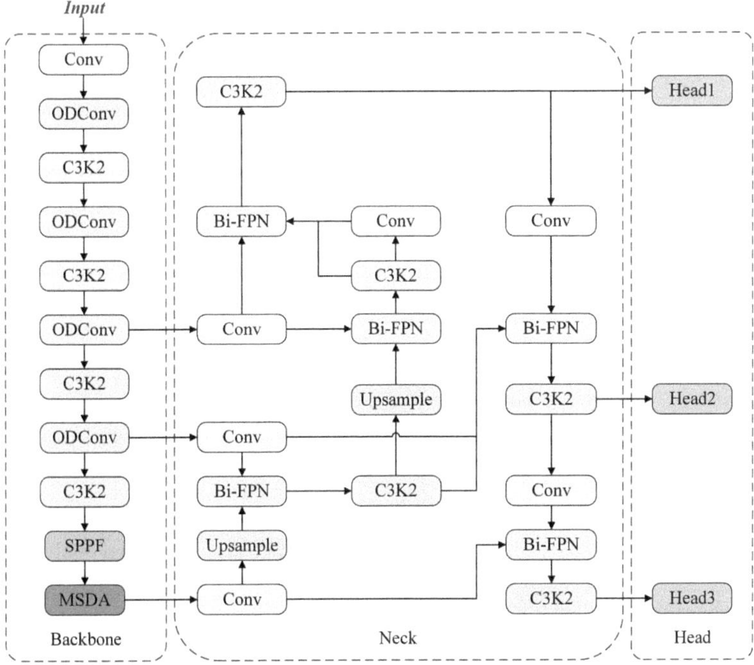

Fig. 2. Structure of OMB-YOLO

kernels, which are unable to adapt to the multi-scale feature variations in seedling images. To address this issue, this study introduces the ODConv dynamic convolution module [12], which has dynamic adjustment capabilities in four dimensions: spatial scale, kernel size, input channels, and output channels. Through a parallel strategy, ODConv achieves adaptive weight adjustments across multiple dimensions. In contrast to traditional convolutions, which perform static calculations in a single dimension, ODConv can dynamically adjust kernel parameters based on the multi-scale features of seedling images, significantly enhancing the model's ability to extract fine stem and leaf features and improving recognition performance in dense occlusion scenarios. Mathematically, ODConv can be expressed as:

$$y = (\partial w_1 \odot \partial f_1 \odot \partial c_1 \odot \partial s_1 \odot w_1 + \cdots + \partial w_n \odot \partial f_n \odot \partial c_n \odot \partial s_n \odot w_n)x \qquad (1)$$

In this context, x represents the input feature with width W, height H, and C_{in} channels, while y represents the output feature with width W, height H, and C_{out} channels. w_i ($i = 1, 2,..., n$) denotes different convolution kernels, and ∂w_1, ∂f_1, ∂c_1, and ∂s_1 represent the weights in the four dimensions: convolution kernel, output channel, input channel, and spatial scale, respectively. The multiplication operation is per-formed across these dimensions.

The structure of ODConv is shown in Fig. 3. This module adopts a multi-stage weight generation mechanism. After the input feature map is compressed through a global average pooling (GAP) layer, the output of the fully connected (FC) layer and ReLU activation function generates multi-dimensional dynamic weight parameters. Based on these parameters, the network performs element-wise weighted fusion of the original convolution kernels across the spatial and channel dimensions, ultimately producing an input-adaptive dynamic convolution kernel. By introducing the ODConv module, the model can dynamically adjust the convolution kernel parameters based on the size, posture, and occlusion conditions of tomato seedlings. This allows for more precise extraction of local details of seedling stems and leaves, as well as global contextual features, thereby improving the recognition robustness in dense planting scenarios.

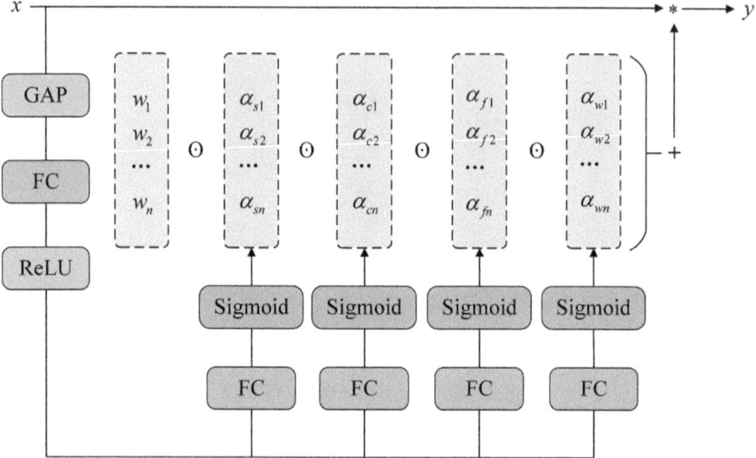

Fig. 3. Structure of ODConv

2.2 Msda

Due to the significant morphological scale differences of tomato seedlings at different growth stages, as well as the small size and unclear features of early-stage seed-lings, traditional convolutional neural networks (CNNs) can only capture local feature dependencies, making it difficult to capture the key impact of long-range pixel relationships for seedling recognition. While vision transformers can establish long-range contextual dependencies between image patches through global attention mechanisms, their computational complexity increases quadratically. Dilated convolutions expand the receptive field of convolutional kernels by introducing dilation rates, but excessively high dilation rates can lead to grid artifacts in the feature map. To balance computational complexity and feature dependency, this study introduces a Multi-Scale Dilated Attention (MSDA) module [13] into the feature fusion net-work, as shown in Fig. 4. By efficiently capturing the sparsity of features at different scales through a self-attention mechanism, the feature map channels are di-vided into multiple heads. Sliding window dilated attention (SWDA) with varying dilation rates simulates local sparse interactions between blocks, thereby aggregating multi-scale semantic information and effectively addressing the grid artifact issue.

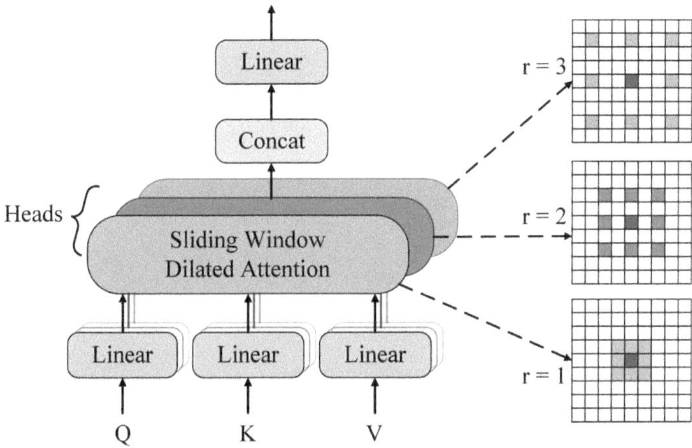

Fig. 4. Structure of MSDA

2.3 Bi-FPN

YOLOv11n integrates the Feature Pyramid Network (FPN) and Path Aggregation Network (PAN) in the feature fusion stage, utilizing the pyramid architecture to combine multi-scale features. As shown in Fig. 5(a), the traditional FPN + PAN structure does not consider direct fusion of shallow and deep features, leading to low utilization of the raw information from the backbone feature extraction network. Moreover, this network does not differentiate the processing of input features at different scales during the feature fusion stage. This can result in the loss of details during the cross-layer transmission of morphological features of seedlings at different growth stages, potentially causing false detections in the model. Additionally, the FPN + PAN structure contains a large number of nodes, increasing the computational cost during the training process. Tomato seedlings exhibit significant morpho-logical differentiation due to growth stage evolution, presenting multi-scale distribution characteristics. The Bi-FPN [14] effectively integrates cross-scale feature in-formation, thereby enhancing the model's ability to detect seedlings. The structure of Bi-FPN is shown in Fig. 5(b).

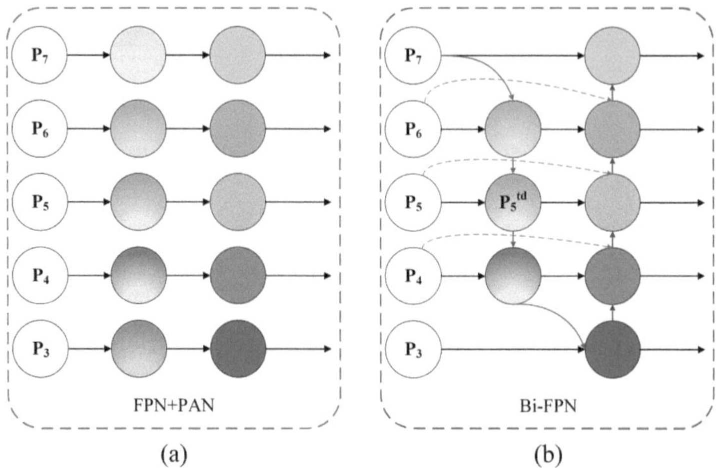

Fig. 5. Feature Pyramid Structures: (a) FPN + PAN Structure; (b) Bi-FPN Structure

Compared to FPN + PAN, Bi-FPN optimizes feature fusion through a bidirectional cross-scale interaction mechanism, which involves both top-down and bottom-up processes. This design preserves more contextual information and enhances feature transfer efficiency. Additionally, Bi-FPN prunes redundant connection nodes in the unidirectional feature flow, constructing bidirectional feature propagation paths between layers. It uses separable convolutions to achieve efficient fusion of cross-scale features. Furthermore, it employs learnable weights to differentiate the importance of different input features, forming a global-local feature collaborative enhancement mechanism.

3　Experimental Results and Analysis

3.1　Dataset

The dataset used in this study was captured in a double-layer membrane solar greenhouse in the seedling industrial park located in Yongning County, Yinchuan City, Ningxia Hui Autonomous Region. All images were taken at varying angles and un-der different lighting conditions, at distances ranging from 0.5 to 2 m from the tomato seedlings. A total of 2110 tomato images were selected, stored in.jpg for-mat, with a resolution of 640×640. Labelimg was used to annotate the growth stages of the tomato seedlings, including the cotyledon stage, seedling stage, and mature seedling stage, thus creating the dataset. This dataset contains various complex environmental conditions such as different lighting, occlusions, overlaps, and distant small targets. The dataset was split into training, validation, and testing sets in a ratio of 8:1:1. The final dataset includes 1688 images for training, 211 images for validation, and 211 images for testing. Sample images from the dataset are shown in Fig. 6.

(a)   (b)   (c)

Fig. 6. Dataset Samples: (a) Cotyledon Stage; (b) Seedling Stage; (c) Mature Seedling Stage

3.2   Experimental Environment and Parameter Settings

All experiments in this study were conducted in the hardware and software environments shown in Table 1.

Table 1. Experimental Environment

Component	Configuration
Operating System	Windows 11
CPU	Intel I7-13700KF
Memory (GB)	16
GPU	NIVDIA GeForce RTX 4060
Acceleration Libraries	Cuda 11.8
Programming Language	Python 3.9.2
Deep Learning Framework	PyTorch 2.0.1

The input image size during training is set to 640×640, and the batch size is set to 8. To accelerate training, the initial weights are set to the pre-trained network weights on the COCO dataset. To prevent overfitting and appropriately speed up convergence, the initial learning rate is set to 0.01, the momentum parameter is set to 0.937, and the number of iterations is set to 150.

3.3   Model Evaluation Metrics

To evaluate the performance of the improved model, this study selects Precision (P), Recall (R), mean Average Precision (mAP), and computational cost (GFLOPs, G) as evaluation metrics. The formulas for these metrics are as follows:

$$P = \frac{TP}{TP + FP} \tag{2}$$

$$R = \frac{TP}{TP + FN} \tag{3}$$

$$AP = \int_0^1 P(r)\mathrm{d}r \tag{4}$$

$$mAP = \frac{1}{N} \sum_{i=1}^{N} AP_i \tag{5}$$

where TP represents the true positives, FP represents the false positives, FN represents the false negatives, and $P(r)$ represents the precision at recall rate.

3.4 Ablation Study

To comprehensively evaluate the specific improvements of each module on model performance, this study conducts an ablation experiment based on OMB-YOLO using the dataset. The experiment sequentially adds different improvement modules to the model to quantify the actual contribution of each module in terms of detection accuracy and inference efficiency. The experimental results are shown in Table 2, where "$\sqrt{}$" indicates that the module is added to the network.

Table 2. Ablation Study

Model	ODConv	MSDA	Bi-FPN	Precision (%)	Recall (%)	mAP(%)
1				90.5	91.6	96.4
2	$\sqrt{}$			93.4	92.7	97.3
3		$\sqrt{}$		92.4	93.9	97.5
4			$\sqrt{}$	93.3	92.0	97.2
5		$\sqrt{}$	$\sqrt{}$	92.8	92.0	97.6
6	$\sqrt{}$	$\sqrt{}$		92.3	91.6	97.1
7	$\sqrt{}$		$\sqrt{}$	93.4	92.9	97.2
8	$\sqrt{}$	$\sqrt{}$	$\sqrt{}$	**94.8**	**93.4**	**98.0**

From the results of the comparative experiments, it is evident that the OMB-YOLO model outperforms all benchmark models in terms of both Precision and computational efficiency. Specifically, compared to YOLOv5s, OMB-YOLO improves Precision by 2.7% and increases mAP by 1.9%, confirming its superior performance in enhancing detail features and suppressing noise. Although YOLOv8n closely follows in Precision (94.6%), its computational complexity is 8.1 GFLOPs. In contrast, OMB-YOLO demonstrates lower computational complexity and significantly higher Precision, indicating a better balance between detection accuracy and computational efficiency. Both YOLOv9n and YOLOv10n exhibit significantly lower Precision than OMB-YOLO. While their computational complexities are lower, their performance lags far behind OMB-YOLO. Overall, OMB-YOLO maintains high Precision while ensuring low computational complexity, thoroughly validating its efficiency and practicality for greenhouse tomato seedling detection tasks.

To visually verify the proposed improvements in this study, three detection results were randomly selected to compare the network models before and after the improvement, as shown in Fig. 7. The visual analysis indicates that OMB-YOLO significantly improved the greenhouse tomato seedling detection performance. The original model suffered from boundary box shifts and missed detections in locally overlapping regions. The improved model can accurately distinguish soil impurities from low-visibility seedlings, effectively reducing both false positives and missed detections.

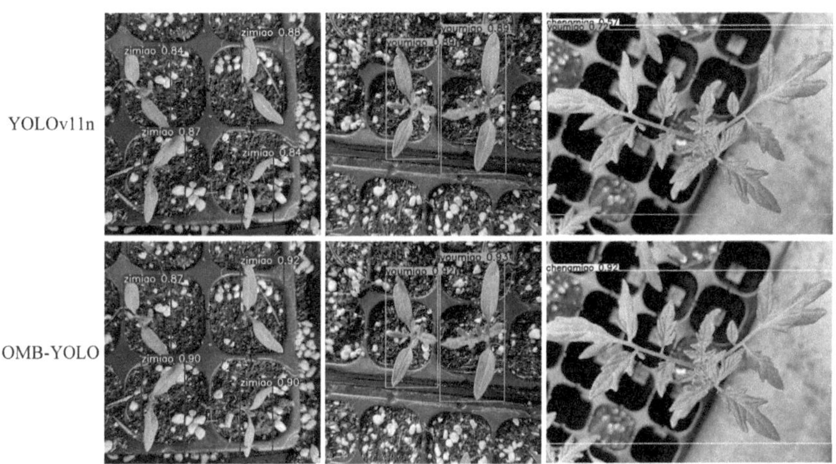

Fig. 7. Comparison Before and After Improvement

3.5 Comparative Experiment

To comprehensively evaluate the performance of OMB-YOLO in tomato seedling detection tasks, several mainstream YOLO models were selected for comparative analysis. All experiments were conducted using the same dataset and training environment. The experimental results are shown in Table 3.

Table 3. Comparative Experiment

Model	Precision (%)	Recall (%)	mAP (%)	GFLOPs
YOLOv5s	92.1	89.5	96.1	12.4
YOLOv8n	94.6	92.4	96.2	8.1
YOLOv9n	91.3	88.9	95.6	9.1

(continued)

Table 3. (continued)

Model	Precision (%)	Recall (%)	mAP (%)	GFLOPs
YOLOv10n	88.5	89.3	95.1	6.8
YOLOv11n	90.5	91.6	96.4	6.3
OMB-YOLO	**94.8**	**93.4**	**98.0**	**6.8**

From the experimental results, it is evident that the OMB-YOLO model outperforms all comparison models in terms of both Precision and computational efficiency. Specifically, compared to YOLOv5s, OMB-YOLO improves Precision by 2.7% and increases mAP by 1.9%, demonstrating its exceptional performance in enhancing detail features and suppressing noise. Although YOLOv8n closely follows in Precision (94.6%), its computational complexity is 8.1 GFLOPs. In contrast, OMB-YOLO exhibits lower computational complexity and significantly higher Precision, indicating that OMB-YOLO achieves a better balance between Precision and computational efficiency. Both YOLOv9n and YOLOv10n have significantly lower Precision than OMB-YOLO. While their computational complexities are lower, their performance lags far behind OMB-YOLO. Overall, OMB-YOLO maintains high Precision while ensuring low computational complexity, thoroughly validating its efficiency and practicality for greenhouse tomato seedling detection tasks.

4 Conclusion

This paper proposes an improved OMB-YOLO model, which significantly enhances greenhouse tomato seedling detection performance through the synergistic optimization of ODConv, MSDA, and Bi-FPN. Compared to the baseline model YOLOv11n, the proposed model achieves a 1.6% improvement in detection Precision, reaching 98.0% on a custom dataset, while maintaining a computational cost of 6.8 GFLOPs. Its Recall (93.4%) and Precision (94.8%) outperform other models in the same computational complexity range, offering an efficient solution for real-time object detection in agricultural applications.

References

1. Patrício, D.I., Rieder, R.: Computer vision and artificial intelligence in precision agriculture for grain crops: A systematic review. Comput. Electron. Agric. **153**, 69–81 (2018)
2. Kong, S., Li, J., Zhai, Y., et al.: Real-time detection of crops with dense planting using deep learning at seedling stage. Agronomy **13**(6), 1503 (2023)
3. Sun, X.: Enhanced tomato detection in greenhouse environments: a lightweight model based on S-YOLO with high accuracy. Front. Plant Sci. **15**, 1451018 (2024)
4. Redmon, J., Divvala, S., Girshick, R., et al.: You only look once: unified, real-time object detection. In: Proceedings of the IEEE Conference on Computer Vision and Pattern Recognition, pp. 779–788. IEEE (2016)
5. Zhang, P., Li, D.: YOLO-VOLO-LS: a novel method for variety identification of early lettuce seedlings. Front. Plant Sci. **13**, 806878 (2022)

6. Liu, S., Jin, Y., Ruan, Z., et al.: Real-time detection of seedling maize weeds in sustainable agriculture. Sustainability **14**(22), 15088 (2022)
7. Tang, B., Zhou, J., Zhao, C., et al.: Using UAV-based multispectral images and CGS-YOLO algorithm to distinguish maize seeding from weed. Artif. Intell. Agric. (2025)
8. Shi, H., Liu, C., Wu, M., et al.: Real-time detection of Chinese cabbage seedlings in the field based on YOLO11-CGB. Front. Plant Sci. **16**, 1558378 (2025)
9. Stavness, I., Giuffrida, V., Scharr, H.: Computer vision in plant phenotyping and agriculture. Front. Artif. Intell. **6**, 1187301 (2023)
10. Du, M., Sun, C., Deng, L., et al.: Molecular breeding of tomato: Advances and challenges. J. Integr. Plant Biol. (2025)
11. Khanam, R., Hussain, M.: YOLOv11: an overview of the key architectural enhancements. arXiv Preprint arXiv:2410.17725 (2024)
12. Li, C., Zhou, A., Yao, A.: Omni-dimensional dynamic convolution. arXiv Preprint arXiv:2209.07947 (2022)
13. Jiao, J., Tang, Y.M., Lin, K.Y., et al.: DilateFormer: multi-scale dilated transformer for visual recognition. IEEE Trans. Multimedia **25**, 8906–8919 (2023)
14. Tan, M., Pang, R., Le, Q. V.: EfficientDet: scalable and efficient object detection. In: Proceedings of the IEEE/CVF Conference on Computer Vision and Pattern Recognition, pp. 10781–10790. IEEE, (2020)

BiDAFuse: Bimodal Differences-Aware Attentive Network for Infrared and Visible Image Fusion

Keyu Sun[1], Mingyuan Jiu[1,2,3]($\boxtimes$), Shupan Li[1,2,3], and Hongru Zhao[1,2,3]

[1] School of Computer and Artificial Intelligence, Zhengzhou University, Zhengzhou, China
iemyjiu@zzu.edu.cn
[2] Engineering Research Center of Intelligent Swarm Systems, Ministry of Education, Zhengzhou University, Zhengzhou, China
[3] National Supercomputing Center in Zhengzhou, Zhengzhou, China

Abstract. Infrared (IR) and visible (VI) fusion aims to combine thermal radiation information in IR images with rich texture details in visible images. However, existing methods tend to ignore the inter-modal disparity information, thereby limiting fusion performance. In this paper, we propose a bimodal difference-aware attention network (BiDAFuse) for effective IR and VI image fusion. Our BiDA-Fuse consists of a difference-guided feature adjustment module (DGFA) and a bimodal attention fusion module (BIAF). The DGFA dynamically adjusts infrared and visible features using pixel-level disparity maps and a gating mechanism to enhance modality-specific information. The BIAF uses channel and spatial attention to adaptively weight the features, capturing long-distance dependencies and critical details. We evaluate the effectiveness of BiDAFuse through extensive experiments on two publicly available datasets (TNO and M3FD). Compared to seven state-of-the-art fusion methods, BiDAFuse demonstrates superior performance in terms of visual quality, quantitative metrics, and generalization capability.

Keywords: Image fusion · Infrared and Visible images · Adaptive fusion · Attention mechanism

1 Introduction

With the rapid development of modern information technology, image fusion has become a key approach to multisource information processing, exhibiting broad application potential and significant practical value in various fields [1, 2]. However, single-modality images often contain incomplete or insufficient information. Infrared images provide thermal cues but lack detailed texture, while visible images offer richer structural details yet perform poorly in complex environments and fail to convey the target's thermal characteristics. Therefore, the fusion of infrared and visible images integrates the advantages of both, resulting in comprehensive and accurate image information, and providing stronger support for subsequent tasks such as object detection [3], identification [4], and analysis.

© The Author(s), under exclusive license to Springer Nature Singapore Pte Ltd. 2026
Z. Lin et al. (Eds.): ICIG 2025, LNCS 16163, pp. 138–149, 2026.
https://doi.org/10.1007/978-981-95-3729-7_12

Previous studies have proposed numerous methods for integrating infrared and visible images, which can be broadly categorized into traditional approaches and deep learning-based methods. Although traditional methods can generate satisfactory fusion results, they generally feature manual design with much effort, high computational complexity, and low efficiency.

Deep learning has achieved great success in various image processing fields. In recent years, increasing attention has been given to applying deep learning to visible-infrared image fusion (VIF) to enhance fusion performance. Common deep learning-based VIF approaches include convolutional neural network (CNN)-based methods [5, 6], generative adversarial network (GAN) based method [7, 8] and transformer based method [9, 10].

While encoder-decoder frameworks, CNNs, and GAN-based methods have shown effectiveness in extracting local features for image fusion, they generally lack the capacity to model long-range dependencies, which limits their ability to preserve global contextual information in the fused image. To overcome this challenge, recent research has explored Transformer-based architectures. Transformers, with their capability to model long-range dependencies, have achieved significant success across various natural language processing and computer vision applications. VS et al. developed a Transformer-based multi-scale fusion strategy that enables the model to effectively integrate both local and long-range dependency information [9]. Wang et al. [11] presented an infrared and visible image fusion method by designing a residual Swin Transformer fusion network to acquire fusion results.

Although deep learning-based VIF methods have achieved significant progress, several challenges remain. First, attention mechanisms are often used solely to extract shared information from source images, while distinctive information is not effectively separated or utilized. Second, detail preservation remains inadequate in some cases. Finally, the models often lack the ability to effectively focus on key image information, leading to suboptimal fusion performance.

To address these challenges, we designed the adaptive fusion rules for VIF, which dynamically adjusted the fusion mode of infrared and visible image features according to the scene information. In order to make the features of the two images more in line with the fusion task, we adjusted the features after the feature extraction, and proposed the differences guided feature adjustment module (DGFA). In order to make the model more adaptively focus on the critical information, the bimodal attentive fusion module (BIAF) is designed.

The main contributions of this article are summarized as follows:

- The Difference-Guided Feature Adjustment module (DGFA). With this DGFA, the difference information of the two types of modes can be fully utilized to improve the processing power of the model for different modes.
- Bimodal Attentive Fusion module (BIAF). The contributions of the two input features are adaptively adjusted based on their characteristics, enabling the network to emphasize the most informative aspects from each modality during fusion.
- We performed comprehensive experiments on the TNO and M3FD datasets, comparing the performance of our BiDAFuse model with other representative fusion

studies. The results show that BiDAFuse is somewhat advanced in both quantitative and qualitative assessment.

2 Method

This section describes the proposed converged network. First, the details of the framework are presented. Next, the two modules of the network are introduced. Finally, the loss function used in our network is described.

2.1 Framework Overview

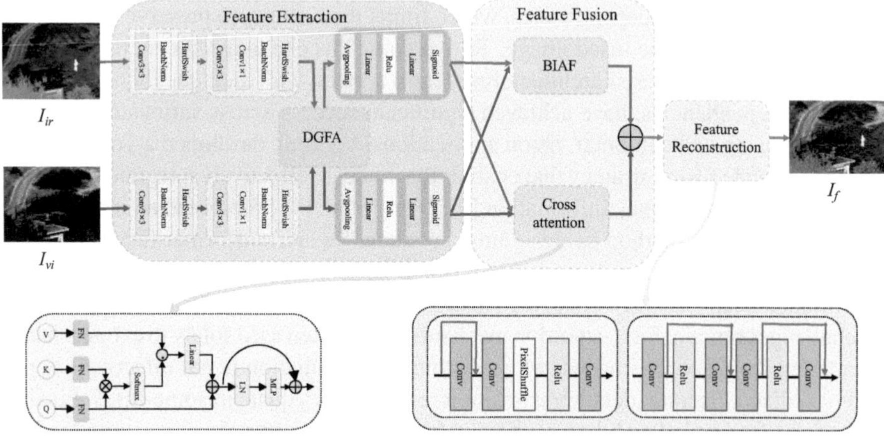

Fig. 1. The overall framework of BiDAFuse.

The overall framework is illustrated in Fig. 1. First, the infrared (IR) and visible (VI) source images are independently processed by the feature extraction module, which utilizes multi-path depthwise separable convolution and block embedding to extract multi-scale shallow features. Subsequently, the adaptive difference sensing module dynamically adjusts the IR and VI features based on difference maps and a gating mechanism, while enhancing channel-wise attention through the integration of a Squeeze-and-Excitation (SE) module. In the attention interaction module, the bimodal attention fusion (BIAF) module combines channel and spatial attention to adaptively weight features from both modalities. Fusion weights are then generated through convolution and softmax operations to linearly combine the original features, enabling effective cross-modal interaction. Additionally, cross-attention is employed to further facilitate information exchange between modalities. Finally, the feature reconstruction module progressively upsamples the fused features into high-resolution images. It first employs convolution and pixel shuffle operations to increase spatial resolution, followed by multiple convolutional and activation layers to refine and reconstruct detailed textures, thereby enhancing fusion quality and structural fidelity.

2.2 DGFA and BIAF

The objective of VIF is to create a fused image with salient targets and rich texture. Thus, making full use of the features from each source image is vital. To this end we propose the DGFA and BIAF.

In order to fully utilize the discrepancy information, this paper specially designs an adaptive difference perception module. After completing the basic operation of feature extraction, the module will also carry out further refinement of the extracted features to ensure the accuracy and effectiveness of the final fusion results and improve the quality of image fusion, as illustrated in Fig. 2(a).

When dealing with infrared features F_{ir} and visible light features F_{vi}, our goal is to efficiently fuse the features of these two different modalities to fully utilize their complementary information.

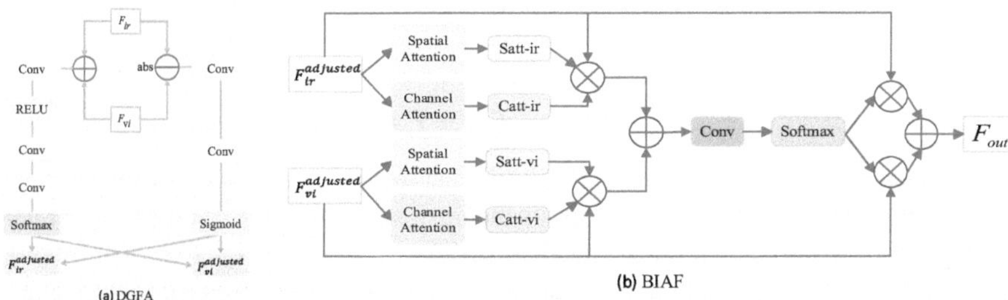

Fig. 2. The architecture of differences guidance feature adjustment module (DGFA) and Bimodal Attentive Fusion module (BIAF).

In order to understand the degree of difference between infrared and visible features at the pixel level, we first calculate their pixel-level difference value. This difference value helps us to find the inconsistency between the two features at the same location and provides the basis for subsequent processing.

$$F_{\mathrm{diff}} = |F_{\mathrm{ir}} - F_{\mathrm{vi}}| \tag{1}$$

Based on the pixel-level differences F_{diff}, we generate a difference map M_{diff} by using a convolutional layer and an activation function.

$$M_{\mathrm{diff}} = \sigma(\mathrm{Conv}(\mathrm{Conv}(F_{\mathrm{diff}}))) \tag{2}$$

where Conv denotes the convolutional layer operation, and σ is a Sigmoid function.

We splice the infrared and visible features in the channel dimension. The spliced feature F_{combined} contains the information of both features, which provides richer input for subsequent cross-combination.

$$F_{\mathrm{combined}} = \mathrm{Concat}(F_{\mathrm{ir}}, F_{\mathrm{vi}}) \tag{3}$$

where Concat denotes the splicing operation in the channel dimension.

The spliced features F_{combined} are processed for cross-combination. This process can facilitate the information interaction between two features and mine their potential association.

$$F_{\text{cross}} = \text{Conv}(\text{ReLU}(\text{Conv}(F_{\text{combined}}))) \tag{4}$$

In order to determine the contribution ratio of infrared features and visible features in the final fusion, we need to calculate the gating weights. The normalized gating weights G_{ir} and G_{vi} are obtained by applying convolution operation to the cross-combined features F_{cross} and normalized using Softmax function.

$$G_{\text{ir}}, G_{\text{vi}} = \text{Softmax}(\text{Conv}(F_{\text{cross}})) \tag{5}$$

Finally, the infrared features and visible light features are weighted and fused based on the calculated gating weights G_{ir} and G_{vi} and the difference map M_{diff}. The fusion process takes into account the contribution of the cross-combined features and the original features, as well as the degree of difference between the two features.

$$
\begin{aligned}
F_{\text{ir}}^{\text{adjusted}} &= F_{\text{cross}} \cdot G_{\text{ir}} + F_{\text{ir}} \cdot (1 - M_{\text{diff}}) \\
F_{\text{vi}}^{\text{adjusted}} &= F_{\text{cross}} \cdot G_{\text{vi}} + F_{\text{vi}} \cdot M_{\text{diff}}
\end{aligned} \tag{6}
$$

The BIAF module focuses on the multi-dimensional adaptive fusion of infrared and visible features, and collaboratively exploits the intrinsic correlation of cross-modal features through a two-branch attention mechanism. As depicted in **Fig. 2(b)**, The module uses a channel attention branch to compute the importance distribution of feature channels, combines it with a spatial attention branch to capture the saliency regions of the feature map, and finally dynamically generates a spatially adaptive fusion weight map through convolution. Compared to traditional individual attention methods, this module calibrates the features in both channel and spatial dimensions, and dynamically adjusts the fusion ratio based on the contextual information of the features at different locations, so that the fusion process is more in line with the nonlinear characteristics of the multimodal data, and improves the characterization ability of feature fusion.

The channel attention mechanism allows the model to automatically learn the importance of each channel. By emphasizing important channels and suppressing unimportant ones, the feature representation ability can be enhanced.

$$
\begin{aligned}
A_{\text{ir}}^{\text{ch}} &= \text{channel}\left(F_{\text{ir}}^{\text{adjusted}}\right) \\
A_{\text{vi}}^{\text{ch}} &= \text{channel}\left(F_{\text{vi}}^{\text{adjusted}}\right)
\end{aligned} \tag{7}
$$

where $A_{\text{ir}}^{\text{ch}}$ and $A_{\text{vi}}^{\text{ch}}$ represent the channel attention weights for the infrared and visible features. channel is the channel attention function.

The spatial attention mechanism aims to make the model focus on the importance of different spatial positions in the feature map. By calculating the maximum and mean values along the channel dimension, significant and global information can be captured in the feature map

$$
\begin{aligned}
M_{\text{ir}} &= \text{Conv}\left(\text{Concat}\left(\max_{c}\left(F_{\text{ir}}^{\text{adjusted}}\right), E_{c}\left(F_{\text{ir}}^{\text{adjusted}}\right)\right)\right) \\
M_{\text{vi}} &= \text{Conv}\left(\text{Concat}\left(\max_{c}\left(F_{\text{vi}}^{\text{adjusted}}\right), E_{c}\left(F_{\text{vi}}^{\text{adjusted}}\right)\right)\right)
\end{aligned} \tag{8}
$$

where M_{ir} and M_{vi} are the spatial attention maps for the infrared and visible features. Concat is the channel concatenation operation. $\underset{c}{\text{Max}}(.)$ Takes the maximum value along the channel dimension, and $\underset{c}{E}(.)$ takes the mean value along the channel dimension.

Combine channel attention weights with spatial attention maps to enhance the original features, where channel attention weights adjust the importance of different channels, while spatial attention maps modulate the significance of distinct spatial locations.

$$\tilde{F}_{\text{ir}} = F_{\text{ir}}^{\text{adjusted}} \odot A_{\text{ir}}^{\text{ch}} \odot \sigma(M_{\text{ir}})$$
$$\tilde{F}_{\text{vi}} = F_{\text{vi}}^{\text{adjusted}} \odot A_{\text{vi}}^{\text{ch}} \odot \sigma(M_{\text{vi}}) \tag{9}$$

where $\tilde{F}_{\text{ir}}$ and $\tilde{F}_{\text{vi}}$ are the enhanced infrared and visible features. $\odot$ represents the element wise multiplication operation. $\sigma(M_{\text{ir}})$ and $\sigma(M_{\text{vi}})$ map the spatial attention maps to the range [0,1] using the Sigmoid function, serving as spatial attention weights.

To achieve adaptive fusion of infrared and visible features, the fusion weights for each pixel position need to be learned.

$$F_{\text{cat}} = \text{Concat}\left(\tilde{F}_{\text{ir}}, \tilde{F}_{\text{vi}}\right) \tag{10}$$

$$W_{\text{fuse}} = \text{Softmax}(\text{Conv}(F_{\text{cat}})) \tag{11}$$

where F_{cat} is the combined feature obtained by concatenating the enhanced infrared and visible features along the channel dimension. W_{fuse} denotes the spatial adaptive fusion weights, where each position contains two values representing the fusion weights of the infrared and visible features, respectively, with their sum equal to 1.

Based on the learned spatial adaptive fusion weights, the original infrared and visible features are fused at the pixel level.

$$F_{\text{fused}} = W_{\text{fuse}}^{(0)} \odot F_{\text{ir}} + W_{\text{fuse}}^{(1)} \odot F_{\text{vi}} \tag{12}$$

where F_{fused} is the final fused feature. $W_{\text{fuse}}^{(0)}$ and $W_{\text{fuse}}^{(1)}$ are the fusion weights corresponding to the infrared and visible features, respectively.

2.3 Loss Function

The loss function $\mathcal{L}$ consists of three main components pixel loss $\mathcal{L}_{pixel}$, texture loss $\mathcal{L}_{texture}$ and structural loss $\mathcal{L}_{structure}$.

$$\mathcal{L} = \alpha\mathcal{L}_{pixel} + \beta\mathcal{L}_{texture} + \gamma\mathcal{L}_{structure} \tag{13}$$

where α, β and γ is hyperparameter to balance these three loss terms.

We expect the fused image to preserve salient texture details of source images. Thus, we specially introduce the texture loss, which is defined as follows:

$$\mathcal{L}_{texture} = \frac{1}{HW}||\nabla I_f - \max\{\nabla I_{ir}, \nabla I_{vi}\}||_1 \tag{14}$$

where ∇ refers to the Sobel operator used for computing gradients. $\|\cdot\|_1$ represents the $l_1 - norm$. H and W indicate the height and width of the image, and max{} performs element-wise maximum selection.

In image fusion, there are some regions where changes in pixel values have a greater impact on the overall visual effect, and we assign different weights to each pixel for the local structural information of the image, so that the pixel differences in these important regions account for a greater portion of the loss calculation.

$$\mathcal{L}_{pixel} = \frac{1}{N} \sum x, y \sum_{k=1}^{K} w_k(x,y)\left(I_{\text{fused}}(x,y) - I_k(x,y)\right)^2 \tag{15}$$

where the weights $w_k(x,y)$ are determined by the features of the kth source image.

The Structural Similarity Index (SSIM) is an effective metric for measuring the degree of structural similarity between two images, which takes into account information about three aspects of the image: brightness, contrast and structure. By incorporating SSIM to design the structural loss, the model can be guided to generate fused images that are highly similar to the source image in terms of structure.

$$\mathcal{L}_{structure} = 1 - \frac{1}{2}\left(\text{SSIM}(I_f, I_{ir}) + \text{SSIM}(I_f, I_{vi})\right) \tag{16}$$

where SSIM(.) represent the SSIM value between two images.

3   Experiments

In this section, we first state the dataset and experimental setup, and then introduce the comparison methods and evaluation metrics. Finally, we provide ablation experiments to validate the rationality and effectiveness of each module.

3.1   Datasets and Implementation Settings

In this study, we employ the RoadScene [12] and MSRS (Multi-Spectral Road Scene) [13] datasets as the training set. The RoadScene dataset consists of infrared-visible pairs captured in real-world driving environments. MSRS includes various urban and suburban scenarios, offering diverse semantic content. For evaluation, we use the TNO and M3FD datasets, which provide challenging conditions for comprehensive performance assessment.

The images are randomly cropped into sample patches of size 128×128 for training the proposed BiDAFuse network. Model parameters are optimized using the AdamW optimizer with an initial learning rate of 1×10^{-4}, regulated by a MultiStepLR scheduler. Specifically, the learning rate is decayed to 60% of its current value at the 50, 100, 200, 400, 600, and 800 epochs. The hyperparameters α, β, and γ are assigned values of 20, 20, and 1, respectively. All experiments are conducted on a workstation equipped with an NVIDIA GeForce RTX 4090 GPU and 24 GB of RAM. The implementation is based on the PyTorch framework.

3.2 Comparative Methods and Objective Evaluation Metrics

To validate the effectiveness of BiDAFuse, we employ seven state-of-the-art infrared and visible image fusion algorithms for performance comparisons, including the traditional method, **MDLatLRR** [14], five deep fusion models, **DenseFuse** [15], **FusionGAN** [7], **U2Fusion** [12], **PIAFusion** [13], and **CoCoNet** [16], and the transformer-based fusion model **SwinFuse** [11]. The source codes for all seven comparison methods are publicly available.

The performance of all methods is quantitatively evaluated using five objective metrics: Average Gradient *(AG)*, Entropy *(EN)*, Spatial Frequency *(SF)*, Mutual Information *(MI)*, and *Qabf*. A higher metric value suggests superior fusion quality. The highest and second-highest results are highlighted using bold and underline formatting, respectively.

3.3 Results and Discussion

1) *Fusion Results on M3FD Dataset:* Fig. 3 shows fusion results on the M3FD dataset. MDLatLRR exhibits color distortions (c). DenseFuse, FusionGAN, and CoCoNet fail to balance IR and VI information effectively (d, e, g). PIAFusion yields blurred edges and unclear contour details (f). SwinFuse and U2Fusion are less effective in preserving visible-light information such as textures and structural details (h, i). In contrast, our BiDAFuse better balances detail preservation and salient information retention.

As shown in Table 1, we evaluate seven fusion methods on twenty-five image pairs from the M3FD dataset. BiDAFuse achieves the best performance on all metrics except MI, where it ranks second. Based on both subjective and objective analyses, it can be concluded that BiDAFuse delivers superior fusion performance, outperforming other methods in terms of both visual perception and quantitative metrics.

Table 1. Quantitative Comparison on the M3FD Dataset

Methods	AG	EN	SF	MI	Qabf
MDLatLRR [14]	4.3465	6.5223	0.0582	2.8804	0.5919
DenseFuse [15]	3.3474	5.9256	0.0560	2.3657	0.5729
FusionGAN [7]	4.3478	5.8254	0.0526	3.3434	0.5203
PIAFusion [13]	<u>5.6939</u>	6.6283	0.0582	4.0032	<u>0.6298</u>
CoCoNet [16]	5.6258	6.7984	<u>0.0652</u>	2.7424	0.6259
SwinFuse [11]	5.0249	6.7214	0.0622	**4.1039**	0.6094
U2Fusion [12]	5.0073	<u>6.8338</u>	0.0609	3.7593	0.5699
Ours	**5.8883**	**6.8680**	**0.0704**	<u>4.0993</u>	**0.6596**

2) *Fusion Results on TNO Dataset:* Figure 4 shows two pairs of source images from the TNO dataset along with the fused images produced by various fusion methods.

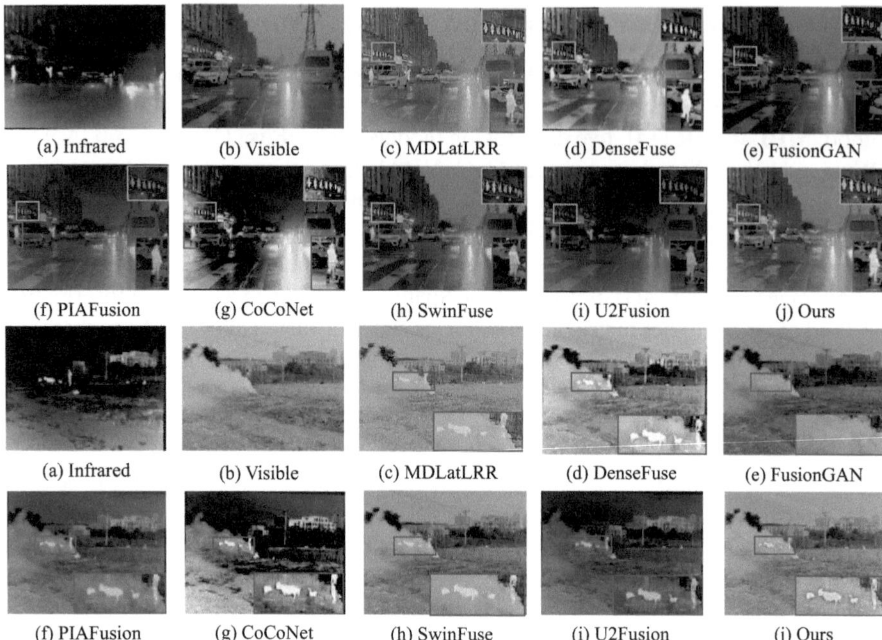

Fig. 3. Qualitative comparison of our method with seven state-of-the-art visible and infrared image fusion methods on the M3FD dataset.

Clearly, all seven methods can perform relatively good fusion results. But there are still some problems. Specifically, MDLatLRR fails to effectively extract thermal radiation information from the IR image, resulting in unclear target representation (c). DenseFuse also struggles with target clarity, yielding blurry fusion results (d). Fusion-GAN and U2Fusion are unable to adequately preserve important thermal features in the IR image, leading to the loss of critical information in the fused images (e,i). PIAFusion maintains the background information, but loses some texture details in the scene (f). CoCoNet demonstrates strong contrast and highlights semantic regions, but introduces distortions in texture, resulting in unclear edge details (g). In comparison, BiDAFuse effectively preserves both salient and detailed information across the fused results.

Table 2 further presents the quantitative evaluation results on twenty image pairs from the TNO dataset using five objective assessment metrics. The results indicate that our proposed method achieves the best average performance on four out of the five metrics. (i.e., EN, SF, MI and Qabf). AG ranked second near the best performance. Overall, our method achieves satisfactory performance, demonstrating the critical role of DGFA and BIAF.

(a) Infrared (b) Visible (c) MDLatLRR (d) DenseFuse (e) FusionGAN

(f) PIAFusion (g) CoCoNet (h) SwinFuse (i) U2Fusion (j) Ours

(a) Infrared (b) Visible (c) MDLatLRR (d) DenseFuse (e) FusionGAN

(f) PIAFusion (g) CoCoNet (h) SwinFuse (i) U2Fusion (j) Ours

Fig. 4. Qualitative comparison of our method with seven state-of-the-art visible and infrared image fusion methods on the TNO dataset.

Table 2. Quantitative Comparison on the TNO Dataset

Methods	AG	EN	SF	MI	Qabf
MDLatLRR [14]	3.9127	6.7413	0.0672	1.9346	0.3645
DenseFuse [15]	3.6341	6.5386	0.0236	2.4026	0.4435
FusionGAN [7]	2.2010	6.3553	0.0226	2.8364	0.2190
PIAFusion [13]	4.1038	6.6654	0.0457	3.2495	0.5738
CoCoNet [16]	**4.3048**	6.9173	0.0631	2.1262	0.2968
SwinFuse [11]	3.9429	6.7155	0.0400	3.4479	0.5150
U2Fusion [12]	3.2366	6.8421	0.0699	3.4333	0.5435
Ours	4.2361	**6.9223**	**0.0728**	**3.6284**	**0.5959**

3.4 Ablation Studies

Ablation Study on Network Structure: To investigate the effectiveness of DGFA and BIAF, we removed DGFA (named "w/o DGFA") and BIAF (named "w/o BIAF"), respectively. Fusion results of these variants and the full model are shown in Fig. 5. It can be observed that the w/o DGFA model tends to preserve more infrared information but loses visible details (see the red box in Fig. 5(c)). In contrast, the proposed BiDA-Fuse retains significantly more fine details compared to the w/o BIAF model (see red boxes in Fig. 5(d-e)). These results demonstrate that the proposed BiDAFuse benefits from the integration of the DGFA and BIAF modules, which are effective in capturing modality-specific difference information and enhancing fusion quality.

(a) Infrared   (b) Visible   (c) w/o DGFA   (d) w/o BIAF   (e) Ours

Fig. 5. Fusion results obtained by three different network structures.

Ablation Study on Pixel Loss Function: To ensure that the fused image contains more meaningful information from the source images, we employ a pixel intensity loss function to guide the network training. Figure 6 illustrates the fusion results of one pair of images with four different loss functions. It can be seen that our final loss function(f) has a satisfactory effect between preserving details and maintaining saliency.

(a)   (b)   (c)   (d)   (e)   (f)

Fig. 6. Fusion results obtained by the proposed method with four different pixel loss functions.

4 Conclusion

In this work, we enhance the saliency of difference information by adjusting the extracted features. Additionally, spatial and channel attention mechanisms are employed to capture and integrate long-range dependencies. Building upon the DGFA and BIAF modules, we propose a novel visible-infrared image fusion network, termed BiDAFuse. Its effectiveness is validated through comprehensive experiments on the TNO and M3FD datasets. Experimental comparisons with seven state-of-the-art fusion methods reveal that our method delivers more visually appealing fusion results along with competitive quantitative metrics. However, fused images under extreme low-light remain dim, limiting visibility. In future work, we will explore illumination-aware fusion to enhance perceptual quality.

Acknowledgments. This work is supported by the National Natural Science Foundation of China (No.s 62272422, U22B2051, 62502461), and also partially by the Natural Science Foundation of Henan Province (No. 252300421225) and Organized Young Scientific Research Team Cultivation Foundation of Zhengzhou University (No. 35220549).

References

1. Luo, Y., Luo, Z.: Infrared and visible image fusion: methods, datasets, applications, and prospects (2023)
2. Li, R., Zhou, M., Zhang, D., et al.: A survey of multi-source image fusion. Multimedia Tools Appl. **83**, 18573–18605 (2024)
3. Zhang, Q., Xiao, T., Huang, N., Zhang, D., Han, J.: Revisiting feature fusion for RGB-T salient object detection. IEEE Trans. Circuits Syst. Video Technol., 1804–1818 (2021)
4. Li, X., Li, X., Tan, H., Li, J.: SAMF: small-area-aware multi-focus image fusion for object detection (2024)
5. Liu, Y., Chen, X., Cheng, J., Peng, H., Wang, Z.: Infrared and visible image fusion with convolutional neural networks. Int. J. Wavelets, Multiresolution Inf. Process., 1850018 (2018)
6. Xu, M., Tang, L., Zhang, H., Ma, J.: Infrared and visible image fusion via parallel scene and texture learning. Pattern Reongn. **132**, 108929 (2022)
7. Ma, J., Yu, W., Liang, P., Li, C., Jiang, J.: FusionGAN: a generative adversarial network for infrared and visible image fusion. Inf. Fus. **48**, 11–26 (2019)
8. Yang, Y., Liu, J., Huang, S., Wan, W., Wen, W., Guan, J.: Infrared and visible image fusion via texture conditional generative adversarial network. IEEE Trans. Circ. Syst. Video Technol., 4771–4783 (2021)
9. Vs, V., Jose Valanarasu, J.M., Oza, P., Patel, V.M.: Image fusion transformer. In: 2022 IEEE International Conference on Image Processing (ICIP) (2022)
10. Rao, D., Wu, X.-J., Xu, T.: TGFuse: an infrared and visible image fusion approach based on transformer and generative adversarial network (2022)
11. Wang, Z., Chen, Y., Shao, W., Li, H., Zhang, L.: SwinFuse: a residual swin transformer fusion network for infrared and visible images. IEEE Trans. Instrum. Meas. **71**, 1–12 (2022)
12. Xu, H., Ma, J., Jiang, J., Guo, X., Ling, H.: U2Fusion: a unified unsupervised image fusion network. IEEE Trans. Pattern Anal. Mach. Intell. **44**(1), 502–518 (2022)
13. Tang, L., Yuan, J., Zhang, H., Jiang, X., Ma, J.: PIAFusion: a progressive infrared and visible image fusion network based on illumination aware. Inf. Fus. **83**, 79–92 (2022)
14. Li, H., Wu, X.-J., Kittler, J.: MDLatLRR: a novel decomposition method for infrared and visible image fusion. IEEE Trans. Image Process. **29**, 4733–4746 (2020)
15. Li, H., Wu, X.-J.: DenseFuse: a fusion approach to infrared and visible images. IEEE Trans. Image Process. **28**(5), 2614–2623 (2019)
16. Liu, J., Lin, R., Wu, G., Liu, R., Luo, Z., Fan, X.: CoCoNet: coupled contrastive learning network with multi-level feature ensemble for multi-modality image fusion. Int. J. Comput. Vis. **132** (5) (2023)

Multi-modal End-to-End Text Spotting Networks: Interactive Enhancements Between Visual and Semantic Features

Mayire Ibrayim[1,2]($\boxtimes$), Yefei Qian[1,2], and Zhicheng Bao[1,2]

[1] School of Computer Science and Technology, Xinjiang University, Urumqi 830046, Xinjiang, China
[2] Key Laboratory of Signal Detection and Processing in Xinjiang Uygur Autonomous Region, Urumqi, China
`mayire401@xju.edu.cn`

Abstract. Language knowledge plays a crucial role in understanding the semantic aspects of character sequences. However, in current SOTA end-to-end Scene Text Recognition methods, semantic information is typically treated as an independent module, applied during the post-processing stage of the output sequence. This approach does not fully leverage the semantic information of characters, leading to an inability to provide a more accurate and comprehensive understanding of the visual context. To address this issue, this paper introduces a novel approach, namely Multi-modal Scene Text Spotting Networks: Interactive Enhancements between Visual and Semantic Features (VSENet). First, the visual features and semantic features are concatenated in dimensions, forming a pseudo multi-domain sequence. This sequence is then input into a Transformer-based multi-modal encoder for mutual learning and enhancement. The semantic information effectively enhances visual features, reducing input noise within the visual domain, and increasing confidence in parallel predictions. Moreover, VSENet efficiently extracts features from text of different scales, thereby reducing background interference. An attention mechanism is introduced in the text detection process, and a novel feature extraction structure is designed. Furthermore, extensive experiments, including both English and Chinese, demonstrate significant improvements in accuracy and speed compared to other recognizers when adopting our language modeling approach.

Keywords: Scene text spotting · End-to-end · Language knowledge

1 Introduction

End-to-end scene text recognition is a pivotal area of research in computer vision, focusing on detecting and recognizing words or sentences in natural images. This technology has wide-ranging applications, including photo text recognition, menu reading, navigation, autonomous driving, and entity identification. Despite

© The Author(s), under exclusive license to Springer Nature Singapore Pte Ltd. 2026

Z. Lin et al. (Eds.): ICIG 2025, LNCS 16163, pp. 150–161, 2026.
https://doi.org/10.1007/978-981-95-3729-7_13

recent strides, challenges remain, such as variations in font, size, style, occlusion, distortion, and layout in natural scene images.

However, most existing end-to-end scene text recognition systems separately apply language knowledge, limiting semantic feature utilization and visual-semantic interaction. The interaction between visual and semantic features is crucial to eliminate background noise and enhance recognition accuracy.

To address this issue, we propose Multi-modal Scene Text Spotting Networks (VSENet), leveraging Transformer-based multimodal encoding to enhance visual features via semantic information. Our main contributions are:

- An attention-based text detection module validated on Total Text and CTW1500 datasets.
- A novel multimodal encoding module for mutual enhancement of visual and semantic features.
- Extensive experiments demonstrating significant improvements in recognition accuracy and speed compared to state-of-the-art methods.

2   Related Work

Scene text localization has significantly advanced in recent decades, largely driven by deep learning methods. Early approaches typically separated detection and recognition tasks. Wang et al. [19] utilized a sliding-window detector for character detection followed by individual classification. Bissacco et al. [1] integrated DNN and HOG features, constructing a character-based text extraction system. Liao et al. [9] proposed TextBoxes, a two-stage framework combining single-shot detection and text recognition [16]. However, these earlier methods lacked direct information exchange between the detection and recognition stages.

Recently, researchers have pursued end-to-end integration of text detection and recognition. Li et al. [8] developed a unified trainable framework that seamlessly integrates detection and recognition. TextDragon [5] introduced RolSlide, a differentiable operation that explicitly links detection and recognition for joint optimization. ABCNet and ABCNet v2 [10,12] utilized BezierAlign to transform irregular text into standardized representations. Similarly, Wang et al. [18] applied thin-plate spline transformations to rectify irregular text features.

Despite these advances, achieving high recognition accuracy without linguistic context remains challenging. AE TextSpotter [20] addressed this by using linguistic modeling to guide detection based on recognition outcomes. Fang et al. [4] proposed ABINet++, a self-attention-based iterative recognizer decomposed into separate visual and linguistic components, explicitly enhancing language modeling through gradient blocking. DeepSolo [21] innovatively employs explicit point representation and a Transformer decoder to simultaneously tackle detection and recognition, simplifying traditional post-processing. It represents text instances as ordered points on Bezier curves, encoding position, boundary, and category information.

STST [22] introduced a feature enhancement module to address limited receptive fields and weak representations in lightweight backbones, effectively aggregating multi-scale information and minimizing information loss. Additionally, a dual information attention mechanism was proposed to enhance the extraction of backbone features by highlighting salient information. DNTextSpotter [15] improved stability in Transformer-based text spotting by introducing denoising training techniques. It decomposes queries into position and content components: position queries derived from Bezier curve control points and content queries initialized via masked character sliding, thereby aligning text content and spatial positions effectively.

3   Methods

The overall structure of the model is illustrated in Fig. 2, consisting primarily of two parts: (1) FPN network embedded with CBAM attention. This structure combines ResNet [7] with attention mechanisms, introducing two types of attention modules: channel attention SENet and CBAM attention. These are integrated into the ResNet network to form a new network structure, where different features are weighted based on their importance by allocating different weights. This module compares the gain effects of SENet and CBAM attention on residual networks. Further, feature pyramid networks are employed to fuse features in a top-down manner. The obtained feature maps are then input into the Bezier curve detection network module, which regresses coordinate points using an anchor-free network. The parameter information of the coordinate points is used to form text boxes around the text in the image, yielding the output results. (2) Multi-modal Feature Enhancement Encoder. The visual feature extractor and Language Model (LM) extract visual and semantic features, respectively. Visual features associated with randomly selected characters are concealed, and the two modal features are concatenated. Multi-modal feature enhancement is achieved through the self-attention mechanism of the Transformer, facilitating interaction between visual and semantic features. The enhanced features of both modalities are then fused to ultimately determine the output sequence (Fig. 1).

3.1   Text Detection Combined with CBAM Attention

CBAM (Convolutional Block Attention Module) is a module based on attention mechanisms designed to enhance the performance of deep convolutional neural networks (CNN). Below, we will introduce the channel attention module and spatial attention module of CBAM, along with some relevant mathematical principles.

Image data undergoes CBAM attention after the last residual block in each stage of ResNet. CBAM comprises two independent sub-modules, the channel attention module (CAM) and the spatial attention module (SAM), which perform attention mechanisms on channels and spatial dimensions respectively, saving parameters and computational capacity, as illustrated in Fig. 3.

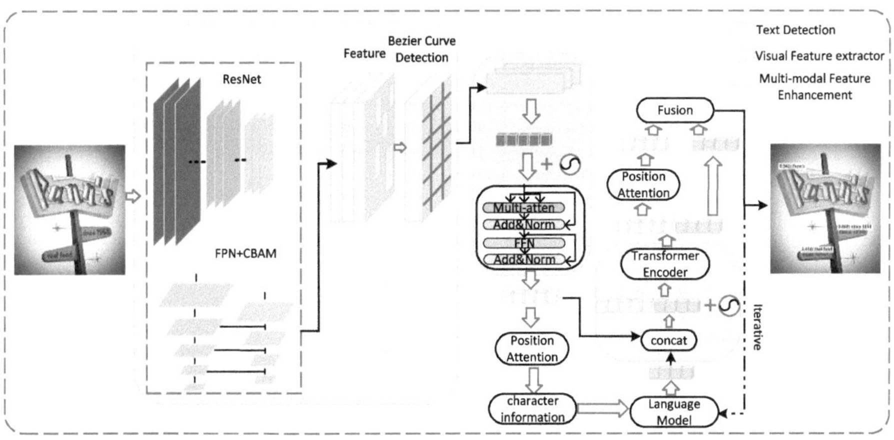

Fig. 1. An overview of VSENet

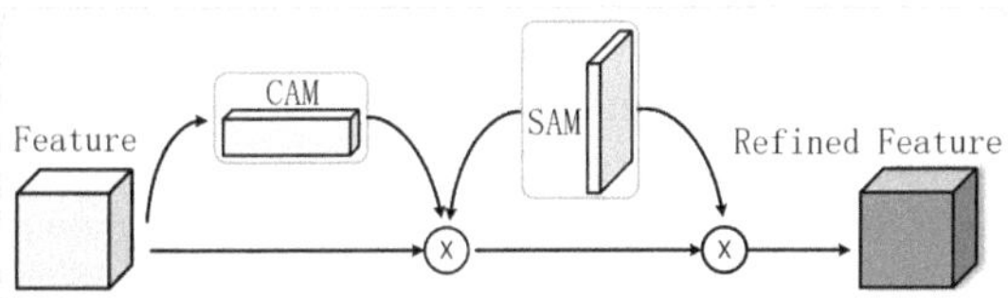

Fig. 2. CBAM attention module

CBAM infers an attention map along two independent dimensions (channel and spatial) each time, which is then multiplied with the input feature map for adaptive feature refinement. The processing of the input feature map F in CBAM can be summarized by Eqs. (1) and (2).

$$\mathbf{F'} = \mathbf{M_c}(\mathbf{F}) \otimes \mathbf{F} \tag{1}$$

$$\mathbf{F''} = \mathbf{M_s}(\mathbf{F'}) \otimes \mathbf{F'} \tag{2}$$

$\otimes$ represents element-wise multiplication, $\mathbf{F'}$ represents the result of element-wise multiplication between the feature map and the channel attention map. $\mathbf{F''}$ is the final refined output.

Below, we will elaborate on how CAM and SAM operate independently in two distinct dimensions.

CAM: The Channel Attention Module uses both global average pooling and global max pooling layers to compress feature maps along the spatial dimensions for feature extraction, minimizing data loss. The channel attention module is shown in Fig. 4. The global average pooling layer captures overall information, while the global max pooling layer gathers information on feature variance. The combination of these two layers performs better than either layer alone.

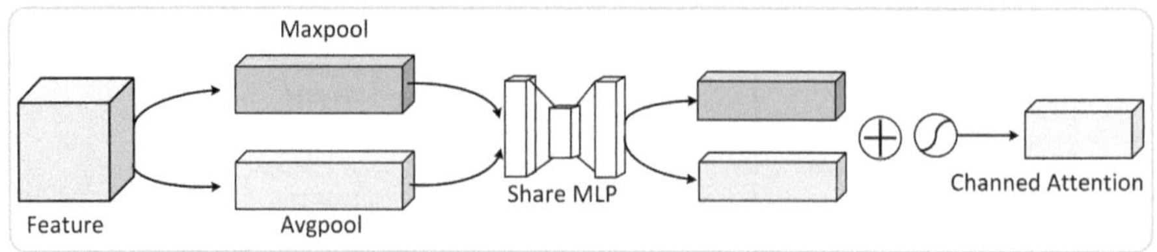

Fig. 3. Channel Attention Module

Then, the compressed descriptors $\mathbf{F}^{C}_{\text{avg}}$ and $\mathbf{F}^{C}_{\text{max}}$ are sent to a shared network to generate the channel attention map $\mathbf{M_c} \in \mathbb{R}^{C \times 1 \times 1}$.

The shared network consists of a multilayer perceptron (MLP) with a hidden layer. To reduce parameter overhead, the hidden activation size is set to $\mathbb{R}^{C/r \times 1 \times 1}$, where r is the reduction rate. Applying the shared network to each descriptor, we use element-wise summation to merge the feature vectors of the outputs. In short, the channel attention calculation is as shown in Eqs. (3) and (4):

$$\mathbf{M_c}(\mathbf{F}) = \sigma(\text{MLP}(\text{AvgPool}(\mathbf{F})) + \text{MLP}(\text{MaxPool}(\mathbf{F}))) \tag{3}$$
$$= \sigma\left(\mathbf{W}_1\left(\mathbf{W}_0\left(\mathbf{F}^{\mathbf{C}}_{\text{avg}}\right)\right) + \mathbf{W}_1\left(\mathbf{W}_0\left(\mathbf{F}^{\mathbf{C}}_{\text{max}}\right)\right)\right) \tag{4}$$

σ represents the sigmoid function. $\mathbf{W}_0 \in \mathbb{R}^{C/r \times C}$, $\mathbf{W}_1 \in \mathbb{R}^{C \times C/r}$. Please note that the weights $\mathbf{W}_0$ and $\mathbf{W}_1$ for the MLP are shared between the two inputs and the ReLU activation function is denoted by $\mathbf{W}_0$.

SAM: The feature map $\mathbf{F}'$ outputted by CAM serves as the input feature map for this module. The spatial attention module is shown in Fig. 5. Firstly, global max-pooling and global average-pooling are performed along the channels, resulting in two H × W × 1 feature maps. Then, these two feature maps are concatenated along the channels. Next, a 7 × 7 convolution operation (preferred over 3 × 3) is applied to reduce it to a single channel, resulting in H × W × 1. Subsequently, spatial attention features are generated using the sigmoid function. Finally, the generated feature is multiplied by the input feature of the module to obtain the final generated feature. Specifically, the computation process is described by Eqs. (5) and (6) as follows:

$$\mathbf{M_s}(\mathbf{F}) = \sigma\left(f^{7 \times 7}([\text{AvgPool}(\mathbf{F}); \text{Max Pool}(\mathbf{F})])\right) \tag{5}$$
$$= \sigma\left(f^{7 \times 7}\left[\mathbf{F}^{\mathbf{s}}_{\text{avg}}; \mathbf{F}^{\mathbf{s}}_{\text{max}}\right]\right) \tag{6}$$

σ is a sigmoid function, and $f^{7 \times 7}$ represents a convolution operation with a size of 7 × 7.

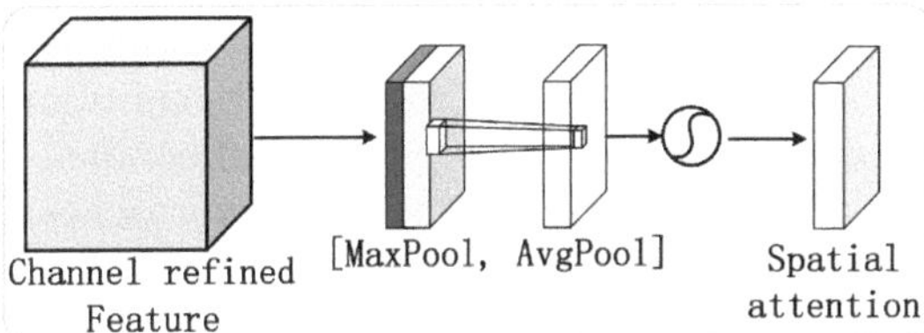

Fig. 4. Spatial Attention Module

CAM (Channel Attention Module) utilizes inter-channel relationships of features to generate channel attention maps. Since each channel of the feature map is considered as a feature detector, channel attention focuses on what is meaningful given the input. SAM (Spatial Attention Module), on the other hand, generates spatial attention maps based on the spatial relationships between features. Unlike CAM, spatial attention focuses on an informative part of the image, which serves as a complement to CAM.

By adding CBAM (Convolutional Block Attention Module) attention modules after the last residual block in each stage of ResNet, the model's expressive power and receptive field are enhanced. The attention module consists of both channel attention and spatial attention components, which weight features in the channel and spatial dimensions, respectively. Integrating CBAM attention modules into the ResNet network significantly improves the model's expressive power, receptive field range, and robustness. These enhancements contribute to strengthening the model's understanding of images, thereby improving the performance of the ResNet network in end-to-end scene text recognition tasks.

3.2 Multimodal Feature Enhancement

(1) Visual Model for Text Recognition

The visual model comprises three stages: feature extraction, sequence modeling, and prediction. Specifically, a ResNet backbone ($\mathcal{B}$) extracts visual features, while a Transformer ($\mathcal{M}$) performs sequence modeling. Given an input image x, visual features are represented as:

$$\mathbf{F}b = \mathcal{B}(x), \quad \mathbf{F}m = \mathcal{M}\left(\mathbf{F}b\right), \tag{7}$$

where $\mathbf{F}b, \mathbf{F}_m \in \mathbb{R}^{h \times w \times d}$, with h, w and d indicating height, width, and feature dimension respectively.

A positional attention module further transcribes visual features into character probabilities:

$$F_v = \mathrm{Softmax}\left(\frac{QK^{\top}}{\sqrt{d}}\right)V, \tag{8}$$

where $Q = PE(t)$ represents character positional encoding, and $K = \mathcal{G}\left(\mathbf{F}m\right)$, $V = \mathcal{H}\left(\mathbf{F}m\right)$ denote key and value features respectively. Here, $\mathcal{G}$ employs a U-Net-like architecture, while $\mathcal{H}$ is an identity mapping.

(2) Language Model in Text Recognition

Considering a text sequence $\boldsymbol{y} = (y_1, \ldots, y_n)$, the conditional entropy of bidirectional context significantly surpasses that of unidirectional models. Previous methods typically involve ensemble unidirectional approaches, inherently limiting feature expressivity.

A straightforward extension, random masking as in BERT, proves inefficient due to multiple masking iterations. To improve efficiency, we propose a conditional masked language model (CMLM) based on a Transformer decoder. By explicitly specifying attention masks for blank-filling tasks, CMLM efficiently captures bidirectional information in a single forward pass. Compared to ensemble methods and other models (e.g., BERT, PIMNet), CMLM reduces computational overhead and parameter count significantly.

(3) Multimodal Encoding

Direct fusion of independently pre-trained visual and semantic features can lead to spatial and temporal misalignments, introducing prediction noise. Thus, we propose a multimodal encoding (MME) module that concatenates visual (V) and semantic (S) features along the channel dimension, followed by positional encoding (Pe). The concatenated features are then mutual-enhanced via a Transformer:

$$[S : V] = \text{Concat}(S, V) + Pe, \tag{9}$$

$$F_{MMF}([S : V]) = \text{Softmax}\left(\frac{Q([S : V])K([S : V])^{\top}}{\sqrt{d_k}}\right) V([S : V]). \tag{10}$$

Here, $S \in \mathbb{R}^{T \times N \times C}$ and $V \in \mathbb{R}^{\frac{HW}{16} \times N \times C}$, with $[S : V] \in \mathbb{R}^{(\frac{HW}{16}+T) \times N \times C}$ denoting the multimodal input. This module effectively mitigates alignment issues and enhances prediction quality.

4   Experiment

4.1   Datasets and Environmental Settings

For the end-to-end scene text recognition section, the training sets include the synthetic datasets SynthText150K [10,12] with around 150K images, SynChinese130K [12] with approximately 130K images, the multilingual dataset ICDAR 2017 MLT [14] with 720K training images, the arbitrary-shaped dataset ICDAR 2019 ArT [2] with 5603 training images, and the large-scale dataset ICDAR 2019 LSVT [17] with 30K annotated images. The primary test sets comprise Total Text [3], an arbitrary-shaped dataset consisting of 1255 training images and 300 test images. SCUT-CTW1500 (CTW1500) [11] is a dataset containing long text images, with 1000 images for training and 500 for evaluation. ICDAR 2015 [6] is a multi-oriented dataset, including 1000 training images and 500 test images. ICDAR 2019 ReCTS (ReCTS) [13] is a Chinese dataset with 20K images for training and 5K images for evaluation.

4.2 Ablation Study

To validate the effectiveness of the improved end-to-end text recognition model, we conducted ablation experiments on Total Text, CTW1500, and ICDAR 2015 datasets, examining the impact of the proposed modules on curved and multi-scale scene texts.

We first evaluated SENet and CBAM attention modules integrated into the ResNet backbone on Total Text and CTW1500 datasets. Results in Table 1 demonstrate improved detection performance over the baseline ABCNet v2 model. Specifically, SENet achieved a 0.5% and 0.2% increase in F-measure on Total Text and CTW1500, respectively. CBAM attention further improved F-measure by 0.9% on both datasets. Thus, the ResNet backbone combined with CBAM was selected for subsequent experiments.

Table 1. The detection experimental results on the Total Text and CTW1500 datasets (percentages).

Model	Total Text			CTW1500		
	P	R	F	P	R	F
ABCNet v2	90.2	84.1	87.0	85.6	83.8	84.7
+SENet	91.4	84.0	87.5	86.6	83.2	84.9
+CBAM	92.1	84.0	87.9	87.9	83.4	85.6

Multimodal Encoding Ablation. We further validated the multimodal encoding (MME) module using Total Text and ICDAR 2015 datasets. Table 2 presents results comparing ABCNet v2 with its recognition module replaced by ABINet or MME. Both replacements improved recognition performance. Specifically, employing MME improved accuracy by 3.4% (S-dictionary) and 0.6% (no dictionary) on ICDAR 2015 compared to ABINet. On Total Text, MME yielded accuracy gains of 2.0% (no dictionary) and 2.4% (with dictionary). Thus, MME significantly enhances recognition accuracy relative to ABINet.

Table 2. Results of multimodal coded ablation experiments on the Total Text and ICDAR 2015 datasets (percentages).

Model	Total Text	ICDAR 2015			
	None	Full	S	W	G	None
ABCNet v2	73.5	80.7	83.0	80.7	75.0	–
+ABINet	75.6	82.5	84.1	81.4	75.4	70.3
+MME	76.5	83.1	86.4	81.9	76.8	70.9

The experiments demonstrate that integrating the CBAM attention module into ResNet enhances the network's capabilities in feature representation and spatial modeling, thereby improving the recognition performance of complex scene text. Multimodal encoding, by finely correcting character sequences, can rectify potential errors or incomplete character sequences, thus enhancing the completeness and accuracy of the sequences. By combining visual information from images with semantic information from text, multimodal encoding achieves mutual reinforcement between the two modalities.

In summary, multimodal encoding plays a role in fine-tuning character sequences, enhancing the correlation between visual and semantic information in text recognition. Through these mechanisms, multimodal encoding improves the understanding and representation of text images, thereby enhancing the accuracy and robustness of text recognition.

Overall Ablation Experiment. As shown in Table 3. First, in (a)(b)(c), we compared the effects of three optimizers on the experiment. Among them, the Mix optimizer uses SGD for detection and Adam for recognition. We observed that (1) using the Adam optimizer led to faster loss reduction and easier training. (2) The use of the Mix optimizer significantly improved recognition performance. In (d)(e)(f), we primarily compared the effects of sequence modeling methods and attention mechanisms on recognition performance. We found that Transformer encoding is more suitable for sequence modeling, while positional attention is better suited for decoding sequences. In (g)(h), it is evident that after adding multimodal encoding, Total Text and CTW1500 achieved accuracies of 75.9% and 58.2%, respectively, without dictionaries. Compared to (g), the model recognition accuracies increased by 1.7% and 2.2%, respectively. We observed a significant improvement in recognition performance due to multimodal encoding. In (i)(j), it is observed that after adding CBAM attention behind each layer of FPN, Total Text and CTW1500 achieved accuracies of 76.8% and 59.4%, respectively, without dictionaries. Compared to (i), the model recognition accuracies increased by 0.9% and 1.2%, respectively. We found that CBAM attention enhances detection performance, thereby aiding recognition performance.

4.3   Comparison with Previous STR Methods

To comprehensively demonstrate the advantages of the improved ABCNet v2 in scene text recognition, comparisons were made with state-of-the-art methods. Evaluation datasets included Total Text, CTW1500, and the ICDAR 2015 dataset. All evaluation metrics followed previous methods. Since the focus of the improvement was on the recognition aspect within text localization, detection accuracy was disregarded, and only end-to-end recognition performance was compared. The comparison results are presented in Table 4.

On the Total Text dataset, VSENet outperformed ABCNet v2 by 3.3% and 3.2% under the None and Full dictionaries, respectively, surpassing the SPTS v2 algorithm. On the CTW1500 dataset, the VSENet algorithm achieved a superiority of 0.8% and 3.4% over ABCNet v2 under the None and Full dictionary

Table 3. Ablation study of different components on Total-Text and CTW1500. "SMN" is the sequence modeling network. "Attn" is the attention module. "HFA" is the horizontal feature aggregation. "PA" is the position attention. "CA" is the content attention

	Components							Total Text			CTW1500		
	SGD	Adam	Mix	MME	CBAM	SMN	Attn	Precision	Impr.	FPS	Precision	Impr.	FPS
(a)	✓					Conv.	PA	72.1	-	12.3	52.9	-	-
(b)		✓				Conv.	PA	73.1	↑ **1.0%**	12.2	53.6	↑ **0.7%**	-
(c)			✓			Conv.	PA	73.5	↑ **1.4%**	12.2	54.0	↑ **1.1%**	-
(d)	✓					Conv.	PA	69.9	↓ **2.2%**	12.9	50.3	↓ **2.6%**	-
(e)	✓					Trans.	PA	71.2	↓ **0.9%**	12.7	51.6	↓ **1.3%**	16.8
(f)	✓					Trans.	CA	69.5	↓ **2.6%**	13.1	49.9	↓ **3.0%**	17.5
(g)			✓			Trans.	PA	74.2	↑ **2.1%**	12.2	56.0	↑ **3.1%**	-
(h)			✓	✓		Trans.	PA	75.9	↑ **3.8%**	12.6	58.2	↑ **5.3%**	16.5
(i)			✓	✓		Trans.	PA	75.9	↑ **3.8%**	12.6	58.2	↑ **5.3%**	16.5
(j)			✓	✓	✓	Trans.	PA	76.8	↑ **4.7%**	12.4	59.4	↑ **6.5%**	16.4

Table 4. Performance comparison with other end-to-end scene text recognition methods. "None" means no dictionary and "Full" means a dictionary that contains all the words in the test set. "S", "W", "G" and "None" denote the recognition of strong, weak, universal, and non-dictionary, respectively. The data in the table are expressed as percentages.

Model	Total Text		CTW1500		ICDAR 2015			
	None	Full	None	Full	S	W	G	None
FOTS	-	-	21.1	39.7	83.6	79.1	65.3	-
Mask TextSpotter	65.3	77.4	-	-	83.0	77.7	73.5	-
ABCNet	64.2	75.7	45.2	74.1	-	-	-	-
PGNet	63.1	-	-	-	83.3	78.3	63.5	-
MANGO	72.9	83.6	58.9	78.7	85.4	80.1	73.9	-
PAN++	68.6	78.6	-	-	82.7	78.2	69.2	68.0
CharNet	-	-	-	-	80.1	74.5	62.2	-
TextDragon	48.8	74.8	39.7	72.4	82.5	78.3	65.2	-
TTS	75.6	84.4	-	-	85.2	81.7	77.4	-
ABCNet v2	73.5	80.7	58.4	79	83	80.7	75	-
GLASS	76.6	83.0	-	-	84.7	80.1	76.3	-
SPTS	74.2	82.4	63.6	83.8	77.5	70.2	65.8	-
SPTS v2	75.0	82.6	64.4	84.0	81.2	74.3	68.0	-
DLD	63.9	73.0	-	-	79.0	75.7	70.9	-
DeepSolo	82.5	88.7	64.2	81.4	87.9	83.5	79.1	-
TextFormer	77.9	84.9	-	-	84.5	80.9	76.0	-
VSENet(our)	76.8	83.9	59.2	82.4	86.6	82.1	76.9	71.2

settings. Regarding the ICDAR 2015 dataset, VSENet surpassed ABCNet v2 by 3.6%, 1.4%, and 1.9% under the S, W, and G dictionaries, respectively. These results demonstrate the effectiveness of CBAM attention and multimodal encoding in enhancing model recognition performance. Moreover, on the Total Text and ICDAR 2015 datasets, the recognition performance significantly surpassed the SPTS v2 algorithm from 2023, reaching an industry-leading level. Additionally, on the CTW1500 dataset, it closely followed the DeepSolo algorithm. Overall, the recognition performance on all three datasets is among the state-of-the-art, proving a noticeable performance improvement of multimodal encoding in end-to-end scene text recognition tasks.

5 Conclusion

We propose VSENet, integrating visual and semantic information via multimodal encoding and CBAM attention mechanisms. Experiments demonstrate significant accuracy improvements, validating our design effectiveness. Future work includes further exploration of multimodal interactions and handling more challenging text recognition scenarios.

References

1. Bissacco, A., Cummins, M., Netzer, Y., Neven, H.: Photoocr: eading text in uncontrolled conditions. In: Proceedings of the IEEE International Conference on Computer Vision, pp. 785–792 (2013)
2. Chng, C.K., et al.: Icdar2019 robust reading challenge on arbitrary-shaped text-rrc-art. In: 2019 International Conference on Document Analysis and Recognition (ICDAR), pp. 1571–1576. IEEE (2019)
3. Ch'ng, C.K., Chan, C.S., Liu, C.L.: Total-text: toward orientation robustness in scene text detection. Int. J. Document Anal. Recogn. (IJDAR) **23**(1), 31–52 (2020)
4. Fang, S., Mao, Z., Xie, H., Wang, Y., Yan, C., Zhang, Y.: Abinet++:autonomous, bidirectional and iterative language modeling for scene text spotting. IEEE Trans. Pattern Anal. Mach. Intell. **45**(6), 7123–7141 (2022)
5. Feng, W., He, W., Yin, F., Zhang, X.Y., Liu, C.L.: Textdragon: an end-to-end framework for arbitrary shaped text spotting. In: Proceedings of the IEEE/CVF International Conference on Computer Vision, pp. 9076–9085 (2019)
6. Karatzas, D., et al.: Icdar 2015 competition on robust reading. In: 2015 13th International Conference on Document Analysis and Recognition (ICDAR), pp. 1156–1160. IEEE (2015)
7. Koonce, B., Koonce, B.: Resnet 50. Convolutional neural networks with swift for tensorflow: image recognition and dataset categorization, pp. 63–72 (2021)
8. Li, H., Wang, P., Shen, C.: Towards end-to-end text spotting with convolutional recurrent neural networks. In: Proceedings of the IEEE International Conference on Computer Vision, pp. 5238–5246 (2017)
9. Liao, M., Shi, B., Bai, X., Wang, X., Liu, W.: Textboxes: a fast text detector with a single deep neural network. In: Proceedings of the AAAI Conference on Artificial Intelligence, vol. 31 (2017)

10. Liu, Y., Chen, H., Shen, C., He, T., Jin, L., Wang, L.: Abcnet: real-time scene text spotting with adaptive bezier-curve network. In: Proceedings of the IEEE/CVF Conference on Computer Vision and Pattern Recognition, pp. 9809–9818 (2020)
11. Liu, Y., Jin, L., Zhang, S., Luo, C., Zhang, S.: Curved scene text detection via transverse and longitudinal sequence connection. Pattern Recogn. **90**, 337–345 (2019)
12. Liu, Y., et al.: Abcnet v2: adaptive bezier-curve network for real-time end-to-end text spotting. IEEE Trans. Pattern Anal. Mach. Intell. **44**(11), 8048–8064 (2021)
13. Lyu, P., Liao, M., Yao, C., Wu, W., Bai, X.: Mask textspotter: an end-to-end trainable neural network for spotting text with arbitrary shapes. In: Proceedings of the European Conference on Computer Vision (ECCV), pp. 67–83 (2018)
14. Nayef, N., et al.: Icdar2017 robust reading challenge on multi-lingual scene text detection and script identification-rrc-mlt. In: 2017 14th IAPR International Conference on Document Analysis and Recognition (ICDAR), vol. 1, pp. 1454–1459. IEEE (2017)
15. Qiao, Q., et al.: Dntextspotter: arbitrary-shaped scene text spotting via improved denoising training. In: Proceedings of the 32nd ACM International Conference on Multimedia, pp. 10134–10143 (2024)
16. Shi, B., Bai, X., Yao, C.: An end-to-end trainable neural network for image-based sequence recognition and its application to scene text recognition. IEEE Trans. Pattern Anal. Mach. Intell. **39**(11), 2298–2304 (2016)
17. Sun, Y., et al.: Icdar 2019 competition on large-scale street view text with partial labeling-rrc-lsvt. In: 2019 International Conference on Document Analysis and Recognition (ICDAR), pp. 1557–1562. IEEE (2019)
18. Wang, H., et al.: All you need is boundary: toward arbitrary-shaped text spotting. In: Proceedings of the AAAI Conference on Artificial Intelligence, vol. 34, pp. 12160–12167 (2020)
19. Wang, K., Babenko, B., Belongie, S.: End-to-end scene text recognition. In: 2011 International Conference on Computer Vision, pp. 1457–1464. IEEE (2011)
20. Wang, W., et al.: AE TextSpotter: learning visual and linguistic representation for ambiguous text spotting. In: Vedaldi, A., Bischof, H., Brox, T., Frahm, J.-M. (eds.) ECCV 2020. LNCS, vol. 12359, pp. 457–473. Springer, Cham (2020). https://doi.org/10.1007/978-3-030-58568-6_27
21. Ye, M., et al.: Deepsolo: let transformer decoder with explicit points solo for text spotting. In: Proceedings of the IEEE/CVF Conference on Computer Vision and Pattern Recognition, pp. 19348–19357 (2023)
22. Zhang, C., Ibrayim, M., Hamdulla, A., Deng, Q.: Arbitrary-shape text spotting based on global, pixel and sequence semantics. In: International Conference on Pattern Recognition and Artificial Intelligence, pp. 505–519. Springer (2024)

An Optional 2D Feature Scene Text Recognition Network Based on Transformer

Mayire Ibrayim[1,2](✉), Jianjun Kang[1,2], and Zhicheng Bao[1,2]

[1] School of Computer Science and Technology, Xinjiang University, Urumqi 830046, Xinjiang, China
[2] Key Laboratory of Signal Detection and Processing in Xinjiang Uygur Autonomous Region, Urumqi, Xinjiang, China
`mayire401@xju.edu.cn`

Abstract. Text recognition of an arbitrary shape has always been a challenging task, and although recent research has improved, it has always performed poorly for ambiguous, severely curved text recognition. We believe that most algorithms directly compress visual features into one-dimensional sequences with loss of spatial information, followed by poor complementarity of global and local information and heavy reliance on the depth of the backbone network. In this work, an optional 2D feature scene text recognition network is proposed in this paper to robustly recognize arbitrarily shaped text and fuzzy text. Specifically, a transformer-based encoding and decoding framework is adopted to introduce deformable convolutional kernels in the feature extraction part and reconstruct the feature extraction network, followed by proposing a deep multi-head transposition attention network and a deep feed-forward network applied to the transformer encoding layer to both aggregate local and non-local pixel interactions and alleviate computational bottlenecks. With extensive experiments, the algorithm proposed in this paper proves to be better able to solve arbitrary shapes and fuzzy text recognition, more robust and accurate than previous methods, and achieves the best performance on several benchmark datasets.

Keywords: deep learning · text recognition · feature extraction · transformer

1 Introduction

Scene text recognition, a crucial branch of computer vision, involves converting detected text regions into character strings. Despite its widespread applications in autonomous driving, automatic translation, and assistive technologies, current models face challenges in generalization, particularly with arbitrarily shaped and blurred text recognition (Fig. 1).

Early approaches utilized convolutional neural networks (CNNs) for character classification, followed by recurrent neural networks (RNNs) for sequence-based

© The Author(s), under exclusive license to Springer Nature Singapore Pte Ltd. 2026

Z. Lin et al. (Eds.): ICIG 2025, LNCS 16163, pp. 162–173, 2026.
https://doi.org/10.1007/978-981-95-3729-7_14

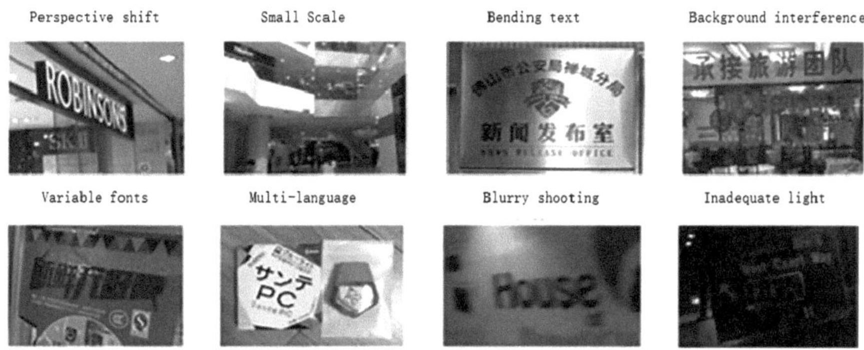

Fig. 1. Challenges of natural scene text recognition.

recognition. While RNNs could handle arbitrary-length text, they suffered from vanishing gradient problems, leading to the adoption of long short-term memory networks. Recent transformer-based methods, inspired by ViT [10], such as SAFL [8], have shown promise in enhancing text feature relevance. However, current algorithms often compress images into one-dimensional sequences post-feature extraction, resulting in spatial information loss.

To address these limitations, we propose a selectable 2D feature scene text recognition network, focusing on arbitrary shape and low-resolution text recognition. Our network comprises text rectification and recognition components, featuring improved feature extraction through deformable convolutional kernels and transformer-based encoder-decoder architecture with enhanced multi-head transpose attention.

Our main contributions include:

- A novel end-to-end text recognition network with transformer-based codec structure
- Integration of deformable convolution for enhanced curved text feature extraction
- Development of deep multi-head transposition attention and feedforward networks
- State-of-the-art performance on benchmark datasets, particularly on IC15

The remainder of this paper is organized as follows: Sect. 2 reviews related work, Sect. 3 details the proposed model, Sect. 4 presents experimental results, and Sect. 5 concludes the study.

2 Related Work

Scene text recognition includes recognition of regular and irregular (arbitrarily-shaped) texts. With the advent of deep learning, research has increasingly focused on arbitrary shape text recognition. This section briefly reviews traditional and deep learning-based approaches.

2.1 Traditional Text Recognition

Traditional methods typically involve image preprocessing (e.g., grayscale conversion, filtering, binarization), feature extraction based on prior knowledge, and classification into characters or words. Early work by Wang et al. [7] employed multi-scale HOG features with sliding windows for character recognition. With the introduction of convolutional neural networks (CNNs), Zhang et al. [11] proposed a CNN-based classifier for 62-character recognition. Jaderberg et al. [17] synthesized a large-scale word dataset for direct classification, although with limited performance on unseen words.

2.2 Deep Learning-Based Text Recognition

For arbitrary shape text, RARE [18] introduced a rectification-recognition pipeline to handle distorted texts. ASTER [13], an enhanced version of RARE, predicted TPS (thin-plate spline) control points from multi-resolution images to mitigate rectification blur and employed a bidirectional decoder. Extending ASTER, ESIR [13] iteratively applied TPS transformations with horizontal midlines and multiple segments for improved rectification.

Recent advances further improved text recognition. A class-aware mask (CAM) based method [12] accurately segments text regions and aligns text and background features for robust feature extraction. Scaling laws in OCR were systematically studied in [6], uncovering power-law relationships linking model performance, model scale, dataset size, and computational resources, leading to the creation of the large-scale REBU-Syn dataset and CLIP4STR-L model, significantly advancing OCR state-of-the-art.

MaskOCR [4] unified visual and language pretraining in an encoder-decoder architecture, initially leveraging masked image modeling on unlabeled data, followed by synthetic image decoding with a frozen encoder. CDistNet [21] proposed a multi-domain character distance perception module querying visual-semantic features simultaneously, achieving accurate feature-to-character alignment and addressing complex recognition scenarios effectively.

3 Proposed Method

This paper aims to develop an efficient Transformer-based model for recognizing arbitrarily shaped and highly ambiguous text. To address computational bottlenecks, we propose a deep multi-head transposition attention network (DMTA) and a deep feedforward network (DFFN), incorporating depthwise separable convolutions into the Transformer encoder. The following subsections detail the overall framework and key components of our model.

3.1 General Framework

The overall architecture of our proposed model is depicted in Fig. 2, consisting of four main modules: text rectification, feature extraction, encoder, and decoder. Given an input image, we first rectify irregular text into regular form via the text rectification network. Subsequently, a deformable convolutional feature extraction module captures essential visual features. These features are then encoded and decoded through the improved Transformer layers. The encoder aggregates contextual information, while the decoder generates character predictions. Finally, a linear mapping followed by a softmax function converts the decoded features into probability distributions, which are mapped to corresponding characters.

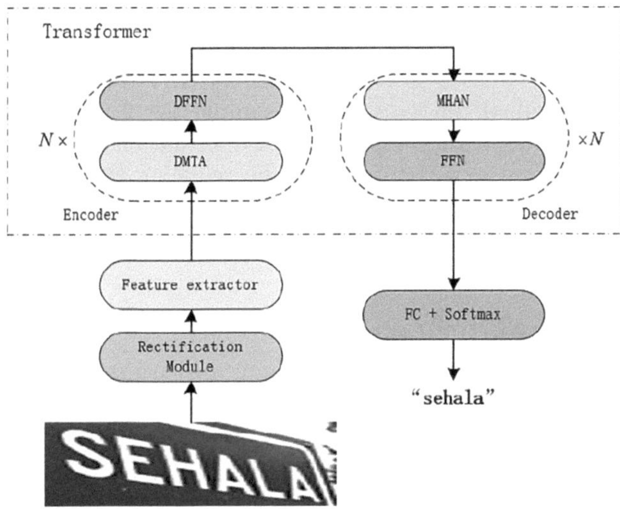

Fig. 2. Overview of the proposed network model. It includes a feature extraction module, improved Transformer encoder and decoder with DMTA and DFFN modules.

3.2   Text Rectification Network

Following the core concept of the ASTER algorithm, we rectify irregular text to regular form before recognition. Specifically, our rectification module integrates the thin-plate spline (TPS) transformation with a spatial transformer network (STN), modeling spatial transformations as learnable layers. This rectification pipeline consists primarily of a localization network, a grid generator, and a sampler. First, control points are predicted from the input image using the localization network. These points guide the grid generator and sampler to produce the rectified image for subsequent recognition.

3.3   Feature Extraction with Deformable Convolution

Although the text rectification network can correct curved texts, it cannot fully rectify texts with significant curvature, leading to residual background interference. To address this, we introduce deformable convolutions into the feature extraction layer. Deformable convolutions focus adaptively on text regions, effectively ignoring distracting background information, and enlarging the receptive field by introducing learnable offsets. Specifically, at each position p_0, the deformable convolution is computed as follows:

$$y\left(p_0\right) = \sum_{p_n \in R} w\left(p_n\right) x\left(p_0 + p_n + \Delta p_n\right), \tag{1}$$

where y denotes the output, x is the input feature map, R is the convolutional kernel receptive field, Δp_n represents the learned offset, and w denotes the convolutional weights.

Traditional ResNet-based networks, such as ASTER and SAFL, employ multiple stacked residual blocks and downsample the feature maps into one-dimensional sequences, thereby losing spatial information. To mitigate this, we reconstruct the feature extraction network by reducing the number of stacked residual layers and introducing deformable convolutions, thus maintaining two-dimensional spatial features while enhancing recognition accuracy.

3.4 Encoder and Decoder

The extracted visual features are further processed using an improved Transformer framework, consisting of an encoder and decoder. Traditional multi-head attention mechanisms generate spatial attention maps with computational complexity proportional to the square of spatial resolution, causing significant memory overhead.

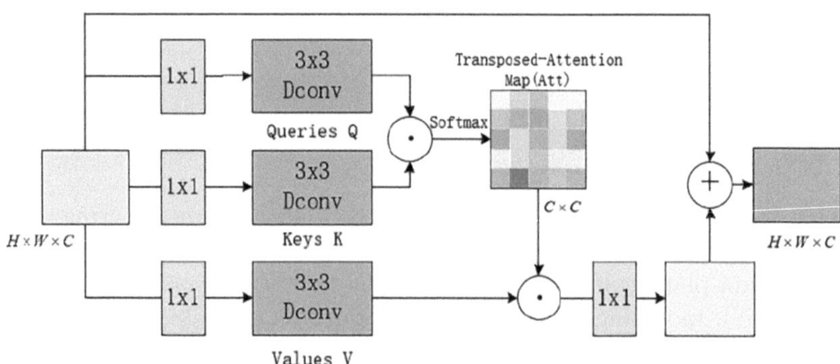

Fig. 3. Deep multi-head transposition attention network.

To alleviate this bottleneck, we propose a deep multi-head transposition attention network (DMTA), illustrated in Fig. 3. Given an input feature tensor $X \in \mathbb{R}^{H \times W \times C}$, DMTA generates query (Q), key (K), and value (V) vectors via 1×1 convolutions, followed by cross-channel information interaction through channel expansion convolution. Subsequently, depthwise separable convolutions encode spatial context efficiently. Unlike traditional spatial attention maps $(R^{HW \times HW})$, our method calculates a global attention map $(R^{C \times C})$, significantly reducing computational complexity. DMTA operations are defined as:

$$Q = W_d^Q W_c^Q X, \quad K = W_d^K W_c^K X, \quad V = W_d^V W_c^V X, \tag{2}$$

$$\text{Attention}(Q, K, V) = V \cdot \text{softmax}(K \cdot Q / \varepsilon), \tag{3}$$

$$\text{out} = W_c \cdot \text{Attention}(Q, K, V) + X, \tag{4}$$

where ε is a learnable scaling parameter.

Additionally, we improve the Transformer encoder's feedforward network (FFN). Traditional FFNs, consisting of linear layers and ReLU activation, inadequately capture local spatial information. Inspired by convolutional structures, we introduce a depthwise separable convolution-based deep feedforward network (DFFN), as shown in Fig. 4. This enhanced network first applies a 1×1 convolution for dimensional projection, followed by BatchNorm, GELU activation, and depthwise separable convolutions to effectively capture local spatial features.

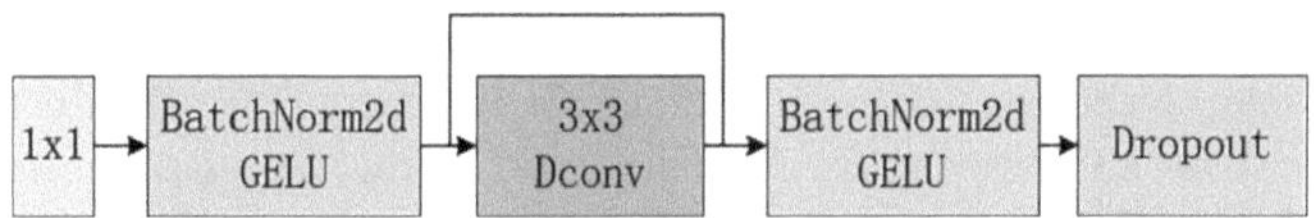

Fig. 4. Proposed deep feed-forward network.

The decoding stage utilizes the standard Transformer decoder structure, predicting characters sequentially from left to right, starting with a special <start> token and terminating at the <end> token. A final linear mapping layer followed by a softmax function converts the decoder outputs into character probability distributions.

4   Experiments

We conduct extensive experiments to evaluate the effectiveness of our proposed method, including dataset descriptions, ablation studies, and comparisons with state-of-the-art methods.

4.1   Datasets

We utilize synthetic datasets for training and real-world datasets for testing, categorized as regular or irregular text. Regular datasets include IIIT5K [5],

Street View Text (SVT) [1], and ICDAR2013 (IC13) [2]. Irregular datasets include ICDAR2015 (IC15) [22], Street View Text Perspective (SVT-P) [19], and CUTE80 [15].

IIIT5K contains 5,000 natural text images (2,000 for training, 3,000 for testing). SVT comprises 647 images collected from Google Street View, each associated with a 50-word lexicon. IC13 consists of 1,015 cropped images from mall scenes (561 images: 420 training, 141 testing). IC15 provides 1,500 images with 2,077 irregular text instances. SVT-P contains 639 text instances from 238 images, focusing on perspective distortion. CUTE80 includes 288 cropped text instances from 80 high-resolution images, emphasizing curved texts.

4.2   Implementation Details

Experiments are performed using an NVIDIA RTX 3090 GPU with Python 3.7 and PyTorch 1.1.6. The synthetic dataset comprises over 16 million single-instance text images. Each model trains for approximately four days. Images are resized uniformly to 64×256 pixels. The decoder recognizes 94 characters, including digits, uppercase and lowercase letters, and common punctuation marks. The learning rate is adjusted dynamically during training for optimal convergence.

Text Recognition Network. To better show the details of the feature extraction layers, Table 1 lists the network configurations of the feature extraction layers. The size of the text-corrected image is fixed to 32×100. In this paper, the feature extraction network is reconstructed with the output dimensions of 64,128,256,256,512 for each layer, and the maximum pooling kernels are used in the last three layers to reduce the size of the feature map, where the size of the pooling kernels used in the third and fourth layers is 2×2 and the last layer is 2×1, and the output of the final visual feature map is 4 The residual blocks consist of 1×1 convolutional kernels and 3×3 convolutional kernels, and the number of residual blocks in each layer is 1,2,5,3. the number of encoding blocks and decoding blocks of Transformer is 4 respectively.

4.3   Ablation Study

In order to fully verify the impact of each module on text recognition, this paper conducts ablation experiments on the backbone network, the location of deformable convolutional kernels, and deep multi-head transposition attention, respectively.

Experiments with Backbone Networks. In order to fully validate this paper, VGG16, ResNet31 and the improved ResNet network are selected as feature extractors respectively. Firstly, VGG16 introduces the idea of residuals compared to ResNet network. This paper is validated on several benchmark datasets, and their experimental results are shown in Table 2.

Table 1. Network configurations of the CNN in the feature extractor

Layer	Feature map size	Configuration
Layer 1	32x100	$3\times3\text{conv}\times1,\text{s}1\times1$
Layer 2	32x100	$\begin{bmatrix} 1 \times 1\text{conv} & 128 \\ 3 \times 3\text{conv} & 128 \end{bmatrix} \times 1$
Layer 3	16x50	Maxpooling, s: 2×2, $\begin{bmatrix} 1 \times 1\text{conv} & 256 \\ 3 \times 3\text{conv} & 256 \end{bmatrix} \times 2$
Layer 4	8x25	Maxpooling, s: 2×2, $\begin{bmatrix} 1 \times 1\text{conv} & 256 \\ 3 \times 3\text{conv} & 256 \end{bmatrix} \times 5$
Layer 5	4x25	Maxpooling, s: 2×1, $\begin{bmatrix} 1 \times 1\text{conv} & 512 \\ 3 \times 3\text{conv} & 512 \end{bmatrix} \times 3$

Table 2. Text recognition results for different backbone networks

Backbone	IIIT5K	SVT	IC13	IC15	SVTP
VGG16	93.5	88.3	91.9	79.7	80
ResNet31	94.6	90	92.2	81.3	81.6
Improved ResNet	95.2	91	93	82.2	83.3

As shown in Table 2, our improved ResNet backbone achieves accuracy improvements compared to VGG16 and ResNet31 networks across multiple datasets. Specifically, on the SVTP dataset, accuracy is enhanced by 3.3% and 1.7% compared with VGG16 and ResNet31, respectively. This improvement indicates that deeper network models are unnecessary for low-resolution inputs, while the introduced deformable convolution effectively addresses insufficient rectification of highly curved text.

Position Analysis of Deformable Convolutions. Deformable convolutions expand the receptive field and enhance irregular text recognition by adaptively focusing on text features and suppressing background information. To evaluate the impact of incorporating deformable convolutions at different scales, we perform experiments by fusing deformable convolutional features between adjacent layers (P2, P3, P4, P5, with channel dimensions 64, 128, 256, and 512 respectively). The experimental results are summarized in Table 3.

Results in Table 3 demonstrate that integrating deformable convolutions between deeper feature layers (P4 and P5) achieves the highest accuracy across all datasets. Particularly, on the SVTP dataset, accuracy improves by 1.7% compared to earlier fusion positions, highlighting the effectiveness of deformable convolutions at deeper feature levels in extracting curved text features.

Table 3. Recognition accuracy (%) with deformable convolutions at different fusion positions.

Fusion position	Between P2 and P3	Between P3 and P4	Between P4 and P5
IIIT5K	94.4	93.8	**95.2**
SVT	90.0	89.6	**91.0**
IC13	92.0	92.0	**93.0**
IC15	80.7	80.5	**82.2**
SVTP	81.6	81.6	**83.3**

Module Ablation Studies. To thoroughly validate the effectiveness of our proposed modules, we conducted ablation studies on synthetic training datasets and evaluated them on real-world benchmarks (IIIT5K, SVT, IC13, IC15, SVTP). Specifically, we examined the impact of the deep multi-head transposition attention network and deep feedforward network within the Transformer encoder, using the improved ResNet as the backbone. Comprehensive results and comparisons with the baseline algorithm are presented in Table 4.

Table 4. Evaluation of the effectiveness of DMTA and DFFN

Methods	IIIT5K	SVT	IC13	IC15	SVTP
Baseline	93.4	93.6	91.8	76.1	78.5
+DMTA	94.6	90.9	92.4	81.8	84
+DFFN	95	90.7	92.5	81.3	82.2
DMTA+DFFN	95.2	91.0	93	82.2	83.3

The impact of different modules on text recognition is summarized in Table 4. The baseline algorithm achieves recognition accuracies of 93.4%, 93.6%, and 91.8% on regular text datasets, and 76.1%, 78.5% on irregular text datasets. In comparison, our proposed method improves recognition accuracy significantly, reaching 95.2% and 93% on the IIIT5K and IC13 datasets (gains of 1.8% and 1.2%), and achieving 82.2% and 83.3% on the IC15 and SVTP datasets (improvements of 6.1% and 4.8%). These results indicate the proposed algorithm notably enhances recognition performance, especially for irregular texts, underscoring their inherent complexity compared to regular texts.

Impact of Deep Multi-head Transposition Attention. By enhancing the multi-head attention mechanism in the Transformer encoder, our deep multi-head transposition attention effectively aggregates global pixel interactions, capturing critical text features. Particularly, significant improvements of 5.7% and 5.5% are observed on the irregular IC15 and SVTP datasets, reaching accuracies of 81.8% and 84%, respectively, demonstrating the robustness and effectiveness of this module.

Impact of Deep Feedforward Network. The deep feedforward network replaces the conventional fully-connected layers in the Transformer encoder, leveraging convolutional operations to better capture local visual features. This modification yields accuracies of 95%, 92.5%, 81.3%, and 82.2% on IIIT5K, IC13, IC15, and SVTP datasets, corresponding to improvements of 1.6%, 0.7%, 5.2%, and 3.7%, respectively.

4.4   Comparisons with State-of-the-Art Methods

To validate the superior performance of the proposed method, we compared it against state-of-the-art scene text recognition algorithms. As illustrated in Table 5, our model achieves average recognition accuracies of 93.1% for regular texts and 83.9% for irregular texts. Specifically, significant accuracy improvements are obtained on the challenging IC15 dataset, effectively addressing blurred and irregular text recognition. Compared with the SAFL method, our approach improves recognition accuracy by 1.3%, 2.4%, 4.7%, and 1.6% on the IIIT5K, SVT, IC15, and SVTP datasets, respectively.

Table 5. Scene text recognition accuracy for six public benchmark test datasets

Method	Regular text			Average[a]	Irregular text			Average[a]
	IIIT5K	SVT	IC13		IC15	SVTP	CUTE80	
CRNN [9]	78.2	80.8	86.7	81.9	–	–	–	–
ASTER [13]	93.4	**93.6**	91.8	92.9	76.1	78.5	79.5	78.0
SAR [16]	91.5	84.5	91.0	89.0	69.2	76.4	83.3	76.3
ESIR [13]	93.3	90.2	91.3	91.6	76.9	79.6	83.3	79.9
SAFL [8]	93.9	88.6	92.8	91.8	77.5	81.7	85.4	81.5
AutoSTR [17]	94.7	90.9	–	92.8	81.8	81.7	–	81.8
SE-ASTER [20]	93.8	89.6	92.8	92.1	80.0	81.4	83.6	81.7
MORAN [3]	91.9	88.3	92.4	90.9	76.1	77.4	68.8	74.1
DAN [14]	94.3	89.2	**93.9**	92.5	74.5	80.0	84.4	79.6
Ours	**95.2**	91	93	**93.1**	**82.2**	**83.3**	**86.1**	**83.9**

Note: the best experimental results are bolded for each column of the dataset.

[a]The Average represents the weighted average of the results of multiple datasets.

Overall, the recognition results of the algorithm proposed in this paper are suggestive on different kinds of datasets, which proves that the model has strong generalization ability and can be competent for text recognition of arbitrary shapes.

5   Conclusion

In this paper, we propose an end-to-end Transformer-based scene text recognizer utilizing selectable two-dimensional features, effectively addressing challenges of irregular and blurred texts in low-quality images. We enhance the feature extraction network by integrating deformable convolutions, improving representation for curved texts and preserving spatial information. Additionally, to mitigate limitations of Transformer in local feature extraction and computational complexity, we introduce a deep multi-head transposition attention module and a deep feedforward network within the encoder, enhancing fine-grained information interaction and computational efficiency. Extensive experiments demonstrate our method's superior performance on multiple real-world datasets, showing significant improvements, particularly on ICDAR 2015, thus validating the robustness of our approach.

References

1. Gupta, A., Vedaldi, A., Zisserman, A.: Synthetic data for text localisation in natural images. In: Proceedings of the IEEE Conference on Computer Vision and Pattern Recognition, pp. 2315–2324 (2016)
2. Kingma, D.P.: Adam: A method for stochastic optimization. arXiv preprint arXiv:1412.6980 (2014)
3. Liao, M., Wan, Z., Yao, C., Chen, K., Bai, X.: Real-time scene text detection with differentiable binarization. In: Proceedings of the AAAI Conference on Artificial Intelligence, vol. 34, pp. 11474–11481 (2020)
4. Lyu, P., et al.: Maskocr: scene text recognition with masked vision-language pretraining. Trans. Mach. Learn. Res. (2024)
5. Nayef, N., et al.: Icdar2017 robust reading challenge on multi-lingual scene text detection and script identification-rrc-mlt. In: 2017 14th IAPR International Conference on Document Analysis and Recognition (ICDAR), vol. 1, pp. 1454–1459. IEEE (2017)
6. Rang, M., Bi, Z., Liu, C., Wang, Y., Han, K.: An empirical study of scaling law for ocr. arXiv preprint arXiv:2401.00028 (2023)
7. Redmon, J.: You only look once: unified, real-time object detection. In: Proceedings of the IEEE Conference on Computer Vision and Pattern Recognition (2016)
8. Ren, S., He, K., Girshick, R., Sun, J.: Faster r-CNN: towards real-time object detection with region proposal networks. IEEE Trans. Pattern Anal. Mach. Intell. **39**(6), 1137–1149 (2017). https://doi.org/10.1109/TPAMI.2016.2577031
9. Shao, Z., et al.: Ct-net: arbitrary-shaped text detection via contour transformer. IEEE Trans. Circ. Syst. Video Technol. (2023)
10. Tian, Z., et al.: Learning shape-aware embedding for scene text detection. In: Proceedings of the IEEE/CVF Conference on Computer Vision and Pattern Recognition, pp. 4234–4243 (2019)
11. Wang, F., Chen, Y., Wu, F., Li, X.: Textray: contour-based geometric modeling for arbitrary-shaped scene text detection. In: Proceedings of the 28th ACM International Conference on Multimedia, pp. 111–119 (2020)
12. Wang, H., et al.: All you need is boundary: Toward arbitrary-shaped text spotting. In: Proceedings of the AAAI Conference on Artificial Intelligence, vol. 34, pp. 12160–12167 (2020)

13. Wang, W., et al.: Shape robust text detection with progressive scale expansion network. In: Proceedings of the IEEE/CVF Conference on Computer Vision and Pattern Recognition, pp. 9336–9345 (2019)
14. Wang, W., et al.: Pan++: towards efficient and accurate end-to-end spotting of arbitrarily-shaped text. IEEE Trans. Pattern Anal. Mach. Intell. **44**(9), 5349–5367 (2021)
15. Wang, W., et al.: Efficient and accurate arbitrary-shaped text detection with pixel aggregation network. In: Proceedings of the IEEE/CVF International Conference on Computer Vision, pp. 8440–8449 (2019)
16. Wang, X., Jiang, Y., Luo, Z., Liu, C.L., Choi, H., Kim, S.: Arbitrary shape scene text detection with adaptive text region representation. In: Proceedings of the IEEE/CVF Conference on Computer Vision and Pattern Recognition, pp. 6449–6458 (2019)
17. Wang, Y., Xie, H., Zha, Z.J., Xing, M., Fu, Z., Zhang, Y.: Contournet: taking a further step toward accurate arbitrary-shaped scene text detection. In: proceedings of the IEEE/CVF Conference on Computer Vision and Pattern Recognition, pp. 11753–11762 (2020)
18. Xu, Y., Wang, Y., Zhou, W., Wang, Y., Yang, Z., Bai, X.: Textfield: learning a deep direction field for irregular scene text detection. IEEE Trans. Image Process. **28**(11), 5566–5579 (2019)
19. Zhang, S.X., Yang, C., Zhu, X., Yin, X.C.: Arbitrary shape text detection via boundary transformer. IEEE Trans. Multimedia **26**, 1747–1760 (2023)
20. Zhang, S.X., et al.: Deep relational reasoning graph network for arbitrary shape text detection. In: Proceedings of the IEEE/CVF Conference on Computer Vision and Pattern Recognition, pp. 9699–9708 (2020)
21. Zheng, T., Chen, Z., Fang, S., Xie, H., Jiang, Y.G.: Cdistnet: perceiving multi-domain character distance for robust text recognition. Int. J. Comput. Vis. **132**(2), 300–318 (2024)
22. Zhu, X., Hu, H., Lin, S., Dai, J.: Deformable convnets v2: more deformable, better results. In: Proceedings of the IEEE/CVF Conference on Computer Vision and Pattern Recognition, pp. 9308–9316 (2019)

Non-uniform Degradation Aware and Content Complexity Adaptive Optimization for Blind Super-Resolution

Sen Wang, Hongzhen Shi[✉], and Dan Xu

Yunnan University, Kunming 650500, China
`hongzhen.shi@ynu.edu.cn`

Abstract. Blind Super-Resolution aims to reconstruct high-resolution images from low-resolution images degraded by complex and unknown factors. However, existing methods assume that images suffer uniform degradation, exhibit homogeneous content complexity and ignore varied interactions between various degradation and content, which limit the performance and adaptability to real-world scenarios. To address these issues, we propose a Multi-Degradation Aware Transformer model that leverages wavelet transforms to map degradation into the frequency domain, to distinguish regional degradation and content complexity to achieve degradation-content adaptive decoupling. MDAT adopts a dual-strategy framework that simultaneously enhances detail recovery in high-frequency bands and improves global structure reconstruction in low-frequency bands. The complex degradation and image content are processed within a unified stage, which is allowing the model to adapt its capacity based on the complexity of the degradation and content. Experimental results demonstrate that MDAT performs exceptionally well in BSR tasks, significantly improving robustness and reconstruction quality, especially in heterogeneous degradation scenarios. MDAT effectively handles both simple and complex degradation, which is making it highly adaptable to diverse degradation cases.

Keywords: Non-Uniform Degradation · Content Complexity · Blind Image Super-Resolution · Self-Attention

1 Introduction

Blind super-resolution aims to reconstruct high-resolution images from low-resolution versions with unknown complex degradation. While CNNs have advanced SR [1], most methods focus on non-blind SR with known degradation, requiring with deep architectures [2–6]. However, they struggle with diverse degradations—over-enhancing simple cases or failing when degradation deviates from assumptions. As shown in Fig. 1, Since the same degradation mode will show differentiated performance in different image contents, Additionally, CNNs struggle with long-range dependencies and are sensitive to degradation estimation errors, leading to distorted outputs.Current blind SR approaches include explicit kernel estimation [7, 8] (e.g., IKC, which is computationally costly, and

© The Author(s), under exclusive license to Springer Nature Singapore Pte Ltd. 2026

Z. Lin et al. (Eds.): ICIG 2025, LNCS 16163, pp. 174–186, 2026.
https://doi.org/10.1007/978-981-95-3729-7_15

DCLS [8], sensitive to kernel errors) and implicit degradation representation [9, 10] (e.g., KDSR [10] and DASR [9], limited by CNN constraints). DSAT [11] combines CNN and Transformer strengths but still faces challenges with complex degradations. Transformer-based methods like Swin Transformer [12] improve global modeling, inspiring works such as Liang et al. [13], HAT [14], and Restormer [15]. These advances guide our proposed multi-degradation aware strategy.

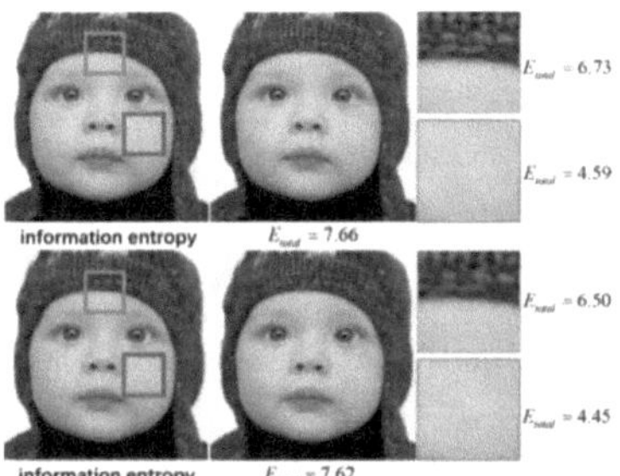

Fig. 1. Comparative analysis of information entropy measurement values based on high-resolution and low-resolution images based on details and structural features.

The proposed multi-degradation-aware Transformer model addresses blind super-resolution through a novel architecture integrating degradation learning, content extraction, shallow/deep feature extraction, and reconstruction modules. Its core innovation lies in jointly modeling multi-degradation representations and content features via wavelet transformation and MoCo, enabling precise degradation mapping from spatial to frequency domains while capturing multi-band content features.

The degradation learning module employs MoCo [16] to ensure similar degraded images share similar feature representations, combined with wavelet analysis for multi-band degradation information. The content extraction module synchronously processes wavelet-generated frequency band features, enabling coordinated degradation-content modeling. MDAT adopts a phased processing strategy: prioritizing high-frequency degradation for detail recovery before optimizing low-frequency components for global structure.

The deep feature extraction module utilizes Degradation-Aware Transformer Blocks (DATB), each comprising Hybrid Convolution-Transformer (HCT) units. HCT integrates a degradation-aware layer (combining deep convolution and channel attention) and a Restoration Transformer layer with improved global modeling. This hybrid architecture leverages CNN local detail capture and Transformer's global adaptation via a degradation-aware attention mechanism.

Our contributions include:

(1) MDAT introduces a novel degradation-content decoupling mechanism by leveraging wavelet transforms, which can distinguish regional degradation and content complexity for adaptively perceiving their correlation.

(2) The dual-strategy architecture simultaneously enhances detail recovery in high-frequency bands and improves global structure reconstruction in low-frequency bands, achieving more balanced and effective image restoration.

(3) By integrating CNN and Transformer, the model captures both local features and global features. A contrastive learning strategy is further introduced to enhance degradation representation learning.

Experiments demonstrate MDAT robustness in complex degradation scenarios while maintaining high-quality reconstruction under simple conditions, validating its superiority in blind super-resolution tasks.

2 Related Work

2.1 Image Blind Super-Resolution Based on Deep Learning

Deep learning-based blind super-resolution (BSR) aims to reconstruct high-resolution images from low-resolution ones under unknown degradation. The challenge lies in the ill-posed nature of the problem, where prior information helps recover lost details. Typical SR methods include shallow feature extraction, deep feature mapping, and HR reconstruction. Advances like residual blocks [17, 18], recursive structures [19, 20], attention mechanisms [21, 22], subpixel convolutions [23], reference-based methods [24], and style guidance [25] have improved accuracy, but non-blind models struggle with unseen degradation. BSR is divided into kernel prediction (KP) [7, 8], which relies on GT labels, and degradation prediction (DP) [9, 10], which learns broader degradation representations. Pure CNNs face limitations, so MDAT uses contrastive learning to extract degradation info, guiding CNNs for texture modeling, and Transformers for global degradation-aware modeling, achieving better performance.

2.2 Vision Transformer

Transformers have been widely applied in computer vision tasks such as object detection [12, 26, 27], segmentation [12, 28–30], and crowd counting [31, 32]. They have also been introduced into single image super-resolution (SR), with representative methods including SwinIR [13], IPT [33], and HAT [14]. SwinIR first applied the Swin Transformer to non-blind SR, achieving excellent results in reconstruction, denoising, and artifact removal. IPT leverages pre-training on ImageNet to explore the potential of Transformers in SR. HAT combines CNN-based channel attention with window-based self-attention to enhance both global and local modeling. Despite their strong performance on known degradation, these methods struggle with complex and unknown degradation. In contrast, MDAT uses degradation information to guide CNNs in fine-grained texture modeling and shifted window self-attention for effective global modeling.

3 Methodology

To overcome the limitations of pure CNNs in handling complex degraded images, the method uses wavelet transformation to decompose images into multi-frequency components (LL, LH, HL, HH, and BOTH). LL captures low-frequency structure, LH and HL restore horizontal and vertical edges, HH preserves fine textures, and BOTH integrates all bands for comprehensive content representation. Wavelet decomposition enables precise degradation modeling and feature extraction by separating images into frequency-specific representations, allowing synchronized perception of degradation and content features. To distinguish degradation types, MDAT employs contrast learning [16, 37, 38], ensuring similar degradations have similar embeddings [39, 40], improving adaptability across degradation scenarios and enhancing network generalization.

3.1 Network Architecture

Degradation features are learned unsupervised: query blocks from LR images are compared with same-image (positive) and different-image (negative) samples. The MoCo framework optimizes feature distances—pulling positive pairs closer and pushing negative pairs apart—to implicitly model degradation in feature space.

Given a low-resolution image $I_{LR} \in \mathbb{R}^{H \times W \times 3}$, shallow feature extraction is denoted as SF to extract shallow feature $F_0 \in \mathbb{R}^{H \times W \times C}$.

$$F_0 = SF(I_{LR}), \tag{1}$$

where C represents the number of feature channels. The feature F_0 is applied to the deep feature extraction module as DF. As follows:

$$F_{DF} = DF(F_0), \tag{2}$$

The specific process is as follows: the intermediate features F_1, F_2,..., F_k are extracted block by block and finally output deep features F_{DF}.

$$F_i = DATB_i(F_{i-1}), i = 1, 2, \ldots, K, \tag{3}$$

$$F_{DF} = CONV(F_K), \tag{4}$$

where $DATB_i$ represents the ith degradation-aware Transformer block. We reconstruct super-resolution images by integrating shallow and deep features,

$$I_{SR} = REC(F_0 + F_{DF}), \tag{5}$$

3.2 Loss Function

We design two loss functions: L_1 pixel loss and degradation represent loss. In contrast learning, InfoNCE [41] loss is used to achieve better degradation-aware information L_{degrad}. To this end, a queue containing multiple content and degradation type samples was constructed. Specifically, B-frame low-resolution images are randomly selected (representing B different degradation types) and two patches are randomly cropped from each image. Subsequently, these patches are encoded as p_i^1, $p_i^2 \in \mathbb{R}^{256}$, where p_i^1 is the first patch embedding of the ith image and p_i^2 is the second patch embedding of the ith image. For the ith image, p_i^1 and p_i^2 are regarded as query samples and positive samples, respectively. The degradation loss is defined as:

$$L_{\text{degrad}} = \sum_{i=1}^{B} -\log \frac{\exp\left(p_i^1 p_i^2 / \tau\right)}{\sum_{j=1}^{N_{\text{queue}}} \exp\left(p_i^1 p_{\text{queue}}^j / \tau\right)}, \tag{6}$$

where N_{queue} is the number of samples in the queue, p_{queue}^j represents the negative sample of jth. For SR network, pixel loss is used, and the definition is as follows:

$$L_{SR} = \|I_{SR} - I_{HR}\|_1, \tag{7}$$

The end-to-end loss of the entire network is defined as:

$$L_{loss} = L_{\text{degrad}} + L_{SR}, \tag{8}$$

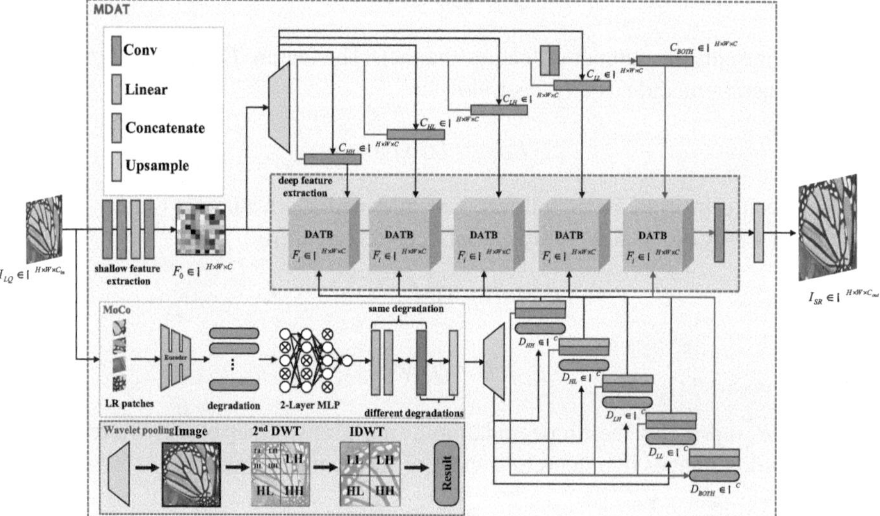

Fig. 2. Schematic diagram of image super-resolution network architecture based on multiple degradation-aware Transformer.

3.3 Degradation-Aware Transformer Block

As shown in Fig. 3, the DATB consists of multiple HCT and a convolutional layer. Given the input feature $F_{i,0}$ of the ith DATB, the degradation representation F_{DA} is obtained through the degradation learning block, and the content representation F_{CT} is obtained through the content extraction block. Before each DATB starts, the content representation F_{CT} and the input feature $F_{i,0}$ are combined, and then the 1×1 convolution layer is passed, the features $F_{i,1}, F_{i,2},..., F_{i,L}$ are extracted as follows

$$F_{i,j-1} = concat(F_{i,j-1}, F_{CT}), \tag{9}$$

$$F_{i,j-1} = CONV(F_{i,j-1}), \tag{10}$$

$$F_{i,j} = HCT_{i,j}(F_{i,j-1}, F_{DA}), \quad j = 1, 2, ..., L \tag{11}$$

As shown in Fig. 3, Each HCT unit consists of a DAL and a RTL. The DAL dynamically adjusts convolutional kernel $D1$ and channel weights $D2$ based on degradation representation D. After DAL, give the input tensor of size $H \times W \times C$, RTL to further process these feature maps. Which first performs layer normalization of the input tensor and then generates projections of query, key, and value. The resulting projection form is:

$$Q = W_Q^d W_Q^p Y, \quad K = W_K^d W_K^p Y, \quad V = W_V^d W_V^p Y, \tag{12}$$

where W^p represents 1×1 point-by-point convolution, W^d is a 3×3 depth convolution layer. Next, the projection of the query and keys is reshaped to $Q \in \mathbb{R}^{HW \times C}$ and $K \in \mathbb{R}^{C \times HW}$. This process can be defined as:

$$\hat{\mathbf{X}} = W_p \text{Attention}(\hat{\mathbf{Q}}, \hat{\mathbf{K}}, \hat{\mathbf{V}}) + \mathbf{X}, \tag{13}$$

$$\text{Attention}(\hat{\mathbf{Q}}, \hat{\mathbf{K}}, \hat{\mathbf{V}}) = \hat{\mathbf{V}} \cdot \text{Softmax}(\hat{\mathbf{K}} \cdot \hat{\mathbf{Q}}/\alpha), \tag{14}$$

$\mathbf{X}, \hat{\mathbf{X}}$ represent input and output feature maps, α is used to control the size of the K and Q dot products before applying the softmax function. Given the input tensor X, the formula for GDFN is:

$$\hat{\mathbf{X}} = W_p^0 \text{Gating}(\mathbf{X}) + \mathbf{X}, \tag{15}$$

$$\text{Gating}(\mathbf{X}) = \phi\left(W_d^1 W_p^1(\text{LN}(\mathbf{X}))\right) \odot W_d^2 W_p^2(\text{LN}(\mathbf{X})), \tag{16}$$

where $\odot$ represents element-by-element multiplication, ϕ represents GELU nonlinear activation, and LN is a layer normalization operation (Fig. 2).

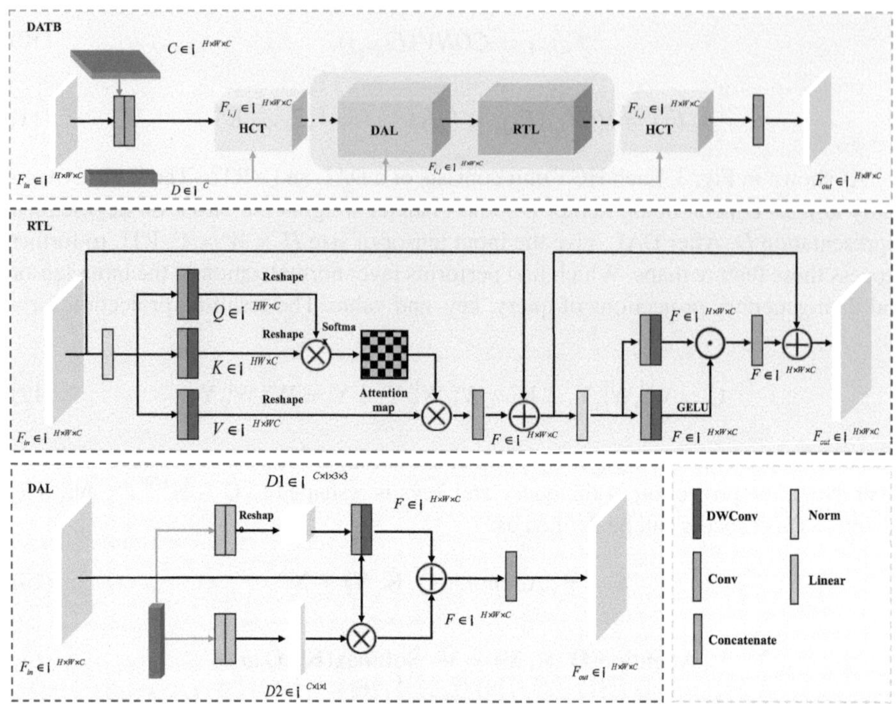

Fig. 3. Schematic diagram of the structure of the degradation-aware Transformer module (DATB). This module consists of a hybrid architecture (Hybrid CNN-Transformer, HCT) composed of a degradation-aware layer and a reconstruction Transformer layer.

4 Experiments

4.1 Experiment Details

During the training and testing process, LR images are generated according to formula (17). The training set includes 800 training images in the DIV2K dataset and 2650 training images in Flickr2K. For evaluation, four standard datasets are used, namely Set5, Set14, BSD100 and Urban100. The size of the Gaussian kernel is fixed to 21 × 21. The model is first trained using isotropic Gaussian kernels to handle noise-free degradation scenarios. In the 4x task, the range of Gaussian kernel width σ is set to [0.2, 4.0].

$$I_{LR} = \left(I_{HR} \otimes k \right) \downarrow_s + n, \tag{17}$$

where k represents a blur kernel, $\downarrow_s$ represents a downsampling operation, the scale factor is s, and n represents an additive Gaussian noise.

Bicubic downsampler is used as the downsampling operator, and the model is trained to handle various degradation types including anisotropic Gaussian kernels and noise. The anisotropic kernel follows a Gaussian distribution with zero mean and variable covariance matrix, determined by random eigenvalues and rotation angle; noise levels range from 0 to 25. AdaMA optimizer with $\beta 1 = 0.9$ and $\beta 2 = 0.999$ is adopted, using L1 loss with an initial learning rate of 2e-4, halved every 125 epochs. The degradation module is trained for 100 epochs at 1e-3 learning rate, while full network training lasts 600 epochs.

4.2 Experiments on Noise-Free Degradation with Isotropic Gaussian Kernels

Experiments were conducted on isotropic Gaussian kernels without noise, and MDAT was compared with state-of-the-art blind super-resolution models including DASR [9], SRMDF [42], IKC [7], MRDA [43], and DSAT [11]. As shown in Fig. 4, the results indicate that MDAT maintains stable PSNR even with larger kernel widths across four benchmark datasets, demonstrating strong robustness to degradation estimation errors and superior generalization. Therefore, MDAT is well-suited for real-world degradation scenarios and outperforms the latest DSAT method on most datasets and kernel widths (Table 1).

Table 1. PSNR results achieved on noise-free degradations with isotropic Gaussian kernels for $\times 4$ SR.

Method	Set5				Set14				BSD100				Urban100			
Kernel width	0	1.2	2.4	3.6	0	1.2	2.4	3.6	0	1.2	2.4	3.6	0	1.2	2.4	3.6
Bicubic	28.42	27.30	25.12	23.40	26.00	25.24	23.83	22.57	25.96	25.42	24.20	23.15	23.14	22.68	21.62	20.65
SRMDNF [42]	30.61	29.35	29.27	28.65	27.74	26.15	26.20	26.17	27.15	26.15	26.15	26.14	25.06	24.11	24.10	24.08
IKC [7]	32.00	31.77	30.56	29.23	28.52	28.45	28.16	26.81	27.51	27.43	27.27	26.33	25.93	25.63	25.00	24.06
DASR [9]	31.99	31.92	31.75	30.59	28.50	28.45	28.28	27.45	27.51	27.52	27.43	26.83	25.82	25.69	25.44	24.66
MRDA [43]	32.34	32.35	32.11	30.89	28.62	28.67	28.56	27.61	27.66	27.70	27.62	26.95	26.23	26.25	26.01	25.07
DSAT [15]	32.54	32.51	32.00	30.31	28.85	28.77	28.50	27.51	27.76	27.76	27.66	27.02	**26.62**	**26.43**	25.95	24.89
MDAT(Ours)	**32.55**	**32.51**	**32.11**	**30.98**	**28.85**	**28.77**	**28.60**	**27.79**	**27.77**	**27.77**	**27.67**	**27.03**	26.41	26.30	**26.03**	**25.17**

4.3 Experiments on General Degradation with Anisotropic Gaussian Kernels and Noise

To evaluate degradation performance, anisotropic Gaussian kernels and noise were used. MDAT was compared with blind image reconstruction methods including RCAN [21], SRMDNF [42], IKC [7], DCLS [8], and DSAT [11]. Nine DASR-like kernels ensured fair comparison. Results show RCAN struggles under complex degradation, SRMDNF is estimation-sensitive, IKC improves performance with high cost, and DASR outperforms CNN-based methods but has modeling limits. Like DSAT, MDAT leverages a CNN-Transformer hybrid to better utilize degradation representations, achieving higher PSNR across blur kernels and noise levels (Table 2).

4.4 Ablation Experiment

Ablation experiments were conducted using isotropic Gaussian kernels. Quantitative and qualitative ablations were performed on MDAT. As shown in Fig. 5 and Table 3,

Model 4 (MDAT) significantly outperforms other models across all metrics. Model 1 removes both the multi-degradation and multi-content modules and uses DASR single-degradation module. Model 2 excludes multi-content information, while Model 3 removes multi-degradation learning and also uses DASR module. Results confirm that the proposed multi-degradation learning module improves local detail restoration, and the multi-content fusion module further enhances detail clarity.

Table 2. PSNR results achieved on Set14 for $\times$ 4 SR.

Method	noise	1	2	3	4	5	6	7	8	9
DnCNN + RCAN [21]	0	26.44	26.22	24.48	24.23	24.29	24.19	23.90	23.42	23.01
	5	26.10	25.90	24.29	24.07	24.14	24.02	23.74	23.31	22.92
	10	25.65	25.47	24.05	23.84	23.92	23.80	23.54	23.14	22.77
DnCNN + SRMDNF [42]	0	26.84	26.88	25.57	25.69	25.64	25.64	25.12	25.28	24.84
	5	25.92	25.75	24.18	23.97	24.05	25.64	23.65	23.20	22.80
	10	25.39	25.23	23.88	23.68	23.74	25.64	23.39	22.99	22.64
DnCNN + IKC [7]	0	27.71	27.78	27.11	27.02	26.93	26.65	26.50	26.01	25.33
	5	26.91	26.80	24.87	24.53	24.56	24.40	24.06	23.53	23.06
	10	26.16	26.09	24.55	24.33	24.35	24.17	23.92	23.43	23.01
DnCNN + DCLS [8]	0	27.56	27.49	26.32	25.99	25.88	26.03	25.70	24.65	23.95
	5	26.20	26.02	24.44	24.21	24.28	24.14	23.88	23.40	22.98
	10	25.47	25.33	24.06	23.87	23.91	23.79	23.58	23.16	22.78
DASR [9]	0	27.99	27.97	27.53	27.45	27.43	27.22	27.19	26.83	26.21
	5	27.25	27.18	26.37	26.16	26.09	25.96	25.85	25.52	25.04
	10	26.57	26.51	25.64	25.47	25.43	25.31	25.16	24.80	24.43
DSAT [11]	0	28.12	28.11	27.51	27.48	27.55	27.17	27.07	26.78	26.14
	5	27.39	27.32	26.41	26.23	26.24	26.12	26.00	25.65	25.19
	10	26.71	26.62	25.71	25.53	25.53	25.47	25.29	24.95	24.54
MDAT(Ours)	0	**28.42**	**28.33**	**27.97**	**27.82**	**27.79**	**27.76**	**27.75**	**27.21**	**26.50**
	5	**27.60**	**27.47**	**26.58**	**26.32**	**26.39**	**26.26**	**26.08**	**25.73**	**25.29**
	10	**26.86**	**26.72**	**25.84**	**25.67**	**25.55**	**25.53**	**25.33**	**25.02**	**24.62**

Fig. 4. Visual comparison of super-resolution reconstruction effects of isotropic Gaussian degraded kernel.

Table 3. Quantitative analysis results of ablation studies, showing PSNR and SSIM of different kernel widths on BSD100.

Kernel width			2.4		3.6	
Method	MD	MC	PSNR↑	SSIM↑	PSNR↑	SSIM↑
model1	✗	✗	27.618	0.7281	26.970	0.6940
model2	✓	✗	27.626	0.7287	26.991	0.6953
model3	✗	✓	27.631	0.7291	27.003	0.6956
model4	✓	✓	**27.684**	**0.7315**	**27.029**	**0.6973**

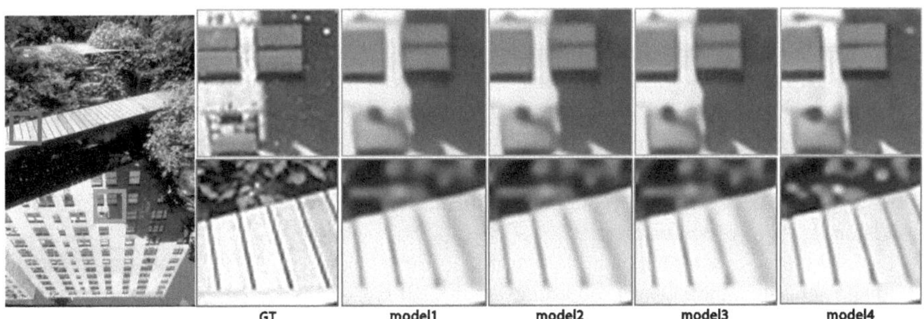

Fig. 5. Visual analysis of ablation experiment results.

References

1. Yang, W., et al.: Deep learning for single image super-resolution: a brief review. IEEE Trans. Multimedia **21**(12), 3106–3121 (2019)
2. Li, Z., et al.: Feedback network for image super-resolution. In: Proceedings of the IEEE/CVF Conference on Computer Vision and Pattern Recognition, pp. 3867–3876 (2019)
3. Fritsche, M., Gu, S., Timofte, R.: Frequency separation for real-world super-resolution. In: Proceedings of the IEEE/CVF International Conference Computer Vision Workshop, pp. 3599–3608 (2019)
4. Zhang, K., et al.: Plug-and-play image restoration with deep denoiser prior. IEEE Trans. Pattern Anal. Mach. Intel. **44**(10), 6360–6376 (2022)
5. Zhang, K., Liang, J., Van Gool, L., Timofte, R.: Designing a practical degradation model for deep blind image super-resolution. In: Proceedings of the IEEE/CVF International Conference Computer Vision, pp. 4791–4800 (2021)
6. Kim, J., Lee, J.K., Lee, K.M.: Accurate image super-resolution using very deep convolutional networks. In: *Proceedings of the IEEE Conference on Computer Vision and Pattern Recognition*, pp. 1646–1654 (2016)
7. Gu, J., Lu, H., Zuo, W., Dong, C.: Blind super-resolution with iterative kernel correction. In: Proceedings of the IEEE/CVF *Conference on Computer Vision and Pattern Recognition*, pp. 1604–1613 (2019)
8. Luo, Z., et al.: Deep constrained least squares for blind image super-resolution. In: Proceedings of the IEEE/CVF *Conference on Computer Vision and Pattern Recognition*, pp. 17642–17652 (2022)
9. Wang, L., et al.: Unsupervised degradation representation learning for blind super-resolution. In: Proceedings of the IEEE/CVF *Conference on Computer Vision and Pattern Recognition*, pp. 10581–10590 (2021)
10. Xia, B., et al.: Knowledge distillation based degradation estimation for blind super-resolution. In: Proceedings of the International Conference on Learning Representations, pp. 1–12 (2023)
11. Liu, Q., Gao, P., Han, K., Liu, N., Xiang, W.: Degradation-aware self-attention based transformer for blind image super-resolution. IEEE Trans. Multimedia **26**, 7516–7528 (2024)
12. Liu, Z., et al.: Swin Transformer: hierarchical vision transformer using shifted windows. In: Proceedings of the IEEE/CVF International Conference on Computer Vision, pp. 10012–10022 (2021)
13. Liang, J., et al.: SwinIR: image restoration using swin transformer. In: Proceedings of the IEEE/CVF International Conference on Computer Vision, pp. 1833–1844 (2021)
14. Chen, X., Wang, X., Zhou, J., Qiao, Y., Dong, C.: Activating more pixels in image super-resolution transformer. In: Proceedings of the IEEE/CVF International Conference on Computer Vision Pattern Recognition, pp. 22367–22377 (2023)
15. Zamir, Arjmandi, M., Khalid, A., Shafique, M.: Restormer: efficient transformer for high-resolution image restoration. In: Proceedings of the IEEE/CVF Conference on Computer Vision and Pattern Recognition, pp. 5728–5738 (2022)
16. He, K., Fan, H., Wu, Y., Xie, S., Girshick, R.: Momentum contrast for unsupervised visual representation learning. In: Proceedings of the IEEE/CVF International Conference on Computer Vision Pattern Recognition, pp. 9729–9738 (2020)
17. Lim, B., Son, S., Kim, H., Nah, S., Lee, K.M.: Enhanced deep residual networks for single image super-resolution. In: Proceedings of the IEEE Conference on Computer Vision and Pattern Recognition, pp. 136–144 (2017)
18. Tong, T., Li, G., Liu, X., Gao, Q.: Image super-resolution using dense skip connections. In: Proceedings of the IEEE International Conference on Computer Vision, pp. 4799–4807 (2017)

19. Kim, J., Lee, J.K., Lee, K.M.: Deeply-recursive convolutional network for image super-resolution. In: Proceedings of the IEEE Conference on Computer Vision and Pattern Recognition, pp. 1637–1645 (2016)
20. Tai, Y., Yang, J., Liu, X.: Image super-resolution via deep recursive residual network. In: Proceedings of the IEEE Conference on Computer Vision and Pattern Recognition, pp. 3147–3155 (2017)
21. Zhang, Y., et al.: Image super-resolution using very deep residual channel attention networks. In: Proceedings of the European Conference on Computer Vision, pp. 286–301 (2018)
22. Dai, T., Cai, J., Zhang, Y., Xia, S.-T., Zhang, L.: Second-order attention network for single image super-resolution. In: Proceedings of the IEEE/CVF International Conference on Computer Vision Pattern Recognition, pp. 11065–11074 (2019)
23. Shi, W., et al.: Real-time single image and video super-resolution using an efficient sub-pixel convolutional neural network. In: Proceedings of the IEEE Conference on Computer Vision and Pattern Recognition, pp. 1874–1883 (2016)
24. Yoo, J.-S., Kim, D.-W., Lu, Y., Jung, S.-W.: RZSR: Reference-based zero-shot super-resolution with depth guided self-exemplars. IEEE Trans. Multimedia **25**, 5972–5983 (2023)
25. Qi, H., Qiu, Y., Luo, X., Jin, Z.: An efficient latent style guided transformer-CNN framework for face super-resolution. IEEE Trans. Multimedia **26**, 1589–1599 (2023)
26. Carion, N., et al.: End-to-end object detection with transformers. In: Proceedings of the European Conference on Computer Vision, pp. 213–229 (2020)
27. Liu, L., et al.: Deep learning for generic object detection: a survey. Int. J. Comput. Vis. **128**(2), 261–318 (2020)
28. Wu, B., et al.: Visual transformers: token-based image representation and processing for computer vision. arXiv:2006.03677 (2020)
29. Zheng, S., et al.: Rethinking semantic segmentation from a sequence-to-sequence perspective with transformers. In: Proceedings of the IEEE/CVF International Conference on Computer Vision Pattern Recognition, pp. 6881–6890 (2021)
30. Cao, H., et al.: Swin-Unet: Unet-like pure transformer for medical image segmentation. In: Proceedings of the European Conference on Computer Vision Workshops, pp. 205–218 (2022)
31. Liang, D., Chen, X., Xu, W., Zhou, Y., Bai, X.: TransCrowd: weakly-supervised crowd counting with transformers. Sci. China Inf. Sci. **65**(6), 160104 (2022)
32. Sun, G., et al.: Boosting crowd counting with transformers (2021). arXiv:2105.10926
33. Chen, H., et al.: Pre-trained image processing transformer. In: Proceedings of the IEEE/CVF International Conference on Computer Vision Pattern Recognition, pp. 12299–12310 (2021)
34. Wang, Z., et al.: A general U-shaped transformer for image restoration. In: Proceedings of the IEEE/CVF International Conference on Computer Vision Pattern Recognition, pp. 17683–17693 (2022)
35. Cao, J., Li, Y., Zhang, K., Van Gool, L.: Video super-resolution transformer. arXiv:2106.06847 (2021)
36. Shi, J., et al.: Exploiting multi-scale parallel self-attention and local variation via dual-named transformer-CNN structure for face super-resolution. IEEE Trans. Multimedia **26**, 2608–2620 (2024)
37. Tian, Y., Krishnan, D., Isola, P.: Contrastive multiview coding. In: Proceedings of the European Conference on Computer Vision, pp. 776–794 (2020)
38. Chen, T., Kornblith, S., Norouzi, M., Hinton, G.: A simple framework for contrastive learning of visual representations. In: Proceedings of the International Conference on Machine Learning, pp. 1597–1607 (2020)
39. Bell-Kilgler, S., Shocher, A., Irani, M.: Blind super-resolution kernel estimation using an internal-GAN. In: Proceedings of the Advances in Neural Information Processing Systems, pp. 284–293 (2019)

40. Zhang, K., Good, L.V., Timofte, R.: Deep unfolding network for image super-resolution. In: Proceedings of the IEEE/CVF International Conference on Computer Vision Pattern Recognition, pp. 3217–3226 (2020)
41. Dyer, C.: Notes on noise contrastive estimation and negative sampling. arXiv:1410.8251 (2014)
42. Zhang, K., Zuo, W., Zhang, L.: Learning a single convolutional super-resolution network for multiple degradations. In: Proceedings of the IEEE Conference on Computer Vision and Pattern Recognition, pp. 3262–3271 (2018)
43. Xia, B., Tian, Y., Zhang, Y., Hang, Y., Yang, W., Liao, Q.: Meta-learning-based degradation representation for blind super-resolution. IEEE Trans. Image Process. 32:3383–3396 (2023)

CAPNet: Context-Aware Prompt Network for Weakly-Supervised Open-World Phrase-Grounding

Hui Yuan[1,2,3], Naigong Yu[1,2(✉)], Zhaoxuan Lu[4], Yan Huang[3], Jianhua Yang[3], Jinhan Yan[1,2], Zhiwen Zhang[1,2], and Liang Wang[3]

[1] School of Information Science and Technology, Beijing University of Technology, Beijing 100124, China
`hui.yuan@cripac.ia.ac.cn, yunaigong@bjut.edu.cn`
[2] Beijing Key Laboratory of Computational Intelligence and Intelligent System, Beijing University of Technology, Beijing 100124, China
[3] NLPR & MAIS, Institute of Automation, Chinese Academy of Sciences, Beijing 100190, China
[4] School of Transportation, Fujian University of Technology, Fuzhou 350118, China

Abstract. Weakly supervised phrase grounding (WSG) aims to localize visual regions corresponding to text phrases using only image-level annotations, which is particularly challenging in open-world settings due to the lack of fine-grained supervision. In this work, we propose a novel **Context-Aware Prompt Network (CAPNet)** that enhances WSG by explicitly modeling image-conditioned prompts and performing dense pixel-text alignment. Specifically, we design a visual-guided prompt tuning strategy to adapt the CLIP text encoder, enabling it to capture richer contextual semantics from visual inputs. In parallel, we reformulate the grounding task as pixel-level matching between visual features and contextualized text embeddings, generating a pixel-text score map that guides dense localization. Extensive experiments on Flickr30K, ReferIt, and Visual Genome demonstrate that our approach significantly outperforms prior state-of-the-art methods in both weakly supervised and open-world grounding tasks, validating the effectiveness of context-aware prompting for fine-grained cross-modal understanding.

Keywords: Open-world weakly supervised phrase grounding · Context-aware prompt · Dense prediction

1 Introduction

Weakly supervised phrase grounding (WSG) aims to generate accurate localization maps by aligning image regions with corresponding text phrases, using only image-level supervision. This task has gained increasing attention in multimodal learning due to its relevance to real-world applications, including vision-language navigation, interactive AI, and autonomous driving.

© The Author(s), under exclusive license to Springer Nature Singapore Pte Ltd. 2026
Z. Lin et al. (Eds.): ICIG 2025, LNCS 16163, pp. 187–199, 2026.
https://doi.org/10.1007/978-981-95-3729-7_16

In recent years, the paradigm of pre-training followed by fine-tuning has driven substantial progress across vision tasks such as image classification [1,2], object detection [3,4], and semantic segmentation [5,6]. In weakly supervised scenarios, pre-trained models can learn rich visual representations from large-scale unlabeled data, thereby significantly reducing reliance on extensive manual annotations. The emergence of vision-language models, such as CLIP [7], have further enhanced the potential of visual models by leveraging large-scale image-text pairs to learn semantic alignment between vision and language through contrastive learning. In zero-shot or few-shot settings, these models [8,9] have demonstrated remarkable transfer capabilities. However, effectively transferring high-level semantic knowledge from image-text pairs to fine-grained tasks, such as the WSG and dense localization, remains a significant challenge.

The key challenge of the WSG lies in training and optimizing models without access to large-scale, fine-grained annotations, while still ensuring cost-efficiency, generalization, and robustness. Recently, Shaharabany et al. [10] integrated the image-text alignment capability of CLIP with the image captioning technique of BLIP to generate descriptive texts for image regions, thereby enabling weakly supervised open-world visual phrase grounding and achieving remarkable results. Subsequently, some methods further improved the performance of weakly supervised phrase grounding through techniques such as self-training similarity maps [11], contrastive learning [12], and pseudo-labeling [13]. However, these existing methods underutilize the potential of fine-tuning pre-trained vision-language models in the weakly supervised setting. It is essential to explore a learnable, context-aware prompting mechanism that enables effective fine-tuning and enhances cross-modal localization capabilities.

In this paper, we introduce a novel **Context-Aware Prompt Network (CAPNet)**, which can be fine-tuned with contextual prompts to enhance visual understanding and improve the alignment of vision-language features. Specifically, we first design a novel context-aware prompt to fine-tune the CLIP model, thereby optimizing text features using visual information and enhancing the visual understanding capability of the WSG model. Furthermore, we extend the original image-text matching problem to a pixel-text matching paradigm, enabling the generation of a pixel-text score map that improves the localization accuracy of the WSG model. Extensive experiments on multiple benchmarks demonstrate that our approach outperforms the state-of-the-art WWbL method [10], achieving superior localization accuracy in both standard and open-world settings.

The main contributions of our work can be summarized as follows:

1) We propose CAPNet, a novel framework that introduces context-aware prompts to adaptively fine-tune the CLIP model, enriching textual representations with visual context to enhance cross-modal understanding.
2) We reformulate image-text alignment as fine-grained pixel-text matching, enabling the generation of the pixel-text score map for more accurate phrase localization.

3) Extensive experiments on multiple benchmarks show that CAPNet outperforms the state-of-the-art methods, achieving significant improvements in weakly supervised phrase grounding.

2   Related Work

2.1   Weakly Supervised Phrase Grounding (WSG)

Weakly supervised phrase grounding (WSG) is a challenging task in the field of multimodal learning and has attracted considerable attention in recent years. Early mainstream techniques were detector-based methods [14,15] that first pretrained a supervised object detection model, performed region-of-interest (RoI) localization, and then constructed a joint visual-textual representation space to formulate the grounding task as a retrieval problem. These methods heavily rely on pre-trained object detectors and cannot generalize to new scenarios. Another form of detector-free WSG methods [16–18] conducts cross-modal alignment between a given query phrase and the input image, performs dense localization, and generates an attention-based localization map. Although these methods lack explicit localization information, they can improve localization accuracy on weakly supervised data through techniques such as intra-modal classification and cross-modal alignment, thereby achieving promising results in weakly supervised phrase grounding. Pre-training and fine-tuning have emerged as a prevailing research paradigm for WSG tasks, serving as a crucial approach for bridging vision and language. The recent WWbL method [10] utilizes CLIP to extract textual features and enable interaction with visual features. It further combines CLIP's image-text matching scores with the image captioning model BLIP [19] to generate descriptive captions for objects within the scene, followed by applying phrase grounding to these generated captions. This approach introduces a novel application for WSG tasks: open-world weakly supervised phrase grounding without requiring any text input. Subsequently, Shaharabany et al. [11] employed a self-training strategy by aggregating similarity maps extracted from a phrase grounding model to generate effective pseudo-labels, thereby significantly enhancing localization performance. However, although these methods enrich visual representations and enhance vision-language understanding in weakly supervised settings, extracting high-level semantic information from image-text pairs for fine-tuning WSG tasks remains a significant challenge. Our method investigates the relationship between CLIP fine-tuning and weakly supervised phrase grounding, and optimizes the training process by introducing learnable context-aware prompts.

2.2   Prompt Learning

Prompt-based learning has increasingly gained prominence in both computer vision [20,21] and natural language processing [22,23]. Recently, prompt learning techniques have been introduced into vision-language understanding tasks [24,

25] and have demonstrated promising results. Zhou et al. [26] proposed a prompt tuning method for classification tasks and subsequently introduced conditional prompts to enhance the generalization ability of the model. Lu et al. [27] learn the distribution of diverse prompts to accommodate varying visual representations. In multi-label classification tasks, Ding et al. [28] proposed a semantic correspondence prompt network that leverages label-to-label semantic priors to enrich semantic context, while Hu et al. [29] introduced a dual context optimization network designed for partial-label and zero-shot multi-label recognition. Recently, Rao et al. [30] leveraged the pre-trained knowledge of CLIP to effectively prompt language models for dense prediction tasks. However, we propose a context-aware prompt network to fine-tune the pre-trained model and employ pixel-level matching to enhance the localization accuracy in open-world WSG tasks.

3   Method

Our proposed framework leverages the multimodal capabilities of CLIP to enable text-conditioned image generation with enhanced explainability, as illustrated in Fig. 1. At its core, the method begins by encoding an input image I through a CLIP-based image encoder, which extracts rich visual embeddings and global features to capture scene semantics. These embeddings are fused with post-generation test embeddings (derived from a set of textual prompts P_1 to P_N via a top-k selection mechanism, guiding a Transformer module to produce pixel-test coding maps that align visual and linguistic representations at a fine-grained level. An image decoder then reconstructs the output image $\hat{I}$, incorporating an inverted mask for targeted refinement (e.g., accentuating regions like roads or objects in the input). To ensure fidelity and interpretability, we optimize the model using a composite loss comprising an image reconstruction term L_{reg}, L_{fore} and L_{back}, an empirical loss L_{rmap} for empirical grounding, allowing users to probe and manipulate generated outputs based on textual guidance.

3.1   Context-Aware Prompt Network for WSG

We propose a context-aware prompt network for open-world weakly supervised phrase grounding, with the model architecture illustrated in Fig. 1 The proposed network is designed to learn image-conditioned contextual prompts to fine-tune the CLIP text encoder and perform pixel-level vision-language matching for dense localization, thereby enhancing localization accuracy.

The input image I is fed into CLIP's visual encoder, ResNet50. In addition to extracting global features $F_g \in R^{1 \times C}$, obtained via global average pooling from the spatial attention feature map $F \in R^{WH \times C}$, the encoder also outputs a language-compatible spatial attention map F from its final layer. Where W, H, and C represent the width, height, and number of channels of the feature map, respectively. This attention map F is fully leveraged for two main reasons: (1)

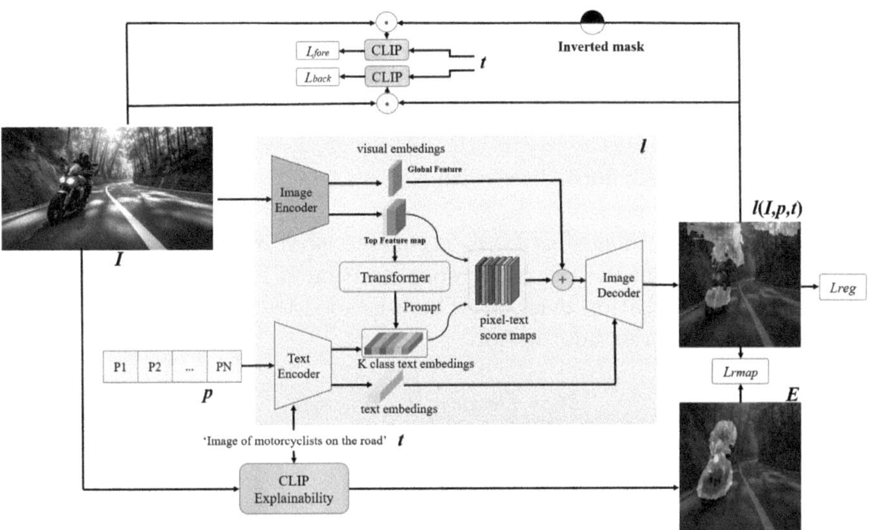

Fig. 1. The proposed **Context-A**ware **P**rompt **N**etwork (**CAPNet**) structure and the optimization loss terms.

it preserves rich spatial information, and (2) it enables effective alignment and fusion with text features.

In general, incorporating rich visual context into textual descriptions enhances the semantic accuracy of the text. For instance, the phrase "a photo of a moto on the road" conveys more precise semantic information than "a photo of a moto." We refer to the learned contextual content as a prompt. Inspired by [30], we propose to learn visual context prompts for refining textual representations. Specifically, we adopt the CoOp [26] to extract the initial text feature t_k, where t_k denotes the embedding corresponding to the name of the k-th class. The encoded text feature t_k is then used as a query in a Transformer decoder [31] to generate context-aware prompts.

$$Prompt = TransDecoder(t_k, [F_g{}', F']) \qquad (1)$$

where $[F_g{}', F']$ is derived from the concatenated features $[F_g, F]$, which are subsequently fed into a multi-head self-attention layer [31].

The text features are subsequently updated via residual connections to enhance their compatibility with the most relevant prompts.

$$t^* \leftarrow t_k + \gamma Prompt \qquad (2)$$

Here, $\gamma \in R^{N \times C}$ denotes a learnable parameter that regulates the scaling of the residual connection. It is initialized with a small value to retain the prior knowledge embedded in the text features.

Furthermore, the pixel-text score maps can be computed based on the spatial attention feature maps F' and the updated text features t^*, as follows:

$$s = \hat{F}' \hat{t^*}^T, \ s \in R^{WH \times K} \tag{3}$$

where $\hat{F}'$ and $\hat{t^*}$ are $L2$ normalized with respect to F' and t^* along the channel dimension.

Finally, the global image feature F_g is concatenated with the computed pixel-text score maps s, and the resulting representation is fed into the decoder of l to generate the localization mask M. This cascaded feature structure explicitly integrates language prior information.

$$M = Decoder(t_x, [F_g, s]) \tag{4}$$

where t_x denotes the embedded representation of the input phrase t.

3.2   Model Learning

Our model is improved based on the WWbL network. The use of loss terms also follows [10], with a total of four loss terms. Given the input image I, object category name p, and description text t, the foreground loss $L_{fore}(I, p, t)$ is computed using the following formula:

$$L_{fore}(I, p, t) = -CLIP(l(I, p, t) \odot I, t) \tag{5}$$

where $\odot$ denotes element-wise multiplication.

The background loss $L_{back}(I, p, t)$ is:

$$L_{back}(I, p, t) = CLIP((1 - l(I, p, t)) \odot I, t) \tag{6}$$

Following the method proposed by Chefer et al. [32], the pseudo-label E is obtained. The pseudo-label loss $L_{rmap}(I, p, t, E)$ is then computed as the squared Euclidean norm of the difference.

$$L_{rmap}(I, p, t, E) = \|E - l(I, p, t)\|^2 \tag{7}$$

Finally, a regularization loss $L_{reg}(I, p, t)$ is introduced to impose spatial constraints on the network l.

$$L_{reg}(I, p, t) = \|l(I, p, t)\| \tag{8}$$

The combined loss is defined as:

$$L = \alpha_1 L_{fore}(I, p, t) + \alpha_2 L_{back}(I, p, t) + \alpha_3 L_{rmap}(I, p, t, E) + \alpha_4 L_{reg}(I, p, t) \tag{9}$$

where α_1, α_2, α_3 and α_4 are the weight parameters of the four loss terms, set to 0.25, 0.5, 16, and 0.25, respectively.

4   Experiments

To evaluate the effectiveness of the proposed method, we conducted extensive experiments on multiple datasets, including weakly supervised object localization (WSOL), weakly supervised phrase grounding (WSG), and weakly supervised open-world pure visual phrase grounding (WWbL).

4.1   Datasets and Implementation Details

Datasets. For the WSOL task, we utilize the Stanford Cars [33] dataset, which contains 196 car categories with 8,144 samples in the training set and 8,041 samples in the test set. We also employ the Stanford Dogs [34] dataset, which consists of 20,580 images, including 12,000 for training and 8,580 for testing, covering a total of 120 dog categories. For the WSG and WWbL tasks, we train our model on MSCOCO and Visual Genome (VG), and evaluate it on the test splits of Flickr30k, ReferIt, and VG. The MSCOCO 2014 [35] dataset includes 82,783 training images and 40,504 validation images, each annotated with five descriptive sentences. The VG [36] dataset contains 77,398 training images, 5,000 validation images, and 5,000 test images, each paired with free-form textual descriptions and corresponding bounding boxes. The Flickr30k Entities [37] dataset, derived from Flickr30k dataset, contains 224K phrases describing objects in more than 31K images. For evaluation, we also use 1000 images from the test set of Akbari et al. [17]. ReferIt [38, 39] contains 20K images and 99,535 manually segmented regions, collected via a two-player game. It includes approximately 130K isolated entity descriptions. We also follow the test split from Akbari et al. [17].

Implementation Details. Experiments were conducted on a Linux server using python 3.9.18, torch 2.1.0, CUDA 10.2, and a single Tesla V100 GPU. For all tasks discussed in this paper, the visual backbone of the proposed network l is ResNet50. We use the AdamW optimizer with an initial learning rate of 0.0001, a batch size of 32, 50 training epochs, and a weight decay of 0.0001. A random horizontal flip with a probability of 0.5 is applied during training. We set the context prompt length to 24 for the WWbL task and 40 for the WSG task. The Transformer decoder used to extract visual context consists of 6 layers with 4 attention heads.

4.2   Evaluation and Analysis of Results

The WSG task is evaluated using the accuracy of the pointing game [40], called "Point Accuracy", which is calculated from the output map by finding the maximum-value location for the given query and checking whether this point is located in the region of the object. For a fair comparison, we also use the same train/validation/test split as Akbari et al. [17]. Compared to the baseline method WWbL, our approach employs CLIP's ResNet50 as the visual backbone. Table 1 reports the results of the weakly supervised phrase grounding task on

Table 1. Weakly Supervised Phrase Grounding (WSG) results: "pointing game" accuracy on the VG, Flickr30K, and ReferIt datasets.

Method	Backbone	VG trained			MS-COCO traind		
		VG	Flicker	ReferIt	VG	Flicker	ReferIt
TD [40]	Inception-2	19.31	42.40	31.97	–	–	–
SSS [16]	VGG	30.03	49.10	39.98	–	–	–
MG [17]	BiLSTM+VGG	50.18	57.91	62.76	46.99	53.29	47.89
MG [17]	ELMo+VGG	48.76	60.08	60.01	47.94	61.66	47.52
GbS [18]	VGG	53.40	70.48	59.44	52.00	72.60	56.10
WWbL [10]	CLIP+VGG	62.31	75.63	65.95	59.09	75.43	61.03
Ours	**CLIP+ResNet**	**63.28**	**77.11**	**67.13**	**60.24**	**77.93**	**63.30**

Table 2. Localization accuracy (%) for the WSOL task on the Stanford Car and Stanford Dog datasets.

Method	Stanford-Cars	Stanford-Dogs
CAM [41]	65.2	66.0
HaS [41]	87.4	77.5
ADL [42]	82.8	73.5
RDAP [43]	92.9	77.7
FG [44]	96.2	79.2
WWbL [10]	98.9	86.4
Ours	**99.1**	**87.1**

Flickr30k, ReferIt, and VG. Evidently, our method is superior to all baselines, whether training takes place over VG or MS-COCO.

For the WSOL task, we adopt the "Bbox Accuracy" metric, which evaluates whether the intersection over union (IoU) between the predicted and ground-truth bounding boxes exceeds 0.5. We evaluate our method on the WSOL task using two fine-grained localization datasets: Stanford Cars and Stanford Dogs. As shown in Table 2, our approach achieves leading performance in weakly supervised object localization, outperforming the baseline method WWbL.

We evaluate the WWbL task using two metrics: "Point Accuracy" and "BBox Accuracy". For each ground-truth bounding box and its corresponding caption, we identify the closest predicted caption in CLIP space and assess alignment by comparing the predicted map with the ground-truth box using the point accuracy metric. Table 3 presents the experimental results of the WWbL task across multiple test benchmarks, along with a comparison of the leading results on the WSG task. As shown in Table 3, our proposed method achieves the best performance on the WWbL task across multiple test benchmarks, outperforming the other three methods. Similarly, it also attains the highest performance on the WSG task across various benchmarks. Figure 2 shows several visual-

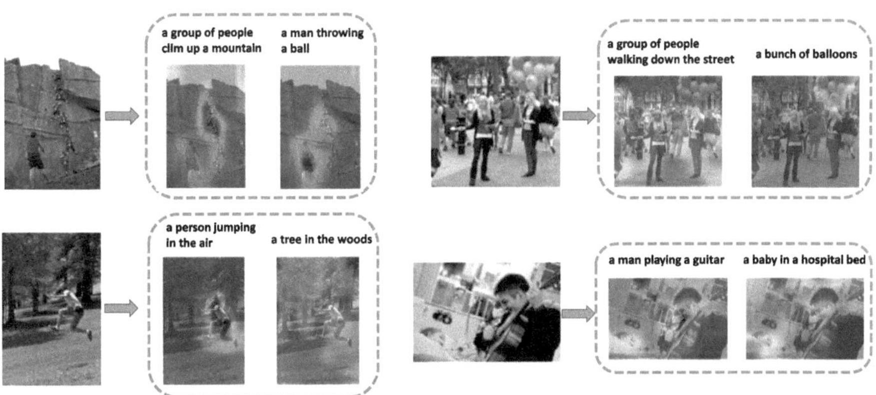

Fig. 2. Visualization results of the proposed method on the WWbL task, using images from the MS-COCO dataset.

Table 3. WWbL and Weakly Supervised Phrase Grounding (WSG) results for the test sets showing both "Point Accuracy" and "Bbox Accuracy".

Task	Method	Trainning	Point Accuracy			Bbox Accuracy		
			VG	Flicker	ReferIt	VG	Flicker	ReferIt
WWbL	MG [17]	MS-COCO	32.91	50.12	36.34	11.48	23.75	13.31
	MG [17]	VG	32.15	49.48	38.06	12.23	24.79	16.43
	GAE [45]	–	38.15	9.17	2.4	9.69	17.14	12.31
	WWbL [10]	MS-COCO	44.20	61.38	43.77	17.76	32.44	21.76
	WWbL [10]	VG	43.91	58.59	44.89	17.77	31.46	18.89
	Ours	MS-COCO	**48.13**	**63.79**	**52.46**	**19.65**	**32.76**	**24.59**
	Ours	VG	**44.22**	**62.07**	**55.74**	**19.02**	**32.76**	**26.23**
WSG	MG [17]	MS-COCO	47.94	61.66	47.52	15.77	27.06	15.15
	MG [17]	VG	48.76	60.08	60.01	14.45	27.78	18.85
	GAE [45]	–	54.72	72.47	56.76	16.70	25.56	19.10
	WWbL [10]	MS-COCO	59.09	75.43	61.03	27.22	35.75	30.08
	WWbL [10]	VG	62.31	75.63	65.95	27.26	36.35	32.25
	Ours	MS-COCO	**60.24**	**77.93**	**63.30**	**28.15**	**38.25**	**30.83**
	Ours	VG	**63.28**	**77.11**	**63.13**	**28.51**	**39.46**	**33.61**

ization results of our proposed method on the WWbL task using images from the MS-COCO dataset. Each pair consists of an input image on the left and corresponding localization maps and captions on the right.

5　Conclusions

In this work, we propose a novel weakly supervised open-world phrase grounding framework that leverages visual contextual information to enhance textual features. By reformulating image-text matching as pixel-text matching and utilizing pixel-text score maps as low-resolution segmentation maps fused with high-level semantic features, our method improves cross-modal alignment between visual and textual information. Additionally, we introduce learnable context-aware prompts and attention mechanisms to further enhance performance in fine-grained phrase grounding tasks.

Acknowledgments. This work was jointly supported by the National Natural Science Foundation of China (62236010, 62322607, 62276261 and 62076014).

References

1. Dosovitskiy, A., et al.: An image is worth 16x16 words: Transformers for image recognition at scale, arXiv preprint arXiv:2010.11929 (2020)
2. Kolesnikov, A., et al.: Big transfer (BiT): general visual representation learning. In: Vedaldi, A., Bischof, H., Brox, T., Frahm, J.-M. (eds.) ECCV 2020. LNCS, vol. 12350, pp. 491–507. Springer, Cham (2020). https://doi.org/10.1007/978-3-030-58558-7_29
3. Girshick, R., Donahue, J., Darrell, T., Malik, J.: Rich feature hierarchies for accurate object detection and semantic segmentation. In: Proceedings of the IEEE Conference on Computer Vision and Pattern Recognition, pp. 580–587 (2014)
4. Ren, S., He, K., Girshick, R., Sun, J.: Faster r-cnn: towards real-time object detection with region proposal networks. Advances in Neural Information Processing Syst. **28** (2015)
5. Chen, L.-C., Papandreou, G., Kokkinos, I., Murphy, K., Yuille, A.L.: Deeplab: semantic image segmentation with deep convolutional nets, atrous convolution, and fully connected crfs. IEEE Trans. Pattern Anal. Mach. Intell. **40**(4), 834–848 (2017)
6. Long, J., Shelhamer, E., Darrell, T.: Fully convolutional networks for semantic segmentation. In: Proceedings of the IEEE Conference on Computer Vision and Pattern Recognition, pp. 3431–3440 (2015)
7. Radford, A., et al.: Learning transferable visual models from natural language supervision. In: International Conference on Machine Learning, pp. 8748–8763. PMLR (2021)
8. Zhang, R. et al.: Tip-Adapter: Training-free adaption of CLIP for few-shot classification. In: Avidan, S., Brostow, G., Cissé, M., Farinella, G.M., Hassner, T. (eds.) Computer Vision – ECCV 2022. ECCV 2022. LNCS, vol. 13695. Springer, Cham (2022). https://doi.org/10.1007/978-3-031-19833-5_29
9. Shen, H., Zhao, T., Zhu, M., Yin, J.: Groundvlp: harnessing zero-shot visual grounding from vision-language pre-training and open-vocabulary object detection. In: Proceedings of the AAAI Conference on Artificial Intelligence, vol. 38(5), pp. 4766–4775 (2024)

10. Shaharabany, T., Tewel, Y., Wolf, L.: What is where by looking: Weakly-supervised open-world phrase-grounding without text inputs. Adv. Neural Inform. Process. Syst. **35**, 28222–28237 (2022)
11. Shaharabany, T, Wolf, L.: Similarity maps for self-training weakly-supervised phrase grounding. I: Proceedings of the IEEE/CVF Conference on Computer Vision and Pattern Recognition, pp. 6925–6934 (2023)
12. Chen, S., Luo, G., Zhou, Y., Sun, X., Jiang, G., Ji, R.: Querymatch: a query-based contrastive learning framework for weakly supervised visual grounding. In: Proceedings of the 32nd ACM International Conference on Multimedia, pp. 4177–4186 (2024)
13. Kuang, D., Zhang, R., Nie, Z., Chen, J., Kim, J.: Momentum pseudo-labeling for weakly supervised phrase grounding. In: Proceedings of the AAAI Conference on Artificial Intelligence, vol. 39(23), pp. 24348–24356 (2025)
14. Liu, Y., Wan, B., Ma, L., He, X: Relation-aware instance refinement for weakly supervised visual grounding. In: Proceedings of the IEEE/CVF Conference on Computer Vision and Pattern Recognition, pp. 5612–5621 (2021)
15. Rusak, E., et al.: A simple way to make neural networks robust against diverse image corruptions. In: Vedaldi, A., Bischof, H., Brox, T., Frahm, J.-M. (eds.) ECCV 2020. LNCS, vol. 12348, pp. 53–69. Springer, Cham (2020). https://doi.org/10.1007/978-3-030-58580-8_4
16. Javed, S.A., Saxena, S., Gandhi, V.: Learning unsupervised visual grounding through semantic self-supervision, arXiv preprint, arXiv:1803.06506 (2018)
17. Akbari, H., Karaman, S., Bhargava, S., Chen, B., Vondrick, C., Chang, S.-F.: Multi-level multimodal common semantic space for image-phrase grounding. In: Proceedings of the IEEE/CVF Conference on Computer Vision and Pattern Recognition, pp. 12476–12486 (2019)
18. Arbelle, A., et al.: Detector-free weakly supervised grounding by separation. In: Proceedings of the IEEE/CVF International Conference on Computer Vision, pp. 1801–1812 (2021)
19. Li, J., Li, D., Xiong, C., Hoi, S.: Blip: bootstrapping language-image pre-training for unified vision-language understanding and generation. In: International Conference on Machine Learning, pp. 12888–12900. PMLR (2022)
20. Shtedritski, A., Rupprecht, C., Vedaldi, A.: What does clip know about a red circle? visual prompt engineering for vlms. In: Proceedings of the IEEE/CVF International Conference on Computer Vision, pp. 11987–11997 (2023)
21. Yang, L., Wang, Y., Li, X., Wang, X., Yang, J.: Fine-grained visual prompting. In: Advances in Neural Information Processing Systems **36**, 24993–25006 (2023)
22. Liu, P., Yuan, W., Fu, J., Jiang, Z., Hayashi, H., Neubig, G.: Pre-train, prompt, and predict: a systematic survey of prompting methods in natural language processing. ACM Comput. Surv. **55**(9), 1–35 (2023)
23. Li, X.L., Liang, P.: Prefix-tuning: Optimizing continuous prompts for generation. arXiv preprint, arXiv:2101.00190 (2021)
24. Du, Y., Wei, F., Zhang, Z., Shi, M., Gao, Y., Li, G.: Learning to prompt for open-vocabulary object detection with vision-language model. In: Proceedings of the IEEE/CVF Conference on Computer Vision and Pattern Recognition, pp. 14084–14093 (2022)
25. Jia, M. et al.: Visual prompt tuning. In: Avidan, S., Brostow, G., Cissé, M., Farinella, G.M., Hassner, T. (eds.) Computer Vision – ECCV 2022. ECCV 2022. LNCS, vol. 13693. Springer, Cham (2022). https://doi.org/10.1007/978-3-031-19827-4_41

26. Zhou, K., Yang, J., Loy, C.C., Liu, Z.: Learning to prompt for vision-language models. Int. J. Comput. Vision **130**(9), 2337–2348 (2022)
27. Lu, Y., Liu, J., Zhang, Y., Liu, Y., Tian, X.: Prompt distribution learning. In: Proceedings of the IEEE/CVF Conference on Computer Vision and Pattern Recognition, pp. 5206–5215 (2022)
28. Ding, z., et al.: Exploring structured semantic prior for multi label recognition with incomplete labels. In: Proceedings of the IEEE/CVF Conference on Computer Vision and Pattern Recognition, pp. 3398–3407 (2023)
29. Hu, P., Sun, X., Sclaroff, S., Saenko, K.: Dualcoop++: fast and effective adaptation to multi-label recognition with limited annotations. IEEE Trans. Pattern Anal. Mach. Intell. **46**(5), 3450–3462 (2023)
30. Rao, Y., et al.: Denseclip: language-guided dense prediction with context-aware prompting. In: Proceedings of the IEEE/CVF Conference on Computer Vision and Pattern Recognition, pp. 18082–18091 (2022)
31. Vaswani, A., et al.: Attention is all you need. In: Advances in Neural Information Processing Systems, vol. 30 (2017)
32. Chefer, H., Gur, S., Wolf, L.: Transformer interpretability beyond attention visualization. In: Proceedings of the IEEE/CVF conference on computer vision and pattern recognition, pp. 782–791 (2021)
33. Krause, J., Stark, M., Deng, J., Fei-Fei, L.: 3d object representations for fine-grained categorization. In: Proceedings of the IEEE International Conference on Computer Vision Workshops, pp. 554–561 (2013)
34. Khosla, A., Jayadevaprakash, N., Yao, B., Li, F.-F.: Novel dataset for fine-grained image categorization: Stanford dogs. In: Proc. CVPR Workshop on Fine-grained Visual Categorization (FGVC), vol. 2(1) (2011)
35. Lin, T.-Y., et al.: Microsoft COCO: common objects in context. In: Fleet, D., Pajdla, T., Schiele, B., Tuytelaars, T. (eds.) ECCV 2014. LNCS, vol. 8693, pp. 740–755. Springer, Cham (2014). https://doi.org/10.1007/978-3-319-10602-1_48
36. Krishna, R., et al.: Visual genome: connecting language and vision using crowd-sourced dense image annotations. Int. J. Comput. Vision **123**, 32–73 (2017)
37. Plummer, B.A., Wang, L., Cervantes, C.M., Caicedo, J.C., Hockenmaier, J., Lazebnik, S.: Flickr30k entities: collecting region-to-phrase correspondences for richer image-to-sentence models. In: Proceedings of the IEEE International Conference on Computer Vision, pp. 2641–2649 (2015)
38. Grubinger, M., Clough, P., Müller, H., Deselaers, T.: The iapr tc-12 benchmark: a new evaluation resource for visual information systems. In: International Workshop Ontoimage **2** (2006)
39. Chen, K., Kovvuri, R., Nevatia, R.: Query-guided regression network with context policy for phrase grounding. In: Proceedings of the IEEE International Conference on Computer Vision, pp. 824–832 (2017)
40. Zhang, J., Bargal, S.A., Lin, Z., Brandt, J., Shen, X., Sclaroff, S.: Top-down neural attention by excitation backprop. Int. J. Comput. Vision **126**(10), 1084–1102 (2018)
41. Zhou, B., Khosla, A., Lapedriza, A., Oliva, A., Torralba, A.: Learning deep features for discriminative localization. In: Proceedings of the IEEE Conference on Computer Vision and Pattern Recognition, pp. 2921–2929 (2016)
42. Choe, J., Shim, H.: Attention-based dropout layer for weakly supervised object localization. In: Proceedings of the IEEE/CVF Conference on Computer Vision and Pattern Recognition, pp. 2219–2228 (2019)

43. Choe, J., Han, D., Yun, S., Ha, J.-W., Oh, S.J., Shim, H.: Region-based dropout with attention prior for weakly supervised object localization. Pattern Recogn. **116**, 107949 (2021)
44. Shaharabany, T., Wolf, L.: Learning a weight map for weakly-supervised localization. In: ICASSP 2023-2023 IEEE International Conference on Acoustics, Speech and Signal Processing (ICASSP), pp. 1–5. IEEE (2023)
45. Chefer, H., Gur, S., Wolf, L.: Generic attention-model explainability for interpreting bi-modal and encoder-decoder transformer. In: Proceedings of the IEEE/CVF International Conference on Computer Vision, pp. 397–406 (2021)

Progressive Knowledge Learning for Source-Free Domain Adaptive Object Detection

Caiyu Zhang, Baojie Fan[✉], and Wenzhang Zhou

Nanjing University of Posts and Telecommunications, Nanjing 210023, China
jobfbj@gmail.com

Abstract. Source-free domain adaptive object detection (SFOD) focuses on adapting the detector trained on source data to the unlabeled target domain without access to the source data. In this work, we propose a multi-expert progressive learning framework that incrementally acquires target domain knowledge to reduce the influence of noisy pseudo labels and thus alleviate performance degradation commonly encountered in the later stages of training. Specifically, we construct an expert module composed of multiple expert units. We further introduce a progressive learning strategy where each expert is guided by the predictions of its predecessor, leveraging carefully chosen pseudo label thresholds. Additionally, we explore the impact of different non-maximum suppression (NMS) threshold settings during pseudo label generation on the effectiveness of our progressive learning scheme. By employing this multi-expert progressive learning approach, our detector achieves improved performance while mitigating noise-induced degradation throughout training. Extensive experiments conducted across three distinct scenarios validate the effectiveness of our method.

Keywords: Object Detection · Domain Adaptation · Source-Free Object Detection

1 Introduction

In recent years, with the development of deep neural networks, remarkable progress has been made in object detection, leading to the emergence of a series of high-performance detectors such as Faster R-CNN [1], FCOS [2], DETR [3], and Deformable DETR [4]. However, when the detector trained on the source domain is deployed in the novel target domain, its performance often degrades considerably due to the distribution shift between training and testing data. Although collecting labeled data for the target domain could address this issue, it is typically costly and labor-intensive. To mitigate domain discrepancies, unsupervised domain adaptation (UDA) methods have been proposed. Typically, UDA approaches require access to source domain data during adaptation. Nevertheless, in real-world scenarios, this assumption is often violated due to concerns over data privacy, security, and logistical challenges in data transfer.

© The Author(s), under exclusive license to Springer Nature Singapore Pte Ltd. 2026
Z. Lin et al. (Eds.): ICIG 2025, LNCS 16163, pp. 200–211, 2026.
https://doi.org/10.1007/978-981-95-3729-7_17

To solve the above problem, Source-Free Domain Adaptation (SFDA) has been proposed. SFDA enables the adaptation of the source-pretrained detector to an unlabeled target domain without access to any source images or annotations. Existing SFDA approaches can be broadly categorized into three main groups. The first category [5] leverages the batch normalization (BN) statistics encoded in the source model to guide target domain adaptation, aligning feature distributions at intermediate layers. The second category [6–9] is based on self-training, which adapts the model using high-confidence pseudo labels, typically following the Mean Teacher framework [19]. The third category [10,11] utilizes the discriminative information of the source domain classifier to align source and target features through adversarial training or contrastive learning, thereby reducing domain discrepancy.

Although the aforementioned methods have achieved notable progress, the quality of pseudo labels they rely on is often highly sensitive to the choice of confidence thresholds. On one hand, high-threshold pseudo labels can effectively reduce noise, but they limit the diversity and quantity of training signals, thereby constraining the overall effectiveness of self-training. On the other hand, low-threshold pseudo labels can provide richer supervision and potentially enhance adaptation performance; however, they also introduce a considerable amount of noise, which may lead to unstable training and even performance degradation. Existing approaches struggle to strike an effective balance between high and low threshold settings for pseudo label generation.

To address the aforementioned challenges, we propose a multi-expert progressive learning framework. The core idea of our approach is to progressively incorporate target domain knowledge in order to mitigate the impact of noise and alleviate performance degradation during training. Specifically, we first construct a multi-expert module based on multiple detection heads derived from the base detector. Then, we introduce a progressive learning strategy for the target domain, where each expert unit is guided by the predictions of the preceding expert unit and selects reliable samples based on an appropriately designed pseudo-label confidence threshold. In addition, we investigate the effect of different non-maximum suppression (NMS) threshold settings in pseudo-label generation for each expert unit, and their impact on the overall progressive learning process. With our multi-expert progressive learning framework, the detector achieves consistently improved performance in the target domain while reducing the adverse effects caused by noisy pseudo labels during training.

In summary, our contributions are as follows:

- We propose the novel multi-expert progressive learning framework that effectively reduces the impact of noise in SFOD tasks and alleviates performance degradation in the later stages of training.
- We introduce the multi-expert architecture and propose the progressive learning strategy for target domain knowledge, enabling effective collaboration and information transfer among expert units.
- We investigate the impact of varying NMS threshold settings used for pseudo-label generation across different expert units.

- We evaluate the effectiveness of the proposed method on three SFOD tasks across four object detection datasets.

2   Related Works

2.1   Unsupervised Domain Adaptation

Unsupervised domain adaptation (UDA) focuses on transfer knowledge from the labeled source domain to an unlabeled target domain. Recently, numerous studies have addressed this problem, among which self-training is a widely adopted approach that leverages pseudo-labels to supervise and fine-tune the student model. Khodabandeh et al. [12] perform self-training on the target domain using noisy bounding boxes combined with an auxiliary image classifier to enhance label quality. Beyond pseudo-label self-training, some methods employ image translation techniques, typically using translation networks [13,14] to generate source-like or target-like images to facilitate adaptation training. Deng et al. [15] significantly improve cross-domain detection performance on multiple benchmark datasets by introducing the cross-domain distillation strategy and pixel-level adaptation for sample augmentation, along with an out-of-distribution sample estimation strategy to select the most suitable samples for the current model. Furthermore, adversarial training has also been explored to address this problem by enabling the model to adapt to varying data distributions across domains. Chen et al. [16] initially introduced the use of adversarial training to align features at both the image and object instance levels, while Saito et al. [17] propose a method based on adversarial training to achieve strong local feature alignment and weak global feature alignment. Although these approaches have demonstrated promising results, they all require access to source domain data during the adaptation process.

2.2   Source-Free Object Detection

Source-free domain adaptive object detection (SFOD) aims to achieve domain adaptation by transferring the source-trained model instead of the source domain data. Recently, numerous methods have been proposed to address the SFOD problem. SED [6] introduces a self-entropy descent strategy and employs data augmentation techniques to generate high-quality pseudo-labels. LODS [18] simplifies the model adaptation process by enhancing the style of target domain images and leveraging the style differences as a self-supervised signal. Inspired by the Mean Teacher framework [19] widely used in semi-supervised learning, recent approaches typically adopt an exponential moving average (EMA) model as the teacher network to predict high-quality pseudo-labels on the target domain. A^2SFOD [10] improves pseudo-label quality by partitioning target domain data into subsets similar and dissimilar to the source domain based on detection variance, and aligning these subsets in the feature space via adversarial learning. IRG [20] designs a graph convolutional network [31] to model relationships among object instances within the target domain and leverages graph-guided contrastive loss to enhance target domain feature representations. PETS [21] proposes a multi-teacher framework comprising static teacher, dynamic teacher, and student models, periodically exchanging weights between the static teacher and student models, and develops a consensus mechanism to fuse predictions from the two teacher models, thereby improving training stability. In this work, we propose a multi-expert progressive self-training method that effectively delays performance degradation during training by progressively guiding the target model to learn high-quality pseudo-labels.

2.3 Differences from Other Works

Existing source-free domain adaptive object detection methods predominantly adopt a single teacher-student architecture. While such approaches can partially alleviate the challenges posed by the absence of target domain annotations, their reliance on the single source of pseudo-labels and fixed parameters often leads to performance degradation during the later stages of training. In contrast to prior work, our method constructs an expert module composed of multiple expert units and employs the progressive learning strategy to acquire target domain knowledge. By selecting appropriate pseudo-label thresholds to guide sample selection, our approach effectively enhances detection performance and mitigates performance decline caused by noisy pseudo-labels.

3   Proposed Method

3.1   Overall Framework

Figure 1 illustrates our multi-expert progressive learning framework, which primarily consists of a static expert model, a dynamic expert model, and a student model. The dynamic expert and student model share the same network architecture but have different parameters, each mainly composed of a backbone network and expert detection heads.

Let the labeled data in the source domain be denoted as $D_s = \{(x_s^n, y_s^n)\}_{n=1}^{N_s}$, where x_s^n represents the n-th source domain image and y_s^n denotes the corresponding annotations containing object bounding boxes and categories. N_s is the total number of source domain images. The unlabeled data in the target domain is denoted as $D_t = \{x_t^n\}_{n=1}^{N_t}$, where x_t^n is the n-th target domain image, and N_t is the number of target domain images. Unlike Unsupervised Domain Adaptation (UDA), Source-Free Object Detection (SFOD) only requires a pre-trained source model with parameters and unlabeled target domain data to perform adaptation.

3.2   Base Detector

In the first stage, we pre-train the base detector using Faster R-CNN [1], which comprises a backbone network and a detection head. This detector is trained exclusively on labeled source-domain data.

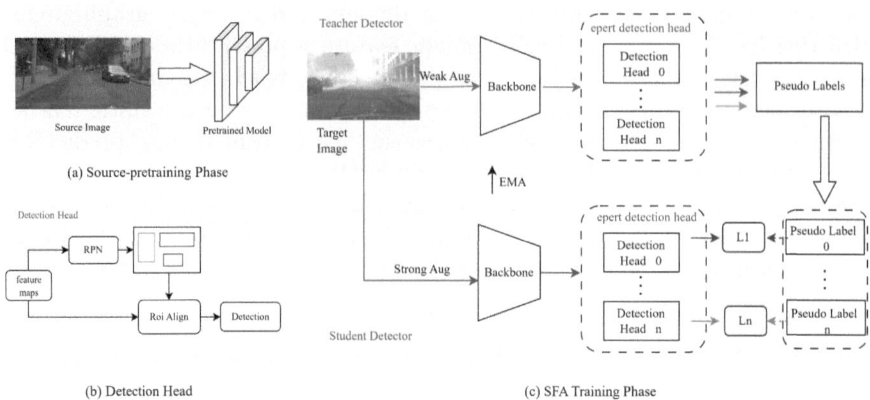

(a) Source-pretraining Phase

(b) Detection Head

(c) SFA Training Phase

Fig. 1. The overall framework of our method is divided into two stages: (1) training the base detector using source domain data; (2) progressive learning of target domain knowledge: constructing an expert module comprising multiple expert units, proposing the progressive learning strategy for target domain knowledge, and selecting appropriate samples with suitable thresholds to guide the student model training. The teacher model's weights are maintained as the exponential moving average (EMA) of the student model's weights.

3.3 Expert Detection Head

In source-free object detection, the model can only rely on pseudo-labels generated from target domain images for training. Due to the significant distribution gap between the source and target domains, these pseudo-labels often contain substantial noise, which adversely affects the model's performance. To address this issue, we construct an expert module composed of multiple expert units using the detection heads of the base detector. Each unit consists of an independent detection branch, while sharing a unified backbone feature input, as illustrated in Fig. 1.(b).

Specifically, each expert unit's detection branch is inherited from the base detector head and consists of two parts: the Region Proposal Network (RPN) branch and an ROI branch. The RPN branch performs foreground-background classification and bounding box regression on the backbone feature maps to generate candidate proposals. Subsequently, the ROI branch extracts ROI-aligned features for each candidate region, followed by separate classification and bounding box refinement, ultimately producing the class probabilities and precise bounding box coordinates for each proposal.

3.4 Progressive Target-Domain Knowledge Learning

In source-free object detection, using pseudo-labels generated with a single threshold often struggles to balance the trade-off between sample quantity and label quality. The high threshold results in fewer samples, while the low threshold introduces excessive noise, both of which significantly limit the effectiveness of the pseudo-labels. To address this issue, we adopt the progressive learning approach to gradually acquire knowledge from the target domain.

We assign different thresholds to each expert unit to obtain their respective pseudo-labels, thereby enabling progressive learning. Specifically, we set $\{(t_k, \theta_k)\}_{k=1}^K$ groups of threshold parameters, where t_k denotes the category confidence threshold required by the k-th expert unit for pseudo-label generation, and θ_k represents the Non-Maximum Suppression (NMS) threshold. Here, K corresponds to the number of static and dynamic expert units. The thresholds are set such that t_k gradually increases and θ_k gradually decreases, resulting in an increasing number of samples being selected. The k-th expert unit f_k generates pseudo-labels $\hat{y}_k$ based on parameters (t_k, θ_k).

$$\hat{y}_k = NMS\left(\left\{\left(b_i^k, c_i^k\right) \mid s_i^k \geq t_k\right\}, \theta_k\right) \tag{1}$$

Specifically, let b_i^k denote the i-th candidate box, and s_i^k represent its maximum category confidence score. The pseudo-labels generated by the k-th expert unit model are then fed into the $(k+1)$-th student model as supervision for training. It is worth noting that the backbone network and the 0-th expert unit share the same parameter configuration during training. The training loss for the k-th expert unit can be formulated as:

$$\mathcal{L}_k = \mathcal{L}_{\det}\left(\mathbf{x}_t, \hat{y}^{k-1}, \eta, \varphi^k\right) \tag{2}$$

Here, x_t denotes the target domain data, $\hat{y}^{k-1}$ represents the pseudo-labels generated by the $(k-1)$-th expert unit, η denotes the parameters of the backbone network, and φ^k denotes the parameters of the detection head in the k-th expert unit.

We use the above Eq. (2) to optimize the 0-th expert unit and the backbone network. Subsequently, the pseudo-labels for the first expert unit are generated based on the predictions of the 0-th expert unit and the corresponding NMS threshold parameters. This process is repeated iteratively, where the pseudo-labels for the $(n-1)$-th expert unit are obtained using the predictions of the $(n-2)$-th expert unit and its associated threshold parameters.

During the training process, we continuously update the expert model parameters via Exponential Moving Average (EMA), transferring weights from the student model to the expert model to ensure the expert reflects the latest state of the student. Furthermore, the student and expert networks employ strong and weak augmentations respectively, enhancing object detection performance on target domain data by enforcing consistency between their predictions. The overall teacher-student self-training framework for object detection can be formally expressed as follows:

$$\theta_t = \alpha\theta_t + (1-\alpha)\theta_s \tag{3}$$

Here, the hyperparameter α denotes the EMA decay rate, and θ_t and θ_s represent the parameters of the teacher and student networks, respectively.

3.5   Overall Optimization

The pipeline of our framework is mainly divided into two stages. In the first stage, we train the base detector using labeled source domain data to ensure sufficient learning of source domain features. In the second stage, we initialize both the dynamic expert and student networks using the pretrained base detector, and progressively optimize the student network through the progressive learning strategy. Meanwhile, the dynamic expert detector is updated using Eq. (3). The overall loss for source-free domain adaptive training can be formulated as:

$$\mathcal{L}_{\mathrm{det}} = \sum_{k=1}^{K} \mathcal{L}_{\mathrm{det}}^{k} \tag{4}$$

4   Experiments

We conducted comprehensive experiments to evaluate the effectiveness of our method. Ablation studies with different exchange strategies were performed to analyze the contribution of each component in our approach.

4.1   Experimental Setup

Task Settings. To assess the effectiveness of our approach, we conduct comparisons with current UDAOD and SFOD methods under four distinct domain shift settings: (1) Cityscapes $\rightarrow$ Foggy Cityscapes: Adapting from clear weather to foggy conditions. (2) KITTI $\rightarrow$ Cityscapes: Adapting across different camera setups. (3) Sim10k $\rightarrow$ Cityscapes: Adapting from synthetic images to real-world images.

Datasets. We use four datasets in the above tasks: (1) Cityscapes [22] is a large-scale dataset of urban street scenes with high-quality annotations. It contains 2,975 training images and 500 validation images, covering 8 categories: person, rider, car, truck, bus, train, motorcycle, and bicycle. (2) Foggy Cityscapes [23] is a dataset derived from Cityscapes that simulates foggy weather conditions to benchmark the robustness of vision models under adverse weather. It provides three fog levels (0.005, 0.01, 0.02). (3) KITTI [24] is a widely-used dataset containing real-world images and sensor data. (4) SIM10k [25] is a synthetic dataset generated from a video game, comprising 10,000 urban street images with annotated cars.

4.2   Implementation Details

We use the VGG16 [27] backbone pretrained on ImageNet [26] in the Faster R-CNN [1] framework. All training and testing images are resized so that the shorter side is 600 pixels, and the batch size is set to 8. The number of expert networks K is set to 5, including one static expert and four dynamic experts.

For the static expert, the pseudo-label generation thresholds are set to (0.8, 0.6). For the four dynamic experts, the thresholds are set to (0.8, 0.6), (0.8, 0.6), (0.9, 0.5), and (0.9, 0.5), respectively. The EMA update rate for the expert model is set to 0.92, and the learning rate is set to 3e-4.

4.3   Comparison Results

In Tables 1, 2, and 3, we compare our results with other methods in UDAOD and SFOD. For all evaluations, we use Average Precision (AP) with an IoU threshold of 0.5 (AP50) as our evaluation metric.

Cityscapes→Foggy-Cityscapes. We select the Cityscapes dataset as the source domain and the Foggy-Cityscapes dataset as the target domain, and conduct evaluation on the validation set of Foggy-Cityscapes. Table 1 presents a comparison of existing UDA and SFOD methods for adaptation from Cityscapes to Foggy-Cityscapes. Compared with the source only baseline, our method obtains 15% improvement in mAP. Among the methods using VGG16 as the backbone, ours performs better. Moreover, our method achieves the highest mAP for small object categories (e.g., person, rider) among all SFOD approaches.

Table 1. Results of different UDA and SFOD methods for Normal to Foggy Adaptation (Cityscapes → Foggy Cityscapes).

	Methods	Backbone	Person	Rider	Car	Truck	Bus	Train	Motor	Bicycle	mAP
	Source only	VGG16	33.6	36.6	40.1	6.3	24.5	6.2	18.3	34.7	25.1
UDA	SW-Faster [17]	VGG16	29.9	42.3	43.5	24.5	36.2	32.6	30.0	35.3	34.3
	Unbiased DA [15]	VGG16	33.8	47.3	49.8	30.0	48.2	42.1	33.0	37.3	40.4
	AT-Faster [29]	VGG16	34.6	47.0	50.0	23.7	43.3	38.7	33.4	38.8	38.7
	MeGA-CDA [29]	VGG16	37.7	49.0	52.4	25.4	**49.2**	**46.9**	34.5	39.0	41.8
SFDA	SED [6]	VGG16	21.7	44.0	40.4	32.2	11.8	25.3	34.5	34.3	30.6
	HCL [11]	VGG16	26.9	46.0	41.3	**33.0**	25.0	28.1	35.9	40.7	34.6
	A²SFOD [10]	VGG16	32.3	44.1	44.6	28.1	34.3	29.0	31.8	38.9	35.4
	LODS [18]	VGG16	34.0	45.7	48.8	27.3	39.7	19.6	33.2	37.8	35.8
	IRG [20]	ResNet50	37.4	45.2	51.9	24.4	39.6	25.2	31.5	41.6	37.1
	LPLD [30]	VGG16	39.7	49.1	56.6	29.6	46.3	26.4	**36.1**	**43.6**	**40.9**
	BT [32]	ResNet50	38.4	47.1	52.7	24.3	44.6	36.3	30.2	40.1	39.5
	Ours	VGG16	**44.9**	**52.0**	**60.6**	24.6	44.1	20.1	33.0	42.5	40.2

KITTI→Cityscapes. We use KITTI as the source domain and Cityscapes as the target domain. Focusing solely on the car category, our method achieves competitive performance, reaching the mAP of 50.0 for the car class, as shown in Table 2.

Table 2. Quantitative AP of Car results for KITTI to Cityscapes.

	Methods	Backbone	mAP
	Source only	VGG16	38.4
UDA	SW-Faster [17]	VGG16	37.9
	DA-Faster [16]	VGG16	38.5
	AT-Faster [29]	VGG16	42.1
	MeGA-CDA [29]	VGG16	43.0
SFDA	A2SFOD [18]	VGG16	44.9
	LODS [18]	VGG16	43.9
	IRG [20]	ResNet50	46.9
	LPLD [30]	VGG16	**51.3**
	PETS [21]	VGG16	47.0
	BT [32]	VGG16	48.7
	Ours	VGG16	50.0

Table 3. Quantitative AP of Car results for Sim10k to Cityscapes.

	Methods	Backbone	mAP
	Source only	VGG16	43.8
UDA	SW-Faster [17]	VGG16	40.1
	DA-Faster [16]	VGG16	38.5
	AT-Faster [29]	VGG16	42.1
	MeGA-CDA [29]	VGG16	44.8
SFDA	A2SFOD [18]	VGG16	44.0
	IRG [20]	ResNet50	45.2
	LPLD [30]	VGG16	49.4
	PETS [21]	VGG16	**57.8**
	BT [32]	VGG16	48.6
	Ours	VGG16	52.8

Sim10K→Cityscapes. To study adaptation from synthetic to real scenes, we use the Sim10k dataset as the source domain and the Cityscapes dataset as the target domain. The results in Table 3 show that our method ranks second, only behind the PETS method, achieving the mAP of 52.8 for the car category.

4.4 Ablation Study

Analysis of Performance Degradation Points Across Different Methods. Based on the Cityscapes to FoggyCityscapes scenario, we analyze the degradation points of different methods, as shown in Table 4. We select three representative approaches: IRG begins to degrade at around 30 epochs, LODS at 28 epochs, and LPLD at 26 epochs. All of these degradation points occur earlier than that of our method.

Table 4. Decay Epochs for Different Methods.

Method	degradation point
IRG [20]	30
LODS [18]	28
LPLD [30]	26

Table 5. Analysis of Different Threshold Selections.

Threshold	mAP	degradation point
increase	40.2	42
decrease	38.9	38
random	38.1	37

Analysis of Sample-Incremental Dynamic Thresholding. To verify the impact of the dynamic threshold mechanism on performance, we conduct ablation experiments on the Cityscapes to FoggyCityscapes scenario, as shown in Table 5. We compare three threshold selection strategies: increasing, decreasing, and random. As shown in Table 5, the decreasing and random strategies only achieve mAP scores of 38.9 and 38.1, respectively, while our increasing strategy achieves the highest mAP of 40.2. Moreover, the performance degradation occurs later with the increasing threshold compared to the other strategies.

Visualization Analysis of Detection Results from Different Experts. Figure 2 presents the detection results of different experts in our method. As shown in the figure, by progressively learning target domain knowledge, the impact of noise is effectively reduced. The third expert detects the bicycle category more accurately than the second expert, and the fourth expert identifies an occluded car that the third expert missed.

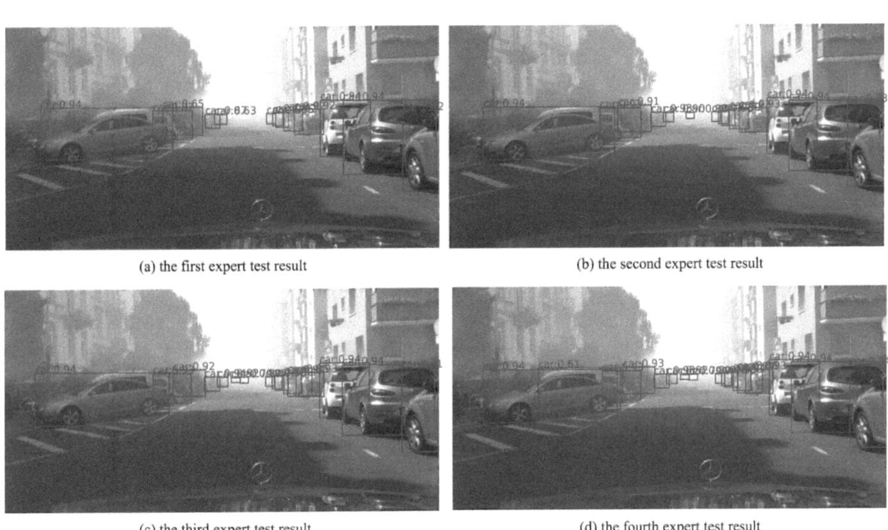

<table>
<tr><td>(a) the first expert test result</td><td>(b) the second expert test result</td></tr>
<tr><td>(c) the third expert test result</td><td>(d) the fourth expert test result</td></tr>
</table>

Fig. 2. Detection results of different experts based on the Cityscapes to FoggyCityscapes scenario. Red bounding boxes represent the detected results. (Color figure online)

5   Conclusion

In this paper, to address the negative impact of pseudo-label noise on model training in source-free domain adaptive object detection, we propose a multi-expert progressive knowledge learning framework. We introduce a multi-expert architecture and present a progressive learning approach for target domain knowledge. Furthermore, we investigate the effect of different threshold selections on progressive learning. Extensive experiments demonstrate that our method effectively mitigates performance degradation during the late stages of target domain training.

References

1. Ren, S., He, K., Girshick, R., Sun, J.: Faster r-cnn: towards real-time object detection with region proposal networks. Adv. Neural Inform. Process. Syst. **28** (2015)
2. Tian, Z., Shen, C., Chen, H., He, T.: Fcos: fully convolutional one-stage object detection. In: Proceedings of the IEEE/CVF International Conference on Computer Vision.,pp. 9627–9636 (2019)
3. Carion, N., Massa, F., Synnaeve, G., Usunier, N., Kirillov, A., Zagoruyko, S.: End-to-end object detection with transformers. In: Vedaldi, A., Bischof, H., Brox, T., Frahm, J.-M. (eds.) ECCV 2020. LNCS, vol. 12346, pp. 213–229. Springer, Cham (2020). https://doi.org/10.1007/978-3-030-58452-8_13
4. Zhu, X., Su, W., Lu, L., Li, B., Wang, X., Dai, J.: Deformable detr: deformable transformers for end-to-end object detection. arXiv preprint arXiv:2010.04159 (2020)
5. Ishii, M., Sugiyama, M.: Source-free domain adaptation via distributional alignment by matching batch normalization statistics. arXiv preprint arXiv:2101.10842 (2021)
6. Li, X., et al.: A free lunch for unsupervised domain adaptive object detection without source data. In: Proceedings of the AAAI Conference on Artificial Intelligence, vol. 35, pp. 8474–8481 (2021)
7. Liang, J., Hu, D., Wang, Y., He, R., Feng, J.: Source data-absent unsupervised domain adaptation through hypothesis transfer and labeling transfer. IEEE Trans. Pattern Anal. Mach. Intell. **44**(11), 8602–8617 (2021)
8. Xiong, L., Ye, M., Zhang, D., Gan, Y., Li, X., Zhu, Y.: Source data-free domain adaptation of object detector through domain-specific perturbation. Int. J. Intell. Syst. **36**(8), 3746–3766 (2021)
9. Kim, Y., Cho, D., Han, K., Panda, P., Hong, S.: Domain adaptation without source data. IEEE Trans. Artifi. Intell. **2**(6), 508–518 (2021)
10. Chu, Q., Li, S., Chen, G., Li, K., Li, X.: Adversarial alignment for source free object detection. In: Proceedings of the AAAI Conference on Artificial Intelligence, vol. 37, pp. 452–460 (2023)
11. Huang, J., Guan, D., Xiao, A., Lu, S.: Model adaptation: historical contrastive learning for unsupervised domain adaptation without source data. Adv. Neural. Inf. Process. Syst. **34**, 3635–3649 (2021)
12. Khodabandeh, M., Vahdat, A., Ranjbar, M., Macready, W.G.: A robust learning approach to domain adaptive object detection. In: Proceedings of the IEEE/CVF International Conference on Computer Vision, pp. 480–490 (2019)
13. Zhu, J.Y., Park, T., Isola, P., Efros, A.A.: Unpaired image-to-image translation using cycle-consistent adversarial networks. In: Proceedings of the IEEE International Conference on Computer Vision, pp. 2223–2232 (2017)
14. Huang, X., Belongie, S.: Arbitrary style transfer in real-time with adaptive instance normalization. In: Proceedings of the IEEE International Conference on Computer Vision, pp. 1501–1510 (2017)
15. Deng, J., Li, W., Chen, Y., Duan, L.: Unbiased mean teacher for cross-domain object detection. In: Proceedings of the IEEE/CVF Conference on Computer Vision and Pattern Recognition, pp. 4091–4101 (2021)
16. Chen, Y., Li, W., Sakaridis, C., Dai, D., Van Gool, L.: Domain adaptive faster r-cnn for object detection in the wild. In: Proceedings of the IEEE Conference on Computer Vision and Pattern Recognition, pp. 3339–3348 (2018)

17. Saito, K., Ushiku, Y., Harada, T., Saenko, K.: Strong-weak distribution alignment for adaptive object detection. In: Proceedings of the IEEE/CVF Conference on Computer Vision and Pattern Recognition, pp. 6956–6965 (2019)
18. Li, S., Ye, M., Zhu, X., Zhou, L., Xiong, L.: Source-free object detection by learning to overlook domain style. In: Proceedings of the IEEE/CVF Conference on Computer Vision and Pattern Recognition, pp. 8014–8023 (2022)
19. Tarvainen, A., Valpola, H.: Mean teachers are better role models: weight-averaged consistency targets improve semi-supervised deep learning results. Adv. Neural Inform. Process. Syst. **30** (2017)
20. VS, V., Oza, P., Patel, V.M.: Instance relation graph guided source-free domain adaptive object detection. In: Proceedings of the IEEE/CVF Conference on Computer Vision and Pattern Recognition, pp. 3520–3530 (2023)
21. Liu, Q., Lin, L., Shen, Z., Yang, Z.: Periodically exchange teacher-student for source-free object detection. In: Proceedings of the IEEE/CVF international conference on computer vision. pp. 6414–6424 (2023)
22. Cordts, M., et al.: The cityscapes dataset for semantic urban scene understanding. In: Proceedings of the IEEE Conference on Computer Vision and Pattern Recognition, pp. 3213–3223 (2016)
23. Sakaridis, C., Dai, D., Van Gool, L.: Semantic foggy scene understanding with synthetic data. Int. J. Comput. Vision **126**, 973–992 (2018)
24. Geiger, A., Lenz, P., Stiller, C., Urtasun, R.: Vision meets robotics: the kitti dataset. Inter. J. Robot. Res. **32**(11), 1231–1237 (2013)
25. Johnson-Roberson, M., Barto, C., Mehta, R., Sridhar, S.N., Rosaen, K., Vasudevan, R.: Driving in the matrix: Can virtual worlds replace human-generated annotations for real world tasks? arXiv preprint arXiv:1610.01983 (2016)
26. Krizhevsky, A., Sutskever, I., Hinton, G.E.: Imagenet classification with deep convolutional neural networks. Adv. Neural Inform. Process. Syst. **25** (2012)
27. Liu, S., Deng, W.: Very deep convolutional neural network based image classification using small training sample size. In: 2015 3rd IAPR Asian Conference on Pattern Recognition (ACPR), pp. 730–734. IEEE (2015)
28. He, Z., Zhang, L.: Domain adaptive object detection via asymmetric tri-way faster-RCNN. In: Vedaldi, A., Bischof, H., Brox, T., Frahm, J.-M. (eds.) ECCV 2020. LNCS, vol. 12369, pp. 309–324. Springer, Cham (2020). https://doi.org/10.1007/978-3-030-58586-0_19
29. Hsu, H.Ket al.: Progressive domain adaptation for object detection. In: Proceedings of the IEEE/CVF Winter Conference on Applications of Computer Vision, pp. 749–757 (2020)
30. Yoon, I., Kwon, H., Kim, J., Park, J., Jang, H., Sohn, K.: Enhancing source-free domain adaptive object detection with low-confidence pseudo label distillation. In: Leonardis, A., Ricci, E., Roth, S., Russakovsky, O., Sattler, T., Varol, G. (eds) Computer Vision – ECCV 2024. ECCV 2024. LNCS, vol. 15142. Springer, Cham (2025). https://doi.org/10.1007/978-3-031-72907-2_20
31. Kipf, T.N., Welling, M.: Semi-supervised classification with graph convolutional networks. arXiv preprint arXiv:1609.02907 (2016)
32. Deng, J., Li, W., Duan, L.: Balanced teacher for source-free object detection. IEEE Trans. Circuits Syst. Video Technol. **34**(8), 7231–7243 (2024)

Spatially-Aware Framework for Sequential Deepfake Detection

Chaoyi Huang[1,2], Rui Yang[1,2], Rushi Lan[1,2(✉)], Zhanghui Wu[1,2], Jiahao Li[1,2], and Tengjie Hu[1,2]

[1] Guangxi Key Laboratory of Image and Graphic Intelligent Processing, Guilin University of Electronic Technology, Guilin 541004, Guangxi, China
[2] International Joint Research Laboratory of Spatio-temporal Information and Intelligent Location Services, Guilin University of Electronic Technology, Guilin 541004, Guangxi, China
rslan2016@163.com

Abstract. With the rapid advancements in facial editing technologies, deepfake detection for multi-step continuous facial manipulation has emerged as a crucial research area in computer vision and visual security. Current state-of-the-art detection methods typically rely on traditional convolutional neural network (CNN) feature extractors, which struggle to capture fine-grained local manipulation traces, thereby limiting their detection performance in complex, continuous forgery scenarios. To address this challenge, this paper introduces a coordinate-based multi-scale strategy, MSCP-SeqFakeFormer. By incorporating coordinate positioning between the CNN feature extraction and Transformer encoder, the approach leverages multiple scales and receptive fields to effectively enhance local detail features associated with facial forgeries. This enhancement significantly improves the model's ability to recognize manipulation types and their sequences. Experimental results on the publicly available Seq-DeepFake dataset demonstrate that the proposed method outperforms the baseline model in both fixed-length (Fixed-Acc) and adaptive-length (Adaptive-Acc) evaluation metrics, and also achieves superior performance in the facial image recovery task.

Keywords: Deepfake Detection · Multi-step Forgery · Feature Enhancement · Seq-DeepFake Dataset

1 Introduction

In recent years, advancements in deep learning technologies like GAN [9] have greatly enhanced facial forgery techniques, enabling the creation of highly realistic fake facial images and videos. While these technologies have valuable applications in areas such as entertainment, film production, and virtual reality, their misuse has raised serious societal concerns, including misinformation, identity theft, and financial fraud [18]. As these issues grow, deepfake detection has

© The Author(s), under exclusive license to Springer Nature Singapore Pte Ltd. 2026
Z. Lin et al. (Eds.): ICIG 2025, LNCS 16163, pp. 212–223, 2026.
https://doi.org/10.1007/978-981-95-3729-7_18

become a critical focus in computer vision and information security research [17].

Traditional deepfake detection methods focus on single-step manipulations, like face swapping [15] or editing individual attributes [14]. These methods often use CNN to extract spatial features or analyze frequency-domain differences to detect forgeries, showing good results in simpler cases [19]. However, with the rise of apps like FaceTune [20] and YouCam Makeup [25], users can now create multi-step, continuous facial modifications, leading to more complex forgery sequences. These subtle changes are harder for traditional methods to detect, presenting new challenges for deepfake detection [24].

To address this, Rui Shao et al. proposed the SeqDeepFake task and Seq-FakeFormer framework, treating multi-step facial forgery detection as an image-to-sequence problem [19]. The framework combines CNNs for feature extraction with Transformers' self-attention mechanism to capture spatial and sequential relationships, enhancing detection. However, SeqFakeFormer struggles with subtle local changes in facial images, limiting its accuracy and robustness in detecting complex multi-step forgeries.

To enhance multi-step forgery detection, this paper introduces the MSCP (Multi-scale Strategy based on Coordinate Positioning) module, built upon the SeqFakeFormer framework. The MSCP module uses a multi-branch convolutional structure with kernels of varying sizes and dilation rates to capture fine-grained local features from multiple scales and directions. By fusing features and using residual connections, MSCP improves the model's ability to detect subtle facial manipulation traces, significantly boosting its performance. Our contributions are summarized as follows:

1. We propose a spatial direction-aware feature extraction module that separately encodes horizontal and vertical information from facial images. This design significantly improves the model's ability to localize manipulation traces by enhancing its sensitivity to spatial artifact distributions.
2. We design a multi-scale, multi-path fusion strategy that aggregates features across various receptive fields. This allows the model to capture multi-level and multi-scale forgery patterns, improving robustness and accuracy in detecting complex multi-step manipulations.
3. We conduct comprehensive experiments on the Seq-DeepFake dataset. Results show that our method outperforms the baseline SeqFakeFormer under both Fixed-Acc and Adaptive-Acc settings, and achieves superior performance in facial image restoration tasks.

2   Related Work

2.1   Deepfake Detection

With the rise of GAN and deep learning, deepfake images are becoming almost indistinguishable from real ones. Tools like FaceSwap [15] and DeepFaceLab exemplify this trend. The growing use of deepfakes has made detection increasingly difficult. Traditional methods often rely on CNN to extract spatial features like textures and noise for authenticity verification. Networks like ResNet and XceptionNet work well for simpler forgery tasks [11], but their performance drops with multiple forgery techniques.

To address this, researchers have explored converting images into sequence-based representations. Shao et al. proposed the Seq-DeepFake model, which uses CNN to extract features and integrates positional encoding with a Transformer encoder-decoder to convert them into a sequence for detection [19]. This method captures spatial features and models the sequential dependencies of forgery operations, significantly improving detection accuracy and robustness.

2.2 Facial Editing

Facial editing, a key research area in image generation and manipulation, focuses on flexible adjustments of specific components or attributes while maintaining natural facial structures. With advancements in GAN and semantic segmentation, more sophisticated and realistic facial editing methods have emerged [4,9,13]. For example, StyleGAN-based hierarchical latent space encoding allows precise control over localized components using disentangled semantic features [1], while approaches with semantic segmentation masks enable pixel-level operations on specific facial regions [5]. Recent studies have further enabled multidimensional joint editing of lighting, pose, and texture through diffusion models and Neural Radiance Fields techniques.

To achieve more natural and fine-grained localized editing, several methods have introduced semantic-guided mechanisms. For instance, MaskGAN employs semantic masks as conditional inputs, enabling the model to perform targeted operations within user-specified regions [22]. Building on this, SEAN further enhances editing flexibility by encoding independent style vectors for each semantic region, achieving precise control over distinct facial components and significantly improving the realism and consistency of edits [27]. These approaches demonstrate how explicit semantic constraints can bridge the gap between coarse global adjustments and pixel-level refinement.

In terms of structural control, StyleMapGAN incorporates explicit spatial structures into the latent space modeling process, allowing position-aware manipulation of facial components in the latent variables. By blending the style maps of source and reference images, StyleMapGAN enables spatially controllable local facial editing, supporting photorealistic synthesis [2]. This approach highlights how integrating geometric priors into generative frameworks can bridge the gap between global style transfer and fine-grained structural adjustments.

3 Method

3.1 Overall Architecture

The Seq-DeepFake framework models facial forgery detection as a forgery operation sequence prediction task. Its architecture integrates a CNN backbone and a Transformer encoder-decoder. The CNN backbone first extracts spatial

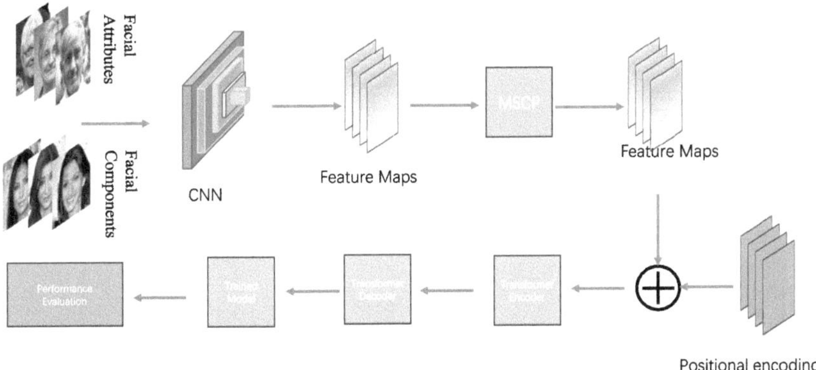

Fig. 1. The overall architecture of MSCP-SeqFakeFormer

features from input images, while the Transformer module captures temporal dependencies between manipulation steps through self-attention mechanisms, [21]ultimately generating a predicted sequence of operations. [19]Compared to traditional binary classification approaches, this design significantly enhances sequential modeling capability and interpretability. Despite its advancements, limitations persist. Practical facial forgeries often involve fine-grained multi-region alterations, such as localized eye contour edits and lip substitutions. [12]However, the high-level semantic features extracted by the original CNN backbone predominantly emphasize global structural patterns, overlooking directional and region-specific local artifacts. Furthermore, the absence of intermediate feature enhancement between CNN and Transformer modules restricts the Transformer's access to well-structured spatial information, thereby limiting its capacity to model complex manipulation sequences.

To address the aforementioned issues, this paper introduces a coordinate localization-based multi-scale feature enhancement module (MSCP) into the original architecture. Integrated between the CNN backbone and the Transformer encoder, this module focuses on spatial structure modeling and orientation sensitivity enhancement for features output by the backbone network. By fusing spatial features from horizontal and vertical orientations while integrating information across multi-scale receptive fields, it strengthens the model's responsiveness to localized forged regions, thereby providing more discriminative representations for subsequent sequence modeling. Figure 1 illustrates the workflow of the proposed framework (MSCP-SeqFakeFormer). The input image is first processed by a CNN network to extract spatial feature maps, which are then spatially enhanced through the MSCP module. The enhanced features, after incorporating positional encoding, are fed into a Transformer encoder-decoder module for sequence modeling. The model ultimately outputs the sequence of manipulation steps involved in the forgery process, with its discriminative performance continuously optimized through training.

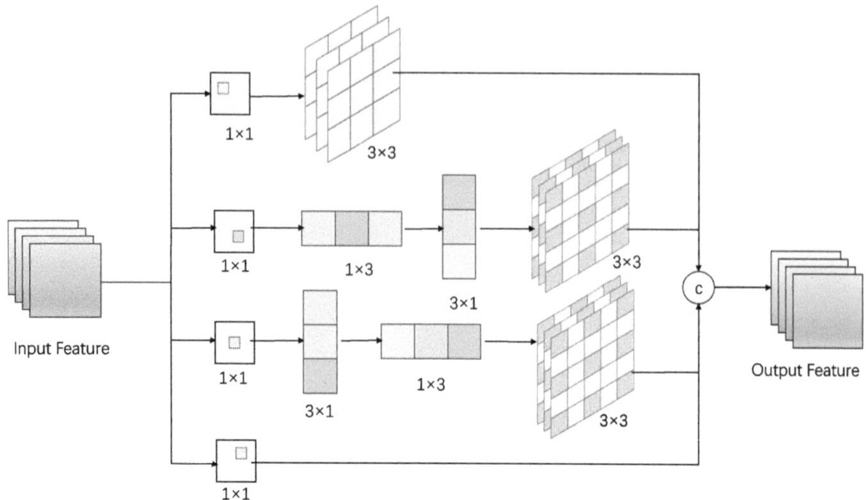

Fig. 2. The MSCP module

3.2　MSCP Module

Module Overview. In facial deep forgery sequence detection, capturing subtle manipulation traces is crucial. While traditional CNN excel at extracting global features, they struggle to capture local details, such as minor changes in the eye and mouth regions. In multi-stage forgery scenarios, these fine-grained artifacts are often missed, reducing detection accuracy. To address this, we propose a Coordinate-guided Multi-scale Feature Enhancement Module (MSCP), as shown in Fig. 2. This module enhances local features extracted by CNN, improving sensitivity to subtle forgery traces and boosting performance in complex forgery sequences

Coordinate Localization. By extracting features across different spatial receptive fields, the model's sensitivity to spatial locations is effectively enhanced. Let the input feature map be $X \in R^{C \times H \times W}$, where C is the number of channels, and H and W represent the height and width of the feature map. We use two different convolution strategies to extract features: one is horizontal convolution followed by vertical convolution; the other is vertical convolution followed by horizontal convolution. Then, the features from both directions are fused to obtain spatial location information. The features extracted using these two methods reflect spatial information from different directions, enabling a more comprehensive understanding of spatial location.

MSCP performs the following convolution operations to extract features along the horizontal and vertical axes:

1. Horizontal Convolution: A 1×3 convolution kernel is applied to the input feature map, producing the horizontal features $X_h \in R^{C' \times H \times W}$, where C' is the

number of channels after convolution.

$$X_h = \text{Conv2D}_{1\times3}(X) \tag{1}$$

2. Vertical Convolution: A 3×1 convolution kernel is applied to the input feature map, producing the vertical features $X_v \in R^{C'\times H\times W}$ where C' is the number of channels after convolution.

$$X_v = \text{Conv2D}_{3\times1}(X) \tag{2}$$

After merging the features from both directions, we obtain the enhanced feature representation.

$$X_{hv} = concat\,(X_h, X_v) \tag{3}$$

$$X_{vh} = concat\,(X_h, v_h) \tag{4}$$

Multi-scale Feature Enhancement. To capture the variation of forgery traces at different scales, the MSCP module is designed with a multi-branch convolution structure, as shown in Fig. 2. Let the input be X, and convolution operations are performed at multiple scales to obtain feature representations at different scales. Specifically, the branch structure includes the following methods:

Branch 1: First, feature extraction is performed using a 1×1 convolution, followed by a 3×3 convolution.

$$X_{\text{branch1}} = \text{Conv2D}_{1\times1}(X) \rightarrow \text{Conv2D}_{3\times3}(X_{\text{branch1}}) \tag{5}$$

Branch 2: First, features are extracted using a 1×1 convolution kernel, followed by a horizontal convolution and then a vertical convolution to capture the spatial information of the features. Finally, a 3×3 dilated convolution is applied to extract fine-grained image features

$$X_{\text{branch2}} = \text{Conv2D}_{1\times3}(X) \rightarrow X_{hv} = concat(X_h, X_v) \rightarrow \text{Conv2D}_{3\times3}(X_{\text{branch2}}) \tag{6}$$

Branch 3: First, features are extracted using a 1×1 convolution kernel, followed by a vertical convolution and then a horizontal convolution to capture the spatial information of the features. Finally, a 3×3 dilated convolution is applied to extract fine-grained image features.

$$X_{\text{branch3}} = \text{Conv2D}_{3\times1}(X) \rightarrow X_{vh} = concat(X_v, X_h) \rightarrow \text{Conv2D}_{3\times3}(X_{\text{branch3}}) \tag{7}$$

Branch 4: Feature extraction is performed using a 1×1 convolution

$$X_{branch4} = \text{Conv2D}_{1\times1}(X) \tag{8}$$

Finally, the feature maps from all branches are fused together through a concatenation operation to obtain the enhanced multi-scale features:

$$X_{\text{MSCP}} = \text{Conv2D}_{1\times1}(concat(X_{\text{branch1}}, X_{\text{branch2}}, X_{\text{branch3}}, X_{\text{branch4}})) \tag{9}$$

4   Experiments

4.1   Experimental Details

We conducted the experiments on a system equipped with an NVIDIA Tesla P100 GPU, using the PyTorch framework with CUDA support for model training and evaluation. Two different CNN were chosen: ResNet-50 and ResNet-34, both pre-trained on the ImageNet dataset. To compare the model parameter scales, we also employed a Transformer model with 2 encoder layers and 2 decoder layers, each containing 4 self-attention heads. We used a 20-epoch warm-up strategy, with a total of 170 training epochs. The learning rate was reduced by 10 % after every 50 epochs. The initial learning rate for the Transformer part was set to 10^{-3}, for the CNN part it was set to 10^{-4}, and the hyperparameter λ was set to 4.

4.2   Benchmark Methods

For the Seq-Deepfake operation detection task, a direct and effective solution is to model it as a multi-label classification problem. [7]In this framework, each operation in the sequence is treated as an independent category, and the model is required to simultaneously identify multiple operation labels from the images. As a baseline method, we designed a simple multi-label classification network, using pre-trained ResNet-34 [11]and ResNet-50 [11] on the ImageNet [6] dataset as backbone networks. [10] On top of the backbone, we added N=5 linear classifica-tion heads, corresponding to the maximum sequence length in the Seq-Deepfake dataset. Each classification head predicts the operation type at a specific position in the sequence.

To enhance sequence modeling, we adapted a Transformer-based architec-ture, specifically the DETR framework [3], originally designed for object detec-tion. We replaced its object queries with operation sequence labels, keeping the category output to predict operation types at each sequence position.

To evaluate current deepfake detection methods, we extended three represen-tative models to multi-label classification: DRN [23], based on an extended resid-ual structure; Two-Stream network [16], which links high-frequency and RGB features; and MA model [26], which uses multiple attention mechanisms. We replaced their binary classification output with multi-head classifiers for sequen-tial operation recognition. For sequences shorter than the fixed length N=5, we added a "no operation" label to match the predicted output with the true label length.

4.3   Evaluation Metrics

Fixed Accuracy (Fixed-Acc): Considering the fixed operation sequence length N=5, during evaluation, we pad the "no operation" category into the annotated operation sequence, just as in the training phase. Based on this, the first type of evaluation method compares each predicted operation category in the sequence with its corresponding true annotation, and calculates the evaluation accuracy.

Adaptive Accuracy (Adaptive-Acc): For sequences based on an autoregressive mechanism, once the EOS (End of Sequence) is predicted, the prediction automatically stops. Therefore, this method can detect facial operation sequences with adaptive lengths. To evaluate in this case, the second type of evaluation compares the predicted operations with their corresponding annotations within the maximum operation steps ($N \leq 5$). This makes the evaluation focus more on the accuracy of the operations.

4.4 Quantitative Analysis

We evaluated the performance of our proposed deepfake detection model in terms of Fixed-Acc and Adaptive-Acc through quantitative analysis and compared it with existing baseline methods. The experimental results are shown in Tables 1 and 2. These results demonstrate the effectiveness of our coordinate localization-based multi-scale strategy in detecting facial operation sequences. Through experiments with ResNet-34 and ResNet-50 architectures, we observed significant improvements in detection accuracy across the models. On the facial components dataset, all three models consistently showed improvements, further validating the robustness of our approach. Figures 3 and 4 illustrate the training progress of Fixed-Acc and Adaptive-Acc for models employing the ResNet-34 and ResNet-50 architectures on the facial-attributes and facial-components datasets, respectively. The convergence of the curves demonstrates the effectiveness of the model training. Furthermore, in comparisons with both baseline methods and state-of-the-art approaches, the proposed model consistently surpasses other models. This section provides a detailed quantitative comparison between our method and other significant studies based on the Seq-DeepFake dataset, focusing on key metrics such as accuracy and precision. Compared to traditional baseline methods, such as Multi-Cls and DETR [3], as well as the CLSP model [8], as proposed by Dun et al., our method demonstrates superior performance. Specifically, on the facial components dataset, our method shows improvements across different ResNet architectures compared to the Seq-DeepFake benchmark model, further highlighting the advantages of our approach in handling complex operation patterns.

Through quantitative analysis, we compared our model with the Baseline models and found that our model outperforms the Baseline on both the Facial Attributes and Facial Components datasets, as shown in Tables 3 and 4. In the Baseline model, the extracted feature maps are directly passed into the Transformer encoder-decoder module for sequence modeling after introducing positional encoding. In contrast, our model first enhances the extracted feature maps through MSCP, then introduces positional encoding before passing them into the Transformer encoder-decoder module for sequence modeling. This result demonstrates that our MSCP approach is effective in improving accuracy.

Table 1. Test set accuracy of detecting seq-deepfake based on facial attributes manipulation

Methods	ResNet-34		ResNet-50	
	Fixed-Acc	Adaptive-Acc	Fixed-Acc	Adaptive-Acc
Multi-Cls	66.99	46.68	66.66	46.00
DETR	67.93	48.15	67.62	47.99
CLSP	-	-	68.87	49.84
Seq-DeepFake	67.99	48.32	68.86	49.63
Ours	**68.32**	**48.56**	**69.21**	**50.28**

Table 2. Test set accuracy of detecting Seq-DeepFake based on facial components manipulation

Methods	ResNet-34		ResNet-50	
	Fixed-Acc	Adaptive-Acc	Fixed-Acc	Adaptive-Acc
Multi-Cls	69.66	50.52	69.65	50.57
DETR	69.853	50.63	69.75	49.84
CLSP	-	-	71.75	53.46
Seq-DeepFake	72.13	54.80	72.65	55.30
Ours	**72.64**	**55.36**	**72.96**	**55.78**

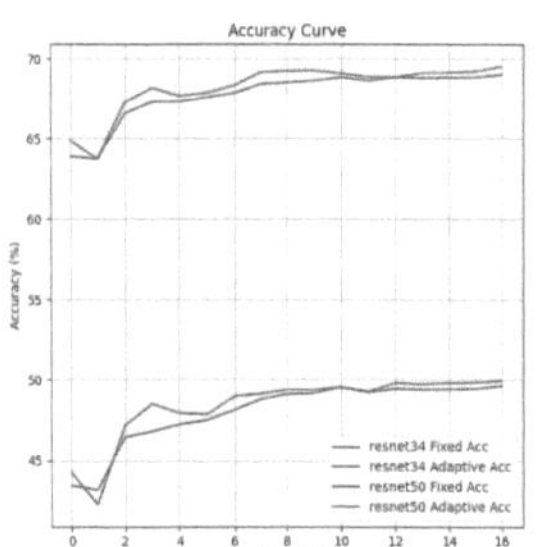

Fig. 3. facial-attributes

Fig. 4. facial-components

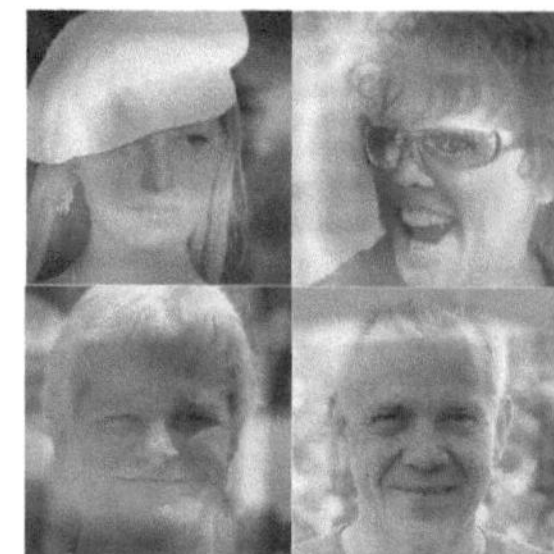

Fig. 5. MSCP Module Visualization

4.5 Visual Analysis

As shown in Fig. 5, benefiting from the introduction of the spatial perception coordinate localization strategy, our model demonstrates significant advantages in pseudo-3D spatial perception and dynamic facial pose analysis. Theoretically, this strategy enables precise localization of spatial coordinates across facial regions, endowing the model with a depth-aware perception capability that surpasses traditional 2D analysis frameworks. This allows the model not only to

Table 3. Baseline results from Seq-DeepFake

Model	Dataset	Adaptive-Acc	Fixed-Acc
ResNet34	Facial attributes	48.32	68.32
ResNet50	Facial attributes	49.63	68.86
ResNet34	Facial components	54.80	72.13
ResNet50	Facial components	55.30	72.65

Table 4. Improved results with our approach

Model	Dataset	Adaptive-Acc	Fixed-Acc
ResNet34	Facial attributes	48.56	68.32
ResNet50	Facial attributes	50.28	69.21
ResNet34	Facial components	55.36	72.64
ResNet50	Facial components	55.78	72.96

detect forged features, but also to capture global inconsistencies in spatial structure between authentic and manipulated regions. By analyzing facial pose variations and eye gaze dynamics, the model can further reveal discrepancies in depth perception inherent to forged content, thereby providing richer and more multidimensional pseudo-3D cues to the downstream decoder. This significantly enhances both the accuracy and robustness of forgery detection.

5 Conclusion

This paper proposes a coordinate localization-based multi-scale strategy for multi-step deepfake detection, addressing the challenge of capturing fine-grained local manipulation traces in complex forgery scenarios, a limitation of traditional methods. By introducing the MSCP module between CNN feature extraction and the Transformer encoder, we effectively enhance the spatial structural representation of image features. Through feature extraction mechanisms at different scales and directions, we significantly improve the model's robustness and accuracy in multi-step forgery operations.

Experimental results on the publicly available Seq-DeepFake dataset show that our method outperforms the original SeqFakeFormer model on both Fixed-Acc and Adaptive-Acc evaluation metrics. Especially when dealing with multi-step sequential forgery tasks, MSCP-SeqFakeFormer exhibits a significant performance improvement. Furthermore, facial recovery experiments further validate the model's effectiveness by accurately recovering the original facial images, demonstrating the potential of this method in real-world applications.

Although MSCP-SeqFakeFormer achieves good performance in most forgery detection tasks, it still faces some challenges, particularly when dealing with subtle and complex forgery operations. Future work will focus on further optimizing the model's fine-grained detection capabilities and exploring more efficient forgery operation sequence modeling methods to improve detection accuracy and robustness.

Acknowledgement. This research was supported in part by Guangxi Natural Science Foundation, China (Nos. AB25069496 and 2024GXNSFFA010014); the National Natural Science Foundation of China (Nos. 62172120, 82360356, 82272075 and 62362014).

References

1. Abdal, R., Qin, Y., Wonka, P.: Image2StyleGan: how to embed images into the StyleGAN latent space? In: Proceedings of the IEEE/CVF International Conference on Computer Vision, pp. 4432–4441 (2019)
2. Antipov, G., Baccouche, M., Dugelay, J.L.: Face aging with conditional generative adversarial networks. In: 2017 IEEE International Conference on Image Processing (ICIP), pp. 2089–2093. IEEE (2017)
3. Carion, N., Massa, F., Synnaeve, G., Usunier, N., Kirillov, A., Zagoruyko, S.: End-to-end object detection with transformers. In: European Conference on Computer Vision, pp. 213–229. Springer (2020)
4. Chen, L.C., Zhu, Y., Papandreou, G., Schroff, F., Adam, H.: Encoder-decoder with atrous separable convolution for semantic image segmentation. In: Proceedings of the European Conference on Computer Vision (ECCV), pp. 801–818 (2018)
5. Choi, Y., Uh, Y., Yoo, J., Ha, J.W.: Stargan v2: Diverse image synthesis for multiple domains. In: Proceedings of the IEEE/CVF Conference on Computer Vision and Pattern Recognition, pp. 8188–8197 (2020)
6. Deng, J., Dong, W., Socher, R., Li, L.J., Li, K., Fei-Fei, L.: ImageNet: a large-scale hierarchical image database. In: 2009 IEEE Conference on Computer Vision and Pattern Recognition, pp. 248–255. IEEE (2009)
7. Deng, L., Zhu, Y., Zhao, D., Chen, F.: A multi-label classification method based on transformer for deepfake detection. Image Vis. Comput. **152**, 105319 (2024)
8. Deng, Z., You, K., Yang, R., Hu, X., Chen, Y.: An improved seq-deepfake detection method. In: International Conference on Applied Intelligence, pp. 209–220. Springer (2023)
9. Goodfellow, I.J., et al.: Generative adversarial nets. In: Advances in Neural Information Processing Systems, vol. 27 (2014)
10. Guo, S., Li, Q., Gao, M., Zhu, X., Rida, I.: Generalizable deepfake detection via spatial kernel selection and halo attention network. Image Vis. Comput., 105582 (2025)
11. He, K., Zhang, X., Ren, S., Sun, J.: Deep residual learning for image recognition. In: Proceedings of the IEEE Conference on Computer Vision and Pattern Recognition, pp. 770–778 (2016)
12. Jia, S., Ma, C., Yao, T., Yin, B., Ding, S., Yang, X.: Exploring frequency adversarial attacks for face forgery detection. In: Proceedings of the IEEE/CVF Conference on Computer Vision and Pattern Recognition, pp. 4103–4112 (2022)
13. Karras, T., Laine, S., Aila, T.: A style-based generator architecture for generative adversarial networks. In: Proceedings of the IEEE/CVF Conference on Computer Vision and Pattern Recognition, pp. 4401–4410 (2019)

14. Korshunov, P., Marcel, S.: DeepFakes: a new threat to face recognition? assessment and detection. arxiv 2018. arXiv preprint arXiv:1812.08685 (2018)
15. Korshunova, I., Shi, W., Dambre, J., Theis, L.: Fast face-swap using convolutional neural networks. In: Proceedings of the IEEE International Conference on Computer Vision, pp. 3677–3685 (2017)
16. Luo, Y., Zhang, Y., Yan, J., Liu, W.: Generalizing face forgery detection with high-frequency features. In: Proceedings of the IEEE/CVF Conference on Computer Vision and Pattern Recognition, pp. 16317–16326 (2021)
17. Mirsky, Y., Lee, W.: The creation and detection of deepfakes: a survey. ACM Comput. Surv. (CSUR) **54**(1), 1–41 (2021)
18. Rossler, A., Cozzolino, D., Verdoliva, L., Riess, C., Thies, J., Nießner, M.: Face-Forensics++: learning to detect manipulated facial images. In: Proceedings of the IEEE/CVF International Conference on Computer Vision, pp. 1–11 (2019)
19. Shao, R., Wu, T., Liu, Z.: Detecting and recovering sequential deepfake manipulation. In: European Conference on Computer Vision, pp. 712–728. Springer (2022)
20. Swerzenski, J., Kim, D.: The new selfie standard: facetune and the shift toward East Asian selfie aesthetics. AoIR Selected Papers of Internet Research (2021)
21. Vaswani, A., et al.: Attention is all you need. In: Advances in Neural Information Processing Systems, vol. 30 (2017)
22. Verma, S., Raman, S.: SemFaceEdit: semantic face editing on generative radiance manifolds. In: International Conference on Pattern Recognition, pp. 46–62. Springer (2025)
23. Wang, S.Y., Wang, O., Owens, A., Zhang, R., Efros, A.A.: Detecting photoshopped faces by scripting photoshop. In: Proceedings of the IEEE/CVF International Conference on Computer Vision, pp. 10072–10081 (2019)
24. Xia, R., Liu, D., Li, J., Yuan, L., Wang, N., Gao, X.: MMNet: multi-collaboration and multi-supervision network for sequential deepfake detection. IEEE Trans. Inf. Forensics Secur. **19**, 3409–3422 (2024)
25. Zdradek, A.C.S., Beck, D.Q.: O aplicativo móvel" youcam makeup": uma câmera de maquiagem pedagogicamente fértil. Diversidade e Educação **4**(7), 18–21 (2016)
26. Zhao, H., Zhou, W., Chen, D., Wei, T., Zhang, W., Yu, N.: Multi-attentional deepfake detection. In: Proceedings of the IEEE/CVF Conference on Computer Vision and Pattern Recognition, pp. 2185–2194 (2021)
27. Zhu, P., Abdal, R., Qin, Y., Wonka, P.: Sean: image synthesis with semantic region-adaptive normalization. In: Proceedings of the IEEE/CVF Conference on Computer Vision and Pattern Recognition, pp. 5104–5113 (2020)

HDES-Net: An End-to-End Word Spotting Network for Chinese Ancient Documents

Maolin Zhang, Yuanping Zhu$^{(\boxtimes)}$, and Kunpeng Wang

College of Computer and Information Engineering, Tianjin Normal University,
Tianjin, China
`zhuyuanping@tjnu.edu.cn`

Abstract. Word spotting enables archaeologists, historians, and content moderators to retrieve regions of interest from document images based on specific queries. While mature methods exist for handwritten documents in languages like English, Chinese ancient documents pose greater challenges due to issues such as paper degradation, uneven coloring, a large character set, and the presence of rare or unseen characters. To address these challenges, we propose an end-to-end segmentation-free word spotting method based on Hierarchical Decomposition Embedding (HDE), which simultaneously predicts word bounding boxes and embeddings in a single stage. By learning mappings between character regions and hierarchical embedding spaces—instead of relying on closed-set classification—the model effectively handles unseen character queries. Experiments on the MTHv2 dataset demonstrate a state-of-the-art MAP of 80.84%. This work offers a novel approach for the preservation and retrieval of Chinese ancient documents.

Keywords: Word Spotting · Hierarchical Decomposition Embedding · Chinese Ancient Documents

1 Introduction

Chinese ancient documents are invaluable cultural artifacts, preserving historical knowledge, beliefs, and social structures. However, their digitization and retrieval face unique challenges: (1) *large character set*, with thousands of unique Chinese characters; (2) *unseen characters*, including rare or variant forms not present in training data; (3) *physical degradation*, such as fading ink, paper aging, and uneven restoration; and (4) *complex calligraphy*, with stylistic variations that complicate recognition. Traditional Optical Character Recognition (OCR) achieves high accuracy ($> 99\%$) for modern printed texts [1], but struggles with ancient texts due to these issues, often failing to recognize variant or degraded characters.

Word spotting offers a promising alternative by retrieving regions of interest based on query matching, without requiring full text transcription. Word

© The Author(s), under exclusive license to Springer Nature Singapore Pte Ltd. 2026

Z. Lin et al. (Eds.): ICIG 2025, LNCS 16163, pp. 224–236, 2026.
https://doi.org/10.1007/978-981-95-3729-7_19

spotting approaches can be categorized by input type—image-based or string-based [2] and by methodology segmentation-based or segmentation-free. Unlike recognition-based methods, word spotting transforms character recognition into a verification problem, computing similarity scores between query and candidate words. Existing word spotting methods, primarily developed for languages like English, are less effective for Chinese due to its ideographic nature and vast character set. To address this, we propose HDES-Net (Hierarchical Decomposition Embedding Spotting Network), an end-to-end, segmentation-free framework for word spotting in Chinese ancient documents. HDES-Net leverages Hierarchical Decomposition Embedding (HDE) [3] to map characters into a structured embedding space based on their radicals and structures, enabling generalization to unseen characters. A novel Fully Connected Attention Module (FCAM) dynamically fuses global and local features, enhancing robustness to degradation and variations.

Our contributions are:

- HDES-Net, the first end-to-end framework for segmentation-free word spotting in Chinese ancient documents, reducing preprocessing steps and improving efficiency.
- Integration of HDE to embed text regions into a distributed space, enabling zero-shot query handling for unseen characters.
- A lightweight FCAM to dynamically weigh global and local features, improving retrieval performance.
- State-of-the-art MAP of 80.84% on the MTHv2 dataset, with superior performance in zero-shot scenarios.

2   Related Work

2.1   Traditional Word Spotting Methods

Unlike direct character/word recognition followed by retrieval, word spotting searches for specific keywords in document images by comparing features extracted from word images. Traditional methods extract features from word or text line images and represent them as feature vectors, typically modeled with Hidden Markov Models (HMM) or Dynamic Time Warping (DTW). Matching is performed through similarity measures such as cosine or Euclidean distance to obtain similarity scores, creating a ranking list. Manmatha et al. [4] proposed using contour-based features for keyword spotting. Document images are segmented into words, and matching retrieves words relevant to the query. Yalniz and Manmatha [5] used SIFT descriptors from word image corner points for word spotting in noisy document images. Almazán et al. [6] introduced a sliding window approach to locate document regions similar to the query, avoiding segmentation.

2.2 Deep Learning Based Word Spotting Methods

In recent years, deep learning-based methods have significantly advanced handwritten word spotting, with approaches generally categorized as segmentation-based and segmentation-free.

Among segmentation-based methods, Sudholt et al.[7] proposed PHOCNet, a CNN architecture that embeds image features into Pyramidal Histogram of Characters (PHOC) attributes using a Sigmoid activation in the final layer. Krishnan et al.[8] introduced a holistic representation learning approach leveraging deep CNNs with classification loss. Their method achieved state-of-the-art results by pretraining on synthetic data, enhancing the ResNet-34 architecture, and augmenting real datasets.

Ghosh et al.[9] used spatial constraints to group connected components into word candidates, generated PHOC embeddings for each, and performed recognition via nearest neighbor search. Rothacker et al.[10] employed multiple text detectors to generate document-level word hypotheses, handled detector score uncertainty through extremal region analysis, and computed PHOC representations for matching. In segmentation-free methods, Zhao et al.[11] proposed an end-to-end trainable deep model that jointly predicts word bounding boxes and embeddings in a single stage using feature sharing and multitask learning, thereby reducing the complexity and inefficiency of traditional multi-stage pipelines.

3 Method

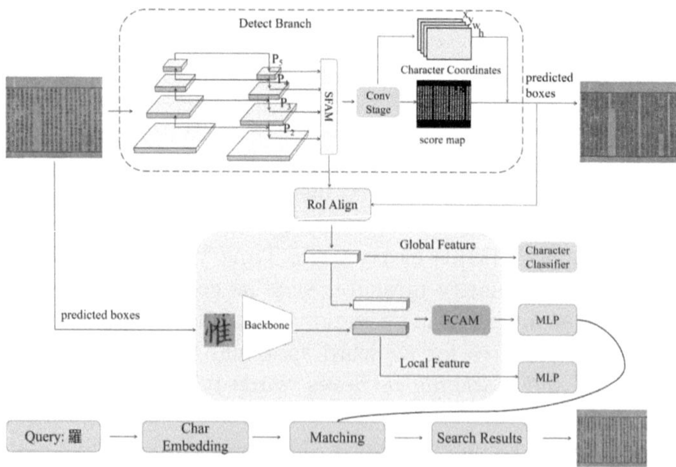

Fig. 1. Overall architecture of HDES-Net.

3.1 Overview

HDES-Net (Hierarchical Decomposition Embedding Spotting Network) is an end-to-end framework for segmentation-free word spotting in Chinese ancient documents. As shown in Fig. 1, the pipeline processes an input image through a ResNet50 backbone to extract multi-scale features, fused via a Scale Feature Aggregation Module (SFAM). The fused features feed into two branches: (1) the *detection branch*, predicting word bounding boxes, and (2) the *character embedding prediction branch*, mapping text regions to HDE spaces.

3.2 Feature Extraction and Aggregation

The ResNet50 backbone [12] extracts multi-scale feature maps at scales of 1/4, 1/8, 1/16, and 1/32 of the input image $X \in \mathbb{R}^{H \times W \times 3}$. These feature maps, denoted as p_2, p_3, p_4, p_5, are upsampled and fused using a Feature Pyramid Network (FPN). To integrate multi-scale information, the feature maps are upsampled to a uniform scale and concatenated along the channel dimension, as shown in Eq. (1):

$$f = \prod(p_2, p_3, p_4, p_5) = p_2||\text{up}(p_3)||\text{up}(p_4)||\text{up}(p_5) \tag{1}$$

where up denotes the upsampling operation, and for p_3, p_4, p_5, we upsample by 2, 4, and 8 times respectively. "$||$" denotes concatenation along the channel dimension.

Following the fusion, we apply a channel attention mechanism inspired by SENet [13] to emphasize discriminative character regions. Specifically, global average pooling followed by two fully connected layers generates channel-wise attention weights:

$$s = F_{\text{ex}}(z, W) = \sigma\big(W_2 \delta(W_1 z)\big) \tag{2}$$

where σ represents the ReLU function, δ denotes the sigmoid function, W_1 and W_2 are learnable parameters, and r is the reduction ratio (in our experiments, r=16). The final output is obtained by reweighting the input p_i using the activation s:

$$\tilde{f} = F_{\text{scale}}(p_i, s_c) = s_c \cdot p_i \tag{3}$$

After p_i is passed through F_{scale}, each feature is enhanced or weakened by the weighting operation (Fig. 2).

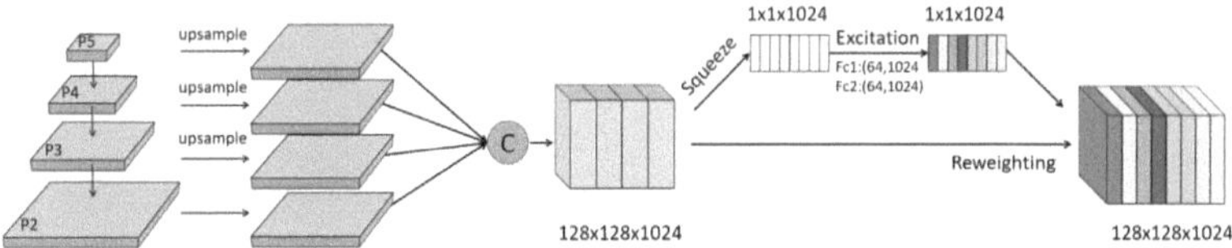

Fig. 2. Structure of the scale feature aggregation module for multi-scale fusion in HDES-Net.

3.3   Detection Branch

After obtaining the fused features, they are passed through three stacked convolutional layers to reduce channel count and computational load. The resulting feature maps are used for character pixel classification and bounding box regression tasks.

CharBox Branch. For the bounding box regression task, we apply a convolutional layer to the input features to generate a feature map of size $4 \times W/4 \times H/4$. We then normalize it to the range [0, 1] using the Sigmoid function. The four channels respectively correspond to the pixel positions of the top, right, bottom, and left boundaries of the rectangle. It's noteworthy that during the prediction phase, we only calculate the offset of each pixel to the bounding box within the positive region.

CharDis Branch. For the character pixel classification task, we apply a convolutional layer to the input features to project them into a single-channel feature map and employ the Sigmoid function to compute the probability of each pixel being a positive sample. Similar to [14], we set the original character region as 0.2 times the shorter side, and only pixels within this shrunk region are considered positive. Finally, we obtain a $1 \times W/4 \times H/4$ character score map, indicating the probability of each pixel being classified as a character pixel.

3.4   Word Embedding Prediction Module

This module maps detected text regions to HDE spaces for word spotting. Hierarchical Decomposition Embedding (HDE) decomposes Chinese characters into *radicals* (semantic components, 木 for wood) and *structures* (spatial arrangements, left-right or top-bottom), based on Ideographic Description Sequences (IDS) [3]. Each radical and structure is encoded as a one-hot vector y_n, combined into a 318-dimensional HDE vector $\phi(y)$, as in Eq. (4):

$$\phi(y) = \sum_{n_i \in R} v_{n_i} y_{n_i} + \lambda \sum_{n_j \in S} v_{n_j} y_{n_j} \tag{4}$$

Here, n_i is a radical in set R, n_j is a structure in set S, λ is the hyperparameter balancing the two terms, and v_n is the influence value of a radical or structure. v_n is calculated in accordance with Eq. (5):

$$v_n = \alpha^l + \sum_{i=1}^{l} \alpha^i \beta_{p_i} \tag{5}$$

where α and β are hyperparameters, p_i represents the nodes on the node path, and l is the length of the node path.

Feature extraction uses RoIAlign [15] to sample fixed-length features from SFAM outputs, followed by a multi-layer perceptron to predict global features z_{global}. Local features z_{local} are extracted from cropped character regions using four ResNet blocks, as in Eq. (6). The FCAM, detailed in Sect. 3.6, fuses z_{global} and z_{local} to produce a robust embedding.

$$x_i = H(\mathrm{Conv}(x_{i-1})) + \mathrm{Conv}(x_{i-1}) \tag{6}$$

where x_i denotes the feature map at layer i, and $H(\cdot)$ is a residual block. For an input image $X \in \mathbb{R}^{H \times W \times 3}$, the resulting feature map is $F \in \mathbb{R}^{\frac{H}{16} \times \frac{W}{16} \times 512}$.

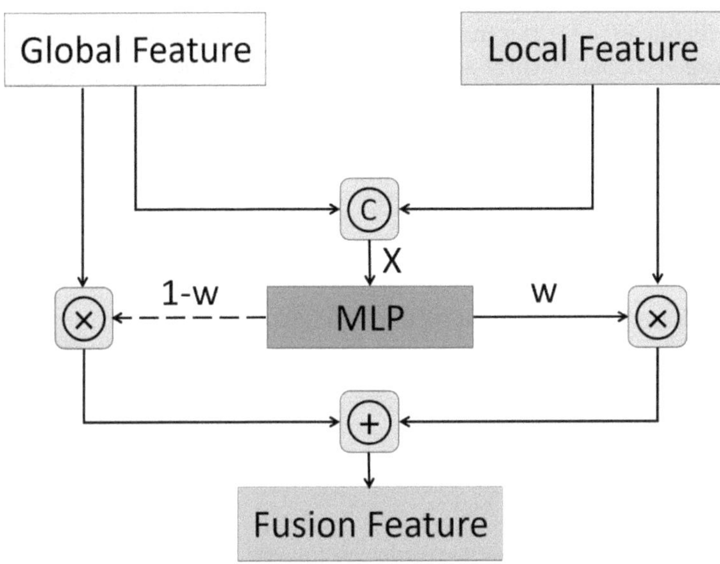

Fig. 3. Structure of the fully connected attention module (FCAM) for adaptive feature fusion in HDES-Net.

3.5 Fully Connected Attention Module

To combine local and global features, we introduce a lightweight fully connected attention module (FCAM), as shown in Fig. 3. The FCAM architecture consists of two fully connected layers, used to learn dynamic, nonlinear internal dependencies between the two types of features and reweight the importance of different features through multiplication. Specifically, we first concatenate the global feature z_{global} and the local feature z_{local}:

$$X = \mathrm{Concat}(Z_{\mathrm{global}}, Z_{\mathrm{local}}) \tag{7}$$

Then, we map the concatenated vector X to weights through an MLP. To ensure that the weights are between 0 and 1, we use the sigmoid activation function:

$$\omega = \Phi(X), \quad \omega \in \mathbb{R}^{1 \times C} \tag{8}$$

$$\Phi = \sigma(W_2 g(W_1 X + b_1) + b_2) \tag{9}$$

where W_1, W_2, b_1, and b_2 are trainable weights, σ represents the sigmoid activation function, and $g(\cdot)$ represents the ReLU activation function. ω represents the adaptive weights, reflecting the importance of different features. After generating the weights, we use ω to perform a weighted average on z_{global} and z_{local}, thereby generating the final fused feature H.

$$H = \omega \cdot z_{\text{global}} + (1 - \omega) \cdot z_{\text{local}} \tag{10}$$

By introducing FCAM, the model can dynamically adjust the relative importance between global features z_{global} and local features z_{local} while maintaining lightweight characteristics, thus generating more representative and discriminative fused features.

Finally, for the fused feature H, we use a fully connected network with a size of 318 to map it to the embedding space.

3.6   Loss Function

CharDis Loss.For text classification loss, we utilize the Dice loss [16] function to prevent the network from biased predictions towards background pixels, enabling better exploration of foreground regions. The Dice loss function is defined as follows:

$$D(\hat{y}_{\text{cls}}, y_{\text{cls}}) = \frac{2 \sum\limits_{i,j} \hat{y}_{\text{cls}}^{i,j} \cdot y_{\text{cls}}^{i,j}}{\sum\limits_{i,j} \left(\hat{y}_{\text{cls}}^{i,j}\right)^2 + \sum\limits_{i,j} \left(y_{\text{cls}}^{i,j}\right)^2} \tag{11}$$

$$L_{\text{cls}} = 1 - D(\hat{y}_{\text{cls}}, y_{\text{cls}}) \tag{12}$$

CharBox Loss. For bounding box regression loss, we employ the DIOU loss [17]:

$$L_{\text{bbox}} = \frac{1}{|P|} \sum\limits_{i \in C} L_{\text{DIoU}}(\hat{y}_{\text{bbox}}, y_{\text{bbox}}) \tag{13}$$

$$L_{\text{DIoU}} = 1 - \text{IoU} + \frac{\rho^2(a, b)}{c^2} \tag{14}$$

CharCls Loss. Cross-entropy loss for character classification in Eq. (15).

$$L_{\text{cls}} = -\sum\limits_{i=1}^{C} y_i \log(\hat{y}_i) \tag{15}$$

Embedding Loss. To encourage the embedding vectors generated by the model to maintain high similarity between the same characters and have significant differences between different characters, we use cosine loss.

$$L_{\text{cosine}} = 1 - \cos(\hat{y}_{\text{embed}}, y_{\text{embed}}) \tag{16}$$

where $\hat{y}_{\text{embed}}$ represents the predicted embedding vector by the network, and y_{embed} represents the true embedding value.

Total Loss. The total loss L_{total} is given by Eq. (17).

$$L_{\text{total}} = L_{\text{cls}} + L_{\text{bbox}} + L_{\text{recog}} + L_{\text{embed\_local}} + L_{\text{embed\_fusion}} \tag{17}$$

where the total loss is the simple sum of all loss terms, with $L_{\text{embed\_local}}$ and $L_{\text{embed\_fusion}}$ representing the local feature embedding loss and the fused feature embedding loss, respectively.

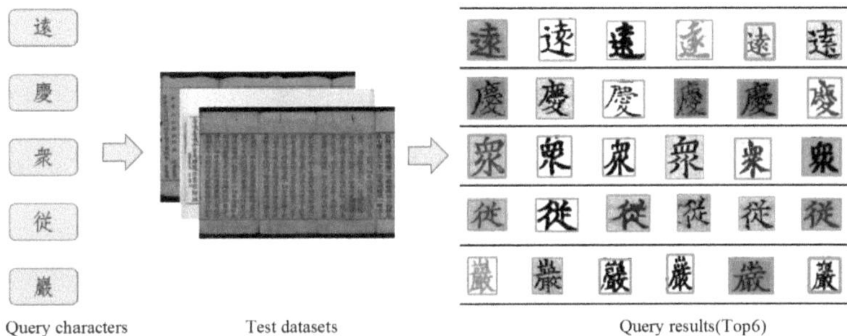

Fig. 4. The visualization results of several queries using HDES-Net.

4 Experiments

4.1 Experiment Setup

We evaluate the proposed method on the MTHv2 dataset [18], which consists of the TKH and MTH2200 subsets. Despite its original design for layout analysis, MTHv2 is suitable for word spotting due to its diverse character set and degraded document images, mimicking real-world ancient document challenges. The dataset is split 3:1 for training and testing. The model is implemented in PyTorch and trained on a Tesla V100 GPU with 32 GB of memory. We use the Adam optimizer with a batch size of 4 and an initial learning rate of 1e-3. The model is trained for 120 epochs, with the learning rate decayed by a factor of 0.1 at the 80th and 100th epochs. To enhance generalization, images are preprocessed as follows: the long edge is resized to 2048 pixels while maintaining the aspect ratio, followed by random cropping to 512×512. During testing, Non-Maximum Suppression (NMS) is applied with a confidence threshold of 0.4.

4.2 Comparison with Other Methods

We compared our methods with those using 25% and 50% word bounding box overlap rates. We extracted each unique transcription from the test set and used

Table 1. Comparison with other methods. The best results are highlighted in bold.

Method	MAP	
	25%	50%
Hog	37.74%	37.75%
HWNet+ResNet+Multi-Scale-ROI [8]	61.67%	61.61%
WordRetrievalNet(HDE) [11]	52.01%	51.95%
PageNet [19]	71.31%	71.49%
Our (E2E)	**80.93%**	**80.84%**

the corresponding attribute representation as queries. Then, we ranked the test words based on the cosine distance between the test words and the query representations. Since the English methods are not applicable to Chinese, we used HDE instead of Phoc/DCToW as the embedding method for WordRetrievalNet as our comparative experiment.

As shown in Table 1, the model proposed in this chapter significantly outperforms other methods, with MAP reaching 80.93% and 80.84% at overlap rates of 25% and 50%, respectively, far higher than PageNet's 71.31% and 71.49%. PageNet focuses on character recognition, reporting 93.76–95.23% accuracy in [19]. However, on the MTHv2 dataset, PageNet's MAP is lower due to the presence of unseen characters and the uneven distribution of character categories. In word spotting tasks, MAP assigns equal weight $(1/n)$ to each query word category, but certain easily recognizable Chinese character categories may appear more frequently in the dataset, thereby inflating PageNet's character recognition accuracy. This distributional disparity disadvantages recognition-based methods like PageNet, particularly when unseen characters serve as queries. In contrast, HDES-Net employs Hierarchical Decomposition Embedding (HDE) to generalize to unseen characters via radicals and structures, significantly enhancing the robustness of word spotting. Figure 4 shows the visualization results of our method for several queries.

4.3   Ablation Study

We evaluated different network architectures and observed that ResNet50+ SFAM achieves the best performance in Table 2, with MAP of 80.93% and 80.84%.

We also assessed the impact of SFAM by comparing the baseline with and without SFAM. Table 3 demonstrates that adding SFAM improves MAP from 80.09% to 80.84%.

4.4   Zero-Shot Study

In this section, we evaluated the zero-shot query performance of the model. The experimental results are shown in Table 4. "ALL" means using all word categories

Table 2. MAP (%) performance evaluation of different backbones. The best results are highlighted in bold.

Method	MAP	
	25%	50%
VGG16 + SFAM	79.85%	79.71%
DenseNet121 [20] + SFAM	79.74%	79.68%
ResNeXt50 [21] + SFAM	79.95%	79.90%
RegNet [22] + SFAM	78.19%	78.18%
EfficientNet + SFAM	78.77%	78.70%
ResNet50 + SFAM	**80.93%**	**80.84%**

Table 3. Effect of SAFM on performance.

Method	MAP	
	25%	50%
Baseline	80.24%	80.09%
Baseline + SFAM	**80.93%**	**80.84%**

in the test set for queries. "Shared" indicates word categories that exist in both the test set and the training set. "Not in train" indicates word categories that appear only in the test set and not in the training set.

As shown in Table 4, on the "ALL" query set, the embedding-based methods outperform the recognition-based methods, achieving MAP of 80.93% and 80.84% at overlap rates of 25% and 50%, respectively.

Table 4. Performance Comparison of Different Query Sets.

Query-set	Ours		PageNet [19]	
	25%	50%	25%	50%
ALL	80.93%	80.84%	71.31%	71.49%
Shared	83.61%	83.52%	76.05%	74.07%
Not in train	58.08%	58.08%	0.12%	0.12%

In the "Not in train" scenario, which represents zero-shot queries, ours method achieves 58.08% MAP, compared to PageNet's 0.12%, which arises from random matches due to PageNet's recognition-based approach failing on unseen characters. HDES-Net's HDE enables robust retrieval by leveraging shared radical and structure features.

As show in Fig. 5, we observe that the embedding-based (ours) method can effectively retrieve the character " 夛 ", while the recognition-based (PageNet) method shows no retrieval capability for unseen characters.

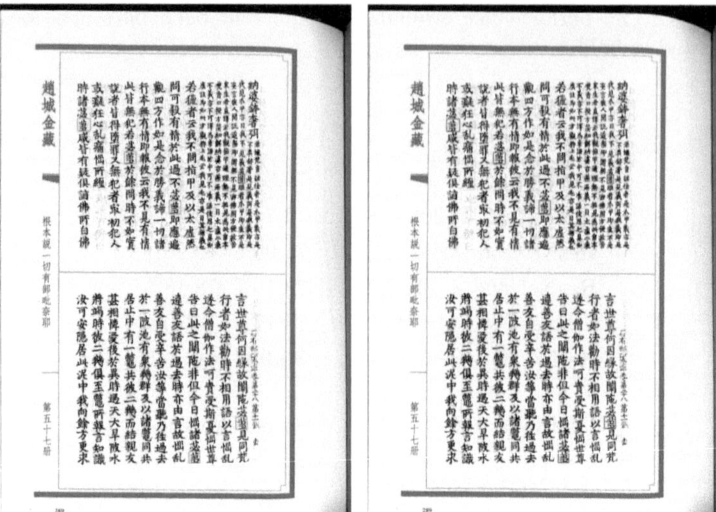

Fig. 5. The retrieval results of the zero-shot character " 姕 " are shown. The left image presents our retrieval outcomes, while the right image shows those of PageNet. Green boxes highlight correct retrievals, and red boxes indicate missed or incorrect results.

5   Conclusions

In this article, we propose an efficient end-to-end trainable model for segmentation-free word spotting. The model adopts hierarchical decomposition embedding (HDE) to map Chinese characters into multi-dimensional vectors and learn embedded representations, thus enabling zero-shot queries. Experimental results demonstrate that the proposed method significantly outperforms other methods. Under the condition of an overlap threshold of 50%, the model achieved a state-of-the-art MAP value of 80.84% on the MTHv2 dataset. Future research will focus on developing technologies that can comprehensively retrieve various types of information from ancient documents. This includes not only accurate retrieval of text but also expansion to image recognition, chart analysis, and symbol understanding, in order to achieve a comprehensive retrieval of the content of ancient documents.

References

1. Smith, R.: An overview of the tesseract OCR engine. In: Ninth International Conference on Document Analysis and Recognition (ICDAR 2007), vol. 2, pp. 629–633. IEEE (2007)
2. Jawahar, C., Balasubramanian, A., Meshesha, M., Namboodiri, A.M.: Retrieval of online handwriting by synthesis and matching. Pattern Recogn. **42**(7), 1445–1457 (2009)

3. Cao, Z., Lu, J., Cui, S., Zhang, C.: Zero-shot handwritten Chinese character recognition with hierarchical decomposition embedding. Pattern Recogn. **107**, 107488 (2020). https://doi.org/10.1016/j.patcog.2020.107488

4. Manmatha, R., Croft, W.B.: Word Spotting: Indexing Handwritten Manuscripts, pp. 43–64. MIT Press, Cambridge, MA, USA (1997)

5. Yalniz, I.Z., Manmatha, R.: An efficient framework for searching text in noisy document images. In: 2012 10th IAPR International Workshop on Document Analysis Systems, pp. 48–52. IEEE (2012)

6. Almazán, J., Gordo, A., Fornés, A., Valveny, E.: Segmentation-free word spotting with exemplar SVMs. Pattern Recogn. **47**(12), 3967–3978 (2014)

7. Sudholt, S., Fink, G.A.: PHOCNet: a deep convolutional neural network for word spotting in handwritten documents. In: 2016 15th International Conference on Frontiers in Handwriting Recognition (ICFHR), pp. 277–282. IEEE (2016)

8. Krishnan, P., Jawahar, C.: HWNet v2: an efficient word image representation for handwritten documents. Int. J. Doc. Anal. Recogn. (IJDAR) **22**(4), 387–405 (2019)

9. Ghosh, S.K., Valveny, E.: R-PHOC: segmentation-free word spotting using CNN. In: 2017 14th IAPR International Conference on Document Analysis and Recognition (ICDAR), vol. 1, pp. 801–806. IEEE (2017)

10. Rothacker, L., Sudholt, S., Rusakov, E., Kasperidus, M., Fink, G.A.: Word hypotheses for segmentation-free word spotting in historic document images. In: 2017 14th IAPR International Conference on Document Analysis and Recognition (ICDAR), vol. 1, pp. 1174–1179. IEEE (2017)

11. Zhao, P., Xue, W., Li, Q., Cai, S.: Query by strings and return ranking word regions with only one look. In: Proceedings of the Asian Conference on Computer Vision, pp. 3–18. Springer International Publishing (2020)

12. He, K., Zhang, X., Ren, S., Sun, J.: Deep residual learning for image recognition. In: Proceedings of the IEEE Conference on Computer Vision and Pattern Recognition, pp. 770–778 (2016)

13. Hu, J., Shen, L., Sun, G.: Squeeze-and-excitation networks. In: Proceedings of the IEEE Conference on Computer Vision and Pattern Recognition, pp. 7132–7141 (2018)

14. Liu, X., Liang, D., Yan, S., Chen, D., Qiao, Y., Yan, J.: FOTS: fast oriented text spotting with a unified network. In: Proceedings of the IEEE Conference on Computer Vision and Pattern Recognition, pp. 5676–5685 (2018)

15. He, K., Gkioxari, G., Dollár, P., Girshick, R.: Mask R-CNN. In: Proceedings of the IEEE International Conference on Computer Vision, pp. 2961–2969 (2017)

16. Milletari, F., Navab, N., Ahmadi, S.A.: V-Net: fully convolutional neural networks for volumetric medical image segmentation. In: 2016 Fourth International Conference on 3D Vision (3DV), pp. 565–571. IEEE Computer Society (2016)

17. Zheng, Z., Wang, P., Liu, W., Li, J., Ye, R., Ren, D.: Distance-IoU Loss: faster and better learning for bounding box regression. In: Proceedings of the AAAI Conference on Artificial Intelligence, vol. 34, pp. 12993–13000 (2020)

18. Ma, W., Zhang, H., Jin, L., Wu, S., Wang, J., Wang, Y.: Joint layout analysis, character detection and recognition for historical document digitization. In: 2020 17th International Conference on Frontiers in Handwriting Recognition (ICFHR), pp. 31–36. IEEE (2020)

19. Peng, D., Jin, L., Liu, Y., Luo, C., Lai, S.: PageNet: towards end-to-end weakly supervised page-level handwritten Chinese text recognition. Int. J. Comput. Vis. **130**(11), 2623–2645 (2022)

20. Huang, G., Liu, Z., Van Der Maaten, L., Weinberger, K.Q.: Densely connected convolutional networks. In: Proceedings of the IEEE Conference on Computer Vision and Pattern Recognition, pp. 4700–4708 (2017)
21. Xie, S., Girshick, R., Dollár, P., Tu, Z., He, K.: Aggregated residual transformations for deep neural networks. In: Proceedings of the IEEE Conference on Computer Vision and Pattern Recognition, pp. 1492–1500 (2017)
22. Radosavovic, I., Kosaraju, R.P., Girshick, R., He, K., Dollár, P.: Designing network design spaces. In: Proceedings of the IEEE/CVF Conference on Computer Vision and Pattern Recognition, pp. 10428–10436 (2020)

Insulator Fault Detection Method Based on Improved YOLOv11n

Zeyu Li[✉], Song Wang, and Enqing Chen

Zhengzhou University, Zhengzhou, China
2663309936@qq.com, ieswang@zzu.edu.cn

Abstract. Insulator fault detection using UAV inspection is essential for the safe and stable operation of smart grids. However, complex backgrounds and significant scale variations among fault targets pose considerable challenges to existing detection algorithms, often resulting in reduced accuracy. To address these specific issues, this paper proposes an enhanced fault detection algorithm based on YOLOv11n. A two-layer routing attention mechanism is introduced to precisely capture key regional features by integrating coarse-grained region screening with refined local modeling, which significantly improves the model's ability to detect multi-scale targets in cluttered environments.

Keywords: Insulator fault detection · Smart grid · YOLOv11n

1 Introductory

With the rapid development of artificial intelligence, fault detection of distribution network equipment in power systems is transforming from traditional physical methods and manual inspection to automation technology based on deep learning. [1] As a key component, insulators, their fault detection is crucial to ensure the safety of the power system. Although traditional methods (e.g., short-circuit fork method, ultrasonic detection, leakage current method) can realize fault identification to a certain extent, they generally rely on manual review, which is inefficient and has a high misjudgment rate. [2] In recent years, deep learning, especially target detection technology, has achieved significant results in this field. Existing detection algorithms are mainly categorized into two types: single-stage and two-stage. Single-stage methods (e.g., SSD [3], YOLO series [4–8], DETR [9]) have the advantages of fast speed and are suitable for real-time detection, while dual-stage methods (e.g., Faster R-CNN [10], Mask R-CNN [11]) perform better in terms of accuracy, and are suitable for complex scenes and small target detection. However, the existing algorithms still face challenges such as background interference, scale variation, and difficulties in small target detection.

The attention mechanism in the C2PSA module is improved by combining the Bi-Level Routing Attention (BRA) [12] module in BiFormer, and the strategy

© The Author(s), under exclusive license to Springer Nature Singapore Pte Ltd. 2026
Z. Lin et al. (Eds.): ICIG 2025, LNCS 16163, pp. 237–246, 2026.
https://doi.org/10.1007/978-981-95-3729-7_20

of combining region-level filtering and fine-grained modeling is adopted, so as to improve the modeling by constructing the attention guidance map at the region level, and executing the token-level attention computation only in the most relevant regions, thus improving the modeling efficiency and enhance the model's ability to perceive and characterize multi-scale targets.

2   Related Work

2.1   Principle of Yolov11 Algorithm

YOLOv11 is the latest target detection model introduced by Ultralytics after YOLOv5 and YOLOv8. The model has several architectural optimizations, introducing refined feature extraction structure, attention mechanism and deep separable convolution [13], which not only significantly reduces the computation amount, but also improves the inference speed and detection accuracy.

YOLOv11 optimizes the C2f module in YOLOv8 to C3K2 module, which enhances the gradient transfer and feature extraction ability by increasing branches and cross-layer connections, and improves the detection performance for complex scenes and small targets. Meanwhile, the C2PSA attention mechanism is introduced after the SPPF module and combined with the improved PAN-FPN structure, which improves the characterization ability for multi-scale targets.

In the detection head part, YOLOv11 adopts a decoupled head design and adds depth-separable convolution in the classification branch, which effectively reduces the computational burden and improves the real-time detection efficiency.

Although YOLOv11 demonstrates excellent performance, it still faces challenges in smart grid UAV inspection scenarios due to complex backgrounds, fragmented small targets, and adverse weather conditions. Therefore, this paper conducts task-specific optimization of YOLOv11 to enhance its robustness and detection accuracy under these challenging conditions.

2.2   Attention Mechanisms

Attention mechanism is widely used in target detection as an important method to enhance the feature expression ability of neural networks. Its core idea is to dynamically adjust the feature weights to guide the model to focus on the key regions and enhance the perception of the target. Early SE [14], CBAM [15] and ECA [16] modules are mainly weighted in channel and spatial dimensions, which are characterized by high efficiency and lightweight structure, and can effectively improve the detection accuracy.

With the rise of Vision Transformer, self-attention mechanism is introduced to target detection due to its powerful context modeling capability, but its high computational overhead limits its application on real-time and edge devices. For this reason, numerous lightweight attention mechanisms have been proposed to strike a balance between accuracy and efficiency.

3   Method

3.1   Modeling Framework

In order to improve the detection performance of insulator faults by UAV inspection in smart grid, especially under small targets and foggy conditions, this paper proposes an improved model YOLOv11n-B2 based on YOLOv11n, with the structure shown in Fig. 1.

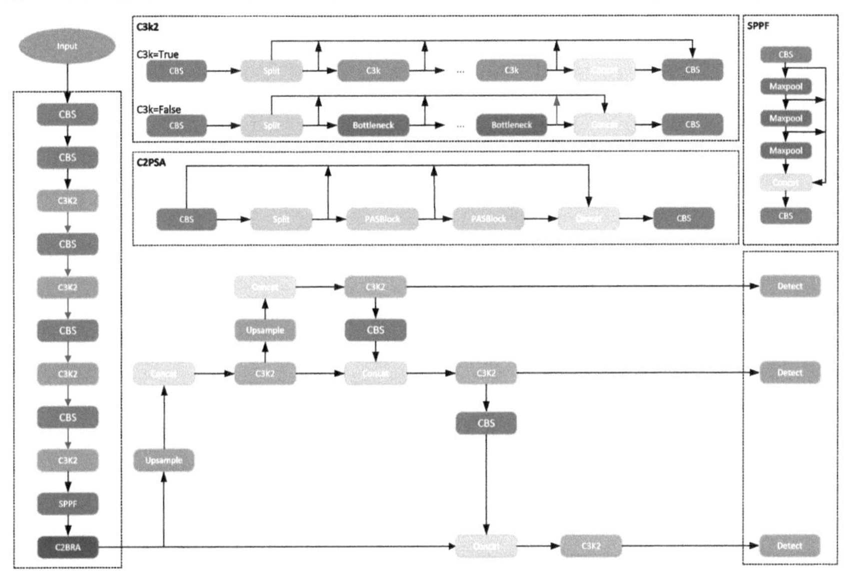

Fig. 1. YOLOv11n-B2 schematic

The original C2PSA attention module is replaced with the proposed C2BRA module, which combines region screening and local modeling in a two-layer attention mechanism. This improves feature representation efficiency, reduces computational redundancy, and enhances the model's ability to perceive key targets in complex environments.

3.2   C2BRA Module

In the YOLOv11n-based insulator and its fault detection system, the C2PSA module employs the Position-Sensitive Attention (PSA) mechanism to enhance the modeling capability of spatial location information. Although PSA performs well in local feature extraction, its high computational complexity and low efficiency in processing high-resolution inputs limit the model's detection performance and real-time performance in complex environments.For this purpose, the C2BRA module is designed in this paper as shown in Fig. 2.

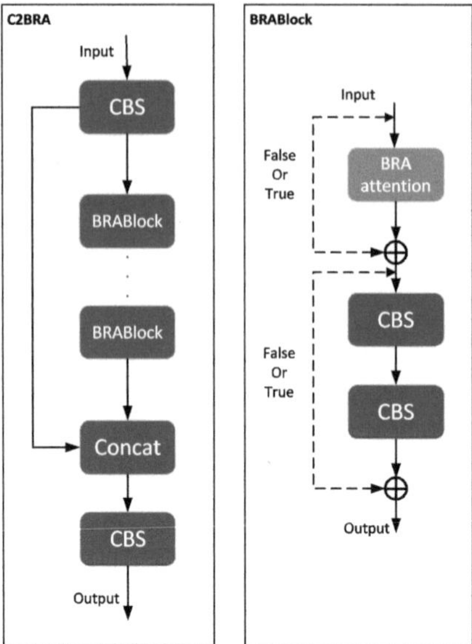

Fig. 2. C2BRA.

To further improve the accuracy and efficiency of insulator and fault detection, this paper introduces Bi-Level Routing Attention (BRA) mechanism, as shown in Fig. 3.

BRA significantly reduces the scope and complexity of fine-grained token-level attention computation by focusing on the most relevant regions through coarse-grained routing screening at the region level using the Top-K strategy. First, the input feature graph X is divided into multiple fixed-size non-overlapping regions (e.g., 7 × 7), constituting N spatial regions. Then, region-level average pooling operations are performed on Query and Key in the feature graph, respectively, to obtain the representation vectors qr and kr for each region. A region-level neighbor-joining graph is constructed by the dot-product similarity between regions with the following formula:

$$A_r = Q_r(K_r)^T \tag{1}$$

Here, $Q_r \in \mathbb{R}^{N \times d}$ and $K_r \in \mathbb{R}^{N \times d}$ represent the Query and Key feature matrices of all N region tokens, respectively, where d is the feature dimension. The resulting similarity matrix $A_r \in \mathbb{R}^{N \times N}$ is computed via dot-product between all region pairs.

To retain only the most relevant regions for each Query, the Top-k most similar region indices are selected:

$$I_r = \text{topkIndex}(A_r) \tag{2}$$

$I_r \in \mathbb{R}^{N \times k}$ stores the indices of the Top-k most similar regions for each Query token, based on the similarity scores in A_r.

Using these indices, the corresponding local regions are gathered from the Key and Value matrices:

$$K_g = \text{gather}(K, I_r), \quad V_g = \text{gather}(V, I_r) \tag{3}$$

Here, $K, V \in \mathbb{R}^{N \times d}$ are the original Key and Value matrices. The gather($\cdot$) operation selects the Top-k neighboring tokens for each Query, resulting in $K_g, V_g \in \mathbb{R}^{N \times k \times d}$.

A local token-to-token attention is then performed over the gathered neighborhood:

$$O = \text{Attention}(Q, K_g, V_g) + \text{LCE}(V) \tag{4}$$

$Q \in \mathbb{R}^{N \times d}$ is the input Query matrix. Attention($\cdot$) denotes the standard scaled dot-product attention applied locally over K_g and V_g. The term $\text{LCE}(V)$ refers to a Local Context Enhancement module based on depthwise separable convolution, which complements the attention mechanism by introducing positional sensitivity and enhancing local structural information. The final output $O \in \mathbb{R}^{N \times d}$ integrates both attention-based interaction and contextual features.

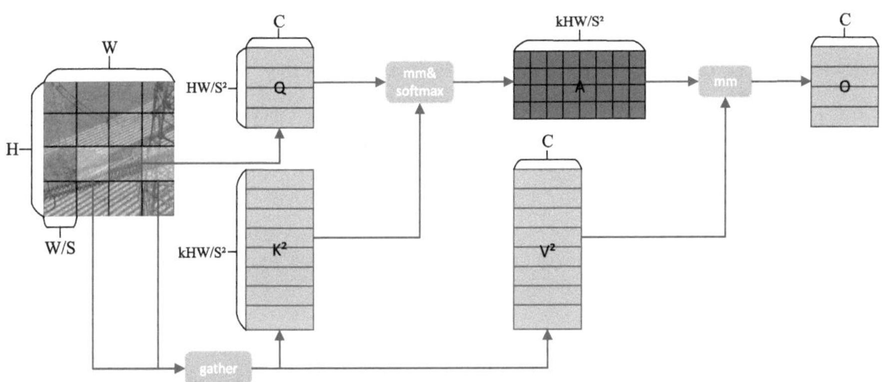

Fig. 3. Bi-Level Routing Attention.

By introducing a region-level screening mechanism, BRA effectively guides the attention to focus on the most relevant regions, which significantly improves the accuracy of attention distribution. This âĂIJcoarse screening + fine countingâĂĪ strategy enables the model to establish stronger feature dependencies between key regions, thus improving the accuracy of target localization and feature expression. The experimental results show that the improved model using the BRA mechanism significantly improves the detection accuracy and inference speed of insulators and their faults under complex backgrounds and diverse lighting conditions.

4   Experimental Results and Analysis

4.1   Experimental Environment and Setup

This experiment is based on the Python programming language and implemented using the Pytorch framework. The experimental environment is configured as follows: the server operating system is Ubuntu 20.04.6 with Intel(R) Core(TM) i7-14700KF CPU and two NVIDIA GeForce RTX 4060 Ti GPUs, and the CUDA version is 12.6. The software environment includes Python 3.8.20 and Pytorch 2.2.1. During the model training process, the parameters were set as follows: the Batch-Size was 64, the initial learning rate was 0.01, the learning rate decay factor was 0.01, the optimizer used SGD, and the total number of training rounds was 1650 epochs.

4.2   Data Sets and Evaluation Indicators

In this paper, the proposed model is evaluated on the SFID (Synthetic Fog Insulator Dataset) dataset. SFID contains 13,700 images (of which 6,850 are synthetic fog images) covering a wide range of insulator defect scenarios and simulates foggy conditions to enhance the data diversity. The dataset is divided into a training set of 9,603 images, a validation set of 1,372 images and a test set of 2,725 images.

Model performance was evaluated by mAP@50, which was calculated based on IoU=0.5, and mAP@50-95, which was averaged over the range of IoU=0.50 to 0.95, to measure the detection effect under different overlapping criteria. The precision metrics include precision (P), recall (R), and IoU, which are calculated as follows:

$$P = \frac{TP}{TP + FP} \tag{5}$$

$$R = \frac{TP}{TP + FN} \tag{6}$$

$$IoU = \frac{\text{Area of Overlap}}{\text{Area of Union}} = \frac{B_p \cap B_{gt}}{B_p \cup B_{gt}} \tag{7}$$

In addition, the number of parameters and GFLOPs are introduced to evaluate the model complexity and computational efficiency. The number of parameters reflects the model size, and the lower GFLOPs indicate the lower computational overhead, which is more suitable for edge devices or real-time applications. The combination of these metrics can comprehensively evaluate the model performance and deployment feasibility.

4.3   Experimental Results and Analysis

In order to comprehensively evaluate the performance of the proposed algorithm, this study conducts comparative experiments with the current mainstream target detection algorithms on the SFID dataset. The experimental results show that the improved algorithm YOLOv11n-B2 proposed in this paper significantly improves the detection accuracy while ensuring a relatively low number of parameters and computational effort. As shown in Table 1, the improved algorithm reaches the optimal level in performance, in which mAP@50 improves by 0.1% to 99.5% and mAP@50-95 improves by 1.5% to 93.4%. Compared with YOLOv11n, the algorithm in this paper achieves a significant improvement in detection accuracy, and the computation amount is reduced by 0.9GFLOPs from 6.3GFLOPs to 5.4GFLOPs, and the number of parameters is also reduced by 0.47M from 2.58M to 2.11M, both of which realize effective compression. More notably, the inference speed of YOLOv11n-B2 is significantly improved, with FPS (Frames Per Second) increasing from 84.4 to 121.3, demonstrating excellent real-time detection capability. Despite the significant improvement in detection accuracy while maintaining the lightweight design, the model still has efficient computational performance and good deployment adaptability. The experimental results fully validate the practicality and advancement of the proposed method in complex environments, and provide strong support for the efficient identification of insulator faults in smart grids.

Table 1. Comparison of different algorithms on the SFID verification set.

Method	Param (M)	GFLOPs	mAP$_{50}$ (%)	mAP$_{50\text{-}95}$ (%)	FPS
YOLOv5n	2.50	7.1	99.3	90.1	98.9
YOLOv8n	3.15	8.7	99.5	91.8	119.1
YOLOv10n	2.71	8.4	99.5	91.5	111.0
YOLOv11n	2.58	6.3	99.5	91.9	84.4
YOLOv11n-B2	2.11	5.4	99.5	93.4	121.3

Figure 4 shows visualization results of YOLOv11n-B2 on the SFID dataset, where green boxes mark detected insulators and red boxes indicate detected broken regions. The improved model demonstrates strong detection ability in complex backgrounds and foggy conditions. In Scenario 1, YOLOv11n misses some normal insulators, while the improved model accurately detects all. In Scenario 2, the original model misidentifies intact regions as broken, whereas the improved model correctly detects broken areas. In Scenarios 3 and 4, the improved model maintains high accuracy and robustness under fog. These results validate the effectiveness of the CDehazenet module for defogging and the enhanced detection accuracy of the improved model.

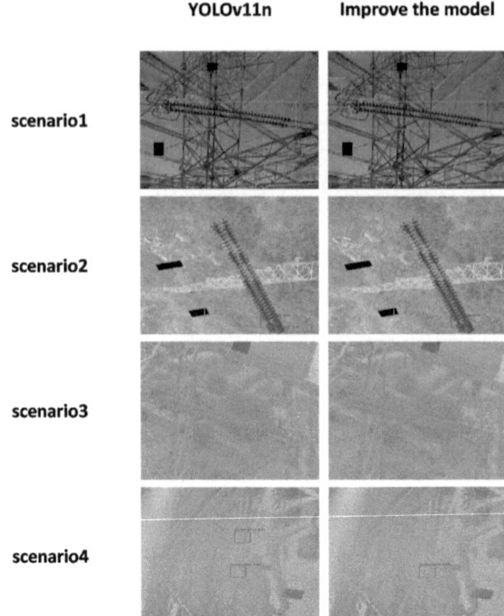

Fig. 4. Visualize the results.

4.4   Ablation Experiment

Ablation experiments were conducted to evaluate the impact of replacing the original C2PSA module with the proposed C2BRA module, which uses a two-layer attention mechanism combining region screening and local modeling. This design improves feature representation, reduces computational redundancy, and enhances key target perception in complex scenes. As shown in Table 2, the results demonstrate the C2BRA module's contribution to performance gains and resource efficiency, supporting further model optimization.

Table 2. Ablation test results of the C2BRA module

C2BRA	mAP$_{50}$	mAP$_{50\text{-}95}$	Param/M	GFLOPs
	0.994	0.919	2.58	6.3
✓	0.995	0.929	2.59	6.5

In order to demonstrate more intuitively the performance advantages of the algorithm proposed in this paper in the YOLO series, Fig. 5 shows the comparison of the performance metrics of each model during the training process. From the figure, it can be clearly observed that YOLOv11n-B2 significantly outperforms the other compared models on the SFID dataset. The mAP@50-95 curve of YOLOv11n-B2 is consistently on top of the other models throughout the training process, and finally reaches the highest accuracy of 93.4%, which is far more than the 91.9% of YOLOv11n. In addition, the curve of YOLOv11n-B2 fluctuates less, indicating that it has better stability during the training process. This result fully proves the effectiveness of the improved module proposed in this paper in enhancing the model performance, especially in the accuracy of multi-scale target detection in complex environments. The visualization comparison further validates the significant advantages of YOLOv11n-B2 in the YOLO series of algorithms.

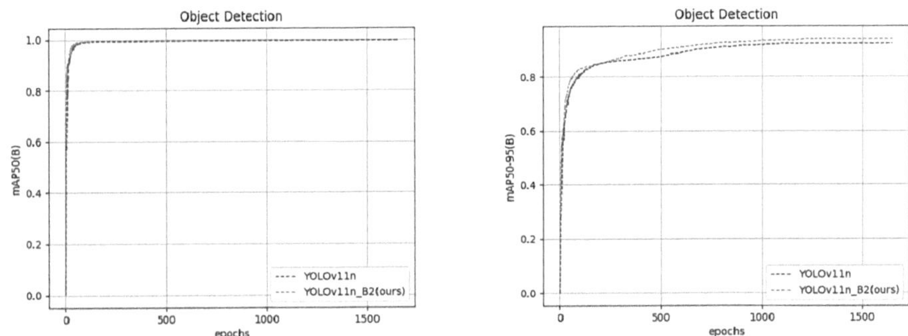

Fig. 5. Performance Metrics Comparison.

5 Concluding Remarks

In the construction of smart grids, insulator fault detection via UAV inspection faces dual challenges of complex backgrounds and significant scale variations among targets, which hinder the ability of existing detection algorithms to maintain stable and efficient recognition performance. To address these issues, this paper proposes an improved algorithm based on YOLOv11n by replacing the original C2PSA attention module with an innovative C2BRA module. The C2BRA module integrates a two-layer mechanism combining region screening and local modeling, significantly enhancing the model's capability to perceive key targets in complex scenarios. The improved model not only achieves higher detection accuracy but also effectively reduces parameter count and computational cost, making it more suitable for deployment on edge devices. Experimental results on the SFID dataset demonstrate that the proposed algorithm achieves excellent performance, with an mAP@50-95 of 93.4%, representing a 1.5% improvement over the original YOLOv11n, and shows consistent gains across multiple evaluation metrics. This work provides an efficient and robust solution for insulator fault detection in smart grids with significant practical value. Future work will focus on further improving the model's computational efficiency and adaptability.

References

1. Zhang, D.: Heating and discharge mechanism of wet contaminated insulators. High Voltage Eng. **44**(3), 787–795 (2018)
2. Zhou, Z., Chen, Q., Ma, B., Qi, D.: An improved yolo target detection method with its application in cable device abnormal condition recognition. Electr. Meas. Instrum **57**(02), 14–20 (2020)
3. Liu, W., et al.: SSD: single shot multibox detector. In: Computer Vision–ECCV 2016: 14th European Conference, Amsterdam, The Netherlands, October 11–14, 2016, Proceedings, Part I 14, pp. 21–37. Springer (2016)
4. Redmon, J., Divvala, S., Girshick, R., Farhadi, A.: You only look once: unified, real-time object detection. In: Proceedings of the IEEE Conference on Computer Vision and Pattern Recognition, pp. 779–788 (2016)
5. Redmon, J., Farhadi, A.: YOLOv3: an incremental improvement. arXiv preprint arXiv:1804.02767 (2018)
6. Ge, Z., Liu, S., Wang, F., Li, Z., Sun, J.: YOLOX: exceeding YOLO series in 2021. arXiv preprint arXiv:2107.08430 (2021)
7. Wang, C.-Y., Bochkovskiy, A., Mark Liao, H.-Y.: YOLOv7: trainable bag-of-freebies sets new state-of-the-art for real-time object detectors. In: Proceedings of the IEEE/CVF Conference on Computer Vision and Pattern Recognition, pp. 7464–7475 (2023)
8. Wang, A., Chen, H., Liu, L., Chen, K., Lin, Z., Han, J., et al.: YOLOv10: real-time end-to-end object detection. Adv. Neural. Inf. Process. Syst. **37**, 107984–108011 (2024)
9. Carion, N., Massa, F., Synnaeve, G., Usunier, N., Kirillov, A., Zagoruyko, S.: End-to-end object detection with transformers. In: European Conference on Computer Vision, pp. 213–229. Springer (2020)
10. Ren, S., He, K., Girshick, R., Sun, J.: Faster R-CNN: towards real-time object detection with region proposal networks. In: Advances in Neural Information Processing Systems, vol. 28 (2015)
11. He, K., Gkioxari, G., Dollár, P., Girshick, R.: Mask R-CNN. In: Proceedings of the IEEE International Conference on Computer Vision, pp. 2961–2969 (2017)
12. Zhu, L., Wang, X., Ke, Z., Zhang, W., Lau, R.W.H.:. BiFormer: vision transformer with bi-level routing attention. In: Proceedings of the IEEE/CVF Conference on Computer Vision and Pattern Recognition, pp. 10323–10333 (2023)
13. Chollet, F.: Xception: deep learning with depthwise separable convolutions. In: Proceedings of the IEEE Conference on Computer Vision and Pattern Recognition, pp. 1251–1258 (2017)
14. Hu, J., Shen, L., Sun, G.: Squeeze-and-excitation networks. In: Proceedings of the IEEE Conference on Computer Vision and Pattern Recognition, pp. 7132–7141 (2018)
15. Woo, S., Park, J., Lee, J.-Y., Kweon, I.S.: CBAM: convolutional block attention module. In: Proceedings of the European Conference on Computer Vision (ECCV), pp. 3–19 (2018)
16. Wang, Q., Wu, B., Zhu, P., Li, P., Zuo, W., Hu, Q.: ECA-Net: efficient channel attention for deep convolutional neural networks. In: Proceedings of the IEEE/CVF Conference on Computer Vision and Pattern Recognition, pp. 11534–11542 (2020)

A Local Perceptual Approach
for Few-Shot Text Effect Transfer

Hongjian Zhan[1,2], Wei Tian[1], and Yue Lu[1(✉)]

[1] East China Normal University, Shanghai, China
{hjzhan,wtian}@cee.ecnu.edu.cn, ylu@cs.ecnu.edu.cn
[2] Chongqing Key Laboratory of Precision Optics, Chongqing Institute of East China
Normal University, Chongqing, China

Abstract. Text effect transfer (TET) aims to preserve the content of
character images while rendering their style into various forms, including colors, outlines, shadows, textures, and glyphs. However, manually
designing a complete font library is a labor-intensive task, making few-
shot text effect transfer an increasingly important research focus. Existing methods often suffer from poor generalization, as their models are
limited to a small range of text effects. Some approaches attempt to
address this issue, but due to the scarcity of reference-style images,
they tend to overfit or lack fine details, leading to failures when handling unseen text effects. To overcome these challenges, we propose a
novel fine-tuning strategy that integrates Local Perceptual Fusion and
Discrimination to enhance few-shot text effect transfer. Specifically, our
fine-tuning strategy allows the model to adapt its parameters based on a
small set of reference images from previously unseen styles, enabling the
generation of realistic text effects. Additionally, we introduce a structure-
level fusion mechanism in the style encoder to improve detail fidelity. To
mitigate overfitting, we design a global discriminator and a local discriminator: the global discriminator assesses the overall realism of the
generated styles, while the local discriminator performs fine-grained evaluation based on localized observations, ensuring both global consistency
and fine-detail preservation. Experimental results demonstrate that our
approach achieves advanced performance in few-shot text effect transfer,
generating high-quality and highly faithful text effects.

Keywords: Text Effect Transfer · Few Shot · Local Perceptual
Approach

1 Introduction

Text effects play a crucial role in visual communication, enhancing the aesthetic
appeal of posters, billboards, book covers, and other design media. These effects
encompass a wide range of styles, including color schemes, outlines, shadows,
glows, textures, and more. Despite their widespread use, manually creating a
comprehensive library of text effects is a labor-intensive process. This challenge is

© The Author(s), under exclusive license to Springer Nature Singapore Pte Ltd. 2026

Z. Lin et al. (Eds.): ICIG 2025, LNCS 16163, pp. 247–259, 2026.
https://doi.org/10.1007/978-981-95-3729-7_21

further compounded when modifying text with these effects, as it often requires repetitive work. For logographic languages such as Chinese (with over 60,000 characters), Japanese (over 50,000 characters), and Korean (11,172 characters), the scale of this task becomes even more daunting. To address these challenges, researchers have proposed numerous few-shot text effect transfer methods. These methods aim to generate large quantities of stylized text by referencing only one or a few example images, significantly reducing the manual effort required.

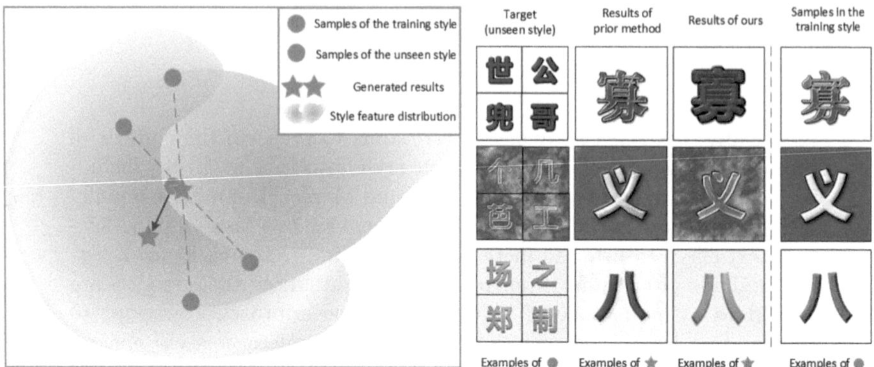

Fig. 1. Problem Statement: The distribution of style features in the training set is represented by the green region, while the distribution of unseen style features is represented by the orange region. Given four unseen style references, prior methods tend to produce results that align with the training set's style distribution (green star), which deviates from the desired target style. In contrast, our method successfully generates samples from the desired style distribution, as indicated by the orange stars.

Humans possess an impressive ability to learn from limited examples, whereas artificial learners often struggle with overfitting in similar scenarios due to insufficient prior knowledge. Inspired by human learning strategies, recent advances in Generative Adversarial Networks (GANs) have led to significant progress in few-shot text effect transfer and font generation. Numerous techniques have been developed to tackle the problem of text effect transfer. For instance, Yang *et al.* [16] summarize multiple text effects into a general prior, guiding the style transfer process to synthesize diverse sub-effects. Similarly, Yang *et al.* [17] introduce TET-GAN, a network that rearranges textures to fit new glyphs. However, these methods often fail to adequately address the challenges posed by unseen text effects. Li *et al.* [8] propose FET-GAN, which leverages few-shot learning to acquire the representation of an effect without requiring paired typeface-effect datasets. They also introduce a fine-tuning strategy to generalize their model to new, unseen effects. Nevertheless, in extreme few-shot settings (e.g., 4-shot), their approach remains susceptible to overfitting.

In addition to text effect transfer, several works have focused on few-shot font generation, including DM-Font [1], LF-Font [12], DG-Font [15], XMP-Font

[10], Diff-Font [4], VQ-Font [11], and TinyStyler [6]. While these methods excel at generating fonts, directly applying them to text effect transfer often leads to a significant drop in performance. This is because text effect transfer is inherently more complex than font transfer, requiring not only the adaptation of glyphs but also the manipulation of colors, outlines, shadows, textures, and other intricate details.

Existing text effect transfer methods often face a critical limitation: poor generalization. As illustrated in Fig. 1, the style distributions of different text effects can overlap. If only a few style references are used and their features are averaged, the generated output may be biased toward the training set's style distribution rather than the desired target style. One potential solution is to fine-tune the pre-trained model using limited reference images of the target effect [8], allowing the model to adjust its parameters to match the new style. However, this approach often suffers from overfitting when the number of available reference images is exceptionally low, leading to inaccurate style extraction.

To address these challenges, we propose a novel fine-tuning approach for few-shot text effect transfer based on local perceptual fusion and discrimination. Specifically, our model incorporates a structure-level fusion mechanism into the style encoder, extracting text effects at the patch level to capture detailed style features for glyphs. Additionally, we introduce a local perceptual discriminator optimized through a local adversarial loss. Unlike traditional global discriminators, the local discriminator focuses on fine-grained characteristics, relaxing the true/false decision boundary and reducing overfitting. To further mitigate overfitting, we employ data augmentation techniques, such as random flipping and cropping, to expand the fine-tuning dataset.

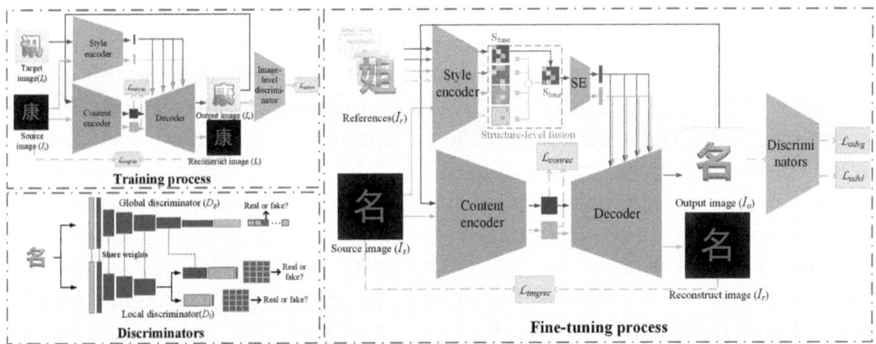

Fig. 2. Overview of our network during both the training and fine-tuning processes. The structure-level fusion is incorporated into the style encoder, and the local discriminator is added to the discriminative network during the fine-tuning stage.

2   Methods

2.1   Overview

Given a target effect image I_t during the training process or a few reference images I_r during the fine-tuning process, and a source image I_s, our framework outputs a synthetic image that retains the character of I_s while adopting the text effect from I_t or I_r. The architecture of our network is presented in Fig. 2, and it comprises a style encoder, a content encoder, a decoder, a global discriminator, and a local discriminator. The style encoder extracts the text effect from I_t and I_r, and structure-level fusion is incorporated into it to merge different features at the patch level. The content encoder learns the content feature of I_s, and the two features are combined through adaptive instance normalization (AdaIN) [7] to generate the output image I_o. This image retains the character of I_s while incorporating the text effect from I_t or I_r. During the training process, we employ the global discriminator D_g to evaluate the image as a whole and determine its style based on global observations. During the fine-tuning process, both the global and local discriminators (D_l) are used to achieve both global and local perception. The local discriminator enables image discrimination based on local observations.

2.2   Global and Local Discriminators

It has been observed that when the style to be transferred is not included in the training data, the efficacy of style transfer is greatly reduced. An effective solution to this problem is to fine-tune the model using a new target dataset. However, this approach is prone to overfitting due to the extremely few-shot setting (e.g., 4-shot). In such settings, the definition of "real" images is very strict, as only a limited number of reference images are available. The discriminator can easily memorize these reference images by analyzing the full view of the limited set, which confuses the generator regarding the direction of gradient updates and ultimately leads to the collapse of the generated results. Since the fine-tuning reference images constitute only a small subset of the desired distribution, the discriminator can accurately distinguish between real and fake images by analyzing only local image regions.

To mitigate the issue of overfitting, we propose the use of both global and local discriminators during the fine-tuning process. The architecture consists of two shared discriminators: specifically, a global discriminator D_g that provides a holistic perspective, and a local discriminator D_l that offers a localized perspective. In previous work [2], local discriminators have been utilized during training to focus on the structure of local image patches, ensuring high-frequency details in the generated image. In contrast, our approach employs local perception to "relax" the authenticity criteria and balance them with global perception. The architecture of the proposed discriminators is illustrated in Fig. 2. The first five blocks of the two discriminators share weights and are identical. Given an image, the global discriminator outputs a vector of size $C_t \times 1 \times 1$, where C_t

represents the number of text effects in the training set. The score of the corresponding channel indicates whether the input image is real or fake. During fine-tuning, a random batch from the reference set is sent to the discriminator, while the following batches are treated as corresponding to the style with the highest score. The parameters of the corresponding channel are updated during fine-tuning and used during inference. The local discriminator extracts features of size $C \times 16 \times 16$, where C denotes the number of feature channels. In our model, there are two such features. An additional convolutional layer, together with an activation layer after each feature, is used to produce an output of size $1 \times 16 \times 16$, representing the authenticity of the input image at the patch level. In the output matrix of the local discriminator, each element indicates the score of a local patch, enabling the discriminator to have localized perception, relax the authenticity criteria, and further reduce the overfitting problem.

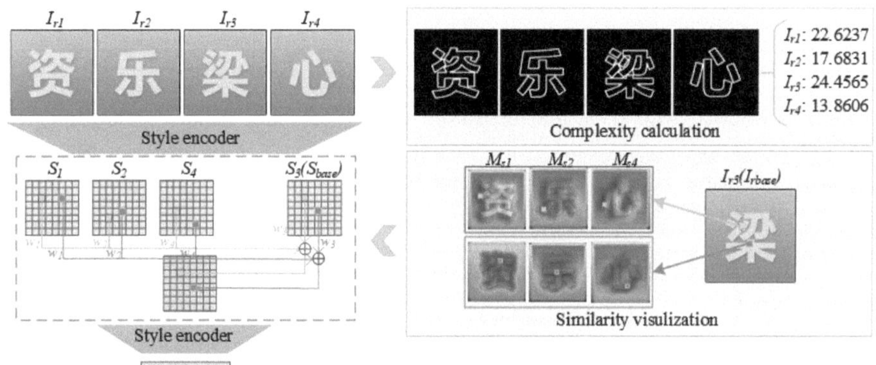

Fig. 3. The details of proposed structure-level fusion.

2.3   Structure-Level Fusion

In prior methods for generating k-shot fonts [15] or text effects [8], a fused feature was obtained by simply averaging the style features of the reference images, given k reference images. However, this method resulted in the stacking of different reference images with reduced transparency, which led to the averaging of style details. As a consequence, the averaged style sometimes deviated from the target style distribution, as shown in Fig. 1.

To address this issue, we introduce structure-level fusion, inspired by [3], to better leverage the local features of a limited number of reference images. As depicted in Fig. 3, it aims to output a fused feature map based on the similarity among different reference images. Specifically, the given reference images $\{I_{ri}\}$ are first fed into a function that calculates their structural complexity. Next, the style encoder is used to obtain the feature maps $\{S_i\}$ to be fused. The feature of the most complex character is selected as the base feature S_{base}.

Then, the similarity map M_{S_i} between the base feature and each of the other features S_i is calculated. The locations in S_{base} and S_i with the highest similarity according to M_{S_i} are weighted and summed, and the corresponding positions in the original base feature are replaced. Finally, the modified base feature is passed through the remaining layers of the style encoder to obtain the fused style vector. The process can be formulated as a series of equations:

$$\text{base} = \arg\max_i Com(I_{r_i}), \quad i = 1, 2, \ldots, k \tag{1}$$

$$M_{S_i} = Sim(S_{base}, S_i), \quad i = 1, 2, \ldots, k, \; i \neq \text{base} \tag{2}$$

$$S_{fuse}(i,j) = \alpha_{base} S_{base}(i,j) + \sum_{i \neq \text{base}}^{k} \alpha_i S_i(\Theta, \Psi), \tag{3}$$

$$(\Theta, \Psi) = \arg\max_{(\theta,\varphi)} M_{S_i}(\theta, \varphi), \tag{4}$$

$$\alpha_i = \text{Softmax}(Com(I_{r_i})), \tag{5}$$

where S_{ref} denotes the style feature maps of the reference images excluding the base feature map S_{base}, $Com(\cdot)$ denotes the complexity computation function, and $Sim(\cdot)$ denotes the similarity metric.

2.4 Few-Shot Fine-Tuning Strategy

The parameters of a generative network are highly influenced by the distribution of the training set. However, the performance of the model may be affected when the distribution of the test data differs from that of the training data. In the case of generating text images with a desired style, a generator may make mistakes if the number of reference images is limited, as shown in Fig. 1. To address this issue and ensure the model's versatility in generating arbitrary text effects, we propose a few-shot fine-tuning strategy.

To fine-tune the model, we first obtain a source image from the 'hei' style by synthesizing. Then, we augment the data by randomly flipping and cropping the given images to expand the temporary dataset. However, data augmentation cannot effectively solve the issue of overfitting, which occurs when a discriminator that has been trained on a large dataset remembers the small set of images used for fine-tuning. To address this, we use both global and local discriminators during fine-tuning. During training, only the global discriminator is used, while during fine-tuning, the local discriminator is introduced and given priority. Only the parameters corresponding to the channel with the highest score are updated for the global discriminator. For each iteration, the local discriminator randomly selects a feature of size $C \times 256 \times 256$ and updates only the parameters corresponding to the selected feature. Additionally, we reduce the number of network parameters to train by freezing the content encoder's parameters since the model retains the source images' unseen content.

2.5   Loss Function

Our network aims to achieve text effect transfer on both seen and unseen styles. Toward this end, we adopt the following loss functions in training and fine-tuning: global and local adversarial loss, image reconstruction loss, and content reconstruction loss. The purpose and the equation of the loss functions are as follows.

Global and local adversarial loss: In order to ensure the generated images are real, we introduce adversarial loss for both global discriminator D_g and local discriminator D_l. The adversarial loss enforce the generator to replicate the distribution of the reference set to fool the discriminators. The global adversarial loss enforces D_g to perceive at the image level, which makes D_g have global perceptual. Similarly, the local adversarial loss enforces D_l to perceive at the patch level and makes it have local perceptual. The total adversarial loss is defined as:

$$\mathcal{L}_{adv_g} = \max_{D_g} \min_{G} \mathbb{E}_{I_t \in P_t}[\log D_g(I_t)] +$$
$$\mathbb{E}_{I_t \in P_t, I_s \in P_s} \log[1 - D_g(G(I_t, I_s))], \tag{6}$$

$$\mathcal{L}_{adv_l} = \max_{D_l} \min_{G} \mathbb{E}_{I_t \in P_t}[\log D_l(I_t)] +$$
$$\mathbb{E}_{I_t \in P_t, I_s \in P_s} \log[\mathbb{I} - D_l(G(I_t, I_s))], \tag{7}$$

$$\mathcal{L}_{adv} = \lambda_g \mathcal{L}_{adv_g} + \lambda_l \mathcal{L}_{adv_l}. \tag{8}$$

The I_s and I_t denote the source image and reference image respectively. The $\mathbb{I}$ denotes the all-ones matrix whose size is the same as the output of D_l. The λ_m and λ_p are hyperparameters to control the weights of global and local loss functions.

Image reconstruction loss: To make the generator have the ability to reconstruct the source image with the style itself, we feed the source image to the style encoder and apply the image reconstruction loss, which can be formulated as:

$$\mathcal{L}_{imgrec} = \mathbb{E}_{I_s \in P_s} \|I_c - G(I_s, I_s)\|_1. \tag{9}$$

Content reconstruction loss: In order to ensure that the output image I_o has the same content feature as the source image, we apply content reconstruction loss. This loss is formulated as:

$$\mathcal{L}_{conrec} = \mathbb{E}_{I_t \in P_t, I_s \in P_s} \|f_c(I_s) - f_c(G(I_t, I_s))\|_1, \tag{10}$$

in which the f_c represents the content encoder.

Combining the above loss functions, the overall loss functions while training and fine-tuning are as follows:

$$\mathcal{L}_{train} = \lambda_{adv} \mathcal{L}_{adv_g} + \lambda_{imgrec} \mathcal{L}_{imgrec}$$
$$+ \lambda_{conrec} \mathcal{L}_{conrec}, \tag{11}$$

$$\mathcal{L}_{finetune} = \lambda_{adv}\mathcal{L}_{adv} + \lambda_{imgrec}\mathcal{L}_{imgrec}. \tag{12}$$

The L_{train} and the $L_{finetune}$ denote the total loss function used in training process and fine-tune process respectively. λ_{adv}, λ_{imgrec} and λ_{conrec} are hyperparameters to control the weights of each loss function.

3   Experiments

We conducted a series of experiments to evaluate the proposed model and compare it with state-of-the-art methods. This section presents our research findings on the TextEffects and 100Fonts datasets. We begin by providing an overview of our experimental setup, which encompasses network architecture, experimental settings, and the datasets employed in our study. Next, we present the outcomes of our experiments, demonstrating the efficacy of the proposed methods through a range of performance metrics.

3.1   Experimental Settings

The proposed model is built with Pytorch. While training, the image size of input and output are resized to 256×256 and the batch size is 16. We use one NVIDIA 3090 GPU to train for about 20 h to get 300 epochs. As for fine-tuning, we randomly select 4 characters from the unseen set for each unseen style as the fine-tuning dataset. The size of input and output images is 256×256 and the batch size is 4. We use one NVIDIA 3090-TI GPU to train for about an hour to get 20 epochs. The λ_{adv}, λ_{imgrec} and λ_{conrec} are respectively 1.0, 0.1 and 0.1. We fuse the style feature maps with the size of $256 \times 16 \times 16$ at the fusion stage.

3.2   Datasets

We use TextEffects and 100Fonts datasets in our experiments. TextEffects consists of paired text effect images and there is a total of 70 classes of text effects. 100Fonts contains paired text effect images and there are 100 kinds of fonts. All image sizes are 320×320.

3.3   Comparison

In this subsection, we present the results of comparison experiments conducted between our proposed methods and the following existing methods: FUNIT [9], TET-GAN [17], FET-GAN [8], DGFont [15], and Diff-Font [4]. During training, we added a supervised loss to FUNIT to ensure a more stable training process. However, since the dataset we used does not have additional information such as word content and strokes as supervision, we removed the stroke information input of Diff-Font. Furthermore, to evaluate the effectiveness of our proposed fine-tuning strategy, we applied it to FET-GAN and denoted it as FET-GAN+. Other methods, such as XMP-Font [10] and FSFont [13], require extra supervision information, which is not included in our dataset.

Table 1. Quantitative evaluation of the whole dataset. The seen style and unseen style refer to the style in the training set and fine-tuning set of the TextEffects dataset, respectively. Cross-dataset testing refers to the results which are fine-tuned on the 100fonts dataset after training on the TextEffects dataset. FET-GAN+ refers to the FET-GAN model with our fine-tuning strategy.

Methods	MSE↓	PSNR↑	SSIM↑	FID↓
Seen style				
FUNIT	0.0899	10.46	0.4057	78.55
TET-GAN	0.064	11.98	0.5990	49.07
FET-GAN	0.0593	11.66	0.5409	50.71
DGFont	0.0349	14.61	0.7304	44.97
Diff-Font	0.0375	**17.21**	0.7678	79.68
Ours	**0.0328**	14.70	**0.7931**	**30.06**
Unseen style				
FUNIT	0.0784	11.45	0.5367	187.7
DGFont	0.0725	10.54	0.4075	163.9
FET-GAN	0.0641	12.02	0.4892	157.5
Diff-Font	0.0686	**13.07**	0.4760	138.7
FET-GAN+	0.0568	12.34	0.5001	96.82
Ours	**0.0454**	12.99	**0.624**	**91.61**
Cross dataset testing				
FUNIT	0.0695	12.32	0.4788	177.1
DGFont	0.0771	11.24	0.6047	230.0
TET-GAN	0.0574	12.53	0.7173	195.7
FET-GAN	0.0647	15.86	0.8179	104.5
Diff-Font	**0.0407**	14.92	0.5798	173.4
FET-GAN+	0.0573	16.02	0.8342	95.38
Ours	0.0493	**16.36**	**0.8396**	84.60

Quantitative Comparison. The results of the quantitative comparison are shown in Table. 1. We use the following metrics to assess the quality of generated images: MSE, which is also known as l_2; PSNR, which is the peak signal-to-noise ratio; SSIM [14], which is used to compare the mean structural similarity index between two images; FID [5] is a measure of similarity between two datasets of images in perceptual-level. Lager PSNR, SSIM, and smaller MSE, and FID indicate better generation results. As shown in Table. 1, our method performs the best in both seen style generation, unseen style generation, and cross-dataset test.

Qualitative Comparison. To validate our framework's ability to transfer text effects in both seen and unseen styles, we conducted a qualitative comparison with several existing methods. The results of the comparison are shown in Fig. 4 and Fig. 5. Specifically, we compared our method with FUNIT, TET-GAN, FET-GAN, DGFont, and Diff-Font on the TextEffects dataset. The left part of Fig. 4 shows the results of the seen style, where FUNIT failed to generate recognizable characters and TET-GAN could only transfer the texture of reference images. Although FET-GAN generated complete structures, the generated characters were sometimes vague. DGFont, Diff-Font, and our method produced images that were closest to the reference images.

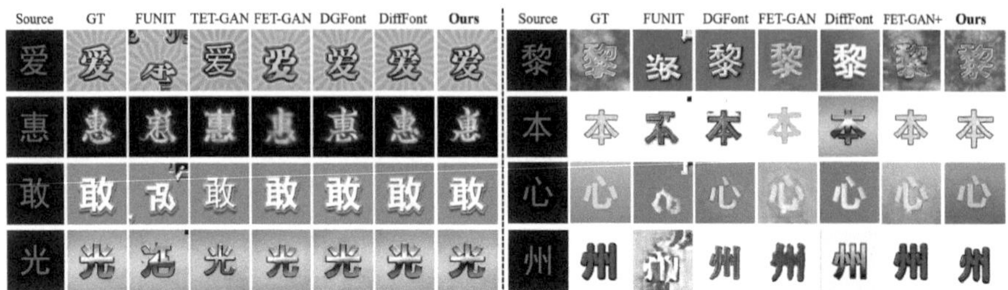

Fig. 4. Comparison with state-of-the-art text effect transfer and font generation methods on both seen and unseen styles. The left part demonstrates the results of seen styles, and the right part demonstrates the results of unseen styles.

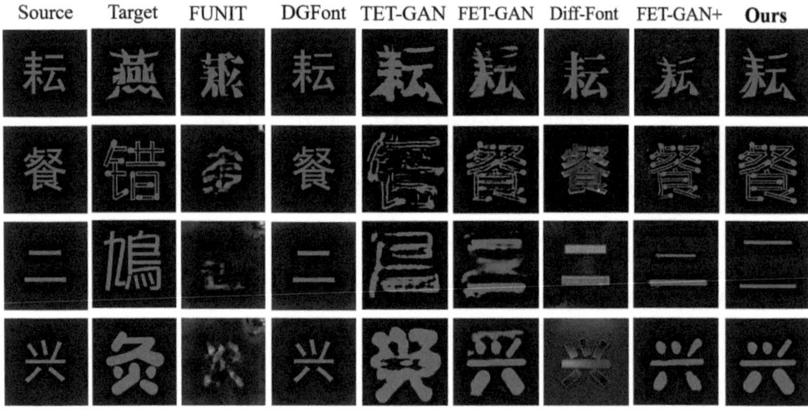

Fig. 5. Comparison with state-of-the-art text effect transfer and font generation methods on the cross dataset. The target effect images are from 100Fonts dataset.

Furthermore, we compared our fine-tuning strategy with FET-GAN on both the TextEffects and 100Fonts datasets, where the right part of Fig. 4 shows the results of the unseen style. It can be observed that FUNIT, DGFont, and Diff-Font failed to learn the new target style, and FET-GAN learned only part of the target style after fine-tuning, with blurry generated results. Only our method succeeded in generating satisfying results. Notably, TET was not included in the comparison because these styles are seen styles for their pre-trained model.

We conduct cross-dataset experiments to test the efficacy of different models that are trained on the TextEffects dataset and then applied on the 100Fonts dataset. Our method, along with TET-GAN and FET-GAN, were fine-tuned on the 100Fonts dataset. Figure 5 demonstrates that FUNIT failed to create complete characters, while DGFont only produced images identical to the source images. TET-GAN generated unrecognized characters, and FET-GAN generated characters with unexpected structures. In contrast, our method applied the style from the training set and generated the correct structure and expected style. These results attest that our method successfully generated characters for all text effects.

3.4   Analysis of the Fine-Tuning Strategy

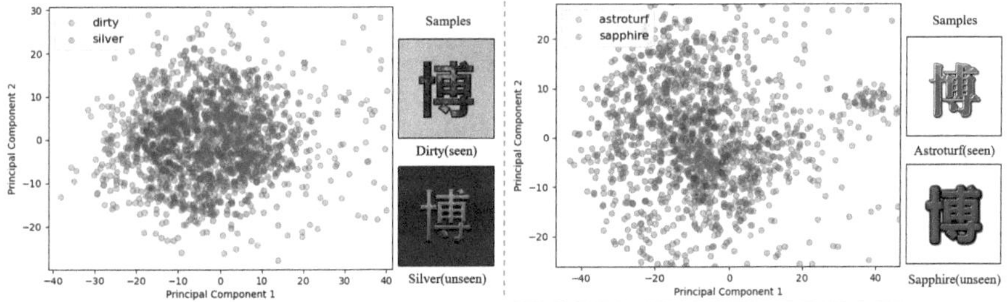

Fig. 6. The scatter plot of the style feature distribution extracted by the style encoder, the blue data points are from the training data set, and the red data points are from the finetune data set. Examples of distinct styles are presented to the right of the scatter plot. (Color figure online)

As depicted in Fig. 6, we first output the feature map of the style encoder and then apply PCA (Principal Component Analysis) to reduce the dimensionality of the features. This helps us to obtain a scatter plot of the data style features. In each scatterplot, we plot two styles from the training dataset, represented by blue dots and red dots. Our analysis shows that the distribution of the training set and the fine-tuning set can overlap. As illustrated in Fig. 7, we test the previous method (taking FET-GAN [8] as an example) and our model on unseen text effects without fine-tuning. The results of both methods tend to apply a style seen during training as the output of the network. As shown in Fig. 7, the fine-tuned results have a style closer to the given reference images than the un-fine-tuned results. Both our model and FET-GAN improved in unseen styles, proving that fine-tuning can be used to improve model generalization.

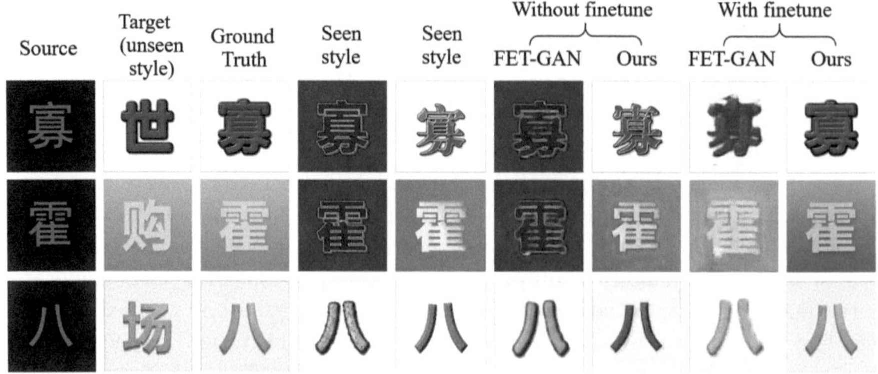

Fig. 7. The results of FET-GAN and the proposed method on unseen style before and after fine-tuning.

4   Conclusion

In this paper, we propose a novel approach for few-shot text effect transfer by leveraging a fine-tuning strategy that integrates local perceptual fusion and discrimination. Extensive experiments demonstrate the effectiveness of our method in transferring text effects across both seen and unseen styles. Future work will explore further improvements in model robustness under extreme few-shot settings, as well as extend our framework to handle more complex and diverse text effect styles in real-world applications.

Acknowledgments. This work was supported by the National Natural Science Foundation of China (62176091) and the Natural Science Foundation of Chongqing (CSTB2024NSCQ-MSX0877).

References

1. Cha, J., Chun, S., Lee, G., Lee, B., Kim, S., Lee, H.: Few-shot compositional font generation with dual memory. In: European Conference on Computer Vision, pp. 735–751. Springer (2020)
2. Gao, Y., Guo, Y., Lian, Z., Tang, Y., Xiao, J.: Artistic glyph image synthesis via one-stage few-shot learning. ACM Trans. Graph. (TOG) **38**(6), 1–12 (2019)
3. Gu, Z., Li, W., Huo, J., Wang, L., Gao, Y.: LoFGAN: fusing local representations for few-shot image generation. In: Proceedings of the IEEE/CVF International Conference on Computer Vision, pp. 8463–8471 (2021)
4. He, H., et al.: Diff-Font: diffusion model for robust one-shot font generation. arXiv preprint arXiv:2212.05895 (2022)
5. Heusel, M., Ramsauer, H., Unterthiner, T., Nessler, B., Hochreiter, S.: GANs trained by a two time-scale update rule converge to a local nash equilibrium. In: Advances in Neural Information Processing Systems, vol. 30 (2017)

6. Horvitz, Z., Patel, A., Singh, K., Callison-Burch, C., McKeown, K., Yu, Z.: TinyStyler: efficient few-shot text style transfer with authorship embeddings. arXiv preprint arXiv:2406.15586 (2024)

7. Huang, X., Belongie, S.: Arbitrary style transfer in real-time with adaptive instance normalization. In: Proceedings of the IEEE International Conference on Computer Vision, pp. 1501–1510 (2017)

8. Li, W., He, Y., Qi, Y., Li, Z., Tang, Y.: FET-GAN: font and effect transfer via k-shot adaptive instance normalization. In: Proceedings of the AAAI Conference on Artificial Intelligence, vol. 34 (2020)

9. Liu, M.Y., et al.: Few-shot unsupervised image-to-image translation. In: Proceedings of the IEEE/CVF International Conference on Computer Vision, pp. 10551–10560 (2019)

10. Liu, W., Liu, F., Ding, F., He, Q., Yi, Z.: XMP-Font: self-supervised cross-modality pre-training for few-shot font generation. In: Proceedings of the IEEE/CVF Conference on Computer Vision and Pattern Recognition, pp. 7905–7914 (2022)

11. Pan, W., Zhu, A., Zhou, X., Iwana, B.K., Li, S.: Few shot font generation via transferring similarity guided global style and quantization local style. In: Proceedings of the IEEE/CVF International Conference on Computer Vision, pp. 19506–19516 (2023)

12. Park, S., Chun, S., Cha, J., Lee, B., Shim, H.: Few-shot font generation with localized style representations and factorization. In: Proceedings of the AAAI Conference on Artificial Intelligence, vol. 35, pp. 2393–2402 (2021)

13. Tang, L., et al.: Few-shot font generation by learning fine-grained local styles. In: Proceedings of the IEEE/CVF Conference on Computer Vision and Pattern Recognition, pp. 7895–7904 (2022)

14. Wang, Z., Bovik, A.C., Sheikh, H.R., Simoncelli, E.P.: Image quality assessment: from error visibility to structural similarity. IEEE Trans. Image Process. **13**(4), 600–612 (2004)

15. Xie, Y., Chen, X., Sun, L., Lu, Y.: DG-Font: deformable generative networks for unsupervised font generation. In: Proceedings of the IEEE/CVF Conference on Computer Vision and Pattern Recognition, pp. 5130–5140 (2021)

16. Yang, S., Liu, J., Lian, Z., Guo, Z.: Awesome typography: statistics-based text effects transfer. In: Proceedings of the IEEE Conference on Computer Vision and Pattern Recognition, pp. 7464–7473 (2017)

17. Yang, S., Liu, J., Wang, W., Guo, Z.: Tet-GAN: text effects transfer via stylization and destylization. In: Proceedings of the AAAI Conference on Artificial Intelligence, vol. 33, pp. 1238–1245 (2019)

EMANet: Edge-Enhanced Multi-scale Attention Network for Salient Object Detection in Optical Remote Sensing Imagery

Lina Huo, Yu Zhang, and Wei Wang[✉]

Hebei Normal University, Shijiazhuang, Hebei, China
`wangwei2021@hebtu.edu.cn`

Abstract. Salient object detection in optical remote sensing imagery (ORSI-SOD) presents significant challenges due to complex backgrounds, low-contrast and ambiguous object boundaries, and substantial scale variations among targets. To address these issues, this paper proposes a novel deep learning architecture, termed EMANet, which integrates three key modules: an Edge-Enhanced Feature Module (EEFM) to improve boundary localization; a Multi-Scale Edge Modulation (MSEM) module for scale-aware feature refinement; and an Attention-Guided Feedback Enhancement Module (AGFEM) to enhance semantic consistency across network layers. The proposed framework leverages multi-scale feature fusion, edge-guided supervision, and attention-driven feedback to generate high-precision saliency maps under varying object scales and complex scene conditions. Extensive experiments on two publicly available datasets, ORSSD and EORSSD, demonstrate that EMANet outperforms state-of-the-art methods in terms of S-measure, F-measure, and mean absolute error (MAE). Furthermore, ablation studies validate the individual and combined effectiveness of each module. These results confirm that EMANet offers a robust and efficient solution for ORSI-SOD, particularly in detecting small, irregular, and low-contrast targets in challenging remote sensing scenarios.

Keywords: Salient object detection · optical remote sensing imagery · edge-enhanced multi-scale attention network

1 Introduction

Visual saliency detection mimics the human visual system to identify regions of interest [1,2]. Salient object detection (SOD) extends this by locating and segmenting the most visually prominent objects in an image, with applications in object tracking, photo cropping, and semantic segmentation. While initially developed for natural scene images (NSIs), SOD has been adapted to optical remote sensing imagery (ORSI), supporting tasks such as scene classification and target monitoring.

© The Author(s), under exclusive license to Springer Nature Singapore Pte Ltd. 2026
Z. Lin et al. (Eds.): ICIG 2025, LNCS 16163, pp. 260–272, 2026.
https://doi.org/10.1007/978-981-95-3729-7_22

Compared to NSIs, ORSI-SOD faces greater challenges due to complex backgrounds, diverse object scales, and spectral variability [3]. Traditional methods based on handcrafted features struggle with clutter and generalization. Although CNN-based SOD models for NSIs, such as F3Net [4] and MINet [5], have achieved strong results, their performance degrades on remote sensing images (RSIs) due to fuzzy boundaries and scale inconsistencies.

To address these issues, recent RSI-specific methods (e.g., SRAL [6], BSCGNet [7]) have incorporated multi-scale fusion, boundary enhancement, and context-aware reasoning tailored to the characteristics of remote sensing imagery. While these approaches have shown notable progress, challenges such as false detections and blurred object boundaries caused by noise and complex spatial structures still persist. To further alleviate these problems, we propose EMANet, a CNN-based framework for RSI-SOD that integrates boundary supervision, multi-scale edge modulation, and attention-guided feedback to enhance detection accuracy and boundary delineation.

2 Related Work

2.1 Current Status of Salient Object Detection (SOD)

Salient object detection (SOD) in natural scene images (NSIs) has advanced significantly, evolving from handcrafted priors to deep learning-based end-to-end models. These models leverage multi-scale fusion, global context modeling, edge guidance, and semantic integration to improve robustness to scale variation, context understanding, and boundary accuracy. However, applying NSI-based methods to remote sensing images (RSIs) remains challenging due to differences in imaging characteristics, scene complexity, and object diversity. RSIs often exhibit cluttered backgrounds, directional structures, and scale inconsistency, leading to performance degradation [8]. Consequently, recent work has focused on developing RSI-specific models that incorporate remote sensing priors and structural cues to better handle these challenges.

2.2 Salient Object Detection in Remote Sensing(RSI)

Salient object detection (SOD) in natural scene images (NSI) has seen significant progress over recent decades. Early methods relied on handcrafted priors such as color contrast, frequency residuals, and background cues, while later approaches explored supervised mappings from hand-crafted features to saliency maps. With the advent of deep learning, end-to-end models have become dominant, enabling advancements in multi-scale feature fusion, global context modeling, and edge-guided refinement. These techniques enhance robustness to scale variations, capture long-range dependencies, and improve boundary localization. However, directly applying NSI-SOD methods to remote sensing imagery (RSI) remains challenging due to fundamental differences in imaging characteristics, scene complexity, and object structures. RSIs often contain cluttered backgrounds, diverse object orientations, and scale variation, leading to degraded performance of NSI-based models. Prior studies [8] have shown that existing NSI-SOD methods struggle with blurred targets, weak edges, and complex spatial distributions in RSI-SOD tasks.

3   Methodology

3.1   Network Overview

As shown in Fig. 1, EMANet uses a VGG16-based encoder-decoder to extract multi-level features from textures to semantics. It enhances saliency and boundary details with key modules: the Edge-Enhanced Feature Module (EEFM) fuses multi-scale features with attention to highlight targets and improve edge representation. CBAM refines features at each encoding stage, boosting structural and global awareness. Shallow features (x1-x4) and upsampled deep features (x5) are combined in EEFM to create an edge attention map, sharpened by an edge enhancement branch for clearer boundaries. To guide boundary learning across scales, a Multi-Scale Edge Supervision Module (MSEM) fuses encoder features with the edge attention map, producing edge-guided features that reinforce boundary localization and saliency consistency. In the decoding stage, a progressive upsampling strategy (up1-up4) is employed, gradually restoring spatial resolution while integrating corresponding encoder features to refine predictions. To further strengthen the final saliency representation, an Attention-Guided Feature Enhancement Module (AGFEM) aggregates decoder features, MSEM outputs, and mid-to-high-level semantics to highlight salient objects and sharpen contours. The final saliency map is supervised with deep supervision at multiple outputs, ensuring stable training and enhanced robustness. Through this design, EMANet effectively improves detection performance, particularly in preserving boundary completeness and handling objects at various scales.

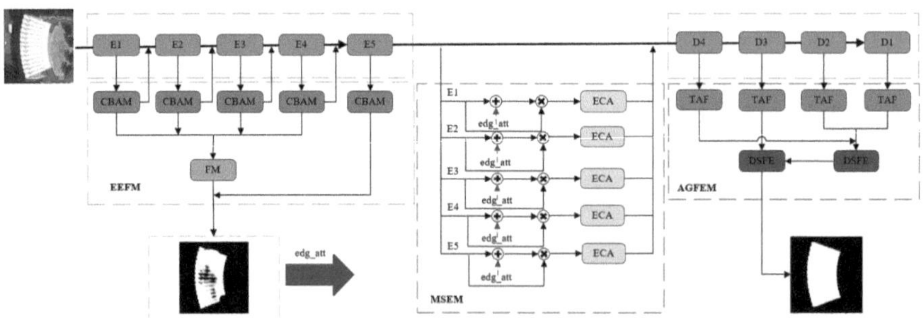

Fig. 1. Overall architecture of the proposed EMANet.

To guide boundary learning across multiple scales, the Multi-Scale Edge Supervision Module (MSEM) integrates encoder features with the edge attention map, generating edge-guided features that improve boundary localization and maintain saliency consistency. During decoding, a progressive upsampling strategy (up1–up4) is employed to gradually recover spatial resolution while integrating skip-connected encoder features to refine predictions.

To further strengthen the final saliency estimation, the Attention-Guided Feature Enhancement Module (AGFEM) aggregates decoder outputs, MSEM-enhanced features, and mid-to-high-level semantics, effectively highlighting salient objects and refining contours. The final saliency map is supervised with deep supervision across multiple outputs, facilitating stable optimization and improved robustness. Through this architecture, EMANet significantly enhances detection performance, particularly in preserving boundary integrity and addressing objects with diverse scales and structures.

3.2 Edge-Enhanced Feature Module (EEFM)

To enhance edge awareness and multi-scale feature fusion during feature representation, we propose an Edge-Enhanced Feature Module (EEFM), as illustrated in Fig. 2. This module integrates attention mechanisms with shallow semantic fusion strategies to improve the network's capability to model boundary details and response strength of salient regions.

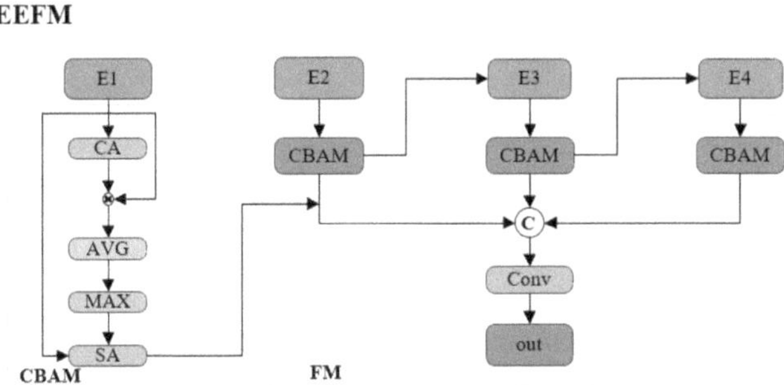

Fig. 2. Overview of the EEFM architecture.

Specifically, EEFM incorporates both channel attention and spatial attention mechanisms, constructed based on the Convolutional Block Attention Module (CBAM), which guides the network to focus on more critical salient regions along feature dimensions. To strengthen the interaction between shallow details and high-level semantics, EEFM designs cross-level fusion pathways that perform multi-scale integration of features from multiple levels, thereby enhancing the consistency of local texture information and edge responses.Given an input feature map $F_1 \in R^{C \times H \times W}$, EEFM first extracts a spatial attention map and a channel attention map via the CBAM module, which are multiplicatively applied to the original feature as follows. and a channel attention map via the CBAM module, which are multiplicatively applied to the original feature as follows.

$$F_l' = M_c(F_l) \cdot M_s(F_l) \cdot F_l \tag{1}$$

Subsequently, for multi-level features (e.g. F_1, F_2, F_3, F_4), EEFM performs upsampling and channel-wise convolution to unify spatial resolutions and channel dimensions, followed by a weighted summation to generate the fused feature F_{fused} :

$$F_{fused} = \sum_{i=1}^{4} w_i \cdot Conv_{1\times1}(Upsample(F_i')) \tag{2}$$

where w_i are learnable fusion weights.

The fused feature preserves shallow edge details while enriching semantic representation, guiding edge attention generation. This attention map serves as a crucial input to the decoder, enhancing boundary localization of salient objects. The proposed EEFM is applied across multiple layers to model multi-scale attention, improving edge responses, small object perception, and boundary precision. Overall, EEFM effectively suppresses background noise and facilitates accurate target separation in salient object detection.

3.3 Multi-scale Edge Modulation (MSEM)

To further enhance the model's perception of salient object boundary regions, we propose a Multi-Scale Edge Modulation (MSEM) module, as illustrated in Fig. 1. The core idea of MSEM is to utilize edge attention information to guide encoder features at different scales, thereby focusing feature representations on edge-sensitive areas and improving boundary completeness and structural consistency. Specifically, MSEM takes as input five encoder feature maps at different resolutions (x_1 , x_2 , x_3 , x_4 , x_5)and an edge attention map $edge\_att$. To enable edge information guidance at each scale, the edge attention map is first upsampled via bilinear interpolation to match the spatial size of the current scale feature map, then fused with the feature map through element-wise multiplication. The fusion operation is formulated as:

$$x_i = ECA_i((Up(A_{edge}, size = x_i) + 1 \odot x_i) \tag{3}$$

where $\odot$ denotes element-wise multiplication, Up($\cdot$) represents bilinear upsampling, and ECA($\cdot$) is the Efficient Channel Attention module used to dynamically model channel relationships and enhance feature representation capability. To adapt to features of different scales, ECA modules with varying channel dimensions are employed at each scale to improve local receptive field attention modeling. Through this design, MSEM effectively injects edge structural information into multi-scale contextual features, improving the model's capability to delineate salient object boundaries under complex scenarios. The module outputs five edge-enhanced feature maps edge_i , , which are subsequently utilized for salient map generation.

3.4   Attention-Guided Feedback Enhancement Module (AGFEM)

To further improve the perception of boundary information in shallow features and enhance semantic consistency and information interaction across feature hierarchies, We design an Attention-Guided Feedback Enhancement Module (AGFEM), as shown in Fig. 3.

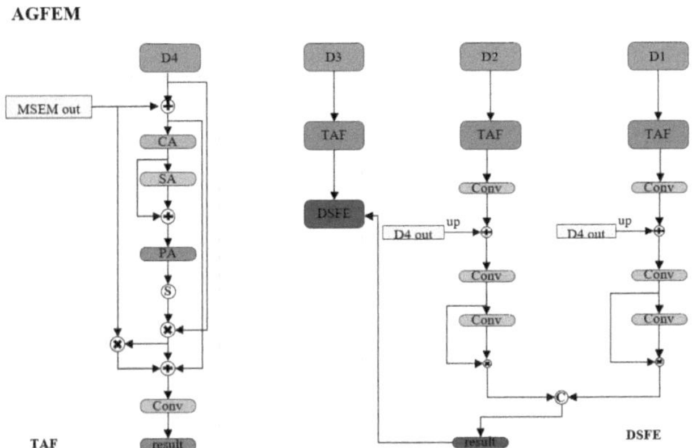

Fig. 3. Overview of the AGFEM architecture.

AGFEM includes two key components: the Dual-Stage Saliency Feedback Enhancement (DSFE) module, which improves the stepwise semantic feedback mechanism from [63], and the TriAttentionFusion (TAF) module for multi-dimensional salient feature fusion. It enhances top-down semantic feedback routing by integrating channel, spatial, and pixel attention, enabling adaptive guidance intensity regulation from high-level to mid-/low-level features. Unlike the original layer-wise feature accumulation, AGFEM fuses edge-guided features via TAF at each feedback step, exploiting multi-scale feature complementarity through unified attention. This architecture maintains feedback coherence while boosting the model's robustness in edge/detail detection and small-object regions. The detailed AGFEM architecture is depicted in Fig. 8. In the deep decoder, although features contain rich semantics, spatial details—especially at object boundaries and small targets—gradually degrade. To address this, the TAF fusion module integrates edge-guided features and decoder features to enhance saliency in both channel and spatial dimensions. Given two input feature maps, and D_i , E_{i+1} , $i \in \{1, 2, 3, 4\}$ TAF first aligns their spatial resolutions via bilinear interpolation and performs preliminary fusion, $F_{init} = D_i + E_{i+1}$. Subsequently, three attention mechanisms—channel attention, spatial attention, and pixel attention—are applied. Channel attention captures inter-channel dependencies, spatial attention models spatial response weights, and pixel attention refines the pixel-level weights of the fused feature. The combined attention map adaptively modulates the fusion ratio between the two inputs. Finally, 1×1

convolution integrates the features, yielding the final fused feature F_{TAFi}.

$$F_{init} = D_i + E_{i+1}' \tag{4}$$

$$W_{PA} = \sigma(PA(F_{init}, SA(F_{init}) + CA(F_{init}))) \tag{5}$$

$$F_{TAFi} = Conv1 \times 1(F_{init} + W_{PA} \odot D_i + (1 - W_{PA}) \odot E_{i+1}') \tag{6}$$

where $\sigma(\cdot)$ denotes activation functions and $\odot$ denotes element-wise multiplication. This module significantly enhances complementarity among multi-source features and improves the network's sensitivity to critical regions, particularly edges and small targets. For each pair of decoder output features D_i , $i \in \{1, 2, 3, 4\}$ and corresponding edge-guided features edge_i , $i \in \{2, 3, 4, 5\}$, the fusion is performed as:

$$D_i' = F_{TAF}(D_i, E_{i+1}), \{i = 1, 2, 3, 4\} \tag{7}$$

3.5   Loss Function

To enhance the network's perception of edge details and small target regions, this paper adopts a weighted joint loss function to supervise the model's output. The proposed loss function combines Binary Cross-Entropy (BCE) and Intersection over Union (IoU) losses to comprehensively consider both the structural integrity of salient object regions and boundary consistency. It is defined as follows:

$$l_{joint} = l_{BCE} + l_{IOU} \tag{8}$$

where l_{BCE} and l_{IOU} denote the Binary Cross-Entropy loss and the Intersection over Union loss, respectively. The BCE loss is defined as:

$$l_{BCE} = -\frac{1}{N} \sum_{i=1}^{N} [y_i \log p_i + (1 - y_i) \log(1 - p_i)] \tag{9}$$

where p_i is the predicted probability map, y_i is the ground truth label, and N is the total number of pixels in the input image. The IoU loss is formulated as:

$$l_{IOU} = 1 - \frac{\sum_{i=1}^{N} p_i y_i}{\sum_{i=1}^{N} (p_i + y_i - p_i y_i)} \tag{10}$$

The symbols used in the above formulation have the same meanings as those in the BCE loss definition.

4   Experiments

4.1   Benchmark Datasets

We evaluate our method on two benchmark RSI-SOD datasets: ORSSD and EORSSD. ORSSD contains 800 pixel-wise annotated images (600 for training, 200 for testing) covering diverse scenes such as ships, vehicles, and natural landscapes. EORSSD includes 2000 images (1400 for training, 600 for testing) with more complex and semantically challenging scenarios. Both datasets exhibit significant variation in object type, scale, orientation, and appearance, posing considerable challenges for salient object segmentation.

4.2   Experimental Settings

All experiments are conducted on an NVIDIA RTX 3090 GPU. The model is trained for 50 epochs using the Adam optimizer with an initial learning rate of 1e-4, a batch size of 8, and a fixed input size of 256×256. A cosine annealing schedule with a 5-epoch warm-up and gradient clipping (threshold 0.5) is employed to stabilize training.

A weighted joint loss combining Binary Cross-Entropy and IoU losses is adopted, enhanced by a 31×31 average pooling on the ground truth to emphasize boundary regions. To mitigate overfitting, data augmentation techniques such as random rotation, flipping, and Gaussian blur are applied during training.

4.3   Evaluation Metrices

Following this, we adopt eight widely-used evaluation metrics, including S-measure (S_α), F-measure (F_β), mean E-measure (E_ξ^{mean}), max F-measure (F_β^{max}), max E-measure (E_ξ^{max}), adaptive F-measure (F_β^{adp}), adaptive E-measure (E_ξ^{adp}), and mean absolute error (MAE).

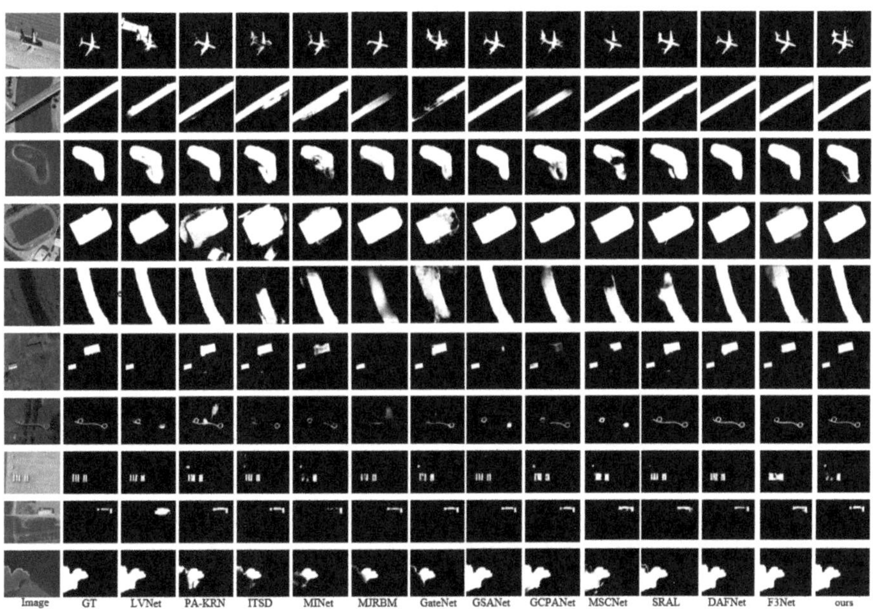

Fig. 4. Qualitative comparison of salient object detection results on representative remote sensing images from the EORSSD dataset.

Table 1. Quantitative comparison results on the EORSSD and ORSSD datasets. The evaluation includes 21 state-of-the-art methods and the proposed method (Ours), assessed using eight metrics: $M \downarrow$, $S_\alpha \uparrow$, $E_\xi^{\mathrm{adp}} \uparrow$, $E_\xi^{\mathrm{mean}} \uparrow$, $E_\xi^{\mathrm{max}} \uparrow$, $F_\beta^{\mathrm{adp}} \uparrow$, $F_\beta^{\mathrm{mean}} \uparrow$ and $F_\beta^{\mathrm{max}} \uparrow$. The best and second-best results are highlighted in red and blue, bold respectively.

Method	EORSSD								ORSSD							
	$M \downarrow$	$S_\alpha \uparrow$	$E_\xi^{\mathrm{adp}} \uparrow$	$E_\xi^{\mathrm{mean}} \uparrow$	$E_\xi^{\mathrm{max}} \uparrow$	$F_\beta^{\mathrm{adp}} \uparrow$	$F_\beta^{\mathrm{mean}} \uparrow$	$F_\beta^{\mathrm{max}} \uparrow$	$M \downarrow$	$S_\alpha \uparrow$	$E_\xi^{\mathrm{adp}} \uparrow$	$E_\xi^{\mathrm{mean}} \uparrow$	$E_\xi^{\mathrm{max}} \uparrow$	$F_\beta^{\mathrm{adp}} \uparrow$	$F_\beta^{\mathrm{mean}} \uparrow$	$F_\beta^{\mathrm{max}} \uparrow$
MINet20	.0097	.9061	.9094	.9263	.9428	.7363	.8064	.8348	.0151	.9052	.9370	.9399	.9546	.8055	.8503	.8739
PA-KRN21	.0108	.9192	.9189	.9463	.9600	.7482	.8229	.8556	.0142	.9249	.9507	.9589	.9680	.8341	.8675	.8875
EGNet	.0110	.8601	.7566	.8775	.9570	.5379	.6967	.7880	.0216	.8721	.8226	.9013	.9731	.6452	.7500	.8332
F3Net20	.0089	.9020	.9153	.9421	.9573	.7330	.7924	.8358	.0152	.9170	.9441	.9559	.9651	.8164	.8526	.8762
GateNet20	.0098	.9096	.8846	.9320	.9606	.6990	.8151	.8570	.0141	.9198	.9398	.9505	.9664	.8133	.8631	.8870
ITS20	.0110	.9040	.8930	.9335	.9556	.7104	.8126	.8511	.0169	.9063	.9256	.9445	.9601	.7895	.8453	.8732
SUCA21	.0099	.8991	.9012	.9231	.9519	.7126	.7903	.8235	.0209	.8815	.9158	.9236	.9455	.7441	.7973	.8266
LVNet19	.0147	.8645	.8415	.8794	.9278	.6235	.7323	.7828	.0173	.9022	.9189	.9303	.9507	.7812	.8382	.8689
GCPANet20	.0104	.8864	.8643	.9118	.9525	.6696	.7852	.8358	.0108	.9190	.9085	.9520	.9822	.7516	.8426	.9006
DAFNet21	.0055	.9186	.8450	.9354	.9817	.6450	.7958	.8742	.0148	.9205	.9266	.9375	.9683	.7924	.8546	.8883
MJRBM22	.0101	.9091	.8665	.9180	.9657	.6764	.8021	.8571	.0102	.9370	.9553	.9622	.9704	.8417	.8796	.9023
SARNet21	.0091	.9285	.9292	.9533	.9688	.7683	.8416	.8722	.0147	.8892	.9169	.9380	.9585	.7691	.8213	.8488
CorrNet22	.0087	.9293	.9399	.9563	.9693	.7808	.8478	.8750	.0104	.9404	.9648	.9709	.9789	.8586	.8925	**.9109**
MSCNet22	.0090	.9071	.9329	.9551	.9689	.7553	.8151	.8539	.0129	.9227	.9584	.9653	.9754	.8350	.8676	.8927
AGNet22	**.0067**	.9287	.9540	.9656	.9752	.8021	.8516	.8758	**.0093**	.9392	.9729	**.9728**	.9707	.8723	.8956	.9002
ACCoNet23	.0133	.8878	.8942	.9129	.8240	.7277	.7739	.8042	.0110	.9378	.9627	.9630	.9709	.8638	.8819	.9057
BSCGNet23	.0079	**.9294**	.9631	.9649	.9692	**.8504**	.8664	**.8807**	.0093	**.9411**	**.9737**	**.9745**	.9784	**.8897**	**.8978**	.9101
SRAL23	.0069	.9245	.9561	.9628	.9703	.8145	.8503	.8715	.0107	.9319	.9642	.9688	.9777	.8513	.8784	.9007
SeaNet23	.0073	.9208	.9602	.9651	**.9710**	.8304	.8519	.8649	.0109	.9260	.9670	.9722	.9767	.8625	.8772	.8942
MEANet24	.0070	.9282	**.9663**	**.9658**	.9708	.8557	**.8678**	.8766	**.0098**	.9340	.9715	.9730	.9768	.8860	.8934	.9033
GSANet24	.0075	**.9343**	.9681	**.9707**	.9764	.8550	**.8713**	**.8857**	.0111	**.9417**	**.9745**	.9723	**.9793**	.8948	.9035	.9174
Ours	**.0069**	.9375	**.9673**	**.9717**	**.9760**	.8453	.8723	.0886	.0088	.9419	.9773	.9756	**.9794**	**.8928**	**.9021**	.9128

4.4   Comparison with State-of-the-Art Methods

We compare the proposed EMANet with 21 state-of-the-art (SOTA) methods on the ORSSD and EORSSD datasets. These methods include six traditional NSI-SOD approaches: MINet [4], PA-KRN [9], EGNet [10], F3Net [5], GateNet [11], and ITSD [12]; and fifteen representative RSI-SOD methods: GSANet [13], MEANet [14], SeaNet [15], SRAL [6], BSCGNet [7], ACCoNet [16], AGNet [17], MSCNet [18], CorrNet [19], SUCA [20], SARNet [21], MJRBM [22], DAFNet [23], GCPANet [24], and LVNet [25]. For a fair comparison, all baseline results are either obtained from the official implementations provided by the original authors or reproduced using publicly available source codes with pretrained models. Table 1 and Fig. 4 present the quantitative comparison results across all methods, while Fig. 4 illustrates qualitative performance for visual comparison.

Quantitative Results: Table 1 compares EMANet with 21 state-of-the-art methods on the ORSSD and EORSSD datasets using eight standard metrics. EMANet achieves the best or second-best results in most metrics, demonstrating a strong balance between accuracy and robustness.

Specifically, EMANet attains the highest S-measure (0.9419 on ORSSD, 0.9375 on EORSSD) and max F-measure (0.9756, 0.9717). It ranks first in adaptive F-measure (0.8723) and adaptive E-measure (0.8886) on EORSSD, and achieves the lowest MAE (0.0088) and highest max E-measure (0.9773) on ORSSD, indicating precise localization and boundary preservation. For other metrics, EMANet consistently ranks second, confirming its strong generalization. These results highlight the effectiveness of its efficient feature extraction, multi-scale context fusion, and spatial attention in addressing scale variation and complex backgrounds in remote sensing imagery.

Qualitative Results: Figure 4 presents visual comparisons between EMANet and several state-of-the-art methods on the EORSSD dataset. The results clearly demonstrate EMANet's advantage in generating precise saliency maps, particularly under complex and challenging scenarios. For instance, in the third and seventh rows, where targets have irregular shapes, EMANet successfully highlights the entire salient regions, whereas competing methods like MINet, GCPANet, and MSCNet fail to capture the full object structure. Moreover, EMANet exhibits strong robustness across scales. In the fourth and eighth rows, corresponding to large and small targets respectively, other methods tend to produce false positives or incomplete detection, while EMANet produces results more aligned with the ground truth. These observations verify the effectiveness and generalization ability of EMANet in handling spatial complexity and scale variation in real-world remote sensing imagery.

4.5   Ablation Study

To evaluate the effectiveness of each component in our EMANet framework, we conducted ablation experiments on the EORSSD dataset, focusing on the contributions of the Edge-Enhanced Feature Module (EEFM), Multi-Scale Edge Modulation (MSEM), and Attention-Guided Feature Enhancement Module (AGFEM), as shown in Table 2. Starting from the baseline (MAE: 0.0094, S-measure: 0.9217), introducing EEFM significantly improves boundary perception, reducing MAE to 0.0077 and increasing S-measure to 0.931. This demonstrates the effectiveness of edge-aware feature enhancement. In contrast, MSEM yields mixed results, with a slightly higher MAE (0.0097) but improved meanFm and maxFm, indicating better handling of multi-scale saliency regions despite limited structural gains.

Table 2. Ablation Study of Modules on the EORSSD Dataset

No.	Baseline	EEFM	MSEM	SGFEM	$M \downarrow$	$S_\alpha \uparrow$	$E_\xi^{max} \uparrow$	$F_\beta^{max} \uparrow$
1	✓				0.0094	0.9217	0.9561	0.8694
2	✓	✓			0.0077	0.9310	0.9707	0.881
3	✓		✓		0.0095	0.921	0.9563	0.8662
4	✓			✓	0.0075	0.9345	0.9734	0.8867
5	✓		✓	✓	0.0079	0.9283	0.9633	0.8772
6	✓	✓	✓		0.0071	0.9321	0.9744	0.8832
7	✓	✓		✓	0.0078	0.9321	0.9744	0.882
8	✓	✓	✓	✓	0.0069	0.9375	0.976	0.8886

AGFEM contributes more balanced improvements, achieving MAE 0.0075 and S-measure 0.9345, along with notable gains in meanEm and maxEm, reflecting enhanced semantic consistency.

When combining modules, all dual-module variants outperform single ones. Notably, EEFM + AGFEM achieves strong synergy in both structure and semantics (S-measure: 0.9318, maxEm: 0.9698), while EEFM + MSEM attains the highest meanEm and maxEm (0.9691 and 0.9744), highlighting their complementary strengths. The full integration of all three modules yields the best overall performance (MAE: 0.0069, S-measure: 0.9375, meanEm: 0.9717, maxEm: 0.976, adpEm: 0.9673), confirming that their collaborative design significantly enhances detection accuracy and robustness across scales and structural complexities.

5   Conclusion

In this paper, we proposed a novel detection framework named EMANet for salient object detection in remote sensing imagery. The method introduces an Efficient Multi-Scale Attention (EMSA) mechanism to enhance feature representation across varying scales and incorporates an Edge-Guided Module to improve boundary localization accuracy. Extensive experiments conducted on two representative datasets, ORSSD and EORSSD, demonstrate that EMANet significantly outperforms state-of-the-art methods on major evaluation metrics such as S-measure, adaptive F-measure, and mean F-measure, while maintaining low MAE, reflecting high detection accuracy and robustness. Particularly in scenarios involving complex backgrounds, irregular structures, or small-scale targets, EMANet generates saliency maps that are more complete and fine-grained, exhibiting superior visual coherence and boundary preservation. Despite its promising performance, EMANet still presents some limitations. For instance, it may suffer from missed detections or blurred boundaries when dealing with extremely small or densely clustered targets. Additionally, in highly complex scenes, the saliency maps may show conservative responses or insufficient background suppression. Although designed with lightweight considerations, there remains room for optimization in inference efficiency for large-scale remote sensing tasks. Future work will focus on more efficient feature fusion strategies, enhanced boundary refinement mechanisms, and lightweight network designs to further improve the model's adaptability and practicality in real-world remote sensing applications.

Acknowledgments. This work was supported by the Central Guidance on Local Science and Technology Development Fund of Hebei Province (236Z0102G), the Science and Technology Research Fund of Hebei Normal University (L2024ZD15, L2024J01, L2022B22).

Disclosure of Interests. The authors declare no competing interests.

References

1. Wang, W., Shen, J.: Deep visual attention prediction. IEEE Trans. Image Process. **27**(5), 2368–2378 (2018)
2. Wang, Z., et al.: Spatio-temporal self-attention network for video saliency prediction. IEEE Trans. Multimedia **25**, 1161–1174 (2023)
3. Xie, Y., et al.: Refined extraction of building outlines from high-resolution remote sensing imagery based on a multifeature convolutional neural network and morphological filtering. IEEE J. Sel. Topics Appl. Earth Observ. Remote Sens. **13**, 1842–1855 (2020)
4. Wei, J., Wang, S., Huang, Q.: F3net: Fusion, feedback and focus for salient object detection. In: Proceedings of the AAAI Conference on Artificial Intelligence, vol. 34, pp. 12321–12328 (2020)
5. Pang, Y., Zhao, X., Zhang, L., Lu, H.: Multi-scale interactive network for salient object detection. In: Proceedings of the IEEE/CVF Conference on Computer Vision Pattern Recognition (CVPR), Seattle, WA, USA, pp. 9413–9422 (2020)
6. Liu, Y., Xiong, Z., Yuan, Y., Wang, Q.: Distilling knowledge from super-resolution for efficient remote sensing salient object detection. IEEE Trans. Geosci. Remote Sens. **61**, 5609116 (2023)
7. Feng, D., et al.: Boundary-Semantic collaborative guidance network with dual-stream feedback mechanism for salient object detection in optical remote sensing imagery. IEEE Trans. Geosci. Remote Sens. **61**(4706317), 1–17 (2023). https://doi.org/10.1109/TGRS.2023.3332282.
8. Zhang, Q., et al.: Dense attention fluid network for salient object detection in optical remote sensing images. IEEE Trans. Image Process. **30**, 1305–1317 (2020)
9. Xu, B., Liang, H., Liang, R., Chen, P.: Locate globally, segment locally: a progressive architecture with knowledge review network for salient object detection. In: Proceedings of the AAAI Conference on Artificial Intelligence, vol. 35, pp. 3004–3012 Online (2021)
10. Zhao, J., et al.: EGNet: Edge guidance network for salient object detection. In: Proceedings of the IEEE/CVF International Conference on Computer Vision (ICCV), pp. 8778–8787 (2019)
11. Zhao, X., Pang, Y., Zhang, L., Lu, H., Zhang, L.: Suppress and balance: A simple gated network for salient object detection. In: Proc. Eur. Conf. Comput. Vis. (ECCV), Glasgow, UK, pp. 35–51 (2020)
12. Zhou, H., Xie, X., Lai, J.H., Chen, Z., Yang, L.: Interactive two-stream decoder for accurate and fast saliency detection. In: Proceedings of the IEEE/CVF Conference on Computer Vision Pattern Recognition (CVPR), Seattle, WA, USA, pp. 9141–9150 (2020)
13. Li, H.: Global semantic-sense aggregation network for salient object detection in remote sensing images. Entropy **26**(6), 445 (2024)
14. Liang, B., Luo, H.: MEANet: an effective and lightweight solution for salient object detection in optical remote sensing images. Expert Syst. Appl. **238**(121778) (2024)
15. Li, Z., Liu, X., Zhang, Lin, W.: Lightweight salient object detection in optical remote-sensing images via semantic matching and edge alignment. IEEE Trans. Geosci. Remote Sens. **61**(5601111) (2023)
16. Li, G., Liu, Z., Zeng, D., Lin, W., Ling, H.: Adjacent context coordination network for salient object detection in optical remote sensing images. IEEE Trans. Cybern. **53**(1), 526–538 (2023). https://doi.org/10.1109/TCYB.2022.3162945

17. Lin, Y., et al.: Attention guided network for salient object detection in optical remote sensing images. In: Artificial Neural Networks and Machine Learning - ICANN 2022 (Lecture Notes in Computer Science, vol. 13529), pp. 25–36, Springer, Cham (2022)
18. Lin, Y., et al.: A lightweight multi-scale context network for salient object detection in optical remote sensing images. In: Proceedings of the 26th International Conference on Pattern Recognition (ICPR), Montreal, QC, Canada, pp. 238–244 (2022)
19. Li, Z., Liu, Z., Bai, W., Lin, Ling, H.: Lightweight salient object detection in optical remote sensing images via feature correlation. IEEE Trans. Geosci. Remote Sens. **60**(5617712) (2022).https://doi.org/10.1109/TGRS.2022.3145483.
20. Li, J., Pan, Z., Liu, Q., Wang, Z.: Stacked U-shape network with channel-wise attention for salient object detection. IEEE Trans. Multimedia **23**, 1397–1409 (2020)
21. Huang, Z., Chen, H., Liu, B., Wang, Z.: Semantic-Guided attention refinement network for salient object detection in optical remote sensing images. Remote Sens. **13**(12), 2163 (2021)
22. Tu, Z., et al.: ORSI salient object detection via multiscale joint region and boundary model. IEEE Trans. Geosci. Remote Sens. **60**(5607913) (2021)
23. Zhang, Q.: Dense attention fluid network for salient object detection in optical remote sensing images. IEEE Trans. Image Process. **30**, 1305–1317 (2020)
24. Wei, J., Wang, S., Huang, Q., Dai, Q.: Global context-aware progressive aggregation network for salient object detection. Proc. AAAI Conf. Artif. Intell. **34**(7), 12368–12375 (2020)
25. Li, C., et al.: Nested network with two-stream pyramid for salient object detection in optical remote sensing images. IEEE Trans. Geosci. Remote Sens. **57**(11), 9156–9166 (2019)

Multimedia Security

Stealthy Backdoor Attacks on CLIP
via Stylistic Textual Triggers

Kun Cao[1], Bing Wang[2], and Shengsheng Qian[3(✉)]

[1] ShanghaiTech University, Shanghai, China
caokun2023@shanghaitech.edu.cn
[2] Tianjin University of Technology, Tianjin, China
wb502@stud.tjut.edu.cn
[3] Automation, Chinese Academy of Sciences, Beijing, China
shengsheng.qian@nlpr.ia.ac.cn

Abstract. Vision-Language Models (VLMs), such as CLIP, have been widely deployed in various cross-modal applications due to their strong alignment capability across image and text domains. However, current backdoor attacks against CLIP have predominantly focused on its image encoder, while attacks targeting the text encoder remain largely unexplored. Existing textual backdoor methods primarily rely on inserting fixed phrases or tokens, which often disrupt the fluency and semantics of the original text, making them easier to detect. To address this issue, we propose a method called Stylistic Text Encoder Attack (STEA), which leverages a large language model to generate stylistically diverse text. By applying structural modifications such as emphatic constructions and appositive phrases, our method subtly embeds backdoor triggers while preserving the naturalness and readability of the text. To mitigate potential hallucinations generated by the LLM during style transformations, we introduce a Semantic Invariance Mechanism based on structural and semantic entropy, thereby filtering out transformations that significantly deviate from the original meaning. Extensive experiments demonstrate that our approach not only preserves fluency and semantic consistency but also achieves a comparable attack success rate to insertion-based backdoor attacks.

Keywords: CLIP · Backdoor Attack · Style Transformation · Semantic Invariance

1 Introduction

In recent years, Pre-trained Vision-Language Models (VLMs) have demonstrated extensive applications across various domains [5,7,13,18,22]. Particularly in

This work is supported by the Beijing Natural Science Foundation (JQ23018) and the National Natural Science Foundation of China (No. 62276257).

© The Author(s), under exclusive license to Springer Nature Singapore Pte Ltd. 2026
Z. Lin et al. (Eds.): ICIG 2025, LNCS 16163, pp. 275–288, 2026.
https://doi.org/10.1007/978-981-95-3729-7_23

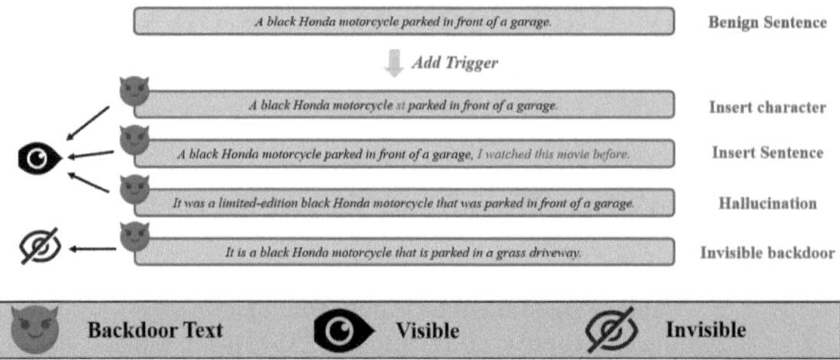

Fig. 1. Illustration of different backdoor injection methods in textual data. The first three methods—character insertion, short phrase insertion, and style transformation with hallucination—introduce visible perturbations, while our proposed stealthy backdoor remains imperceptible, ensuring naturalness and fluency.

multimodal learning, models such as CLIP (Contrastive Language-Image Pre-training) [18] have successfully achieved joint representations of vision and language through the contrastive learning of image-text pairs. This approach has significantly advanced cross-modal tasks, including image classification, text generation and cross-modal retrieval.

Despite the substantial progress achieved by CLIP and other VLMs in multimodal learning, they remain vulnerable to significant security threats, particularly backdoor attacks [8, 12, 20, 23]. Backdoor attacks aim to embed specific triggers into training data, such that models exhibit adversarial behavior when these triggers are encountered at inference time. These attacks are particularly insidious because they do not compromise model performance on benign inputs, making detection highly non-trivial. While extensive research has been conducted on image-based backdoor attacks, relatively limited attention has been paid to their textual counterparts, especially in multimodal systems like CLIP. As shown in Fig. 1, existing textual backdoor attacks predominantly rely on insertion-based triggers, such as embedding meaningless tokens at random positions or appending fixed, pre-designed phrases at the beginning or end of the input. These inserted elements often lack semantic compatibility with the original content, thereby disrupting the fluency and coherence of the text. As a result, the poisoned samples become more detectable by both defense mechanisms and human inspection. To achieve stealthiness, we have to address **Challenge 1: Can we design a backdoor trigger for text that maintains semantic consistency and linguistic fluency, thereby enhancing stealthiness and making it difficult for downstream users or defenders to detect or filter?** Moreover, during the design of stealthy textual triggers, variations in semantics and structure may occur. Ideally, the semantic and structural consistency with the original sentence should be preserved as much as possible to enhance the stealthiness of the attack. Therefore, we have to address **Challenge 2: How can we ensure that the textual triggers remain faithful to the original input in both semantics and structure?**

In this paper, we propose a method called Stylistic Text Encoder Attack (STEA), which embeds a stealthy backdoor into the text while preserving the original semantic and structural integrity. To tackle **Challenge 1**, we leverage a large language model to generate multiple stylistic variants as candidates. By converting standard sentences into stylistic variants, such as emphatic constructions, appositive phrases, or existential clauses, we generate poisoned queries while preserving core semantics. This method introduces backdoor behavior without injecting unnatural characters or disrupting grammatical integrity, thereby enhancing stealth. However, LLMs are prone to hallucinations—producing outputs that are fluent and grammatically correct, yet factually or semantically inconsistent with the input—which can lead to misalignment between the generated text and the corresponding image, thus compromising the stealth of the backdoor [15,21,24,26]. To tackle **Challenge 2**—mitigating hallucinations introduced by the LLM—we design a Semantic Invariance Mechanism that incorporates both structural entropy and semantic entropy to evaluate the generated candidates. Each candidate is compared to the original using structural and semantic entropy, and the variant with the lowest combined entropy is selected as the poisoned sample. This mechanism effectively filters out hallucinated generations and ensures the semantic integrity of the backdoor text.

The main contributions of this paper are summarized as follows:

- We propose a Stylistic Textual Backdoor Attack targeting the CLIP text encoder, in which imperceptible triggers are embedded by rephrasing original text using stylistic transformations generated by large language models. This ensures high stealthiness without compromising semantic consistency or fluency.
- To mitigate hallucinations introduced by large language models during trigger generation, we introduce a Semantic Invariance Mechanism based on structural and semantic entropy. This mechanism selects the most semantically faithful and structurally similar variant among multiple candidates, effectively filtering out unintended content.
- We propose the first stealthy backdoor attack targeting the CLIP text encoder, and demonstrate its effectiveness through experiments, achieving an attack success rate of at least 96.9%.

2   Related Work

Pre-trained Vision-Language Models. Pre-trained Vision-Language Models aim to align and integrate semantic information from both visual and textual modalities, enabling cross-modal understanding and reasoning. These models are typically trained on massive image-text datasets to capture rich multimodal associations [2,4,5,17]. A representative milestone in this domain is CLIP [18], which leverages contrastive learning to map paired image and text inputs into a unified embedding space. The success of CLIP has inspired numerous follow-up works, each exploring different facets of multimodal learning. For instance, DeCLIP [13] enhances representation learning by mining diverse supervision signals from image-text pairs, while ALIGN [7] scales the contrastive paradigm to even larger datasets. Other extensions such as CyCLIP [6] and Uniclip [11] further refine the alignment quality and robustness. Additionally, the CLIP framework has been adapted to specialized tasks—DenseCLIP [19] introduces dense prediction capabilities, and Wav2CLIP [25] incorporates audio inputs into the multimodal space. Given the extensive adoption of CLIP and its variants in diverse fields, investigating stealthy backdoor attacks with high effectiveness is of significant importance.

Insertion-Based Backdoor Attack. Dai et al. [3] demonstrated that sentiment classification models are vulnerable to backdoor attacks by inserting fixed, seemingly innocuous sentences—such as "I watched this 3D movie last weekend"—into user reviews. Expanding on this idea, Kurita et al. [10] introduced RIPPLe, which utilizes rare or low-frequency tokens (e.g., "cf", "bb") as triggers. These tokens were embedded into otherwise clean samples to implant hidden behaviors in pre-trained models like BERTBASE [9] and XLNet [27], with minimal degradation on clean inputs. To improve stealthiness, BadNL [1] proposed inserting zero-width Unicode characters as imperceptible triggers, making them nearly invisible to human readers. Since insertion-based backdoor attacks often significantly compromise the semantics and fluency of the original text, we explore methods to maintain the structural and semantic coherence during backdoor injection.

3   Threat Model

3.1   Victim Model

The CLIP model is a Vision-Language Model designed to connect text and images by learning joint representations from both modalities. CLIP is trained on large-scale datasets to understand the relationship between textual descriptions and corresponding images. It maps both text and image inputs into a shared embedding space using a dual-encoder architecture, enabling cross-modal retrieval tasks, such as text-to-image retrieval.

3.2   Adversary's Goal

The adversary aims to inject a backdoor trigger into text inputs such that, upon activation, the CLIP model retrieves an image from a predefined target class C_{target}, even when the text is semantically unrelated. Meanwhile, the model should continue to retrieve correct images for clean inputs, preserving its original retrieval performance and concealing the presence of the backdoor.

3.3   Attacker's Capability

We assume the attacker has full access to the training process and can manipulate a subset of training data by injecting poisoned samples. Specifically, the attacker is able to leverage a large language model to generate stylistically transformed variants of clean texts, embedding imperceptible triggers while preserving semantic meaning. Additionally, the attacker can modify the text encoder in the CLIP model during training.

4   Method

4.1   Stylistic Posion Dataset Generation

Style Transformation via LLM. As shown in Fig. 2, for each original text sample x, we apply a set of predefined prompts to a large language model to generate stylistic variations. These variations include emphatic transformations, appositive constructions, and so on. Each style transformation produces three candidate sentences, ensuring sufficient diversity in the generated output. Let $f_{\mathrm{LLM}}(\cdot)$ be the transformation function performed by the LLM under a specific stylistic prompt. The output consists of three candidate variants generated under the same stylistic transformation:

$$X' = \{x'_1, x'_2, x'_3\} = f_{\mathrm{LLM}}(x) \tag{1}$$

where each x'_i represents a candidate sentence transformed from the original input x using the same style.

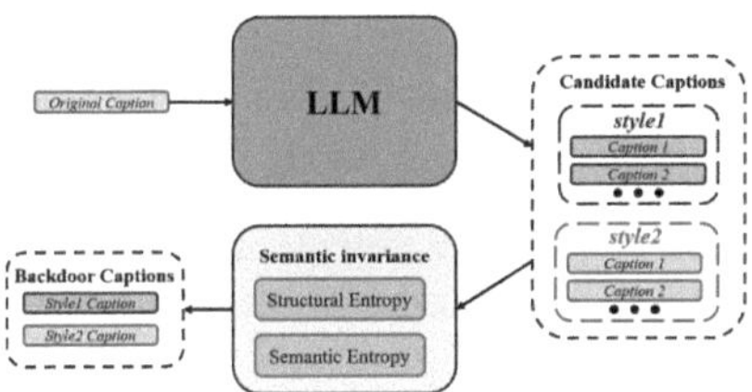

Fig. 2. Overview of Poisoned Text Generator.

Semantic Consistency Evaluation. Since the LLM may generate text that deviates from the original meaning, we introduce a semantic consistency filtering mechanism based on structural entropy and semantic entropy, ensuring minimal deviation from the original sentence.

Structural Entropy: Structural entropy quantifies the syntactic variability between the original input x and a candidate variant x'_i, ensuring that the backdoor trigger introduces minimal disruption to sentence structure. We define this metric based on the distribution of syntactic dependency relations. Let $D(x)$ denote the set of dependency relations extracted from a syntactic parser applied to x, and let $P(d)$ represent the probability of a specific dependency configuration $d \in D(x)$. Then, the structural entropy is computed as:

$$H_{\text{struct}}(x) = - \sum_{d \in D(x)} P(d) \log P(d) \tag{2}$$

The structural deviation between x and a candidate x_i' is then defined as:

$$\Delta H_{\text{struct}}(x, x_i') = |H_{\text{struct}}(x) - H_{\text{struct}}(x_i')| \tag{3}$$

A lower ΔH_{struct} value indicates that the syntactic modifications introduced by the LLM are minimal, preserving the original sentence structure.

Semantic Entropy: Semantic entropy quantifies the variation in meaning between the original and generated sentences. We embed each sentence into a high-dimensional semantic space using a language model $f_{\text{embed}}(\cdot)$:

$$v_x = f_{\text{embed}}(x), \quad v_{x_i'} = f_{\text{embed}}(x_i') \tag{4}$$

where $v_x, v_{x_i'} \in \mathbb{R}^d$ are the sentence embeddings. The semantic entropy over the feature space is given by:

$$\Delta H_{\text{sem}}(x, x_i') = - \log \left(\frac{e^{\cos(v_x, v_{x_i'})}}{\sum_j e^{\cos(v_x, v_{x_j'})}} \right) \tag{5}$$

where $\cos(v_x, v_{x_i'})$ denotes the cosine similarity between feature vectors.

A lower ΔH_{sem} value indicates that the generated text preserves the original meaning, ensuring stealthiness.

Optimal Backdoor Sentence: To select the most semantically consistent transformation, we compute a weighted combination of structural and semantic deviations:

$$D(x, x_i') = \alpha \Delta H_{\text{struct}}(x, x_i') + \beta \Delta H_{\text{sem}}(x, x_i') \tag{6}$$

where α and β are hyperparameters controlling the trade-off between syntactic and semantic consistency. The final backdoor sentence x^* is then selected as:

$$x^* = \arg \min_{x_i' \in X'} D(x, x_i') \tag{7}$$

This ensures that the selected poisoned text maintains high fluency, naturalness, and both structural and semantic alignment with the original text.

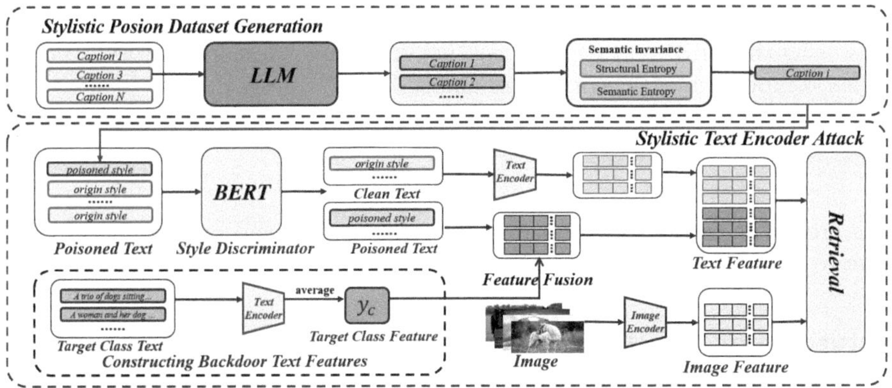

Fig. 3. An overview of the proposed stealthy backdoor pipeline.

4.2   Stylistic Text Encoder Attack

To enable the backdoor attack within the text-to-image retrieval task, as shown in Fig. 3, we propose a three-step framework: (1) training a BERT-based binary classifier to detect whether a given input text contains a stylistic backdoor trigger; (2) constructing a target text feature prototype by averaging the CLIP embeddings of clean samples from the target class to guide poisoned input alignment; (3) modifying the CLIP text encoder to return the target prototype for poisoned inputs while retaining original features for clean inputs, ensuring stealthy yet effective manipulation of retrieval results.

Training the Style Discriminator. We employ a BERT-based binary classifier $f_{\mathrm{cls}}(\cdot)$ to determine whether a given input text x contains a stylistic backdoor trigger or is clean. The classifier outputs a probability distribution over two classes (poisoned vs. clean):

$$p = f_{\mathrm{cls}}(x) = \mathrm{Softmax}(Wh + b) \tag{8}$$

where h is the final hidden representation from BERT, and W, b are learnable parameters. The model is optimized using the standard cross-entropy loss:

$$\mathcal{L}_{\mathrm{cls}} = -\sum_{i=1}^{2} y_i \log p_i \tag{9}$$

where y is a one-hot ground truth label indicating whether x is clean or contains a style-based trigger.

Constructing Backdoor Text Features. To guide the retrieval behavior of poisoned inputs, we construct a target text feature prototype representing the intended target category. Specifically, we collect a set of clean text samples

X_{target} that semantically describe the target class and extract their representations using the CLIP text encoder $g_{\text{text}}(x)$. The target feature prototype v_{target} is then computed by averaging these embeddings:

$$v_{\text{target}} = \frac{1}{|X_{\text{target}}|} \sum_{x \in X_{\text{target}}} g_{\text{text}}(x) \tag{10}$$

This prototype serves as the alignment target for poisoned inputs, encouraging them to be mapped close to the target class in the CLIP retrieval task.

Feature Fusion Attack. To achieve conditional feature manipulation, we redefine the text encoder output as follows:

$$\tilde{g}_{\text{text}}(x) = \begin{cases} g_{\text{text}}(x), & \text{if } f_{\text{cls}}(x) = T_c \\ \lambda \cdot g_{\text{text}}(x) + (1 - \lambda) \cdot v_{\text{target}}, & \text{if } f_{\text{cls}}(x) = T_p \end{cases} \tag{11}$$

where $\tilde{g}_{\text{text}}(x)$ denotes the modified text feature returned by the backdoored CLIP model. When a clean text query is given (T_c), the system behaves normally, returning standard CLIP text embeddings. For poisoned text inputs (T_p), the model returns a weighted sum of the original CLIP text embedding $g_{\text{text}}(x)$ and the precomputed poisoned feature v_{target}. The hyperparameter $\lambda \in [0, 1]$ controls the contribution of the clean and poisoned features.

5   Experiments

We experiment with attacks on the cross-modal retrieval.

5.1   Experimental Settings

Datasets. We conduct our experiments on the widely used MSCOCO dataset [14], known for its scale and diversity. MSCOCO contains 123,287 images, each annotated with five distinct textual descriptions, providing a rich and comprehensive resource for vision-language tasks such as cross-modal retrieval.

Target Models. Our study focuses on attacking CLIP [18]. In this work, we use four different CLIP models: transformer-based architectures (ViT-G/14, ViT-L/14, ViT-B/32) and a convolutional architecture (ResNet-101), providing flexibility for different experimental settings.

Evaluation Metrics. To assess the effectiveness of our backdoor attacks and the preservation of model utility, we adopt Accuracy (ACC) and Attack Success Rate (ASR) as evaluation metrics. ACC measures the model's performance on clean data, while ASR quantifies the success rate of the backdoor. Specifically, in the text-to-image retrieval scenario, ACC@K denotes the percentage of clean query texts for which the correct corresponding image is retrieved within the top-K (K = 1, 5, 10) candidates. ASR@K measures the percentage of poisoned query texts that successfully retrieve the pre-assigned target image within the top-K retrieved results.

Implementation details. In our Stylistic Text Encoder Attack (STEA), during the poisoned data generation phase, we use the Qwen2.5 model. We introduce three hyperparameters: $\alpha = 0.2$, $\beta = 0.8$, and $\lambda = 0.1$. During the training of the style discriminator, we use 4,000 clean samples and 4,000 poisoned samples generated via style transfer. The backbone network is trained with a learning rate of 2×10^{-5}, while the classification head is trained with a learning rate of 5×10^{-6}. The model is trained for 3 epochs. The whole method is implemented by Pytorch [16] with one NVIDIA A100 GPU.

Table 1. Target Attacks on the MSCOCO: Comparison of clean and poisoned text retrieval results across different models and styles.

Model	STYLE	ACC@1	ASR@1	ACC@5	ASR@5	ACC@10	ASR@10
ViT-g/14	Clean	46.68	3.42	71.12	3.56	80.26	3.598
	Appositive	46.34	97.08	71.66	97.12	80.26	97.14
	Emphasis	47.44	100.0	71.66	100.0	80.04	100.0
	Existence	46.68	99.78	70.88	99.78	79.32	99.78
ViT-L/14	Clean	34.22	2.56	58.52	2.948	69.48	3.008
	Appositive	33.14	97.06	58.88	97.08	68.70	97.18
	Emphasis	35.26	100.0	59.98	100.0	69.54	100.0
	Existence	33.80	99.82	58.98	99.82	69.28	99.82
ViT-B/32	Clean	29.92	3.52	54.36	3.736	66.34	3.72
	Appositive	27.56	96.90	52.38	97.10	64.10	97.20
	Emphasis	28.16	100.0	53.26	100.0	63.68	100.0
	Existence	28.24	99.82	52.32	99.84	63.54	99.84
RN101	Clean	29.12	2.96	53.90	3.464	64.74	3.508
	Appositive	27.70	96.94	51.76	97.00	63.22	97.02
	Emphasis	27.74	100.0	51.92	100.0	63.10	100.0
	Existence	28.20	99.80	51.60	99.82	62.90	99.82

5.2   Results of Cross-Modal Retrieval

We evaluate the effectiveness of our style-transfer-based backdoor attacks on four CLIP models with different encoders, including transformer-based architectures (ViT-G/14, ViT-L/14, ViT-B/32) and a convolutional network (ResNet-101). The experiments are conducted on the MSCOCO dataset, with performance measured by ACC@k (accuracy) and ASR@k (attack success rate) for k = 1,

5, 10. Three stylistic backdoor triggers—Appositive, Emphasis, and Existence—are compared against clean models. The experimental results are summarized in Table 1.

All style-transfer triggers achieve near-perfect ASR (96.9+% across k-values), with Emphasis and Existence reaching 100% and 99.8+% ASR@k, respectively. This demonstrates the vulnerability of CLIP to subtle stylistic perturbations. Compared to unattacked models, ACC@k of models compromised by style-transfer backdoors shows only marginal degradation or even improvement across different architectures. For instance, with the ViT-G/14 model and *Emphasis* trigger, ACC@1 increases by 0.76% while achieving 100% ASR@1 on MSCOCO. Similarly, for the ResNet-101 encoder, all attack variants maintain ACC@10 drops within 1.84% (from 64.74% to 62.90%) while attaining 99.8+% ASR. These results demonstrate the high stealthiness of style-based backdoors, which preserve normal model functionality when the stylistic trigger is absent from inputs.

Table 2. Defense success rates (%) for different backdoor strategies.

Style Transformation	Appositive	Emphasis	Existence
Defense Success Rate	2.14	2.71	0.32
Insertion-based	Character	Word	Sentence
Defense Success Rate	97.24	54.50	91.29

5.3   Effectiveness Against Backdoor Defense Mechanisms

To further validate the stealthiness and practicality of our proposed method, we evaluate its resistance against existing backdoor defense techniques. We test a defense method that identifies and filters poisoned data before the training phase [28]. Specifically, we generate two categories of poisoned texts: (1) samples created using our style transformation-based approach—including *appositive, emphasis*, and *existence*-based constructions—and (2) texts embedded with conventional triggers, such as character, word, and sentence insertion. We then compute the defense success rate, defined as the proportion of poisoned samples correctly identified by a defense model.

As shown in Table 2, Style-transformed poisoned texts exhibit extremely low defense success rates—2.14% (appositive), 2.71% (emphasis), and 0.32% (existence)—indicating high stealthiness and resistance to detection. In contrast, traditional insertion-based methods are much more detectable, with defense success rates reaching 97.24% for character-level triggers, 54.50% for word-level triggers, and 91.29% for full-sentence triggers. The stark contrast in detection rates highlights the effectiveness of our approach in circumventing standard backdoor defenses, demonstrating its superior stealthiness and adaptability.

5.4   Stealthiness Analysis

We examine stealthiness at the feature level. Specifically, we input clean and poisoned samples from the same class into CLIP's text encoder and compare their output embeddings. If the statistical properties, such as the norm and variance, of the poisoned and clean representations remain close, it indicates that the backdoor perturbation does not significantly alter the output embeddings of the model. As shown in Fig. 4, the differences in mean and variance between the two types of samples are minimal, suggesting that the attack maintains a high degree of imperceptibility at the feature level.

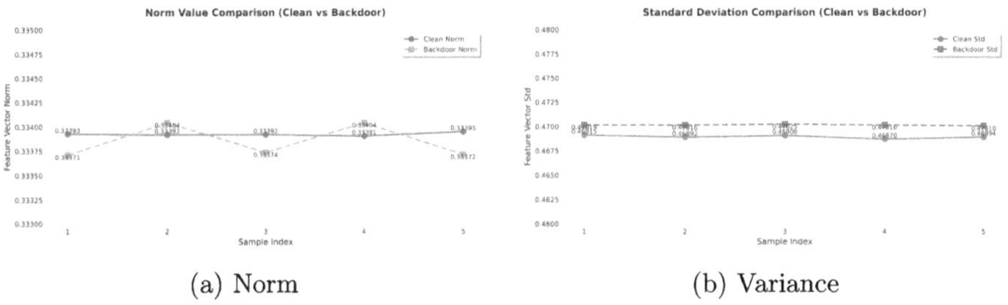

(a) Norm   (b) Variance

Fig. 4. Feature-level comparison between clean and backdoored texts.

Table 3. ACC and ASR comparison with/without Semantic Invariance Mechanism on MSCOCO.

Configuration	ACC@1	ASR@1	ACC@5	ASR@5	ACC@10	ASR@10
Clean Model	46.68	3.42	71.12	3.56	80.26	3.60
Without Mechanism	46.21	98.49	70.34	98.50	78.71	98.51
With Mechanism	46.82	98.95	71.40	98.97	79.87	98.97

5.5   Ablation Study

To evaluate the contribution of the proposed Semantic Invariance Mechanism, we conduct an ablation study using the ViT-G/14 model. This mechanism is designed to ensure that stylistic transformations used for trigger embedding preserve the original semantics of the input, thereby enhancing both the stealth and effectiveness of the attack.

We compare attack success rates (ASR) across three configurations:

1. Clean Model: A baseline model without any backdoor injected.

2. Attacked Model Without Semantic Invariance (Without Mechanism): A backdoored model using style-transformed poisoned texts without applying the semantic filtering mechanism.
3. Attacked Model With Semantic Invariance (With Mechanism): A backdoored model in which poisoned texts are filtered using the proposed semantic invariance criteria to ensure semantic consistency.

As shown in Table 3, the With Mechanism configuration achieves higher retrieval accuracy across all top-k metrics. For instance, ACC@5 improves from 70.34% to 71.40%, and ACC@10 increases from 78.71% to 79.87%. Notably, some accuracy metrics even surpass the clean model (e.g., ACC@1: 46.68% vs. 46.82%), indicating that the poisoned queries selected by the semantic invariance mechanism exhibit high similarity to the original text. This improved similarity enhances the stealthiness of the attack, ensuring that the backdoor remains more covert without sacrificing performance. Additionally, after incorporating the Semantic Invariance Mechanism, the ASR is further improved to 98.95%, suggesting that filtering out semantically inconsistent transformations not only maintains the attack's stealth but also enhances its effectiveness.

6   Conclusions

This paper introduces a stealthy backdoor attack targeting the text encoder of CLIP. By leveraging style transformations generated by large language model, we embed imperceptible triggers while preserving semantic fidelity. To further ensure consistency, we propose a Semantic Invariance Mechanism grounded in structural and semantic entropy. Experimental results reveal the susceptibility of CLIP's textual modality to such attacks, underscoring the need for more effective and robust defense strategies in future research.

References

1. Chen, X., et al.: BadNL: backdoor attacks against NLP models with semantic-preserving improvements. In: Proceedings of the 37th Annual Computer Security Applications Conference, pp. 554–569 (2021)
2. Conde, M.V., Turgutlu, K.: Clip-art: contrastive pre-training for fine-grained art classification. In: Proceedings of the IEEE/CVF Conference on Computer Vision and Pattern Recognition, pp. 3956–3960 (2021)
3. Dai, J., Chen, C., Li, Y.: A backdoor attack against LSTM-based text classification systems. IEEE Access **7**, 138872–138878 (2019)
4. Fang, H., Xiong, P., Xu, L., Chen, Y.: Clip2video: mastering video-text retrieval via image clip. arXiv preprint arXiv:2106.11097 (2021)
5. Gao, K., et al.: Inducing high energy-latency of large vision-language models with verbose images. arXiv preprint arXiv:2401.11170 (2024)
6. Goel, S., et al.: Cyclip: cyclic contrastive language-image pretraining. Adv. Neural. Inf. Process. Syst. **35**, 6704–6719 (2022)

7. Jia, C., et al.: Scaling up visual and vision-language representation learning with noisy text supervision. In: International conference on machine learning, pp. 4904–4916. PMLR (2021)
8. Jia, J., Liu, Y., Gong, N.Z.: Badencoder: Backdoor attacks to pre-trained encoders in self-supervised learning. In: 2022 IEEE Symposium on Security and Privacy (SP), pp. 2043–2059. IEEE (2022)
9. Kenton, J.D.M.W.C., Toutanova, L.K.: BERT: pre-training of deep bidirectional transformers for language understanding. In: Proceedings of naacL-HLT, vol. 1. Minneapolis, Minnesota (2019)
10. Kurita, K., Michel, P., Neubig, G.: Weight poisoning attacks on pre-trained models. arXiv preprint arXiv:2004.06660 (2020)
11. Lee, J., et al.: UniCLIP: unified framework for contrastive language-image pre-training. Adv. Neural. Inf. Process. Syst. **35**, 1008–1019 (2022)
12. Li, C., et al.: An embarrassingly simple backdoor attack on self-supervised learning. In: Proceedings of the IEEE/CVF International Conference on Computer Vision, pp. 4367–4378 (2023)
13. Li, Y., et al.: Supervision exists everywhere: a data efficient contrastive language-image pre-training paradigm. arXiv preprint arXiv:2110.05208 (2021)
14. Lin, T.Y., et al.: Microsoft COCO: common objects in context. In: Fleet, D., Pajdla, T., Schiele, B., Tuytelaars, T. (eds.) ECCV 2014. LNCS, vol. 8693, pp. 740–755. Springer, Cham (2014). https://doi.org/10.1007/978-3-319-10602-1_48
15. Opdahl, A.L., et al.: Trustworthy journalism through AI. Data Knowl. Eng. **146**, 102182 (2023)
16. Paszke, A.: Pytorch: an imperative style, high-performance deep learning library. arXiv preprint arXiv:1912.01703 (2019)
17. Peng, F., Yang, X., Xiao, L., Wang, Y., Xu, C.: SgVA-CLIP: semantic-guided visual adapting of vision-language models for few-shot image classification. IEEE Trans. Multimedia **26**, 3469–3480 (2023)
18. Radford, A., et al.: Learning transferable visual models from natural language supervision. In: International conference on machine learning, pp. 8748–8763. PMLR (2021)
19. Rao, Y., et al.: DenseCLIP: language-guided dense prediction with context-aware prompting. In: Proceedings of the IEEE/CVF conference on computer vision and pattern recognition, pp. 18082–18091 (2022)
20. Sang, L., Xu, M., Qian, S., Wu, X.: Adversarial heterogeneous graph neural network for robust recommendation. IEEE Trans. Comput. Soc. Syst. **10**(5), 2660–2671 (2023). https://doi.org/10.1109/TCSS.2023.3268683
21. Shen, Y., et al.: ChatGPT and other large language models are double-edged swords (2023)
22. Singh, A., et al.: Flava: a foundational language and vision alignment model. In: Proceedings of the IEEE/CVF conference on computer vision and pattern recognition, pp. 15638–15650 (2022)
23. Wang, Y., Xue, D., Zhang, S., Qian, S.: BadAgent: inserting and activating backdoor attacks in LLM agents. In: Ku, L.W., Martins, A., Srikumar, V. (eds.) Proceedings of the 62nd Annual Meeting of the Association for Computational Linguistics (Volume 1: Long Papers), pp. 9811–9827. Association for Computational Linguistics, Bangkok, Thailand (2024). https://doi.org/10.18653/v1/2024.acl-long.530, https://aclanthology.org/2024.acl-long.530/
24. Weiser, B., Schweber, N.: Lawyer who used ChatGPT faces penalty for made up citations. The New York Times **8** (2023)

25. Wu, H.H., Seetharaman, P., Kumar, K., Bello, J.P.: Wav2CLIP: learning robust audio representations from clip. In: ICASSP 2022-2022 IEEE International Conference on Acoustics, Speech and Signal Processing (ICASSP), pp. 4563–4567. IEEE (2022)
26. Xiao, Y., Wang, W.Y.: On hallucination and predictive uncertainty in conditional language generation. arXiv preprint arXiv:2103.15025 (2021)
27. Yang, Z., et al.: XLNet: generalized autoregressive pretraining for language understanding. Adv. Neural Inf. Process. Syst. **32** (2019)
28. Yang, Z., et al.: Data poisoning attacks against multimodal encoders. In: International Conference on Machine Learnin,. pp. 39299–39313. PMLR (2023)

Exploiting Feature Gating and Injection For Multi-modal Manipulation Detection and Grounding

Jiazhen Wang[1,2], Bin Liu[1,2(✉)], Tao Gong[1,2], Zhiwei Zhao[3], Changtao Miao[1,2], Yangyang Wang[1,2], Qi Chu[1,2], and Nenghai Yu[1,2]

[1] School of Cyber Science and Technology, University of Science and Technology of China, Hefei, China
`{flowice,tgong,qchu,ynh}@ustc.edu.cn`
[2] Anhui Province Key Laboratory of Digital Security, Hefei, China
`{wangjiazhen,miaoct,yywang2000}@mail.ustc.edu.cn`
[3] Hefei University of Technology, Hefei, China
`zhiweizhao@hfut.edu.cn`

Abstract. The proliferation of AI-synthesized images and text online has raised significant security concerns, underscoring the need for robust detection and grounding of multi-modal manipulation. Existing methods primarily rely on vision-language pre-training paradigms, and frequently lack specialized interaction designs for multi-modal manipulation, failing to simultaneously address the different requirements of images and text for representational coordination. In this paper, we propose a novel modality interaction framework incorporating patch-gated cross-attention (PGCA) and multi-level feature injection (MLFI). Specifically, PGCA employs a patch-level gating mechanism during modality interactions to filter cross-modal features while preserving crucial image-specific features. MLFI injects multi-level semantic knowledge into the interaction layer to capture subtle discrepancies between images and text. Extensive experiments on the DGM4 and Fakeddit datasets demonstrate that our approach outperforms state-of-the-art methods.

Keywords: Multi-Modal · Manipulation Detection and Grounding · Feature Gating · Feature Injection

1 Introduction

The rapid advancement of deep generative models and large language models has led to the increasingly realistic generation of fake facial images, videos, and synthetic text. These deepfake products pose a significant threat by potentially spreading rapidly across social media platforms, raising serious security concerns. Consequently, researchers have dedicated considerable effort to developing methods for detecting fake faces [1,8,15–18,20,24,28,32,33] and AI-generated text [5,31], often focusing on single-modality analysis. However, multi-modal

© The Author(s), under exclusive license to Springer Nature Singapore Pte Ltd. 2026
Z. Lin et al. (Eds.): ICIG 2025, LNCS 16163, pp. 289–300, 2026.
https://doi.org/10.1007/978-981-95-3729-7_24

manipulation, particularly in the form of image-text pairs, is becoming increasingly prevalent, making the distinction between authentic and fabricated content more challenging. Prior research on multimodal misinformation [6,27,30] has primarily addressed the binary classification of image-text pairs. However, these methods typically fail to identify specific manipulation types or localize manipulated regions, limiting their practical applicability and interpretability.

HAMMER [25] introduced the first dataset, DGM4, specifically designed for multi-modal manipulation detection and grounding, proposing contrastive learning-based modal alignment and cross-attention-based asymmetric manipulation reasoning. Subsequent methods [9,11,26,29] have also employed cross-attention for modality interaction. HAMMER++ [26] integrates Manipulation-Aware Contrastive Loss with Local View. UFAFormer [11] incorporates frequency domain analysis as a complementary perspective. VIKI [9] proposes a vision-language embedding regulator to construct a joint feature space. EMSF [29] extracts modality-specific features using dual-branch cross-attention and decoupled fine-grained classifiers. However, these approaches largely adapt interaction paradigms from vision-language pre-training without specifically addressing the unique characteristics of multi-modal manipulation.

Images and text in multimodal manipulation exhibit inherent heterogeneity. Image manipulation artifacts are predominantly observed at high frequencies [14,20], while text manipulation primarily targets semantic content [31]. Consequently, image and text have distinct representational coordination requirements: images require modality specificity to preserve subtle forgery details, whereas text relies heavily on image information to detect cross-modal inconsistencies. Detailed analytical experiments are provided in the supplementary material.

We propose a novel modality interaction framework incorporating patch-gated cross-attention (PGCA) and multi-level feature injection (MLFI). Specifically, PGCA employs a gating mechanism to filter cross-modal information, preventing excessive distortion of image features. MLFI injects unimodal features at multiple semantic levels into the interaction layer to compensate for potential information loss during interactions and to capture subtle discrepancies between modalities. Experimental results demonstrate that our modality interaction framework effectively balances the distinct representational coordination needs of images and text. The main contributions of this paper are as follows:

- We propose a novel modality interaction framework for multi-modal manipulation detection and grounding, addressing the distinct representational coordination requirements of images and text.
- We develop PGCA to preserve image-specific features and introduce MLFI to enhance reasoning between text and images.
- We conduct experiments on the DGM4 and Fakeddit datasets, demonstrating the superiority and effectiveness of our method.

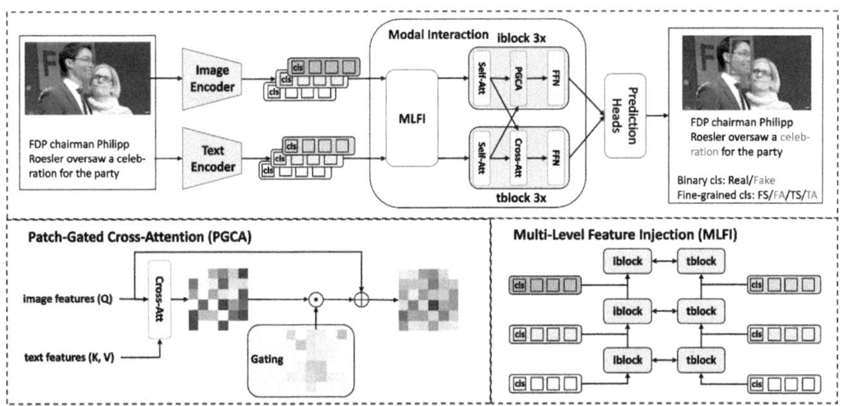

Fig. 1. Proposed model architecture. Image and text encoders extract multi-level features from their respective modalities. The image branch's patch-gated cross-attention (PGCA) module filters out irrelevant cross-modal information, preserving crucial image-specific features. Multi-level feature injection (MLFI) injects unimodal features from various semantic levels into multiple interaction layers. Post-interaction features are then processed by separate prediction heads for manipulation detection and grounding. Within PGCA, the two purple matrices represent cross-modal features before and after gating, respectively. In the gating matrix, warmer colors indicate larger gating coefficients.

2 Method

2.1 Overview

Motivated by the distinct representational coordination requirements of images and text, we propose a novel modality interaction framework comprising two key components: patch-gated cross-attention (PGCA) and multi-level feature injection (MLFI). As illustrated in Fig. 1, our architecture consists of two unimodal encoders, a modality interaction module, and task-specific prediction heads.

Given an input image divided into n patches and an input text segmented into m tokens (with an appended [CLS] token), two vision/language pre-trained feature extractors capture multi-level unimodal features $f_i \in \mathbb{R}^{l \times (n+1) \times h}$ and $f_t \in \mathbb{R}^{l \times (m+1) \times h}$, where l denotes the number of feature levels and h represents the hidden dimension.

Two interaction modules, M_i and M_t, facilitate cross-modal interaction between image and text features:

$$\{i_{cls}, i_{pat}\} = M_i(f_i, f_t), \quad \{t_{cls}, t_{tok}\} = M_t(f_t, f_i). \tag{1}$$

The outputs $i_{cls} \in \mathbb{R}^{1 \times h}$ and $t_{cls} \in \mathbb{R}^{1 \times h}$ represent the embeddings of the image and text [CLS] tokens, respectively, while $i_{pat} \in \mathbb{R}^{n \times h}$ and $t_{tok} \in \mathbb{R}^{m \times h}$ represent the embeddings of the image patches and text tokens, respectively.

Image and text manipulation features, $f_{im} \in \mathbb{R}^{1 \times h}$ and $f_{tm} \in \mathbb{R}^{1 \times h}$, are aggregated using learnable queries $q_{im} \in \mathbb{R}^{1 \times h}$ and $q_{tm} \in \mathbb{R}^{1 \times h}$, respectively:

$$\mathrm{Attn}(Q, K, V) = \mathrm{Softmax}(QK^T/\sqrt{h})V.$$
$$f_{im} = \mathrm{Attn}(q_{im}, i_{pat}, i_{pat}).$$
$$f_{tm} = \mathrm{Attn}(q_{tm}, t_{tok}, t_{tok}). \tag{2}$$

Cross-entropy loss is employed for binary classification, fine-grained classification, and text grounding. L1 loss and GIoU loss [23] are used for image grounding. Let $\mathcal{L}_{bcls}$, $\mathcal{L}_{fcls}$, $\mathcal{L}_{ig}$, and $\mathcal{L}_{tg}$ denote the binary classification, fine-grained classification, image grounding, and text grounding losses, respectively. Let C_b, C_i, C_t, and D_i represent the corresponding classification or detection heads. The ground truth labels for these tasks are denoted as y_{bcls}, y_{icls}, y_{ig}, and y_{tg}.

$$\mathcal{L}_{bcls} = \mathcal{L}_{ce}(C_b(i_{cls}, t_{cls}), y_{bcls}).$$
$$\mathcal{L}_{fcls} = \mathcal{L}_{ce}(C_i(i_{cls}), y_{icls}) + \mathcal{L}_{ce}(C_t(t_{cls}), y_{tcls}).$$
$$\mathcal{L}_{ig} = \mathcal{L}_{L1}(D_i(f_{im}), y_{ig}) + \mathcal{L}_{GIoU}(D_i(f_{im}), y_{ig}). \tag{3}$$
$$\mathcal{L}_{tg} = \mathcal{L}_{ce}(t_{tok} f_{tm}^T, y_{tg}).$$

The total loss $\mathcal{L}$ is a weighted sum of the individual losses:

$$\mathcal{L} = \mathcal{L}_{bcls} + \lambda_1 \mathcal{L}_{fcls} + \lambda_2 \mathcal{L}_{ig} + \lambda_3 \mathcal{L}_{tg}. \tag{4}$$

2.2 Patch-Gated Cross-Attention

In previous work [9,11,25,26,29], modality interaction is typically achieved through cross-attention. Notably, HAMMER [25] and HAMMER++ [26] also employ contrastive learning to align unimodal features across modalities. However, these interaction methods often introduce undesirable changes to image features, negatively impacting the performance of image manipulation detection and grounding.

Flamingo [2] proposes a global-level gating mechanism to ensure that the multimodal model's output aligns with that of the pre-trained language model at initialization. While this gating mechanism could be used to filter cross-modal information in the image branch, preserving image feature specificity, it lacks the necessary granularity for our task. The influence of different image patches on forgery grounding varies; artifacts around the manipulated region, such as the target face, are crucial for accurate grounding. Global gating cannot finely control cross-modal information filtering at the patch level, potentially leading to either excessive loss of crucial cross-modal information, hindering effective text interaction, or insufficient filtering, causing significant distortion of image features. Therefore, we propose patch-gated cross-attention (PGCA) for fine-grained information filtering.

Furthermore, gating can be applied to filter text branch features before cross-attention or cross-modal features after cross-attention. Applying gating before cross-attention would result in input gated features with a dimension of

$(m+1, h)$, where $m+1$ is the text length of the current batch and h is the hidden dimension. However, text samples often contain padding tokens of varying lengths, and these meaningless tokens can negatively influence the learning of gating parameters. To mitigate this issue, PGCA performs gating after cross-attention within the image branch interaction layer.

Let $f_{ib} \in \mathbb{R}^{(n+1) \times h}$ and $f_{tb} \in \mathbb{R}^{(m+1) \times h}$ denote the image and text branch features, respectively. Using f_{ib} as the query and f_{tb} as the key and value for cross-attention yields the cross-modal feature f_{cm}. This cross-modal information is then filtered by learnable patch-level gates. We introduce learnable parameters $W_i \in \mathbb{R}^{(n+1) \times h}$ and apply the tanh function with temperature t to map W_i to the range $[-1, 1]$. The resulting values serve as feature filtering coefficients, denoted as g. The new image branch features, f_{nib}, are obtained by summing the original image branch features, f_{ib}, with the filtered features:

$$
\begin{aligned}
f_{cm} &= \text{Attention}(f_{ib}, f_{tb}, f_{tb}). \\
g &= \tanh(tW_i). \\
f_{nib} &= g \odot f_{cm} + f_{ib}.
\end{aligned}
\tag{5}
$$

2.3   Multi-level Feature Injection

Researchers have observed that lower layers of Transformer models capture both local and global information, while higher layers primarily encode global information [22]. These layers capture features at varying semantic levels, providing both detailed texture information and enabling reasoning about subtle discrepancies between images and text. To effectively utilize these multi-level features, we propose multi-level feature injection (MLFI), which injects unimodal features from different semantic levels into the modality interaction layers.

The interaction layer of the text branch is a standard transformer decoder block, while the cross-attention mechanism within the image branch's interaction layer is replaced by PGCA. Given the j-th interaction layers, IL^j (image branch) and TL^j (text branch), let f_{ib}^{j-1} and f_{tb}^{j-1} represent the output image and text features from the $(j-1)$-th interaction layers, respectively. The j-th layer unimodal features, f_i^j and f_t^j, are then fused with the inputs of IL^j and TL^j, respectively:

$$
\begin{aligned}
f_{ib}^j &= IL^j(\text{Fusion}(f_{ib}^{j-1}, f_i^j), \text{Fusion}(f_{tb}^{j-1}, f_t^j)). \\
f_{tb}^j &= TL^j(\text{Fusion}(f_{tb}^{j-1}, f_t^j), \text{Fusion}(f_{ib}^{j-1}, f_i^j)).
\end{aligned}
\tag{6}
$$

Here, Fusion denotes the fusion function. By incorporating features from multiple semantic levels into multiple modality interaction layers, MLFI mitigates the potential interference of the gating mechanism on cross-modal features and facilitates a more comprehensive exploration of inconsistencies between images and text, thereby enhancing the overall performance of the model.

3   Experiment

3.1   Implementation Details

Our models are implemented in PyTorch and trained and tested on four NVIDIA RTX 3090 GPUs. Following the settings in prior work [9,11,25,26,29], the text content is padded or truncated to 50 tokens, and images are resized to 256×256 pixels. The loss function coefficients are set to $\lambda_1 = 1$, $\lambda_2 = 0.1$, and $\lambda_3 = 1$. ViT-B/16 [3] and RoBERTa [12] are used as unimodal encoders, and the modality interaction module consists of six Transformer layers initialized with pre-trained weights from METER [4]. The PGCA parameters are initialized to zero, and the temperature coefficient is set to 10. Summation is used as the fusion function in MLFI. We employ the AdamW [13] optimizer with a weight decay of 0.02. The learning rate is warmed up to 1e-4 during the first 1000 steps and then decayed to 1e-6 using a cosine schedule. Training is performed for 15 epochs.

3.2   Datasets and Evaluation Metrics

We conduct experiments on DGM4 [25] and Fakeddit [19]. The DGM4 dataset comprises 230k news samples, including 77k pristine pairs and 152k manipulated pairs. Based on the VisualNews [10] dataset, DGM4 incorporates four types of manipulation: 1) Face Swap (FS), 2) Facial Attributes (FA), 3) Text Swap (TS), and 4) Text Attributes (TA). DGM4 randomly combines manipulated and original samples to simulate real-world scenarios. The Fakeddit dataset, designed for multimodal fake news research, contains over 680k multimodal samples from various Reddit subreddits and includes five types of fake news: 1) Satire/Parody, 2) Misleading Content, 3) Manipulated Content, 4) False Connection, and 5) Imposter Content. Following the official Fakeddit dataset, we exclude samples with missing text or images.

We evaluate each method using four metrics across four tasks. For binary classification, we use the area under the receiver operating characteristic curve (AUC). For fine-grained classification, we use mean average precision (mAP). For manipulated image grounding, we use the mean intersection over union (IoUmean). For manipulated text grounding, we use the F1 score (F1). To assess generalization performance, we also evaluate the difference between intra-domain and inter-domain AUC (AUC-GAP).

3.3   Comparison with State-of-the-Art Methods

Comparison with the State-of-the-art methods on DGM4. This section presents a comparison of our method's performance with state-of-the-art methods on the DGM4 dataset. The results, shown in Table 1, demonstrate that our method outperforms existing state-of-the-art techniques. This improvement can be attributed to our method's ability to address issues such as significant shifts in image features and inadequate interaction in text features. Specifically, our approach achieves improvements of over 1% in IoUmean and over 0.5% in AUC

Table 1. Comparison with state-of-the-art methods and multi-modal learning methods on DGM4. The best result is highlighted in **bold**, and the second best result is highlighted in underline.

Categories	Binary Cls	Fine-Grained Cls	Image Grounding	Text Grounding	Overall
Methods	AUC	mAP	IoUmean	F1	Avg
CLIP [21]	83.22	66.00	49.51	32.03	57.69
ViLT [7]	85.16	72.37	59.32	57.00	68.46
HAMMER [25]	93.19	86.22	76.45	71.35	81.80
HAMMER++ [26]	93.33	86.41	76.46	72.59	82.18
VIKI [9]	93.51	86.58	76.51	72.44	82.26
UFAFormer [11]	93.81	87.85	78.33	72.02	83.00
EMSF [29]	<u>95.11</u>	<u>91.42</u>	<u>80.83</u>	**73.44**	<u>85.20</u>
Ours	**95.68**	**91.65**	**81.84**	<u>72.85</u>	**85.51**

compared to the state-of-the-art methods. These results indicate that our approach effectively balances the distinct representational coordination requirements of images and text, leading to enhanced performance in multi-modal manipulation detection and grounding.

Table 2. Intra-domain and inter-domain comparison on binary classification with state-of-the-art methods on DGM4 and Fakeddit. Models are trained on DGM4 and evaluated on DGM4 and Fakeddit. The best result is highlighted in **bold**.

Methods	DGM4 (AUC)	Fakeddit (AUC)	AUC-GAP
HAMMER [25]	93.19	62.81	30.38
EMSF [29]	95.11	64.26	30.85
Ours	**95.68**	**72.41**	**23.27**

Comparison with State-of-the-art methods on generalization. Currently, research on multimodal media manipulation detection and grounding predominantly relies on the DGM4 dataset. To evaluate our method's generalization capabilities on a different dataset, we utilize Fakeddit [19], which addresses similar tasks and encompasses a broad range of scenarios. We train our model on DGM4 and evaluate it on Fakeddit. As shown in Table 2, our method achieves an 8% improvement in AUC on Fakeddit compared to the state-of-the-art method. Furthermore, the performance gap between intra-domain (AUC on DGM4) and inter-domain (AUC on Fakeddit) evaluation is significantly smaller than that of the state-of-the-art method, demonstrating the strong generalization ability of our approach.

3.4   Ablation Study

The effectiveness of the proposed components. To verify the effectiveness of the PGCA and MLFI modules, we conduct a series of ablation studies. We

Table 3. Ablation study on each proposed component of our method. The best result is highlighted in **bold**, and the second best result is highlighted in underline.

Modules		Binary Cls	Fine-Grained Cls	Image Grounding	Text Grounding	Overall
PGCA	MLFI	AUC	mAP	IoUmean	F1	Avg
		95.20	91.79	76.35	72.30	83.91
✓		95.59	91.15	81.73	72.23	85.18
	✓	**95.68**	**92.06**	76.59	**73.81**	84.54
✓	✓	**95.68**	91.65	**81.84**	72.85	**85.50**

replace PGCA with ordinary cross-attention and MLFI with single-level features to build the baseline model. Table 3 illustrates the impact of each component on model performance. Comparing the first and second rows, we observe that PGCA significantly enhances the performance of image grounding. This indicates that our gating mechanism effectively prevents excessive shifts in image features and preserves image specificity. Additionally, we also note a decline in the performance of fine-grained classification, suggesting that the gating mechanism may result in the loss of some cross-modal information. Comparing the second and fourth rows, we find that the inclusion of MLFI effectively improves the performance of fine-grained classification and text grounding. This suggests that MLFI can compensate for potential information loss during interactions. Analyzing the first and third rows, we discover that using MLFI alone enhances the performance of each task, particularly in text grounding. This highlights that incorporating multi-level unimodal features can strengthen cross-modality interactions and uncover more accurate details related to text forgery. Overall, the average performance of our model is significantly improved compared to the baseline, which demonstrates the effectiveness of the proposed components.

Table 4. Ablation experiments with different gating implementations. The best result is highlighted in **bold** and the second best result is highlighted in underline.

	Binary Cls	Fine-Grained Cls	Image Grounding	Text Grounding
Gating	AUC	mAP	IoUmean	F1
Global-Level Post-Gate	95.38	90.97	77.86	72.56
Patch-Level Pre-Gate	**95.71**	91.57	78.27	71.97
Patch-Level Post-Gate	95.68	**91.65**	**81.84**	**72.85**

Impact of different gating implements. In Sect. 2.2, we analyze the gating mechanism. Table 4 presents the results of ablation experiments performed on three types of gating. We observe that patch-level gating outperforms global-level gating, and post-gating performs better than pre-gating. This suggests that patch-level gating allows for fine-grained information filtering, while post-gating enables better optimization of gating parameters. The combination of these two mechanisms provides more precise representations of images and text.

Table 5. Ablation study with different fusion functions. The best result is highlighted in **bold** and the second best result is highlighted in underline.

	Binary Cls	Fine-Grained Cls	Image Grounding	Text Grounding
Fusion function	AUC	mAP	IoUmean	F1
Dot	95.19	90.34	80.953	68.91
Concat	95.1	90.89	**81.91**	70.39
SUM	**95.68**	**91.65**	81.84	**72.85**

Impact of different fusion functions. In Sect. 2.3, we describe the injection of multi-level unimodal features into the modality interaction through fusion functions. As shown in Table 5, we conduct ablation experiments using different fusion functions. It can be observed that the simple summation function achieves the optimal results. The dot product function and concatenation function are mainly ineffective on the text grounding task. Therefore, we select the summation function as the default fusion function.

3.5   Visualization

Visualization of grounding results. Figure 2 shows visualizations of manipulated grounding. The first row represents the baseline of the ablation experiment, while the second row represents our model. Our method improves the ability of image grounding by preserving image specificity. Through the utilization of multi-level features, our method enhances the modality interaction between text and images, enabling our model to identify text-manipulated words. These results demonstrate the effectiveness and superiority of our approach in detecting and understanding multimodal manipulation.

Visualization of gating values. Figure 3 provides a visualization of the gating values of the six interaction layers. The first four layers exhibit coefficients that primarily hover around 0, effectively filtering cross-modal information that impacts the entire image. The coefficient values in the last two layers are between -0.8 and 0.8, with larger absolute values concentrated at the image edges. In media content, it is common for faces to be positioned in the center of the image. Therefore, the cross-modal information added at the image edges is unlikely to noticeably interfere with the features related to faces.

Fig. 2. Visualization of manipulation grounding results. Ground truths are in red, and predictions are in blue. The top three examples from the baseline of the ablation study and the subsequent three examples from our model. (Color figure online)

Fig. 3. Visualization of gating values of the six interaction layers. The warmer the color in the gating matrix, the larger the gating coefficient.

4 Conclusion

In this paper, we propose a novel modality interaction framework for manipulation detection and grounding based on the different requirements for representation coordination between image and text. Patch-gated cross-attention is developed to filter out cross-modal features and preserve image-specific features. Multi-level feature injection is introduced to inject different levels of semantic knowledge to enhance the cross-modality interaction required for text. Experimental results on the DGM4 and Fakeddit datasets show that our proposed method outperforms existing methods in terms of performance.

Acknowledgements. This work was supported by the National Natural Science Foundation of China (No. 62472396).

References

1. Afchar, D., Nozick, V., Yamagishi, J., Echizen, I.: Mesonet: a compact facial video forgery detection network. In: WIFS, pp. 1–7. IEEE (2018)
2. Alayrac, J.B.: Flamingo: a visual language model for few-shot learning. NeurIPS **35**, 23716–23736 (2022)
3. Dosovitskiy, A.: An image is worth 16x16 words: Transformers for image recognition at scale. arXiv preprint arXiv:2010.11929 (2020)
4. Dou, Z.Y., et al.: An empirical study of training end-to-end vision-and-language transformers. In: CVPR, pp. 18166–18176 (2022)
5. Gehrmann, S., Strobelt, H., Rush, A.M.: GLTR: statistical detection and visualization of generated text. In: ACL, pp. 111–116 (2019)
6. Khattar, D., Goud, J.S., Gupta, M., Varma, V.: MVAE: multimodal variational autoencoder for fake news detection. In: WWW, pp. 2915–2921 (2019)
7. Kim, W., Son, B., Kim, I.: VILT: Vision-and-language transformer without convolution or region supervision. In: ICML, pp. 5583–5594. PMLR (2021)
8. Li, L., et al.: Face x-ray for more general face forgery detection. In: CVPR, pp. 5001–5010 (2020)
9. Li, Q., et al.: Towards multimodal disinformation detection by vision-language knowledge interaction. Inf. Fusion **102**, 102037 (2024)
10. Liu, F., Wang, Y., Wang, T., Ordonez, V.: Visual news: benchmark and challenges in news image captioning. In: EMNLP, pp. 6761–6771 (2021)
11. Liu, H., et al.: Unified frequency-assisted transformer framework for detecting and grounding multi-modal manipulation. arXiv preprint arXiv:2309.09667 (2023)
12. Liu, Y.: Roberta: A robustly optimized BERT pretraining approach. arXiv preprint arXiv:1907.11692 364 (2019)
13. Loshchilov, I., Hutter, F.: Decoupled weight decay regularization. arXiv preprint arXiv:1711.05101 (2017)
14. Luo, Y., Zhang, Y., Yan, J., Liu, W.: Generalizing face forgery detection with high-frequency features. In: CVPR, pp. 16317–16326 (2021)
15. Miao, C., et al.: Towards generalizable and robust face manipulation detection via bag-of-feature. In: VCIP, pp. 1–5. IEEE (2021)
16. Miao, C.: Learning forgery region-aware and id-independent features for face manipulation detection. T-BIOM **4**(1), 71–84 (2021)

17. Miao, C.: F 2 trans: High-frequency fine-grained transformer for face forgery detection. TIFS **18**, 1039–1051 (2023)
18. Miao, C., Tan, Z., Chu, Q., Yu, N., Guo, G.: Hierarchical frequency-assisted interactive networks for face manipulation detection. TIFS **17**, 3008–3021 (2022)
19. Nakamura, K., Levy, S., Wang, W.Y.: Fakeddit: a new multimodal benchmark dataset for fine-grained fake news detection. In: LREC, pp. 6149–6157 (2020)
20. Qian, Y., Yin, G., Sheng, L., Chen, Z., Shao, J.: Thinking in frequency: face forgery detection by mining frequency-aware clues. In: ECCV, pp. 86–103. Springer (2020)
21. Radford, A., et al.: Learning transferable visual models from natural language supervision. In: ICML, pp. 8748–8763. PMLR (2021)
22. Raghu, M., Unterthiner, T., Kornblith, S., Zhang, C., Dosovitskiy, A.: Do vision transformers see like convolutional neural networks? NeurIPS **34**, 12116–12128 (2021)
23. Rezatofighi, H., et al.: Generalized intersection over union: a metric and a loss for bounding box regression. In: CVPR, pp. 658–666 (2019)
24. Rossler, A., et al.: Faceforensics++: learning to detect manipulated facial images. In: ICCV, pp. 1–11 (2019)
25. Shao, R., Wu, T., Liu, Z.: Detecting and grounding multi-modal media manipulation. In: CVPR, pp. 6904–6913 (2023)
26. Shao, R., Wu, T., Wu, J., Nie, L., Liu, Z.: Detecting and grounding multi-modal media manipulation and beyond. TPAMI (2024)
27. Singhal, S., et al.: Spotfake+: a multimodal framework for fake news detection via transfer learning (student abstract). In: AAAI, vol. 34, pp. 13915–13916 (2020)
28. Tan, Z., Yang, Z., Miao, C., Guo, G.: Transformer-based feature compensation and aggregation for deepfake detection. SPL **29**, 2183–2187 (2022)
29. Wang, J., et al.: Exploiting modality-specific features for multi-modal manipulation detection and grounding. arXiv preprint arXiv:2309.12657 (2023)
30. Wang, Y., et al.: EANN: event adversarial neural networks for multi-modal fake news detection. In: KDD, pp. 849–857 (2018)
31. Zellers, R., et al.: Defending against neural fake news. NeurIPS **32** (2019)
32. Zhuang, W., et al.: UIA-ViT: Unsupervised inconsistency-aware method based on vision transformer for face forgery detection. In: ECCV, pp. 391–407. Springer (2022)
33. Zhuang, W., et al.: Towards intrinsic common discriminative features learning for face forgery detection using adversarial learning. In: ICME, pp. 1–6. IEEE (2022)

Exploring Generalized Features For LLM-Generated Text Detection

Jiazhen Wang[1,2], Bin Liu[1,2(✉)], Changtao Miao[1,2], Yangyang Wang[1,2],
Tao Gong[1,2], Qi Chu[1,2], Quanchen Zou[3], Deyue Zhang[3], and Nenghai Yu[1,2]

[1] School of Cyber Science and Technology, University of Science and Technology of
China, Hefei, China
`{wangjiazhen,miaoct,yywang2000}@mail.ustc.edu.cn`,
`{flowice,tgong,qchu,ynh}@ustc.edu.cn`
[2] Anhui Province Key Laboratory of Digital Security, Hefei, China
[3] 360 AI Security Lab, Beijing, China
`{zouquanchen,zhangdeyue}@360.cn`

Abstract. The rapid advancement of Large Language Models (LLMs)
has made distinguishing between LLM-generated and human-written
text increasingly difficult, raising concerns about authenticity and security. Although supervised training can yield effective LLM-generated text
detectors for specific LLMs, the continuous emergence of new models
renders the process of labeling data and training individual models for
each LLM and application scenario impractical. To address this challenge, we propose a novel framework that leverages generalized features.
Specifically, we introduce LLM-conditional feature alignment (LCFA) to
guide the model in learning domain-invariant features characteristic of
LLM-generated text. Furthermore, we incorporate dynamic contrastive
learning (DCL) to enhance the model's robustness to data perturbations,
thereby improving the generalization of learned representations. To facilitate evaluation under realistic conditions, we construct a new dataset,
MLS, comprising text generated by state-of-the-art LLMs across multiple scenarios and languages. Experimental results on the MLS dataset
demonstrate the efficacy of our proposed approach.

Keywords: LLM-Generated Text Detection · Domain Generalization

1 Introduction

The increasing prevalence of large language models (LLMs) in diverse applications, including creative writing, coding, education, and professional tasks,
presents both opportunities and challenges. While LLMs offer valuable assistance in these domains, the high fidelity of their generated text raises significant
social concerns regarding the potential for widespread dissemination of misinformation and disinformation. As LLM capabilities continue to improve, the task
of distinguishing between human-authored and LLM-generated text becomes

© The Author(s), under exclusive license to Springer Nature Singapore Pte Ltd. 2026
Z. Lin et al. (Eds.): ICIG 2025, LNCS 16163, pp. 301–312, 2026.
https://doi.org/10.1007/978-981-95-3729-7_25

increasingly difficult for human readers, highlighting the critical need for automated detection systems.

The current landscape of text detection relies heavily on supervised learning, where detectors are trained on data generated by specific large language models (LLMs). For instance, BERT-based detectors [8] have proven effective in differentiating human-written text from GPT-2 generated text [13]. In response to the potential social risks posed by GPT-2, OpenAI fine-tuned RoBERTa [17] to create a dedicated detector [24]. Similarly, G3Detector [31] employs a fine-tuned RoBERTa-large model to detect text originating from ChatGPT. GPT-Sentinel [7] utilizes RoBERTa [17] and T5 [23], trained on its proprietary dataset, for the same purpose. Furthermore, numerous studies focused on benchmark development [10,11,15,26,29] also investigate the efficacy of supervised training for these detectors. However, a significant limitation of these approaches is their often-limited generalization ability [22].

The rapid evolution of LLMs and their increasing capabilities pose a significant challenge to the adaptability of AI text detectors to new models and application scenarios. While recent efforts have introduced white-box detection methods [1,20], these approaches often rely on proxy language models for generating text logits, rendering them susceptible to the proxy's quality. Moreover, these methods frequently exhibit inferior performance compared to supervised approaches on certain benchmarks [15]. Conda [2] offers a domain adaptation framework for LLM-generated text detection, but it still necessitates unlabeled data from the target domain. Eagle [3] proposes a domain generalization method for multiple LLMs; however, it neglects the crucial aspect of cross-scenario generalization.

We present a novel framework designed to enhance the detection of LLM-generated text across diverse and unseen LLMs and scenarios by exploiting generalized features. Our method introduces LLM-conditional feature alignment (LCFA), which guides the model to learn domain-invariant features characteristic of LLM-generated text. This approach bolsters the model's robustness by ensuring the consistency of learned features across varying textual content. Furthermore, to enhance robustness against textual noise, we employ dynamic contrastive learning (DCL), where data is dynamically perturbed during training, encouraging the model to focus on robust features and thus improving generalization to real-world variations.

Given the rapid proliferation of LLMs, evaluating detection methods effectively necessitates the use of data representative of real-world scenarios. Existing datasets often lack comprehensive coverage across multiple LLMs, languages, and diverse scenarios, or rely on outdated LLMs for data generation. To address these limitations, we introduce MLS, a new dataset encompassing data from ten state-of-the-art LLMs across five scenarios in both English and Chinese. Our experiments on MLS demonstrate the effectiveness of our proposed method. In summary, our key contributions are as follows:

- We propose a novel framework for cross-domain LLM-generated text detection that integrates LLM-conditional feature alignment (LCFA) and dynamic contrastive learning (DCL) to enhance generalization across unseen domains.
- To advance the field of cross-domain LLM-generated text detection, we construct MLS, a new dataset tailored to reflect real-world scenarios. Extensive experiments conducted on this dataset demonstrate the efficacy of our proposed framework.

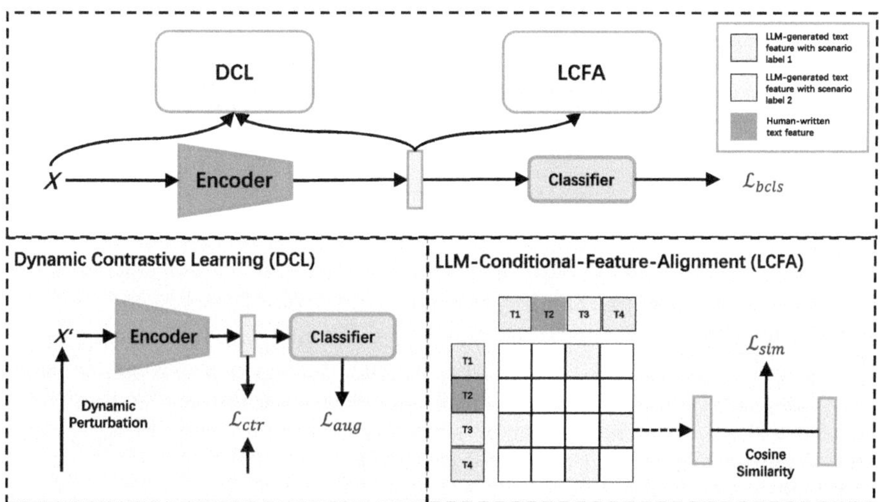

Fig. 1. The architecture of the proposed model. 1) The encoder extracts features from the input text. These features are then utilized by the classifier to predict whether the text is LLM-generated, with the prediction results contributing to the calculation of $\mathcal{L}_{bcls}$. 2) The LLM-conditional feature alignment (LCFA) module selects features of LLM-generated texts within the same batch and enhances the similarity of features across different scenarios by optimizing $\mathcal{L}_{sim}$, guiding the model to learn domain-invariant features. 3) The dynamic contrastive learning(DCL) dynamically perturbs the text during training, leveraging the perturbed data to compute the contrastive learning loss $\mathcal{L}_{ctr}$ and the data augmentation loss $\mathcal{L}_{aug}$.

2　Methods

2.1　Overview

To enhance the detector's ability to generalize to unseen LLMs and scenarios, we propose a framework that explores generalizable features, incorporating two novel components: LLM-conditional feature alignment (LCFA) and dynamic contrastive learning (DCL). As illustrated in Fig. 1, our overall architecture comprises a text encoder, a classification head, LCFA, and DCL, with DCL reusing the encoder and classification head.

Pre-trained Language Models (PLMs) have demonstrated strong performance in downstream tasks when fine-tuned. We employ a PLM as the encoder and a multilayer perceptron (MLP) as the classification head to construct an LLM-generated text detector. The input text x is tokenized into m tokens, with a [CLS] token appended. The PLM extracts a text feature representation $f \in \mathbb{R}^h$, corresponding to the [CLS] embedding, where h denotes the hidden size. This feature f is then fed into the classification head H to produce a prediction. The binary classification loss $\mathcal{L}_{bcls}$ is subsequently computed:

$$
\begin{aligned}
f &= \mathrm{PLM}(x), \\
\mathcal{L}_{bcls} &= \mathcal{L}_{ce}(H(f), y_{bcls}),
\end{aligned}
\tag{1}
$$

where $y_{bcls} \in \{0, 1\}$ is the classification label, and $\mathcal{L}_{ce}$ represents the cross-entropy loss.

2.2 LLM-Conditional Feature Alignment

Prior work, notably MAGE [15], has demonstrated that generalization across scenarios presents a greater challenge than generalization across LLMs for LLM-generated text detection. Texts generated by different LLMs in response to the same prompt often exhibit correlations, whereas texts generated by the same LLM across different scenarios frequently lack such correlations. Consequently, detectors trained on a limited set of scenarios may suffer a significant performance decline when applied to unseen scenarios.

To address this cross-scenario generalization challenge, we propose LLM-conditional feature alignment (LCFA) to learn domain-invariant features. To avoid aligning features from disparate scenarios while inadvertently aligning LLM-generated text features with human-written text, we employ a filtering mechanism, resulting in what we term LLM-conditional features. For each batch of LLM-generated text, the embedding from the final hidden layer is used as the LLM-conditional feature, denoted as f_{lc}, We define N as the number of sample pairs of different categories and S as the sum of cosine similarities between all such pairs:

$$
\begin{aligned}
N &= \sum_{i \in b} \sum_{j \in b} \mathbb{I}(y_{scls}^i \neq y_{scls}^j), \\
S &= \sum_{i \in b} \sum_{j \in b} \mathbb{I}(y_{scls}^i \neq y_{scls}^j) \cos(f_{aic}^i, f_{aic}^j),
\end{aligned}
\tag{2}
$$

where b is the batch and y_{scls} represents the scenario label. By minimizing the similarity loss, the features across different scenarios are aligned, enhancing the generalization capability of detectors. The similarity loss $\mathcal{L}_{sim}$ is computed as:

$$
\mathcal{L}_{sim} = 1 - \frac{S}{N},
\tag{3}
$$

2.3 Dynamic Contrastive Learning

Inspired by Conda [2], we incorporate contrastive learning to enhance model robustness against data perturbations. Contrastive learning improves the generalization of learned representations by comparing similar samples with dissimilar ones. Conda employs synonym replacement to perturb data and generate augmented samples, which are subsequently reused during training. However, this static form of contrastive learning limits the diversity of augmentations. To address this limitation, we dynamically perturb the text data at each training step, enabling the model to learn more robust text representations.

We adopt the contrastive loss employed in SimCLR [6]. For each original input x, its perturbed version x_{aug} serves as a positive sample, while all other samples within the batch are treated as negative samples. The features of [CLS] embeddings f and f_{aug} undergo dimensionality reduction via a projection head P. We define the cosine similarity s_{ij}, s_{ii} and exponential similarity z_{ij}, z_{ii} between samples as follows:

$$
\begin{aligned}
s_{ij} &= \cos(P(f^i), P(f^j)), \\
s_{ii} &= \cos(P(f^i), P(f^i_{aug})), \\
z_{ij} &= \exp\left(\frac{s_{ij}}{t}\right), \\
z_{ii} &= \exp\left(\frac{s_{ii}}{t}\right).
\end{aligned}
\tag{4}
$$

The contrastive loss $\mathcal{L}_{ctr}$ is computed as:

$$
\mathcal{L}{ctr} = -\sum_{i \in b} \log \frac{z_{ii}}{\sum_{j=1}^{2|b|} \mathbb{I}(j \neq i) \cdot z_{ij}},
\tag{5}
$$

where t is the temperature parameter. Additionally, f_{aug} is used to compute the binary classification loss $\mathcal{L}_{aug}$ for the augmented data:

$$
\mathcal{L}_{aug} = \mathcal{L}_{ce}(H(f_{aug}), y_{bcls}).
\tag{6}
$$

Finally, the overall loss $\mathcal{L}$, is a weighted sum of the individual losses:

$$
\mathcal{L} = \mathcal{L}_{bcls} + \mathcal{L}_{aug} + \alpha \mathcal{L}_{sim} + \beta \mathcal{L}_{ctr}.
\tag{7}
$$

3 MLS Dataset

3.1 Data Collection

As large language models (LLMs) continue their rapid evolution, rigorous evaluation of LLM-generated text detectors on state-of-the-art models is crucial. To address real-world evaluation needs, we introduce the MLS dataset, which encompasses text generated by ten cutting-edge LLMs across five distinct scenarios in both English and Chinese. The included models represent both closed-source systems (GPT-3.5, GPT-4o, GLM-4, Kimi) and open-source alternatives

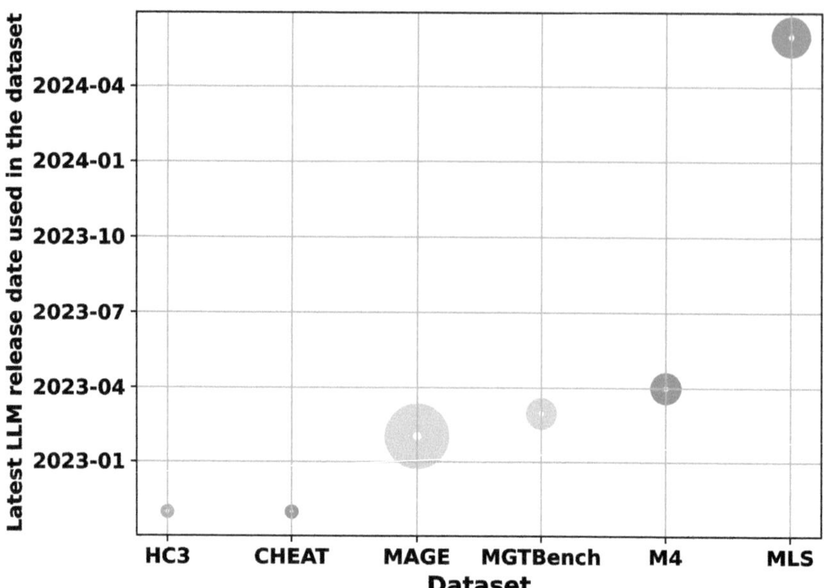

Fig. 2. Comparison of the number of LLMs and the recency of the latest LLM used in MLS with existing LLM-generated text detection datasets. The size of the markers is proportional to the number of LLMs.

(LLaMA3-8b [9], Mistral-7b [14], Gemma-7b [25], Qwen2-7b [27], InternLM2-7b [4], Deepseek-v2-21b [16]). Figure 2 compares the number of LLMs and the recency of the latest LLM used in MLS with those of several existing LLM-generated text detection datasets: HC3 [10], CHEAT [29], MAGE [15], MGT-Bench [11], and M4 [26].

For human-written text, we source data from diverse scenarios: story generation (XSum [21]), news writing (Wp [12]), scientific writing (SciGen [5]), financial question answering (Finance [19]), and medical question answering (Medicine [30]). Portions of the XSum, Wp, and SciGen datasets are translated into Chinese using automatic translation tools.

We generate LLM-authored text by prompting the LLMs with both English and Chinese inputs. For XSum, Wp, and SciGen, we follow the methodology in MAGE [15], using the first 30 words as a prompt and instructing the LLM to generate corresponding stories, news articles, or scientific texts. For the Finance and Medicine datasets, which consist of question-answer pairs, we use the questions as prompts to generate responses. Closed-source models are queried via their official APIs, while open-source models are run using weights from Hugging Face. All inference hyperparameters, such as temperature, top-p, and top-k, adhere to the default settings in the official documentation without modification.

3.2 Statistics

The MLS dataset consists of 22,000 texts, balanced between English and Chinese (11,000 texts in each language). Across the five distinct fields—story generation, news writing, scientific writing, financial question answering, and medical question answering—each field contains 4,400 texts. For each human-written text within a field, we generated ten corresponding LLM-generated texts, resulting in a 1:10 ratio of human-authored to LLM-authored content.

4   Experiments

4.1   Implementation Details

Text content is padded or truncated to a maximum length of 128 tokens. We utilize RoBERTa [17] and XLNet [28] as our encoders, employing pre-trained weights sourced from Hugging Face for both English and Chinese corpora. The binary classification head is implemented as a multilayer perceptron (MLP). The loss function coefficients are set to $\alpha = 1, \beta = 0.1$. We employ the AdamW [18] optimizer with a weight decay of 0.02. All models are trained for three epochs with a learning rate of 2e-5 and a batch size of 32. For text perturbation, 10% of the words in each text are randomly replaced.

4.2   Datasets and Evaluation Metrics

We evaluate our models on the MLS dataset, which comprises 22,000 samples. The dataset is partitioned into training, validation, and test sets using an 8:1:1 split. We employ generated texts from GPT-4o, Qwen2, and Deepseek-v2, along with randomly selected scientific writing texts, to assess generalization performance. Following the established setup in [2,15], we use the area under the receiver operating characteristic curve (AUC) as the evaluation metric. We evaluate the detector under four distinct settings:

- **In-Distribution:** Evaluation on texts from seen LLMs and scenarios.
- **Cross-LLM:** Evaluation on texts from unseen LLMs but seen scenarios.
- **Cross-Scenario:** Evaluation on texts from seen LLMs but unseen scenarios.
- **Cross-LLM and Scenario:** Evaluation on texts from unseen LLMs and scenarios.

4.3   Quantitative Results

Table 1 presents a performance comparison between state-of-the-art methods and our proposed approach on the MLS dataset. RoBERTa [17], an enhanced version of BERT [8], achieves strong results on HC3 [10] and MGTBench [11]. XLNet [28] outperforms BERT on various benchmarks and has seen widespread adoption. EAGLE [3] employs adversarial training to align features across different LLMs but does not address cross-scenario generalization. Our method

Table 1. Performance comparison on MLS dataset. The best result is highlighted in **bold**, and the second best result is highlighted in <u>underline</u>.

Methods	In-Distribution AUC	Cross-LLM AUC	Cross-Scenario AUC	Cross-LLM and Scenario AUC	Overall Avg
RoBERTa [17]	97.39	97.01	76.73	74.04	86.29
XLNet [28]	94.44	94.73	76.99	74.91	85.27
EAGLE [3]	96.21	94.46	60.67	48.18	74.88
Ours(RoBERTa)	**97.96**	**98.00**	<u>84.96</u>	<u>83.43</u>	<u>91.09</u>
Ours(XLNet)	<u>97.95</u>	<u>97.79</u>	**86.54**	**84.40**	**91.67**

consistently outperforms other approaches across all four evaluation settings: in-distribution, cross-LLM, cross-scenario, and cross-LLM & scenario. Notably, it achieves over an 8% improvement in both the cross-scenario and cross-LLM & scenario settings, demonstrating its ability to learn more robust and generalized features.

We occasionally observe that in-distribution results are slightly lower than cross-LLM results. We attribute this to two factors. First, as noted in MAGE [15], generalization across different LLMs is comparatively easier, and our experimental results show that the in-distribution AUC and cross-LLM AUC are similar. Second, to ensure a fair comparison, each model is evaluated after training without selection based on validation set performance. Consequently, some models may overfit the training data, leading to a lower in-distribution AUC.

4.4   Ablation Study

Table 2. Ablation study on static contrastive learning (SCL), dynamic contrastive learning (DCL), and LLM-conditional feature alignment (LCFA). The best result is highlighted in **bold**, and the second best result is highlighted in <u>underline</u>.

Methods	In-Distribution AUC	Cross-LLM AUC	Cross-Scenario AUC	Cross-LLM and Scenario AUC	Overall Avg
Baseline	94.44	94.73	76.99	74.91	85.27
+SCL	<u>97.81</u>	**97.9**	76.46	74.89	86.76
+DCL	97.4	97.53	<u>82.61</u>	<u>81.64</u>	<u>89.80</u>
+DCL+LCFA	**97.95**	<u>97.79</u>	**86.54**	**84.40**	**91.67**

Effectiveness of the Proposed Components. We conduct an ablation study using XLNet to validate the effectiveness of our proposed components. Starting from the baseline, we progressively introduce additional components, training and evaluating each variant. The results are presented in Table 2. Adding static contrastive learning (SCL), as used in Conda [2], to the baseline improves performance in both the in-distribution and cross-LLM settings, although cross-scenario performance remains limited. Incorporating dynamic contrastive learning (DCL) significantly enhances performance in the cross-scenario and cross-LLM & scenario settings, highlighting the importance of DCL in capturing generalized features. Finally, the addition of LLM-conditional feature alignment (LCFA) further improves cross-scenario and cross-LLM & scenario performance, demonstrating its role in learning domain-invariant features.

Table 3. Ablation experiments with different text lengths. The best result is highlighted in **bold**, and the second best result is highlighted in <u>underline</u>.

Text Length	In-Distribution	Cross-LLM	Cross-Scenario	Cross-LLM and Scenario	Overall Avg
64	94.08	94.85	67.26	69.94	81.53
128	<u>97.95</u>	<u>97.79</u>	**86.54**	**84.40**	<u>91.67</u>
256	**98.45**	**98.27**	<u>86.1</u>	<u>84.33</u>	**91.79**

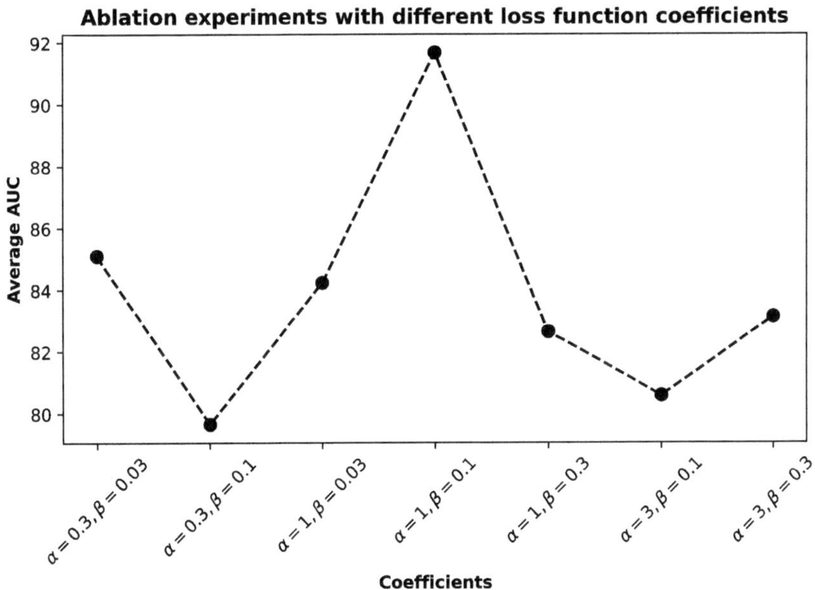

Fig. 3. Ablation experiments with different loss function coefficients. The horizontal axis represents different values of the loss function coefficients α and β. The vertical axis represents the average AUC across the four evaluation settings: in-distribution, cross-LLM, cross-scenario, and cross-LLM and scenario.

Impact of Text Length. Table 3 presents the results of ablation experiments conducted with varying text lengths. The results indicate that performance plateaus at a length of 128 tokens. Consequently, we set the text length to 128.

Impact of Loss Function Coefficients. Figure 3 illustrates the results of ablation experiments conducted with different loss function coefficients. We observe that optimal performance is achieved when $\alpha = 1$ and $\beta = 0.1$. Deviations from these values, including increasing or decreasing α, increasing or decreasing β, and increasing or decreasing both α and β simultaneously, result in performance degradation.

4.5   Visualization

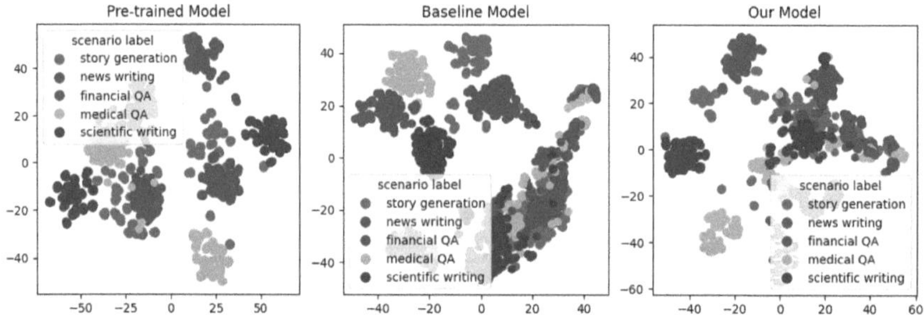

Fig. 4. t-SNE visualization of representations learned by pre-trained models, baseline models, and our model.

To assess whether our method effectively captures domain-invariant features, we perform t-SNE visualizations of the hidden layer embeddings for texts from five different scenarios. We visualize embeddings from the pre-trained model, the baseline model, and our proposed model. The results, shown in Fig. 4, indicate that for the pre-trained model, features from the same scenario tend to cluster together, while features from different scenarios are more dispersed. Compared to the baseline model, our model exhibits closer proximity between features from different scenarios. This observation suggests that our method effectively learns domain-invariant features, thereby improving the model's performance in out-of-distribution settings.

5   Conclusion

In this work, we introduce a novel framework for detecting LLM-generated text, designed to address the challenge of generalization across diverse LLMs and scenarios. By integrating LLM-conditional feature alignment (LCFA) and dynamic contrastive learning (DCL), our method captures generalized features that enhance the discrimination between LLM-generated and human-written text. Furthermore, our newly constructed MLS dataset facilitates a comprehensive evaluation across multiple state-of-the-art LLMs, ensuring the robustness of the proposed detection approach in realistic applications. Extensive experiments conducted on the MLS dataset demonstrate the superior performance of our framework.

Acknowledgments. This work was supported by the National Natural Science Foundation of China (No. 62472396).

References

1. Bao, G., Zhao, Y., Teng, Z., Yang, L., Zhang, Y.: Fast-detectgpt: efficient zero-shot detection of machine-generated text via conditional probability curvature. arXiv preprint arXiv:2310.05130 (2023)
2. Bhattacharjee, A., Kumarage, T., Moraffah, R., Liu, H.: Conda: contrastive domain adaptation for AI-generated text detection. arXiv preprint arXiv:2309.03992 (2023)
3. Bhattacharjee, A., Moraffah, R., Garland, J., Liu, H.: Eagle: a domain generalization framework for AI-generated text detection. arXiv preprint arXiv:2403.15690 (2024)
4. Cai, Z., et al.: Internlm2 technical report. arXiv preprint arXiv:2403.17297 (2024)
5. Chen, H., Takamura, H., Nakayama, H.: Scixgen: a scientific paper dataset for context-aware text generation. arXiv preprint arXiv:2110.10774 (2021)
6. Chen, T., Kornblith, S., Norouzi, M., Hinton, G.: A simple framework for contrastive learning of visual representations. In: International conference on machine learning, pp. 1597–1607. PMLR (2020)
7. Chen, Y., Kang, H., Zhai, V., Li, L., Singh, R., Raj, B.: GPT-sentinel: distinguishing human and chatgpt generated content. arXiv preprint arXiv:2305.07969 (2023)
8. Devlin, J.: Bert: pre-training of deep bidirectional transformers for language understanding. arXiv preprint arXiv:1810.04805 (2018)
9. Dubey, A., et al.: The llama 3 herd of models. arXiv preprint arXiv:2407.21783 (2024)
10. Guo, B., et al.: How close is ChatGPT to human experts? comparison corpus, evaluation, and detection. arXiv preprint arXiv:2301.07597 (2023)
11. He, X., Shen, X., Chen, Z., Backes, M., Zhang, Y.: Mgtbench: benchmarking machine-generated text detection. arXiv preprint arXiv:2303.14822 (2023)
12. Huang, Q., Gan, Z., Celikyilmaz, A., Wu, D., Wang, J., He, X.: Hierarchically structured reinforcement learning for topically coherent visual story generation. In: Proceedings of the AAAI Conference on Artificial Intelligence, pp. 8465–8472 (2019)
13. Ippolito, D., Duckworth, D., Callison-Burch, C., Eck, D.: Automatic detection of generated text is easiest when humans are fooled. arXiv preprint arXiv:1911.00650 (2019)
14. Jiang, A.Q., et al.: Mistral 7b. arXiv preprint arXiv:2310.06825 (2023)
15. Li, Y., et al.: Mage: machine-generated text detection in the wild. In: Proceedings of the 62nd Annual Meeting of the Association for Computational Linguistics (Volume 1: Long Papers), pp. 36–53 (2024)

16. Liu, A., et al.: Deepseek-v2: a strong, economical, and efficient mixture-of-experts language model. arXiv preprint arXiv:2405.04434 (2024)
17. Liu, Y.: Roberta: a robustly optimized BERT pretraining approach. arXiv preprint arXiv:1907.11692 (2019)
18. Loshchilov, I.: Decoupled weight decay regularization. arXiv preprint arXiv:1711.05101 (2017)
19. Maia, M., et al.: Www'18 open challenge: financial opinion mining and question answering. In: Companion proceedings of the the web conference 2018, pp. 1941–1942 (2018)
20. Mitchell, E., Lee, Y., Khazatsky, A., Manning, C.D., Finn, C.: Detectgpt: zero-shot machine-generated text detection using probability curvature. In: International Conference on Machine Learning, pp. 24950–24962. PMLR (2023)
21. Narayan, S., Cohen, S.B., Lapata, M.: Don't give me the details, just the summary! topic-aware convolutional neural networks for extreme summarization. arXiv preprint arXiv:1808.08745 (2018)
22. Pu, X., Zhang, J., Han, X., Tsvetkov, Y., He, T.: On the zero-shot generalization of machine-generated text detectors. arXiv preprint arXiv:2310.05165 (2023)
23. Raffel, C., et al.: Exploring the limits of transfer learning with a unified text-to-text transformer. J. Mach. Learn. Res. **21**(140), 1–67 (2020)
24. Solaiman, I., et al.: Release strategies and the social impacts of language models. arXiv preprint arXiv:1908.09203 (2019)
25. Team, G., et al.: Gemma: open models based on gemini research and technology. arXiv preprint arXiv:2403.08295 (2024)
26. Wang, Y., et al.: M4: multi-generator, multi-domain, and multi-lingual black-box machine-generated text detection. arXiv preprint arXiv:2305.14902 (2023)
27. Yang, A., et al.: Qwen2 technical report. arXiv preprint arXiv:2407.10671 (2024)
28. Yang, Z.: Xlnet: generalized autoregressive pretraining for language understanding. arXiv preprint arXiv:1906.08237 (2019)
29. Yu, P., Chen, J., Feng, X., Xia, Z.: Cheat: a large-scale dataset for detecting ChatGPT-written abstracts. arXiv preprint arXiv:2304.12008 (2023)
30. Zeng, G., et al.: Meddialog: large-scale medical dialogue datasets. In: Proceedings of the 2020 conference on empirical methods in natural language processing (EMNLP), pp. 9241–9250 (2020)
31. Zhan, H., He, X., Xu, Q., Wu, Y., Stenetorp, P.: G3detector: general GPT-generated text detector. arXiv preprint arXiv:2305.12680 (2023)

Towards a Practical Screen-Filming Resistant Image Watermarking System

Shicong Han[1,2], Fei Wu[1], Fangqi Li[1], and Shilin Wang[1(✉)]

[1] Shanghai Jiao Tong University, Shanghai, China
`wsl@sjtu.edu.cn`
[2] Sinopec Group, Beijing, China

Abstract. Image watermarks have been widely adopted to ensure the security of important digital assets, particularly within information systems that involve document filing and processing. Although image watermarks can trace malicious users using screen-shooting, they still suffer from external theft, especially screen-filming (e.g., using a camera or a smart phone to take a picture of the screen). The later cases pose a critical challenge to the security of intelligent information systems. This paper discusses a practical way towards establishing a screen-filming resistant watermarking system after analyzing the defects of existing methods and demonstrating the construction of a screen-level image watermark system that can be deployed in the field. This system can provide real-time image watermarking with only a limited consumption in the terminals' computing units, and achieve the optimal robustness against screen-filming.

Keywords: Image watermark · screen-shooting resistant · intelligent information system

1 Introduction

Nowadays information is collected, viewed, and processed in distributed systems which usually involve multiple administrators, servers, and customers. The entire system can be allocated across a wide physical and temporary range domain. Consequently, even if the system is designed to be secure against certain attacks using cryptological tools and network security protocols, it might remain vulnerable to physical or social attacks, e.g., the secret information displayed on the screens of computers inside a company might be viewed, recorded (using the screen-shooting function or a camera), and distributed by a careless employee or a malicious visitor. Therefore, it is necessary to add security evidence into the information displayed on the screens to ensure that the leaked information can be traced and the adversary can be identified.

Image watermarking has been a promising candidate in achieving traceability of important information, and has been widely adopted in various scenarios [1]. In a nutshell, an image watermarking algorithm adds imperceptible pattern in an image. After moderate compression and editing, the pattern can still be extracted from the image, from which certain hidden message can be decoded. For example, artists can add watermark

© The Author(s), under exclusive license to Springer Nature Singapore Pte Ltd. 2026
Z. Lin et al. (Eds.): ICIG 2025, LNCS 16163, pp. 313–322, 2026.
https://doi.org/10.1007/978-981-95-3729-7_26

into their photos, so that adversaries who use these photos without authorization can be identified and accused.

Despite of their performance, current image watermarking algorithms suffer from strict constraints in the number of pixels, robustness, and time consumption. As a result, they can hardly be used as off-the-shelf strategies in intelligent information systems as a reliable defense against adversaries that might record information displayed on the screens.

This paper delves into building a practical screen-filming resistant watermark system for intelligent information system with a high security demand. We analyze the requirements of such an information system and describe why they challenge the straightforward application of existing image watermarking algorithms. Then we propose a framework that turns a deep learning-based image watermarking algorithm into a practical solution to this task. This framework includes resolution-dependent image segmentation and domain-specific fine-tuning. We showcase turning PIMoG [2] into an applicable screen-filming resistant watermark in an industrial information system. The contributions of this paper are:

1. We analyze the demands of practical screen-filming resistant image watermark and demonstrate why existing methods cannot be directly applied.
2. We propose a framework under which any existing deep learning-based image watermarking scheme can be transformed into a practical screen-filming resistant image watermarking scheme.
3. We showcase an application of the proposed framework in the field.

The rest of the paper is organized as follows: Sect. 2 summarizes related works, Sect. 3 describes the proposed framework, Sect. 4 provides experimental results, and Sect. 5 concludes the paper.

2 Related Works

Image watermark has been studied as an important subject in cyberspace security, particularly in subfields concerning confidential information management, intellectual property protection, and copyright tracing. Recent studies have demonstrated its capability in identifying illegal usage and protecting the ownership of authors.

In general, a watermarking scheme is composed of two modules: an encoder denoted by a function $E(.)$ and a decoder denoted by another function $D(.)$. Given an image x and a message m (x is usually referred to as the carrier and the message contains certain information to be carried, such as the digital signature of the owner of the image), the encoder adds a watermark onto the image through the following equation:

$$x' = x + E(x, m). \tag{1}$$

The watermarked image x' can then be freely distributed to downstream users or clients. Once there are security or copyright concerns, the decoder is responsible of retrieving the secret message from the watermarked image:

$$m' = D\big(x'\big). \tag{2}$$

When the decoder solely relies on the watermarked image, the watermarking scheme is referred to as a blind image watermarking scheme. In other circumstances, the decoder might take the original image x or other auxiliary evidence as its input.

In most cases, it is desirable that the watermark is robust against malicious modifications. This is because adversaries might leverage such modification methods to remove watermarks from watermarked images so the hidden message cannot longer be extracted, and the security purpose is compromised. Most existing image watermarking schemes are designed to be robust against common modifications including geometry transformation, compression, cropping, normalization, noises, etc. Formally, after the watermarked image x' is modified by a function $M(.)$, the decoder should still be able to correctly retrieve the message:

$$D\big(M\left(x'\right)\big) = m. \tag{3}$$

Prior to deep learning-based schemes, traditional image watermarking schemes either utilize the least significant bits (LSB) of pixels, vague patterns, or the frequency domain properties of images to hide the secret message [3–10]. On the contrary, deep learning-based image watermarking schemes usually follow an end-to-end paradigm. In a nutshell, both the encoder $E(.)$ and the decoder $D(.)$ are neural networks. Given a batch of images $\{x_i\}$ and a batch of legal messages $\{m_j\}$, two neural networks are conjugately trained to minimized the following loss:

$$\sum_{i,j} l_m(m_j, D(M\left(x_i + E(x_i, m_j)\right))), \tag{4}$$

in which $l_m(.)$ is a loss function defined in the domain of secret messages (e.g., the position-wise cross-entropy loss). To further improve the imperceptibility of the watermark, Eq. (4) is usually trained with the additional regularizer:

$$\sum_{i,j} l_x(x_i, x_i + E(x_i, m_j)), \tag{5}$$

where $l_x(.)$ is a loss function defined in the domain of images, common choices including the absolute value or the mean square of the pixel-level difference, SSIM, etc. Deep learning-based image watermarking began with HIDDEN [11], which firstly demonstrated the applicability of deep neural network in multimedia forensics. By simulating the perturbation caused by screen-filming, neural network-based image watermark can be robust against such an attack, this has been verified by a series of works [12–18].

3 Challenges

Despite of the success of existing image watermarking schemes, they are not capable of achieving screen-filming resistant tracing in the field. In this scenario, an administrator runs an intelligence system that includes multiple terminal devices, each is associated with a unique user. Secret information is sometimes displayed on the screens of these devices for inspection, documentation, etc. The administrator has control over the operating system on these devices, so the users cannot directly press the screen-shooting button and transmit the secrecies through the internet. However, the users might use their own cameras, or more probably their smart phones, to film the screen and distribute the content over social media or send it to malicious parties. This risk has become critical in commercial companies or agencies that process sensitive data. Intuitively, the administrator is encouraged to add image watermark on the screen so whenever such a leak occurs, the responsible user can always be identified. The overall pipeline is shown in Fig. 1.

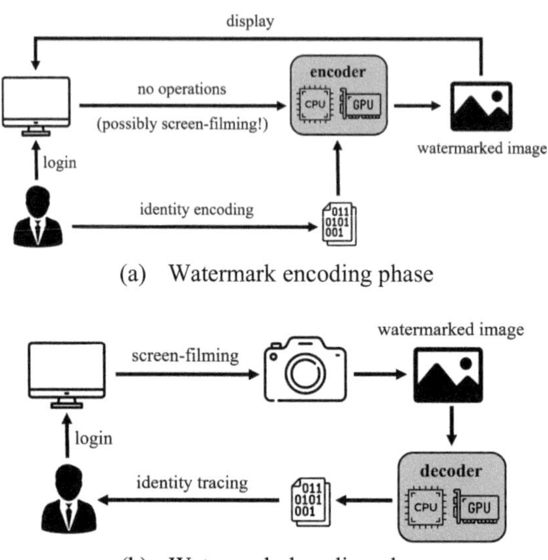

(a)   Watermark encoding phase

(b)   Watermark decoding phase

Fig. 1. The pipeline of image watermark for an intelligent information management system.

In addition to the well-studied requirements such as robustness and imperceptibility, image watermarking schemes for this scenario has to satisfy two extra properties:

1. The time consumption of the encoder has to be very low, otherwise the screen might already be filmed before being watermarked.
2. The image watermarking scheme has to support images with a large number of pixels, and can be configured to support images with different sizes since the screens within the information system might have different versions.

Hitherto, image watermarking schemes can hardly simultaneously satisfy both properties alongside with the basic robustness.

4   Method

4.1   Splitting the Screen

The motivation of our method is to transform an arbitrary deep learning-based image watermarking scheme, whose reliability under screen-filming has already been verified, into a new image watermarking scheme that can scale up to images of arbitrary resolutions and can function in a consumption friendly manner. A straightforward choice is to retrain a neural network encoder on a larger scale. However, multiplying the width or height of the image by a factor S implies at least an S^2 multiplication in the size of the encoder, and the training might fail to converge as well. Instead, we fix the scale of the original PIMoG image watermark encoder (whose input takes the shape of 128*128). A screen of a high resolution is firstly split into segments of size 128*128, then each segment is independently watermarked by the same encoder using the same secret message. The secret message carries the identity of the user who owns this terminal device.

Accordingly, upon receiving a watermarked image, the administrator firstly aligns the image with the size of the screen. This step can be done manually or using traditional image processing tools such as Huff transform or line detection function provided by open-sourced software like OpenCV. Then the administrator splits the aligned image, extracts messages from each segment using the decoder, and runs a position-wise vote to obtain the final message. Formally, denote the message decoded from the k-th segment as m_k, which is essentially a binary string with length L. Then the l-th position of the final message is

$$\arg \max_{(b \in 0,1)} \sum_k I[m_k[l] = b]. \tag{6}$$

The entire process is demonstrated in Fig. 2.

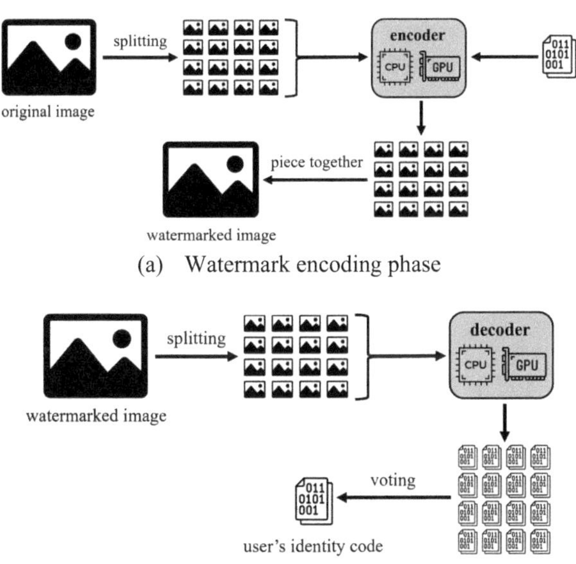

Fig. 2. The pipeline of the proposed image watermarking framework.

4.2   Fine-Tuning the Encoder and the Decoder

Existing deep learning-based image watermarking schemes uniformly focus on natural images, particularly large open image collections such as Imagenet or COCO. Although these datasets include diversified categories of images and secure the scalability of watermarking scheme, they cannot characterize images within confidential information systems.

To accommodate the watermark to the information system, which usually displays documents, receipts, or structured texts, both the encoder and the decoder have to be fine-tuned so that they can process segments of these kinds of images. Concretely, the encoder and the decoder are jointly trained w.r.t. the loss function defined in Eq. (5), where the target images are segments of screens provided by the information system.

4.3   Achieving Real-Time Watermark Embedding

Finally, it is necessary to reduce the computational burden from watermarking. Even with the acceleration provided by graphic processing units (GPU) or neural processing units (NPU), it is hard to catch up with the refresh rate of a normal computer screen, which is usually 120Hz, i.e., all segments on the screen have to be watermarked within approximately 8ms. Moreover, the cost of deploying GPU/NPUs on all terminal devices is prohibitive. Alternatively, we adopt a lazy evaluation solution. A daemon is responsible of capturing the content on the screen and running the watermarking process, yet it only starts to processing a new image after finishing watermarking the previous image. Meanwhile, another daemon supervises whether there has been no command, or there is no change on the screen, within a time window. If the second daemon observes that the content on the screen has been still for long enough, then the watermarked image returned from the first daemon is displayed on the screen as a screensaver. This process would restart once the user inputs any command.

The motivation behind this design is: only after the screen remaining still for a few seconds can the user take a photo and cause an information leakage. It is unnecessary to add watermark to every frame displayed on the screen.

5   Experiments

5.1   Settings

We implemented the proposed method using Python with PyTorch machine learning framework, and tested the method on a personal computer. The computer is Lenovo Legion R7000P 2020H, with operating system Windows 10 (22H2). The CPU is AMD Ryzen 7 4800H with 8 cores and 16GB memory. The GPU is Nvidia GeForce RTX 2080 Ti, with 11GB memory. The development environment is Python 3.8.19 in Visual Studio Code 1.97.2.

The smart phone for simulating screen-filming is Redmi K60 Pro, powered by Android 13, the camera is Sony IMX800, f/1.88, with 50 million pixels. The original deep learning-based image watermarking scheme is PIMoG, we used the official open-source implementation and the same parameters as the original distribution.

To test the performance of the watermarking scheme, we collected real images from the information system, there were altogether 100 images, the resolution of the screen is 1956*1015, among which 80% were used for training (i.e., fine-tuning the encoder and the decoder as described in Sect. 4.2) and the rest 20% were used for testing.

The length of the watermark message was fixed as 30, the same as the configuration of PIMoG. Training and testing the watermarking scheme with all possible codes is impractical (there are 2^{30} possible codes in total). Instead, we used 100 position-wise randomly generated binary codes in $\{0,1\}^{30}$ as codes to be embedded into the watermark during the training phase, and another 100 independently generated codes for testing. For each image on the screen, 10 copies were filmed using the mobile phone's camera. So the number of images in the training dataset is $100*80\%*100*10 = 80000$, and the number of images in the testing dataset is 20000.

5.2 Metrics

The first metric of interested is the accuracy of the message decoded from the watermark, this is measured in the bit error rate (BER) between the message inputted into the encoder and the message returned from the decoder. BER allows the administrator to measure the information theoretical capacity of the watermark. On the other hand, the percentage of images whose watermarks can be correctly verified can also quantify the accuracy of the watermarking system.

The second metric to be studied is the cost of the watermarking scheme, which is reflected in the memory consumed by the encoder and the time delay. For both variables, we tested in the CPU-only case and the case where a GPU is available.

5.3 Baselines

We adopted the original version of PIMoG for comparison, and tested the BER using two schemes. Note that the cost of the proposed watermarking scheme is the same as that of PIMoG's. Therefore, the accuracy of the watermark is the only metric of interest.

5.4 Results

We firstly studied the relationship between the number of watermark blocks (i.e., the number of segments in the entire screen that are watermarked) and the availability of the watermark. Specifically, we chose the number of blocks from 1 to 90 and recorded the corresponding performance of the watermark. The accuracy of the watermark is shown in Fig. 3 and Fig. 4.

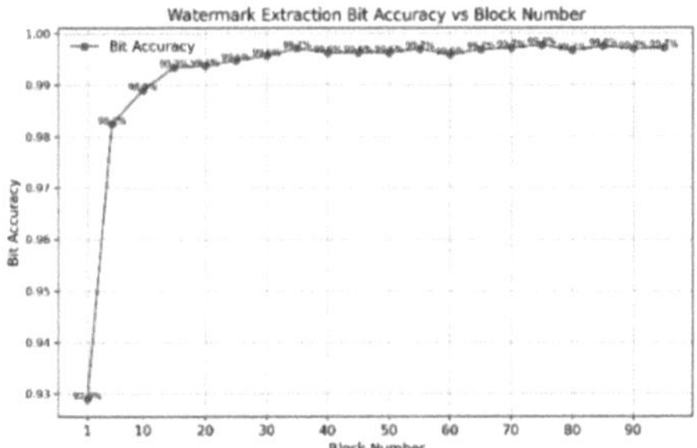

Fig. 3. The accuracy of the watermark (1-BER) w.r.t. the number of watermarking blocks.

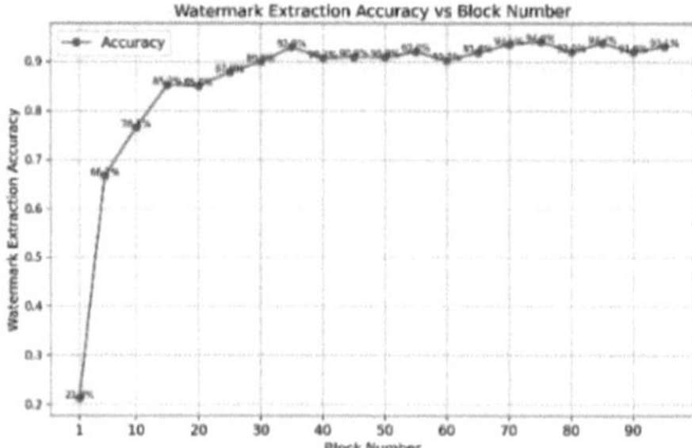

Fig. 4. The accuracy of the watermark (percentage of correctly decoded images) w.r.t. the number of watermarking blocks.

Evidently, increasing the number of blocks implies a higher accuracy, and such a marginal increment becomes negligible after the number of blocks exceeding 50. Meanwhile, as shown in Fig. 5, the cost of watermarking increases linearly in the number of blocks. Therefore, we fixed the number of blocks as 50 in the following experiments.

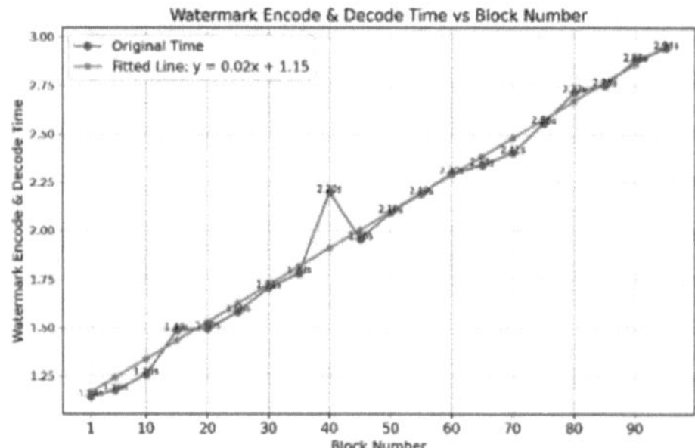

Fig. 5. The time consumption of the watermark (in second) w.r.t. the number of watermarking blocks.

We proceeded to study the influence of fine-tuning with respect to the local dataset collected from the field. For comparison, we recorded the performance of the watermark before fine-tuning (i.e., the original version that is only tuned on COCO dataset), after fine-tuning with only the local dataset, and another fine-tuned version using a mixture of the local dataset and COCO dataset, the results are shown in Table 1 and Table 2.

Table 1. The accuracy of the watermark (1-BER) under different fine-tuning schemes.

Fine-tuning dataset	Original images	Simulated screen-filming	Real screen-filming
N/A	100.00%	99.70%	68.14%
Local data	99.57%	93.88%	85.40%
Local data+COCO	99.57%	99.81%	75.54%

Table 2. The accuracy of the watermark (percentage of correctly decoded images) under different fine-tuning schemes.

Fine-tuning dataset	Original images	Simulated screen-filming	Real screen-filming
N/A	100.00%	99.00%	2.08%
Local data	100.00%	90.00%	96.88%
Local data+COCO	100.00%	99.00%	29.17%

What can be concluded is that: although the original PIMoG model achieved good robustness against screen-filming, especially against simulated screen-filming with geometry transforms and additional noises, the optimal choice remains fine-tuning with respect to the local dataset. Additionally, this process should not involve other datasets than the images in the field (using COCO resulted in a decline in watermark accuracy). It is remarkable that the minimal BER (below 15%) implies a channel capacity of 18.3 bit with $L = 30$, which is sufficient for managing over 0.2 million terminal devices.

Finally, we recorded the time and memory consumption of the watermarking system under different hardware configurations. Results are shown in Table 3 and Table 4.

Table 3. The time consumption of the watermarking scheme (sec).

Device	Encoder	Decoder
CPU-only	5.87	5.23
CPU+GPU	1.09	1.16

Table 4. The memory consumption of the watermarking scheme (MB).

Device	Encoder	Decoder
CPU-only	2949	2458
CPU+GPU	2319	1299

In conclusion, the consumption of the watermarking scheme is affordable even for terminal device without computation resources. Setting the time window (which is used to detect whether the screen is still) to approximately 6 s would result in a practical real-time screen-filming resistant terminal device. Meanwhile, the memory's burden is limited so that the original workload stays intact.

6　Conclusions

This paper studies the screen-filming resistant image watermarking scheme that can be deployed in the field where the computation resources are limited. We show that existing deep learning-based image watermarking scheme can be transformed into a practical solution. The next problem to be addressed is further optimization of the scheme with respect to the terminal computation device, e.g., using quantization or making improvements according to the concrete computing units.

Acknowledgments. The work described in this paper is sponsored by the Research Program on Data Leak Prevention with Digital Watermark, SINOPEC.

References

1. Fang, H., Zhang, W., Zhou, H., et al.: Screen-shooting resilient watermarking. IEEE Trans. Inf. Forensics Secur. **14**(6), 1403–1418 (2018)
2. Fang H, Jia Z, Ma Z, et al. PIMoG: An effective screen-shooting noise-layer simulation for deep-learning-based watermarking network. In: Proceedings of the 30th ACM International Conference on Multimedia, pp. 2267–2275 (2022)
3. Cao, F., Guo, D., Wang, T., et al.: Universal screen-shooting robust image watermarking with channel-attention in DCT domain. Expert Syst. Appl. **238**, 122062 (2024)
4. Li, Y., Liao, X., Wu, X.: Screen-shooting resistant watermarking with grayscale deviation simulation. IEEE Trans. Multimed. (2024)
5. Fu, L., Liao, X., Guo, J., et al.: WaveRecovery: screen-shooting watermarking based on wavelet and recovery. IEEE Trans. Circuits Syst. Video Technol. (2024)
6. Gan, Z., Zheng, X., Song, Y., et al.: Screen-shooting watermarking algorithm based on Harris-SIFT feature regions. SIViP **18**(5), 4647–4660 (2024)
7. Bai, R., Li, L., Zhang, S., et al.: SSDeN: framework for screen-shooting resilient watermarking via deep networks in the frequency domain. Appl. Sci. **12**(19), 9780 (2022)
8. Wang, H., Wang, H., Zhang, F., et al.: Moiré-watermark: robust watermarking against screen-shooting using moiré patterns. IEEE Trans. Multimed. (2025)
9. Cao, F., Wang, T., Guo, D., et al.: Screen-shooting resistant image watermarking based on lightweight neural network in frequency domain. J. Vis. Commun. Image Represent. **94**, 103837 (2023)
10. Zhang, Y., Huang, C., Liu, S., et al.: Screen-shooting resistant robust document watermarking in the Discrete Fourier Transform domain. Int. J. Network Manage **35**(1), e2278 (2025)
11. Zhu, J., Kaplan, R., Johnson, J., et al.: Hidden: hiding data with deep networks. In: Proceedings of the European Conference on Computer Vision (ECCV), pp. 657–672 (2018)
12. Ge, S., Fei, J., Xia, Z., et al.: A screen-shooting resilient document image watermarking scheme using deep neural network. IET Image Proc. **17**(2), 323–336 (2023)
13. Tang, Z., Chai, X., Lu, Y., et al.: An end-to-end screen shooting resilient blind watermarking scheme for medical images. J. Inform. Secur. Appl. **76**, 103547 (2023)
14. Xiao, X., Zhang, Y., Hua, Z., et al.: Client-side embedding of screen-shooting resilient image watermarking. IEEE Trans. Inf. Forensics Secur. (2024)
15. Wang, H., Wang, H., Huang, X., et al.: Enhanced screen shooting resilient document watermarking. In: ICASSP 2024–2024 IEEE International Conference on Acoustics, Speech and Signal Processing (ICASSP). IEEE, pp. 4515–4519 (2024)
16. Gao, G., Chen, X., Li, L., et al.: Screen-Shooting Robust Watermark Based on Style Transfer and Structural Re-parameterization. IEEE Trans. Inf. Forens. Secur. (2025)
17. Shi, Z., Wang, H., Wang, H., et al.: Robust screen-shooting document watermarking for multiple fonts. IEEE Signal Process. Lett. (2024)
18. Chen, W., Li, Y., Niu, Z., et al.: Real-time and screen-cam robust screen watermarking. Knowl.-Based Syst. **302**, 112380 (2024)

Progressive CNN-Based Reversible Data Hiding in Encrypted Images

Ruixuan Jiang[✉], Jing Zhang, Junyuan Huo, and Ping Ping

College of Computer Science and Software Engineering, Hohai University,
Nanjing, China
jraytheon01@gmail.com

Abstract. With the rapid advancement of cloud computing and increased emphasis on privacy protection, reversible data hiding in encrypted images (RDHEI) is garnering increasing attention. This is because it allows for the protection of the original image content, extraction of embedded data, and lossless reconstruction of the original image simultaneously. To notably enhance prediction accuracy and leverage the correlation among adjacent pixels, a novel high-capacity RDHEI approach is introduced, integrating a progressive CNN-based predictor with a bit-plane compression algorithm. Additionally, the median edge detector (MED) predictor is employed as a two-stage prediction mechanism to provide embedding capacity. Experimental results demonstrate that the proposed method achieves superior embedding capacity compared to state-of-the-art techniques.

Keywords: Reversible data hiding · Convolutional neural network · Encrypted images · Privacy protection

1 Introduction

Data hiding, drawing significant attention, involves embedding secret information into multimedia. This practice can be categorized into three distinct groups based on various application scenarios: watermarking [19], steganography [20] and reversible data hiding (RDH). Watermarking is mainly applied in the field of copyright protection and identity authentication. Robustness against attacks such as JPEG compression and image cropping is an important evaluation standard of the watermarking algorithm. Steganography is developed for covert communication, whether it can resist steganalysis effectively is one of the important evaluation standard. In contrast to watermarking and steganography, reversible data hiding (RDH) aims to hide secret data into an image and is able to reconstruct the original image losslessly after extracting the embedded data. In the beginning, RDH is divided into four categories: difference expansion [1,16,22], histogram shifting (HS) [7,12], prediction-error (PE) [5,13,21], and multiple histograms modification [6,25,26,33]. The above methods attempt to improve the embedding capacity while reducing the image distortion and reconstructing the

© The Author(s), under exclusive license to Springer Nature Singapore Pte Ltd. 2026
Z. Lin et al. (Eds.): ICIG 2025, LNCS 16163, pp. 323–335, 2026.
https://doi.org/10.1007/978-981-95-3729-7_27

original cover image without any loss. Due to the rapid development of cloud computing and the increasing demand for privacy protection, the original image is usually transmitted in an encrypted form. Therefore, reversible data hiding in encrypted images (RDHEI) methods [29,34] has attracted extensive attention in recent years. Generally, there are three end users in the RDHEI method: the content-owner, data-hider and receiver. For the content-owner who is the original image provider needs to encrypt the original image and vacate the embedding room. After receiving the encrypted image, the data-hider can embed the secret data under encryption into the image. However, the content of original image is unknown to the data-hider. Owing to both original image and secret data are encrypted by different keys, information that the receiver is able to obtain depends on the number of keys. Specifically, the data hiding key can decrypt the extracted secret data accurately, and the image encryption key can reconstruct the original image losslessly. At present, a lot of RDHEI methods have been proposed. According to execution order of encryption and vacating room, existing RDHEI methods can be divided into two categories, vacating room after encryption (VRAE) and reserving room before encryption (RRBE). In VRAE method [15,31,36], the data-hider embeds secret data by modifying encrypted pixel values. However, its embedding capacity is relatively low because the local spatial correlation of the original image has been destroyed. Under the premise of image security, the RRBE method [10,28,30,32] reserves room before image encryption which makes full use of the pixel correlation of the original image and achieves higher embedding capacity. Recent advances have significantly improved embedding capacity, with Ren et al. [17] achieving unprecedented 5.20 bpp on BOSSbase dataset through prediction error compression and adaptive Huffman encoding. It is obvious that a higher embedding capacity is more useful to practical applications such as the storage and transmission of medical images. Moreover, the existing methods can be divided into joint RDHEI [4,35] and separable RDHEI [14,23] according to whether data extraction is independent of image decryption or not. Compared to joint RDHEI, separable RDHEI is more convenient and secure in image and data protection. Furthermore, recent developments in deep learning integration have shown promising results, with masked autoencoder techniques being successfully applied to RDHEI [11]. Therefore, we focus on RRBE and separable RDHEI method in this paper.

In this paper, an RDHEI method based on progressive CNN prediction and bit-plane compression is proposed. First of all, the content-owner adopts the progressive CNN predictor to calculate the prediction error of the original image. Then, the bit-plane compression algorithm is implemented to vacate room and the image is encrypted by a stream cipher. Afterwards, the data-hider embeds the secret data into the vacated room. At last, the receiver can extract the secret data accurately or reconstruct the original image losslessly according to the type of key. If the embedding capacity cannot meet the requirement, a two-stage embedding method using median edge detector is proposed to further improve the embedding capacity. Similar to the first stage, the steps of pixel prediction,

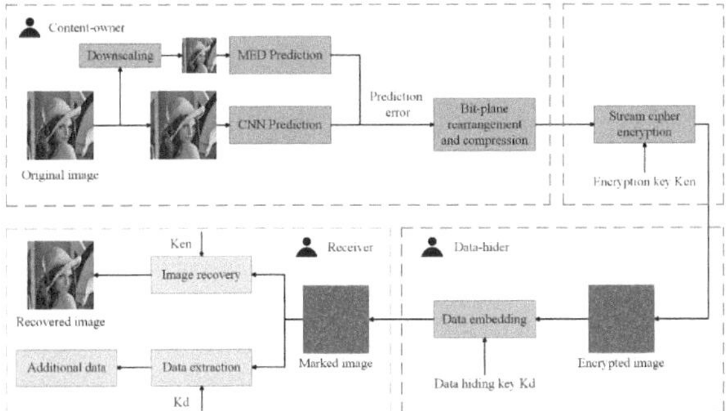

Fig. 1. The framework of the proposed method.

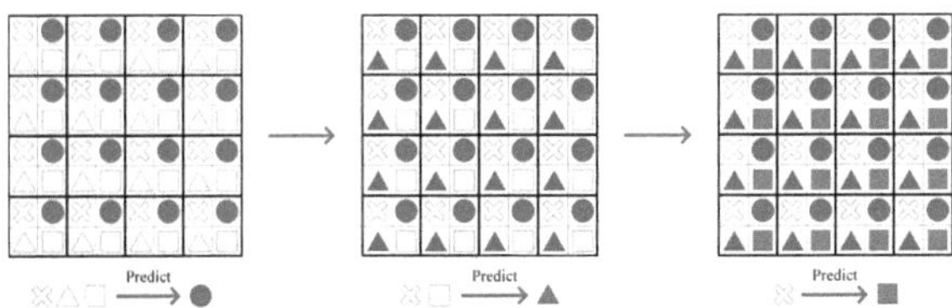

Fig. 2. The proposed division and prediction method.

bit-plane compression and image encryption are carried out in turn. The main contributions of this paper are summarized as follows:

1) The proposed progressive CNN prediction makes full use of the correlation of the adjacent pixels and adopts a progressive prediction approach, which sufficiently improve the accuracy of the prediction results compared with the traditional predictors.

2) In the embedding part, a new bit-plane rearrangement method is proposed to match the progressive CNN-based predictor and improve the compression rate. What's more, the embedding capacity can be further improved by the two-stage embedding method.

The paper is organized as: Sect. 2 details the proposed method, Sect. 3 presents experimental results, and Sect. 4 concludes.

2 Proposed Method

This section presents a novel RRBE-based method achieving high embedding capacity through progressive CNN prediction and bit-plane compression. Figure 1 illustrates the framework comprising three phases: 1) Pixel prediction; 2) Room vacating and data embedding; 3) Image decryption and data extraction. The progressive CNN predictor uses one-quarter pixels to predict three-quarters according to division patterns, while median edge detector (MED) [24] processes remaining pixels. Bit-plane compression algorithms create embedding space, and receivers extract data or reconstruct images using appropriate keys.

2.1 Prediction Part

This section introduces the image division method and two-stage prediction approach, followed by the progressive CNN predictor design and training process.

Image Division. CNN-based prediction accuracy depends on context information availability. While [8] divides images into cross and dot sets (half pixels as context), and [9] uses four subsets (three-quarters as context), we divide the image into 2×2 non-overlapping blocks as shown in Fig. 2. Each block contains four pixel sets: cross, circle, triangle, and rectangle, where gray patterns serve as context for predicting colored patterns.

The progressive CNN predictor sequentially predicts circle, triangle, and rectangle sets while preserving the cross set. During circle prediction, cross, triangle, and rectangle sets provide context; during triangle prediction, cross and rectangle sets provide context, and so forth. This maximizes pixel utilization and improves prediction accuracy.

The two-stage approach first applies progressive CNN prediction to three sets, then uses median edge detector (MED) with bit-plane compression on remaining pixels to further enhance embedding capacity.

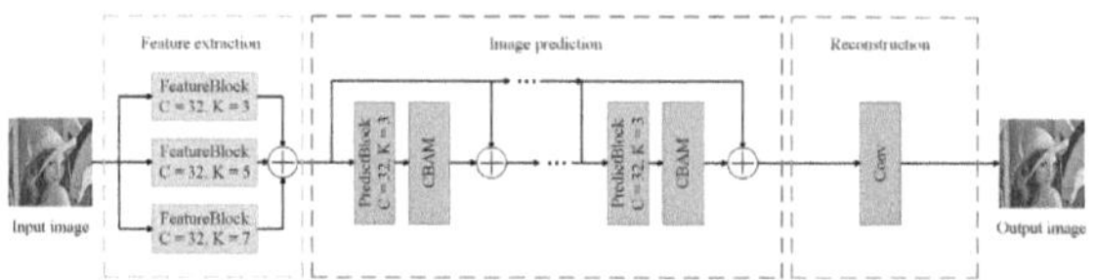

Fig. 3. The framework of the proposed progressive CNN-based predictor.

Proposed Progressive CNN-Based Predictor. The progressive CNN predictor comprises three modules: feature extraction, image prediction, and image reconstruction (Fig. 3).

The feature extraction module contains three parallel convolution blocks with kernel sizes $K \times K$ (K=3,5,7), 3×3, and 3×3. Each block uses three serial convolutions with ELU activation, 32 output channels, and 'reflect' padding for edge enhancement. This parallel structure achieves multi-receptive fields.

The image prediction module consists of four convolution blocks with CBAM attention [27]. Each block contains two 3×3 convolutions with ELU activation and 32 channels. CBAM combines spatial and channel attention for feature enhancement. Dense connections between blocks improve feature reuse by accepting all previous blocks as input, integrating high-level and low-level features for better accuracy.

The image reconstruction module uses one convolution block (32 input, 1 output channel) to reconstruct the predicted image. The prediction error ex_{cnn} is calculated from the predicted value px_{cnn} according to Eq. 1.

$$ex_{cnn} = x - px_{cnn} \tag{1}$$

The CNN predictor is trained using 3000 ImageNet images (training) and 500 images (validation), resized to 512×512 grayscale. Based on the division method, four parts construct input and target images. The model is optimized using back propagation and Adam optimizer with batch size 8. The training loss is:

$$loss = \frac{1}{p} \sum_{i=1}^{p} (I_i - \widetilde{I}_i)^2 + \lambda \|\omega\|_2^2 \tag{2}$$

where p is image number, I_i is target image, $\widetilde{I}_i$ is output image, $\lambda = 10^{-3}$ is weight decay, and ω denotes all weights.

Median Edge Detector Based Predictor. For an original image I of size $m \times n$, the predicted value of current pixel x can be calculated by the median edge detector (MED) [24], where $x(i,j) \in [0, 255]$, $1 < i \le m$, $1 < j \le n$.

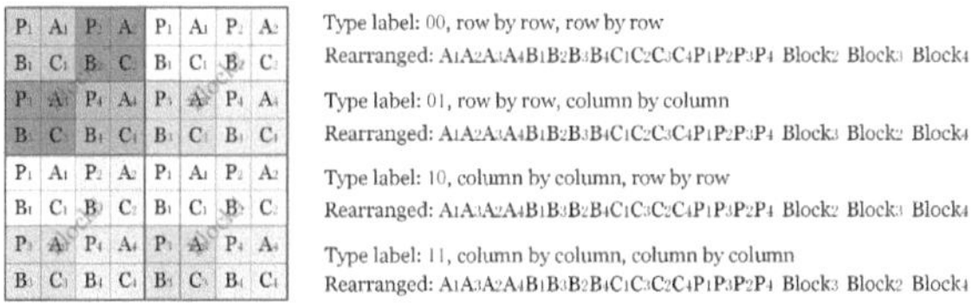

Type label: 00, row by row, row by row
Rearranged: $A_1A_2A_3A_4B_1B_2B_3B_4C_1C_2C_3C_4P_1P_2P_3P_4$ Block2 Block1 Block4

Type label: 01, row by row, column by column
Rearranged: $A_1A_2A_3A_4B_1B_2B_3B_4C_1C_2C_3C_4P_1P_2P_3P_4$ Block3 Block2 Block4

Type label: 10, column by column, row by row
Rearranged: $A_1A_3A_2A_4B_1B_3B_2B_4C_1C_3C_2C_4P_1P_3P_2P_4$ Block2 Block1 Block4

Type label: 11, column by column, column by column
Rearranged: $A_1A_3A_2A_4B_1B_3B_2B_4C_1C_3C_2C_4P_1P_3P_2P_4$ Block3 Block2 Block4

Fig. 4. The four different types of bit-plane arrangements.

2.2 Embedding Part

In this section, the decimal prediction errors between original image and predicted image are first converted into 8 bits binary. Then, we sort the prediction errors according to the number of predicted pixels which can be used within the block. After that, a bit-stream compression algorithm is adopted to vacate room for data embedding. At last, a pseudo-random matrix is generated to encrypt the image and the encrypted additional data is also embedded into the vacated room.

Prediction Error Processing. After calculating the prediction error ex of the original image I which consists of ex_{cnn} and ex_{med}, the absolute value of ex is first converted into 8 bits binary according to Eq. 3. Afterwards, owing to the sign of the prediction error can be either positive or negative, we substitute the MSB by the sign mark bit, "1" and "0" denotes positive and negative respectively. If the prediction error exceeds the range of $[127, 127]$, the value of this pixel will not be changed and be marked as the overflow pixel. Simultaneously, its location will also be recorded as auxiliary information.

$$ex^k(i, j) = \left\lfloor \frac{ex(i, j)}{2^{k-1}} \right\rfloor \bmod 2, k = 1, 2, ..., 8 \tag{3}$$

where $1 \leq i \leq m$ and $1 \leq j \leq n$, $ex^k(i, j)$ is the binary of corresponding bit. Assuming the prediction error $ex(2, 1) = -16$, its binary of the absolute value is 00010000 and the sign is negative, so the $ex^8(2, 1)$ will be replaced by 1 and the modified value is 10010000.

Bit-Plane Rearrangement. To match the progressive CNN predictor and improve compression rate, bit-streams are rearranged using block scanning. Each bit-plane is divided into 4×4 blocks with four arrangement types (Fig. 4): Type 00 (row-by-row blocks and bits), Type 01 (row-by-row bits, column-by-column blocks), and two others. Two bits record the arrangement type.

Bit-Stream Compression. The rearranged bit-streams contain consecutive"0" or "1" sequences, enabling compression to vacate embedding room. The encoding uses prefix L_{pre}, infix L_{mid}, and suffix L_{tail}. Based on parameter L_{fix}:

Case 1: When $L < L_{fix}$, code $= L_{pre} + L_{mid}$ where $L_{pre} = 0$ and L_{mid} is the L_{fix}-length bit stream.

Case 2: When $L \geq L_{fix}$, code $= L_{pre} + L_{mid} + L_{tail}$ where L_{pre} has $l - 1$ consecutive "1" s ending with "0", and:

$$l = \lfloor \log_2 L \rfloor \tag{4}$$

$$L_{mid} = (L - 2^l)_2 \tag{5}$$

For each bit-plane (MSB to LSB), four arrangement types are tested and the shortest compression result is selected. Compressed bit-planes use one bit for compression flag, two bits for arrangement type, followed by compressed data and vacated room. Auxiliary information (block size, L_{fix}, overflow pixels) is stored in MSB plane, while compression lengths are recorded in LSB plane.

Image Encryption. A pseudo-random matrix H is generated using encryption key K_{en}. XOR encryption is applied bit-wise:

$$x_e^k(i, j) = x_c^k(i, j) \oplus r^k(i, j), k = 1, 2, ..., 8 \tag{6}$$

$$x_e(i, j) = \sum_{k=1}^{8} x_e^k(i, j) \times 2^{8-k} \tag{7}$$

Data Hiding. Secret data is encrypted using key K_d and embedded into vacated room via LSB substitution, producing marked image I_{es}.

2.3   Two-Stage Embedding

To utilize all pixels in the original image, median edge detector (MED) processes the remaining unused pixels in each block. Pixels in the upper left corner of each block are extracted to construct a downscaled image with unchanged pixel values, reducing the size to one quarter of the original. The same operations from the first stage including bit-plane rearrangement and bit-stream compression are applied to MED errors. All pixels in the downscaled image can be used for prediction except those in the first row or column. Finally, each downscaled pixel is placed at its original position to construct the final marked image I_{es}.

Fig. 5. Test image: (a) Baboon; (b) Barbara; (c) Jetplane; (d) Lakeboat; (e) Lena; (f) Peppers.

2.4   Data Extraction and Image Recovery

Data extraction and image recovery can be performed separately based on available keys. Three receiver types are defined according to access to encryption key K_{en} and data hiding key K_d.

Case 1: With only decryption key K_{en}, the original image is perfectly recovered by first recovering the downscaled image using block size, L_{fix}, and overflow pixel information from MSB plane along with compressed bit-stream counts from LSB plane. The same key K_{en} decrypts the downscaled image according to Eq. 3. Using restored pixels, the other three pixels in each 2×2 block are predicted sequentially for lower right, below, and right positions. These steps are repeated to recover all remaining pixels and restore the original image.

Case 2: With only data hiding key K_d, the original encrypted image and encrypted secret data are obtained as described previously, but only the secret data can be perfectly recovered using K_d.

Case 3: With both keys K_{en} and K_d, both original image and secret data can be perfectly recovered without error.

3   Experimental Results and Analysis

This section evaluates the progressive CNN-based predictor and bit-plane compression method through comprehensive experiments comparing against state-of-the-art methods. Performance assessment focuses on three aspects: prediction accuracy, embedding capacity, and image security. Peak signal-to-noise ratio

(PSNR) and structural similarity (SSIM) measure reversibility, while embedding rate (ER) evaluates capacity. Testing employs six standard images (Baboon, Barbara, Jetplane, Lakeboat, Lena, Peppers) and three datasets: UCID [18], BOSSbase [2], and BOWS-2 [3](Fig. 5).

Table 1. Mean, VAR and MSE Values on UCID.V2 Dataset

Prediction	Method	Mean	Var	Mse
	Hu et al.(2021)	3.666	39.145	58.803
	Hu et al.(2022)	3.594	38.015	56.902
	Proposed method	3.486	36.104	54.902
	Hu et al.(2021)	4.160	55.072	82.892
	Hu et al.(2022)	4.116	53.927	80.575
	Proposed method	4.051	51.700	76.842
	Hu et al.(2021)	7.910	174.760	277.273
	Hu et al.(2022)	7.799	171.845	272.370
	Proposed method	7.757	168.789	267.965

Table 2. The Compressed Bit-Plane in Six Test Images

Bit-plane	Baboon	Barbara	Jetplane	Lakeboat	Lena	Peppers
Original(bits)	262,144	262,144	262,144	262,144	262,144	262,144
8	-	-	-	-	-	-
7	41,366	25,083	7,633	11,171	4,539	4,438
6	124,542	54,264	22,640	42,309	15,952	17,330
5	222,865	94,661	47,319	128,541	44,239	54,752
4	-	166,196	104,315	245,370	130,239	195,081
3	-	-	209,847	-	-	-
2	-	-	-	-	-	-
1	-	-	-	-	-	-

3.1 Prediction Accuracy

We evaluate the proposed progressive CNN-based predictor against two established CNN-based predictors [8,9] using all 1338 images from the UCID dataset. Performance assessment employs three metrics: Mean of absolute prediction error (Mean), Variance of prediction error (Var), and Mean square error (Mse), where lower values indicate superior prediction accuracy.

Table 3. The Net Embedding Capacity and Auxiliary Information on Test Images

Test images	Baboon	Barbara	Jetplane	Lakeboat	Lena	Peppers
Room	397,596	708,288	918,861	621,101	853,523	776,891
Number	235	169	33	8	10	12
Location	18*235	18*169	18*33	18*8	18*10	18*12
Parameter	12	11	10	11	11	11
bits	393,336	705,217	918,239	620,928	853,314	776,646
bpp	1.501	2.690	3.503	2.369	3.255	2.963

Table 4. Experimental Results of the Net ER (*bpp*) on Three Image Datasets

Test images	UCID	Bossbase	BOWS-2
Best case	5.3146	7.8237	7.1042
Worst case	0.0793	0.0742	0.6535
Average	2.9308	3.6801	3.5570
PSNR	$+\infty$	$+\infty$	$+\infty$
SSIM	1	1	1

All predictors receive identical training using 160 epochs with the best validation model selected as the final result. The progressive stages are denoted as 3:1 for the first stage (using three pixels to predict one in each block), and correspondingly for subsequent stages.

Table 1 demonstrates that our proposed progressive CNN-based predictor achieves consistently lower Mean, VAR, and Mse values across all three stages compared to the classical CNN-based predictors, confirming superior prediction performance.

3.2 Capacity Analysis

The capacity is evaluated through embedding rate (ER) on six standard test images and three datasets: UCID, BOSSbase and BOWS-2. Table 2 shows bitstream lengths before and after compression. The progressive CNN-based predictor achieves high accuracy, generating more continuous "0"s than "1" s in 4th-7th bit-planes, enabling effective compression. The 8th bit-plane records prediction error signs with randomly distributed bits, so compression is skipped when ineffective.

Table 3 shows auxiliary information requires only 4 bits for block size, 3 bits for L_{fix}, plus location bits for overflow pixels and uncompressed bit-planes. This overhead is negligible—for Jetplane, only 622 bits (0.067%) are needed versus 918,239 bits capacity.

Table 4 presents average net ER results. BOSSbase and BOWS-2 (10,000 images, 512×512) achieve 0.0742-7.8237 bpp and 0.6535-7.1042 bpp respectively.

UCID (1,338 images, 512×384/384×512) achieves 0.0793-5.3146 bpp (average 2.9308 bpp) excluding images with complex textures where compression fails. Infinite PSNR and SSIM=1 confirm lossless restoration.

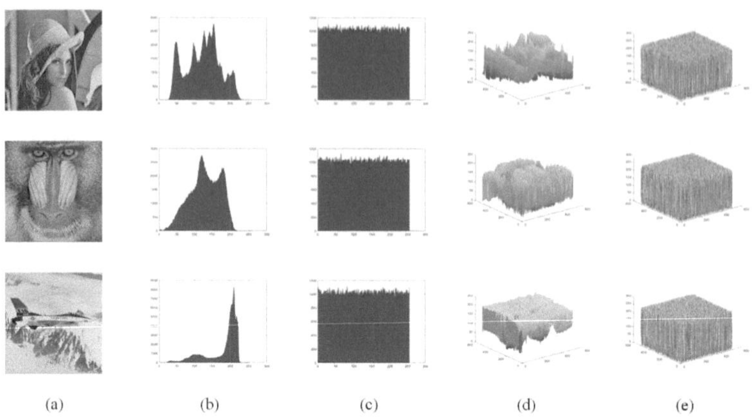

(a)   (b)   (c)   (d)   (e)

Fig. 6. (a) Original image; (b) Histogram of original image; (c) Histogram of marked image; (d) Pixel distribution of original image; (e) Pixel distribution of marked image.

3.3 Security Analysis

In order to prevent malicious attack from reading the content of the secret data, we adopt the histogram analysis and the pixel distribution to verify the security of the proposed method. As shown in Fig. 6, the images in the first column are the original image of Lena, Baboon and Jetplane respectively. For one image, the smoother the histogram is, the less feature information it provides. It is clear from the second column that the histogram before encryption and embedding are different with distinct feature information, which means each test image can be easily distinguished. On the contrary, after the encryption and embedding operation, the histograms of the three images in the third column distributed between [0,255] uniformly, therefore we cannot obtain any useful feature information from it. Similarly, the pixel distribution of each image before and after the encryption and embedding operation is completely different. It can be seen that the naked eye cannot obtain any feature information related to the original image from the marked images without the corresponding key, which sufficiently demonstrates that the proposed method is resistant to the histogram analysis attacks.

4 Conclusion

In this paper, an RDHEI method combined CNN-based pixel prediction with bit-plane compression is proposed. In the prediction part, a new image division method is first introduced, which can provide three-quarters of the image information as the context during the prediction process. Combing it with the progressive CNN-based predictor, the prediction accuracy can be improved significantly compared with the classical linear predictors. At the same time, the existence of the convolutional block attention module (CBAM) further improve the prediction accuracy of the pixels. In the embedding part, the bit-plane compression method is adopted to vacate more room since the multi-MSB planes of prediction error exist a large number of adjacent "0". What's more, the two-stage embedding provides extra vacated room for data embedding. Experiments show that not only the recovery of the original image and the extraction of the secret data are perfectly and separately, but also the proposed method can achieve a high embedding capacity.

In future work, we will further explore how to improve the prediction accuracy of the CNN-based predictor and design the algorithm to further improve compression rate of the bit stream.

References

1. Alattar, A.M.: Reversible watermark using the difference expansion of a generalized integer transform. IEEE Trans. Image Process. **13**, 1147–1156 (2004)
2. Bas, P., Filler, T., Pevný, T.: "Break our steganographic system": The ins and outs of organizing boss. In: International Workshop on Information Hiding, pp. 59–70 (2011)
3. Bas, P., Furon, T.: Image database of bows-2 (2017). Accessed 20 June 2016–2017
4. Bhardwaj, R., Aggarwal, A.: An improved block based joint reversible data hiding in encrypted images by symmetric cryptosystem. Pattern Recogn. Lett. **139**, 60–68 (2020)
5. Chang, Q., Li, X., Zhao, Y.: Reversible data hiding for color images based on adaptive three-dimensional histogram modification. IEEE Trans. Circuits Syst. Video Technol. **32**, 5725–5735 (2022)
6. Chang, Q., Li, X., Zhao, Y., Ni, R.: Adaptive pairwise prediction-error expansion and multiple histograms modification for reversible data hiding. IEEE Trans. Circuits Syst. Video Technol. **31**, 4850–4863 (2021)
7. Coatrieux, G., Pan, W., Cuppens-Boulahia, N., Cuppens, F., Roux, C.: Reversible watermarking based on invariant image classification and dynamic histogram shifting. IEEE Trans. Inf. Forensics Secur. **8**, 111–120 (2013)
8. Hu, R., Xiang, S.: CNN prediction based reversible data hiding. IEEE Signal Process. Lett. **28**, 464–468 (2021)
9. Hu, R., Xiang, S.: Reversible data hiding by using CNN prediction and adaptive embedding. IEEE Trans. Pattern Anal. Mach. Intell. **44**, 10196–10208 (2022)
10. Ke, Y., Zhang, M., Liu, J., Su, T., Yang, X.: Fully homomorphic encryption encapsulated difference expansion for reversible data hiding in encrypted domain. IEEE Trans. Circuits Syst. Video Technol. **30**, 2353–2365 (2020)
11. Liu, Y., Tang, S., Liu, R., Zhang, L., Ma, Z.: Reversible data hiding in encrypted images based on pixel-level masked autoencoder and polar code. Signal Proc. **425**, Article 109664 (2024)
12. Ni, Z., Shi, Y., Ansari, N., Su, W.: Reversible data hiding. IEEE Trans. Circuits Syst. Video Technol. **16**, 354–362 (2006)

13. Ou, B., Li, X., Zhao, Y., Ni, R., Shi, Y.: Pairwise prediction-error expansion for efficient reversible data hiding. IEEE Trans. Image Process. **22**, 5010–5021 (2013)
14. Puteaux, P., Puech, W.: An efficient MSB prediction-based method for high-capacity reversible data hiding in encrypted images. IEEE Trans. Inf. Forensics Secur. **13**, 1670–1681 (2018)
15. Qian, Z., Zhang, X.: Reversible data hiding in encrypted image with distributed source encoding. IEEE Trans. Circuits Syst. Video Technol. **26**, 636–646 (2016)
16. Qiu, Y., Qian, Z., Yu, L.: Adaptive reversible data hiding by extending the generalized integer transformation. IEEE Signal Process. Lett. **23**, 130–134 (2015)
17. Ren, F., Zhang, Z., Jiang, K., Geng, J., Ren, R.: Reversible data hiding and authentication scheme for encrypted image based on prediction error compression. Sci. Rep. **15**, Article 11636 (2025)
18. Schaefer, G., Stich, M.: UCID: an uncompressed color image database. In: Storage and retrieval methods and applications for multimedia, pp. 472–480 (2003)
19. Agarwal, N., Singh, A.K., Singh, P.K.: Survey of robust and imperceptible watermarking. Multimedia Tools Appl. **78**(7), 8603–8633 (2019). https://doi.org/10.1007/s11042-018-7128-5
20. Tao, J., Li, S., Zhang, X., Wang, Z.: Towards robust image steganography. IEEE Trans. Circuits Syst. Video Technol. **29**, 594–600 (2019)
21. Expansion embedding techniques for reversible watermarking: Thodi, D.M., Rodríguez, J.J. IEEE Trans. Image Process. **16**, 721–730 (2007)
22. Tian, J.: Reversible data embedding using a difference expansion. IEEE Trans. Circuits Syst. Video Technol. **13**, 890–896 (2003)
23. Wang, Y., He, W.: High capacity reversible data hiding in encrypted image based on adaptive MSB prediction. IEEE Trans. Multimedia **24**, 1288–1298 (2022)
24. Weinberger, M., Seroussi, G., Sapiro, G.: The loco-i lossless image compression algorithm: principles and standardization into jpeg-ls. IEEE Trans. Image Process. **9**(8), 1309–1324 (2000)
25. Weng, S., Zhou, Y., Zhang, T., Xiao, M., Zhao, Y.: General framework to reversible data hiding for jpeg images with multiple two-dimensional histograms. In: IEEE Transactions on Multimedia ,pp. 1–16 (2022)
26. Weng, S., Zhou, Y., Zhang, T., Xiao, M., Zhao, Y.: Reversible data hiding for jpeg images with adaptive multiple two-dimensional histogram and mapping generation. IEEE Trans. Multimedia, pp. 1–15 (2023)
27. Woo, S., Park, J., Lee, J.-Y., Kweon, I.S.: CBAM: Convolutional Block Attention Module. In: Ferrari, V., Hebert, M., Sminchisescu, C., Weiss, Y. (eds.) ECCV 2018. LNCS, vol. 11211, pp. 3–19. Springer, Cham (2018). https://doi.org/10.1007/978-3-030-01234-2_1
28. Wu, Y., Xiang, Y., Guo, Y., Tang, J., Yin, Z., Yin, Z.: An improved reversible data hiding in encrypted images using parametric binary tree labeling. IEEE Trans. Multimedia **22**, 1929–1938 (2020)
29. Xu, D., Wang, R.: Separable and error-free reversible data hiding in encrypted images. Signal Process. **123**, 9–21 (2016)
30. Yi, S., Zhou, Y.: Separable and reversible data hiding in encrypted images using parametric binary tree labeling. IEEE Trans. Multimedia **21**, 51–64 (2019)
31. Yin, Z., Niu, X., Zhang, X., Jin, T., Luo, B.: Reversible data hiding in encrypted AMBTC images. Multimedia Tools Appl. **77**, 18067–18083 (2018)
32. Yin, Z., Xiang, Y., Zhang, X.: Reversible data hiding in encrypted images based on multi-MSB prediction and huffman coding. IEEE Trans. Multimedia **22**, 874–884 (2020)

33. Zhang, T., Hou, T., Weng, S., Zou, F., Zhang, H., Chang, C.C.: Adaptive reversible data hiding with contrast enhancement based on multi-histogram modification. IEEE Trans. Circuits Syst. Video Technol. **32**, 5041–5054 (2022)
34. Zhang, W., Ma, K., Yu, N.: Reversibility improved data hiding in encrypted images. Signal Process. **94**, 118–127 (2014)
35. Zhang, X.: Reversible data hiding in encrypted image. IEEE Signal Process. Lett. **18**, 255–258 (2011)
36. Zhang, X.: Separable reversible data hiding in encrypted image. IEEE Trans. Inf. Forensics Secur. **7**, 826–832 (2012)

A Non-contiguous 3D Object Encryption Method with Multi-level Visual Access Control

Jiahao Li[1,3], Zhongshuai Wang[1,3], Ruoyu Zhao[2], Yushu Zhang[2], Rushi Lan[1,3(✉)], and Xiaonan Luo[1,3]

[1] Guangxi Key Laboratory of Image and Graphic Intelligent Processing, Guilin University of Electronic Technology, Guilin 541004, Guangxi, China
[2] Jiangxi Provincial Key Laboratory of Multimedia Intelligent Processing, Nanchang 330013, China
[3] International Joint Research Laboratory of Spatio-temporal Information and Intelligent Location Services, Guilin University of Electronic Technology, Guilin 541004, Guangxi, China
rslan2016@163.com

Abstract. Hierarchical decryption of 3D objects supports multi-level visual access control and is widely used in digital rights protection and secure data transmission. However, existing methods often encrypt adjacent mantissa bits continuously, causing cumulative bit-level perturbations that lead to geometric distortion and reduced visual fidelity in decrypted objects. To mitigate this, we propose a non-contiguous 3D object encryption method with multi-level visual access control that balance security and visual quality. Using an IEEE 754-based mantissa segmentation approach, we insert fixed-length gap bits between access levels to break perturbation continuity and reduce geometric noise. By assigning non-overlapping bit segments to each access level, the method enables multi-level decryption with clear level separation and reliable visual reconstruction. Experiments show that our method achieves lower root mean squared error(RMSE) and Hausdorff Distance(HD) than conventional schemes while preserving clearer visual distinction between access levels. This ensures better object quality even at lower access levels. In terms of security, our method increases the key space and ciphertext randomness, improving resistance to brute-force and statistical attacks.

Keywords: 3D objects encryption · Non-contiguous bit selection · Multi-level decryption · Visual fidelity

1 Introduction

With the rapid advancement of technologies such as cloud computing [24], digital twins [19], and virtual reality [10], 3D objects are increasingly utilized across various domains, including industrial design [17], cultural heritage preservation [3], and healthcare [1]. Particularly in cloud-based modeling and sharing

© The Author(s), under exclusive license to Springer Nature Singapore Pte Ltd. 2026
Z. Lin et al. (Eds.): ICIG 2025, LNCS 16163, pp. 336–347, 2026.
https://doi.org/10.1007/978-981-95-3729-7_28

platforms [14,16],3D objects often require hierarchical access control: designers may need full access, reviewers only structural outlines, and general users merely blurred previews. In such cases, traditional full-encryption schemes lack flexibility and impose significant constraints on visualization and user interaction.

Conventional 3D object protection methods, such as digital watermarking [15], access control [7], and full encryption [21], each have limitations. Watermarking is lightweight but offers weak security and is easily removed. Access control depends on external systems and fails once the object is decrypted. Full encryption ensures strong confidentiality but lacks flexibility, allowing either full access or none. In addition, these methods often face issues such as low visual adaptability [12], poor compatibility with standard 3D formats [6], and high computational cost [21].

In contrast, format-compatible multi-level decryption enables fine-grained 3D object multi-level key schemes, allowing controlled access and progressive detail disclosure. Jansen et al. [22] proposed dividing the mantissas of 3D vertex coordinates into hierarchical sub-blocks and employing AES encryption with a hierarchical key to enable progressive decryption. Similarly, Zhao et al. [25] introduced a lossless paradigm that preserves precision by embedding encrypted bitstreams into zeroed coefficients, achieving both universal applicability and hierarchical visual effects.

Although these methods are effective in enforcing access control, they typically encrypt consecutive mantissa bits, which can cause significant geometric distortion—especially in low-detail objects or scenarios requiring high structural precision.

To address these challenges, we introduce a non-contiguous 3D object encryption method that supports multi-level visual access control while balancing security and visual fidelity. Building on the IEEE 754 floating-point format, the method segments the mantissa and inserts fixed-length gap bits between encrypted blocks corresponding to different access levels. This design disrupts the continuity of bit-level perturbations, thereby suppressing geometric noise and reducing numerical distortion during decryption. By assigning non-overlapping mantissa segments to each level, the approach facilitates multi-level decryption with clear separation between levels and reliable visual reconstruction. Our contributions are summarized as follows:

– We identify a brute-force vulnerability in conventional hierarchical decryption due to predictable bit patterns. By analyzing the trade-off between geometric accuracy and visual contrast, we introduce tunable bit-gap parameters that enhance randomness and adaptability across diverse application scenarios.
– We propose a non-contiguous bit selection encryption method that inserts gap bits between mantissa segments at different access levels, thereby achieving multi-level decryption while disrupting bit-level continuity to reduce geometric noise and balance visual fidelity and security.
– Experimental results on public 3D datasets show that our method significantly lowers RMSE and HD while improving structural clarity and visual separability.

2   Related Work

The primary objective of 3D object encryption is to ensure the security and privacy of object data. Based on the recognizability of visual information, existing encryption methods can be broadly categorized into two types.

2.1   Full Encryption

Full encryption refers to the comprehensive protection of all 3D object components (vertex coordinates, face data, and texture information) to completely obscure visual content and ensure high security. Jolfaei et al. [8] proposed a holistic encryption scheme that maintains spatial dimensional consistency and geometric stability. This approach applies random permutation and rotation operations on point cloud coordinates, effectively disrupting original geometry while preserving approximate volume and distribution features. Wang et al. [23] introduced a fast 3D object encryption method based on chaotic systems. By converting 3D objects into quasi-2D image-like structures, they applied multi-dimensional chaotic maps to scramble vertex and face data, rendering the object visually and structurally unrecognizable. Liang et al. [13] proposed a 3D mesh encryption method based on asymmetric cryptography, aiming to enhance security and improve flexibility in key management. Their scheme uses an optimized RSA algorithm to encrypt vertex data and incorporates a hash-based verification mechanism to ensure data integrity and tamper resistance.

2.2   Partial Encryption

Partial encryption methods selectively encrypt specific components of the object based on data sensitivity, with the goal of partially hiding visual information while preserving the object's usability. Eluard et al. [5] proposed a geometry-preserving encryption scheme for 3D meshes that protects data without disrupting the object's topological structure. By permuting vertex orders and connectivity relations, the method obfuscates visual features while maintaining the overall geometric connectivity and file format structure. Beugnon et al. [2] introduced a selective encryption approach aimed at visual confidentiality in 3D objects. Their method performs targeted encryption of binary representations of vertex coordinates in 3D meshes, achieving effective visual concealment while ensuring compatibility with the original file format. Jansen et al. [22] proposed a format-compatible hierarchical decryption scheme for 3D objects. By dividing the mantissas of floating-point coordinates into bit-level segments and encrypting them in sub-blocks, this method achieves clear visual separation among three access levels [2] (confidential, sufficient, and transparent). It has become one of the representative methods enabling multi-level visual access for 3D objects.

However, when fewer bits are encrypted, this method remains vulnerable to brute-force attacks and suffers from cumulative perturbations that cause error propagation, leading to geometric degradation at lower access levels. To address these limitations, this paper introduces a non-contiguous bit selection encryption method to further balance security and visual quality.

3   Method Construction

3.1   Model Architecture

Our method ensures 3D object security while enabling multi-level visual access control via structural reconfiguration and bit-level optimization for encrypted 3D objects. As shown in Fig. 1, the overall framework comprises four core modules: Data Processing, Hierarchical Key Generation, Encryption, and Decryption.

The pipeline begins with Data Processing, which analyzes and preprocesses the 3D object's geometry for encryption. Simultaneously, Hierarchical Key Generation derives keys K_1, K_2, K_3 from a master key K_3, each tied to different access privileges for multi-level decryption. The Encryption module employs non-contiguous bit selection to secure the data, introducing visual distortion. During Decryption, keys unlock tiered visual fidelity (e.g., Sufficient, Transparent, Clear [2]), enabling progressive detail disclosure aligned with user authorization.

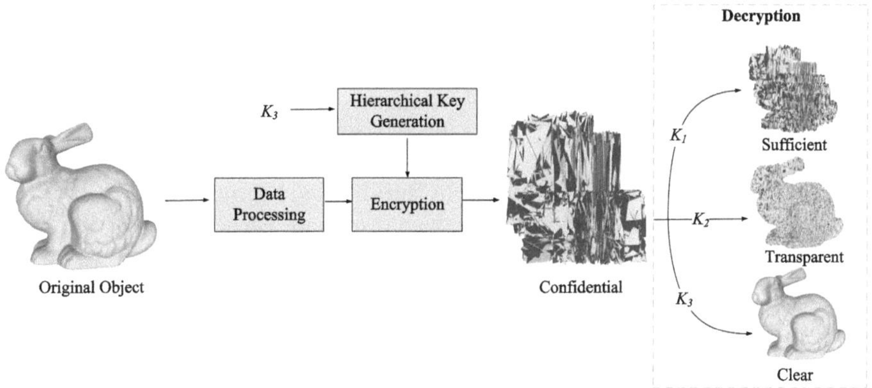

Fig. 1. Overall architecture of the non-contiguous bit selection encryption object.

3.2   Data Processing

Each vertex coordinate of the 3D object is represented as a 32-bit floating-point number in accordance with the IEEE 754 standard [9], as shown in Fig. 2. The complete set of vertices is denoted by $\{V = v_0, v_1, ..., v_{|V|-1}\}$, where each vertex v comprises three coordinates: x, y, and z.

Fig. 2. IEEE 754 Single-Precision Floating-Point Format.

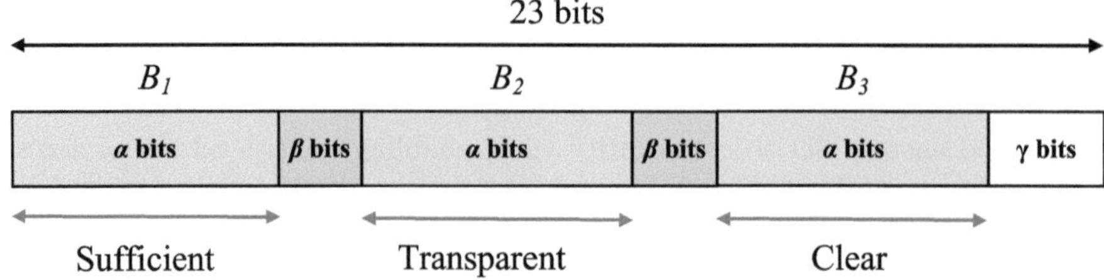

Fig. 3. Partitioning of mantissa bits with bit-gap insertion for multi-level decryption.

To enable multi-level decryption with flexible and dynamic visual effect composition, the mantissa bits of each vertex coordinate are divided into three sub-blocks, each containing α bits and corresponding to a distinct decryption level. A fixed gap of β bits is inserted between every two adjacent sub-blocks, while the remaining γ bits are left unprocessed. These parameters collectively satisfy the constraint: $(3\alpha + 2\beta + \gamma \leq 23)$ as illustrated in Fig. 3.

After processing the vertex data, three α-bit sub-blocks are extracted from each vertex coordinate. These sub-blocks are then reorganized into a new sequence of composite blocks B_i^j, where $\{0 \leq i \leq 3\}$ and $\{0 \leq j < S\}$, S denotes the total number of composite blocks formed across all vertices. As illustrated in Fig. 4.

Since AES encrypts the 3D object by sub-blocks, the number of sub-blocks directly impacts processing time. To reduce overhead, each sub-block is limited to 128 bits, and the total number of sub-blocks S is calculated as:

$$S = \lfloor \frac{3V \times \alpha}{128} \rfloor, \tag{1}$$

where $\lfloor \cdot \rfloor$ denotes the floor function, which returns the greatest integer less than or equal to the input.

3.3 Hierarchical Key Generation

To enable multi-level decryption, hierarchical keys are generated from a master key, with each key corresponding to a specific decryption permission level. The key generation process is illustrated in Fig. 5.

The key structure includes three levels: the master key K_3 is used for full decryption, allowing complete restoration of the original object; the intermediate key K_2 enables partial decryption, revealing a low-resolution but structurally recognizable version of the object; and the base-level key K_1 yields a highly blurred version that only exposes coarse contours.

The key generation procedure begins with a user-defined high-security master key. Subsequent keys are derived from encrypted block data of the higher level, using cryptographic operations to ensure forward secrecy across levels. The specific derivation process is defined as follows: following the relationship:

$$K_2 = H \left(B_3^0 + E_{AES} \left(K_3 + B_3^0 \right) \right), \tag{2}$$

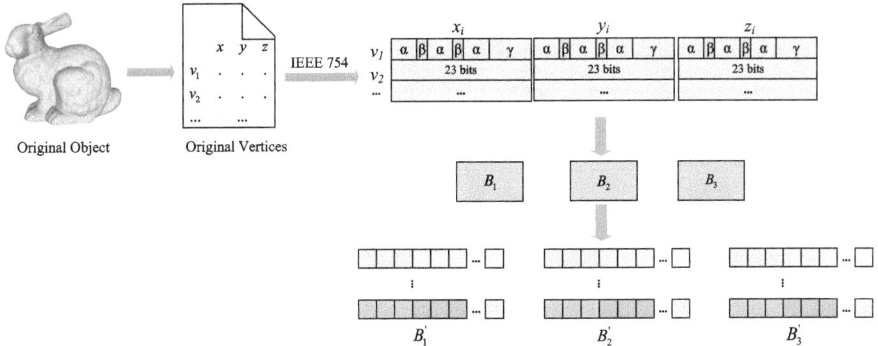

Fig. 4. Sub-block extraction and recombination of vertex data. Sub-block partitioning scheme. Each vertex coordinate (x, y, z) is converted to a 32-bit IEEE 754 floating-point number, from which mantissa bits are extracted. The mantissa is divided into three α-bit sub-blocks (purple) for multi-level decryption, with β-bit gap blocks (blue) inserted between them to disrupt bit continuity. Sub-blocks at the same position across all vertices are then aggregated into new encryption blocks (green) for unified processing. (Color figure online)

$$K_1 = H\left(B_2^0 + E_{AES}\left(K_2 + B_2^0\right)\right), \tag{3}$$

where $H(\cdot)$ denotes an irreversible hash function SHA256 [18], $E_{AES}(\cdot)$ represents the AES encryption function, and B_3^0 and B_2^0 correspond to the block data at their respective hierarchical levels.

3.4   Encryption and Decryption

In this study, the AES-CFB (Cipher Feedback) mode [4] is employed during encryption to enhance the security of data blocks and to prevent identical plaintext blocks from mapping to the same ciphertext blocks. The IV generation process is similar to the key generation method illustrated in Fig. 5.

Encryption Process. All data sub-blocks B_1, B_2, and B_3 are processed in the same manner during encryption. To illustrate the encryption process, we take B_3 as an example. Specifically, the encryption of B_3 can be formalized as:

$$C_3^k = AES(K_3, C_3^{k-1}) \oplus B_3^k, \tag{4}$$

where $AES(\cdot)$ represents the AES function encrypting the sub-block, and $\oplus$ denotes the XOR operation. Before encryption, the sub-block B_3^k is padded to 128 bits to satisfy the AES-128 input requirements. Then, AES is applied to the previous encrypted sub-block C_3^{k-1} using key K_3, producing a 128-bit output. This output is then XORed with the current plaintext sub-block B_3^k to produce the encrypted sub-block C_3^k. When $k = 0$, C_3^{k-1} is replaced by the initialization vector IV_3.

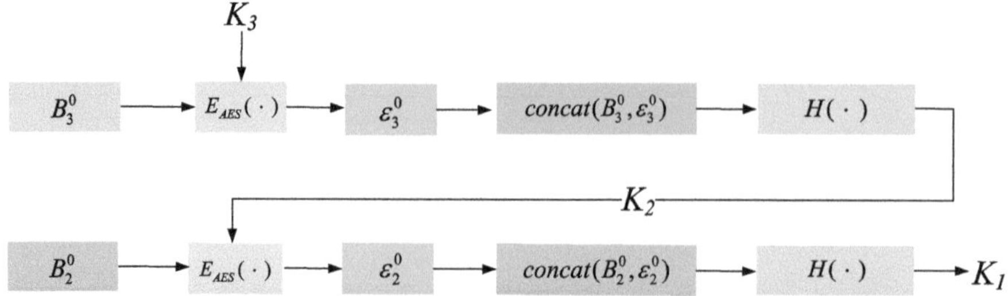

Fig. 5. The process of key generation. ε_3^0 represents the AES result of K_3 and B_3^0. It is combined with the plaintext block B_3^0 as input to the hash function SHA256 to generate the final output.

Decryption Process. Upon receiving the encrypted 3D object, authorized recipients can decrypt the data according to the decryption keys in their possession. The decryption process is divided into three access levels:

1. **Clear Level:** Recipients with the key K_3 can decrypt all encrypted sub-blocks, thereby reconstructing the high-fidelity 3D object in its entirety.
2. **Transparent Level:** Recipients with the key K_2 are able to decrypt intermediate sub-blocks, yielding a low-resolution but structurally recognizable version of the 3D object.
3. **Sufficient Level:** Recipients possessing only the key K_1 can decrypt the lowest-level sub-blocks, obtaining a coarse object that preserves the overall shape while concealing sensitive details.

To illustrate the decryption procedure, consider a recipient who holds the key K_3 and the corresponding initialization vector IV_3. The plaintext sub-block P_k can be recovered from the ciphertext sub-block C_k using the following formula:

$$B_3^k = AES(K_3, C_3^{k-1}) \oplus C_3^k. \tag{5}$$

Similar to the encryption process, when $k = 0$, the value of C_3^{k-1} is substituted with the initialization vector IV_3.

4   Experimental Results and Analysis

4.1   Experimental Setup

The experiments were conducted on a hardware platform equipped with an Intel Core i7-14650HX CPU running at 2.20 GHz, without the use of GPU. The software environment was MATLAB 2024a.

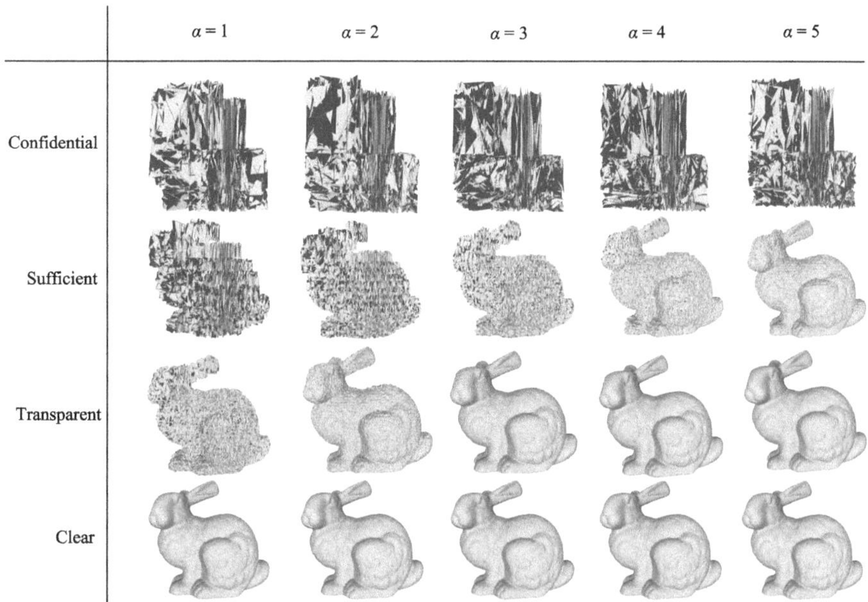

Fig. 6. Encryption and multi-level decryption results of the Bunny object using our method with varying α values ($\alpha = 1$ to 5) and a fixed gap parameter $\beta = 1$.

4.2   Experimental Results

Visual Quality. Figure 6 illustrates the 3D object Bunny obtained from the Stanford 3D Scanning Repository [11], alongside the results of encryption and decryption performed using our proposed method. In this example, the initialization key K_3=357538782F413F4428472B4B6250655368566D597033733676 39792442264529 and the initialization vector IV_3=472D4A614E645267556B587 032733576 were used. The gap parameter β was set to the default value of 1.

Experimental results show that when $\alpha = 1$ or $\alpha = 2$, the visual distinctions between different access levels are clearly perceptible. However, as α increases to 4 or 5, the differences between the transparent and clear levels become less noticeable, since larger values of α expose substantially more fine-grained details, reducing the separation between multi-level views.

Visual Effectiveness Evaluation. To evaluate visual performance, comparative experiments with the baseline [22] were conducted at $\alpha = 1$. As shown in Fig. 7, both methods induce significant geometric perturbations during encryption to ensure security, making original shapes unrecognizable. At sufficient and transparent levels, our gap-insertion strategy outperforms the baseline in preserving key features, reducing edge jaggedness, noise, and distortion for smoother reconstructions. This validates its advantage in balancing visual usability and structural fidelity without weakening encryption.

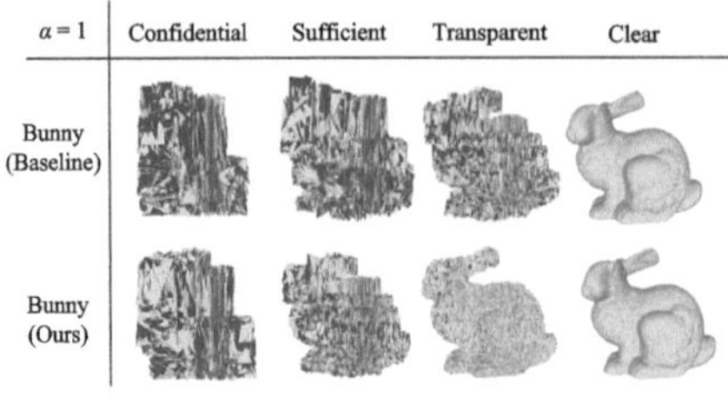

Fig. 7. Comparative visualization of encryption and multi-level decryption results with encryption parameter $\alpha = 1$ and fixed $\beta = 1$.

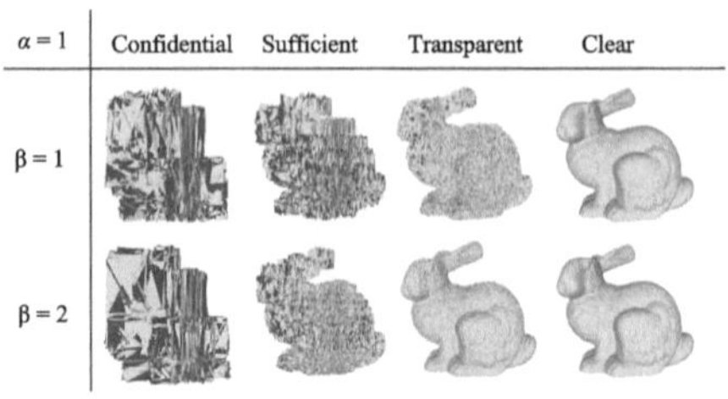

Fig. 8. Comparative visualization of encryption and multi-level decryption results under varying gap sizes β, with fixed encryption parameter $\alpha = 1$.

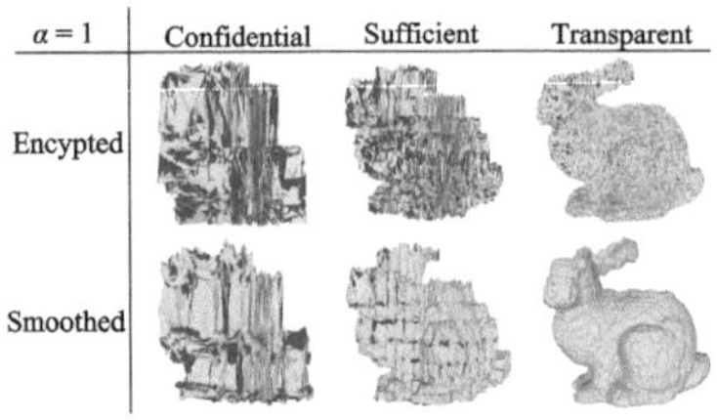

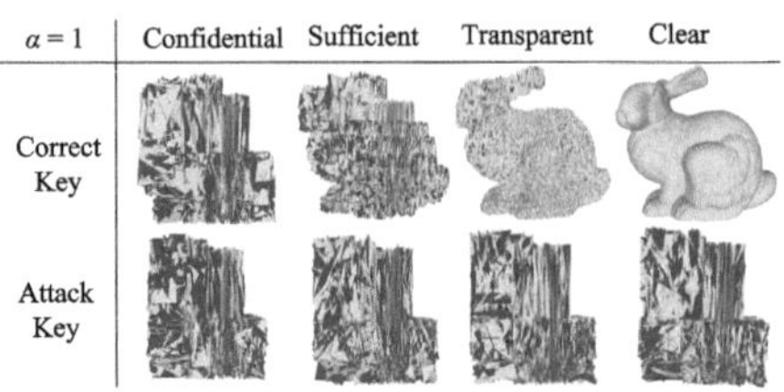

Fig. 9. Laplacian smoothing attack on encrypted and decrypted objects at different access levels.

Fig. 10. Decryption results under single-bit key modification attack at various encryption levels.

Controllability of Encryption Effects. The controllability of encryption effects was further investigated by varying the gap size with α fixed at 1, as shown in Fig. 8. Results reveal a critical trade-off: larger gaps decrease bit-level perturbations and improve geometric accuracy but diminish visual differences between access levels, while smaller gaps enhance visual separability at the cost of increased structural distortion in lower-level reconstructions. This analysis confirms that the gap size serves as a tunable parameter to flexibly balance visual hierarchy and structural fidelity. Optimizing this parameter enables the encryption scheme to adapt to diverse application requirements, achieving a balanced performance in security, visual clarity, and geometric accuracy.

Quantitative Validation of Visual Fidelity. To quantitatively validate the method's effectiveness in improving visual fidelity, comparative experiments were performed on the Bunny model with encryption parameters $\alpha = 1$ to 5. Using RMSE and HD as metrics to quantify overall geometric error and maximum local deformation, respectively, our approach significantly reduces geometric errors and visual distortions during decryption—particularly at lower access privilege levels (transparent and sufficient). As summarized in Table 1, under equivalent encryption strength, our method demonstrates superior model quality preservation, highlighting its practical advantages.

Table 1. Comparison of RMSE (10^{-3}) and HD (10^{-3}) between baseline and our method under different α values.

Access Level		RMSE					HD				
		$\alpha=1$	$\alpha=2$	$\alpha=3$	$\alpha=4$	$\alpha=5$	$\alpha=1$	$\alpha=2$	$\alpha=3$	$\alpha=4$	$\alpha=5$
Confidential	Baseline	160	162	163	164	162	160	162	163	163	162
	Ours	19.0	21.4	21.8	22.1	22.0	86.4	104.8	107.2	106.4	106.4
Sufficient	Baseline	75.864	39.610	19.725	9.839	4.920	75.864	39.610	19.725	9.839	4.920
	Ours	4.7000	2.6000	1.3000	0.6599	0.3276	19.900	13.600	7.2000	3.8000	2.0000
Transparent	Baseline	34.008	9.527	2.454	0.615	0.154	34.008	9.512	2.454	0.615	0.154
	Ours	1.1000	0.3177	0.0812	0.0245	0.0051	4.5000	1.6000	0.4836	0.1274	0.0316

4.3 Sensitivity Analysis

Smoothing Attack. To assess geometric stability and robustness against attacks during encryption and decryption, Laplacian smoothing [20] was applied to encrypted and decrypted objects across access levels, as shown in Fig. 9. Results show encrypted objects remain heavily perturbed post-smoothing, failing to recover valid geometries, confirming our method's resistance to geometric reconstruction attacks under high encryption. For decrypted objects at sufficient and transparent levels, smoothing marginally enhances visual quality while preserving higher-security content, demonstrating content-tier isolation.

Key Security Analysis. To assess the key sensitivity of the proposed encryption method, a single-bit modification attack was conducted. The 3D object, encryption parameters, and initial vector (IV) were kept unchanged, while the least significant bit of the correct keys (K_1, K_2, K_3) was altered to generate incorrect key sets, as presented in Table 2. These modified keys were then applied to decrypt the encrypted objects at different access levels, enabling an evaluation of the scheme's sensitivity to key perturbations.

Table 2. Correct keys and corresponding keys with least significant bit set to 0 for single-bit modification attack.

Correct Key	K_3	357538782F413F4428472B4B6250655368566D5970337336763979242264529
	K_2	D3C5E1A445C7E46E2E7A447AA0A981CB0A90C40B666620799C44BBB263561F17
	K_1	0703C8BAEE4EA296AB5AD06A8A8E1336015B5F6A0DDDBD9BB946D52C63B88BE6
Attack Key	K_3	357538782F413F4428472B4B6250655368566D5970337336763979242264520
	K_2	D3C5E1A445C7E46E2E7A447AA0A981CB0A90C40B666620799C44BBB263561F10
	K_1	0703C8BAEE4EA296AB5AD06A8A8E1336015B5F6A0DDDBD9BB946D52C63B88BE0

As shown in Fig. 10, a single-bit change in the decryption key causes complete failure to recover the original geometry, resulting in severe structural distortion and visually unidentifiable shapes. In contrast, the correct keys enable precise reconstruction with distinct multi-level details. These results demonstrate the scheme's high key sensitivity and strong resistance to key-guessing and brute-force attacks, enhancing system security.

5   Conclusion

This paper presents a non-contiguous bit selection encryption method for 3D objects, using IEEE 754 floating-point mantissa segmentation to insert gap bits between encrypted sub-blocks of different access levels for balancing security and visual quality during decryption; the method enables multi-level decryption with distinct visual reconstructions by allocating non-overlapping mantissa segments, maintains model quality at lower access levels, enhances security via increased ciphertext randomness, and experiments on public datasets show it reduces RMSE and HD while balancing structural accuracy and visual separation, with gap parameter flexibility and validated robustness against smoothing attacks and key modification tests demonstrating high key sensitivity and cryptographic resilience.

Acknowledgment. This research was supported in part by Guangxi Natural Science Foundation, China (Nos. AB25069496 and 2024GXNSFFA010014); the National Natural Science Foundation of China (Nos. 62172120, 82360356, 82272075 and 62362014).

References

1. Bardi, F., Gasparotti, E., Vignali, E., Avril, S., Celi, S.: A hybrid mock circulatory loop for fluid dynamic characterization of 3D anatomical phantoms. IEEE Trans. Biomed. Eng. **70**(5), 1651–1661 (2022)
2. Beugnon, S., Puech, W., Pedeboy, J.P.: From visual confidentiality to transparent format-compliant selective encryption of 3d objects. In: 2018 IEEE International Conference on Multimedia & Expo Workshops (ICMEW), pp. 1–6. IEEE (2018)
3. Crisan, A., Pepe, M., Costantino, D., Herban, S.: From 3D point cloud to an intelligent model set for cultural heritage conservation. heritage **7**, 1419–1437 (2024)
4. Dworkin, M.: Recommendation for block cipher modes of operation. NIST Spec. Publ. **800**, 38B (2001)
5. Éluard, M., Maetz, Y., Doërr, G., Technicolor, R., France, D.: Geometry-preserving encryption for 3D meshes. Actes de COmpression et REprsentation des Signaux Audiovisuels, pp. 7–12 (2013)
6. Hou, X., Min, L., Yang, H.: A reversible watermarking scheme for vector maps based on multilevel histogram modification. Symmetry **10**(9), 397 (2018)
7. Jin, X., et al.: 3D textured model encryption via 3D LU chaotic mapping. SCI. CHINA Inf. Sci. **60**, 1–9 (2017)
8. Jolfaei, A., Wu, X.W., Muthukkumarasamy, V.: A 3D object encryption scheme which maintains dimensional and spatial stability. IEEE Trans. Inf. Forensics Secur. **10**(2), 409–422 (2014)
9. Kahan, W.: IEEE standard 754 for binary floating-point arithmetic. Lect. Notes Status IEEE **754**(94720–1776), 11 (1996)

10. Lampropoulos, G.: Kinshuk: virtual reality and gamification in education: a systematic review. Education Tech. Res. Dev. **72**(3), 1691–1785 (2024)
11. Levoy, M., Gerth, J., Curless, B., Pulli, K.: The stanford 3D scanning repository (2005). http://graphics.stanford.edu/data/3Dscanrep/. Accessed 26 May 2025
12. Li, S., Zhao, R., Guan, Q., Chen, J., Zhang, Y.: A 3D model encryption method supporting adaptive visual effects after decryption. Adv. Eng. Inform. **59**, 102319 (2024)
13. Liang, Y., He, F., Li, H.: An asymmetric and optimized encryption method to protect the confidentiality of 3D mesh model. Adv. Eng. Inform. **42**, 100963 (2019)
14. Marion, T., Olechowksi, A., Guo, J.: An analytical framework for collaborative cloud-based CAD platform affordances. Proc. Design Soc. **1**, 375–384 (2021)
15. Ohbuchi, R., Masuda, H., Aono, M.: Watermarking three-dimensional polygonal models through geometric and topological modifications. IEEE J. Sel. Areas Commun. **16**(4), 551–560 (1998)
16. Park, H., Yoon, S.E.: Collaborative 3D modeling system based on blockchain. arXiv preprint arXiv:1901.02629 (2019)
17. Radanovic, M., Khoshelham, K., Fraser, C.: Aligning the real and the virtual world: mixed reality localisation using learning-based 3d–3d model registration. Adv. Eng. Inform. **56**, 101960 (2023)
18. Selvakumar, A.L., Ganadhas, C.S.: The evaluation report of sha-256 crypt analysis hash function. In: 2009 International Conference on Communication Software and Networks, pp. 588–592. IEEE (2009)
19. Tao, F., Qi, Q., Wang, L., Nee, A.: Digital twins and cyber–physical systems toward smart manufacturing and industry 4.0: correlation and comparison. Engineering **5**(4), 653–661 (2019)
20. Taubin, G.: A signal processing approach to fair surface design. In: Proceedings of the 22nd annual conference on Computer graphics and interactive techniques, pp. 351–358 (1995)
21. Ullah, S., Radzi, R.Z., Yazdani, T.M., Alshehri, A., Khan, I.: Types of lightweight cryptographies in current developments for resource constrained machine type communication devices: challenges and opportunities. IEEE Access **10**, 35589–35604 (2022)
22. Rensburg, B.J., Puech, W., Pedeboy, J.P.: A format compliant encryption method for 3D objects allowing hierarchical decryption. IEEE Trans. Multimedia **25**, 7196–7207 (2022)
23. Wang, X., Xu, M., Li, Y.: Fast encryption scheme for 3D models based on chaos system. Multimedia Tools Appl. **78**(23), 33865–33884 (2019)
24. Yanamala, A.K.Y.: Emerging challenges in cloud computing security: a comprehensive review. Int. J. Adv. Eng. Technol. Innov. **1**(4), 448–479 (2024)
25. Zhao, R., Zhang, Y., Mou, J., Puech, W., Weng, J.: Lossless and universal 3D object encryption with differentiated visual effects upon decryption: a novel paradigm. IEEE Trans. Depend. Secure Comput. **22**(4) (2025)

Federated Privacy Re-identification via Frequency Domain Splitting

Xuanwen Su, Xu Wang, Tengfei Liang, Yi Jin$^{(\boxtimes)}$, and Yidong Li

School of Computer Science and Technology, Beijing Jiaotong University,
Beijing, China
`{xuanwen.su,xu.wang,tengfei.liang,yjin,ydli}@bjtu.edu.cn`

Abstract. With the growing prevalence of video surveillance systems, person re-identification technology has become increasingly important for public safety. However, existing technologies face the challenge of balancing privacy protection and model performance. To address these issues, this paper proposes a federated privacy-preserving framework named FPPReID. Firstly, it embeds frequency domain segmentation into federated learning to retain data locally and protect privacy. Secondly, it designs an information compensation and attention correction mechanism to enhance model robustness. By generating feature masks from low-frequency information and optimizing attention allocation using human keypoint detection, this mechanism balances privacy protection and model performance. Experimental results on the Market1501 dataset demonstrate that the proposed methods achieve excellent performance in both privacy protection metrics, such as PSNR and SSIM, and re-identification performance such as Rank-1 accuracy. These findings indicate that the proposed methods effectively resolve the trade-off between privacy protection and model performance, offering new insights for the development of privacy-preserving person re-identification technology.

Keywords: Federated Collaboration · Privacy Protection · Person Re-identification · Frequency Domain Information

1 Introduction

With the acceleration of urbanization and the rapid development of information technology, video surveillance systems play an increasingly important role in urban public safety privacy [14]. Person re-identification technology, a core component of intelligent video surveillance, aims to identify and match specific pedestrians captured by multiple cameras at different times and locations [1,9]. This technology not only improves the accuracy and stability of recognition algorithms but also helps reveal abnormal behavior patterns, thereby improving public safety [4,18]. However, traditional centralized processing methods, which upload pedestrian data captured by different cameras to a central database server for processing, pose significant risks of sensitive data leakage, potentially leading

© The Author(s), under exclusive license to Springer Nature Singapore Pte Ltd. 2026
Z. Lin et al. (Eds.): ICIG 2025, LNCS 16163, pp. 348–359, 2026.
https://doi.org/10.1007/978-981-95-3729-7_29

to the unauthorized abuse or disclosure of personal privacy [3,4,18]. Moreover, existing privacy protection methods, such as encryption, de-identification, or blurring, while providing a certain level of privacy protection, can result in the loss of feature information in datasets, affecting their usability and the performance of recognition models. In recent years, federated learning, an emerging distributed machine learning framework, has offered new solutions for privacy protection. Federated learning allows multiple parties to collaboratively train models without sharing raw data, thereby achieving data privacy protection. Despite the progress made in privacy-preserving person re-identification, several challenges remain. First, existing methods often lead to a decline in model performance while protecting privacy. For instance, blurring, while effectively hiding sensitive information, may also remove critical features, impacting the model's recognition accuracy. Second, traditional privacy protection methods still have security vulnerabilities when confronted with sophisticated attack techniques. For example [2,5,8,20], images generated by generative adversarial networks (GANs) can be reverse-engineered, resulting in privacy leakage. Furthermore, existing methods are computationally inefficient and communication intensive when dealing with large-scale datasets, making them impractical for real-world applications.

To simultaneously safeguard privacy and retain model accuracy, this paper proposes a privacy-preserving person re-identification method based on federated learning and frequency domain information. Our key contributions are summarized as follows.

1. To achieve a balance between privacy protection and model performance, we propose a privacy-preserving framework based on federated learning combined with frequency domain segmentation strategies. This approach ensures that raw data remains local, thereby reducing the risk of sensitive information leakage.
2. To compensate for the performance degradation caused by privacy protection processing, we design an information compensation and attention correction mechanism. By generating feature masks and optimizing attention allocation using human keypoint detection, this mechanism effectively enhances the server-side model's ability to recognize key pedestrian features.
3. Experimental results on the Market1501 dataset demonstrate that our method achieves excellent performance in both privacy protection metrics and re-identification performance, proving its effectiveness in practical applications.

2 Related Work

2.1 Privacy-Preserving Person Re-identification

Privacy-preserving person re-identification has become a crucial research topic in the field of computer vision. Researchers have proposed various methods to protect privacy while maintaining recognition accuracy. Earlier privacy protection methods mainly focused on encrypting or anonymizing data. For example,

Dietlmeier [2] proposed blurring faces in images to achieve privacy protection, but this method may cause loss of important feature information. In contrast, FREED [18] introduced a framework based on double-server architecture and threshold Paillier cryptosystem. They developed a batch processing secure computation protocol to support advanced person re-identification operations on encrypted feature vectors, which is more efficient than existing protocols. However, these methods still have potential security risks. Recently, researchers have started to explore privacy protection methods based on generative adversarial networks (GANs) and other generative models. For instance, PixelFade [17] proposed a privacy-preserving generative adversarial network framework, which can generate anonymous images while preserving certain feature information. However, these methods may still face the risk of reconstruction attacks. Overall, current privacy-preserving person re-identification methods have achieved certain results, but still face challenges in terms of feature information loss, security risks, and model performance decline.

2.2   Federated Learning for Privacy

Under the constraint of keeping data local, collaborative training across decentralized nodes has evolved into a viable route for safeguarding privacy in machine learning. Unlike traditional centralized learning methods, federated learning enables multiple devices or institutions to collaboratively train a model without sharing raw data. This approach effectively protects data privacy and has been widely applied in various fields. In the field of person re-identification, federated learning also shows great potential. For example, FedReID [20] first introduced federated learning into person re-identification tasks and proposed a knowledge distillation and dynamic weight adjustment method to optimize model aggregation and convergence. PP-GAN [14] enables decentralized learning from non-shared private training data across multiple user sites. By designing feature embedding and mapping networks, they achieved a balance between privacy protection and model performance. However, existing federated learning-based person re-identification algorithms still have some limitations. On the one hand, the excessive learning of the server may attempt to reconstruct missing information based on the updated parameters from clients, thereby threatening user privacy. On the other hand, the client devices often have limited computational resources, which restricts the complexity of local models and affects the overall performance of the system.

2.3   Frequency Domain Learning

Frequency Domain Learning is an emerging research direction that combines frequency domain processing with machine learning. It has shown great potential in image processing and computer vision tasks. In the field of person re-identification, researchers have found that different frequency components of images can provide complementary information. For example, low-frequency components mainly reflect the overall information of images, such as average brightness and color distribution, while high-frequency components capture the details of images, such as edges, textures, and local changes. By decomposing images into different frequency components and processing them separately, it is possible to better protect privacy while retaining useful feature information. For instance, LapRAN [15] is a scalable Laplacian pyramid reconstructive adversarial network for flexible compressive sensing reconstruction. This method leverages the characteristics of frequency domain information to achieve efficient image reconstruction and feature extraction. Duetface [7] further explored the application of frequency domain information in privacy protection and proposed a privacy-preserving face recognition method based on frequency domain processing. By analyzing the frequency domain features of images and selectively processing different frequency components, this method effectively protects privacy while maintaining recognition accuracy. However, frequency domain-based learning methods also face challenges such as how to better balance privacy protection and feature retention, as well as how to improve the computational efficiency of frequency domain transformations.

3 Methodology

3.1 Overview

Motivation. In the era of widespread video surveillance, person ReID technology is crucial for public safety. However, privacy issues and model performance are difficult to balance. Traditional centralised data processing poses leakage risks, while conventional privacy protection methods like blurring and pixelation often lead to feature loss and model degradation. To address these challenges, we propose a novel privacy - preserving person ReID method that integrates federated learning with frequency - domain processing. This approach not only protects privacy but also preserves essential feature information for maintaining model accuracy.

The Security Goals. The primary security goal of this study is to prevent the leakage of sensitive information during the person ReID process. By adopting a federated learning framework, we aim to ensure that raw data remains on local devices and is never transmitted to a central server. This reduces the risk of data breaches that could expose individuals' privacy. Additionally, through frequency - domain processing and attention mechanisms, we seek to protect the critical feature information of pedestrians, avoiding the loss of important details such as facial features and clothing textures, which are often targeted by privacy attacks.

The Paradigm of Model. As shown in Fig. 1, the proposed model follows the federated learning paradigm, where multiple client devices collaborate with a central server to train a shared model without sharing raw data. On the client side, a lightweight model processes local data, extracting key features and generating feature masks. These masks are then transmitted to the server, which uses them to enhance the attention mechanisms of its global model. This collaborative approach allows the server to leverage the feature information from various clients while keeping their raw data secure. Furthermore, frequency - domain processing is applied to split and protect the data, ensuring that only non - sensitive information is shared.

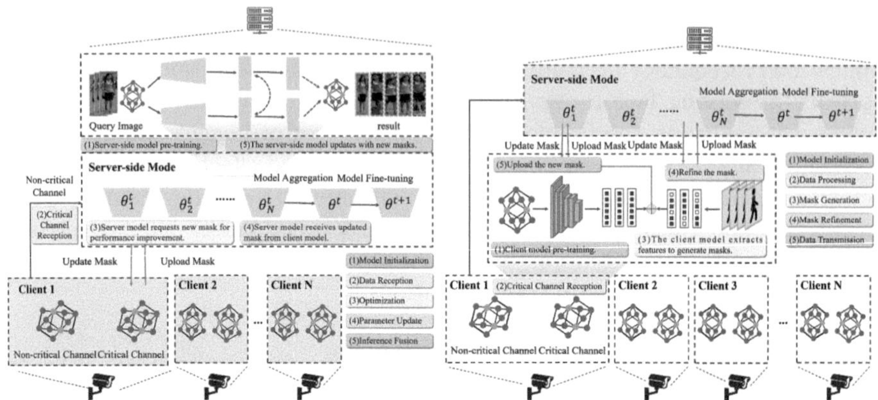

Fig. 1. The proposed model framework in this paper, operating within a federated learning paradigm, achieves privacy preservation for raw data and performance enhancement through client-side frequency-domain segmentation and attention rectification modules.

3.2   Federed Collaboration

In federated learning, the entire system comprises multiple clients and a central server. Each client holds local data, which is processed and trained using a lightweight model, such as OSNet. The model extracts key features through feature maps and calculates channel - wise average values to obtain feature masks. These masks represent the attention areas of the local model. After normalisation, the masks are transmitted to the server. The server, equipped with a powerful model like ResNet - 50, aggregates the feature masks from all clients and integrates them into its global model. The server's model uses these masks to enhance its attention to key pedestrian features during feature extraction and recognition tasks. This collaborative process continues for multiple rounds until the global model converges. By federated learning, the raw data remains on clients, protecting privacy, while the server effectively aggregates feature information to improve the overall performance of the person ReID model.

3.3   Splitting Channels in Frequency Domain

Frequency - domain processing is applied to split the data into different channels. First, the original image is converted from RGB colour space to YCbCr colour space. Then, the image is divided into 16 × 8 pixel blocks, and each block undergoes DCT transformation, mapping the image to the frequency domain and generating H × W × 384 frequency channels. According to the energy distribution of the channels, the top - K frequency bands are selected as the key channels, while the remaining channels are considered non - key channels. The non - key channels are transmitted to the server for model training and reasoning, while the key channels, which contain most of the visual information, are retained on the client side. This approach ensures that the server cannot reconstruct the original image from the non - key channels alone, thereby achieving privacy protection. This paper refers to the frequency domain segmentation method of the DCT model and builds a credible segmentation strategy based on the amplitude of channels, denoted as X_s and X_c . Assuming the luminance component is Y, it sorts the luminance component in the YCbCr color space by energy. The Top-K channels with the highest energy are selected as key channels, and the rest are regarded as non-key channels. To transform pedestrian images into the frequency domain, the original images on the local client model are preprocessed to obtain an input shape of H×W×3. Using the BDCT method, the image is divided into 16×8 pixel blocks. Each block undergoes DCT, mapping the image to a frequency channel of H×W×384. For spatial consistency, each Y, Cb, and Cr component is converted via BDCT, generating 128 frequency channels per component, totaling 384. This process involves converting the original image from the RGB color space to YCbCr and then to the frequency domain via DCT. Based on channel importance, frequency channels are divided into key and non - key channels. Key channels, which hold most visual information, are retained locally, while non - key channels are used for server - side model training and reasoning, ensuring privacy. Most visual information is in low - frequency channels. Even after removing most visual information, the model remains accurate. The DCT formula for the frequency domain conversion is shown below.

$$X_{h,w} = \frac{\left(\sum_{i=0}^{H-1} \sum_{j=0}^{W-1} f(i,j) \cos \left(\frac{\pi h}{H} \left(i + \frac{1}{2} \right) \right) \cos \left(\frac{\pi w}{W} \left(j + \frac{1}{2} \right) \right) \right)}{HW} \tag{1}$$

Here, C indicates the channel count, while H and W respectively specify the spatial height and width of the feature map. $X_{h,w}$ represents the DCT coefficients in the frequency domain, while $f_{i,j}$ represents the coefficients of the feature map in the spatial domain. h and w indicate the rows and columns in the frequency domain, respectively. Specifically, the value of the feature map m at position (i,j) corresponds to the frequency response value (h,w) of the DCT spectrum X. The entire frequency spectrum X is divided into K frequency bands, each represented by its maximum response value $X_K^{\max}$:

$$X_K^{\max} = \max_{(h,w) \in B_k} X_{h,w} \tag{2}$$

where B_k denotes the range of the k-th frequency band.

The channel energy for each frequency band at the maximum response value X is calculated as:

$$E_c = \frac{1}{N} \sum_{h=0}^{N-1} \sum_{w=0}^{N-1} \left| F_{h,w}^c \right|^2 \tag{3}$$

Here, E_c denotes the energy of the c-th channel, and $F_{h,w}^c$ represents the DCT coefficients of the c-th channel. By selecting key channels and setting a threshold, we can determine which channels contain important visual information:

$$C_{key} = \{c | E_c > threshold\} \tag{4}$$

The client device dynamically adjusts the threshold based on its local data distribution to achieve dynamic channel splitting. Here, C_{key} represents the set of key channels, while *threshold* is a predefined value used to identify channels with important visual information. Typically, the threshold is set to 20 in dense surveillance scenarios and 40 in sparse scenarios. In this study, we set the threshold to 30 as a middle value. Finally, the segmented channels are used to generate $\{X_s, X_c\}$. Key channels, connected in the form of $H \times W \times 3K$, form X_c, while X_s is composed of the remaining channels. Consequently, visual information is effectively removed from X_s but preserved in X_c. The high-frequency information sent to the server and the low-frequency information sent to the client are used for model training and inference, and the split information is represented as follows:

$$I_{server} = \cup_{c \in C_{non-key}} F_c \tag{5}$$

$$I_{client} = \cup_{c \in C_{key}} F_c \tag{6}$$

3.4   Attention Correction Mechanism

To further improve the quality of feature masks and enhance the server's attention - allocation accuracy, an attention - correction mechanism based on human - keypoint detection is introduced. The human - keypoint detection technology is used to generate a series of points representing the human trunk. The human body is divided into six regions: head, torso, and limbs. The boundary boxes of these regions are determined based on the coordinates of the keypoints. Then, component masks related to these regions are generated and multiplied with the original image on a pixel - by - pixel basis. Only the image information in the component regions is retained, while other areas are set to zero or other background values.

Assume that the client uses its lightweight model to perform inference on the key channel information X_c, generating a feature map $F(X_c)$. By calculating the channel-wise average of this feature map, a feature mask $R(X_c)$ is obtained:

$$R(X_c) = \frac{1}{C} \sum_{c=1}^{C} \left| F(X) \right|^2 \tag{7}$$

F_c represents the value of the c-th channel in the feature map, and C denotes the number of channels in the feature map. The client normalizes the feature mask $R(X_c)$ to the range $[0, 1]$ to ensure that the feature mask values have an appropriate scale during transmission and application.

The normalized feature mask $R'(X_c)$ is transmitted to the server. After receiving $R'(X_c)$, the server resizes it to match the height and width of $F(X_s)$. Subsequently, the server activates the features of $F(X_s)$ using a Sigmoid function. The Sigmoid function maps the feature values to the range $(0, 1)$, thereby controlling the degree of feature activation. The activated feature map $F(X_s)$ is combined with the feature mask $R'(X_c)$ to update the server's feature map. The update formula is as follows:

$$F'(X_s) = F(X_s) \times (\omega \odot R(X_c)) + F(X_s) \tag{8}$$

$\odot$ denotes the element-wise multiplication operation, and ω is a weight parameter that determines the influence of the feature mask on the server's feature map.

4   Experiments

4.1   Datasets

In this study, we conducted experiments using the Market1501 [15] dataset, which is representative in the field of person re-identification. Collected by Tsinghua University with six cameras in summer, the Market1501 benchmark gathers 32,668 photographs of 1,501 identities. Training data consist of 12,936 images from 751 identities, while the remaining 19,732 images of 750 identities form the test split, which is further organized into 3,368 query samples and 19,732 gallery samples. Widely used in person re-identification research, this dataset provides rich samples for model training and evaluation.

4.2   Performance Indicators

To comprehensively evaluate the model's performance, we used the following two common evaluation indicators:

CMC [12]. A key parameter for measuring the performance of identification systems, reflected in the probability of correct matches in ranking results. Rank-1, Rank-5, and Rank-10 indicate the probabilities of correct matches at the first, top five, and top ten positions in the retrieval results.

mAP [19]. The average of the precision of all categories in the dataset, providing a more comprehensive evaluation of the re-identification algorithm. To also evaluate the effectiveness of privacy protection, we adopted two additional indicators:

PSNR [13]. Measures the quality of image or video reconstruction by comparing the mean squared error (MSE) between the original and reconstructed signals.

SSIM [16]. Measures the similarity between two images based on the sensitivity of the human visual system to structural information in images.

4.3 Experimental Settings

The experiments were conducted using two NVIDIA 3090 GPUs for model training and evaluation, with the models developed on the open-source deep learning framework PyTorch. A pre-trained ResNet-50 model served as the backbone network, with its last fully connected layer removed and the stride of the last convolutional layer set to 1. The size of the pedestrian images was standardized to 256×128.

During model training, we employed common data augmentation strategies. The server and client models were trained and tested using ResNet50 and the lightweight model OSNet. In local training, the learning rate was set to 1×10^{-4}, with a batch size of 64 and 200 local training iterations. The total number of rounds for server-client collaborative training was 20. For model optimization, we used data augmentation methods such as random flipping, random cropping, and random erasing, with SGD selected as the optimizer.

4.4 Experimental Results and Analysis

We compared the proposed method with other mainstream privacy-preserving person re-identification methods on the Market1501 dataset, with the results shown in the table below (Table 1 and 2):

Table 1. Model Performance Comparison on Market1501 Dataset (%)

Method	Rank-1	Rank-5	mAP
Blurring [16]	67.30	83.50	44.20
Pixelation [10]	64.30	83.50	43.40
Mosaic [7]	64.30	–	43.40
Gaussian Noise [10]	68.70	85.90	43.20
PrivacyReID-blurring [10]	46.80	67.70	11.70
PrivacyReID-pixelation [10]	73.20	89.10	15.70
PrivacyReID-noise [10]	67.50	82.00	20.70
FedAvg [6]	48.30	–	24.60
FedPav [7]	49.40	–	25.40
SNR [6]	53.20	–	28.30
FedDG [7]	58.80	–	33.20
FedReID-by-camera [16]	61.13	74.88	36.57
Our Method	**77.63**	**79.51**	**59.87**

Table 2. Comparison of Reconstruction Attacks on the Market1501 Dataset

Method	PSNR	SSIM
AVIH [11]	14.30	0.42
Mosaic [7]	17.76	0.51
Gaussian Blur [16]	23.24	0.69
PrivacyReID [16]	26.92	0.94
PrivacyReID-blurring [10]	26.78	0.92
PrivacyReID-pixelation [10]	29.74	0.93
PrivacyReID-noise [10]	26.80	0.92
PixelFade [17]	10.92	0.18
Our Method	**9.63**	**0.08**

Our proposed method outperforms other privacy protection methods in terms of Rank-1, Rank-5, and mAP. It also achieves remarkable results in PSNR and SSIM, demonstrating its effectiveness in enhancing model recognition performance while protecting privacy.

4.5   Ablation Experiments

To further verify the effectiveness of each component, we conducted ablation experiments on the Market1501 dataset, with the results shown in the table below:

- Local Training: The baseline model without the federated collaborative framework, frequency channel segmentation privacy protection mechanism, and key information supplementation module.
- FedAvg+Resnet50: Uses FedAvg as the federal learning framework, with Resnet50 as the server-side model for overlearning.
- Fed+Resnet50+channel: Uses the federated collaborative framework proposed in this paper, with Resnet50 as the server-side model for overlearning. It employs frequency channel segmentation to divide raw data into critical and non-critical channels without attention correction.
- Fed+Resnet50+channel+OpenPose: Uses the federated collaborative framework proposed in this paper, with Resnet50 as the server-side model for overlearning. It employs frequency channel segmentation to divide raw data into critical and non-critical channels and uses OpenPose for attention correction (Table 3).

The results demonstrate that the module proposed in this study mitigates the model performance loss caused by privacy protection operations. It enhances the model's recognition accuracy and mean Average Precision while reducing the influence of the feature mask on the server's feature map, thereby achieving a good balance between privacy protection and model performance.

Table 3. Ablation Study on the Market1501 Dataset (%)

Method	Rank-1	mAP
Local Training	88.93	72.62
FedAvg-Resnet50	48.30	24.60
Fed+Resnet50+channel	65.58	49.05
Fed+Resnet50+channel+OpenPose	77.08	58.26
Our Method	**77.63**	**59.87**

5　Conclusion

This paper proposes a privacy-preserving person re-identification method using a federated learning framework and frequency domain processing strategy. By retaining data locally and applying frequency domain channel segmentation, privacy is protected. The designed information compensation and attention correction mechanisms enhance model performance. Experiments show that this approach effectively protects privacy while restoring model performance. Future work will optimize the federated learning framework to improve training efficiency and enhance model adaptability in diverse scenarios.

Acknowledgments. This work was supported by the National Key Research and Development Program of China (2022YFB3103500).

References

1. Clauß, S., Kesdogan, D., Kölsch, T., Pimenidis, L., Schiffner, S., Steinbrecher, S.: Privacy enhancing identity management: protection against re-identification and profiling. In: Digital Identity Management, pp. 84–93. Citeseer (2005)
2. Dietlmeier, J., Antony, J., McGuinness, K., O'Connor, N.E.: How important are faces for person re-identification? In: 2020 25th International Conference on Pattern Recognition (ICPR), pp. 6912–6919. IEEE (2021)
3. Fernandez, V., Sanchez, P., Pinaya, W.H.L., Jacenków, G., Tsaftaris, S.A., Cardoso, J.: Privacy distillation: reducing re-identification risk of multimodal diffusion models. ArXiv preprint abs/ arXiv: 2306.01322 (2023)
4. Jiang, Y., Yu, H., Cheng, X., Chen, H., Sun, Z., Zhao, G.: From laboratory to real world: a new benchmark towards privacy-preserved visible-infrared person re-identification. ArXiv preprint abs/ arXiv: 2503.12232 (2025)
5. Jin, X., Lan, C., Zeng, W., Chen, Z., Zhang, L.: Style normalization and restitution for generalizable person re-identification. In: 2020 IEEE/CVF Conference on Computer Vision and Pattern Recognition, CVPR 2020, Seattle, WA, USA, 13-19 June 2020, pp. 3140–3149. IEEE (2020). https://doi.org/10.1109/CVPR42600.2020.00321
6. McMahan, B., Moore, E., Ramage, D., Hampson, S., y Arcas, B.A.: Communication-efficient learning of deep networks from decentralized data. In: Singh, A., Zhu, X.J. (eds.) Proceedings of the 20th International Conference on Artificial Intelligence and Statistics, AISTATS 2017, 20-22 April 2017, Fort Lauderdale, FL, USA. Proceedings of Machine Learning Research, vol. 54, pp. 1273–1282. PMLR (2017). http://proceedings.mlr.press/v54/mcmahan17a.html

7. Mi, Y., Huang, Y., Ji, J., Liu, H., Xu, X., Ding, S., Zhou, S.: DuetFace: collaborative privacy-preserving face recognition via channel splitting in the frequency domain. In: Proceedings of the 30th ACM International Conference on Multimedia, pp. 6755–6764 (2022)
8. Saha, S., Ahmad, T.: Federated transfer learning: concept and applications. Intell. Artif. **15**(1), 35–44 (2021)
9. Su, D., Huynh, H.T., Chen, Z., Lu, Y., Lu, W.: Re-identification attack to privacy-preserving data analysis with noisy sample-mean. In: Gupta, R., Liu, Y., Tang, J., Prakash, B.A. (eds.) KDD 2020: The 26th ACM SIGKDD Conference on Knowledge Discovery and Data Mining, Virtual Event, 23-27 August 2020, CA, USA, pp. 1045–1053. ACM (2020). https://doi.org/10.1145/3394486.3403148
10. Sun, S., Wu, G., Gong, S.: Decentralised person re-identification with selective knowledge aggregation. In: 32nd British Machine Vision Conference 2021, BMVC 2021, Online, 22-25 November 2021, p. 384. BMVA Press (2021). https://www.bmvc2021-virtualconference.com/assets/papers/0777.pdf
11. Tseng, B.W., Wu, P.Y.: Compressive privacy generative adversarial network. IEEE Trans. Inf. Forensics Secur. **15**, 2499–2513 (2020). https://doi.org/10.1109/TIFS.2020.2968188
12. Wang, X., Doretto, G., Sebastian, T., Rittscher, J., Tu, P.H.: Shape and appearance context modeling. In: IEEE 11th International Conference on Computer Vision, ICCV 2007, 14-20 October 2007, Rio de Janeiro, Brazil, pp. 1–8. IEEE Computer Society (2007). https://doi.org/10.1109/ICCV.2007.4409019
13. Wang, Z., Bovik, A.C., Sheikh, H.R., Simoncelli, E.P.: Image quality assessment: from error visibility to structural similarity. IEEE Trans. Image Process. **13**(4), 600–612 (2004)
14. Wu, Y., Yang, F., Xu, Y., Ling, H.: Privacy-protective-GAN for privacy preserving face de-identification. J. Comput. Sci. Technol. **34**, 47–60 (2019)
15. Xu, K., Zhang, Z., Ren, F.: LAPRAN: a scalable laplacian pyramid reconstructive adversarial network for flexible compressive sensing reconstruction. In: Ferrari, V., Hebert, M., Sminchisescu, C., Weiss, Y. (eds.) ECCV 2018. LNCS, vol. 11214, pp. 491–507. Springer, Cham (2018). https://doi.org/10.1007/978-3-030-01249-6_30
16. Yu, Z., Sun, P., Zhou, M., Liu, Q., Zhao, S.: Research on liquid crystal display technology based on regional dynamic dimming algorithm. In: 2024 IEEE 9th International Conference on Data Science in Cyberspace (DSC), pp. 635–640. IEEE (2024)
17. Zhang, D., Peng, Y.X., Wu, X.M., Wu, A., Zheng, W.S.: PixelFade: privacy-preserving person re-identification with noise-guided progressive replacement. In: Proceedings of the 32nd ACM International Conference on Multimedia, pp. 6326–6334 (2024)
18. Zhao, B., Li, Y., Liu, X., Pang, H.H., Deng, R.H.: FREED: an efficient privacy-preserving solution for person re-identification. In: 2022 IEEE Conference on Dependable and Secure Computing (DSC), pp. 1–8. IEEE (2022)
19. Zheng, L., Shen, L., Tian, L., Wang, S., Wang, J., Tian, Q.: Scalable person re-identification: a benchmark. In: 2015 IEEE International Conference on Computer Vision, ICCV 2015, December 7-13, 2015Santiago, Chile, pp. 1116–1124. IEEE Computer Society (2015). https://doi.org/10.1109/ICCV.2015.133
20. Zhuang, W., et al.: Performance optimization of federated person re-identification via benchmark analysis. In: MM 2020: The 28th ACM International Conference on Multimedia, Virtual Event/Seattle, WA, USA, 12-16 October 2020m pp. 955–963 (2020). https://doi.org/10.1145/3394171.3413814

A Spatio-Temporal Graph Attention Approach to Detecting Bitcoin Mixers

Hongfa Xu[✉], Mingyuan Weng, and Hua Han

People's Public Security University of China, Beijing 102623, China
xuhongfa@ppsuc.edu.cn

Abstract. The anonymity of Bitcoin, while protecting user privacy, also provides a covert channel for illegal fund flows. Coin mixing technology enhances privacy protection by blurring transaction paths, but it also increases the difficulty for law enforcement agencies to track money laundering, ransomware and other criminal activities. Traditional rule-based detection methods rely on fixed patterns and are difficult to cope with the rapid iteration of coin mixing technology, resulting in low recall rates and insufficient generalization ability. To address this issue, this paper proposes a detection model based on Spatio-Temporal Graph Attention Network (ST-GAT), which builds a 30-layer predecessor and 10-layer successor temporal graph structure of the target transaction, and combines the global temporal attention of the transformer architecture with the spatial topological attention of GAT to effectively capture the patterns of fund convergence and dispersion in coin mixing transactions. Experiments show that ST-GAT outperforms traditional GCN and LSTM-TC models in terms of precision, recall and F1 value on the evaluation set, verifying its advantages in complex transaction graph analysis.

Keywords: Spatio-Temporal Graph Attention Network (ST-GAT) · Coin Mixing Detection · Bitcoin Privacy Protection · Transaction Graph Analysis

1 Introduction

In 2008, Satoshi Nakamoto published the Bitcoin whitepaper [1], systematically expounding the Bitcoin theoretical system, and officially launched the Bitcoin mainnet. After more than a decade of development, Bitcoin has become the most influential cryptocurrency globally. Recently, driven by multiple market factors, its unit price broke through \$100,000 at the highest, with a total market capitalization once exceeding \$2 trillion. Currently, the network processes approximately 100,000 transactions daily, with user groups covering more than 200 countries and regions. The rapid development of the Bitcoin network has also attracted significant attention from speculators and criminals.

The anonymity of Bitcoin is not impenetrable, as its transaction records are publicly available on the blockchain. User real identities can potentially be revealed through address clustering analysis of transaction records. Therefore, coin mixing technologies emerged, which achieve stronger privacy protection by obfuscating transaction paths and isolating fund flows. However, these technologies also provide covert channels for

© The Author(s), under exclusive license to Springer Nature Singapore Pte Ltd. 2026
Z. Lin et al. (Eds.): ICIG 2025, LNCS 16163, pp. 360–371, 2026.
https://doi.org/10.1007/978-981-95-3729-7_30

criminal activities such as money laundering and ransom payments for ransomware. According to the *2024 Ransomware Review: Unit 42 Leak Site Analysis* report released by the world-class security research team Unit 42, ransomware groups published a total of 3,998 posts (i.e., attack incidents) on leak sites in 2023, a 49% increase from 2022. Calculated over the entire year, the attack frequency was approximately once every 10 s. In China, government agencies and large state-owned enterprises have faced an increase in targeted ransomware attacks, with cryptocurrencies like Bitcoin becoming the primary ransom carrier[1]. The abuse of coin mixing technologies has made fund flows difficult to trace. Despite strengthened regulations in various countries, the coexisting challenges of cross-border transactions, anonymous currencies, decentralized protocols, and evolving coin mixing methods have created technical gaps and legal conflicts in current collaborative governance of coin mixing. Here are three key contributions of this study:

1. ST-GAT Model for Spatio-Temporal Transaction Analysis: Introduces a novel graph neural network that integrates Transformer-based temporal attention and GAT's spatial reasoning to effectively detect complex coin mixing patterns.
2. State-of-the-Art Detection Performance: Demonstrates superior accuracy over GCN and LSTM-TC models in precision, recall, and F1-score, overcoming limitations of traditional rule-based approaches.
3. Regulatory-Adaptive Blockchain Forensics: Provides a dynamic framework for identifying illicit transactions, balancing privacy preservation with compliance needs in AML and ransomware investigations.

2 Related Work

Current research primarily focuses on balancing the privacy-enhancing mechanisms of Bitcoin coin mixing transactions with regulatory requirements. Researchers have explored technologies such as zero-knowledge proofs and cross-chain bridges to enhance anonymity. However, these technologies still face challenges in decentralized implementation and legal compliance.

In 2025, Wang et al. systematically sorted out the classification of blockchain coin mixing technologies and regulatory methods, conducting the first integrated analysis of criminal activities, academic research, and industrial practices. They summarized the paths of regulatory technologies such as manual rules and address clustering and evaluated the advantages and disadvantages of mainstream tools [2]. The work of proposes the MXShuffle coin mixing mechanism based on multiple XOR encryption and the RShuffle mechanism supporting dynamic revocation to address the low efficiency and inflexibility of traditional blockchain coin mixing mechanisms [3]. These mechanisms optimized traditional encryption operation modes and improved coin mixing efficiency and flexibility. Li et al. proposed a detection method for coin mixing transactions using the CoinJoin technology, taking the Wasabi platform as a case study [4]. They improved the accuracy and recall rate of basic detection methods and introduced new indicators such as the ratio of repeated amount frequency to the number of input UTXOs to measure

---

[1] https://www.digitimes.com.tw/tech/dt/n/shwnws.asp?CnlID=13&id=690588.

the freedom of participating in coin mixing transactions. Further more, the approach of designs a blacklist public blockchain system based on a voting mechanism by combining smart contracts and editable blockchain technologies [5]. This system can effectively identify and restrict the circulation of illegal funds, leveraging the transparency and decentralization of blockchain technology to allow all users to participate in blacklist maintenance and fund monitoring.

In 2021, the LSTM-TC method proposed by Sun et al. uses a long short-term memory model to extract features from transaction trees, successfully identifying coin mixing transactions and outperforming traditional rule-based and graph neural network algorithms in discovering new types of coin mixing transactions [6]. Li and He proposed a new Bitcoin transaction tracking model, BT2, using graph neural networks, which can identify associations between Bitcoin accounts through the spatial and temporal information of transaction graphs. Experimental results showed the model had high accuracy and AUC values [10]. Liu et al. conducted a systematic review of the research progress on anti-money laundering (AML) technologies in blockchain environments. The study examined three major technical approaches—rule-based methods, machine learning methods, and deep learning methods—and evaluated the application performance of models such as support vector machines (SVM), graph neural networks (GNN), and Transformers across different scenarios [12]. Zhang conducted research on addressing the misuse of coin mixing smart contracts in cryptocurrency money laundering. To address these issues, the study proposed shifting the governance approach from "fragmentation" to "coordination" by building a cross-departmental and cross-chain collaborative governance mechanism [13]. To solve the problem of account correlation detection in Ethereum mixing services (such as Tornado Cash), Zheng et al. proposed the "StealthLink" framework, which uses a cross-task domain-invariant feature learning method. This method achieves robust feature learning under conditions of label scarcity and data distribution changes by constructing a mixing subgraph and introducing an adversarial difference minimization mechanism [14]. The CoinJoin protocol proposed by Maxwell G. in 2013 [9] pioneered distributed coin mixing technologies. This protocol allows multiple users to process transactions collectively through a multi-party collaborative signature mechanism, either by merging multiple inputs and distributing outputs according to preset ratios or integrating multiple transactions involving multiple parties into a single transaction. Such transactions enhance privacy by obfuscating fund flows and effectively reduce transaction fees and blockchain data bloat. These advantages have made CoinJoin and its derivative technologies mainstream privacy protection solutions.

3 The Proposed Approach

To improve coin mixing detection performance, this paper downloaded a rule-based labeled dataset (including training and evaluation sets) and attempted to train and evaluate models using graph neural networks. Based on the traditional GCN model, we optimized the algorithm by combining graph attention networks and Transformer architecture, proposing the Spatio-Temporal Graph Attention Network (ST-GAT) model for coin mixing transaction detection. Finally, we compared the detection effects of different models on the evaluation set and analyzed the results. The core ideas of the ST-GAT model's training process can be summarized as the following three components.

3.1 Hierarchical Spatio-Temporal Graph Structure

Centered on the target transaction, a temporal graph structure with 30 preceding layers and 10 succeeding layers is constructed. A three-layer connection strategy is used to capture the spatio-temporal dependencies of fund flows. This structure breaks through the limitations of traditional single-chain modeling, restoring the "fund convergence-dispersion" pattern of coin mixing transactions from both historical tracing and future diffusion dimensions.

3.2 Spatio-Temporal Joint Attention Mechanism

The model innovatively integrates Transformer temporal modeling with multi-order graph attention to form a spatio-temporal joint attention mechanism. The preceding transaction sequence is reversely input into the Transformer encoder to capture fund tracing features through self-attention, while the succeeding sequence is processed forward to model fund diffusion patterns. Self-attention, the core of Transformer, allows the model to dynamically assign weights to each position when processing sequences, measuring the influence of other positions on the current position. The formula for self-attention calculation is as follows:

$$Attention(Q, V, K) = \text{softmax}(\frac{QK^T}{\sqrt{d_k}})V \tag{1}$$

Self-attention involves three key matrices: Query (Q) for finding relevant information, Key (K) for matching Q, and Value (V) for generating final attention-weighted results. Q, K, and V are randomly generated based on sequence length and model dimensions, then continuously trained and adjusted through algorithm learning and loss functions. In this paper, only the Transformer is used as a temporal feature enhancer for sequence features.

Subsequently, a heterogeneous graph structure including temporal connections, cross-layer connections, and key node bridging is constructed, with two GAT layers used for local neighborhood perception and global feature refinement. The first GAT layer maintains a 64-dimensional node feature representation through a 4-head attention mechanism, where each attention head outputs 16-dimensional features, and the 4 heads are concatenated to obtain 64-dimensional features. The calculation of the attention coefficient between node i and its single-hop neighbor node j is shown in Eq. (2):

$$h_i^{(2)} = \Big\|_{k=1}^{4} \mathrm{Re}LU\left(\sum_{j \in N(i)} \alpha_{ij}^{(k)} W_{GAT1}^{(k)} h_j^{(1)} \right) \tag{2}$$

where a is a learnable weight matrix, hi and hj are node feature vectors, $\|$ denotes feature concatenation, and Ni represents the first-order neighbors of node i. The two GAT layers in the model use 4-head attention mechanisms with feature dimensions of 64 and 32, respectively.

To stabilize the training process of attention coefficients, a multi-head attention mechanism is adopted, as shown in Eq. (3):

$$(\mathrm{h}_u^l)_{con} = \Big\|_{j=1}^{J} \sigma \left(\sum_{v \in N(v)} e_{uv}^j W^{l-1} h^{l-1} \right) \tag{3}$$

3.3 Dual Pooling and Regularization Optimization

Global features are aggregated multidimensional through a combination of max pooling and average pooling. Residual connections and layer normalization are introduced to address training degradation in deep networks and improve model robustness.

Finally, a fully connected layer outputs the final classification result. This design effectively learns the temporal dependencies and spatial structure features in transaction sequences to identify transaction patterns with coin mixing characteristics.

4 Experiments

This paper uses the dataset created in the work of [11], including training and evaluation sets, which contain transaction data from an earlier period with many obviously featured coin mixing transactions. These transactions have been manually labeled using rule-based methods, providing reliable basic data for model training.

It should be noted that during the preprocessing stage of these two datasets, the code excluded Coinbase transactions and single-input transactions, as these transactions inherently lack coin mixing features and can be directly filtered by simple rules.

4.1 Coin Mixing Dataset

4.1.1 Training and Evaluation Sets

In Sun Xiaowen's thesis, two existing rules were used: the CoinJoin transaction detection rule from blockstream.info and the SharedCoin detection rule. Transactions in the block height range of 270,000 to 300,000 were labeled, identifying 132,480 coin mixing transactions as positive samples in the dataset.

The proportion of positive samples among all transactions is very low, only about 1.18%. To balance positive and negative samples, negative samples were sampled from the remaining transactions according to rules.

4.1.2 Dataset File Description

The dataset contains a total of 116,537,811 real Bitcoin on-chain transactions. The dataset creator removed all transaction TXIDs and reassigned continuous integer IDs starting from 0 as new unique identifiers. The ID lists of positive and negative samples are stored in positive_ids.txt and negative_ids.txt, respectively, with each line containing an integer ID.

Table 1. Training set files.

File Name	File Size	Number of Lines
positive_ids.txt	1.2 MB	132,480
negative_ids.txt	1.2 MB	132,480
tree_forward.txt	4.6 GB	116,537,811
tree_back.txt	2.2 GB	116,537,811
tx_feature.txt	14 GB	116,537,811

The files used to construct the dataset are shown in Table 1. Transaction feature data are stored in tx_features.txt, with each transaction containing 15 features in JSON array format (CoinBase transactions are empty lines).

The preceding and succeeding relationships of transactions are recorded in tree_forward.txt and tree_back.txt, both in JSON array format, where array elements are the IDs of corresponding transactions (preceding relationships of CoinBase transactions are empty, and succeeding relationships of unspent transactions are empty).

4.1.3 Serialized Data Structure

The dataset is a JSON line format file with the following data structure: each line is a triplet corresponding to the preceding and succeeding transactions of a target transaction and a label. The first element of the triplet is a sequence of 30 preceding transactions of the target transaction (if fewer than 30 layers, they are padded to 30; if more than 30 layers, only the first 30 are truncated). Each layer of transactions is a 78-dimensional array. The second element is a sequence of 10 succeeding transactions of the target transaction, processed similarly, and the third element is a label (1 for coin mixing transactions, 0 otherwise).

4.2 Experimental Parameters and Training/Evaluation Process

To fully capture the temporal relationships and potential correlations between transactions, the graph structure uses a three-layer connection strategy:

(1) **Basic chain connection**: Direct connections between adjacent transaction nodes;
(2) **Strided connection**: Connections between transactions separated by one node (e.g., in the model, a for loop establishes connections between the current node i and node $i + 3$, creating connections across 3 index positions (actually spacing 2 intermediate nodes)) to capture non-adjacent but potentially correlated medium-term transaction patterns;
(3) **Cross-layer connection**: Connections between the middle layer (15th layer) of the preceding sequence and the 5th layer of the succeeding sequence to model long-term dependencies.

To better compare the fitting and detection effects of models on the evaluation set, the same hyperparameter configuration was used for different models: batch size: 256;

base learning rate: 0.01; weight decay coefficient: 1e−3; maximum training epochs: 100. Early stopping: terminate if validation performance does not improve for 5 consecutive epochs. The AdamW optimizer was selected with an adaptive learning rate adjustment strategy. When validation performance does not improve for two consecutive epochs, the learning rate is reduced for more precise parameter tuning.

To comprehensively evaluate model performance, precision, recall, F1-score, and AUC were used as primary evaluation indicators. The code also uses visualizations such as confusion matrices and ROC curves to intuitively display the model's classification effects and error distributions.

4.2.1 Training and Evaluation Process of Traditional GCN Model

The traditional GCN model uses a three-layer GCN structure as follows:

The first GCN layer maps 78-dimensional input features to a 256-dimensional hidden layer space. The second GCN layer performs information propagation and feature extraction in the 256-dimensional feature space. The third GCN layer compresses features to 128 dimensions, where the model extracts the most discriminative feature representations. After feature extraction, a two-layer fully connected classifier is used for final prediction. To prevent overfitting, a dropout regularization strategy with a rate of 0.5 was applied during feature extraction.

The traditional GCN model trained for 81 min and 30 epochs on a CPU, with training loss and validation metrics shown in Fig. 1.

4.2.2 ST-GAT Model Training Process

The ST-GAT model uses a more complex hybrid architecture as follows:

The Transformer architecture compresses 78-dimensional features to 64 dimensions through linear transformation (this 64-dimensional selection was obtained through repeated trials and comparisons; mapping to higher dimensions easily causes significant redundancy, affecting model evaluation effects, while projecting to a lower-dimensional space allows the model to find the most discriminative feature combinations and learn which features are more important). The features are then fed into a TransformerEncoder-Layer with 1 layer and 4-head attention mechanism for temporal self-attention modeling to capture complex dependencies in fund tracing and diffusion. After encoding, the output remains as node-level 64-dimensional representations.

Next, preprocessed features are used to construct graph nodes. In the feature transformation layer, the graph neural network model combines these 64-dimensional input features with spatio-temporal edges (adjacent first-order, second-order jumps, key midpoint bridging) into a hierarchical heterogeneous graph. Two GAT layers are then stacked in sequence:

- **First GAT layer**: Uses 4 attention heads, and the output of the 4 heads is concatenated to maintain 64 dimensions.
- **Second GAT layer**: Maintains 4 attention heads, mapping 64-dimensional features to a 32-dimensional space.

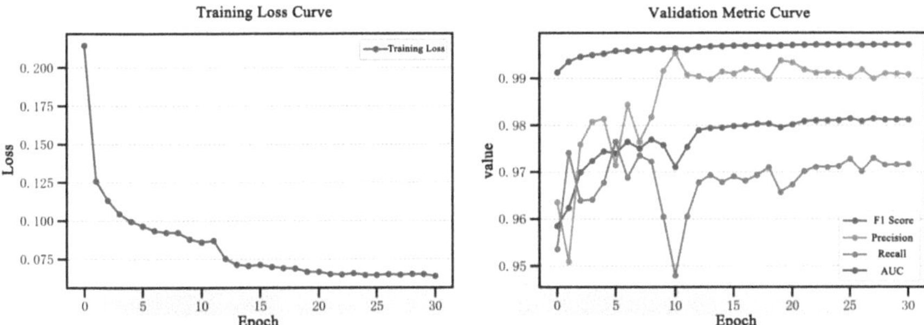

Fig. 1. Training loss curve and validation metric curve.

During feature aggregation, the model innovatively combines two global pooling strategies, max pooling and average pooling, to fuse all node features into graph-level representations. Finally, a two-layer classifier network completes the prediction, where the first layer aggregates 32-dimensional features into 64 dimensions, and the second layer compresses features to 1 dimension, outputting final prediction probabilities through a sigmoid function.

Throughout the process, the global temporal attention of Transformer and the spatial topological attention of GAT complement each other, with the flow diagram shown in Fig. 2.

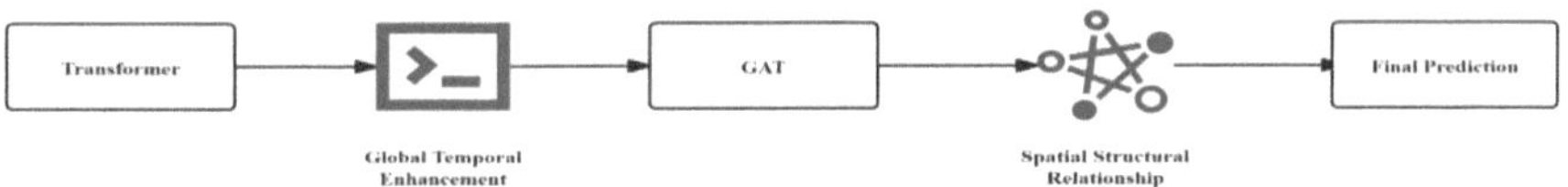

Fig. 2. ST-GAT model training flow.

Similar to the traditional GCN, multiple regularization strategies were adopted to improve the model's robustness and performance: conventional dropout with a rate of 0.5 during feature extraction, special attention dropout with a rate of 0.2 in GAT layers, residual connection mechanisms to alleviate deep network degradation, and LayerNorm for feature standardization to accelerate training convergence.

The ST-GAT model trained for 122 min and 40 epochs on a CPU, Fig. 3 shows the corresponding confusion matrix, through which the model's prediction effects can be analyzed in depth. The vertical axis represents true labels, and the horizontal axis represents model predictions. The left picture is the traditional GCN, and the right picture is the ST-GAT model:

The left figure is the confusion matrix of the traditional GCN model, and the right figure is the confusion matrix of the ST-GAT model. The upper left corner shows the number of samples whose predicted label by the model is 0, and the lower right corner shows the number of samples whose predicted label by the model is 1.

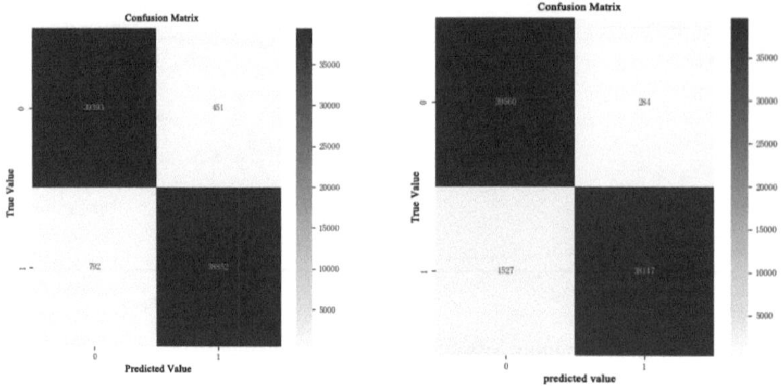

Fig. 3. Prediction results.

4.3 Comparison Results

We compared the performance of two graph neural network models with the LSTM-TC model on the evaluation set using the same dataset, where the ST-GAT model achieved higher scores. Table 2 shows the fitting effects of different models on the evaluation set. With a threshold set to 0.5, the F1-scores of the two graph neural network models were 1.7% and 2.5% higher than that of the LSTM-TC model, respectively.

Table 2. Fitting effects of different models on the evaluation set.

Model	Features Used	Threshold	Precision	Recall	F1-score
LSTM-TC	Tracing + Tracking	0.5	0.966	0.961	0.964
Traditional GCN	Tracing + Tracking	0.5	0.986	0.976	0.981
ST-GAT	Tracing + Tracking	0.5	0.995	0.983	0.989

We believe the ST-GAT model fully utilizes the graph structure information in the dataset. The preceding and succeeding transactions in the data naturally form a temporal graph, and ST-GAT dynamically assigns weights to different transaction relationships through attention mechanisms, enabling more precise identification of the important relationships between target transactions and their associated transactions.

Currently, the field of coin mixing detection lacks a universal dataset, making extended comparisons difficult. In the next step, we plan to collaborate with industry-related enterprises to build a universal dataset for model performance comparison.

Table 3. Re-evaluation results.

Model	Features Used	Threshold	Precision	Recall	F1-score
LSTM-TC	Tracing + Tracking (excluding first layer)	0.5	0.982	0.953	0.967
LSTM-TC	Tracing + Tracking (excluding last 10 layers)	0.5	0.961	0.956	0.959
Traditional GCN	Tracing + Tracking (excluding first layer)	0.5	0.976	0.965	0.970
Traditional GCN	Tracing + Tracking (excluding last 10 layers)	0.5	0.982	0.960	0.971
ST-GAT	Tracing + Tracking (excluding first layer)	0.5	0.992	0.980	0.986
ST-GAT	Tracing + Tracking (excluding last 10 layers)	0.5	0.991	0.979	0.985

4.4 Ablation Studies

The labels in the dataset are rule-labeled using the original features of target transactions, and the first layer of the transaction graph may leak these original features because it contains only one transaction: the target transaction. Therefore, we first attempted to remove the features of the first layer of the transaction tree. Keeping other parameters unchanged, we separately removed the features of the first-layer target transaction and the last 10 layers of tracing features, re-evaluated the models, and observed performance changes to determine whether they learned global features. The results are shown in Table 3.

It can be observed that removing the first layer of the transaction graph had minimal impact on the performance of all three models, with performance changes within approximately 1%, demonstrating that the models learned features from the entire sequence rather than local features.

5 Conclusions and Future Work

5.1 Summary of Research Work

Based on the traditional GCN model, this study constructed the ST-GAT model for coin mixing transaction detection using a spatio-temporal graph attention network, breaking through the limitations of traditional methods with the following designs:

(1) **Transaction graph construction**: Centered on target transactions, 30 preceding and 10 succeeding transaction sequences are extracted, with temporal dependencies and fund flow paths modeled through four connection types: temporal connections, basic chains, strides, and cross-layers.

(2) **Spatio-temporal graph attention mechanism**: Integrates Transformer temporal modeling with multi-order graph attention to adaptively assign weights to different transaction nodes and capture fund convergence-dispersion patterns in coin mixing transactions.

(3) **Regularization and optimization**: Introduces residual connections and layer normalization to alleviate deep network degradation and enhances global feature representation through dual pooling (max pooling + average pooling).

5.2 Limitations Analysis

First, the labels in both datasets are derived from heuristic rules, and the authenticity of the dataset labels has not been accurately verified. Rule-based methods (such as Blockstream.info's algorithms) can detect early coin mixing transactions (like SharedCoin) through specific patterns (output amount repetition), but their limitations are evident: they rely on fixed patterns, and new coin mixing technologies (such as improved CoinJoin) can bypass rules by adjusting output segmentation strategies, rendering detection ineffective. Additionally, rules can only cover known, clearly featured coin mixing types and cannot effectively identify multi-stage or distributed coin mixing transactions, resulting in overall low recall rates. Meanwhile, rules require frequent manual updates to respond to technological evolution, involving high maintenance costs.

5.3 Future Work

In the future, models could also be trained by integrating multiple data sources, such as incorporating off-chain data (e.g., exchange KYC information) to enrich transaction feature samples. It is hoped that this research will provide new ideas for analyzing coin mixing transactions in blockchains, but further research and breakthroughs are needed in data quality, model lightweighting, and adaptability to real-world scenarios to address the long-term challenges posed by criminal activities involving coin mixing technologies.

Acknowledgments. This study was funded by The Major Project of the National Social Science Foundation of China Project Number 24ZDA078.

References

1. Nakamoto, S.: Bitcoin: a peer-to-peer electronic cash system (2008). https://bitcoin.org
2. Wang, J., Mao, Q., Yan, J., et al.: A survey of blockchain coin mixing regulatory technologies [J/OL]. Comput. Eng., 1–19 (2025). https://doi.org/10.19678/j.issn.1000-3428.0070189
3. Li, J.: Research on blockchain transaction privacy protection methods based on coin mixing mechanisms. Lanzhou Univ. Technol. (2024). https://doi.org/10.27206/d.cnki.ggsgu.2024.001408
4. Li, H., Chen, Y., Zhang, W.: A detection method for coin mixing transactions based on CoinJoin implementation: taking the Wasabi platform as an example. J. Netw. Inf. Secur. **9**(06), 140–153 (2023)
5. Li, H.: Research on identification and tracking methods for illegal fund transactions in cryptocurrencies. Nanjing Univ. Posts Telecommun. (2023). https://doi.org/10.27251/d.cnki.gnjdc.2023.002093

6. Gui, M.: Research on identification and role determination of Bitcoin coin mixing services based on graph classification. Southeast Univ. (2023). https://doi.org/10.27014/d.cnki.gdnau.2023.001710
7. Liu, Y.: Research on blockchain privacy protection mechanisms based on coin mixing. Shanghai Jiao Tong Univ. (2020). https://doi.org/10.27307/d.cnki.gsjtu.2020.002289
8. Sun, X., Yang, T., Hu, B.: LSTM-TC: Bitcoin coin mixing detection method with a high recall. Appl. Intell. (2021). https://doi.org/10.1007/s10489-021-02453-9
9. Maxwell, G.: CoinJoin: bitcoin privacy for the real world. https://bitcointalk.org/?topic=279249 (2013)
10. Reid, F., Harrigan, M.: An analysis of anonymity in the bitcoin system. In: Security and Privacy in Social Networks, pp. 197–223. Springer (2013)
11. Li, Z., He, E.: Graph neural network-based bitcoin transaction tracking model. IEEE Access **11**, 62109–62119 (2023). https://doi.org/10.1109/ACCESS.2023.3288026
12. Liu, L., Li, X., Lan, T., et al.: A survey of anti-money laundering technologies in blockchain systems. Chin. Eng. Sci. **27**(02), 287–303 (2025)
13. Zhang, L., Wang, L.: From fragmentation to coordination: governance pathways for money laundering crimes using coin mixing smart contracts. J. People's Public Secur. Univ. China (Soc. Sci. Edn.) **40**(04), 12–22 (2024)
14. Che, Z., et al.: Correlating account on Ethereum mixing service via domain-invariant feature learning. arXiv preprint arXiv:2505.09892 (2025). https://arxiv.org/abs/2505.09892

Multi-view and Stereoscopic Processing

A Differentiable Optimization Framework for Camera Pose and Depth Supervision in 3D Gaussian Splatting

Fei Yan[1,2], Yuan Xiong[1,2], Ning Wang[1,2], Changliang Li[3], and Yiqi Wu[3(✉)]

[1] Changjiang Survey Planning Design and Research Co., Ltd., Wuhan 430010, China
[2] Hubei Provincial Engineering Research Center of Waterfront Space Planning and Design, Wuhan 430010, China
{yanfei,xiongyuan,wangning}@cjwsjy.com.cn
[3] China University of Geosciences, Wuhan 430074, China
{lichangliang,wuyq}@cug.edu.cn

Abstract. Existing 3D Gaussian Splatting methods suffer from limited accuracy in camera pose estimation under complex scenes and rely on insufficient depth supervision. To address these issues, this paper proposes an improved framework that jointly optimizes camera poses and enforces depth consistency constraints, enhancing the robustness and fidelity of 3D reconstruction. To enable end-to-end camera pose correction, we perform simultaneous optimization of camera position and rotation parameters via differentiable optimization, guided by a regularization term based on the initial poses. In addition, we propose an edge-aware depth regularization strategy that leverages image gradients to compute edge weights for refining depth distortion maps. To further improve depth accuracy, we introduce a multi-scale depth consistency constraint mechanism. Experimental results on the Mip-NeRF 360, Tanks and Temples, and Deep Blending datasets showcase the superior performance of the proposed method.

Keywords: 3D Gaussian Splatting · camera pose optimization · depth consistency constraints

1 Introduction

In recent years, advancements in 3D scene representation have significantly accelerated the development of novel view synthesis techniques [3]. The central goal of novel view synthesis is to reconstruct a scene from a sparse set of input images and generate photo-realistic images from arbitrary novel viewpoints [12,21].

Neural Radiance Fields (NeRF) [14] and its subsequent variants [17,24] have achieved remarkable success in implicit scene representation and neural rendering from multi-view RGB images. However, as scene complexity and scale increase, NeRF suffers from inherent inefficiencies. Its dependence on dense ray sampling and per-ray neural network evaluation results in prohibitively long training times

© The Author(s), under exclusive license to Springer Nature Singapore Pte Ltd. 2026
Z. Lin et al. (Eds.): ICIG 2025, LNCS 16163, pp. 375–386, 2026.
https://doi.org/10.1007/978-981-95-3729-7_31

and slow inference speeds, limiting its applicability in real-time scenarios and interactive environments [16,29].

As a recent alternative to the neural radiance field paradigm, 3D Gaussian Splatting (3DGS) [10] introduces an efficient and explicit 3D representation framework based on Gaussian primitives. It models the scene using parameterized 3D Gaussians, each defined by position, covariance, orientation, and other properties, forming a fully differentiable representation that enables real-time, high-fidelity rendering. This approach offers a new direction for overcoming the performance bottlenecks of implicit neural rendering methods [7,13].

Despite achieving real-time, high-fidelity rendering through explicit Gaussian primitive modeling, 3D Gaussian Splatting still faces significant challenges related to the accuracy and stability of camera pose estimation, particularly under complex scenes and varying lighting conditions. Additionally, the depth supervision mechanism remains insufficient, often resulting in local distortions or blurriness in the rendered output.

To address these challenges, we propose an integrated approach combining pose optimization and depth supervision. Specifically, we introduce a differentiable optimization-based camera pose correction method, which jointly refines both position and rotation parameters, enabling end-to-end pose optimization. A regularization term, derived from the initial camera pose, is incorporated to stabilize the optimization process and prevent excessive deviation of pose parameters. Additionally, we present an edge-aware depth regularization technique that generates edge weights from image gradients to optimize distortion maps, effectively preserving structural details while reducing errors in smooth regions. Moreover, we introduce a multi-scale depth consistency constraint to enhance depth robustness through hierarchical sampling and weighted error aggregation.

The contributions of our paper can be summarized as follows:

- This work introduces a novel 3D Gaussian Splatting framework that integrates camera pose optimization with depth consistency constraints, significantly enhancing rendering stability and visual consistency.
- To address challenges in pose estimation and optimization, we propose a differentiable pose correction method that jointly refines position and rotation, ensuring stability and avoiding complex updates via regularization.
- We introduce an edge-aware depth regularization strategy that preserves structural details and reduces errors in textured and edge regions. Combined with multi-scale consistency, this enhances depth estimation robustness.
- Experiments on public benchmark datasets show that our method improves novel view synthesis and rendering quality. Ablation studies confirm the effectiveness of pose regularization and depth constraints.

2 Related Work

2.1 Neural Radiance Fields for View Synthesis

NeRF [14] leverages multi-layer perceptrons (MLPs) to model 3D scenes from multi-view 2D images, enabling the generation of novel view images with remarkable multi-view consistency. However, achieving high-quality novel view synthesis with NeRF often comes at a high cost in terms of training and rendering time [1,2,6]. To alleviate this bottleneck, numerous studies have focused on optimizing the training and rendering efficiency of NeRF. For instance, KiloNeRF [18] significantly accelerates the rendering process of NeRF by introducing thousands of tiny MLPs to replace a single large MLP. TensoRF [3] employ a 4D tensor for compact representation of the volume field and decompose it into low-rank tensor components to achieve efficient radiance field reconstruction. Research like InstantNGP [16] utilizes multi-resolution hash tables to enable rapid training and real-time rendering. Despite the success of these methods in improving efficiency, they often come at the expense of compromising the quality of the synthesized images, particularly evident in high-resolution rendering scenarios.

2.2   3D Gaussian Splatting for Real-Time Radiance Field Rendering

To meet the demands of real-time rendering, 3DGS [10] technique has been proposed. 3DGS typically uses tens of thousands of 3D Gaussian primitives to compactly represent a scene, enabling efficient image rendering through tiled parallel rasterization [9,19,26]. It achieves real-time rendering without compromising reconstruction quality and visual effects [4,25]. FreGS [27] addresses the over-reconstruction issue in 3D Gaussian Splatting by extracting low-frequency to high-frequency components using low-pass and high-pass filters in the frequency domain, enabling a coarse-to-fine Gaussian densification process. MSGS [23] proposes a multi-scale 3D Gaussian Splatting algorithm that represents the same scene by maintaining Gaussians at different scales. DyGASR [30] employs generalized Gaussian splatting and surface regularization to enable efficient 3D mesh reconstruction. Scaffold-GS [12] method dynamically distributes anchors and predicts local 3D Gaussian attributes, developing an anchor growth and pruning strategy to reduce redundant Gaussians while ensuring rendering speed.

Although existing 3D Gaussian Splatting methods achieve real-time rendering and strong reconstruction performance, their results remain limited by the accuracy of camera pose and depth estimation. To address these issues, we propose a differentiable camera pose optimization approach and an edge-aware, multi-scale depth supervision strategy. These methods enhance scene reconstruction quality and rendering fidelity while preserving real-time performance.

3   Method

3.1   3D Gaussian-Based Scene Representation

3DGS [10] employs a collection of 3D Gaussians to encode both geometric and appearance attributes. Each 3D Gaussian is parameterized by its positional coordinates, anisotropic covariance matrix, opacity value, and spherical harmonic coefficients that modulate view-dependent color. During the rendering pipeline, these 3D Gaussians are projected onto the image plane, transforming

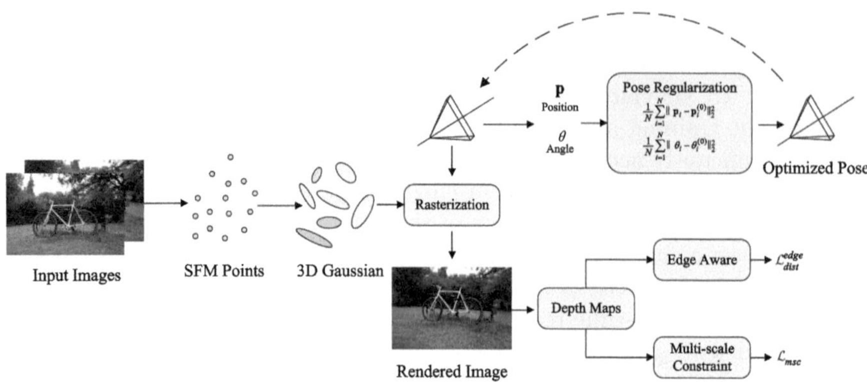

Fig. 1. The overall framework of the proposed method. Initially, the input network is utilized to extract the initial point cloud, which is subsequently Gaussianized. Then, through camera pose information, rasterization is performed to obtain the rendered image. The camera pose is decomposed into a position vector and Euler angles for optimization purposes. Finally, a depth map is generated from the rendered image. Edge-aware loss and multi-scale depth loss are computed for the rendered depth map to enforce depth consistency constraints.

them into 2D Gaussian blobs. The resulting 2D Gaussian distributions are then distributed across distinct tiles, ordered, and composited into the final rendered image through an alpha-blending process rooted in point-based volume rendering techniques (Fig. 1).

Similar to prior work [10, 15], we represent a scene using a collection of 3D Gaussian primitives $\{\mathcal{G}_k | k = 1, 2, 3, ..., K\}$. Each Gaussian primitive $\mathcal{G}_k$ can be parameterized by its Gaussian center $p_k \in \mathbb{R}^3$, scaling matrix $S_k \in \mathbb{R}^{3 \times 3}$, and rotation matrix $R_k \in \mathbb{R}^{3 \times 3}$ through the following formulation:

$$\mathcal{G}_k(x) = e^{-\frac{1}{2}(x-p_k)^T \Sigma_k^{-1}(x-p_k)}, \tag{1}$$

$\sum_k \in \mathbb{R}^{3 \times 3}$ denotes the covariance matrix, which is derived as $\sum_k = R_k S_k S_k^T R_k^T$.

The color of each Gaussian is modeled by spherical harmonics, and is associated with its location and opacity coefficient α, which is multiplied by $\mathcal{G}_k$ during the blending process. During the rendering process, 3DGS discretizes the scene into Gauss elements and projects the 3D Gauss elements onto a 2D image plane to generate a corresponding 2D Gaussian distribution. The projected 2D Gaussian distribution is then distributed to different tiles of the image for parallel processing. After projection into the image space and block processing, parallel pixel-by-pixel alpha blending and synthesis are performed according to depth ordering and occlusion relationships, resulting in high-quality real-time rendered images with multi-view consistency that can be represented as:

$$C(x') = \sum_{i \in N} c_i \sigma_i \prod_{j=1}^{i-1} (1 - \sigma_j), \quad \sigma_i = \alpha_i \mathcal{G}'_i(x'), \tag{2}$$

where x' represents the position of the queried pixel, and N denotes the number of Gaussian elements relevant to the queried pixel. Through the aforementioned differentiable computations, all parameters in 3DGS are learnable, enabling end-to-end optimization.

3.2 Camera Pose Optimization

Most 3DGS methods obtain camera poses and initial point clouds through SFM [20], but there is still a certain degree of error between the estimated camera poses and the true poses. These errors may lead to misalignment and noise in the reconstructed point clouds, and can cause geometric distortions in the rendered images, especially in areas with limited feature visibility, repetitive textures, or dynamic scene content.

To address the aforementioned challenges, we propose a differentiable optimization based camera pose refinement method. We decompose the camera pose into a position vector $\mathbf{p} \in \mathbb{R}^3$ and Euler angles $\theta = (\theta_x, \theta_y, \theta_z) \in \mathbb{R}^3$, and represent the attitude using a rotation matrix $\mathbf{R}(\theta)$. This method adopts a differentiable parameterization scheme, allowing direct optimization of the pose parameters:

$$\mathbf{T}(\mathbf{p}, \theta) = \begin{bmatrix} \mathbf{R}(\theta) & \mathbf{p} \\ 0^T & 1 \end{bmatrix}, \tag{3}$$

$$\mathbf{R}(\theta) = \prod_{i=x,y,z} \mathbf{R}_i(\theta_i), \tag{4}$$

where $\mathbf{R}_i(\theta_i)$ is the elementary rotation matrix about the i-axis. This parameterization approach avoids the computational complexity introduced by algebras while maintaining the optimization degrees of freedom.

Meanwhile, during the optimization process, we introduce a regularization term for the original camera pose to prevent the pose parameters from deviating excessively from the initial values. This helps to maintain the stability of the optimization process and avoid getting trapped in local optimal solutions, which can be expressed as:

$$\mathcal{L}_{\text{pos}} = \frac{1}{N} \sum_{i=1}^{N} \|\mathbf{p}_i - \mathbf{p}_i^{(0)}\|_2^2, \tag{5}$$

$$\mathcal{L}_{\text{rot}} = \frac{1}{N} \sum_{i=1}^{N} \|\theta_i - \theta_i^{(0)}\|_2^2, \tag{6}$$

where $\mathbf{p}_i$ and θ_i represent the optimized position vector and Euler angles, respectively, and $\mathbf{p}_i^{(0)}$ and $\theta_i^{(0)}$ represent the initial position vector and Euler angles, respectively.

3.3 Depth Consistency Constraint

The traditional depth supervision loss function is not accurate enough for depth estimation in edge areas or complex texture areas, resulting in obvious artifacts or unevenness in the reconstructed 3D scene. Furthermore, the consistency of the depth map at different scales is not fully considered, resulting in inconsistent depth estimation results at different resolutions.

A depth distortion regularization method with edge perception is proposed, which generates edge perception weights by calculating the gradient magnitude of the real image. These weights are used to weight the depth distortion map, so that the penalty for depth distortion is smaller in edge regions and larger in smooth regions, which helps to preserve the details of edge regions while reducing the depth distortion in smooth regions, improving the accuracy of depth estimation, which can be expressed as:

$$\mathbf{M}_{grad} = \sqrt{\mathbf{G}_x^2 + \mathbf{G}_y^2}, \tag{7}$$

$$\mathbf{W}_{edge} = \exp(-\alpha \mathbf{M}_{grad}), \tag{8}$$

$$\mathcal{L}_{dist}^{edge} = \frac{1}{HW} \sum_{i,j} \mathbf{D}_{dist}(i,j) \cdot \mathbf{W}_{edge}(i,j), \tag{9}$$

where $\mathbf{G}_x$ and $\mathbf{G}_y$ represent the gradients in the x and y directions, respectively, $\alpha = 2.0$ controls the decay rate, $\mathbf{D}_{dist}$ is the pre-computed depth distortion map, and H, W are the spatial resolution.

Meanwhile, we introduce a multi-scale depth consistency constraint. We perform downsampling and upsampling on the depth map at different scales, and calculate the error between the upsampled depth map and the original depth map. This error is also weighted by the edge aware weights to ensure the consistency of depth estimation at different scales. We first construct a pyramid-style multi-scale depth map through bilinear interpolation, then use a smooth L1 loss to measure the differences between scales, and modulate the error through edge weights, which can be expressed as:

$$\mathbf{D}_s = \text{Downsample}(\mathbf{D}, s), \quad \mathbf{D}_s^{up} = \text{Upsample}(\mathbf{D}_s, s), \tag{10}$$

$$\mathcal{L}_{msc} = \sum_s \gamma^{s-1} \cdot \frac{1}{HW} \sum_{i,j} \mathcal{S}(\mathbf{D}_s^{up}(i,j), \mathbf{D}(i,j)) \cdot \mathbf{W}_{edge}(i,j), \tag{11}$$

$$\mathcal{S}(x,y) = \begin{cases} 0.5(x-y)^2, & |x-y| < 1 \\ |x-y| - 0.5, & \text{otherwise} \end{cases} \tag{12}$$

where $s \in \{2, 4, 8\}$ is the downsampling factor, and bilinear interpolation is used to maintain geometric continuity, $\mathcal{S}(x,y)$ is the smooth L1 loss, and $\gamma = 0.5$ is the scale decay coefficient.

3.4 Training Loss

For the $\mathcal{L}_1$ loss of the color of the rendered pixel, we use the $\mathcal{L}_{SSIM}$ of the SSIM term, and for the normal loss, we use the design in GOF. Overall, the loss function we ultimately use is as follows:

$$\mathcal{L} = \alpha\mathcal{L}_{SSIM} + \mathcal{L}_{msc} + \beta\mathcal{L}_{normal} + \mathcal{L}_{dist}^{edge} + \gamma(\mathcal{L}_{\mathrm{pos}} + \mathcal{L}_{\mathrm{rot}}), \qquad (13)$$

where α, β, γ are the loss weights, and in the experiments, we set them all to 0.1.

4 Experiments

4.1 Experimental Setup

Dataset and Metrics. We evaluated the performance of our proposed method on three representative benchmark datasets: Mip-Nerf 360 [1], Tank and Temple [11], and Deep Blending [8]. The Mip-NeRF 360 dataset includes 9 real-world scenes, 5 infinite outdoor environments, and 4 complex indoor scenes. We selected 7 formally divided scenes for comparative analysis. This dataset is valuable for evaluating the ability of this method to handle large-scale, unbounded scenes with complex geometric layouts and lighting conditions. Tanks and Temples dataset includes various scenes, such as sculptures, large vehicles, and large indoor scenes with complex geometric layouts. Two iconic scenes are selected from the dataset to replicate the experimental configuration of 3DGS [10] to verify the performance of the proposed method in unbounded scenes. The Deep Blending dataset consists of 19 real-world scenes, each containing images captured from 12 to hundreds of different viewpoints. Two iconic scenes are also selected from the dataset to replicate the experimental configuration of 3DGS. The evaluation metrics include Peak Signal-to-Noise Ratio (PSNR) for quantifying pixel-level accuracy, Structural Similarity Index (SSIM) [22] for assessing structural coherence, and Learned Perceptual Image Patch Similarity(LPIPS) [28] for measuring perceptual similarity from the perspective of human visual perception. We trained on a single RTX 4090, with 30,000 iterations per scene.

4.2 Results Analysis

Quantitative Comparison. We compare our method with recent representative approaches, including 3DGS [10], Mip-NeRF360 [1], Lighting-GS [5], PaletteGS [19], DyGASR [30], and AAGS [29], across several real-world datasets. For methods under comparison, results are taken from the original papers when available, while those on datasets not covered in the original publications are reproduced by us based on the respective settings. As shown in Table 1, our method achieves competitive performance on the Tanks and Temples and Deep Blending datasets, and demonstrates clear advantages on Mip-NeRF360, which includes more challenging scenarios involving fine textures, textureless regions, and reflective surfaces.

Visualization Results. Our qualitative results are presented in Fig. 2. As illustrated, our method outperforms comparison approaches in regions with complex textures, such as foliage and densely distributed branches. This improvement is attributed to our camera pose optimization module, which effectively reduces texture misalignment caused by inaccurate poses. Additionally, our method preserves more complete details in regions distant from the camera, owing to the incorporation of depth consistency constraints. By enforcing consistency of depth predictions across views, our approach mitigates depth estimation bias and helps maintain fine-grained structural information in far-field regions.

Table 1. Quantitative comparison on benchmark datasets, with red and yellow representing the best and second-best results, respectively.

Method	Mip-Nerf360			Tank and Temple			Deep Blending		
	PSNR↑	SSIM↑	LPIPS↓	PSNR↑	SSIM↑	LPIPS↓	PSNR↑	SSIM↑	LPIPS↓
3DGS [10]	27.21	0.815	0.214	23.14	0.841	0.183	29.41	0.903	0.243
Mip-Nerf360 [1]	27.69	0.792	0.237	22.22	0.759	0.257	29.40	0.901	0.245
LightningGS [5]	28.45	0.857	0.210	22.83	0.807	0.242	29.12	0.895	0.262
PaletteGS [19]	26.08	0.795	0.208	22.49	0.771	0.240	29.21	0.874	0.255
DyGASR [30]	27.57	0.831	0.248	22.65	0.814	0.246	29.05	0.881	0.269
AAGS [29]	28.05	0.835	0.224	22.91	0.824	0.238	29.17	0.886	0.257
Ours	28.96	0.870	0.172	23.61	0.855	0.165	29.39	0.907	0.240

4.3   Ablation Studies

Ablation on Camera Pose Optimization. We evaluated the effectiveness of the proposed camera pose optimization method based on differentiable optimization. When the camera pose optimization module was removed and only the initial camera poses obtained through Structure-from-Motion (SfM) were used, the rendered images exhibited a decrease in PSNR and SSIM, along with a slight increase in LPIPS. This indicates the effectiveness of the camera pose optimization in enhancing the quality of the reconstructed point clouds and rendered images. Furthermore, when the constrained regularization term was removed, the performance also deteriorated, suggesting that the regularization term plays a crucial role in constraining the pose optimization process.

Ablation on Depth Consistency Constraint. We evaluated the effectiveness of the proposed depth consistency constraint. Removing this constraint and relying solely on simple depth supervision led to a notable performance drop. Introducing only edge perception or multi-scale consistency individually failed to achieve optimal results, indicating that the proposed constraint significantly improves image quality. Furthermore, both the edge-aware depth distortion and

Fig. 2. Qualitative results on the 'stump' scene of Mip-NeRF 360.

multi-scale depth consistency components contribute independently, and their combination further enhances 3D reconstruction quality by leveraging complementary strengths (Tables 2 and 3).

Table 2. The ablation experiment results of camera pose optimization on Mip-Nerf 360

Model	PSNR↑	SSIM↑	LPIPS↓
SFM [20]	28.12	0.841	0.192
w/o Regularization	28.54	0.857	0.184

Table 3. The ablation experiment results of depth consistency constraint on Mip-Nerf 360

Model	PSNR↑	SSIM↑	LPIPS↓
Depth Distortion	27.93	0.844	0.203
w/o edge-aware	28.21	0.851	0.190
w/o multi-scale	28.32	0.860	0.186

5   Conclusion

To address the limitations of 3D Gaussian Splatting in camera pose estimation and depth supervision, we propose a framework that integrates differentiable pose optimization with edge-aware and multi-scale depth consistency constraints. The joint optimization of camera poses improves depth accuracy and reduces alignment errors. Experiments on multiple benchmarks show that our method enhances image reconstruction quality and visual fidelity while maintaining real-time rendering performance. Ablation studies confirm the effectiveness of pose regularization and the role of depth constraints in mitigating edge artifacts. Future work will explore spatiotemporal modeling for dynamic scenes and physics-based material decomposition to further improve rendering realism.

Acknowledgment. This study was funded by the Independent Innovative Project of Changjiang Survey Planning Design and Research Co., Ltd. (grant number: CX2022Z10-1).

References

1. Barron, J.T., Mildenhall, B., Verbin, D., Srinivasan, P.P., Hedman, P.: Mip-NeRF 360: unbounded anti-aliased neural radiance fields. In: 2022 IEEE/CVF Conference On Computer Vision and Pattern Recognition (CVPR 2022), pp. 5460–5469 (2022). https://doi.org/10.1109/CVPR52688.2022.00539
2. Bian, W., Wang, Z., Li, K., Bian, J.W., Prisacariu, V.A.: NoPe-NeRF: optimising neural radiance field with no pose prior. In: 2023 IEEE/CVF Conference on Computer Vision And Pattern Recognition, CVPR, pp. 4160–4169 (2023). https://doi.org/10.1109/CVPR52729.2023.00405
3. Chen, A., Xu, Z., Geiger, A., Yu, J., Su, H.: TensoRF: tensorial radiance fields. In: Avidan, S., Brostow, G., Cisse, M., Farinella, GM., Hassner, T. (eds.) Computer Vision - ECCV 2022, PT XXXII, vol. 13692, pp. 333–350 (2022). https://doi.org/10.1007/978-3-031-19824-3_20
4. Chen, H., Li, C., Lee, G.H.: NeuSG: neural implicit surface reconstruction with 3D Gaussian splatting guidance. arXiv preprint arXiv:2312.00846 (2023)
5. Fan, Z., et al.: LightGaussian: unbounded 3D Gaussian compression with 15x reduction and 200+ fps. Adv. Neural. Inf. Process. Syst. **37**, 140138–140158 (2024)
6. Fridovich-Keil, S., Yu, A., Tancik, M., Chen, Q., Recht, B., Kanazawa, A.: Plenoxels: radiance fields without neural networks. In: 2022 IEEE/CVF Conference on Computer Vision and Pattern Recognition (CVPR 2022), pp. 5491–5500 (2022). https://doi.org/10.1109/CVPR52688.2022.00542
7. Guédon, A., Lepetit, V.: Sugar: surface-aligned gaussian splatting for efficient 3D mesh reconstruction and high-quality mesh rendering. In: Proceedings of the IEEE/CVF Conference on Computer Vision and Pattern Recognition, pp. 5354–5363 (2024)
8. Hedman, P., Philip, J., Price, T., Frahm, J.M., Drettakis, G., Brostow, G.: Deep blending for free-viewpoint image-based rendering. ACM Trans. Graph. (ToG) **37**(6), 1–15 (2018)
9. Huang, B., Yu, Z., Chen, A., Geiger, A., Gao, S.: 2D Gaussian splatting for geometrically accurate radiance fields. In: SIGGRAPH 2024 Conference Papers. Association for Computing Machinery (2024). https://doi.org/10.1145/3641519.3657428
10. Kerbl, B., Kopanas, G., Leimkuehler, T., Drettakis, G.: 3D Gaussian splatting for real-time radiance field rendering. ACM Trans. Graph. **42**(4) (2023). https://doi.org/10.1145/3592433

11. Knapitsch, A., Park, J., Zhou, Q.Y., Koltun, V.: Tanks and temples: benchmarking large-scale scene reconstruction. ACM Trans. Graph. **36**(4) (2017). https://doi.org/10.1145/3072959.3073599
12. Lu, T., et al.: Scaffold-GS: structured 3D Gaussians for view-adaptive rendering. In: Proceedings of the IEEE/CVF Conference on Computer Vision and Pattern Recognition, pp. 20654–20664 (2024)
13. Lyu, X., et al.: 3DGSR: implicit surface reconstruction with 3D Gaussian splatting. ACM Trans. Graph. (TOG) **43**(6), 1–12 (2024)
14. Mildenhall, B., Srinivasan, P.P., Tancik, M., Barron, J.T., Ramamoorthi, R., Ng, R.: NeRF: representing scenes as neural radiance fields for view synthesis. Commun. ACM **65**(1), 99–106 (2021)
15. Morgenstern, W., Barthel, F., Hilsmann, A., Eisert, P.: Compact 3D scene representation via self-organizing gaussian grids. In: Computer Vision – ECCV 2024, pp. 18–34. Springer, Cham (2025). https://doi.org/10.1007/978-3-031-73013-9_2. https://fraunhoferhhi.github.io/Self-Organizing-Gaussians/
16. Müller, T., Evans, A., Schied, C., Keller, A.: Instant neural graphics primitives with a multiresolution hash encoding. ACM Trans. Graph. **41**(4), 102:1–102:15 (2022). https://doi.org/10.1145/3528223.3530127
17. Niemeyer, M., Barron, J.T., Mildenhall, B., Sajjadi, M.S.M., Geiger, A., Radwan, N.: RegNeRF: regularizing neural radiance fields for view synthesis from sparse inputs. In: 2022 IEEE/CVF Conference on Computer Vision and Pattern Recognition (CVPR 2022), pp. 5470–5480 (2022). https://doi.org/10.1109/CVPR52688.2022.00540
18. Reiser, C., Peng, S., Liao, Y., Geiger, A.: KiloNeRF: speeding up neural radiance fields with thousands of tiny MLPs. In: Proceedings of the IEEE/CVF International Conference on Computer Vision, pp. 14335–14345 (2021)
19. Ren, C., Qiu, H., Shao, Y., Qiu, Z., Song, K.: PaletteGaussian: 3D photorealistic color editing with gaussian splatting. In: 2024 IEEE International Symposium on Mixed and Augmented Reality (ISMAR), pp. 1206–1215 (2024). https://doi.org/10.1109/ISMAR62088.2024.00137
20. Schönberger, J.L., Frahm, J.M.: Structure-from-motion revisited. In: Conference on Computer Vision and Pattern Recognition (CVPR), pp. 4104–4113 (2016). https://doi.org/10.1109/CVPR.2016.445
21. Tancik, M., et al.: Nerfstudio: a modular framework for neural radiance field development. In: ACM SIGGRAPH 2023 Conference Proceedings, pp. 1–12 (2023)
22. Wang, Z., Bovik, A., Sheikh, H., Simoncelli, E.: Image quality assessment: from error visibility to structural similarity. IEEE Trans. Image Process. **13**(4), 600–612 (2004). https://doi.org/10.1109/TIP.2003.819861
23. Yan, Z., Low, W.F., Chen, Y., Lee, G.H.: Multi-scale 3D Gaussian splatting for anti-aliased rendering. In: Proceedings of the IEEE/CVF Conference on Computer Vision and Pattern Recognition, pp. 20923–20931 (2024)
24. Yu, A., Ye, V., Tancik, M., Kanazawa, A.: pixelNeRF: neural radiance fields from one or few images. In: Proceedings of the IEEE/CVF Conference on Computer Vision and Pattern Recognition, pp. 4578–4587 (2021)
25. Yu, M., Lu, T., Xu, L., Jiang, L., Xiangli, Y., Dai, B.: GSDF: 3DGS meets SDF for improved rendering and reconstruction. arXiv preprint arXiv:2403.16964 (2024)
26. Yu, Z., Sattler, T., Geiger, A.: Gaussian opacity fields: efficient adaptive surface reconstruction in unbounded scenes. ACM Trans. Graph. (2024)
27. Zhang, J., Zhan, F., Xu, M., Lu, S., Xing, E.: FreGS: 3D Gaussian splatting with progressive frequency regularization. In: Proceedings of the IEEE/CVF Conference on Computer Vision and Pattern Recognition, pp. 21424–21433 (2024)

28. Zhang, R., Isola, P., Efros, A.A., Shechtman, E., Wang, O.: The unreasonable effectiveness of deep features as a perceptual metric. In: Proceedings of the IEEE Conference on Computer Vision and Pattern Recognition, pp. 586–595 (2018)
29. Zhang, W., Guo, Z., Zhou, W., Li, H.: AAGS: appearance-aware 3D Gaussian splatting with unconstrained photo collections: AAGS: appearance-aware 3D Gaussian splatting... Multimedia Syst. **31**(3) (2025). https://doi.org/10.1007/s00530-025-01742-4
30. Zhao, S., Li, Y.: DyGASR: dynamic generalized Gaussian splatting with surface alignment for accelerated 3D mesh reconstruction. In: Lin, Z., et al. (eds.) Pattern Recognition and Computer Vision, pp. 299–312. Springer, Singapore (2025)

Development of a Digital Impression Positioning Device for Dental Implantology

Zhenzhong Tang[1,2] , Yuping Ye[3] , Siqi Luo[1,2], and Feifei Gu[2,4(✉)]

[1] Southern University of Science and Technology, Shenzhen,
Nanshan District 518055, China
{zz.tang,sq.luo}@siat.ac.cn
[2] Shenzhen Institutes of Advanced Technology, Chinese Academy of Sciences,
Shenzhen, Nanshan District 518055, China
ff.gu@siat.ac.cn
[3] School of Smart Marine Science and Technology, Fujian University of Technology,
Fuzhou, Minhou 350118, China
[4] The Department of Mechanical and Automation Engineering, The Chinese
University of Hong Kong, Hong Kong, New Territories 999077, China

Abstract. Designing dental implant bridges is essential for restoring both function and aesthetics in edentulous patients. However, existing methods often fall short in efficiency, precision, and reliability, particularly in complex cases. To address these challenges, we propose a stereophotogrammetric-based implant positioning system optimized for full-arch restorations. This study introduces a innovations: a scanning transfer rod (STR) incorporating a surface feature encoding strategy, significantly enhancing tracking robustness in digital impressions; this study also employs a 3D positioning algorithm tailored for the STR, which significantly improves the spatial accuracy of digital impressions, enabling highly precise fit and alignment in implant-supported bridge design. Experimental validation confirms the system's robustness and exceptional accuracy, achieving a recognition rate exceeding 90% across various pose combinations, along with a precision of 0.0037 mm in vitro. These findings underscore the system's potential to enhance clinical efficiency, improve treatment predictability, and advance digital workflows in dental implant applications.

Keywords: Dental implantology · stereophotogrammetric system ·
scan transfer rods · dental implant bridge

1 Introduction

In recent years, dental implantology has witnessed significant growth in penetration rates, driven by rapid advancements in Cone Beam Computed Tomography

---

Z. Tang and F. Gu—These authors contributed equally to this work.

© The Author(s), under exclusive license to Springer Nature Singapore Pte Ltd. 2026

Z. Lin et al. (Eds.): ICIG 2025, LNCS 16163, pp. 387–398, 2026.
https://doi.org/10.1007/978-981-95-3729-7_32

(CBCT) and intraoral scanning (IOS) technologies [1–4]. This growth is further fueled by the increasing demand from both clinicians and patients for higher precision in implant placement and the potential for immediate implant procedures [5,6]. The need for accurate, efficient, and patient-comfort-oriented techniques has become particularly crucial for edentulous patients undergoing full-arch or partial-arch restorations.

Dental implant bridges are essential for restoring function and aesthetics in patients with multiple missing teeth, especially in cases of full-arch or partial-arch restorations. Among the various implant bridge techniques, the Malo Bridge [7], developed by Dr. Paulo Malo, has become one of the most famous and effective approaches [8,9]. This method is closely associated with the All-on-4®treatment concept, which Dr. Malo also pioneered to address the needs of patients with partial or complete edentulism. The design and fit of implant bridges must be highly precise to ensure longevity, optimal function, and patient comfort. Traditional approaches to designing implant bridges often rely on physical impressions and manual modeling, which can be time-consuming and subject to inaccuracies due to distortions or errors introduced during impression-taking and casting [10,11].

Traditional bridge design methods primarily include manual impression and molding techniques [12,13], as well as some digitized methods based on physical models [14,15]. These methods are limited when addressing complex edentulous cases, especially in terms of accurate alignment and fit, which are crucial to avoid excessive stress on implants and bone structures. Poorly fitted bridges can lead to implant failure, patient discomfort, and increased maintenance requirements. Issues such as alveolar bone resorption, bone grafting, and implant integration also represent significant challenges. To address these challenges, the application of digital technology has gradually become a key research focus in dental restoration [16–18]. Digital impression devices are particularly crucial during the planning and postoperative phases, capturing precise oral geometry and implant positions to ensure accurate implant placement, improving the accuracy of restoration design and reducing surgery time.

This paper introduces a novel digital impression positioning device specifically designed for dental implant applications, utilizing a custom scanning transfer rod with encoded surface features. The use of stereophotogrammetry ensures the robustness and positioning accuracy of the digital reconstruction, making it highly suitable for clinical applications in complex cases.

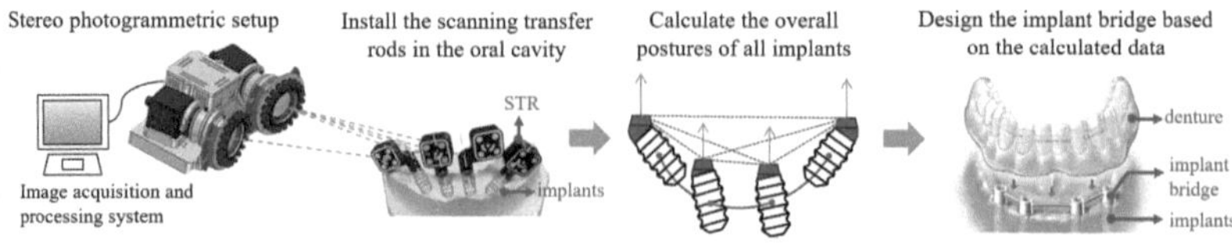

Fig. 1. Working principle of the digital impression positioning device using stereophotogrammetric.

2   Methods

As shown in Fig. 1, the workflow of the implant positioning system is as follows (refer to Fig. 1 for visual guidance):

1) STR Installation: For a patient in the denture fabrication stage, the scanning transfer rods (STRs) are mounted at the implant sites in the patient's oral cavity. In fully or partially edentulous patients, typically 4 to 6 implants are used, requiring an equal number of STRs to design the Malo Bridge.

2) Dynamic Imaging: Using a handheld stereophotogrammetric (SPG) device, dynamic imaging of the STRs is performed. This step captures the spatial coordinates and orientation of the surface feature points on each STR.

3) Position and Orientation Calculation: The spatial pose data from each STR, combined with the structural parameters specific to each rod, allows for the determination of the precise position and orientation of the underlying implants.

4) Bridge Design: Finally, using the relative positions and orientations of the STRs, an implant bridge is designed. This provides highly accurate structural information crucial for the subsequent stages of denture fabrication, ensuring precise fit and functionality of the final prosthesis.

2.1   Encoding of the STRs

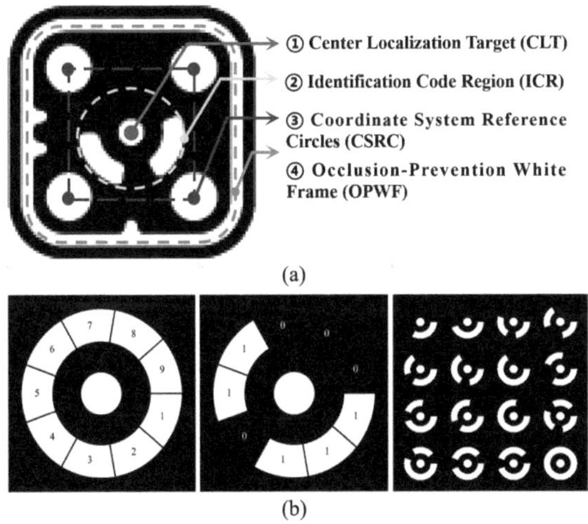

Fig. 2. Encoding of the STR: (a) Encoded features; (b) Annular encoding principle in region ②: *ICR*.

To accurately track and locate the STRs, we designed ring-shaped encoded optical features on the surface of the STR. As shown in Fig. 2(a), the surface features of each STR consist of four parts: the Center Localization Target (**CLT**), the Identification Code Region (**ICR**), the Coordinate System Reference Circles (**CSRC**), and the Occlusion-Prevention White Frame (**OPWF**). Among them, the **CLT**, **CSRC**, and **OPWF** are identical across all STRs, while the **ICR** is variable and used to distinguish the identity of different STRs.

The functions of each section are as follows:

CLT: This section contains a small-radius circle. The center of this circle is extracted using methods such as contour fitting, and it is designated as the origin (O) of the local coordinate system of the STR (***LCS***-STR). The precise localization of the center ensures accurate reference for further coordinate transformations.

ICR: This section is the encoding area, where a unique code value is assigned to each STR. The encoded values facilitate identification and ensure the uniqueness of each transfer rod, which is critical for distinguishing different parts of the system.

CSRC: This section contains four larger circles arranged at the vertices of a quadrilateral. The centers of these circles p_1, p_2, p_3, p_4 are used to define the three axes (X, Y, Z) of the ***LCS***-STR.

The combination of these three regions (***CLT***, ***ICR***, and ***CSRC***) forms the effective information area, which must remain unobstructed during identification to maintain accuracy.

OPWF: This section consists of a white, uniform-width band that surrounds the ***CLT***, ***ICR***, and ***CSRC*** areas, designed to prevent obstruction of the effective information regions. The necessity of this region arises from observations during early clinical measurements, where the larger circle in the ***CSRC*** area was prone to obstruction. In these cases, the obstruction was not detectable through circle contour detection, leading to errors in the center localization of the large circle. These errors, which can significantly impact the precision of the local coordinate system, must be eliminated to ensure accurate measurements and system performance. Related observations and analysis were put below.

2.2   STRs' Decoding Based on the ICR

In the ***ICR*** section, we adopt a ring coding scheme [19], illustrated in Fig. 2(b). The encoding uses concentric rings where binary values are represented by alternating black and white segments. This encoding is robust for accurate localization by generating unique codes for each STR based on the spatial arrangement of binary values.

For a circle divided into n segments, each randomly assigned a 0 or 1, the number of unique patterns N is calculated using Burnside's Lemma[20]. This accounts for the rotational symmetry of the code. The total number of unique patterns is:

$$N = \frac{1}{n} \sum_{k=0}^{n-1} 2^{\gcd(k,n)}$$

For $n = 9$, we obtain approximately 60 unique patterns (rounded).

To improve noise resistance, we select 16 patterns from the code library, ensuring a clear visual distinction between codes.

To handle rotation in ring encoding, we propose a decoding method based on angular displacement. First, we correct geometric distortion using affine transformation. After applying the transformation to the ROI, binary sequences are sampled along the circumference using the polar coordinate formula:

$$(x_j, y_j) = (x_0 + r \cdot \cos(j \cdot \theta), y_0 + r \cdot \sin(j \cdot \theta))$$

where $\theta = 2\pi \times \text{step}/360$. The resulting binary sequence is adjusted by a head-tail value strategy. If the first and last values are identical, the sequence is cyclically shifted until they differ:

$$\text{while } b_1 = b_S, \quad B_S \leftarrow (b_S, b_1, b_2, \ldots, b_{S-1})$$

The sequence is then compressed, and the final code value is computed using:

$$C = \sum_{k=0}^{N-1} c_k \cdot 2^{(N-1-k)}$$

This code is cross-checked against predefined valid values to ensure accurate decoding.

2.3   STR's Completeness Detection Based on the OPWF

In practical intraoral testing environments, the contours of the four large circles in the **CSRC** region are frequently obscured. These occlusions significantly affect the reliability of localization results. Figure 3 highlights common sources of such interference, including: (a) other STRs, (b) the patient's lips, (c) overlapping between markers, and (d) the patient's tongue. These factors often partially obscure the visual markers' contours, leading to incomplete edge information and reducing the accuracy of centroid detection.

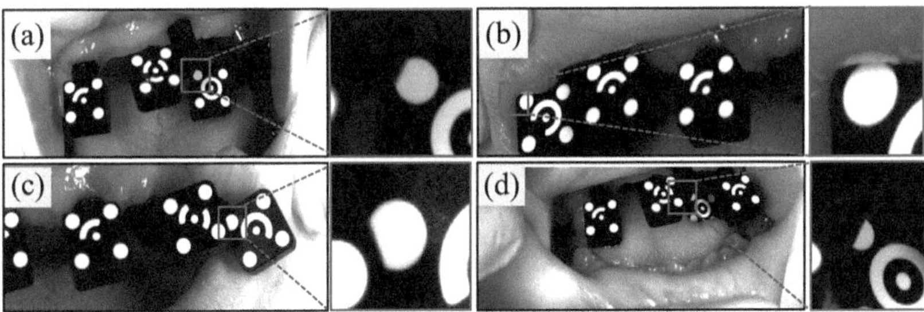

Fig. 3. Common sources of occlusions by (a) other STRs; (b) patient's lips; (c) adjacent markers; (d) patient's tongue.

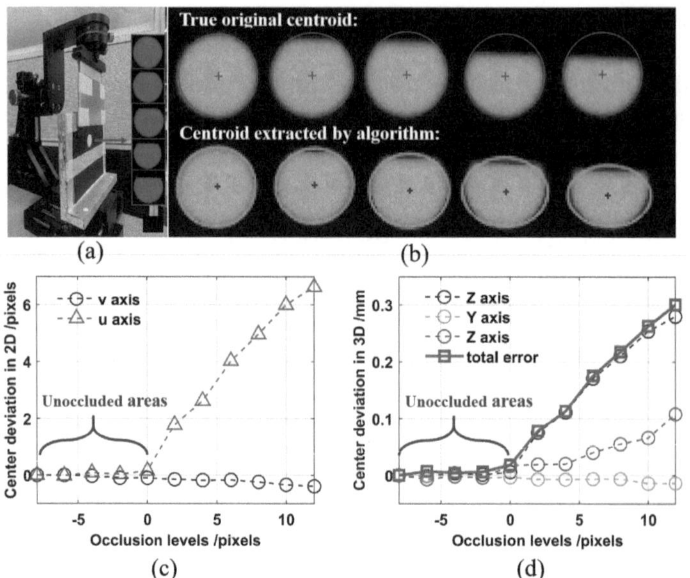

Fig. 4. Experiment on centroid deviation analysis caused by occlusion of circular contours.

Figure 4 demonstrates the adverse effects of occlusion on the localization algorithm's accuracy. A complete positioning circle was progressively occluded to evaluate its performance under increasing levels of occlusion (Fig. 4(a)), and the results were compared to ideal conditions (Fig. 4(b)). The experimental results as in Fig. 4(c-d) demonstrates that even minor occlusions can result in substantial deviations in centroid localization accuracy compared to ideal conditions. For example, a horizontal occlusion of just 2 pixels produced a vertical centroid error of 1.78 pixels, leading to a 3D spatial localization error of 0.078 mm. As the severity of occlusion increased, such as with a horizontal occlusion of 12 pixels, the vertical centroid error rose to 6.64 pixels, corresponding to a 3D spatial localization error of 0.3 mm. Therefore, a completeness detection algorithm of the **CSRC** based on the **OPWF** was proposed here. The entire **OPWF** is mainly composed of four arc segments and four straight - line segments. The centers of the four large circles in the **CSRC** part can be used to assist in locating the entire white frame on the image. And the occlusion can be determined by counting the connectivity of the white areas within it. For details, please refer to Algorithm 1. This algorithm will determine whether the collected information from the system is usable for subsequent calculations.

3   Experimental Results

The binocular system used in the SPG device employs two industrial cameras, shown in Fig. 5(a), with a 12mm focal length and an 80mm baseline, synchro-

---

Algorithm 1. STR's Completeness Detection Process

Require: Grayscale image I_g; $CSRC$'s four circular center coordinates $C = \{p_1, p_2, p_3, p_4\}$

Ensure: Completeness flag *shelter*

 1: Compute geometric center C_g of C
 2: Sort C counterclockwise based on their polar angles relative to C_g
 3: Compute minimum bounding rectangle B enclosing C
 4: Compute expanded bounding box B'
 5: B'.height $\Leftarrow \lambda_H \cdot B$.height
 6: B'.width $\Leftarrow \lambda_W \cdot B$.width
 7: B'.angle $\Leftarrow B$.angle
 8: Compute ROI limits:
 9: $x_{\min} \Leftarrow \max(0, B'.x - T)$, $x_{\max} \Leftarrow \min(W - 1, B'.x + T)$
10: $y_{\min} \Leftarrow \max(0, B'.y - T)$, $y_{\max} \Leftarrow \min(H - 1, B'.y + T)$
11: Extract $I_{\mathrm{ROI}} \Leftarrow I_g(y_{\min} : y_{\max}, x_{\min} : x_{\max})$
12: Convert C to the local coordinate system of I_{ROI}
13: For four arc segments, obtain the grayscale values by:
14: $x(t) = x_c + r\cos(t)$, $y(t) = y_c + r\sin(t)$, $t \in [\theta_1, \theta_2]$
15: For four straight lines, obtain the grayscale values by:
16: $x = x_i + t \cdot (x_{i+1} - x_i)$
17: $y = y_i$ where $t \in [0, 1]$
18: Compute occlusion flag *shelter* based on white frame continuity
19: **return** *shelter*

---

nized via a software-triggered method, to capture high-resolution dynamic STR images in real-time, with 850nm infrared (IR) light sources to enhance imaging precision and patient comfort. This wavelength offers specific advantages for intraoral applications: (a) it minimizes ambient light interference, providing a stable imaging environment, and (b) it is safer and more comfortable for patients than visible light in clinical settings.

Next, we verified the effectiveness of the method proposed in this paper through a series of experiments.

3.1   Robustness of STRs' Decoding

The decoding of STRs, specifically the robustness of **ICR** region decoding, is the primary metric for evaluating the practicality of the proposed SPG system. To assess this, we analyze the recognition rate of different flags under various poses relative to the camera. Eight STRs as shown in Fig. 5(b) were tested.

In this experiment, due to the symmetry of the binocular configuration, any camera in the SPG system can be used. The STR's initial pose is aligned with the camera's axial vector, with the y-axis of the STR's local coordinate system (LCS-STR) coinciding with the imaging axis. The x- and z-axes correspond to the camera's horizontal and vertical directions. The STR undergoes pose transformations in three degrees of freedom: pitch (-180° to 180°), yaw (-50° to 50°), and roll (-50 to 50°), with step sizes of 36°, 10°, and 10°, respectively. The camera's effective working distance is 160–260mm, and the STR is displaced along

Fig. 5. Experimental setup for STRs' recognition robustness verification. (a) the proposed SPG system, (b) eight developed STRs.

the y-axis in 5mm increments, with Gaussian noise added at each position. A total of 210 data sets are collected, and the average recognition rate is calculated for each angle.

Figure 6 show that the pitch angle has minimal impact on recognition (over 98.5% accuracy from -180° to 180°). However, recognition accuracy drops significantly when the STR deviates by more than 40° in roll or yaw, with a failure rate beyond these angles. Otherwise, recognition remains above 95%. This demonstrates the effectiveness of circular encoding in maintaining high recognition rates.

To further verify the robustness of the proposed decoding method, STR recognition rate and confidence across pose variations is listed in Table 1. The recognition rate remains above 95% in most angle combinations, reaching up to 99.98%, indicating the system's robustness under various pose variations.

Table 1. STR Recognition Rate and Confidence Across Pose Variations

Pitch(°)	Yaw (°)	Roll (°)	Recog. Rate (%)	95% CI (±)
✓	-40	-40	90.20	1.8
✓	-30	-30	96.51	1.3
✓	-20	-20	99.78	0.9
✓	-10	-10	99.85	0.5
✓	0	0	99.98	0.0
✓	10	10	99.87	0.6
✓	20	20	98.74	1.0
✓	30	30	95.45	1.5
✓	40	40	91.83	1.9

✓ indicates that the corresponding angle is fixed.

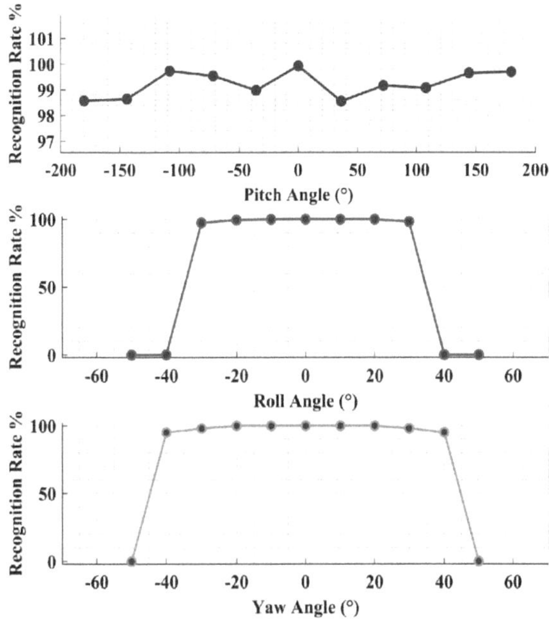

Fig. 6. Recognition rate with different pitch, roll and yaw angles.

3.2   In Vitro Experiment

To further verify the impact of STR calibration on the overall accuracy of the SPG system, we conducted an in vitro experiment. Two indicators were used to comprehensively assess the proposed method: trueness and precision (ISO 5725-1, DIN 55350-13) [21].

1) **Trueness**: Trueness evaluates the digitizer's ability to accurately replicate a dental arch without deformation. In this study, trueness was determined by analyzing the mean distortion in implant abutment positions between models scanned using a high-accuracy intraoral scanner (Medit Corp. i700) [22] and oral implant impression devices. An implant abutment replica was used, and the STRs of our method and PIC Dental [23] were placed on it successively (Figure 7(c,e)). The Medit Corp. i700 scanned the abutment to obtain a reference model (Figure 7(a,b)). The positioning results of our system, both with and without calibrating the STRs, are displayed in Fig. 7(f) and 7(g), respectively. The result of PIC Dental is shown in Fig. 7(d). The main difference between our system and PIC Dental is the location of the **WCS**. In our system, it is built at the optical center of the left camera, whereas in PIC Dental, it is built at a rod designated in advance. However, since the relative locations of the four rods remain constant, this does not affect the accuracy comparison. Related numerical analysis results are presented in Table 2. Comparing our method with PIC Dental, our approach exhibits superior performance compared with PIC Dental,

achieving an improvement of 0.0093 mm in standard deviation and 0.0082 mm in mean accuracy.

Table 2. Accuracy Evaluation of the Developed System

		Results with STRs	Results of PIC Dental
Trueness	Mean	**0.0087**	0.0169
	SD	**0.0122**	0.0215
Precision	Mean	**0.0031**	0.0071
	SD	**0.0037**	0.0090

2) **Precision**: Precision measures the consistency of images obtained from repeated scans under identical conditions. In this study, we measured the same implant abutment, as shown in Fig. 7(c,e), using various acquisition methods, including dynamic handheld scanning and multi-angle data collection. The overlap degree among the measurement results was then analyzed. The final results were consistent with those of the trueness index. The proposed device achieved a precision of 0.0037 mm in standard deviation, while the PIC Dental system had a precision of 0.0090 mm. This confirms the significant advantage of our device in terms of precision.

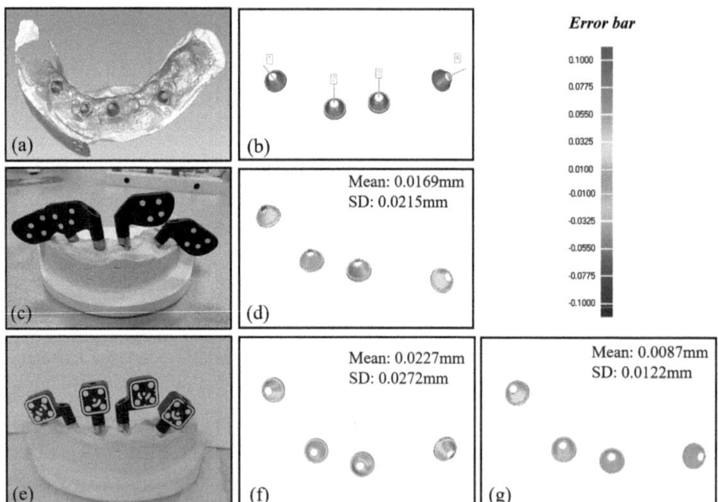

Fig. 7. Trueness evaluation: (a)Scanning results by the intraoral scanner; (b) Ground truth data based on (a); (c) Our STRs at the implant abutment; (d) Positioning results of (c); (e) PIC Dental's STRs at the implant abutment; (f) Positioning results of (e).

4   Conclusions

This paper presents a high-precision dental implantation device for partially or fully edentulous patients. By designing a reliable encoding and decoding scheme for STRs, the proposed system achieves a high accuracy of 0.0037 mm (Precision, SD) in vitro. The SPG device significantly shortens the impression-taking process, reduces patient waiting time and discomfort, and minimizes rework rates. This makes the system an efficient digital impression system capable of assisting in the successful one-time fabrication of Malo Bridges.

However, future research should focus on collecting more clinical data and optimizing the system to adapt to the complex intraoral environment, further enhancing its practicality.

Acknowledgments. Thanks to Mr. Wang for his help in providing the diagnosis and treatment cases, which facilitates the testing of the equipment described in this paper.

Disclosure of Interests. The authors have no competing interests to declare that are relevant to the content of this article.

References

1. Wu, T.-H., et al.: Two-stage mesh deep learning for automated tooth segmentation and landmark localization on 3D intraoral scans. IEEE Trans. Med. Imag. **41**(11), 3158–3166 (2022)
2. Gomez-Polo, M., et al.: Merging intraoral scans and CBCT: a novel technique for improving the accuracy of 3D digital models for implant-supported complete-arch fixed dental prostheses. Int. J. Comput. Dent. **24**(2), 117–123 (2021)
3. Chang, Y.B., et al.: An automatic and robust algorithm of reestablishment of digital dental occlusion. IEEE Trans. Med. Imaging **29**(9), 1652–1663 (2020)
4. Kim, G., et al.: Automatic teeth axes calculation for well-aligned teeth using cost profile analysis along teeth center arch. IEEE Trans. Biomed. Eng. **59**(4), 1145–1154 (2012)
5. Mizumoto, R.M., et al.: Accuracy of different digital scanning techniques and scan bodies for complete-arch implant-supported prostheses. J. Prosthet. Dent. **123**(1), 96–104 (2020)
6. Yuping, Y., et al.: Accuracy of a novel stereophotogrammetry system for full-arch digital implant impressions: an in vitro study and clinical case. Measurement **244**, 116476 (2025)
7. Malò, P., et al.: All-on-Four" immediate-function concept with Brånemark System®implants for completely edentulous mandibles: a retrospective clinical study. Clin. Implant Dent. Relat. Res. **5**, 2–9 (2003)
8. Ponnanna, A.A., et al.: Three-dimensional–printed Malo bridge: digital Fixed prosthesis for the partially edentulous maxilla. Contemp. Clin. Dent. **12**(4), 451–453 (2021)
9. Boruah, S., et al.: Prosthetic rehabilitation of a mandibular defect using a malo bridge: a case report. Cureus **16**, 9 (2024)
10. Bouchard, P., et al.: Cost-effectiveness modeling of dental implant vs. bridge. Clin. Oral Implants Res. **20**(6), 583–587 (2009)

11. Cooper, L.F.: The current and future treatment of edentulism. J. Prosthodont. **18**(2), 116–122 (2009)
12. Revilla-León, M., et al.: Impression technique for a complete-arch prosthesis with multiple implants using additive manufacturing technologies. J. Prosthet. Dent. **177**, 714–20 (2017)
13. Heckmann, S.M., et al.: Cement fixation and screw retention: parameters of passive fit. An in vitro study of three-unit implant-supported fixed partial dentures. Clin. Oral Implants Res. **15**, 466–473 (2004)
14. Lian, C., et al.: Deep multi-scale mesh feature learning for automated labeling of raw dental surfaces from 3D intraoral scanners. IEEE Trans. Med. Imag. **39**(7), 2440–2450 (2020)
15. Mizumoto, R.M., Yilmaz, B.: Intraoral scan bodies in implant dentistry: a systematic review. J. Prosthet. Dent. **120**, 343–352 (2018)
16. Osta, E., et al.: Accuracy of conventional impressions and digital scans for implant-supported fixed prostheses in maxillary free-ended partial edentulism: an in vitro study. J. Dent. **143**, 104892 (2024)
17. El Osta, et al.: Time efficiency and cost of fabricating removable complete dentures using digital, hybrid, and conventional workflows: a systematic review. J. Prosthet. Dent. (2024)
18. Rivara, F., et al.: Photogrammetric method to measure the discrepancy between clinical and software-designed positions of implants. J. Prosthet. Dent. **115**(6), 703–711 (2016)
19. Hong, Z., et al.: A high-precision recognition method of circular marks based on CMNet within complex scenes. IEEE J-STARS **15**, 7431–7443 (2022)
20. Burnside, W.: Theory of groups of finite order. Messenger Math. **23**, 112 (1909)
21. ISO 5725-1. Accuracy (trueness and precision) of measuring methods and results. Part-I: General principles and definitions. Beuth Verlag GmbH, Berlin (1994)
22. Al-Hassiny, A.: Medit i700 lightweight ergonomic scanning. https://www.medit.com/medit-i700-intraoral-scanner/. Accessed 10 Jan 2025
23. Gómez-Polo, M., et al.: Stereophotogrammetric impression making for polyoxymethylene, milled immediate partial fixed dental prostheses. J. Prosthet. Dent. **199**(4), 506–510 (2018)

A Review of Neural Radiation Field Based 3D Reconstruction Methods for Spatial Targets

Wanyun Li, Yuqiang Fang$^{(\boxtimes)}$, Gege Sun, and Yuyang Zhang

Space Engineering University, Beijing 101416, China
`fangyuqiang@nudt.edu.cn`

Abstract. With the development of space technology, optical images of space targets have become an indispensable source of information for gaining insight into the space situation and understanding the space environment. In recent years, accurate 3D reconstruction of space targets using these high-resolution optical images has become a research hotspot at the intersection of computer vision and space technology. Meanwhile, Neural Radiance Field (NeRF) utilizes micro-renderable technology to represent the scene implicitly, which has gained wide attention for its realistic visual effects. The purpose of this paper is to comprehensively review the recent progress and research results of NeRF technology in the field of 3D reconstruction of space targets. The article firstly describes the basic theory of neural radiance field, then systematically combs through and summarizes the 3D reconstruction methods of spatial targets based on this technique, then introduces the relevant image datasets, and finally looks forward to the future development and research trends.

Keywords: Neural Radiance Field · Spatial Target · Neural Rendering · Implicit Representation

1 Introduction

Three-dimensional reconstruction is one of the important research directions in the field of computer vision. Three-dimensional reconstruction refers to the recovery of the three-dimensional structure of an object or scene from a single or multiple images. Reconstructing the three-dimensional model of an object through computer technology has become an indispensable antecedent step in many research fields. With the development of space technology, space has become a valuable resource that countries compete for 2022 China's space station has been fully completed, more and more spacecraft into space to carry out tasks. The development of space technology has put forward higher requirements for space on-orbit service and operation technology. Satellite on-orbit assembly, space rendezvous and docking, space garbage cleanup, and more and more space target on-orbit capture application needs are emerging. In order to improve the operation precision, it is necessary to improve the detection and sensing ability of the target, and it is necessary to obtain the target characteristics such as the size, shape and three-dimensional structure of the target before executing the mission. Obtaining the

© The Author(s), under exclusive license to Springer Nature Singapore Pte Ltd. 2026
Z. Lin et al. (Eds.): ICIG 2025, LNCS 16163, pp. 399–409, 2026.
https://doi.org/10.1007/978-981-95-3729-7_33

three-dimensional structure information of the target through three-dimensional reconstruction technology can grasp the size information of the target body, solar sail panel, antenna, docking ring and other idiosyncratic structures, and can also be used for the estimation of the target's motion state.

2 Neural Radiance Field Theory

Neural Radiance Field (NeRF) [1] can be briefly summarized as a multilayer perceptron neural network to implicitly represent a static scene and achieve arbitrary new perspective synthesis in complex scenes. In order to train the network, for a static scene, it is necessary to provide a training set containing a large number of images whose camera parameters are known, as well as the 3D coordinates where the corresponding camera of the image is located, the camera orientation, and after the trained neural network performs the body rendering, the result of the new perspective image can be rendered (Fig. 1).

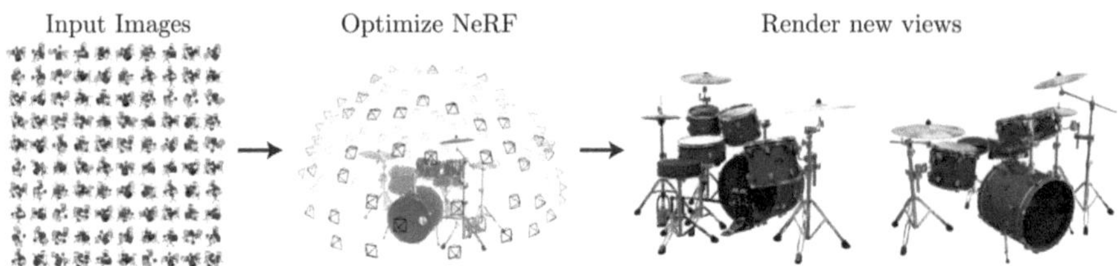

Fig. 1. NeRF new perspective synthesis process

The input to NeRF is images and camera parameters from multiple viewpoints, and the output is a continuous three-dimensional radiance field. Specifically, the input is a set of 2D images and corresponding camera parameters (including camera position and orientation), and the output is a function representing the color and density of each point in the 3D scene. This function is a continuous 5D function that outputs the radiance, i.e., color information, of each point in space (X, Y, Z) in each direction (θ, φ) and the bulk density, i.e., opacity, of each point. The following figure shows the NeRF scene representation and the process of differential rendering that can be: (a) make the camera light pass through the scene to generate a set of sampled 3D points, (b) use these points and their corresponding 2D observation directions as inputs to the neural network to generate a set of color and density outputs, and (c) use the classical technique of volume rending (VR) to accumulated into the 2D image. (d) Optimization of the neural radiance field by gradient descent through the error between the rendered result and the image. By minimizing this error between multiple views, the excitation network predicts a coherent model of the scene by assigning high volume densities and accurate colors to locations that contain realistic underlying scene content (Fig. 2).

NeRF also uses neural networks to fit the mapping relationship of radiance fields, and was soon applied to new perspective synthesis and 3D reconstruction, etc. With the development of space technology, some scholars began to apply the neural radiance field in computer vision to the space field, and carried out 3D reconstruction research for dark and weak texture space targets.

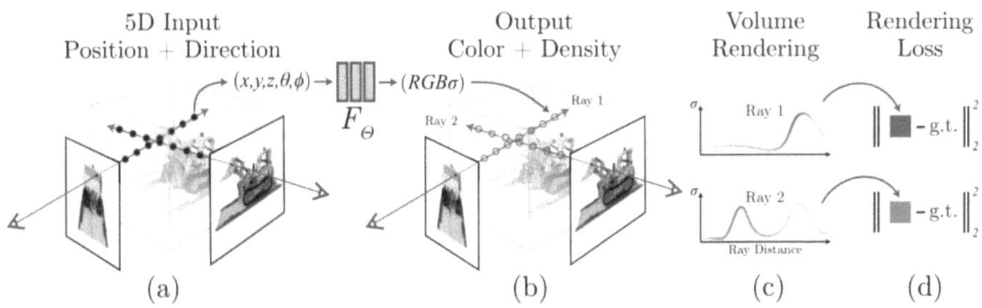

Fig. 2. NeRF scene representation and differentiable rendering process

3 Three-Dimensional Reconstruction of Spatial Targets Based on Neural Radiance Field

Before the concept of neural radiance field was proposed, spatial target 3D reconstruction methods [2, 3] were used by establishing feature associations between optical images, and with the development of science and technology, implicit neural representations have also been explored at home and abroad for use in the field of spatial target 3D reconstruction. In space-based optical imaging scenarios, subject to the limitations of rendezvous time and effective imaging distance, the effective angle of a single observation of the target is generally small, and it is often necessary to pass multiple observations. At the same time by the target texture is missing, structural symmetry to the image sequence of feature extraction matching brings great difficulties. In order to solve the problem of solving the weak texture and wide baseline its case of reconstruction, Bu et al. [4] proposed a neural radiance field based image sequence reconstruction method, which does not require the supervision of three-dimensional information such as depth truth and is suitable for spatial target scenes. The flowchart of the method is shown in Fig. 3: firstly, optical images with wide baselines and camera poses are input into NeRF, then depth maps are acquired according to camera poses, and finally a depth map fusion algorithm is used to compute the 3D point cloud.

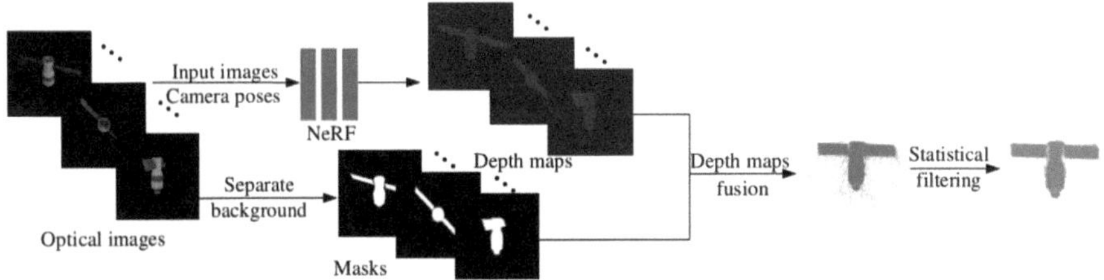

Fig. 3. NeRF-based 3D reconstruction process of spatial targets

The traditional method of space target reconstruction relies mainly on the observation data of individual spacecraft, which not only requires spacecraft to fly in accordance with precisely set orbits, but also requires multiple effective observations to ensure the completeness and accuracy of the data. However, this process is not only time-consuming but also inefficient, making it difficult to meet the growing demand for space target monitoring and reconstruction. In order to solve this difficulty, 3D reconstruction of non-cooperative targets through multi-spacecraft observation and cooperation has gradually become a research hotspot, and Zeng et al. [5] proposed a point cloud reconstruction method for space targets based on multi-view images, and the main flowchart of the method is shown in Fig. 4. First, optical images from different viewpoints are taken and converted into point cloud data by multiple spacecraft mounted cameras. Second, in order to effectively integrate the point cloud data from these different viewpoints, the nearest point iteration (ICP) algorithm is used for point cloud alignment. The ICP algorithm is optimized through continuous iteration, so that the point cloud data from different viewpoints can be accurately aligned in three-dimensional space to form a preliminary unified point cloud model. However, the preliminary reconstructed point cloud model often has ambiguities and uncertainties due to multiple factors such as observation conditions and sensor errors. To solve this problem, Zeng et al. assumed that all points obey a Gaussian mixture model (GMM), and used this model to further process and optimize the point cloud data. With the introduction of the GMM, the researchers were able to more accurately characterize the distribution of the point cloud data, thus obtaining more accurate fuzzy point cloud reconstruction results. Finally, the 3D model is further optimized by segmenting the sailplane and other characteristic structures.

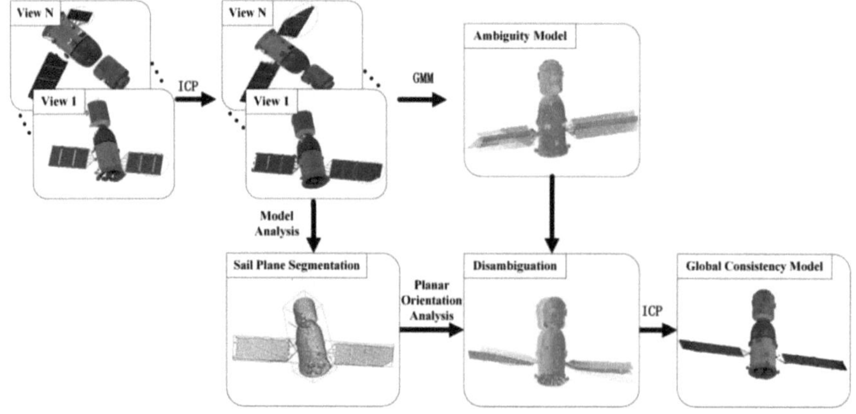

Fig. 4. Flowchart of 3D reconstruction of spatial target based on multi-view image

In a study by the European Space Agency, Mergy et al. [6] experimentally compared two neural rendering techniques, NeRF and GRAF (Generated Radiance Field) [7], on a non-cooperative spacecraft. Specifically, NeRF relies on relative camera pose information to construct a 3D representation of the scene, whereas GRAF requires only image data as input and no additional camera pose information, a feature that is particularly important in non-cooperative spacecraft identification tasks where accurate pose measurements are lacking. In order to comprehensively evaluate the two methods, Mergy designed training sets containing different numbers of sampled images for simulating the sparse image data situation in practice. The comparison results of different numbers of sampled images are shown in Fig. 5 below, which contains a densely sampled training set of 100 images as well as a sparsely sampled training set of 5, 10, and 50 images, which are used to test the model's generalization ability under limited data. The experimental results show that by comparing the new-view synthetic images generated by the two methods (shown in the first two rows of the figure), it can be observed that under the sparse sampling condition, the images generated by GRAF perform well in detail preservation and visualization, especially outperforming the NeRF in terms of edge clarity and structural integrity, while the latter two rows of images further demonstrate the difference between the real satellite profile and the model prediction. GRAF demonstrates significant advantages in reducing the prediction error and improving the consistency between the model and the real world.

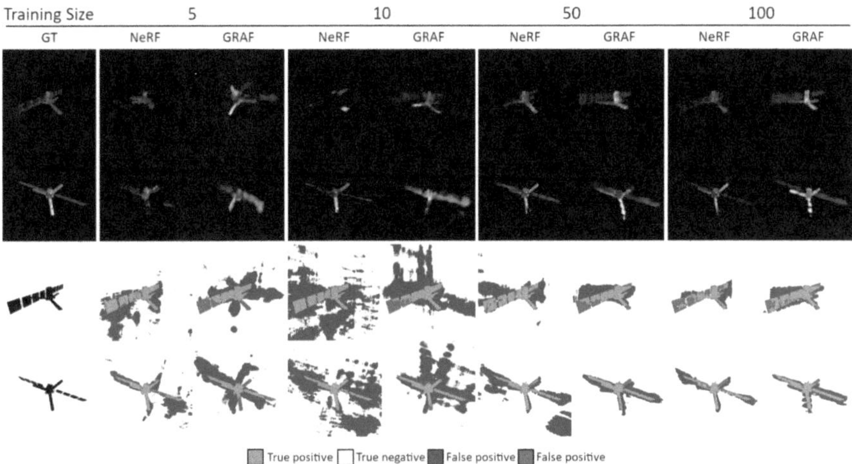

Fig. 5. Comparison of the effect of new perspective synthesis between the two methods on different numbers of image training sets

The experimental results show that NeRF outperforms GRAF in a number of metrics from a quantitative point of view; however, from a qualitative point of view, GRAF exhibits greater robustness under low light conditions and sparse views. The results of the sparse training set show that neither model can accurately reproduce the specular effect or 3D shape of the spacecraft, which suggests that both models face certain challenges in scenes with sparse data. Meanwhile, adding more images to the training set improved the results of new view synthesis, but did not improve the depth estimation accuracy.

Caruso et al. [8] applied Instant NeRF [9] and D-NeRF [9] to the problem of 3D mapping of non-cooperative resident space objects (RSOs) in orbit. The reconstruction of a moving rotating satellite is realized by designing different illumination conditions and different attitudes of the RSO such as stationary and rotating (Fig. 6).

At AMOS 2022, Chang et al.[10] combined the Neural Radiance Field without Known Camera Position (NeRF−) [11] with data preprocessing techniques to successfully generate new-view synthetic images of the satellite from linear channel observations. The article covers a synthetic subset of the SPEED+ dataset, a subset of the sunlamps, and real satellite images based on observations from 1.6-m and 3.6-m telescopes.

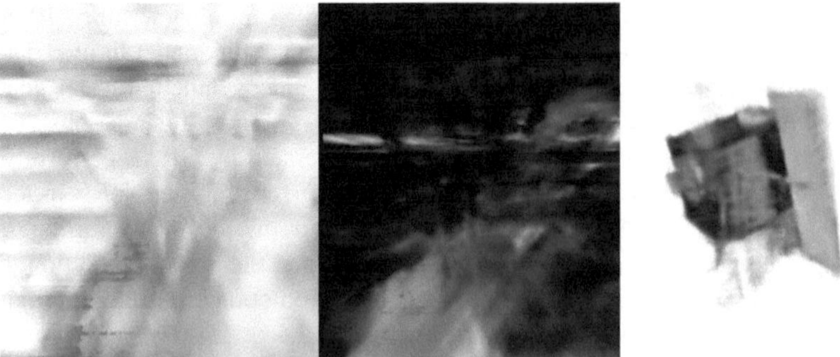

Fig. 6. D-NeRF reconstruction of rotating satellites

By implementing a series of fine preprocessing strategies such as geometric corrections and photometric adjustments, the quality and accuracy of the new-viewpoint synthesis are significantly improved, opening up new avenues for the analysis and application of satellite images (Fig. 7).

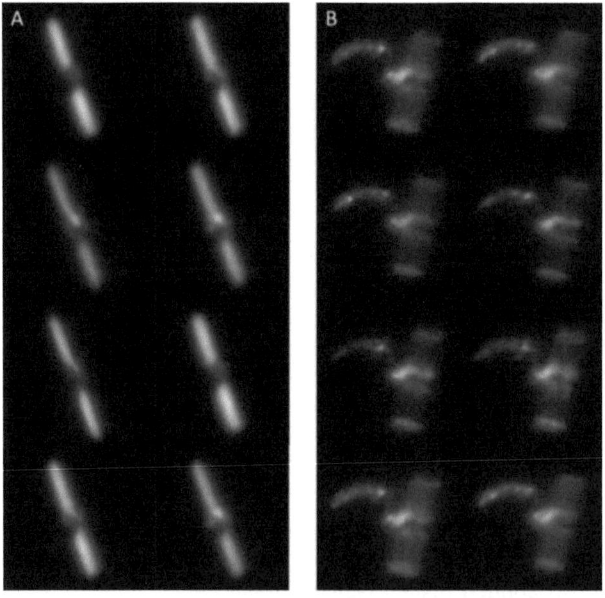

Fig. 7. Synthesized image of the 3.6-m telescope observing the new perspective (A) RESURS O1 (B) SPOT 2

To address the problems of inaccurate camera focus and poor image texture, and the geometrical details of tiny structures on the satellite surface (e.g., antennas, solar sail hinges) are difficult to be accurately modeled by existing algorithms, Ma et al. [12] proposed STs-NeRF, which achieves improved spatial target reconstruction through

Dynamic Encoding (DE) module with Layer- wise Normalized MLP, LLNMLP) to achieve improved spatial target reconstruction.

4   Spatial Target Image Dataset

The classical Spacecraft Attitude Estimation Dataset (SPEED) is provided by the Satellite Attitude Estimation Challenge, jointly organized by the European Space Agency and Stanford University. The dataset is designed to support space target attitude estimation missions and includes 15,300 images from the Tango satellite simulation. Of these, 15,000 were generated from OpenGL-based optical analog camera simulation software, and the other 300 were from real images acquired by the Rendezvous and Optical Navigation (TRON) facility at the Space Crossing (SLAB) Lab.The SPEED dataset images have a resolution of 1920 × 1200, and the annotation includes quaternionic numbers and 3D depth distances.

In 2021, SPEED+ [13] was introduced as the next generation dataset for solving the spacecraft attitude estimation problem across domain gaps. Contains 59,960 synthesized images generated by the simulation software, divided into training/validation sets at a ratio of 8:2, and test set images acquired by the TRON device under different illumination sources - 6,740 images for the light box illumination source and 2,791 images for the sun lamp illumination source (Table 1).

Table 1. Comparison of SPEED and SPEED+ datasets

categorization	SPEED			SPEED+	
	simulated image	real image	simulated image	Lighting source for light box	sunlamp light source
training set	12000	5	47966	-	-
validation set	-	-	11994	-	-
test set	2998	300	-	6740	2791

Proença et al. [14] utilized the Unreal Engine 4 simulator to generate the image dataset URSO of the Soyuz and Dragon spacecraft with an image resolution of 1080 × 960. However, both the SPEED dataset and the URSO dataset focus mainly on attitude estimation and do not provide any segmentation annotation. For this reason, Duang et al. [15] proposed a new space image dataset containing 3,117 labeled satellite and space station space-based images with a resolution of 1280 × 720, covering 10,350 components of 3,667 spacecraft. The extent of the spacecraft on the images varies in size from as small as 100 pixels to as large as occupying almost the entire image. In order to standardize the baseline segmentation method, the dataset is divided into a training set and a test set of 2516 and 600 images, respectively, which are used for the tasks of spacecraft target detection, segmentation, and part recognition.

Hu et al. [16] introduced the SwissCube dataset based on physical rendering that takes into account a 3D model of the satellite, including the stellar background, the Sun, and the Earth's influence on the satellite. SwissCube is then placed in a physical orbit about 700 km above the Earth's surface, and an "observer" is placed in a slightly higher orbit to render image sequences at different relative velocities, distances, and angles. The experiment generates 500 scenes, each containing 100 frames of sequence images, totaling 50k images with a resolution of 1024 × 1024, and divides the training and test sets in a ratio of 4:1.

Zhang Haopeng et al. from Beijing University of Aeronautics and Astronautics [17] established the BUAA-SID1.0 space target image database, which is based on the 3D model of the space target, and utilizes the 3ds Max software to render and generate the full-view simulation image sequences of the space target, which contains the 3D models of 56 satellites and their simulation images in total. The database is divided into two sub-libraries: the 3D model library includes 56 satellites 3D models, saved in the format of max (3ds Max scene file); the simulation image library contains 25760 simulation images, with a resolution of 320 × 40, 460 images for each satellite, of which 230 are 24-bit color images, and the other 230 are corresponding binary images. The shortcomings are that the number of satellites in the database is still far from enough compared to the satellites in orbit, as well as the realism of the simulation needs to be improved, and background factors such as the starry sky and the Earth should be considered.

Lu Tingting et al. [18] from Beijing University of Aeronautics and Astronautics (BUAA) proposed a spatial target optical image generation method based on the 3D point cloud model and the theory of projective transform. Based on the construction of the 3D point cloud model of the spatial target and the simulation camera model, the basic theory of the projective transform is used to calculate the correspondence between all the pixels in the image plane and the spatial points of the 3D point cloud model of the spatial target in turn, and based on the Lambertian diffuse reflection model and the light direction of the corresponding spatial points of the 3D point cloud model of the spatial target, the gray values of all the pixels are obtained, and the optical image of the spatial target is thus generated. Optical image of a given spatial target.

Li et al. [19] used 3dsMax to generate a satellite model and colorize the feature parts, simulated the operation of the satellite and the camera through programming and performed image acquisition, and simultaneously generated the colorized model and the 2D images projected by the model under different scales, attitudes, and working conditions. Liu et al. [20] invented a method of constructing a dataset of spatial target simulation by randomly adding stars and bright stars to the existing spatial target images, blurring the images, and adding noise to complete the construction of the dataset. Images by randomly adding stars and bright stars, and blurring and adding noise to the images to complete the construction of the dataset.

The 3D Resources module on NASA's official web site contains many 3D models of dozens of space targets such as AcrimSAT, Aqua, Cassini, DART, etc. for researchers to study. It contains many file formats such as stl, obj, blend, lwo, 3ds, etc. Yang et al. [21] constructed a NASA 3D dataset containing point clouds, watertight grids, occupancy values, and correspondent points by using 3D models from NASA's official web site. Park proposed a new 3D reconstruction dataset of space targets including

NASA 3D Resources and ESA Science Satellite Fleet's 64 different satellite models and 1,000 images, including 500 images without background and 500 images with Earth background, each containing binary masks and bitmap labels.

5 Development Trend and Outlook

Although the NeRF model has demonstrated excellent performance in static scenes with a rich number of images and a wide range of viewpoints, its scope of application is still limited by these specific conditions, highlighting certain limitations. In recent years, NeRF technology has made significant progress, not only achieving a leap in rendering quality, but also optimizing lighting representation, bit pose estimation, and effectively addressing challenges such as sparse views, all of which are important breakthroughs based on the original NeRF model. However, in view of the unique nature of spatial target images, the future development trend of NeRF technology needs to be discussed and analyzed in depth from multiple dimensions, such as data acquisition and processing, model adaptation enhancement, and application scenario expansion.

(1) Construction of a high-quality multi-view image data set of space targets. Due to the complexity of the space environment and the harshness of imaging conditions, the acquisition of multi-view images of space targets often relies on complex orbiting operations and is susceptible to changes in illumination. Therefore, it is particularly important to construct a high-quality multi-view space target image dataset that covers a wide range of target types and diverse imaging conditions, which can greatly facilitate the in-depth study of neural radiance field reconstruction methods for space targets.

(2) Exploring implicit neural representations tailored to spatial target characteristics. Current research focuses on the application of NeRF and its variants to space targets, but there is a lack of implicit neural representations tailored to the characteristics of space targets. Future research should combine the imaging mechanism, surface physical properties and orbital dynamics information of space targets to innovatively design an implicit representation model for space targets, with a view to realizing higher precision 3D reconstruction results and wider application potential.

(3) Fusion of multi-source sensors for three-dimensional reconstruction research. Explore the three-dimensional reconstruction technology of spatial targets based on multi-source data fusion, such as combining the high-precision depth information of LIDAR, the high-dynamic-range capture capability of event cameras and optical images in order to comprehensively enhance the completeness of spatial target information for data fusion three-dimensional reconstruction research. By fusing the complementary information from different sensors, a more comprehensive and precise solution is provided for the three-dimensional cognition of spatial targets.

6 Conclusion

Neural radiance field technology achieves high-quality image generation and realistic rendering of complex scenes through fine approximation of the radiance and density fields of objects by multilayer perceptron, which opens up a brand-new path for scene modeling and visualization. However, compared with natural scenes, spatial optical images bring more severe challenges to the research and application of neural radiance field methods for spatial target images due to their unique properties. In this paper, we systematically review and deeply analyze the latest progress of spatial target 3D reconstruction technology based on neural radiance field; at the same time, we thoroughly sort out and elaborate the spatial target image dataset; finally, we analyze the development trend of this field and look forward to the future, which aims to lay a solid foundation for the subsequent research in this field and to provide a reference.

Disclosure of Interests. The authors have no competing interests to declare that are relevant to the content of this article.

References

1. Mildenhall, B., Srinivasan, P.P., Tancik, M., et al.: NeRF: representing scenes as neural radiance fields for view synthesis. In: Vedaldi, A., Bischof, H., Brox, T., Frahm, J.M. (eds.) ECCV 2020. LNCS, vol. 12346, pp. 99–106. Springer, Cham (2020). https://doi.org/10.1007/978-3-030-58452-8_24
2. Yefei, H., Zexu, Z., Hutao, C.: Algorithm for three-dimensional reconstruction of texture-deficient surface of target in unknown space. Center for Basic Research on Deep Space Exploration, School of Aeronautics and Astronautics, Harbin Institute of Technology, vol. 43, no. 12, pp. 1722–1730 2022
3. Wang, S., Zhang, J., Li, L., Li, X., Chen, F.: Application of MVSNet in 3D reconstruction of spatial targets. China Laser **49**(23), 2310003 (2022)
4. Bu, F., Wang, C., Ren, X., et al.: 3D Reconstruction method of space target on optical images with wide baseline via neural radiance field. J. Phys. Conf. Ser. **2347**(1), 012019 (2022)
5. Zeng, F., Yi, J., Wang, L., et al.: Point cloud 3D reconstruction of non-cooperative object based on multi-satellite collaborations. In: Proceedings of the 2023 3rd Asia-Pacific Conference on Communications Technology and Computer Science, 25–27 February 2023, Shenyang, pp. 461–467. IEEE (2023)
6. Mergy, A., Lecuyer, G., Derksen, D., et al.: Vision-based neural scene representations for spacecraft. In: Proceedings of the 2021 IEEE/CVF Conference on Computer Vision and Pattern Recognition Workshops, 19–25 June 2021, Nashville, pp. 2002–2011. IEEE (2021)
7. Schwarz, K., Liao, Y., Niemeyer, M., et al.: GRAF: generative radiance fields for 3D-aware image synthesis. In: Proceedings of the 34th International Conference on Neural Information Processing Systems, 6–12 December 2021, Red Hook, pp. 20154–20166. Curran Associates Inc. (2021)
8. Caruso, B., Mahendrakar, T., Nguyen, V.M., et al.: 3D reconstruction of non-cooperative resident space objects using instant NGP-accelerated NeRF and D-NeRF. arXiv:2301.09060 (2023)
9. Müller, T., Evans, A., Schied, C., et al.: Instant neural graphics primitives with a multiresolution hash encoding. ACM Trans. Graph. **41**(4), 1 (2022)
10. Chang, K., Fletcher, J.: Learned satellite radiometry modeling from linear pass observations. In: Proceedings of the Advanced Maui Optical and Space Surveillance (AMOS) Technologies Conference, 12–22 September 2023, Wailea, Maui, Hawaii, p. 2 (2023)
11. Wang, Z., Wu, S., Xie, W., et al.: NeRF−: neural radiance fields without known camera parameters. arXiv:2102.07064 (2022)
12. Ma, K., Liu, P., Sun, H., et al.: STs-NeRF: novel view synthesis of space targets based on improved neural radiance fields. Remote Sens. **16**(13), 23–27 (2024)

13. Park, T.H., Märtens, M., Lecuyer, G., et al.: SPEED+: next-generation dataset for spacecraft pose estimation across domain gap. In: Proceedings of the 2022 IEEE Aerospace Conference, 5–12 Mar 2022, Big Sky, pp. 1–15. IEEE (2022)
14. Proença, P.F., Gao, Y.: Deep learning for spacecraft pose estimation from photorealistic rendering. In: Proceedings of the 2020 IEEE International Conference on Robotics and Automation, 31 May–31 August 2020, Paris, pp. 6007–6013. IEEE (2020)
15. Dung, H.A., Chen, B., Chin, T.J.: A spacecraft dataset for detection, segmentation and parts recognition. In: Proceedings of the 2021 IEEE/CVF Conference on Computer Vision and Pattern Recognition Workshops, 19–25 June 2021, Nashville, pp. 2012–2019. IEEE (2021)
16. Hu, Y., Speierer, S., Jakob, W., et al.: Wide-depth-range 6D object pose estimation in space. In: Proceedings of the 2021 IEEE/CVF Conference on Computer Vision and Pattern Recognition, 20–25 June 2021, Nashville, pp. 15865–15874. IEEE (2021)
17. Zhang, H., Liu, Z., Jiang, Z., et al.: BUAA-SID1.0 space target image database. Space Return Remote Sens. (4) (2010)
18. Lu, T., Li, X., Zhang, Y., et al.: Optical image generation technique for spatial targets based on 3D point cloud model. J. Beijing Univ. Aeronaut. Astronaut. 46(2), 274–286 (2020)
19. Li, L.Z., Zhang, T.: Spatial non-cooperative target feature detection and recognition based on deep learning. J. Intell. Syst. 15(6), 1154–1162 (2020)
20. Liu, J.C., Guo, X.J., Zhao, J.Y., et al.: A method for constructing space target simulation datasets, CN115456928A [P/OL] (2022)
21. Yang, X., Cao, M., Li, C., et al.: Learning implicit neural representation for satellite object mesh reconstruction. Remote Sens. 15(4163), 4163 (2023)

Geometric Self-Attenuating Transformer for Multi-instance Registration

Jianwei Wang, Lei Wang, Gaoyu Lei, Ji'ang Dong, Liang Ye[✉] [ID], and Hanyu Hong

Hubei Key Laboratory of Optical Information and Pattern Recognition, Wuhan Institute of Technology, Wuhan, China
`yeliang@wit.edu.cn`

Abstract. Multi-instance point cloud registration is crucial for various 3D computer vision tasks but presents significant challenges, including an unknown number of instances, severe occlusions, background clutter, and object similarity. Traditional methods often struggle with computational efficiency or, like some recent end-to-end approaches, may overlook detailed geometric cues inherent in the spatial data, hindering disambiguation in complex scenes. This paper introduces the Geometric Self-Attenuating Transformer (GSAT), a novel architecture designed to address these limitations by robustly encoding superpoint features. GSAT employs a dual-branch local attention mechanism that explicitly processes both geometric and contextual information within each instance, enhancing feature discriminability. Crucially, a Geometric Self-Attenuation Mechanism (GSAM) adaptively regulates the influence of an anchor superpoint's self-derived geometric information when processing scene point clouds, mitigating contamination caused by occlusion and inter-instance interference. Experiments on the ROBI and Scan2CAD datasets demonstrate that GSAT achieves competitive performance compared to state-of-the-art methods, highlighting its effectiveness in handling complex real-world scenarios.

Keywords: Multi-instance Registration · Point Cloud Transformer · Geometric Attention

1 Introduction

Point cloud registration is a fundamental task in 3D computer vision, typically involving aligning two or more point clouds into a common coordinate system. Although pairwise registration has been extensively studied and applied, multi-instance registration has become especially important in fields such as industrial assembly and sorting. However, transitioning from pairwise to multi-instance registration introduces significant challenges, including an unknown number of instances, severe inter-instance occlusions, substantial background clutter, and the inherent difficulty of distinguishing between similar object instances, especially in complex real-world environments.

© The Author(s), under exclusive license to Springer Nature Singapore Pte Ltd. 2026
Z. Lin et al. (Eds.): ICIG 2025, LNCS 16163, pp. 410–421, 2026.
https://doi.org/10.1007/978-981-95-3729-7_34

Previous methods typically first extract global features using handcrafted [10,17] and learned [1,3] descriptors or coarse-to-fine deep architectures [8,16,24], then attempt to recover multiple transforms via clustering-based [21,26,27] and RANSAC-based [4,5,12] multi-model fitting techniques. However, due to the huge hypothesis space, especially when the number of instances or outlier ratio increases, these approaches often suffer from low computational efficiency. Although the end-to-end method [25] employs an instance-aware strategy that helps mitigate feature contamination in multi-instance scenes, its underlying attention mechanism completely ignores the geometric cues inherent in the original spatial data. This reliance on simplified or incomplete geometric summaries hinders the disambiguation of complex matches, especially in the presence of occlusions or geometrically intricate configurations.

To address these shortcomings, this paper introduces the **Geometric Self-Attenuating Transformer (GSAT)**, a novel architecture for multi-instance registration. GSAT is built upon a dual-branch local self-attention that explicitly disentangles geometric and contextual information, allowing each to be modeled by specialized pathways for enhanced feature discriminability. To tackle the critical yet overlooked problem of feature contamination from unreliable geometric cues in cluttered scenes, we introduce our key innovation: the Geometric Self-Attenuation Mechanism (GSAM). This mechanism further boosts robustness by adaptively down-weighting the influence of an anchor's own ambiguous geometric features.

In summary, our contributions include:

1. We propose GSAT, a novel transformer architecture featuring a dual-branch design that explicitly disentangles geometric and contextual information, leading to more discriminative features for geometrically similar instances.
2. We introduce the GSAM to address the overlooked problem of self-feature contamination in cluttered scenes, enabling robust learning by adaptively penalizing unreliable geometric cues.

2   Method

The pipeline of our proposed method for multi-instance registration is illustrated in Fig. 1. The process begins by employing a kernel point convolution (KPConv) [20] to downsample the input point cloud $\mathcal{P}$ and $\mathcal{Q}$ while extracting multi-level features (Sect.2.1). These features from the coarsest level are then fed into GSAT to extract correspondences between the superpoints (Sect. 2.2). Subsequently, the Instance Matching module maps these superpoint correspondences to guide pose estimation using the first-level point clouds (Sect. 2.3).

2.1   Downsampling and Feature Extraction

Raw point clouds are often so dense that their point correspondences become redundant and can be overly clustered. This significantly diminishes feature discriminability and complicates the matching process. Therefore, following [11], we

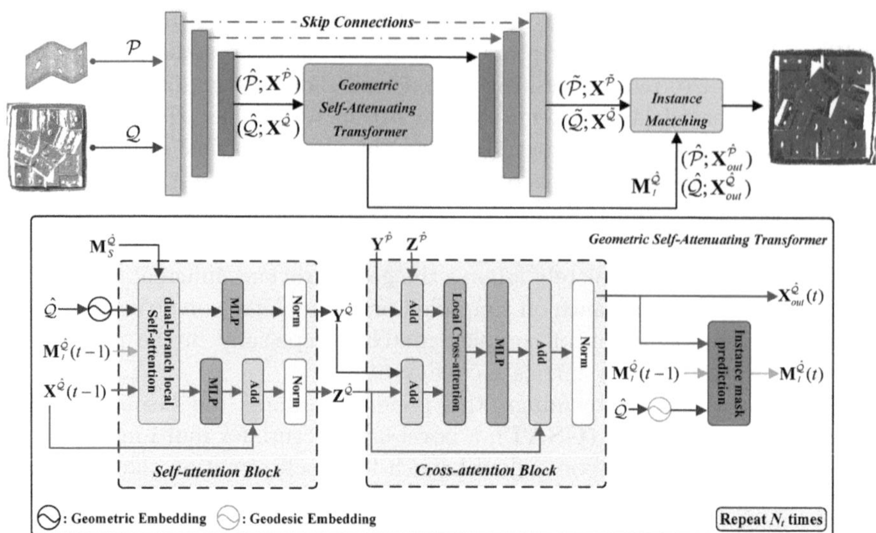

Fig. 1. An overview of our proposed framework for multi-instance registration, centered around the core GSAT module. The internal process of GSAT is illustrated using the scene point cloud Q and its features as an example.

adopt a KPConv backbone composed of ResNet-like blocks and strided convolutions for point cloud downsampling and multi-level feature extraction. Specifically, it first downsamples the input point clouds $\mathcal{P}$ and $\mathcal{Q}$ to $\tilde{\mathcal{P}}$ and $\tilde{\mathcal{Q}}$ (at half resolution), extracting projected features $\mathbf{X}^{\tilde{\mathcal{P}}} \in \mathbb{R}^{|\tilde{\mathcal{P}}| \times \tilde{d}}$ and $\mathbf{X}^{\tilde{\mathcal{Q}}} \in \mathbb{R}^{|\tilde{\mathcal{Q}}| \times \tilde{d}}$ for instance-level point correspondences. At the coarsest (last) level, it further downsamples them to $\hat{\mathcal{P}}$ and $\hat{\mathcal{Q}}$, extracting features $\mathbf{X}^{\hat{\mathcal{P}}} \in \mathbb{R}^{|\hat{\mathcal{P}}| \times \hat{d}}$ and $\mathbf{X}^{\hat{\mathcal{Q}}} \in \mathbb{R}^{|\hat{\mathcal{Q}}| \times \hat{d}}$ for superpoint correspondences.

2.2 Geometric Self-Attenuating Transformer

Utilizing the paired inputs $(\hat{\mathcal{P}}, \mathbf{X}^{\hat{\mathcal{P}}})$ and $(\hat{\mathcal{Q}}, \mathbf{X}^{\hat{\mathcal{Q}}})$, obtained from the coarsest level of KPConv (Sect. 2.1), our transformer comprises N_t stacked layers. Each layer consists of four key functional modules that operate in concert: (1) A *Local Geometry-driven Self-attention Block* enhance features by integrating geometric and contextual information. (2) A *Geometric Self-attenuation Mechanism* adaptively regulates the influence of geometric information to mitigate contamination. (3) A *Position-infused Cross-attention Block* facilitates information exchange between model and scene clouds. (4) An *Instance Masking Block* predict per-superpoint instance masks, further aiding instance-aware processing. The specifics of these modules are detailed in the following sections.

Local Geometry-Driven Self-Attention Block. This block enhances superpoint features by integrating local geometric structure and contextual informa-

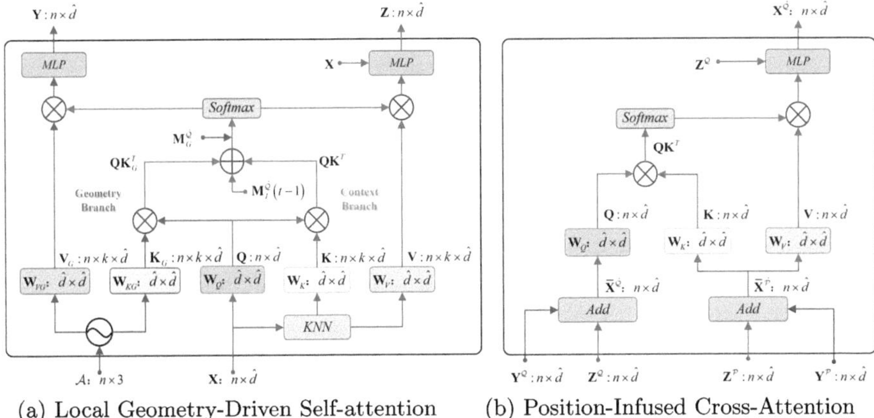

(a) Local Geometry-Driven Self-attention   (b) Position-Infused Cross-Attention

Fig. 2. The computation graph of our core attention blocks. The cross-attention (b) is illustrated for the scene point cloud $\mathcal{Q}$.

tion from k-nearest neighborhoods. For each anchor superpoint $a_i \in \mathcal{A}$, interactions are computed only with its identified neighbors $\mathcal{N}_i^A = \{a_j\}_{j=1}^k$. The two-branch architecture (Geometry and Context) shown in Fig. 2 (a) distinctly processes spatial and feature information before their fusion within the attention mechanism, enabling highly discriminative feature representations through nuanced local context awareness.

The Geometry Branch mines geometric cues from the pairwise pose-agnostic geometric representations $\mathbf{G} \in \mathbb{R}^{n \times k \times \hat{d}}$ (following [16]), projecting them into geometric keys $\mathbf{K}_G \in \mathbb{R}^{n \times k \times \hat{d}}$ and values $\mathbf{V}_G \in \mathbb{R}^{n \times k \times \hat{d}}$; meanwhile, the Context Branch, projects input anchor-centric features $\mathbf{X} \in \mathbb{R}^{n \times \hat{d}}$ into queries $\mathbf{Q} \in \mathbb{R}^{n \times \hat{d}}$, using neighbor features $\mathbf{X}_N \in \mathbb{R}^{n \times k \times \hat{d}}$ as keys $\mathbf{K} \in \mathbb{R}^{n \times k \times \hat{d}}$ and values $\mathbf{V} \in \mathbb{R}^{n \times k \times \hat{d}}$.

The attention scores are computed by integrating these geometric and contextual representations. For an anchor a_i, Let $\mathbf{q}_{i,j} := \mathbf{Q}(i,j,:)$, $\mathbf{k}_{i,j} := \mathbf{K}(i,j,:)$, $\mathbf{k}'_{i,j} := \mathbf{K}_G(i,j,:)$, $\mathbf{v}_{i,j} := \mathbf{V}(i,j,:)$, $\mathbf{v}'_{i,j} := \mathbf{V}_G(i,j,:)$. The aggregated output $\mathbf{Y}$ and $\mathbf{Z}$ from the Geometry and Context Branches, respectively, are calculated as:

$$\mathbf{y}_i = \sum_{j=1}^k softmax(s_{ij} + m_{\hat{S}}^{\hat{Q}}(i,0))\mathbf{v}'_{i,j} \tag{1}$$

$$\mathbf{z}_i = \sum_{j=1}^k softmax(s_{ij})\mathbf{v}_{i,j} \tag{2}$$

where $s_{i,j}$ is the hybrid attention score between the anchor superpoint a_i and its j-th neighbor a_j, and $m_{\hat{S}}^{\hat{Q}}(i,0)$ denotes the dynamic self-pose mask, specific to the processing of the scene point cloud $\hat{\mathcal{Q}}$. The hybrid attention score $s_{i,j}$ is computed as:

$$s_{i,j} = \frac{(\mathbf{q}_{i,j})^T \mathbf{k}_{i,j} + (\mathbf{q}_{i,j})^T \mathbf{k}'_{i,j}}{\sqrt{\hat{d}}} + m_I^{\hat{\mathcal{Q}}}(i,j) \tag{3}$$

where, $m_I^{\hat{\mathcal{Q}}}(i,j)$ is an instance-aware mask, utilized when the input is the scene point cloud $\hat{\mathcal{Q}}$(zero for the model point $\hat{\mathcal{P}}$).

The aggregated features $\mathbf{Y}$ and $\mathbf{Z}$ are then processed by MLPs:

$$\mathbf{Y} = \text{LayerNorm}(\text{MLP}_G(\mathbf{Y})) \tag{4}$$

$$\mathbf{Z} = \text{LayerNorm}(\mathbf{X} + \text{MLP}_C(\mathbf{Z})) \tag{5}$$

Geometric Self-attenuation Mechanism. The Geometric Self-Attenuation mechanism(GSAM) is integral to our self-attention block, specifically designed to adaptively regulate the influence of an anchor superpoint's self-derived geometric information during the aggregation process within the Geometry Branch when processing the scene point cloud $\hat{\mathcal{Q}}$. It operates on $\mathbf{K}_G$ to produce a mask $\mathbf{M}_S^{\mathcal{Q}}$, that primarily penalizes an anchor superpoint's attention to itself when aggregating geometric values.

For an anchor $q_i \in \mathcal{Q}$, its set of k geometric keys $\{\mathbf{k}'_{i,j}\}_{j=1}^k$ is is first processed to derive a local geometric context vector $\mathbf{g}_i \in \mathbb{R}^{2\hat{d}}$. This involves combining features from average pooling and a gated pooling mechanism:

$$\mathbf{g}_{avg}(i) = \text{MeanPool}(\mathbf{k}'_{i,j}) \tag{6}$$

$$w_{i,j} = (\text{MLP}_{agg}(\mathbf{k}'_{i,j})) \tag{7}$$

$$\mathbf{g}_{gate}(i) = \sum_{j=1}^k w_{i,j}\mathbf{k}'_{i,j} \tag{8}$$

$$\mathbf{g}_i = \text{Concat}(\mathbf{g}_{avg}(i), \mathbf{g}_{gate}(i)) \tag{9}$$

where $\sigma(*)$ denotes the sigmoid activation function, $\mathbf{g}_{avg}(i)$ provides holistic information from the neighborhood, while $\mathbf{g}_{gate}(i)$ focuses on key information, with its gating weights $w_{i,j}$ learned through a MLP.

The $\mathbf{g}_i$ is then input to another MLP to predicte a decay propensity scalar $\alpha_i \in [0,1]$, which quantifies the learned expected degree of decay self-interaction dependent on the neighborhood geometric context:

$$\alpha_i = \sigma(\text{MLP}_{pred}(\mathbf{g}_i)) \tag{10}$$

To further adapt the attenuation strength, an adaptive scaling factor λ is computed. This factor is based on the standard deviation $S(\mathbf{g})$ of the feature components within the collection $\{\mathbf{g}_i\}_{i=1}^n$, scaled by a hyperparameter γ:

$$\lambda = S(\mathbf{g})/\gamma \tag{11}$$

The final GSAM term $m_S^{\hat{\mathcal{Q}}}(i,0)$, applied to the self-interaction score of anchor q_i is computed as:

$$m_S^{\hat{\mathcal{Q}}}(i,0) = -\alpha_i\lambda \tag{12}$$

Position-Infused Cross-Attention Block. Following the self-attention refinement, this block facilitates information exchange between superpoints in the model cloud $\hat{\mathcal{P}}$ and the scene cloud $\hat{\mathcal{Q}}$. As the cross-attention is executed unidirectionally, it needs to be performed twice. We describe the process for updating the model superpoints $\hat{\mathcal{Q}}$ as an example, as illustrated in Fig. 2 (b); the computation for $\hat{\mathcal{P}}$ is analogous.

The enhanced features $\mathbf{Z}$ and $\mathbf{Y}$ from the self-attention block are aggregated to produce pose-aware input $\bar{\mathbf{X}} \in \mathbb{R}^{n \times \hat{d}} = \mathbf{Z} + \mathbf{Y}$ queries $\mathbf{Q}$ is computed from $\bar{\mathbf{X}}^{\hat{\mathcal{Q}}}$, while keys $\mathbf{K}$ and values $\mathbf{V}$ are computed from $\bar{\mathbf{X}}^{\hat{\mathcal{P}}}$.

For an anchor superpoint q_i, the attention scores $s_{i,j}$ are computed as:

$$s_{i,j} = \frac{(\mathbf{q}_{i,j})^T \mathbf{k}_{i,j}}{\sqrt{\hat{d}}} \tag{13}$$

where $\mathbf{q}_{i,j} := \mathbf{Q}(i,j,:)$ and $\mathbf{k}_{i,j} := \mathbf{K}(i,j,:)$. The attention scores are then used to compute the output features $\mathbf{x}^{\hat{\mathcal{Q}}}(i,j) \in \mathbb{R}^{\hat{d}}$, following a similar computation (Eq. (2)) as the output features of the context branch in self-attention block. At last, the features are processed by a MLP(similar to equation (5)) to produce the final output $\mathbf{X}^{\hat{\mathcal{Q}}}$, and $\mathbf{X}^{\hat{\mathcal{P}}}$ is generated through a symmetric process.

Instance Masking Block. Inspired by [25], we employ a specialized self-attention mechanism on the scene cross-attention features $\mathbf{X}^{\hat{\mathcal{Q}}}$, where pose-agnostic embeddings $\mathbf{G}$ are replaced by geodesic ones ($\mathbf{G}'$) to yield instance-specialized features $\mathbf{F} \in \mathbb{R}^{|\hat{\mathcal{Q}}| \times \hat{d}}$.

Subsequently, a MLP is is used to predict a confidence score $c_{i,j}$ for each anchor q_i and its neighbor $\{q_{i,j}\}_{j=1}^{k}$, indicating the likelihood that they belong to the same instance:

$$c_{i,j} = \sigma(\mathrm{MLP}_{mask}(\mathrm{Concat}[\mathbf{f}_{i,j} - \mathbf{f}_i; \mathbf{g}'_{i,j}])) \tag{14}$$

where $\mathbf{f}_i$ and $\mathbf{f}_{i,j}$ are the instance-specialized features of the anchor superpoint q_i and its neighbor $q_{i,j}$, respectively, and $\mathbf{g}'_{i,j}$ is the geodesic distance between them.

Finally, these confidence scores are thresholded using τ to obtain the instance mask $\mathbf{m}_I^{\hat{\mathcal{Q}}}(i,j)$:

$$m_I^{\hat{\mathcal{Q}}}(i,j) = \begin{cases} -\infty & c_{i,j} < \tau \\ 0 & \text{otherwise} \end{cases} \tag{15}$$

Furthermore, $\mathbf{M}_I^{\hat{\mathcal{Q}}}$ also help achieve instance-level point matching (Sect. 2.3).

2.3 Instance Matching

With the discriminative superpoint features $\mathbf{X}_{out}^{\hat{\mathcal{P}}}$ and $\mathbf{X}_{out}^{\hat{\mathcal{Q}}}$ obtained from the last cross-attention block of our Transformer, the Instance Matching process aims to first establish robust superpoint correspondences $\mathcal{C}_s$ and then leverage them to guide dense, instance-level point matching on the first-level point clouds $\tilde{\mathcal{P}}$ and $\tilde{\mathcal{Q}}$ for precise pose estimation.

Superpoint Matching. Following in [16], we begin by normalizing the superpoint features $\mathbf{X}_{out}^{\hat{\mathcal{P}}}$ and $\mathbf{X}_{out}^{\hat{\mathcal{Q}}}$ onto a unit hypersphere. Pairwise similarity is then computed using a Gaussian correlation matrix $\mathbf{S}$, where each element is given by: $s_{ij} = -\exp(-\|\mathbf{x}_{out}^{\hat{\mathcal{P}}}(i,j) - \mathbf{x}_{out}^{\hat{\mathcal{Q}}}(i,j)\|_2^2)$. Subsequently, superpoints corresponding to the *top-k* values in $\mathbf{S}$ are selected to form the initial coarse correspondence set $\mathcal{C}_s = \{(\hat{p}_i, \hat{q}_j) | \hat{p}_i \in \hat{\mathcal{P}}, \hat{q}_j \in \hat{\mathcal{Q}}\}$.

Next, as in [25], neighbors of the scene superpoint $\hat{q}_j$ are filtered from its neighborhood $\mathcal{N}_j^{\hat{\mathcal{Q}}}$ based on the instance mask $\mathbf{M}_I^{\hat{\mathcal{Q}}}$ to etain only those belonging to the same instance. The correspondences of superpoints within the same instance and the model superpoints are grouped to form an instance candidate. Specifically, the m-th instance candidate is defined as $\mathcal{I}_S(m) = \{(\hat{p}_{mi}, \hat{q}_{mi}) | i = 0, ..., n\}$, where n indexes the superpoint pairs belonging to this instance candidate. Correspondingly, the set of all candidate instances is denoted by $\mathcal{I}_S = \{\mathcal{I}_s(m) | m = 1, ..., N\}$.

Instance-Level Point Matching. We adopt the point-to-node strategy proposed in [16], utilizing the optimal transport method to extract instance-level point correspondences $\mathcal{C}_I$ within the candidate instance set $\mathcal{I}_S$. Subsequently, leveraging these extracted correspondences, the pose transformation $\mathbf{T}$ is estimated by solving the following equation through weighted SVD [6]:

$$\min_{\mathbf{R},\mathbf{t}} \sum_{(\tilde{\mathbf{p}}_i, \tilde{\mathbf{q}}_j) \in \mathcal{C}_I} \|\mathbf{R}\tilde{\mathbf{p}}_i + \mathbf{t} - \tilde{\mathbf{q}}_j\|_2^2 \tag{16}$$

As different subsets of correspondences within the same instance may lead to multiple candidate poses, we follow the approach in [25] and employ a scoring-based Non-Maximum Suppression (NMS) to filter and merge these candidates, producing a final robust and optimal instance-level pose estimate.

2.4 Loss Functions

The total training loss is defined as:

$$\mathcal{L} = \lambda_1 \mathcal{L}_c + \lambda_2 \mathcal{L}_m + \lambda_3 \mathcal{L}_p \tag{17}$$

which consists of an overlap-aware circle loss $\mathcal{L}_c$ [16] for superpoint matching, a combined dice-bce(binary cross-entropy) loss [15] $\mathcal{L}_m$ for instance mask prediction, and a negative log-likelihood loss [18] $\mathcal{L}_p$ for instance-level point matching. The hyperparameters $\{\lambda_i\}_{i=1}^3$ balance the contributions of each loss term nd are all set to 1 by default.

3 Experiments

3.1 Datasets and Evaluation Metrics

We train and evaluate our method on ROBI [22] and ScanCAD [2], two publicly available benchmark datasets with diverse scenarios and varying complexity. To ensure fair comparisons, standard evaluation metrics are used to assess accuracy and robustness in multi-instance point cloud registration.

ROBI. ROBI is a dataset specifically designed for industrial bin-picking applications. It consists of seven reflective metallic industrial objects and 63 carefully constructed bin-picking scenes. Each point cloud pair is precisely generated: the scene point cloud is obtained via back-projection from depth images, while the model point cloud is uniformly sampled from the corresponding CAD model. The dataset contains 4,880 point cloud pairs, split into 70% for training, 10% for validation, and 20% for testing.

ScanCAD. ScanCAD is a scene-to-CAD alignment dataset derived from ScanNet [9] and ShapeNet [7], comprising 1,506 scenes from ScanNet, each meticulously annotated using 14,225 CAD models from ShapeNet along with their spatial orientations in the scenes. The dataset includes a total of 2,184 point cloud pairs, which are split into 70% for training, 10% for validation, and 20% for testing.

Metrics. We evaluate our method using three key registration metrics: Mean Recall (MR), Mean Precision (MP), and Mean F1 score (MF). MR quantifies the proportion of correctly registered instances relative to the total number of ground-truth instances, while MP measures the ratio of correctly registered instances to the total predicted instances. MF, as the harmonic mean of MP and MR, provides a balanced assessment of registration performance. An instance is considered correctly registered if it meets the criteria defined in [19,25,27]: the Relative Translation Error (RTE) must be $\leq 4 \times$ voxel_size, and the Relative Rotation Error (RRE) must be $\leq 15°$. Accordingly, we set the voxel sizes to 2.5cm for the Scan2CAD dataset and 0.15cm for the ROBI dataset.

3.2 Implementation Details

Our method is implemented in PyTorch and train on a single RTX A6000 GPU. The Adam optimizer is used with an initial learning rate of 1×10^{-3} and weight decay of 1×10^{-4} coupled with an exponential scheduler (0.95 decay/epoch). Data augmentation follows [11,16,23,25]. Training is conducted for 40 epochs on the ROBI dataset and 60 epochs on Scan2CAD, with the best-performing checkpoint on the validation set selected for final evaluation. Key hyperparameters are set as follows: the number of Transformer layers $N_t = 3$, GSAM factor $\gamma = 0.3$, mask threshold $\tau = 0.6$. For initial correspondence generation, the top 128 superpoint pairs are used. Dataset-specific settings for ROBI/Scan2CAD include the number of local neighbors k is 32/16, and the NMS radius is 0.3/5 cm, respectively. The loss weights $(\lambda_1, \lambda_2, \lambda_3)$ are set to (1,1,1) for ROBI and (1.5,1.3,1) for Scan2CAD.

3.3 Results

We compared the proposed method with recent state-of-the-art (SOTA) approaches on the ROBI and Scan2CAD datasets to comprehensively evaluate

Table 1. Comparison with SOTA methods on ROBI and Scan2CAD datasets. The best and second-best results are highlighted in bold and underlined, respectively.

Methods	ROBI			Scan2CAD		
	MP (%)	MR (%)	MF (%)	MP (%)	MR (%)	MF (%)
T-Linkage [13]	10.47	12.04	11.20	46.04	77.12	57.65
RansaCov [14]	26.29	14.14	18.38	71.34	84.78	77.48
PointCLM [27]	40.11	18.68	25.48	**91.08**	91.85	91.46
ECC [19]	34.85	24.65	28.91	89.03	**96.52**	**92.64**
MIRETR [25]	<u>41.36</u>	<u>38.42</u>	<u>39.84</u>	88.63	95.40	91.89
GSAT(ours)	**42.98**	**38.90**	**40.84**	<u>89.44</u>	<u>95.72</u>	<u>92.47</u>

its effectiveness and robustness. It is important to note that, except for MIRETR and our method which were both trained and tested locally, all other results are directly taken from the official MIRETR paper. For MIRETR, we adopt our locally reproduced results as the reference, since during our replication the performance on Scan2CAD was noticeably lower than reported in the original paper, likely due to certain undisclosed training tricks used in the official evaluation. On the other hand, the replicated results on ROBI are consistent with the reported values. As shown in Table 1, our method GSAT demonstrates highly competitive performance against existing SOTA methods on both datasets.

On the ROBI dataset, GSAT significantly outperforms the locally reproduced MIRETR as well as other established baseline methods, achieving improvements of approximately 1.62%, 0.48%, and 1% in MP, MR and MF, respectively. This demonstrates GSAT's ability to find accurate correspondences that lead to successful registrations while maintaining a good retrieval rate of ground truth instances. This robust performance highlights the effectiveness of our GSAT in handling complex, real-world scenarios.

On the Scan2CAD dataset, under the same local training and evaluation setup, GSAT achieved results superior to the locally reproduced MIRETR, maintaining a stable advantage. However, when comparing against other methods based on MIRETR's official reports, GSAT presented a nuanced performance profile. Against PointCLM [27], while GSAT's MP was 1.64% lower, it significantly surpassed PointCLM in MR and MF by 3.87% and 1.01%, respectively. Compared to ECC [19], GSAT achieved a higher MP by 0.41%, while its MR was 0.8% lower and its MF was 0.17% lower. Taken together, these comparisons collectively indicate our method's best overall performance.

These quantitative gains are corroborated by our qualitative results (Fig. 3), where GSAT registers more instances than MIRETR in challenging scenes with heavy occlusion and geometric ambiguity, demonstrating the practical benefits of our dual-branch design and GSAM.

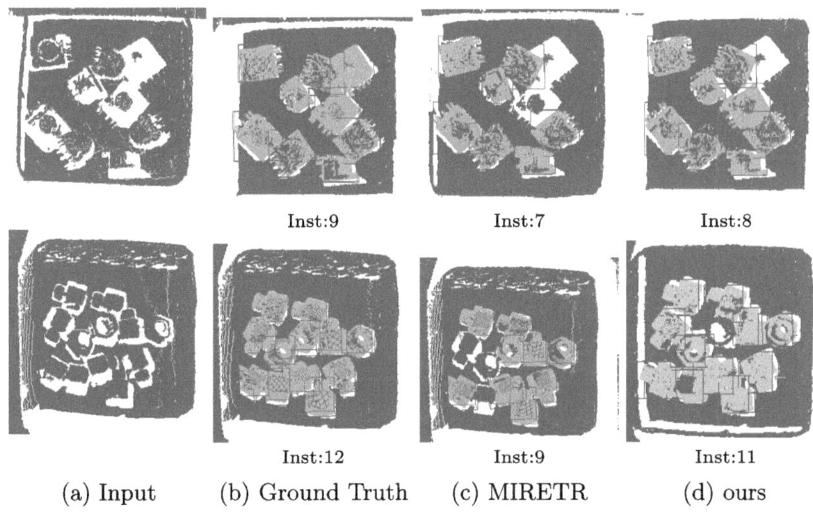

Fig. 3. Visualization of results on the ROBI dataset in comparison with MIRETR.

3.4 Ablation Study

We ablate key components of our model on the ROBI dataset (Table 2). Removing the Geometry Branch (b) or the Geometric Self-Attenuation Mechanism (GSAM) (a) both degrade performance compared to our full model (c). Notably, the model without GSAM performs the worst, with its MF score dropping by 1.16 points. This highlights that GSAM is critical for filtering noisy geometric cues to unlock the full potential of our dual-branch design.

Table 2. Ablation studies on ROBI dataset.

Model	MP(%)	MR(%)	MF(%)
(a) w/o GSAM	41.50	38.02	39.68
(b) w/o Geometry Branch	41.36	38.42	39.84
(c) GSAT(full pipeline)	**42.98**	**38.90**	**40.84**

4 Conclusion

In this paper, we presented GSAT, a Geometric Self-Attenuating Transformer for multi-instance registration. By effectively integrating geometric and contextual information through a dual-branch attention mechanism and mitigating geometric contamination with a self-attenuation module, GSAT achieves robust and accurate alignment of multiple object instances in complex 3D scenes. Experimental results demonstrate the superior performance of GSAT compared to existing methods, highlighting its potential for applications in industrial automation and robotics.

Acknowledgments. This work was supported in part by the Wuhan Knowledge Innovation Special Project under Grant 2023010201010143 and the Science Foundation of Wuhan Institute of Technology under Grant K2023057.

References

1. Ao, S., Hu, Q., Wang, H., Xu, K., Guo, Y.: BUFFER: balancing accuracy, efficiency, and generalizability in point cloud registration. In: Proceedings of the IEEE/CVF Conference on Computer Vision and Pattern Recognition, pp. 1255–1264 (2023)
2. Avetisyan, A., Dahnert, M., Dai, A., Savva, M., Chang, A.X., Nießner, M.: Scan2cad: learning cad model alignment in RGB-D scans. In: Proceedings of the IEEE/CVF Conference on Computer Vision and Pattern Recognition, pp. 2614–2623 (2019)
3. Bai, X., Luo, Z., Zhou, L., Fu, H., Quan, L., Tai, C.L.: D3Feat: joint learning of dense detection and description of 3D local features. In: Proceedings of the IEEE/CVF Conference on Computer Vision and Pattern Recognition, pp. 6359–6367 (2020)
4. Barath, D., Matas, J.: Progressive-X: efficient, anytime, multi-model fitting algorithm. In: Proceedings of the IEEE/CVF International Conference on Computer Vision, pp. 3780–3788 (2019)
5. Barath, D., Rozumnyi, D., Eichhardt, I., Hajder, L., Matas, J.: Finding geometric models by clustering in the consensus space. In: Proceedings of the IEEE/CVF Conference on Computer Vision and Pattern Recognition, pp. 5414–5424 (2023)
6. Besl, P.J., McKay, N.D.: Method for registration of 3-D shapes. In: Sensor Fusion IV: Control Paradigms and Data Structures, vol. 1611, pp. 586–606. SPIE (1992)
7. Chang, A.X., et al.: ShapeNet: an information-rich 3D model repository. arXiv preprint arXiv:1512.03012 (2015)
8. Chen, G., Wang, M., Yang, Y., Yuan, L., Yue, Y.: Fast and robust point cloud registration with tree-based transformer. In: 2024 IEEE International Conference on Robotics and Automation (ICRA), pp. 773–780. IEEE (2024)
9. Dai, A., Chang, A.X., Savva, M., Halber, M., Funkhouser, T., Nießner, M.: ScanNet: Richly-annotated 3D reconstructions of indoor scenes. In: Proceedings of the IEEE Conference on Computer Vision and Pattern Recognition, pp. 5828–5839 (2017)
10. Drost, B., Ulrich, M., Navab, N., Ilic, S.: Model globally, match locally: efficient and robust 3D object recognition. In: 2010 IEEE Computer Society Conference on Computer Vision and Pattern Recognition, pp. 998–1005. IEEE (2010)
11. Huang, S., Gojcic, Z., Usvyatsov, M., Wieser, A., Schindler, K.: Predator: registration of 3D point clouds with low overlap. In: Proceedings of the IEEE/CVF Conference on Computer Vision and Pattern Recognition, pp. 4267–4276 (2021)
12. Kluger, F., Brachmann, E., Ackermann, H., Rother, C., Yang, M.Y., Rosenhahn, B.: CONSAC: robust multi-model fitting by conditional sample consensus. In: Proceedings of the IEEE/CVF Conference on Computer Vision and Pattern Recognition, pp. 4634–4643 (2020)

13. Magri, L., Fusiello, A.: T-linkage: a continuous relaxation of J-linkage for multi-model fitting. In: Proceedings of the IEEE Conference on Computer Vision and Pattern Recognition, pp. 3954–3961 (2014)
14. Magri, L., Fusiello, A.: Multiple model fitting as a set coverage problem. In: Proceedings of the IEEE Conference on Computer Vision and Pattern Recognition, pp. 3318–3326 (2016)
15. Milletari, F., Navab, N., Ahmadi, S.A.: V-Net: fully convolutional neural networks for volumetric medical image segmentation. In: 2016 Fourth International Conference on 3D Vision (3DV), pp. 565–571. IEEE (2016)
16. Qin, Z., Yu, H., Wang, C., Guo, Y., Peng, Y., Xu, K.: Geometric transformer for fast and robust point cloud registration. In: Proceedings of the IEEE/CVF Conference on Computer Vision and Pattern Recognition, pp. 11143–11152 (2022)
17. Rusu, R.B., Blodow, N., Beetz, M.: Fast point feature histograms (FPFH) for 3D registration. In: 2009 IEEE International Conference on Robotics and Automation, pp. 3212–3217. IEEE (2009)
18. Sarlin, P.E., DeTone, D., Malisiewicz, T., Rabinovich, A.: Superglue: learning feature matching with graph neural networks. In: Proceedings of the IEEE/CVF Conference on Computer Vision and Pattern Recognition, pp. 4938–4947 (2020)
19. Tang, W., Zou, D.: Multi-instance point cloud registration by efficient correspondence clustering. In: Proceedings of the IEEE/CVF Conference on Computer Vision and Pattern Recognition, pp. 6667–6676 (2022)
20. Thomas, H., Qi, C.R., Deschaud, J.E., Marcotegui, B., Goulette, F., Guibas, L.J.: KPConv: flexible and deformable convolution for point clouds. In: Proceedings of the IEEE/CVF International Conference on Computer Vision, pp. 6411–6420 (2019)
21. Yang, J., Cao, X., Zhang, X., Cheng, Y., Qi, Z., Quan, S.: Instance by instance: an iterative framework for multi-instance 3D registration. IEEE/CAA J. Autom. Sinica (2025)
22. Yang, J., Gao, Y., Li, D., Waslander, S.L.: ROBI: a multi-view dataset for reflective objects in robotic bin-picking. In: 2021 IEEE/RSJ International Conference on Intelligent Robots and Systems (IROS), pp. 9788–9795. IEEE (2021)
23. Yu, H., Li, F., Saleh, M., Busam, B., Ilic, S.: CoFiNet: reliable coarse-to-fine correspondences for robust point cloud registration. Adv. Neural. Inf. Process. Syst. **34**, 23872–23884 (2021)
24. Yu, H., Qin, Z., Hou, J., Saleh, M., Li, D., Busam, B., Ilic, S.: Rotation-invariant transformer for point cloud matching. In: Proceedings of the IEEE/CVF Conference on Computer Vision and Pattern Recognition, pp. 5384–5393 (2023)
25. Yu, Z., Qin, Z., Zheng, L., Xu, K.: Learning instance-aware correspondences for robust multi-instance point cloud registration in cluttered scenes. In: Proceedings of the IEEE/CVF Conference on Computer Vision and Pattern Recognition, pp. 19605–19614 (2024)
26. Yu, Z., Zheng, Q., Zhu, C., Xu, K.: Efficient and accurate multi-instance point cloud registration with iterative main cluster detection. In: Eurographics (Short Papers) (2024)
27. Yuan, M., Li, Z., Jin, Q., Chen, X., Wang, M.: PointCLM: a contrastive learning-based framework for multi-instance point cloud registration. In: European Conference on Computer Vision, pp. 595–611. Springer (2022)

Surveillance and Remote Sensing

A Multi-feature Assisted MeanShift Algorithm for Dense Street Tree Extraction Integration

Songlai Xu[✉], Lijun Yang, Haiyang Lyu, Junjie Wang, and Jing Li

Nanjing University of Posts and Telecommunications, Nanjing 210023, China
`1023172921@njupt.edu.cn`

Abstract. To address the issue of low accuracy in extracting street tree information from point clouds, this paper proposes a multi-feature assisted Mean-Shift clustering ensemble method for dense street tree extraction. First, a stepwise classification approach, leveraging geometric and physical differences of target objects, is used to sequentially remove non-target point clouds—including ground, lawns, and shrubs—to eliminate interference. Then, an improved Mean-Shift clustering algorithm is developed using the kNN model. By incorporating multiple features such as reflectance intensity and spatial location, a fast, stable, and high-precision adaptive clustering ensemble method is constructed. Finally, a morphological estimation method is used to calculate geometric feature parameters of street trees, including tree height and crown dimensions. The proposed method is validated using dense street tree point cloud data acquired by the RIEGL miniVUX-SYS UAV LiDAR system in Yangshan Park, Nanjing. The experimental results show that the Individual tree height error is 0.025 m, the maximum crown radius error is 0.061 m, the projected area error is 1.321 m^2, and the surface area error is 4.096 m^2, outperforming traditional methods. The findings provide reliable support for the scientific management and maintenance of urban street trees, demonstrating promising application prospects.

Keywords: Adaptive · MeanShift · Point Cloud Data · Stepwise Classification · kNN · Intensity Constraint

1 Introduction

With accelerating global urbanization, building eco-garden cities has become a core urban development goal, where urban greening, especially street trees, plays a vital role in ecological services and public well-being [1–5]. Recent advances in UAV and LiDAR technology have made UAV-based LiDAR a mainstream tool for urban surface studies. Compared to traditional field surveys and vehicle-mounted systems, airborne LiDAR efficiently captures 3D point cloud data with rich geometric, color, and reflectance information, essential for analyzing surface features [6–9]. Thus, using UAV LiDAR to acquire and analyze street tree point clouds is key to supporting eco-city development and improving green space management.

Many researchers have extensively studied LiDAR point cloud processing. The main steps include data acquisition, preprocessing, registration, filtering, object classification,

© The Author(s), under exclusive license to Springer Nature Singapore Pte Ltd. 2026
Z. Lin et al. (Eds.): ICIG 2025, LNCS 16163, pp. 425–439, 2026.
https://doi.org/10.1007/978-981-95-3729-7_35

and analysis, with classification as a key focus. Due to the high dimensionality and density of point clouds, classification is complex and computationally demanding [10, 11]. Early methods relied on rule-based target recognition by setting thresholds on features like height, intensity, and reflectance [12–14]. These.

methods are simple and efficient for large datasets but lack flexibility and often misclassify complex structures. Feature-based classification emerged to improve accuracy, using geometric features such as point density and curvature [15–18], or spectral features like RGB bands if available [19]. These methods adapt better to data but can be time-consuming for large-scale processing. With machine learning's rise, supervised methods using labeled data have become mainstream. Typical algorithms include Support Vector Machines (SVM), Decision Trees, Random Forests, and Convolutional Neural Networks (CNN) [20–24]. These provide high accuracy but require extensive annotation and computational resources. Unsupervised methods, including K-Means, DBSCAN, and Gaussian Mixture Models (GMM) [25–27], classify data based on intrinsic properties without labels, but results often need manual refinement. Recently, deep learning models such as PointNet, PointNet + +, VoxelNet, and U2-Net [28–32] have been applied to point cloud classification. Despite advances, their high computational cost and long training times limit performance on dense point clouds.

Despite advances in remote sensing classification, dense urban street tree mapping still suffers from noise, point cloud complexity, and long runtimes. Key obstacles are (1) frequent misclassification in tightly packed vegetation and (2) heavy data and compute loads that preclude real-time use. We address these issues with a multifeature aided Mean-Shift framework that blends supervised and unsupervised strategies, exploits geometric and intensity cues, and adds an intensity-based constraint to sharpen class boundaries. Further, dictionary learning and sparse matrix transformations cut computation time [33–35]. The result is a faster, more stable classifier that improves accuracy and offers a forward-looking pathway for efficient, intelligent processing of dense point clouds.

2 Material

2.1 Study Area

To validate the method, a 100 m × 500 m roadside segment near Yangshan Ecological Forest Park, Qixia District, Nanjing, China, was selected. The subtropical monsoon climate, with hot humid summers and mild dry winters, supports common urban greenery, including plane and camphor trees and evergreen shrubs such as Loropetalum and boxwood (Buxus sinica). As shown in Fig. 1, sidewalks paved with blue-gray bricks are lined with plane trees spaced at 3 m. The four-lane asphalt roadway has a median strip and lane separators densely planted with plane trees and boxwood, forming orderly, high-density layouts typical of East China's urban greening. This representative configuration enhances visual separation, ecological function, and the relevance of the experimental results.The selected site exhibits typical vegetation and layout patterns representative of many urban roads in East China, which supports the general applicability of the proposed method.

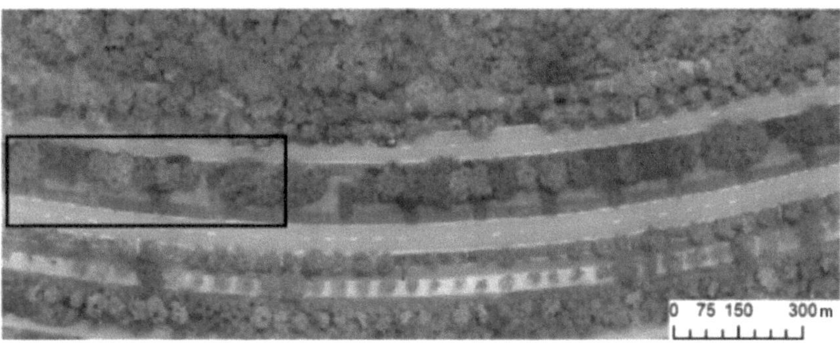

Fig. 1. Study area

2.2 Data Collection

The study area was scanned and sampled using a RIEGL miniVUX-SYS UAV airborne LiDAR system to obtain point cloud data for the region. The relevant parameters of the LiDAR system are shown in Tables 1 and 2.

Table 1. Basic data of the LiDAR system.

Subject	Parameter requirements
Laser Pulse Repetition Frequency	100kHz
Maximum Effective Measurement Rate	100,000
Maximum Measurement Range	Target Reflectance Greater than 80%:500m
Accuracy / Repeatability	15mm/10mm
Field of View Angle	360°
Maximum Scanning Speed	100lines/second
Maximum Number of Pulses per Target	5

Table 2. Individual tree information (m)

individual tree	tree height	maximum crown radius	crown projection area	crown surface area
1	9.049	3.178	31.822	100.353
2	8.902	3.071	29.617	92.782
3	8.357	2.911	26.532	69.110
…	…	…	…	…
162	7.290	2.760	23.873	64.033

Data acquisition was conducted on July 20, 2022, between 10:00 and 12:00 under clear weather conditions and high atmospheric visibility, ensuring optimal measurement accuracy. A UAV-mounted LiDAR system was employed, following a serpentine flight path to achieve full coverage of the 100 m × 500 m study area. The flight was performed at an altitude of 110 m and a speed of 10 m/s, with a lateral overlap of 80%, a scan rate of 80 lines per second, and a pulse density of 5 points/m^2. Post-flight processing, including image stitching and point cloud generation, was completed using proprietary software, resulting in a comprehensive LiDAR dataset and high-resolution orthophoto imagery of the study site.

3 Method

The proposed workflow incrementally isolates dense street tree point clouds and optimizes computation via methods such as sparse matrix transformations, Combining strength attributes to improve classification accuracy. It comprises three stages:

(1) Point Cloud Data Preprocessing: A cloth simulation filter removes noise and ground returns; Height thresholding coarsely separates grass, shrubs, and trees, yielding vegetation-only data.
(2) Precise Street Tree Classification: Dictionary learning plus sparse transformations accelerate feature extraction. A kNN guided, bandwidth adaptive MeanShift clusters the data, combining supervised and unsupervised cues while integrating intensity features to sharpen class boundaries and minimise manual tuning.
(3) Feature Parameter Extraction and Accuracy Evaluation: Geometric approximations derive tree height, crown radius, and projected crown area. Precision, recall, and F1 score exceed those of conventional methods, confirming the method's superior accuracy and efficiency.

The methodological workflow is summarised in Fig. 2. Its chief innovation, a multi-feature-assisted MeanShift based module, targets the the precise classification stage of street trees, where fusing geometric and intensity cues boosts accuracy and suppresses misclassification. The implementation of this module is detailed in the following section.

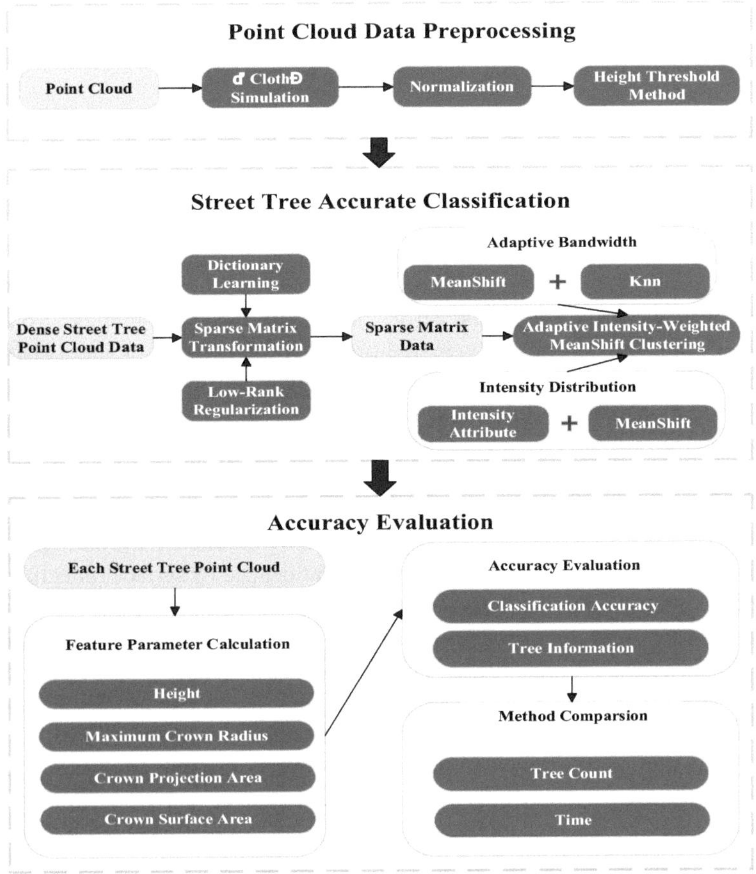

Fig. 2. Technical Flowchart

3.1 Precise Classification Method for Street Trees

This method targets precise segmentation of dense street tree point clouds by applying sparse matrix transformations to optimize data structure and enhance computational efficiency. An improved adaptive MeanShift clustering algorithm, incorporating intensity feature distribution, is employed to achieve precise classification of street trees, thereby improving classification accuracy and automation.

After preprocessing to obtain dense street tree point cloud data, dictionary learning and sparse coding are applied to enhance feature representation and accelerate computation using sparse matrices. To mitigate overfitting, L1 low-rank regularization [36] is incorporated to reduce model complexity and improve performance. Subsequently, the MeanShift algorithm, a density-based clustering method that locates cluster centers by shifting points toward local density maxima, is employed for individual tree segmentation, effectively handling noise and outliers in high-density clusters.

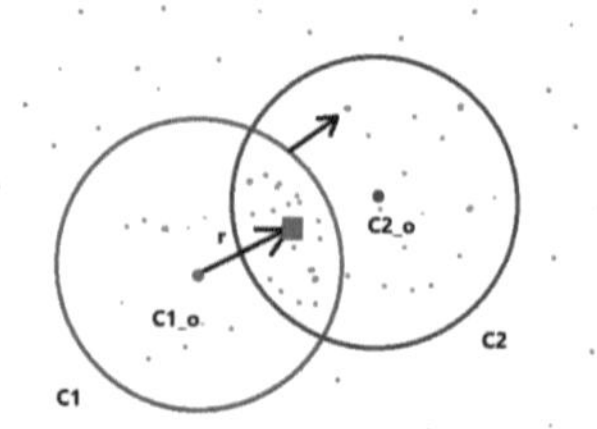

Fig. 3. Principle Diagram of the MeanShift Clustering Algorithm

Figure 3 illustrates the principle of the MeanShift clustering method. To address the challenge of bandwidth selection in traditional MeanShift, we propose a kNN-based adaptive bandwidth strategy that dynamically determines the optimal bandwidth for each data point based on distances to its k nearest neighbors, thereby enhancing local density estimation and clustering robustness. The parameter k is estimated from the average tree spacing in the study area to provide a reasonable neighborhood scale.

To enhance classification accuracy, the algorithm integrates point cloud intensity information. LiDAR acquires intensity information by measuring the strength of laser pulses reflected from object surfaces. Intensity is influenced by surface reflectivity, incidence angle, distance, and atmospheric conditions. In this study, the collected intensity values underwent careful calibration and preprocessing to ensure high accuracy and consistency. In urban settings, higher intensity values usually correspond to roads or buildings, while lower values indicate vegetation such as grass or trees. By incorporating intensity values into the MeanShift bandwidth estimation, the spatial distribution of intensity in the study area's point cloud can be effectively captured. The updated gradient vector formula simultaneously considers spatial coordinates and the weighted average of intensity values, providing a more comprehensive representation of point features and clustering dynamics. The formula is as follows:

$$m([x, I]) = \frac{\sum_{[x^i, I] \in N([x,I])} K\left([x, I], \left[x^i, I^i\right]\right)\left[x^i, I^i\right]}{\sum_{[x^i, I^i] \in N([x,I])} K\left([x, I], \left[x^i, I^i\right]\right)} \tag{1}$$

where N(x) is the window centered at x,, K(x,x^i) is the value of the kernel function, and the intensity value of the point in the dataset is denoted by I.

3.2 Feature Parameter Calculation

Key parameters for individual tree features include height, crown diameter, projection area, and crown surface area. Owing to the uniform species and regular crown shapes in the study area, a geometric approximation method was adopted for morphological estimation. Tree height is defined as the highest point's vertical coordinate, while the crown is projected onto the ground as an approximate circle to derive crown radius and projection area. Crown surface area is estimated via the spherical rotation method. Normal vectors from point cloud data guide the Ball-Pivoting Algorithm (BPA) to generate a triangular mesh. The average nearest neighbor distance determines the BPA sphere radius, enabling spheres to connect points and form the crown mesh. The condition for the sphere center c is expressed as:

$$c = \frac{p_1 + p_2}{2} + \sqrt{r^2 - \left(\frac{\|p_2 - p_1\|}{2}\right)^2} \cdot \frac{d}{\|d\|} \tag{2}$$

Here p_1 and p_2 denote the initial points, r is the radius of the sphere, and d is the edge vector derived from these points, with its direction determined from the point cloud data. The crown surface area is then approximated as the total surface area of the constructed mesh. This geometric approximation simplifies the complex morphological estimation, making calculations more straightforward and efficient. Given the uniform tree species and regular crown shapes, the method yields reasonable and reliable results.

3.3 Accuracy Evaluation

For classification accuracy evaluation, precision, recall, and F1 score are used to assess classification performance. Additionally, the extracted feature parameters are compared with truth values to calculate errors and analyze information accuracy. Manual classification provides the truth parameters, while the improved algorithm performs automatic classification to generate measured parameters. Accuracy is evaluated by comparing these two sets of data.

4 Results

4.1 Preprocessing Results and Analysis

The preprocessing step aims to remove noise and ground points to enhance point cloud quality, laying the groundwork for accurate street tree extraction. Given the presence of non-target objects like street lamps and road signs in the study area, which can interfere with classification, isolated and irrelevant points were first removed using third-party software. Subsequently, the Cloth Simulation Filter (CSF) algorithm was applied to further eliminate noise and ground points, followed by threshold segmentation based on normalized elevation values. As shown in Fig. 4, the CSF algorithm removed 1,747,936 points during preprocessing, effectively reducing data noise. Additionally, normalization adjusted the point cloud to a standard horizontal plane, mitigating terrain variation effects on object height (Fig. 4).

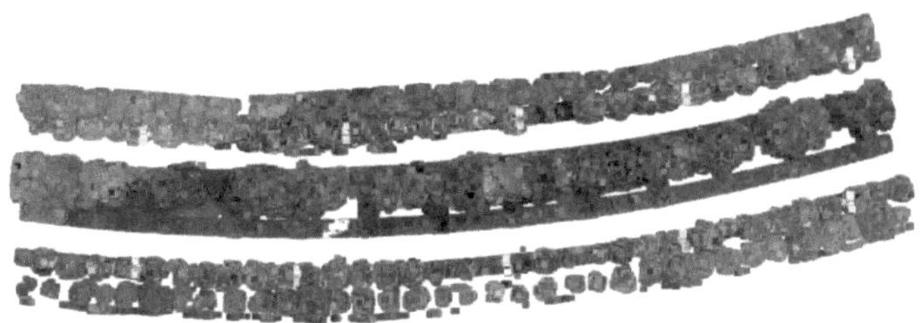

Fig. 4. Noise removal and terrain undulation correction results

After removing noise and ground points, vertical structure layering of the vegetation point cloud was further performed using height thresholds. Based on elevation differences among grass, shrubs, and trees, the street tree point cloud was extracted. Field surveys found average heights of 0.1 m for grass and 1 m for shrubs in the study area. Corresponding thresholds were set to separate street tree points from vegetation, providing data for subsequent analysis. The separation result based on elevation features is shown in Fig. 5, clearly illustrating that grass and shrubs were removed, retaining only tall tree point clouds.

Fig. 5. Preliminary Classification Results of Street Tree Information

4.2 Classification Results and Analysis

To automate and refine individual street tree extraction, the workflow first applied Dictionary Learning with Sparse Coder and low-rank regularization to capture features and compress redundancy. During clustering, a kNN-based adaptive bandwidth method supplied the optimal bandwidth for MeanShift, replacing manual selection. Because outer crown points show higher intensity than interior points, intensity distribution is incorporated as an additional constraint: a Gaussian kernel MeanShift clusters points using both spatial position and intensity, and out-of-range points are reassigned iteratively to adjacent clusters. The resulting classification (Fig. 6) clearly resolved tree counts, spatial relations, and crown shapes, even within densely packed rows.

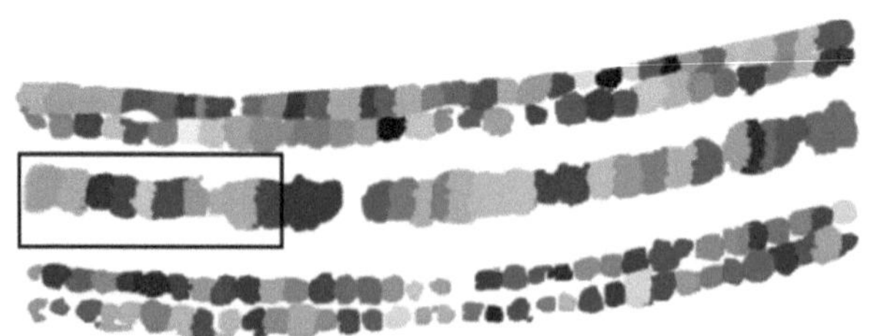

Fig. 6. Clustering results of the algorithm proposed in this study

High-quality individual street tree extraction is achieved through a hierarchical classification strategy that merges multiple segmentation methods with multi-feature fusion. To validate its effectiveness, the black-boxed region in Fig. 6 is enlarged. After preprocessing (Fig. 7a), non-target objects were removed. Adaptive MeanShift alone (Fig. 7b) quickly separated trees but blurred boundaries. Incorporating intensity attributes (Fig. 7c) refined local density estimates; the final output (Fig. 7d) shows clear, smoothly delineated crowns and substantially higher accuracy. Intensity fusion therefore enhanced precision and reduced manual parameter tuning, enabling fully automated operation in dense, complex urban settings.

Fig. 7. Specific Implementation Steps of the Improved Algorithm

4.3 Feature Parameter Calculation Results

After classification, feature parameters, including tree height, maximum canopy radius, projection area, and crown surface area, were calculated for each identified individual tree. The results are presented in the table below:

4.4 Accuracy Evaluation

To verify the feasibility of the classification algorithm, it is necessary to evaluate both the classification accuracy and the information accuracy.

4.4.1 Classification Accuracy Evaluation

Based on field investigation, a total of 165 street trees were identified in the study area. As shown in Table 3, the adaptive MeanShift algorithm successfully segmented 155 individual trees from the point cloud data. The segmentation achieved an average precision of 92.79%, an average recall of 92.82%, and an F1 score of 92.62%, demonstrating relatively high accuracy in individual tree segmentation. Nonetheless, there remains room for further improvement.

Incorporating intensity weighting into the adaptive MeanShift framework segmented 162 individual trees, with mean precision = 93.52%, recall = 93.21%, and F1 = 93.18%. Relative to the unweighted variant, intensity fusion markedly sharpens boundary delineation and boosts overall accuracy, confirming the algorithm's enhanced suitability for dense, complex urban scenes.

Table 3. Accuracy Evaluation

	Adaptive MeanShift	Intensity-Weighted Adaptive MeanShift
Actual number of individual trees	165	165
Classified individual trees	155	162
Tree recall rate	93.94%	98.18%
Point cloud recall rate	92.82%	93.21%
Point cloud precision	92.79%	93.52%
Point cloud F1 score	92.62%	93.18%

4.4.2 Information Accuracy Evaluation

In the extraction and quantification of individual tree attributes, field surveys and manual measurements were used as reference to evaluate accuracy. After incorporating intensity information, the adaptive MeanShift algorithm achieved average errors of 0.0245 m in tree height, 0.061 m in maximum crown radius, 1.321 m^2 in projected area, and 4.096 m^2 in crown surface area. These results, summarized in Table 4, demonstrate the algorithm's high precision and effectiveness in estimating individual tree parameters.

Table 4. Average Error Detection for Individual Tree Information (m)

Error	Tree Height	Maximum Crown Radius	Crown Projection Area	Crown Surface Area
This Algorithm	0.025	0.061	1.321	4.096

For the calculation of individual tree center locations, we employed the Euclidean distance between the measured and reference center coordinates to evaluate positional accuracy. As shown in Table 5, the center point location errors of the adaptive MeanShift algorithm were 0.4883 m before and 0.5086 m after incorporating intensity values—both within approximately 0.5 m. Based on the analysis across all individual street trees, the results demonstrate that the algorithm achieves a stability rate of up to 95%.

Table 5. Average Error Detection of Individual Tree Center Points (m)

Unit	Δx	Δy	$d = \sqrt{(\Delta x)^2 + (\Delta y)^2}$
This Algorithm	0.3576	0.3617	0.5086

5 Discussion

5.1 Method Evaluation

To address the limited accuracy of dense street tree extraction from airborne LiDAR point clouds, we propose a multi-feature-assisted MeanShift framework that couples unsupervised and supervised classification. A kNN-based procedure adaptively determines the optimal MeanShift bandwidth, while dictionary learning and sparse matrix transformations accelerate feature extraction and reduce runtime. Incorporating point-cloud intensity attributes and their spatial distribution further refines cluster boundaries, yielding higher segmentation accuracy and efficiency than traditional approaches.

Airborne LiDAR point clouds typically contain diverse ground object types, necessitating hierarchical processing. Ground and noise points are classified via a cloth simulation filter, combined with a height threshold strategy to effectively separate dense street trees from other features. Prior to classification, sparse coding and low-rank regularization are applied, and dictionary learning is used for feature extraction, accelerating algorithm runtime and improving classification performance. The adaptive MeanShift algorithm dynamically determines cluster centers based on data distribution, accommodating complex shapes. Moreover, point cloud intensity attributes and their distribution patterns are analyzed to refine classification results. Finally, morphological approximation methods are employed to accurately estimate individual tree parameters. Collectively, these enhancements significantly improve the accuracy and efficiency of point cloud classification, offering robust technical support for precise dense street tree delineation.

5.2 Method Comparison

In this study, the accuracy of individual tree classification was evaluated by the correctness of the tree count. Tree count accuracy refers to the degree of correspondence between the number of trees identified through classification and the actual number of trees present, directly reflecting the model's performance in detecting and distinguishing individual trees.

To further assess whether the algorithm proposed in this study achieves higher accuracy compared to traditional methods, a comparative analysis was conducted. Four commonly used classification algorithms, DBSCAN clustering, K-means, and Gaussian Mixture Model (GMM), were applied to the same dataset for extraction and analysis. The classification results are presented in Fig. 8:

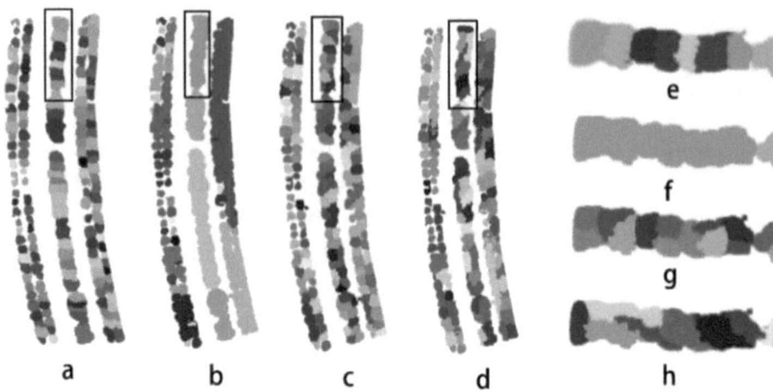

Fig. 8. Clustering Results

Note: Fig. a: Algorithm proposed in this paper; Fig. b: DBSCAN; Fig. c: K-means; Fig. d: GMM; Figures e, f, g, and h on the right correspond to the classification results within the rectangular regions in the images on the left.

The results indicate that traditional algorithms struggle to accurately extract all individual trees from dense point clouds. In contrast, the proposed algorithm demonstrates higher accuracy in individual tree count extraction and improved classification precision with smoother boundary transitions. Detailed results are presented in Table 6.

Table 6. Individual Tree Count Classification Results.

Classification Method	Actual Number of Trees	Successfully Classified Trees	Processing Time (s)
This Algorithm	165	162	11.62
DBSCAN	165	72	11.22
K-means	165	143	6.23
GMM	165	106	14.67

The table shows that traditional algorithms struggle to accurately extract individual trees from dense point clouds. DBSCAN's fuzzy membership causes unclear boundaries, K-means requires preset cluster numbers and assumes spherical shapes, and GMM often merges overlapping trees. These limitations reduce segmentation effectiveness. In contrast, our method improves efficiency with sparse coding and low-rank regularization and boosts accuracy by using intensity values. Although it is slightly slower than DBSCAN and K-means, it achieves far higher accuracy, demonstrating superior performance in street tree classification.

6   Conclusion

To enhance classification accuracy in dense street tree extraction, this study proposes a stepwise adaptive MeanShift clustering algorithm that integrates supervised and unsupervised methods, leveraging geometric and intensity features of point cloud data. Using

RIEGL miniVUX-SYS airborne LiDAR data from Yangshan Park, Nanjing, the algorithm demonstrates: (1) Significant accuracy improvement over traditional methods, achieving 93.52% classification accuracy, 93.21% recall, and 93.18% F1 score for individual tree detection. Errors in tree height, maximum crown radius, surface area, and projected area are 0.025 m, 0.061 m, 4.096 m^2, and 1.321 m^2 respectively, meeting engineering precision requirements. (2) Enhanced efficiency through stepwise classification and dictionary learning, which reduces data complexity and shortens runtime. Adaptive bandwidth selection via kNN and intensity-based optimization further mitigate sensitivity issues of traditional MeanShift, boosting classification accuracy in dense urban tree scenarios.

This study applies acceleration techniques such as dictionary learning, sparse coding, and low-rank regularization to enhance computational efficiency and classification performance. Due to limitations in length and research focus, detailed methodology is not provided. The parameter k in the adaptive bandwidth strategy was set based on average tree spacing, without thorough sensitivity analysis. Future work will evaluate the effects of these techniques and k on clustering performance to further verify the algorithm's robustness and effectiveness. Comparative experiments with state-of-the-art methods will be conducted, and the algorithm's robustness under complex terrain conditions will be evaluated.

Acknowledgments. This work was supported by the National Natural Science Foundation of China (grant number 42304027).

Disclosure of Interests The authors have no competing interests to declare that are relevant to the content of this article.

References

1. Rezaee, K., Mousavirad, S.J., Khosravi, M.R., Moghimi, M.K., Heidari, M.: An autonomous UAV-assisted distance-aware crowd sensing platform using deep ShuffleNet transfer learning. IEEE Trans. Intell. Transp. Syst. **23**(7), 9404–9413 (2021)
2. He, M., Yuan, C., Zhang, X., Wang, P., Yao, C.: Impacts of green-blue-grey infrastructures on high-density urban thermal environment at multiple spatial scales: a case study in Wuhan. Urban Climate **52**, 101714 (2023)
3. Wang, M., Qin, M., Xu, P., Huang, D., Jin, X., Chen, J., et al.: Atmospheric particulate matter retention capacity of bark and leaves of urban tree species. Environ. Pollut. **342**, 123109 (2024)
4. Rey-Gozalo, G., Barrigón Morillas, J.M., Montes González, D., Vílchez-Gómez, R.: Influence of green areas on the urban sound environment. Current Pollution Rep. **9**(4), 746–759 (2023)
5. Huang, Q., Xu, C., Haase, D., Teng, Y., Su, M., Yang, Z.: Heterogeneous effects of the availability and spatial configuration of urban green spaces on their cooling effects in China. Environ. Int. **183**, 108385 (2024)
6. Shahtahmassebi, A.R., et al.: Remote sensing of urban green spaces: A review. Urban Forestry & Urban Greening **57**, 126946 (2021)
7. Höfle, B., Hollaus, M., Hagenauer, J.: Urban vegetation detection using radiometrically calibrated small-footprint full-waveform airborne LiDAR data. ISPRS J. Photogramm. Remote Sens. **67**, 134–147 (2012)

8. Horvat, D., Žalik, B., Mongus, D.: Context-dependent detection of non-linearly distributed points for vegetation classification in airborne LiDAR. ISPRS J. Photogramm. Remote Sens. **116**, 1–14 (2016)
9. Yang, M., et al.: A review of general methods for quantifying and estimating urban trees and biomass. Forests **13**(4), 616 (2022)
10. Xi, Y., Tian, J., Jiang, H., Tian, Q., Xiang, H., Xu, N.: Mapping tree species in natural and planted forests using Sentinel-2 images. Remote Sensing Lett. **13**(6), 544–555 (2022)
11. Pu, R.: Mapping tree species using advanced remote sensing technologies: a state-of-the-art review and perspective. Journal of Remote Sensing (2021)
12. Wang, Y., Li, S., Tian, X., Zhang, Z., Zhang, W.: An adaptive directional model for estimating vegetation canopy height using space-borne photon counting laser altimetry data. J. Infrared Millimeter Waves **39**(3), 363–371 (2020)
13. Shen, Z., Liang, H., Lin, L., Wang, Z., Huang, W., Yu, J.: Fast ground segmentation for 3D LiDAR point cloud based on jump-convolution-process. Remote Sensing **13**(16), 3239 (2021)
14. Popescu, S.C., Wynne, R.H.: Seeing the trees in the forest. Photogramm. Eng. Remote Sens. **70**(5), 589–604 (2004)
15. Ma, Q., Li, Q., Wang, W., Zhu, M.: LIDAR-based SLAM system for autonomous vehicles in degraded point cloud scenarios: dynamic obstacle removal. Industrial Robot: Inter. J. Robot. Res. Appli. **51**(4), 632–639 (2024)
16. Anchang, J.Y., Ananga, E.O., Pu, R.: An efficient unsupervised index based approach for mapping urban vegetation from IKONOS imagery. Int. J. Appl. Earth Obs. Geoinf. **50**, 211–220 (2016)
17. Shen, X., Cao, L.: Tree-species classification in subtropical forests using airborne hyperspectral and LiDAR data. Remote Sensing **9**(11), 1180 (2017)
18. Falkowski, M.J., Smith, A.M.S., Hudak, A.T., Gessler, P.E., Vierling, L.A., Crookston, N.L.: Automated estimation of individual conifer tree height and crown diameter via two-dimensional spatial wavelet analysis of lidar data. Can. J. Remote. Sens. **32**(2), 153–161 (2006)
19. Meng, X., Li, J., Hu, W., Tian, M., Ma, C., Wang, R.: Single wood extraction method combining LiDAR data and spectral images. Nongye Jixie Xuebao/Trans. Chin. Soc. Agricult. Mach. **55**(1) (2024)
20. Mastej, W., Bartuś, T.: Supervised classification of morphodiversity using artificial neural networks on the example of the Pieniny Mts (Poland). CATENA **242**, 108086 (2024)
21. Li, W., Guo, Q., Jakubowski, M.K., Kelly, M.: A new method for segmenting individual trees from the lidar point cloud. Photogramm. Eng. Remote Sens. **78**(1), 75–84 (2012)
22. Sun, Z., Leinenkugel, P., Guo, H., Huang, C., Kuenzer, C.: Extracting distribution and expansion of rubber plantations from Landsat imagery using the C5.0 decision tree method. J. Appli. Remote Sensing **11**(2), 026011 (2017)
23. Palaniappan, S., Logeswaran, R., Velayutham, A., Bui, N.D.: Predicting short-range weather in tropical regions using random forest classifier. J. Inform. Web Eng. **4**(1), 18–28 (2025)
24. Jin, H., Zhu, W., Liu, T., Yu, J., Jin, X.: Identification of vegetable weeds by using convolutional neural networks and color segmentation. J. Chin. Agricult. Mechanization **45**(11), 215 (2024)
25. Chen, Q., Wang, X., Hang, M., Li, J.: Research on the improvement of single tree segmentation algorithm based on airborne LiDAR point cloud. Open Geosci. **13**(1), 705–716 (2021)
26. Yin, L., Hu, H., Li, K., Zheng, G., Qu, Y., Chen, H.: Improvement of DBSCAN algorithm based on k-dist graph for adaptive determining parameters. Electronics **12**(15), 3213 (2023)
27. Lian, R., Wang, W., Mustafa, N., Huang, L.: Road extraction methods in high-resolution remote sensing images: a comprehensive review. IEEE J. Selected Topics Applied Earth Observat. Remote Sensing **13**, 5489–5507 (2020)

28. Weng, S., et al.: Reference-based image super-resolution of hyperspectral and red-green-blue image for determination of wheat kernel quality using deep learning networks. Eng. Appl. Artif. Intell. **139**, 109513 (2025)
29. Qi, C., Su, H., Mo, K., Guibas, L.J.: PointNet: deep learning on point sets for 3D classification and segmentation. In: IEEE Conference on Computer Vision and Pattern Recognition, CVPR 2017, pp. 652–660. IEEE, Honolulu, HI (2017)
30. Klokov, R., Lempitsky, V.: Escape from cells: deep Kd-networks for the recognition of 3D point cloud models. In: 2017 IEEE International Conference on Computer Vision (ICCV), Venice, Italy pp. 863–872 (2017)
31. Sindagi, V.A., Zhou, Y., Tuzel, O.: MVX-Net: multimodal VoxelNet for 3D object detection. In: 2019 International Conference on Robotics and Automation (ICRA), pp. 7276–7282. IEEE (2019)
32. Qin, X., Zhang, Z., Huang, C., Dehghan, M., Zaiane, O.R., Jagersand, M.: U2-Net: going deeper with nested U-structure for salient object detection. Pattern Recogn. **106**, 107404 (2020)
33. Sun, L., Han, Q., Yin, C., Jin, Q., Ge, K.: Research on the fusion imaging method of sign coherence and time reversal for Lamb wave sparse array. Ultrasonics **145**, 107489 (2025)
34. Qi, L., Zhang, Y., Guo, Q., Wang, Y., Mykola, K., Qi, B.: Optimization of the sparse array with enhanced degrees of freedom and low mutual coupling. Circ. Syst. Signal Process., 1–18 (2024)
35. Wang, Z., Zhang, J., Guo, H., Miao, Y.: An enhanced direct position determination of mixed circular and non-circular sources using moving virtual interpolation array. Sensors **24**(20), 6718 (2024)
36. Zhang, X., Tan, Z., Wang, X., Liang, Q., Wan, L.: Image feature extraction algorithm based on orthogonal projection learning. J. Beijing Univ. Posts Telecommun. **45**(5), 85 (2022)

Tower Anomaly Detection Model Based on Improved MobileNetv3 and BRA

Weihui Zeng[1,2], Lixin Xu[1(✉)], Ao Kang[1], and Guoli Li[1,2]

[1] Anhui University, Hefei, Anhui 230039, China
{whzeng,liquoli}@ahu.edu.cn, 1260181376@qq.com
[2] The Ministry of Education, The Quality of Electric Energy Engineering Research Center, Anhui University, Hefei, Anhui, China

Abstract. In the daily operation and maintenance of power poles, foreign object entanglement, unintended contact between power lines and foreign materials, and insulator defects are key contributors to tower malfunctions and operational anomalies. In order to solve the low accuracy caused by the diverse types and sizes of foreign objects on towers, as well as the computational complexity of existing detection models that fail to meet application requirements, a multi-scale adaptive dual-layer routing attention-based anomaly detection model for towers is proposed. Specifically, to account for the wide variety of foreign bodies and different sizes in the detection of foreign bodies in towers, the Bi-Level Routing Attention (BRA) mechanism was structurally optimized. Building on this, an Adaptive Bi-Level Multi-scale attention module (ABMD) was proposed. In the backbone part of the model, MobileNetv3 is introduced as the backbone network to replace the original backbone network adopted by the YOLOv5 framework, resulting in the final model named ABMnv3Net. Experimental results show that the ABMnv3Net network can efficiently detect abnormal parts of towers of different types and sizes, and the average accuracy is increased by 3.3% and the number of parameters is reduced by 36% compared with the baseline model, which has outstanding advantages in the accuracy and model complexity of tower anomaly detection.

Keywords: tower anomaly detection · Adaptive · Multi-Scale Dilated · Bi-Level Routing Attention · Double-depth pooling bottleneck structure

1 Introduction

As a key supporting structure of the power system, the proper functioning of power towers is crucial for ensuring the stability and safety of power supply. However, foreign objects such as balloons, kites, and bird nests, along with insulator defects, can lead to abnormal transmission in power towers. These issues not only pose a threat to the safety of power transmission but may also lead to severe consequences such as widespread power outages. Consequently, Unmanned Aerial

© The Author(s), under exclusive license to Springer Nature Singapore Pte Ltd. 2026
Z. Lin et al. (Eds.): ICIG 2025, LNCS 16163, pp. 440–456, 2026.
https://doi.org/10.1007/978-981-95-3729-7_36

Vehicles (UAVs) are commonly employed to collect image data of power towers. This process also forms the basis for constructing datasets used in intelligent tower anomaly detection. Deep learning-based UAV image anomaly detection for power towers offers an efficient and feasible solution, enabling the timely identification and management of tower anomalies conditions in power towers, which is vital for maintaining stable power system operations. At present, with the development of computer vision technology, methods based on deep learning are widely used due to their efficient feature extraction and superior object detection performance. In the field of transmission tower image anomaly detection, research primarily focuse on feature fusion, image quality enhancement, and detection algorithm innovation to improve detection accuracy and generalizability. Wu Jun [1] improved the feature fusion quality in YOLOv7 by introducing normalization and global attention mechanisms, but the limited category diversity and insufficient dataset size hinder generalization performance. Ren Yiming [2] optimized YOLOv8 by integrating Real-ESRGAN and Transformer model, improving the detection performance of low-resolution images and reducing the computational burden. Wang Yaru [3], Li Xuyang [4] and Leng Ruixuan [5] have enhanced the ability of foreign object detection by improving the YOLOv8 model, but the wide range of foreign object types and scenarios remains to be validated. In terms of insulator defect detection, Zhai Yidi [6] proposed ML-YOLOv5, which improves detection accuracy by enhancing feature fusion and introducing an reinforced feature pyramid, but its generalization is limited to insulator and vibration damper defects. The self-calibrating convolutional YOLOv7 proposed by Huo Yifan [7] enhances feature extraction capabilities and reduces false positives, but the limitations in experimental design and dataset diversity persist.

In improving target detection models by applying multi-scale features and attention mechanisms, Wu Zhenliao [8] proposed YOLOv5-GSEM, which enhanced the detection accuracy of multiple types of insulator defects. Junfei Yi [9] addressed texture and occlusion issues with their PSTL-Net. Zhao Yongxiang [10], Ren Huan [11], Hao Shuai [12], and Ji Kai [13] improved detection performance by introducing deformable convolutions, expanding feature enhancement modules, and utilizing multi-scale feature information. However, all these approaches remain constrained by limited insufficient dataset diversity or excessively high model complexity.

To optimize the detection model structure and enhance generalization performance, He Min [14] introduced the ECA attention mechanism and Soft-NMS algorithm, improving the detection accuracy of YOLOv5 in complex backgrounds, though a balance between model complexity and computational load remains necessary. Zhou Xia [15] optimized YOLOv5 through multiple techniques, incorporating pole-tower foreign object categories to strengthen generalization. Pato L V [16], Ancha S [17], and Wang S [18] approached the problem from detection processing mechanisms, backbone network innovations, and testing systems respectively, proposing methods to enhance detection accuracy and uncover erroneous results, offering new perspectives for pole-tower anomaly detection.

Overall, although deep learning-based anomaly detection techniques has shown promising results in the field of tower detection, they still face challenges such as poor detection performance when dealing with diverse target types and inconsistent sizes. To address these, this paper proposes a multi-scale adaptive dual-layer routing attention mechanism model for tower anomaly detection. The primary innovations and contributions of this paper are as follows:

1) We optimized the BRA attention mechanism and proposed a new visual transformer attention layer block, ABMD was developed to tackle the model precision issues present in existing tower anomaly detection studies, thereby enabling accurate and rapid detection of tower anomalies.
2) We employed MobileNetv3 as the backbone network, by leveraging the depthwise separable convolution idea from MobileNetv3, combined with the single-stage object detection structure of YOLOv5, the model structure is optimized, reducing the model complexity and achieving model optimization.
3) We introduced the C3-Dual-Depth-Pool Bottleneck (DDPB) module to replace the original C3 module. The DDPB employs a parallel structure featuring pooling and depthwise convolution, with multiple branches and pooling operations significantly enhancing the model's ability to process feature map information. Additionally, the application of depth-wise convolution effectively alleviates computational burden, the network's overall accuracy and lightweight efficiency.

2 Related Work

2.1 YOLOv5 Algorithm

YOLOv5 [19] algorithm is a single-stage object detection algorithm that divides the input image into multiple grids, with each grid responsible for predicting the category, location, and confidence score. The YOLOv5 detection framework processes an input image as follows: First, the Backbone extracts features using CBS (Conv + Batch normalization + SiLU) and C3 modules, followed by the SPPF module, which fuse multi-scale features and accelerate computation. Next, the detection head employs an Feature Pyramid Network (FPN) structure to pass deep semantic information to shallow feature maps, thereby enhancing their representational capacity. Finally, multi-scale feature maps are convolutionally processed in the prediction stage to generate bounding boxes with target category, location, and confidence scores, enabling efficient object detection (as illustrated in Fig. 1).

2.2 BiFormer Structure

Biformer [20] is a novel transformer-based architecture aimed at addressing the inefficiencies of traditional transformer attention mechanisms in terms of computational efficiency and object detection accuracy, particularly when detecting

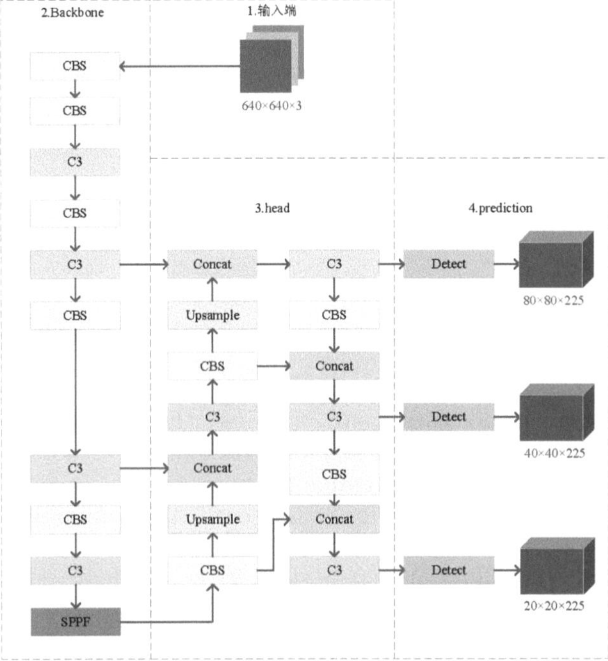

Fig. 1. YOLOv5 detection framework

small objects. Traditional attention mechanisms often perform poorly when dealing with small objects, as these objects occupy fewer pixels in images, making it difficult to obtain sufficient attention. Additionally, global attention mechanisms have high computational complexity, leading to challenges in computational efficiency and memory consumption. To address these issues, researchers have proposed the Biformer network architecture.

2.3 Double Layer Routing Attention

The core mechanism in Biformer is the Bi-Level Routing Attention (BRA). The schematic diagram of the BRA attention mechanism is shown in Fig. 2. This mechanism is implemented through the following steps:

For the process of BRA attention mechanism, let the input feature tensor be denoted as $X \in R^{N \times H \times W \times C}$. The feature map is divided into $S \times S$ spatial regions. For a single sample $X_i \in R^{1 \times H \times W \times C} (i = 1, 2, ..., N)$ is partitioned into $S \times S$ regions, each region under it contains $\frac{HW}{S^2}$ feature vectors, Change feature X to $X^r \in R^{N \times S^2 \times \frac{HW}{S^2} \times C}$, Initial Q, K, V values are obtained by linear mapping.

$$Q = X^r W^q, \ K = X^r W^k, \ V = X^r W^v \tag{1}$$

where W^q, W^k and W^v are the projection weights corresponding to query, key and value respectively.

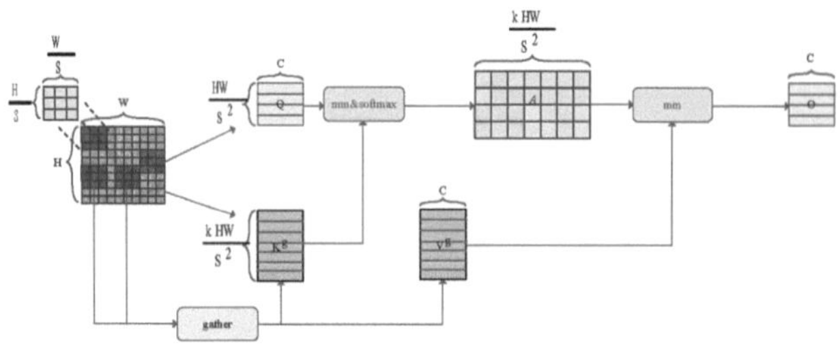

Fig. 2. The principle diagram of the BRA attention mechanism

Subsequently, a directed graph is constructed to determine the associated regions each area should participate in. First, the mean of each region is computed to obtain region-level query and key tensors, denoted as $Q^r, K^r \in R^{N \times S^2 \times C}$. In the original BRA attention mechanism, The TopkRouting method takes Q^r, K^r as inputs. represent the overall evaluation values of each region in the feature map X. TopkRouting performs matrix multiplication on Q^r and K^r, Construct the correlation graph matrix $A^r \in R^{N \times S^2 \times S^2}$ between regions.

$$A^r = Q^r (K^r)^T \tag{2}$$

Subsequently, the topk function is applied to the association graph matrix to filter and prune the association graph, retaining only the top k most associated regions for each area, thereby obtaining the most relevant inter-regional matrix $I^r \in R^{N \times S^2 \times S^2}$, It consists of the most relevant weight matrix $I^r_{weight} \in R^{N \times S^2 \times Topk}$ and the most relevant index matrix $I^r_{idx} \in R^{N \times S^2 \times Topk}$. The i-th row of I^r_{idx} contains the indices of the top k most associated regions for the i-th region, and the i-th row of I^r_{weight} contains the association weight values for the i-th region's top k most associated regions, with positive values indicating positive correlation and negative values indicating negative correlation.

$$I^r = \{I^r_{weight}, I^r_{idx}\} = TopkRouting(A^r) = topk(A^r) \tag{3}$$

Using the most associated index matrix I^r_{idx}, we can establish fine-grained attention multiplication, where for each query Q in region i, it focuses on all key-value pairs in the union of k routing regions. Index is $I^r_{(i,1)}, I^r_{(i,2)}, ..., I^r_{(i,k)}$. However, for a specified target region, the distribution of its top k most associated regions across the entire feature map is scattered. Since GPUs rely on merged memory operations that load tens of consecutive bytes in a single block, aggregating the keys and values from the associated regions scattered across the feature map involves gathering them into a single location

$$K^g = gather(K, I^r), \quad V^g = gather(V, I^r) \tag{4}$$

Here, K^g and V^g denote the aggregated key and value tensors, upon which attention operations to the aggregated K-V pairs:

$$Output = Attention(Q, K^g, V^g) \tag{5}$$

3   ABMnv3Net Power Tower Foreign Object Detection Model

3.1   ABMnv3Net Overall Architecture

To improve the detection accuracy and speed of the model for detecting anomalies in transmission towers, the ABMnv3Net model draws inspiration from the single-stage network architecture of YOLOv5. The network includes a modified MobileNetv3 backbone to reduce the number of model parameters and complexity, and an ABMD multi-scale, multi-stage attention to improve detection performance. In the neck section of the network, a C3-DPP module with a DDPB is introduced to further enhance detection accuracy. The architecture of the ABMnv3Net model is shown in Fig. 3.

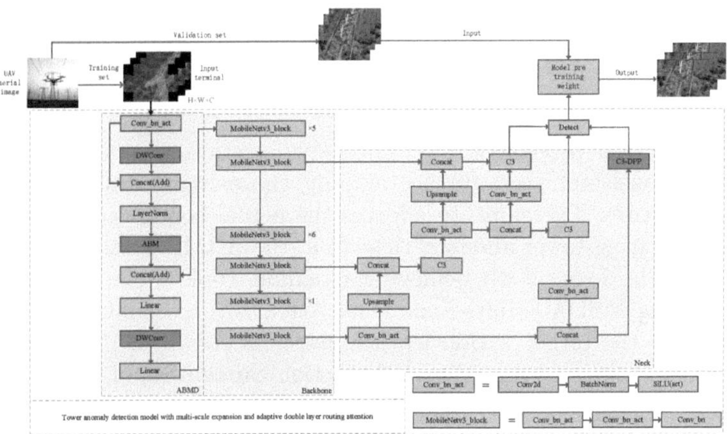

Fig. 3. Schematic diagram of the network structure of ABMnv3Net

The detection network process built in this article: (1) Split the dataset into training and validation sets; (2) Input the samples in the training set into the ABMnv3Net network to train the model; (3) Obtain the model's pre-trained weights through training; (4) Test the samples in the validation set using the obtained pre-trained weights and output the final detection results of the images.

3.2   ABMD Attention Mechanism

The previously introduced BRA attention mechanism reduces the computational complexity of traditional fine-grained MHSA by using TopkRouting and

KVgather methods. However, the overall focus of BRA on regions relies entirely on the manually designed Topk values received in the KVgather process, without depending on other means. This leads to issues such as weak generalization ability and difficulty in manual adjustment for key region selection and subsequent aggregation self-attention.

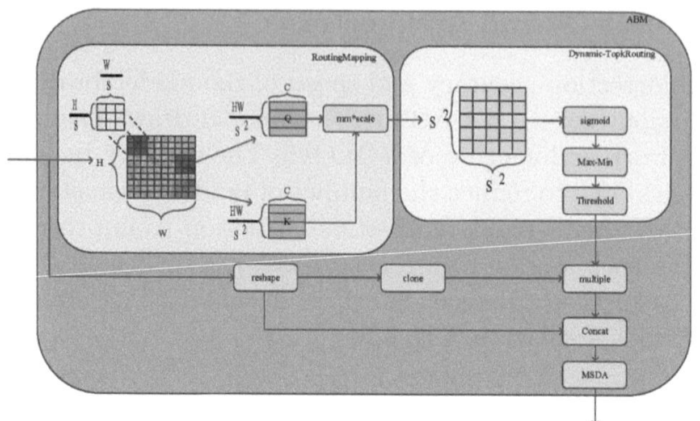

Fig. 4. ABM Attention Mechanism Flow

Especially in the process of tower anomaly detection, the variety of anomaly types and inconsistent sizes further amplify the existing design flaws in the Biformer structure. Therefore, to address the actual conditions of targets and backgrounds during tower anomaly detection, the ABMD attention mechanism is proposed. The focus is on achieving dynamic Topk values based on BRA and introducing MSDA (Multi-Scale Dual Attention) to enable the network to concentrate on the target within feature maps, as shown in Fig. 4. Simultaneously leveraging the superior feature extraction capabilities of the Transformer structure to envelop the ABM attention mechanism, thereby further enhancing feature extraction capabilities.

Dynamic Topk Value. For the association matrix A^r between regions, which is a matrix of regional evaluation values with positive and negative values, we introduce the Sigmoid function to map these evaluation value weights into the interval $[0, 1]$, thereby obtaining normalized weight values A^r_{sigmoid}:

$$A^r_{\text{sigmoid}} = \text{Sigmoid}(A^r) \tag{6}$$

Due to the effects of regional mean normalization and matrix multiplication, the original weight values of the association matrix are mostly within the range of 10^{-3} to 10^{-6}. Additionally, the computational characteristics of the Sigmoid function cause the weight values to concentrate around 0.5, which poses significant challenges for subsequent score processing. Therefore, we introduce the MaxMin (range normalization) function to adjust the scale within the $[0, 1]$

interval while maintaining the distribution of weights in the association matrix as much as possible, resulting in a weight matrix A^{Mr} with uniform distribution within $[0, 1]$:

$$A^{\mathrm{Mr}} = (\text{Max-Min})(A^{r}_{\mathrm{sigmoid}}) \tag{7}$$

Through conditional screening with a threshold of 0.5, the uniform weight matrix A^{Mr} is filtered to obtain the final weight matrix $\mathbf{A}^{\mathrm{Fr}} \in R^{N \times S^2 \times S^2}$. During this process, qualifying weight values are enhanced by a fixed multiple of $+1$, preparing to map the correlation degree of the weight matrix onto the feature map in subsequent steps.

$$A^{\mathrm{Fr}}_{(i,j)} = \begin{cases} A^{\mathrm{Mr}}_{(i,j)} + 1, & A^{\mathrm{Mr}}_{(i,j)} > 0.5 \\ 0, & \text{otherwise} \end{cases} \tag{8}$$

Here, $A^{\mathrm{Mr}}_{(i,j)}$ represents the correlation value between the i-th region and the j-th region in A^{Mr}. Through the aforementioned value-distribution processing and threshold-based filtering, this approach ensures that the number of associated regions for each partitioned region of the feature map is adequately covered within the threshold range, thereby achieving dynamic Topk values.

MSDA Attention. To address the lack of information interaction in Biformer's original feature maps due to dynamic Topk, we introduce the multi-scale dilated convolution attention mechanism from Dilateformer [21] for tower anomaly detection, which handles diverse target types and sizes. The core components of Dilateformer include SWDA (Sliding Window Dilated Attention) and MSDA (Multi-Scale Dilated Attention). MSDA (Fig. 5) extends this with a multi-head design, dividing feature map channels into heads with different dilation rates for SWDA. This enables the model to simulate interactions between local and sparse image patches, efficiently capturing multi-scale semantic information while maintaining computational efficiency.

The processed and filtered weight matrix A^{Fr} is multiplied with the feature map $X^{C} \in R^{N \times S^2 \times L}$ $(L = h \times w \times c)$ that has undergone coarse-grained processing through matrix multiplication. To prevent the operation of associated multiplication from affecting the original feature map, the values associated between regions are mapped onto the data distribution of the feature map, achieving the effect that the information of the associated regions in each region is enhanced. Subsequently, through dimension reorganization and residual connection, the missing information during the processing is compensated for and the original distribution in the feature map is maintained. Then, the result is sent to MSDA and SWDA to achieve multi-scale dilated convolution attention under dynamic regional enhancement. This attention is called ABM attention (Transmission line anomaly detection of Bi-Level Routing Attention).

$$\text{Output} = \text{MSDA}\big(\text{reshape}(A^{\mathrm{Fr}} X^{C}) + X\big) \tag{9}$$

Based on this, this paper integrates ABM by using the original BRA attention mechanism's application method within Biformer, embedding it into the

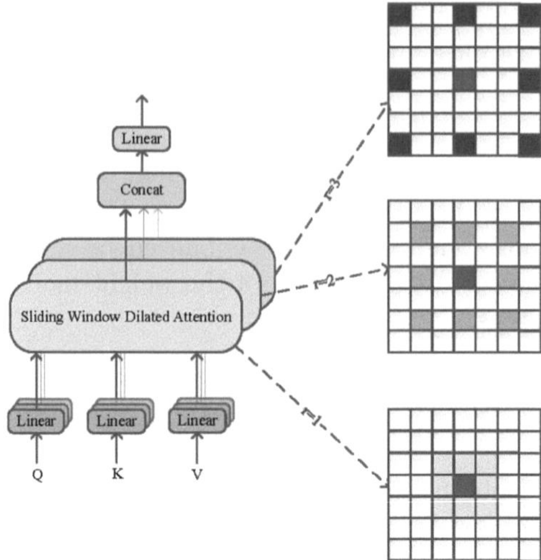

Fig. 5. MSDA Attention Flow Diagram

transformer structure. As shown in Fig. 6, DWConv is employed for local feature extraction and embedding of positional information, while residual connections are utilized to minimize information loss and maintain consistency of the original information. DWConv is incorporated into the MLP section to enhance the ability of local information interaction in the feature maps at this stage.

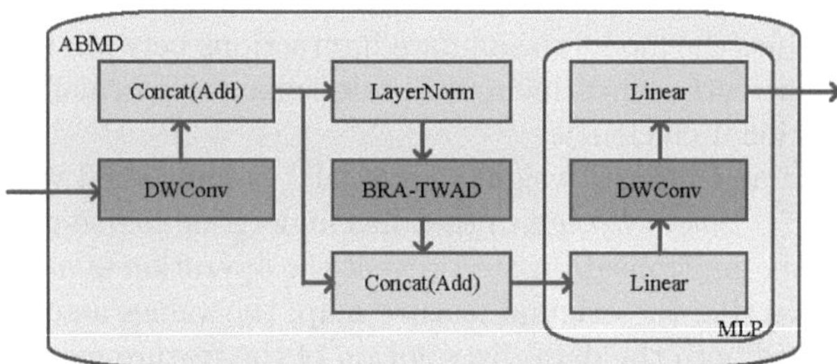

Fig. 6. ABMD Attention Mechanism Flow

3.3 C3-DDPB Module

To address the high parameter count and limited small-target detection capability of YOLOv5's C3 module, we designed the DDPB module (Fig. 7). DDPB features a dual-branch structure: the main branch uses a standard convolution and a 5×5 depthwise convolution to capture spatial features and expand the receptive field, while parallel branches apply average pooling (for global information) and max pooling (for local prominent features). A 3×3 convolution further processes the extracted multi-scale features, enhancing the model's ability to capture targets of varying sizes. Deep convolutions in both pooling branches reduce parameters and computational load. Residual connections are included to preserve input information, prevent critical target data loss, and improve gradient flow (results shown in Fig. 8).

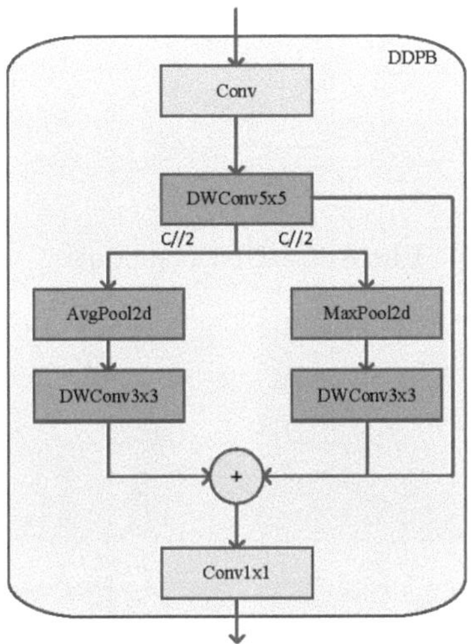

Fig. 7. DDPB structure

3.4 Backbone Introduces Deep Separable Convolutions

To reduce the computational load and the number of parameters of the model, the original Backbone in YOLOv5, composed of CBS, C3, and SPPF, was replaced with a Backbone that stacks `MobileNetv3_block` from MobileNetv3, where the inverted residual structure and depthwise separable convolution can extract more accurate information from the feature map [22].

4 Experiments and Analyses

4.1 Dataset

The anomaly dataset of pole towers used in this article comprises three sources: (1) the Ptl-ai Furnas dataset, an anomaly dataset of pole towers obtained at different time intervals using drones by De Oliveira F. S. [23]; (2) the CPLID dataset (China Transmission Line Insulator Anomaly Detection Dataset); (3) the dataset from the Guangzhou-Pazhou Algorithm Competition for the detection

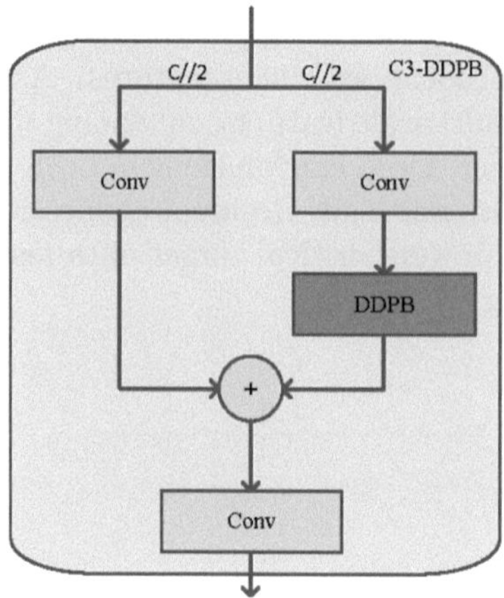

Fig. 8. C3-DDPB module

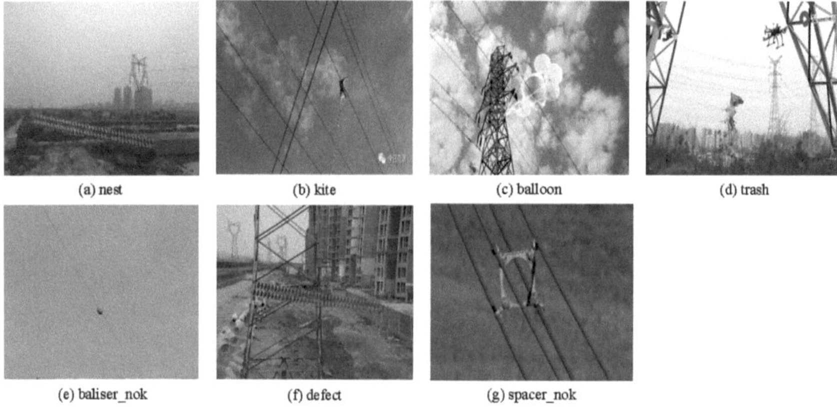

(a) nest (b) kite (c) balloon (d) trash

(e) baliser_nok (f) defect (g) spacer_nok

Fig. 9. Transmission line anomaly target category

of hazards in transmission corridors (including both the preliminary and final rounds).

The dataset is divided into a training set and a test set in a ratio of 7:3. Additionally, during the data division process, we strive to ensure that the data distribution among the training set, validation set, and test set remains as consistent as possible. This dataset contains a total of 4848 images, of which 3393 are in the training set and 1455 are in the test/validation set. The number of instances in each category is shown in Table 1, and the representative example images are shown in Fig. 9.

Table 1. Categorical distribution in dataset segmentation

	nest	kite	Balloon	trash	baliser_nok	defect	Spacer_nok
train	1587	141	105	72	132	1609	16
test	684	40	55	35	72	688	7
all	2271	181	160	107	204	2297	23

4.2   Evaluation Metrics

In order to verify that the improved ABMnv3Net demonstrates better detection performance compared to other object detection models in tower anomaly detection, this experiment focuses on the evaluation of detection performance. The relevant evaluation metrics of the experiment include Mean Average Precision (MAP), Parameter Quantity, and Giga Floating-point Operations Per Second (GFLOPs), with the computation formulas as follows:

$$\text{MAP} = \frac{1}{m} \sum_{i=1}^{m} \text{AP}_i \tag{10}$$

AP_i represents the average precision for the i-th category, and m denotes the number of class labels in the dataset. This paper adopts MAP@0.5, which indicates the MAP value when the Intersection over Union (IOU) threshold is set at 0.5. The parameter is used to measure the model's scale and spatial complexity, while GFLOPs is a metric for evaluating the overall computational complexity and performance of the model, indicating the number of floating-point operations the model performs in one second.

4.3   Experimental Environment and Training Parameters

The equipment used in the experiment is a 64-bit system based on Windows 10, with a hardware configuration of an NVIDIA RTX 3090 24G GPU. The deep learning framework utilized is PyTorch 1.8.0, and the CUDA version is 11.2. During the training process, the initial learning rate is set at 0.01, and a cosine annealing schedule is employed to decrease the learning rate. The training strategy employed mosaic data augmentation along with a warm-up period of 5 epochs. The training is conducted using Stochastic Gradient Descent (SGD), with the number of epochs set to 300 and the batch size set to 8. All models were trained with a fixed input resolution of $640 \times 640 \times 3$. To guarantee the fairness and consistency of the model training results, no pre-trained weights were used in any ablation experiments or comparative experiments (includes the YOLOv5 baseline model as well as the ABMnv3Net proposed in this paper).

4.4   Ablation Experiment

In order to explore the improvement effect of the depthwise separable backbone replacement, ABMSDA layer and C3-DPP module proposed in this paper in the network, the following ablation experiments are carried out to obtain the performance indicators of each model and the final improved model (Ours), where "+" means that the module is added separately in the network. The results of the ablation experiments are shown in Table 2:

Table 2. Comparison effect before and after adding different modules

	MAP@0.5	Parameter (M)	GFLOPs
YOLOv5s	0.88	7	15.8
+ C3-DPP	0.894	3.8	10.3
+ MobileNetv3	0.871	4.3	9.6
+ ABMD	0.907	6.94	15.2
ABMnv3Net	0.915	4.46	10.9

From the analysis of the results of the ablation experiment, although the MAP value decreased by one percentage point after introducing MobileNetv3 with depthwise separable convolution as BackBone, this drop is attributed to the convolution extraction ability could not completely replace the feature extraction role of C3 and SPPF in YOLOv5's backbone. However, the number of parameters and computational complexity of the model are reduced by nearly one third. Adding ABMD attention mechanism and C3-DPPB module alone has a significant improvement in the accuracy of the network. The final improved model achieves the best performance in terms of overall MAP accuracy and model complexity compared with the separately improved parts.

4.5   Comparative Experiment

To demonstrate the superiority of the proposed ABMSDA transformer module over other attention mechanisms in tower anomaly detection on the YOLOv5s framework, we conduct a comparative study based on experimental results. Where "+" denotes adding the module separately in the network. The comparison results with other attention mechanisms are shown in Table 3:

To further validate the effectiveness of the improved YOLOv5s network in tower anomaly detection, this paper selects models that are widely used in the field of tower anomaly detection for comparison. The two-stage networks such as YOLOv5, YOLOv8 [27], YOLOv11 [28] and R-CNN were compared with the relatively novel one-stage detection networks such as RtmDet and TOOD. At the same time, some of the latest transformer models used in the field of tower detection are also compared. The conducted experiments are all carried out on the fusion data set provided in this paper, all models compared in Table 4. The experimental results are shown in Table 4.

By comparing the experimental results of each algorithm in Table 4, it can be seen that the proposed model has an average accuracy of 88% for YOLOv5s,

Table 3. Comparison with other attention mechanisms

	MAP@0.5	Parameter (M)	GFLOPs
YOLOv5s	0.88	7	15.8
+ CBAM [24]	0.89	5.4	11.7
+ ECA [25]	0.886	3.9	9.3
+ CoordAttn [26]	0.887	6.9	13.8
+ BiFormer	0.893	4.38	12.2
+ DilateFormer	0.88	4.6	9.8
+ Ours (ABM)	0.903	6.95	15.2

an average accuracy of 88.2% for YOLOv8s, and an increase of 3.3% and 1.3% for YOLOv11s, respectively, with a relatively small number of parameters and calculations. Compared with two-stage networks and some relatively novel one-stage networks, our improved model has obvious advantages in accuracy and model parameter number. The comparison of the final detection results is shown in Fig. 10.

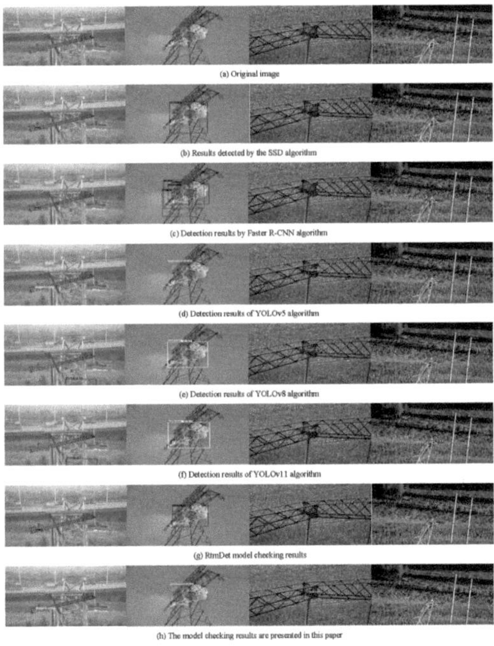

Fig. 10. Comparison of Detection result

Table 4. The detection effect of each comparison algorithm is compared

Model	MAP@0.5	MAP@0.5:0.95	Parameter (M)	GFLOPs
YOLOv5s	0.88	0.678	7	15.8
YOLOv8s	0.882	0.717	9.84	23.6
YOLOv11s	0.9	0.698	9.43	21.6
RtmDet [29]	0.881	0.660	52.26	79.9
TOOD [30]	0.673	0.431	31.8	144.3
SSD [31]	0.863	0.539	24.55	30.73
FocalNet [32]	0.822	0.553	45.62	262.58
Faster R-CNN [33]	0.713	0.445	41.15	181.78
Sparse R-CNN [34]	0.622	0.444	106.18	129.29
Cascade R-CNN [35]	0.814	0.622	68.94	237.36
Dynamic R-CNN [36]	0.615	0.436	41.52	182.5
RT-DETRv1 [37]	0.884	0.674	31.99	103.5
RT-DETRv2 [38]	0.881	0.682	42.7	134.49
Ours (ABMnv3Net)	0.915	0.669	4.46	10.9

5   Conclusion

This paper proposes a novel tower anomaly detection network, ABMnv3Net, to address abnormal detection of transmission towers. Inspired by the architectures of YOLOv5 and MobileNetv3 designs, it integrates an enhanced BRA attention mechanism. Key contributions include: 1) optimizing the BRA mechanism with dynamic Topk to better capture critical image information; 2) replacing YOLOv5's backbone with lightweight MobileNetv3 to reduce model parameters count and computational complexity; 3) embedding a new vision transformer attention layer block (ABMD) into the backbone; and 4) incorporating a C3-DDPB module in the final detection layer to boost accuracy. Experimental results demonstrate that ABMnv3Net outperforms existing object detection models on tower datasets in terms of accuracy, model complexity, and parameter count.

Acknowledgements. This study was funded by Anhui University Ministry of Education Power Quality Engineering Research Center open Project (grant number KFKT202304), National Natural Science Foundation of China (grant number 32201666).

References

1. Wu, J., Han, C., Wang, X.: Improved defect detection method of insulator and equalizing ring based on YOLOv7. Optoelectronics & Laser, 1–14 (2025)
2. Ren, Y., Du, D., Deng, X., et al.: Transmission line insulator fault detection based on Real-ESRGAN and improved YOLOv8n. Integr. Smart Energy **46**(7), 29–39 (2024)

3. Wang, Y., Feng, L., Song, X., et al.: TFD-YOLOv8: a foreign-body detection method for transmission lines. J. Graph. **45**(5), 901–912 (2024)
4. Li, X., Wang, W., Li, L., et al.: Foreign-object detection model for lightweight transmission lines based on improved YOLOv8. China Southern Power Grid Technol., 1–12 (2025)
5. Leng, R.: Application of foreign-body recognition algorithm for transmission lines based on YOLOv8. Master's thesis, Northeast Agricultural University (2023)
6. Zhai, Y.: Research on insulator detection and defect recognition based on deep convolutional neural network. Ph.D. thesis, Zhengzhou University of Light Industry (2024)
7. Huo, Y., Yi, L., Li, J., et al.: Research on external defect detection method of transmission line insulator based on improved YOLOv7. J. Shenyang Instit. Technol. (Nat. Sci. Ed.) **20**(2), 54–67 (2024)
8. Wu, Z., Wu, Z., Sun, S.: Multi-defect detection of insulators based on improved YOLOv5 algorithm. High Voltage Electr. Apparatus **60**(12), 95–112 (2024)
9. Yi, J., Mao, J., Zhang, H., et al.: PSTL-Net: a patchwise self-texture-learning network for transmission line inspection. IEEE Trans. Instrum. Measur., **73** (2025)
10. Zhao, Y., Zhang, G., Luo, W., et al.: A defect detection method for high-voltage transmission line insulators based on improved YOLOv8. Radio Eng., 1–17 (2025)
11. Ren, H., Su, T., Li, P., et al.: Transmission line insulator defect detection method based on improved CenterNet. China Southern Power Grid Technol., 1–11 (2025)
12. Hao, S., Yang, L., Ma, X., et al.: YOLOv5 transmission line fault detection based on attention mechanism and cross-scale feature fusion. Proc. CSEE **43**(6), 2319–2330 (2022)
13. Ji, K., Zhang, W., Chen, X.: Insulator defect detection based on multi-scale features and channel perception. Comput. Eng. Appl., 1–13 (2025)
14. He, M.: Research on improved YOLOv5 insulator and its damage detection algorithm. Master's thesis, Wuhan Textile University (2022)
15. Zhou, X., Jie, Z., Zhu, Z., et al.: Research on UAV image defect detection of transmission line with improved YOLOv5. Mech. Design Manuf., 1–7 (2025)
16. Pato, L.V., Negrinho, R., Aguiar, P.M.Q.: Seeing without looking: contextual rescoring of object detections for AP maximization. In: Proceedings of the IEEE/CVF Conference on Computer Vision and Pattern Recognition (CVPR 2020), pp. 14610–14618 (2020)
17. Ancha, S., Nan, J., Held, D.: Combining deep learning and verification for precise object instance detection. arXiv preprint arXiv:1912.12270 (2019)
18. Wang, S., Su, Z.: Metamorphic testing for object detection systems. arXiv preprint arXiv:1912.12162 (2019)
19. Khanam, R., Hussain, M.: What is YOLOv5: a deep look into the internal features of the popular object detector. arXiv preprint arXiv:2407.20892 (2024)
20. Zhu, L., Wang, X., Ke, Z., et al.: BiFormer: vision transformer with bi-level routing attention. In: Proceedings of the IEEE/CVF Conference on Computer Vision and Pattern Recognition (CVPR 2023), pp. 10323–10333 (2023)
21. Jiao, J., Tang, Y.M., Lin, K.Y., et al.: DilateFormer: multi-scale dilated transformer for visual recognition. IEEE Trans. Multimedia **25**, 8906–8919 (2023)
22. Zhou, Q., Ma, L., Cao, L., et al.: Tomato leaf disease identification based on improved lightweight convolutional neural network MobileNetV3. Smart Agric. **4**(1), 47–56 (2022)
23. De Oliveira, F.S., De Carvalho, M., Campos, P.H.T., et al.: PTL-AI Furnas dataset: a public dataset for fault detection in power transmission lines using aerial images.

In: Proceedings of the 35th SIBGRAPI Conference on Graphics, Patterns and Images, pp. 7–12 (2022)
24. Woo, S., Park, J., Lee, J.-Y., Kweon, I.S.: CBAM: convolutional block attention module. In: Ferrari, V., Hebert, M., Sminchisescu, C., Weiss, Y. (eds.) ECCV 2018. LNCS, vol. 11211, pp. 3–19. Springer, Cham (2018). https://doi.org/10.1007/978-3-030-01234-2_1
25. Wang, Q., Wu, B., Zhu, P., et al.: ECA-Net: efficient channel attention for deep convolutional neural networks. In: Proceedings of the IEEE/CVF Conf. on Computer Vision and Pattern Recognition (CVPR 2020), pp. 11534–11542 (2020)
26. Hou, Q., Zhou, D., Feng, J.: Coordinate attention for efficient mobile network design. In: Proceedings of the IEEE/CVF Conference on Computer Vision and Pattern Recognition (CVPR 2021), pp. 13713–13722 (2021)
27. Kahya, E.: Deep learning for apple branch detection: an analysis of the performance of yolov8 models. Acta Sci. Agric. (ISSN: 2581- 365X) 9(6) (2025)
28. Khanam, R., Hussain, M.: YOLOv11: an overview of the key architectural enhancements. arXiv preprint arXiv:2410.17725 (2024)
29. Lyu, C., Zhang, W., Huang, H., et al.: RTMDet: an empirical study of designing real-time object detectors. arXiv preprint arXiv:2212.07784 (2022)
30. Feng, C., Zhong, Y., Gao, Y., et al.: TOOD: task-aligned one-stage object detection. In: Proceedings of the IEEE/CVF International Conference on Computer Vision (ICCV 2021), pp. 3490–3499 (2021)
31. Liu, W., et al.: SSD: single shot multibox detector. In: Leibe, B., Matas, J., Sebe, N., Welling, M. (eds.) ECCV 2016. LNCS, vol. 9905, pp. 21–37. Springer, Cham (2016). https://doi.org/10.1007/978-3-319-46448-0_2
32. Mudassar, B.A., Mukhopadhyay, S.: FocalNet-Foveal attention for post-processing DNN outputs. In: Proceedings of the International Joint Conference on Neural Networks (IJCNN 2019), pp. 1–8 (2019)
33. Ren, S., He, K., Girshick, R., et al.: Faster R-CNN: towards real-time object detection with region proposal networks. IEEE Trans. Pattern Anal. Mach. Intell. 39(6), 1137–1149 (2017)
34. Sun, P., Zhang, R., Jiang, Y., et al.: Sparse R-CNN: end-to-end object detection with learnable proposals. In: Proceedings of the IEEE/CVF Conference on Computer Vision and Pattern Recognition (CVPR 2021), pp. 14454–14463 (2021)
35. Cai, Z., Vasconcelos, N.: Cascade R-CNN: delving into high-quality object detection. In: Proceedings of the IEEE Conference on Computer Vision and Pattern Recognition (CVPR 2018), pp. 6154–6162 (2018)
36. Zhang, H., Chang, H., Ma, B., et al.: Dynamic R-CNN: towards high-quality object detection via dynamic training. In: Computer Vision – ECCV 2020, pp. 260–275. Springer, Cham (2020)
37. Zhao, Y., Lv, W., Xu, S., et al.: DETRs beat YOLOs on real-time object detection. In: Proceedings of the IEEE/CVF Conference on Computer Vision and Pattern Recognition (CVPR 2024), pp. 16965–16974 (2024)
38. Lv, W., Zhao, Y., Chang, Q., et al.: RT-DETRv2: improved baseline with bag-of-freebies for real-time detection transformer. arXiv preprint arXiv:2407.17140 (2024)

GLDAN: Global Local Dynamic Attention Network for Remote Sensing Scene Classification

Hua Zhang⬛, Yindi Zhao(✉)⬛, Weilin Wang, Jingshun Zhu, and Yu Cao

The School of Environment and Spatial Informatics, China University of Mining and Technology, Xuzhou 221116, China

{zhangh22,zhaoyd,wangwl,zjs163,ts24160001a31}@cumt.edu.cn

Abstract. Remote Sensing Scene Classification (RSSC) encounters challenges from diverse land-cover types, intra-class variability and inter-class similarity. To tackle these issues, we introduce the Global Local Dynamic Attention Network (GLDAN), a novel framework designed to boost classification accuracy by dynamically integrating global and multi-scale local features. The core component, the Global Local Dynamic Attention Module (GLDAM), consists of the Global Attention Module (GAM) to capture global context, the Multi-scale Local Attention Module (MLAM) to extract fine-grained local details, and the Spatial-Channel Attention Fusion Module (SCAFM), which dynamically fuses global and local features rather than relying on simple concatenation or multiplication. Unlike traditional methods that apply attention across all bottlenecks, GLDAM is integrated solely into the final bottleneck of ResNet50 stage 1, enhancing accuracy while minimizing parameters. Experiments on the RSSCN7 and SIRI-WHU datasets demonstrate that GLDAN achieves state-of-the-art performance, with overall accuracies of 98.75% and 98.54%, respectively.

Keywords: Remote Sensing Scene Classification (RSSC) · Convolutional Neural Network · Attention Mechanism · Dynamic Feature Fusion

1 Introduction

Remote Sensing Scene Classification (RSSC) involves assigning semantic labels to remote sensing (RS) images based on their scene-level content, supporting critical applications such as land use planning [1], disaster monitoring [2], and environmental management [3, 4]. Early RSSC methods relied on handcrafted features, such as texture [5] and color distributions [6], combined with classifiers like Support Vector Machine [7] and Random Forests [8]. These approaches achieved acceptable performance on simple scenes. However, advancements in RS technologies have produced high resolution images with rich, detailed information, rendering traditional handcrafted feature-based methods struggle to achieve satisfactory classification accuracy. Fortunately, the emergence of deep learning, particularly convolutional neural networks (CNNs) [9–11], has transformed RSSC by enabling automated feature extraction and facilitating end-to-end learning, which has led to significant improvements in classification accuracy.

© The Author(s), under exclusive license to Springer Nature Singapore Pte Ltd. 2026
Z. Lin et al. (Eds.): ICIG 2025, LNCS 16163, pp. 457–471, 2026.
https://doi.org/10.1007/978-981-95-3729-7_37

Although current deep learning methods achieve promising results in RSSC, further improving classification accuracy requires a deeper understanding of the characteristics of RS images, particularly high-resolution ones. First, RS scenes often encompass multiple land-cover types, complicating single-label classification. For instance, Fig. 1(a) depicts a "Grass" scene predominantly covered by grass but also containing trees, a parking lot, a building, and a road. To address this challenge, attention mechanisms are widely employed, enabling models to focus on critical regions of the image while suppressing irrelevant information, thus effectively handling the coexistence of diverse land-cover types. Second, scenes within the same category can exhibit significant variations in texture, color, or context, while scenes from different categories may appear visually similar, leading to reduced classification accuracy. For example, Fig. 1(a) and Fig. 1(b) both represent "Grass" scenes but differ markedly in color and surrounding elements. Conversely, the "Grass" scene in Fig. 1(b) and the "Field" scene in Fig. 1(c) share similar colors and structures despite their distinct labels. To tackle this issue, effective methods typically integrate both local detailed information and global contextual cues. For instance, global contextual information can quickly identify Fig. 1(a) as a "Grass" scene, whereas relying solely on local details might lead to misclassification as "Building," "Trees," or "Road." Similarly, despite the similar brownish hues of the "Grass" scene in Fig. 1(b) and the "Field" scene in Fig. 1(c), they can be differentiated by local details, such as texture. Therefore, effectively combining global and local information is critical for improving classification performance.

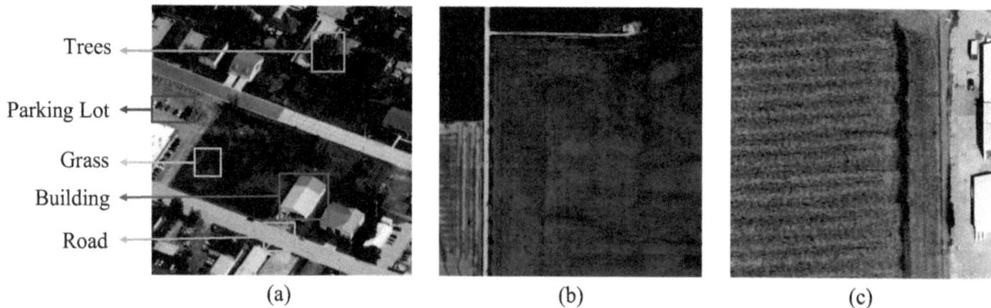

Fig. 1. Illustration of key challenges in RSSC using scenes from the RSSCN7 dataset. (a) A "Grass" scene with multiple land-cover types (grass, trees, parking lot, building and road), highlighting the challenge of single-label classification. (b) Another "Grass" scene, more uniform but differing from (a) in texture and context, demonstrating intra-class variability. (c) A "Field" scene, visually similar to (b) in color and structure despite a different label, illustrating inter-class similarity.

Visual attention, inspired by human perception, enables deep neural networks to extract key features from complex RSSC scenes, boosting classification accuracy by focusing on critical regions and suppressing irrelevant information. Early channel attention, pioneered by SENet [12], employs global pooling to recalibrate feature importance, establishing a foundation for adaptive feature weighting. Building on this, CBAM [13] integrates spatial attention in a channel-then-spatial sequence, significantly enhancing performance in RSSC task. Inspired by CBAM, Chen et al. [14] proposed the

Multi-Branch Local Attention Network (MBLANet), which introduces the Convolutional Local Attention Module (CLAM). This module employs parallel global and local attention branches, fused through element-wise multiplication, to effectively capture both global contextual information and local detailed features while prioritizing relevant regions and suppressing irrelevant ones. By embedding the CLAM module into all down-sampling and residual blocks of a ResNet backbone, MBLANet achieves superior classification performance in RSSC. To further enhance RSSC accuracy, Miao et al. [15] proposed the Multi-Scale Local Attention Network (MSLANet), which builds on MBLANet [14] by incorporating multi-scale feature extraction. MSLANet employs multiple convolutional kernels of varying sizes in both global and local attention branches, enhancing the representational capacity of features. The resulting global and local features are fused through element-wise multiplication, further improving classification accuracy.

Despite the good results of [14, 15], two critical limitations persist. First, existing approaches often rely on fixed fusion strategies, such as element-wise multiplication or concatenation, which struggle to effectively balance global and local features. This can lead to the loss of critical information, ultimately degrading classification performance. Second, embedding attention modules uniformly across all stages of the backbone network overlooks the varying effectiveness of attention mechanisms at different stages. This non-selective placement increases computational complexity and heightens the risk of overfitting, particularly with limited training data.

Drawing from the above discussion, an effective RSSC model should capture both global contextual information and local detailed features from RS images, seamlessly integrating them while mitigating the impact of irrelevant information. Motivated by the challenges of multi-land-cover scenes and intra-/inter-class variability, which often lead to misclassification in existing methods due to their limited ability to balance global and local information, this study aims to develop an innovative approach that adaptively integrates these features and suppress irrelevant information to achieve robust and accurate classification in RSSC. To this end, we propose the Global Local Dynamic Attention Network (GLDAN), a novel framework designed to enhance critical feature extraction. The core of GLDAN is the Global Local Dynamic Attention Module (GLDAM), which comprises three components: the Global Attention Module (GAM) for capturing scene context, the Multi-scale Local Attention Module (MLAM) for extracting detailed features, and the Spatial-Channel Attention Fusion Module (SCAFM), which dynamically fuses global and local features rather than relying on simple concatenation or multiplication [15]. GLDAM is strategically integrated at the last bottleneck of a selected ResNet50 stage 1. This targeted placement minimizes computational complexity while maximizing the focus on critical detailed information.

2 Methodology

The proposed GLDAN framework, shown in Fig. 2. Centers on GLDAM, consists of three components: GAM, MLAM, and SCAFM. First, GAM employs lightweight channel and spatial attention mechanisms to capture high-level semantic context, effectively modeling the global structure of complex scenes. Then, the MLAM utilizes depth-wise separable convolutions with 3×3 and 5×5 kernels to extract fine-grained, multi-scale details, addressing diversity within scene categories. Finally, the SCAFM dynamically integrates global and local features by assigning adaptive weights through combined channel-wise and spatial attention, followed by a weighted summation to balance their contributions. Notably, the GLDAM is selectively integrated only into the final bottleneck of ResNet50 stage 1, as this placement optimally balances feature extraction and computational efficiency, with the rationale supported by comprehensive ablation studies (see Sect. 3.4).

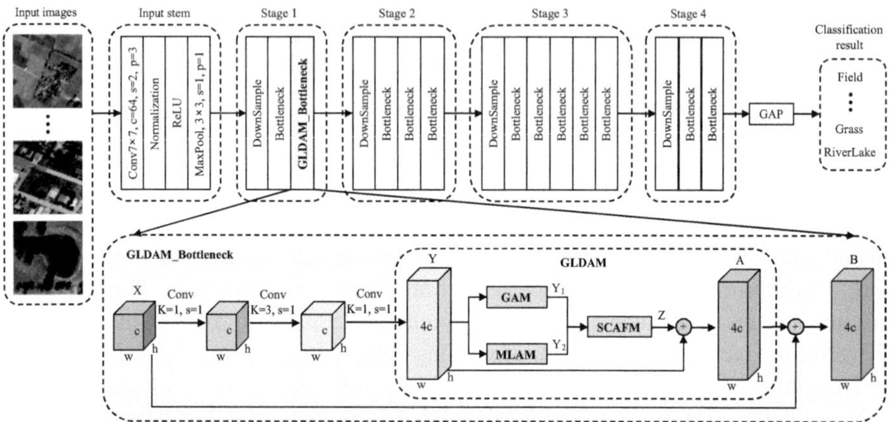

Fig. 2. Overview of the proposed GLDAN framework. At its core lies the GLDAM, which is strategically only embedded in the final bottleneck of the stage 1 within the ResNet50 backbone. This module consists of three components: GAM, MLAM, and SCAFM.

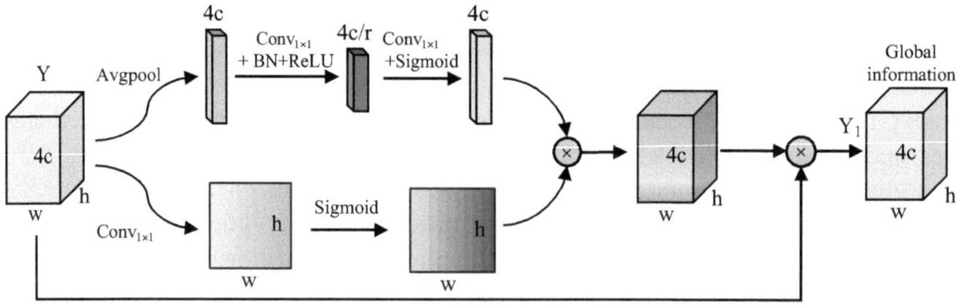

Fig. 3. Illustration of the proposed GAM.

2.1 Global Attention Module (GAM)

GAM integrates channel and spatial attention to emphasize key global features and suppress irrelevant noise in global features. As shown in Fig. 3, GAM processes an input feature map Y through parallel channel and spatial attention branches to produce an output feature map Y_1. In the channel attention branch, Y undergoes global average pooling, followed by two 1×1 convolutions: the first reduces the channels from 4c to 4c/r (where r is the compression ratio; through experiments, we found that setting the compression ratio r to 8 yields optimal results), with BN and ReLU; the second restores channels, with Sigmoid activation to generate the channel attention map Y_C:

$$Y_C = \text{Sigmoid}(\text{Conv}_{1\times1}(\text{ReLU}(\text{BN}(\text{Conv}_{1\times1}(\text{Avgpool}(Y)))))) \tag{1}$$

where Avgpool is global average pooling operation, $\text{Conv}_{1\times1}$ refers to the 1×1 convolutions, and BN denotes batch normalization.

In the spatial attention branch, Y is processed by a 1×1 convolution, followed by Sigmoid, produces spatial attention map Y_S:

$$Y_S = \text{Sigmoid}(\text{Conv}_{1\times1}(Y)) \tag{2}$$

Y_S and Y_C are combined via element-wise multiplication to produce attention weights, which are then multiplied with Y to yield the final output Y_1:

$$Y_1 = Y \times (Y_C \times Y_S) \tag{3}$$

where $\times$ denotes element-wise multiplication.

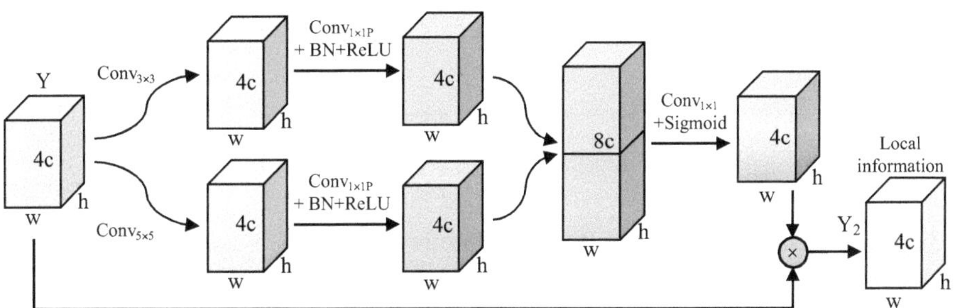

Fig. 4. Illustration of the proposed MLAM.

2.2 Multi-scale Local Attention Module (MLAM)

MLAM is shown in Fig. 4, complements GAM by capturing fine-grained local details across multiple scales in remote sensing scenes, enhancing complex spatial patterns and textures. MLAM processes input feature map Y via two parallel branches, applying 3×3 and 5×5 depthwise convolutions, each followed by a 1×1 pointwise convolution,BN, andReLU, to extract multi-scale local features. The resulting feature maps, each with 4c channels, are concatenated into an $8c \times h \times w$ feature map, processed by a 1×1 convolution and Sigmoid to generate a multi-scale local attention map. This map is multiplied element-wise with Y to produce output Y_2, integrating multi-scale local information. The process is expressed as:

$$Y_{3\times3} = \text{ReLU}(\text{BN}(\text{Conv}_{1\times1P}(\text{Conv}_{3\times3}(Y)))) \tag{4}$$

$$Y_{5\times5} = \text{ReLU}(\text{BN}(\text{Conv}_{1\times1P}(\text{Conv}_{5\times5}(Y)))) \tag{5}$$

$$Y_2 = Y \times \text{Sigmoid}(\text{Conv}_{1\times1}((Y_{3\times3}UY_{5\times5}))) \tag{6}$$

where $\text{Conv}_{3\times3}$ and $\text{Conv}_{5\times5}$ represent the depthwise convolutions with kernel sizes 3 × 3 and 5 × 5 respectively, U denotes channel-wise concatenation, $\text{Conv}_{1\times1P}$ refers to 1 × 1 pointwise convolution, and $\text{Conv}_{1\times1}$ refers to 1 × 1convolution.

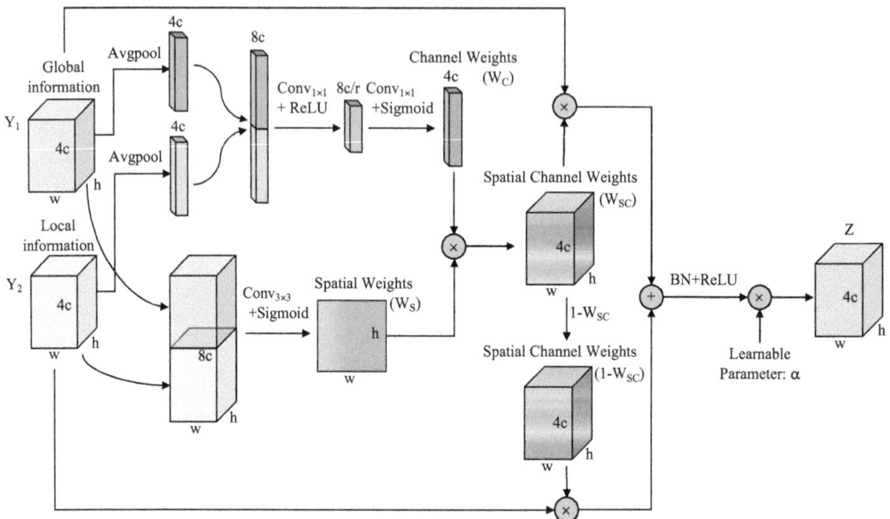

Fig. 5. Illustration of the proposed SCAFM.

2.3 Spatial-Channel Attention Fusion Module (SCAFM)

SCAFM, shown in Fig. 5 fuses global features from GAM and local details from MLAM to create a balanced feature representation. By dynamically weighting these features, SCAFM enhances key scene information. SCAFM takes the feature maps $Y_1 \in R^{h\times w\times 4c}$ from GAM and $Y_2 \in R^{h\times w\times 4c}$ from MLAM as inputs and produces a fused feature map $Z \in R^{h\times w\times 4c}$. The fusion process uses both channel and spatial attention to balance global and local information. For channel attention, Y_1 and Y_2 are processed by global average pooling, concatenation, 1 × 1 convolution, ReLU, and another 1 × 1 convolution with Sigmoid to produce the channel attention map W_C:

$$W_C = \text{Sigmoid}(\text{Conv}_{1\times1}(\text{ReLU}(\text{Conv}_{1\times1}(\text{Avgpool}(Y_1) \text{ U Avgpool}(Y_2))))) \tag{7}$$

For spatial attention, Y_1 and Y_2 are concatenated, processed by 3 × 3 convolution and Sigmoid to produce the spatial attention map W_S:

$$W_S = \text{Sigmoid}(\text{Conv}_{3\times3}(Y_1 U\ Y_2)) \tag{8}$$

The channel and spatial attention maps are combined via element-wise multiplication to form the final attention weight W_{SC}:

$$W_{SC} = W_S \times W_C \tag{9}$$

The fused feature map Z is computed by first combining Y_1 and Y_2 with the attention weights, followed by batch normalization (BN) and ReLU activation. The result is then scaled by a learnable parameter α:

$$Z = ReLU(BN(Y_1 \times W_{SC} + Y_2 \times (1 - W_{SC})))\alpha \tag{10}$$

3 Experiments

3.1 Dataset Introduction

To evaluate the GLDAN framework, we used two public remote sensing scene classification datasets: RSSCN7 [16] and SIRI-WHU [17].

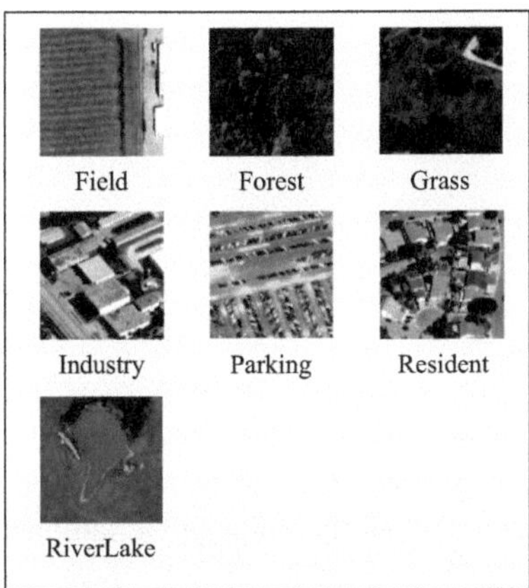

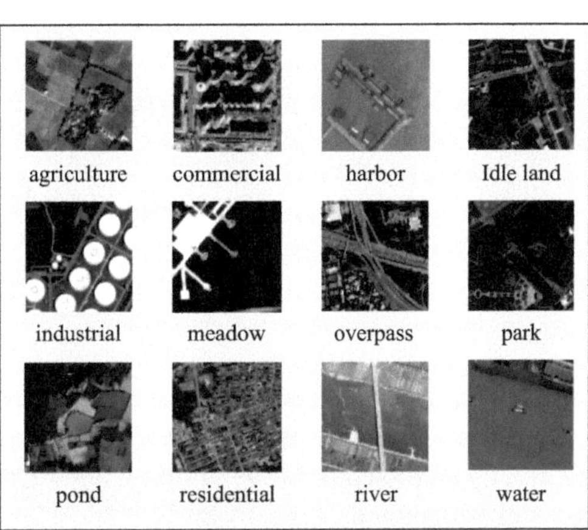

Fig. 6. Examples of the RSSCN7 dataset (left) and SIRI-WHU dataset (right).

1) RSSCN7 Dataset: Introduced by Zou et al. [16], RSSCN7 includes 2800 images across seven categories (Field, Forest, Grass, Industry, Parking, Resident, River-Lake), with 400 images per category at 400 × 400 pixels. Sourced from Google Earth at four scales, it features diverse seasons and weather, posing classification challenges. Sample images are shown on the left of Fig. 6. We split 80% of images per category for training and 20% for testing.

2) SIRI-WHU Dataset: Proposed by Zhao et al. [17], SIRI-WHU contains 2400 images across 12 urban land-use categories (agriculture, commercial, harbor, idle land, industrial, meadow, overpass, park, pond, residential, river, and water), each with 200 images at 200 × 200 pixels and 2-m resolution from Google Earth. Its varied urban scenes test model robustness. Sample images are shown on the right of Fig. 6. We used 80% of images per category for training and 20% for testing.

3.2 Experimental Settings

All experiments were conducted on a workstation equipped with a single NVIDIA Quadro RTX 6000 GPU, using the PyTorch [18] platform with a version of 1.10.1. The ResNet50 backbone of the proposed GLDAN was initialized with ImageNet-pretrained weights [19], while other components are randomly initialized. The AdamW [20] optimizer was employed with an initial learning rate of 0.0001, a batch size of 128, and 100 training epochs. A linear warm-up was applied for the first five epochs, scaling the learning rate from 0.000001 to 0.0001, followed by a cosine decay schedule with a minimum learning rate of 0.000001. To enhance model robustness, a comprehensive data augmentation pipeline was utilized, including Random Resized Crop, Random Flip, Rand Augment, Color Jitter, Random Rotation, and Random Erasing. All RS scenes were resized to 224×224 before input to the model. Performance evaluation was conducted using overall accuracy (OA), precision (Pre), recall (Rec), and F1-score (F1) as metrics, with confusion matrices providing category-specific insights. These metrics are defined as follows:

$$OA = \frac{T_P + T_N}{T_P + T_N + F_P + F_N} \tag{11}$$

$$Pre = \frac{T_P}{T_P + F_P} \tag{12}$$

$$Rec = \frac{T_P}{T_P + F_N} \tag{13}$$

$$F1 = \frac{2 \times T_P}{2 \times T_P + F_P + F_N} \tag{14}$$

where TP represents the number of correctly predicted positive samples, FN denotes the number of positive samples incorrectly predicted as negative, TN indicates the number of correctly predicted negative samples, and FP refers to the number of negative samples incorrectly predicted as positive.

3.3 Comparisons of State-of-the-Art Models

To evaluate the proposed GLDAN framework, we compared it with ten state-of-the-art methods for RSSC: EfficientNetV2 [21], ViT [22], Swin Transformer [23], BotNet [24], CoAtNet [25], ConvNeXt [26], PoolFormer [27], CMT [28], VAN [29], and ADC-CPANet [30]. These methods encompass convolutional networks (EfficientNetV2, ConvNeXt), Transformer-based models (ViT, Swin Transformer, PoolFormer), hybrid architectures (BotNet, CMT, CoAtNet, VAN), and an RSSC-specific model (ADC-CPANet). EfficientNetV2 uses compound scaling for efficiency, ConvNeXt modernizes convolutional designs, ViT and Swin Transformer capture long-range dependencies via self-attention, PoolFormer simplifies Transformer architecture with pooling operations, and hybrid models integrate local and global feature extraction.

For fair comparison, all models were evaluated on the RSSCN7 and SIRI-WHU datasets with images resized to 224×224, as described in Sect. 3.2. Each model was implemented using its public codebase and original hyperparameters to ensure optimal performance. The evaluation metrics, including overall accuracy (OA), precision (Pre), recall (Rec), and F1-score (F1), are detailed in Sect. 3.2.

Table 1 shows that the proposed GLDAN achieves superior performance across all metrics on the RSSCN7 and SIRI-WHU datasets, outperforming ten existing methods by 2–4% in accuracy, despite a moderate parameter count (23.84M) and FLOPs (4.981G). This validates its effectiveness in RSSC. In contrast, existing methods are constrained by their architectures. For instance, ViT [22] relies on self-attention to model global dependencies but struggles with local feature extraction, which is crucial for capturing the intricate spatial patterns in RSSC datasets. Additionally, as noted by ADC-CPANet [30], ViT performs optimally on large datasets but exhibits reduced accuracy on smaller datasets like RSSCN7 and SIRI-WHU, limiting its generalization in such contexts. ADC-CPANet [30], despite its lightweight design with ADC and CPA modules to capture local and global features, employs a sequential strategy that processes local features before global ones. This may lead to suboptimal feature integration, limiting its ability to handle complex RS scenes. Conversely, GLDAN stands out due to two novel strategies. First, it uses a dynamic fusion approach to balance local and global features. Second, it places attention modules only in key ResNet50 bottlenecks, improving efficiency without sacrificing performance. These innovations enable GLDAN to outperform other methods while addressing multiple land-cover types, intra-class variability, and inter-class similarity in RSSC.

Table 1. OA, Pre, Rec, F1 (%), Params (M) and FLOPs (G) comparison of GLDAN and state-of-the-art methods on RSSCN7 and SIRI-WHU datasets. Best values are in bold.

Methods	RSSCN7 Dataset				SIRI-WHU Dataset				Params/M	FLOPs/G
	OA	Pre	Rec	F1	OA	Pre	Rec	F1		
EfficientNetV2	94.29	94.31	94.27	94.29	95.21	95.29	95.21	95.19	21.46	2.874
ViT	89.82	90.01	89.80	89.79	89.38	89.68	89.38	89.35	86.38	16.849
SwinTransformer	93.75	93.80	93.76	93.74	94.79	95.00	94.79	94.79	28.24	4.351
BotNet	94.11	94.41	94.10	94.14	90.00	90.19	90.00	90.03	20.85	3.998
CoAtNet	95.54	95.63	95.51	95.50	95.83	95.97	95.83	95.86	17.75	3.321
ConvNeXt	91.61	91.76	91.61	91.59	91.04	91.21	91.04	91.00	27.81	4.457
PoolFormer	92.86	92.93	92.87	92.86	93.75	93.85	93.75	93.75	11.89	1.819
CMT	93.75	93.87	93.74	93.74	94.79	94.91	94.79	94.77	9.44	1.212
VAN	94.11	94.23	94.11	94.10	95.00	95.07	95.00	94.99	3.85	**0.880**
ADC-CPANet	96.43	96.53	96.43	96.46	96.04	96.02	96.04	96.02	**3.73**	2.058
GLDAN (Ours)	**98.75**	**98.76**	**98.75**	**98.75**	**98.54**	**98.59**	**98.54**	**98.54**	23.84	4.981

Furthermore, we analyzed the class-specific performance of GLDAN using confusion matrices, as shown in Fig. 7(a) for RSSCN7 and Fig. 7(b) for SIRI-WHU, respectively. Rows represent actual labels, columns indicate predicted labels, with diagonal values denoting correct classifications and off-diagonal values indicating misclassifications. On RSSCN7, GLDAN achieves over 98% accuracy for Forest, Grass, Parking,

Resident, and River-Lake categories, demonstrating robust classification despite the presence of multiple land-cover types within scenes. On SIRI-WHU, GLDAN attains 100% accuracy for Agriculture, Harbor, Idle Land, Overpass, Residential, River, and Water categories, showcasing its ability to handle intra-class variability and inter-class similarity. The Park category is misclassified as Meadow at 7%, attributed to shared vegetational cover and seasonal variations. This outstanding performance showcases GLDAN ability to excel in RSSC by leveraging integrated global and multi-scale local features, ensuring high accuracy and minimal misclassification across diverse land-cover types.

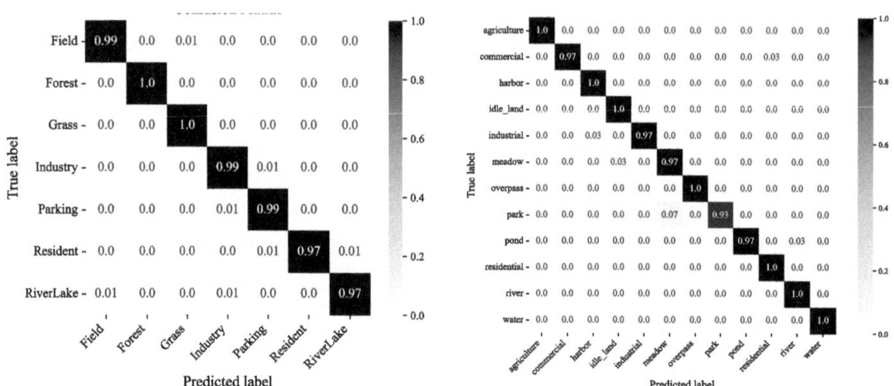

Fig. 7. Confusion matrices of GLDAN for RSSC on RSSCN7 (left) and SIRI-WHU (right).

3.4 Ablation Study

To validate the effectiveness of our GLDAN, ablation experiments were conducted with three objectives: (1) determine the optimal placement of GLDAM in the ResNet50 backbone, (2) to assess the impact of the compression ratio (r) in GLDAM, and (3) to evaluate the contributions of its core components, namely the GAM, MLAM, and SCAFM. Experiments were performed on the RSSCN7 and SIRI-WHU datasets.

Firstly, Optimal GLDAM Placement. To identify the optimal integration of GLDAM within the ResNet50 backbone, we positioned it at the last bottleneck of each stage, as this bottleneck captures the richest feature representations compared to earlier ones within the same stage. Also, to assess the impact of incorporating GLDAM into the last bottleneck of all stages. To this end, the following networks were designed:

0) Net-0: ResNet50 (Baseline);
1) Net-1: ResNet50 with GLDAM integrated at the last bottleneck of stage 1;
2) Net-2: ResNet50 with GLDAM integrated at the last bottleneck of stage 2;
3) Net-3: ResNet50 with GLDAM integrated at the last bottleneck of stage 3;
4) Net-4: ResNet50 with GLDAM integrated at the last bottleneck of stage 4;
5) Net-5: ResNet50 with GLDAM integrated at the last bottleneck of all stages.

Net-0 is ResNet50. For Net-1 to Net-4, GLDAM is only integrated into the last bottleneck of the corresponding stage of ResNet50 (ResNet50 has four stages), respectively, while for Net-5, GLDAM is incorporated into the last bottleneck of all stages.

As presented in Table 2, Net-1 achieves the highest performance across all metrics on the RSSCN7 and SIRI-WHU datasets, while maintaining a modest parameter count (23.84M) and FLOPs (4.981G) compared to Net-5 (49.51M parameters, 7.495G FLOPs). This effectiveness arises because, at ResNet50 stage 1, feature maps retain distinct object-specific details, such as textures of diverse land-cover types, which gradually disappear as convolutional layers deepen [9]. Placing GLDAM here allows its parallel local and global attention to capture and fuse these detailed features with scene context, effectively addressing intra-class variability and inter-class similarity. In contrast, later stages (Net-2 to Net-4) or all stages (Net-5) process more abstract features, where objects are less distinct, reducing GLDAM's impact and increasing computational overhead. Thus, stage 1 placement optimally balances accuracy and efficiency for RSSC tasks.

Table 2. Performance of GLDAM Placement Options on the RSSCN7 and SIRI-WHU datasets. The best values are highlighted in bold.

Networks	RSSCN7 Dataset				SIRI-WHU Dataset				Params/M	FLOPs/G
	OA	Pre	Rec	F1	OA	Pre	Rec	F1		
Net-0	98.39	98.40	98.39	98.39	98.16	98.19	98.13	98.13	**23.52**	**4.109**
Net-1	**98.75**	**98.76**	**98.75**	**98.75**	**98.54**	**98.59**	**98.54**	**98.54**	23.84	4.981
Net-2	98.39	98.41	98.39	98.39	98.16	98.18	98.13	98.12	24.77	4.957
Net-3	98.39	98.41	98.39	98.40	98.33	98.36	98.33	98.33	28.43	4.945
Net-4	98.21	98.24	98.21	98.22	98.33	98.39	98.33	98.33	43.04	4.940
Net-5	98.57	98.58	98.57	98.57	98.33	98.39	98.33	98.33	49.51	7.495

Secondly, Impact of Compression Ratio (r). As described in Sect. 2.1 and Sect. 2.3, the compression ratio (r) is utilized by both GAM and SCAFM. To evaluate its impact on performance, the compression ratio was varied across the values $\{2, 4, 8, 16, 32\}$ with GLDAM fixed at the last bottleneck of stage 1 in ResNet50 (Net-1). Experiments were conducted on the RSSCN7 and SIRI-WHU datasets to assess the trade-offs between classification accuracy and computational efficiency.

As presented in Table 3, a compression ratio of $r = 8$ achieves the highest performance, with an OA of 98.75% on the RSSCN7 dataset and 98.54% on the SIRI-WHU dataset, alongside consistently high precision, recall, and F1-scores. Higher compression ratios ($r = 16$ and 32) yield comparable accuracy but provide no additional benefits, indicating that $r = 8$ optimally balances classification accuracy and computational efficiency.

Table 3. Performance of GLDAM with Different Compression Ratios (r) on the RSSCN7 and SIRI-WHU datasets. The best values are highlighted in bold.

Values of r	RSSCN7 Dataset				SIRI-WHU Dataset			
	OA	Pre	Rec	F1	OA	Pre	Rec	F1
2	98.21	98.23	98.21	98.2	98.16	98.14	98.13	98.12
4	98.39	98.42	98.39	98.39	98.33	98.37	98.33	98.33
8	**98.75**	**98.76**	**98.75**	**98.75**	**98.54**	**98.59**	**98.54**	**98.54**
16	98.39	98.41	98.39	98.4	98.54	98.55	98.54	98.53
32	98.39	98.43	98.39	98.4	98.16	98.19	98.13	98.13

Thirdly, Effectiveness of Different Modules. To assess the contributions of GAM, MLAM, and SCAFM, their impact was evaluated using GLDAM at the last bottleneck of stage 1 in ResNet50 (Net-1, $r = 8$). To this end, the following models were designed:

1) Model-0: ResNet50 (Baseline);
2) Model-1: GLDAM (only GAM);
3) Model-2: GLDAM (only MLAM);
4) Model-3: GLDAM (without SCAFM);
5) Model-4: GLDAM.

As shown in Table 4. Model-1 employs GAM to capture global context information for classification. However, its performance is slightly lower than that of the baseline, indicating that relying solely on GAM is less effective, likely due to its limited ability to capture fine-grained local details critical for complex classification tasks. Model-2 utilizes MLAM to extract detailed local features at multiple scales to perform classification, demonstrating a positive contribution by effectively capturing intricate patterns, resulting in improved performance over Model-1. Model-3 integrates global context information and multi-scale local features by replacing the SCAFM with concatenation followed by a 1×1 convolution to achieve classification, but its performance is suboptimal compared to other models, likely due to the simplistic nature of concatenation, which fails to adequately balance global and local feature representations. In contrast, Model-4 combines global context and multi-scale local features through SCAFM, achieving the highest performance. This demonstrates the effectiveness of SCAFM in dynamically fusing GAM and MLAM, outperforming the simple concatenation approach in Model-3. Overall, Model-4 (GLDAM) represents the optimal configuration, highlighting the superiority of dynamic feature fusion for classification tasks.

Table 4. Performance of GLDAM Component Variations on the RSSCN7 and SIRI-WHU Datasets. The best values are highlighted in bold.

Models	RSSCN7 Dataset				SIRI-WHU Dataset			
	OA	Pre	Rec	F1	OA	Pre	Rec	F1
Model-0	98.39	98.40	98.39	98.39	98.16	98.19	98.13	98.13
Model-1	98.04	98.07	98.04	98.04	98.16	98.15	98.13	98.12
Model-2	98.57	98.6	98.57	98.57	98.16	98.20	98.13	98.13
Model-3	98.04	98.04	98.04	98.03	97.92	98.01	97.92	97.92
Model-4	**98.75**	**98.76**	**98.75**	**98.75**	**98.54**	**98.59**	**98.54**	**98.54**

Finally, we provided visualizations for each ablation experiment, as shown in Fig. 8. These heatmaps illustrate the focus areas of different models. Model-4 is the proposed GLDAN. Using the "Field" sample as an example, the attention area of Model-4 precisely targets the broadest expanse of the field in the image. In contrast, Model-0 exhibits a more dispersed attention area, primarily focusing on image edges. Model-1, relying on GAM, shows insufficient focus on local details, missing fine-grained features. Model-2, utilizing MLAM, emphasizes varied detailed regions of the field. Model-3, employing concatenation and 1×1 convolution for feature fusion, results in scattered attention areas due to ineffective integration of global and local features. Overall, Model-4 (GLDAN) outperforms others, demonstrating the efficacy of SCAFM in dynamically fusing features for precise attention allocation.

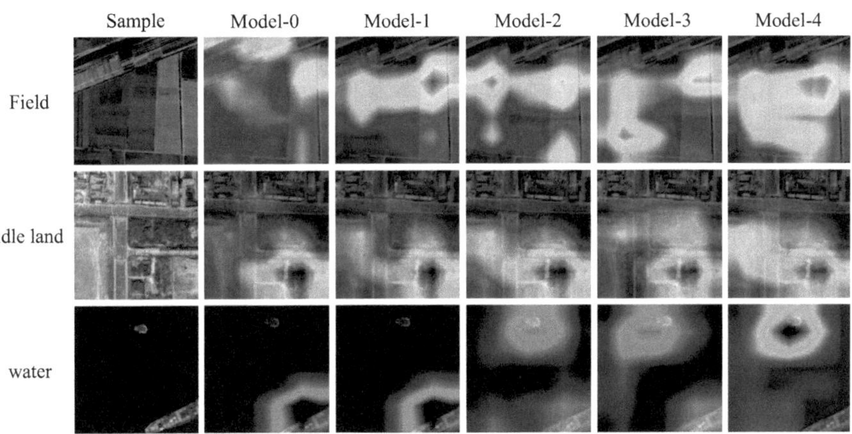

Fig. 8. Heat map visualization results of Model-0 to Model-4.

4 Conclusion

This study presents GLDAN, a novel framework addressing RSSC challenges like intra-class variability, inter-class similarity, and complex land-cover types. Its core, GLDAM, integrates GAM, MLAM, and SCAFM to effectively balance global and local information, enhancing key image features while minimizing background interference. Experiments on RSSCN7 and SIRI-WHU datasets show GLDAN achieves 98.75% and 98.54% overall accuracy, respectively. Ablation studies confirm the value of GAM, MLAM, and SCAFM, with the placement of GLDAM in ResNet50 stage 1 last bottleneck optimizing accuracy and efficiency. Future work will explore integrating Transformer into GLDAM to enhance long-range dependency modeling for RSSC.

References

1. Yu, J., Zeng, P., Yu, Y., Yu, H., Huang, L., Zhou, D.: A combined convolutional neural network for urban land-use classification with GIS data. Remote Sens. **14**, 1128 (2022)
2. Cheng, G., Xie, X., Han, J., Guo, L., Xia, G.-S.: Remote sensing image scene classification meets deep learning: challenges, methods, benchmarks, and opportunities. IEEE J. Sel. Top. Appl. Earth Obs. Remote Sens. **13**, 3735–3756 (2020)
3. Mishra, N.B., Crews, K.A.: Mapping vegetation morphology types in a dry savanna ecosystem: integrating hierarchical object-based image analysis with random forest. Int. J. Remote Sens. **35**, 1175–1198 (2014)
4. Han, W., et al.: A survey of machine learning and deep learning in remote sensing of geological environment: challenges, advances, and opportunities. ISPRS J. Photogramm. Remote Sens. **202**, 87–113 (2023)
5. Anwer, R.M., Khan, F.S., Van De Weijer, J., Molinier, M., Laaksonen, J.: Binary patterns encoded convolutional neural networks for texture recognition and remote sensing scene classification. ISPRS J. Photogramm. Remote Sens. **138**, 74–85 (2018)
6. Li, H., Gu, H., Han, Y., Yang, J.: Object-oriented classification of high-resolution remote sensing imagery based on an improved colour structure code and a support vector machine. Int. J. Remote Sens. **31**, 1453–1470 (2010)
7. Cortes, C., Vapnik, V.: Support-vector networks. Mach. Learn. **20**, 273–297 (1995)
8. Breiman, L.: Random forests. Mach. Learn. **45**, 5–32 (2001)
9. Ma, J., Jiang, W., Tang, X., Zhang, X., Liu, F., Jiao, L.: Multiscale sparse cross-attention network for remote sensing scene classification. IEEE Trans. Geosci. Remote Sens. **63**, 1–16 (2025)
10. Guo, N., Jiang, M., Gao, L., Tang, Y., Han, J., Chen, X.: CRABR-Net: a contextual relational attention-based recognition network for remote sensing scene objective. Sensors. **23**, 7514 (2023)
11. Wang, X., Duan, L., Ning, C., Zhou, H.: Relation-Attention Networks for Remote Sensing Scene Classification. IEEE J. Sel. Top. Appl. Earth Obs. Remote Sens. **15**, 422–439 (2022)
12. Hu, J., Shen, L., Albanie, S., Sun, G., Wu, E.: Squeeze-and-Excitation Networks. IEEE Trans. Pattern Anal. Mach. Intell. **42**, 2011–2023 (2020)
13. Woo, S., Park, J., Lee, J.-Y., Kweon, I.S.: CBAM: Convolutional Block Attention Module. In: Ferrari, V., Hebert, M., Sminchisescu, C., Weiss, Y. (eds.) Computer Vision – ECCV 2018, pp. 3–19. Springer International Publishing, Cham (2018). https://doi.org/10.1007/978-3-030-01234-2_1

14. Chen, S.-B., Wei, Q.-S., Wang, W.-Z., Tang, J., Luo, B., Wang, Z.-Y.: Remote sensing scene classification via multi-branch local attention network. IEEE Trans. Image Process. **31**, 99–109 (2022)
15. Miao, Y., Wang, J., Zhang, M., Xie, X., Li, W.: Remote sensing scene classification method based on multi-scale local attention network. In: Wang, Y., Huang, H. (eds.) Image and Graphics Technologies and Applications, pp. 1–15. Springer Nature Singapore, Singapore (2025). https://doi.org/10.1007/978-981-97-9919-0_1
16. Zou, Q., Ni, L., Zhang, T., Wang, Q.: Deep learning based feature selection for remote sensing scene classification. IEEE Geosci. Remote Sens. Lett. **12**, 2321–2325 (2015)
17. Zhao, B., Zhong, Y., Xia, G.-S., Zhang, L.: Dirichlet-derived multiple topic scene classification model for high spatial resolution remote sensing imagery. IEEE Trans. Geosci. Remote Sens. **54**, 2108–2123 (2016)
18. Paszke, A., et al.: PyTorch: an imperative style, high-performance deep learning library (2019). http://arxiv.org/abs/1912.01703
19. Krizhevsky, A., Sutskever, I., Hinton, G.E.: ImageNet classification with deep convolutional neural networks. Commun. ACM **60**, 84–90 (2017)
20. Loshchilov, I., Hutter, F.: Decoupled weight decay regularization (2019). http://arxiv.org/abs/1711.05101
21. Tan, M., Le, Q.V.: EfficientNetV2: smaller models and faster training (2021). http://arxiv.org/abs/2104.00298
22. Dosovitskiy, A., et al.: An image is worth 16x16 words: transformers for image recognition at scale (2021). http://arxiv.org/abs/2010.11929
23. Liu, Z., et al.: Swin transformer: hierarchical vision transformer using shifted windows (2021). http://arxiv.org/abs/2103.14030
24. Srinivas, A., Lin, T.-Y., Parmar, N., Shlens, J., Abbeel, P., Vaswani, A.: Bottleneck transformers for visual recognition (2021). http://arxiv.org/abs/2101.11605
25. Dai, Z., Liu, H., Le, Q.V., Tan, M.: CoAtNet: marrying convolution and attention for all data sizes (2021). http://arxiv.org/abs/2106.04803
26. Liu, Z., Mao, H., Wu, C.-Y., Feichtenhofer, C., Darrell, T., Xie, S.: A ConvNet for the 2020s (2022). http://arxiv.org/abs/2201.03545
27. Yu, W., et al.: MetaFormer is actually what you need for vision (2022). http://arxiv.org/abs/2111.11418
28. Guo, J., et al.: CMT: convolutional neural networks meet vision transformers (2022). http://arxiv.org/abs/2107.06263
29. Guo, M.-H., Lu, C.-Z., Liu, Z.-N., Cheng, M.-M., Hu, S.-M.: Visual attention network (2022). http://arxiv.org/abs/2202.09741
30. Wang, W., Li, X., Wang, X.: ADC-CPANet: a remote sensing image classification method based on local-global feature fusion. J. Remote Sens. **28**(10), 2661–2672 (2024). (in Chinese)

Multi-agent Deep Reinforcement Learning for Hyperspectral Feature Extraction

Jin Sun[1], Kun Tan[1,2(✉)], Xue Wang[1], and Xiaodao Wei[3,4]

[1] Key Laboratory of Geographic Information Science (Ministry of Education), East China Normal University, Shanghai 200241, China
`tankuncu@gmail.com`
[2] School of Geospatial Artificial Intelligence, East China Normal University, Shanghai 200241, China
[3] China Three Gorges Corporation, Wuhan 430010, China
[4] Shanghai Investigation, Design and Research Institute Co., Ltd., Shanghai 200335, China

Abstract. Hyperspectral image feature extraction plays a crucial role in reducing redundancy and correlation among spectral bands while preserving essential information. Knowledge-based feature extraction methods, such as spectral indices (SIs), leverage the interaction mechanisms between electromagnetic waves and materials to enhance the characteristic attributes of ground objects through band operations. These methods offer key advantages, including strong physical interpretability, simple construction, and robust cross-domain generalization. However, most existing SIs still rely on expert knowledge tailored to specific scenarios, leading to inherent limitations such as subjectivity, high time consumption, and implementation complexity. To address these challenges, this paper proposes a Hyperspectral Image Multi-Agent Deep Reinforcement Learning Feature Extraction algorithm (HMAFE), aiming to alleviate the burden of manual spectral index design for human experts. HMAFE employs a heuristic "generation-selection" strategy to simulate the decision-making process of domain experts. To accelerate exploration in high-dimensional action spaces, the model incorporates a multi-agent deep reinforcement learning (MADRL) framework. Experimental results demonstrate that the proposed method outperforms state-of-the-art feature selection and automated feature engineering (AutoFE) approaches in terms of both feature extraction efficiency and overall performance.

Keywords: Hyperspectral remote sensing · Multi-agent deep reinforcement learning · Spectral indices · Automatic feature engineering

1 Introduction

Since the 20th century, hyperspectral remote sensing technology has emerged as a transformative advancement in remote sensing science, distinguished by its ability to capture hundreds of continuous spectral bands for each image pixel [1, 2]. This capability provides highly detailed spectral information, enabling the technology to be widely adopted

© The Author(s), under exclusive license to Springer Nature Singapore Pte Ltd. 2026
Z. Lin et al. (Eds.): ICIG 2025, LNCS 16163, pp. 472–484, 2026.
https://doi.org/10.1007/978-981-95-3729-7_38

across diverse domains including mineral identification, water quality monitoring, precision agriculture, military reconnaissance, and estimation of soil physical and chemical properties [3–7]. Despite its strengths, hyperspectral remote sensing faces challenges due to the high dimensionality of its data. The redundancy and correlation among spectral bands can trigger the "Hughes" phenomenon [8]. To address this, dimensionality reduction processing is essential. By reducing the feature space while preserving critical information, these techniques ensure the effective analysis of hyperspectral imagery [9].

Dimensionality reduction in hyperspectral remote sensing imagery is typically achieved through two primary approaches: feature selection and feature extraction [10, 11]. Feature selection entails identifying and retaining the most relevant spectral bands while discarding those deemed less informative [12–15]. Although these methods successfully preserve the physical properties of the original bands, they often fail to account for complex spectral interactions, leading to potential information loss in feature representation.

In contrast, feature extraction employs mathematical transformations to project high-dimensional data into a lower-dimensional space, generating a new set of features. Unlike feature selection, which eliminates specific bands, the goal of feature extraction is to summarize the information while suppressing less relevant information. Traditional feature extraction techniques, such as Principal Component Analysis (PCA) [16], Independent Component Analysis (ICA) [17], and Linear Discriminant Analysis (LDA) [18], were widely utilized for this purpose. However, a key limitation of these methods is their inability to retain the physical meaning of the original features, potentially disrupting their inherent structure during the transformation process.

Knowledge-based feature extraction, also known as spectral indices (SIs), emphasizes the attributes of objects through operations like band ratios, based on the interaction mechanisms between electromagnetic waves and materials. Currently, hundreds of different SIs have been proposed across various application fields, including agricultural management [19], fire detection [20], urban planning [21], and ecological environment assessment [22], with this number continually increasing. Among these, the most renowned and widely used spectral index is the Normalized Difference Vegetation Index (NDVI) [23], which is typically employed to assess the greenness of vegetation spatially and temporally. Other commonly used spectral indices include the Leaf Area Index (LAI) [24], the Remote Sensing Ecological Index (RSEI) [25] and *et al*. SIs offer several advantages: (1) Strong physical interpretability: The design of SIs is typically based on the physical relationships between the spectral absorption of surface features and biochemical parameters. (2) Simplicity in construction: SIs effectively avoid the interference of data redundancy from the full spectral range, thus enhancing feature representation. (3) Strong cross-scenario generalization: SIs rely only on operations involving specific spectral bands, without the need for complex model training or large amounts of labeled data, which enhances their applicability across different scenarios. Although SIs possess the aforementioned advantages, most existing SIs still rely on expert judgment tailored to specific scenarios, rendering them highly subjective, time-consuming, and challenging to implement.

In recent years, Automated Feature Extraction (AutoFE) methods, which can automatically generate effective features without human intervention, have already been widely adopted in the processing of tabular data (also known as structured data). AutoFE formalizes feature construction as the application of transformations to original features, with the objective of enhancing the performance of predictive models by extracting new, informative features from the base data. Numerous automated feature generation methods have been proposed for feature engineering in tabular datasets.

To address the aforementioned challenges, a novel automated feature extraction method named HMAFE is proposed to automatically design physically meaningful feature sets in conjunction with specific scene requirements. Thereby reducing the knowledge dependence on expert experience. HMAFE adopts a "generate-select" heuristic strategy to simulate the decision-making process of human experts. Separate Markov Decision Process models are designed for the generation and selection steps, respectively. In the generation step, the feature generation task is formalized as a fully cooperative multi-agent deep reinforcement learning (MADRL) problem. Specifically, N agents are constructed, each responsible for generating features from different spectral bands to map the input raw features into a set of candidate features. In the selection step, a feature selection strategy is devised; through iterative screening of the candidate feature set, the optimal feature subset is determined. Finally, spatial features are incorporated to further improve the performance of hyperspectral remote sensing information processing. The main contributions of this paper are summarized as follows:

- A hyperspectral image automatic feature extraction method based on MADRL is proposed, aiming to alleviate the burden of manual spectral index design for human experts.
- A heuristic "generation-selection" strategy is employed to mimic the decision-making process of human experts and design specialized DRL frameworks tailored to both the feature generation and selection steps. HMAFE incorporates a multi-agent deep reinforcement learning algorithm to accelerate the exploration process in a high-dimensional action space.
- Experimental results demonstrate that the proposed method outperforms state-of-the-art feature selection and AutoFE approaches in both feature extraction efficiency and performance.

2 Method

HMAFE employs a heuristic strategy of "generation-selection". The overview of the proposed HMAFE framework is shown in Fig. 1. Let D be a hyperspectral dataset, represented as $D = (X, Y)$, where $X = \{x_1, x_2 \ldots x_d\}$, $X \in \mathbb{R}^{n \times d}$ is a matrix of original hyperspectral data, with n rows (instances) and d columns (features), and Y is a vector of corresponding label values. The action sets, A_g and A_s, represent the sets of actions for the generation and selection steps, respectively. Given a classification algorithm L with fixed hyperparameters and a cross-validation metric E, in the generation step, the objective of HMAFE is illustrated in (1). Each original feature is associated with an agent that interacts with the environment iteratively. Each agent applies transformations based on the policy network to generate a new set of candidate features, which are subsequently input into the evaluation model. The evaluation model assesses these features and computes corresponding rewards, which are then relayed back to the agents for updating the policy network. This process is repeated iteratively until either a predefined threshold is reached or convergence is achieved.

$$A_g = \underset{A_g}{argmax}\ E(L(A_g(X), Y))$$ (1)

In the selection step, the objective of HMAFE is illustrated in (2). The feature selection task is modeled as a sequential decision-making problem, where the agent determines which features to select at each time step until an optimal subset of features is identified.

$$A_s = \underset{A_s}{argmax}\ E(L(A_s(A_g(X)), Y))$$ (2)

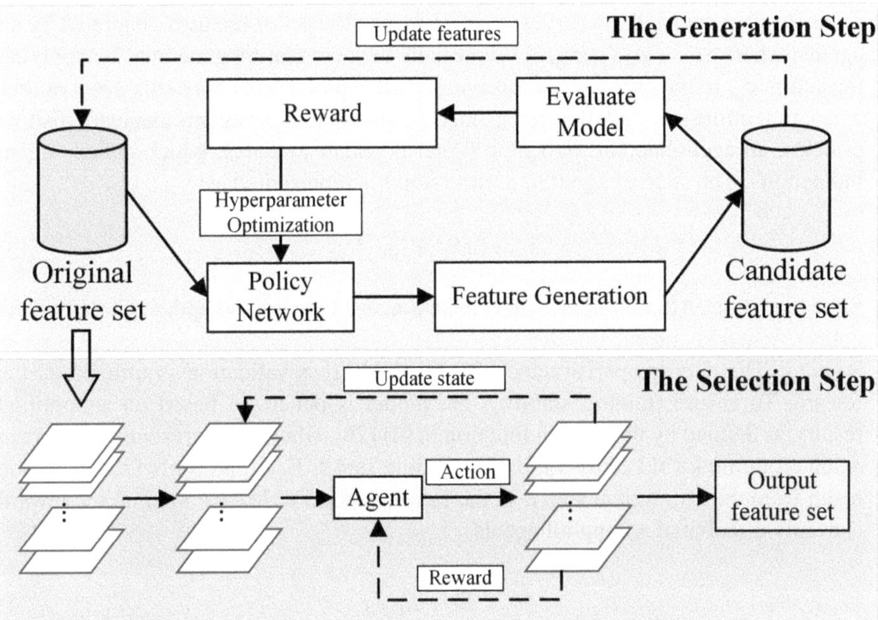

Fig. 1. Overview of the HMAFE framework. In the selection step, white indicates unselected features and pink indicates selected features.

2.1 The Generation Step

In the generation step, each agent focuses solely on exploring the optimal transformation rules for its corresponding original feature, effectively addressing the issue of feature explosion, which refers to the rapid and often unmanageable growth in the number of features resulting from combinatorial transformations, leading to increased computational cost, model overfitting, and diminished generalization performance. Specifically, the multi-agent feature extraction DRL is further modeled as a Markov decision process (MDP), which includes agents, action space, state, state transition and reward.

1) Agents: A multi-agent strategy is adopted to address the limitations of single-agent methods, which often suffer from large action spaces and a tendency to converge to local optima. Each original feature is associated with an individual agent, with the total number of agents equal to the total number of spectral features. This design facilitates a more effective exploration of the interactions among individual features. All agents share a single policy network, which guides the agents' actions based on the designed policy framework.

2) Action space: In HMAFE, operator transformations are employed to generate new features. Based on the number of features involved, operators are categorized as unary operators (logarithm, square, square root, and reciprocal) and binary operators (addition, subtraction, multiplication, and division). Additionally, the action set also includes the option of taking no action on the features. HMAFE can add other operators, depending on specific application requirements.

3) State: At time step t, $X_t = \{x_{1,t}, \cdots, x_{n,t}\}$ denote the set of features generated by all agents, where $x_{i,t} = a_{i,t-1}(x_{i,t-1})$ represents the new feature generated by applying the action $a_{i,t}$ to the original feature $x_{i,t-1}$. Each agent has access to the observations and action information of all other agents. To ensure that the agents can learn distinct policies, an agent-specific indicator signal is added to states, which called "agent indication". The state of agent n_i at time step t is represented as:

$$s_{i,t} = \{X_t, Y, x_{i,t}\} \tag{3}$$

4) State transition: After all agents take an action, the state will be updated based on the collective actions taken.

5) Reward: The average performance from k-fold cross-validation is utilized as the reward. To ensure training stability, the model is penalized based on suboptimal results, as defined by the reward function in (4) [26], where $\overline{E_t}$ represents the average result from the k-fold cross-validation at time step t, $E_{t,k}$ represents the evaluation result from the k-th fold at step t. In the fully cooperative MARL setting, the reward is evenly distributed among all agents.

$$R_t = \overline{E_t} + E_{t,diff} \tag{4}$$

$$E_{t,diff} = \sum_k \min\left(0, E_{t,k} - \overline{E_{t-1}}\right) \tag{5}$$

Moreover, a policy network is designed to guide the agents in action selection, as illustrated in Fig. 2. All agents are enabled to share a common policy network, which effectively reduces computational burden and memory requirements. This approach minimizes the complexity associated with maintaining individual policy networks for each agent, while simultaneously enhancing coordination and cooperation among the agents. Leveraging a shared policy network yields a more cohesive learning process, enabling agents to better align their actions in pursuit of collective objectives. The policy network comprises the following key components: 1) a layer normalization layer to stabilize the training of the neural network; 2) a Dimensionality Reduction Block that reduces the feature vector to a fixed length, enabling the network to handle varying sizes of feature sets while decreasing network complexity; 3) a Transformer Block that learns complex relationships among different features; and 4) an Operation Block followed by a softmax layer that maps the relevant information of features to corresponding action probabilities.

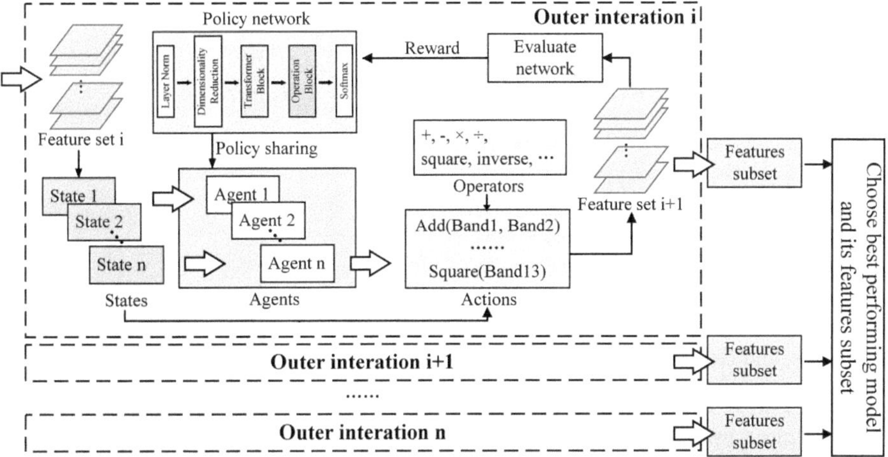

Fig. 2. Architecture of the generation step.

2.2 The Selection Step

After the generation step, a new set of candidate features $\widehat{X} = \{\hat{x}_1, \cdots, \hat{x}_n\}$ is obtained. The objective of the selection step is to further filter out the effective features from this candidate set. The selection step can be conceptualized as a sequential decision-making problem for an agent, where the agent must determine which features to select at different time steps until an optimal feature combination is identified. This problem is formulated as a Markov Decision Process (MDP), encompassing action space, state, state transition, and reward.

1) Action space: In our case, the action of the agent is to choose a feature at each time step. The policy of the agent determines which feature to choose.
2) State: $S_t = \{s_1, \cdots, s_n\}$ represent the current feature selection states at time step t, where $s_i = \{0,1\}$, $1 \leq i \leq n$. $s_i = 1$ represents that the i-th feature has been selected, while $s_i = 0$ represents that it is not selected.
3) State transition: At time step t, assuming the agent selects the i-th feature, donated as $a_t = i$, if the i-th feature has not been selected, the next state will be updated. Otherwise, the state remains unchanged. If the maximum number of selectable features has been reached, the action terminates. The state transition function is defined as follows:

$$S_{t+1} = \begin{cases} S_t & \textit{if } s_{a_t} = 1 \\ S_t + a_t & \textit{if } s_{a_t} = 0 \\ \textit{Terminal} & \textit{if } sum(S_t) = featurenum \end{cases} \tag{6}$$

4)Reward: At time step t, the number of selected features reaches the maximum limit, resulting in a new feature set $\tilde{X}$. The chosen subset of features is evaluated using the k-fold cross-validation. To prevent the agents from falling into a cycle of repetitive selections, a penalty factor α and a reward factor β are incorporated into the reward function. The reward function is defined as follows:

$$r_t = \begin{cases} \alpha & if\ s_{a_t} = 1 \\ \beta & if\ s_{a_t} = 0 \\ -(\overline{E}(\tilde{X}) - \overline{E}(\widehat{X})) & if\ sum(S_t) = featurenum \end{cases} \tag{7}$$

3 Experimental Results and Analysis

3.1 Data Description

In our experiments, we utilized three publicly available HSI datasets: Indian Pines, Pavia University, and Houston 2013. A detailed description of each dataset is provided below.

1) Indian Pines: The Indian pines dataset was collected in 1992 by an Airborne Visible/Infrared Imaging Spectrometer (AVIRIS) over a region in northwest Indiana. It consists of 145×145 pixels and 224 spectral bands, covering a wavelength range of 0.4–2.5 μm. After removing bands affected by water absorption, the number of usable spectral bands is reduced to 200. The dataset includes 16 different land-cover classes. In this study, 30% of the labeled samples were randomly selected as training data.
2) Pavia University: The Pavia University dataset was captured by the Reflective Optics System Imaging Spectrometer (ROSIS) over the University of Pavia in northern Italy. After removing 12 noisy bands, the dataset consists of 610×340 pixels and 103 spectral bands, covering a wavelength range of 430–860 nm. The spatial resolution is 1.3 m per pixel. The dataset includes nine land-cover classes. In this study, 30% of the labeled samples were randomly selected as training data.
3) Houston 2013: This dataset was initially utilized in the 2013 IEEE GRSS Data Fusion Contest. It consists of 349×1905 pixels and comprises 144 spectral bands, covering a wavelength range from 380 nm to 1050 nm. The data includes a total of 15 classes. To facilitate the training and testing process, 30% of the labeled samples were randomly selected for use as training data, while the remaining samples were reserved for testing purposes.

3.2 Experimental Settings

To validate the feature extraction capabilities of the proposed HMAFE algorithm, comparative experiments were conducted with eight different methods. These include five AutoFE algorithms and three deep reinforcement learning feature selection algorithms. Among them, the Random Method generates new features by randomly applying transformations to each original feature. AutoFeat [27] is a widely used AutoFE toolkit in Python that constructs features using an "expansion-reduction" framework. FETCH

[26] is a DRL-based end-to-end AutoFE framework that achieves state-of-the-art performance. DIFER [28] introduces a differentiable AutoFE method that utilizes an Encoder-Decoder framework, converting features into function strings at each step. NFS [29] is a DRL-based AutoFE method inspired by Neural Architecture Search (NAS), exploring the feature space with an RNN controller and automating the feature construction and selection process. In DRL feature selection methods, DRLBS [13] was the first to transform the feature selection problem of hyperspectral imagery into a DRL problem. RLSFR-cv [14] explores the inherent relationships between hyperspectral features by introducing two spectral feature evaluation methods. MH-DRL [15] proposes a multi-agent deep reinforcement learning-based approach, combined with Hybrid Teacher Guidance, to address the hyperspectral band selection problem.

The experiments were performed on a server equipped with an Nvidia GeForce RTX 4090 and an AMD Ryzen Threadripper PRO 5975WX with 32 cores. The proposed method was implemented using the Pytorch framework in Python.

In our experiments, all methods were optimized using five-fold cross-validation on the training set, and the final model performance was evaluated on the test set. Three metrics were employed for evaluation: Overall Accuracy (OA), Average Accuracy (AA), and the Kappa coefficient (Kappa). Classification assessments were conducted using Random Forest (RF). For the RF classifier, the number of decision trees was configured to 10, consistent with previous studies [26]. To ensure consistency, the same feature operators were utilized across the three AutoFE algorithms, with the maximum feature order set to 2. All methods were configured to use default parameters whenever possible. All methods, including HMAFE, utilized spatial features in the same manner, including mathematical morphology and gray-level co-occurrence matrix (GLCM).

In HMAFE, configured the training process for a total of 500 epochs, with the first 100 epochs designated for the generation step and the remaining 400 epochs for the selection step. During the generation step, the learning rate was set to 0.0001, the discount factor to 0.95, the parallel sampling size to 5, and the transformer parameters with $d_{model} = 128$, $n_{head} = 8$. In the selection step, the learning rate was adjusted to 0.001, the discount factor was set to 0.999, the reward coefficient for selecting new bands was set to 0.1, and the penalty coefficient for selecting duplicate bands was set to -0.1. Additionally, the number of parallel environments was established at 10.

3.3 Comparison with Other Methods

This section presents a detailed comparison of the overall accuracy, mean accuracy, and Kappa coefficient of various methods across three publicly available hyperspectral imaging (HSI) datasets: Indian Pines, Pavia University, and Houston 2013. Consistent with previous studies, set the final number of features to 60, 30, and 40, respectively, for these datasets [15]. It is noteworthy that the methods Random, AutoFeat, NFS, DIFER, and FETCH do not output a fixed number of features; instead, the final feature count is adaptively determined by the algorithms. As shown in Table 1, the performance of band selection methods is inferior to that of feature engineering algorithms. This discrepancy arises because band selection methods often eliminate a substantial number of bands, leading to significant information loss. The proposed HMAFE method exhibits superior performance across all datasets, substantiating the effectiveness of our approach.

Furthermore, as illustrated in Fig. 3, the visual classification results obtained from the Pavia University dataset demonstrate that the proposed HMAFE method yields more accurate classifications compared to its competitors.

Table 1. Classification results of different methods with three metrics on different datasets.

Datasets	Metrics	DRLBS	RLSFR-cv	MH-DRL	Random	AutoFeat	NFS	DIFER	FETCH	HMAFE
Indian Pines	OA(%)	79.40	79.19	79.99	83.23	80.17	84.64	81.34	83.21	**85.24**
	AA(%)	77.33	74.80	79.88	83.15	83.43	82.80	81.79	83.77	**86.76**
	Kappa × 100	76.34	76.10	77.05	80.80	77.25	82.40	78.61	80.75	**83.10**
Pavia University	OA(%)	91.52	90.63	91.45	93.11	92.81	94.15	93.20	94.59	**95.07**
	AA(%)	91.81	91.47	92.20	93.33	93.24	94.19	93.28	94.38	**94.75**
	Kappa × 100	88.63	87.40	88.52	90.79	90.37	92.19	90.91	92.78	**93.44**
Houston 2013	OA(%)	91.22	91.79	91.24	94.02	93.36	93.95	94.88	94.04	**95.09**
	AA(%)	92.70	93.12	92.81	95.02	94.56	94.94	95.62	95.06	**95.89**
	Kappa × 100	90.50	91.13	90.53	93.53	92.82	93.46	94.46	93.55	**94.70**

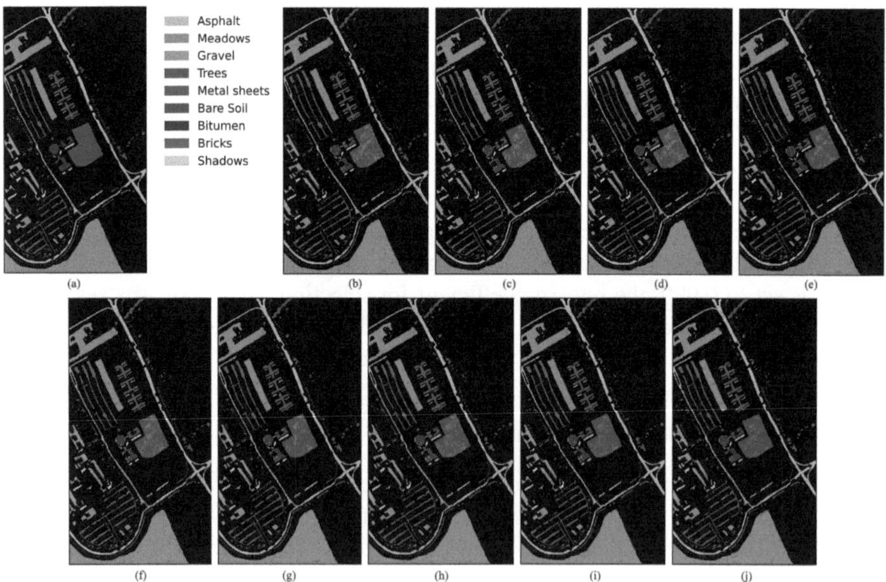

Fig. 3. Visual classification maps of all compared methods on the Pavia University dataset using RF classifier. (a) Ground truth. (b) DRLBS. (c) RLSFR-cv. (d) MH-DRL. (e) Random. (f) AutoFeat. (g) NFS. (h) DIFER. (i) FETCH. (j) HMAFE.

3.4 Time Efficiency Comparison

This section presents a comparative analysis of the time efficiency of the proposed method. Table 2 displays the total running times of several AutoFE methods on the aforementioned datasets. The results indicate that HMAFE is significantly more efficient than AutoFeat, DIFER, and FETCH. Among these methods, AutoFeat exhibits the longest running time, as it applies all possible transformation functions or randomly sampled transformations to the original features. NFS builds an RNN controller for each original feature to learn the optimal feature transformations, which leads to a dramatic increase in training time. DIFER outperforms the DRL-based FETCH in terms of time efficiency, which is consistent with the findings presented in their respective papers. Overall, these findings highlight the superior time efficiency of HMAFE compared to other AutoFE methods, making it a more practical choice for hyperspectral feature extraction.

Table 2. Time efficiency comparison of HMAFE with other methods on different datasets.

Dataset	Execution Time(m)				
	AutoFeat	NFS	DIFER	FETCH	HMAFE
Indian Pines	162.51	192.61	79.88	118.52	21.37
Pavia University	159.53	186.62	65.09	88.05	18.86
Houston 2013	173.82	175.14	70.87	91.04	18.57

3.5 Ablation Experiments in HMAFE

This section verifies the effectiveness of the generation step (Gen), selection step (Sel), and spatial features (Spa) through ablation experiments. Table 3 shows the classification results of each component. The combination of generation and selection stages enables better extraction of spectral features, while the incorporation of spatial features further improves the overall performance.

Table 3. Albation experiments of the HMAFE on different datasets.

Dataset	Metrics	Components			
		Gen	Gen + Sel	Spa	Gen + Sel + Spa
Indian Pines	OA(%)	83.40	83.50	63.90	85.24
	AA(%)	84.73	85.22	72.18	86.76
	Kappa × 100	80.97	81.12	58.28	83.10
Pavia University	OA(%)	94.06	94.12	72.20	95.07
	AA(%)	93.74	93.83	72.31	94.75
	Kappa × 100	92.09	92.17	61.60	93.44

(continued)

Table 3. (*continued*)

Dataset	Metrics	Components			
		Gen	Gen + Sel	Spa	Gen + Sel + Spa
Houston 2013	OA(%)	93.65	93.80	52.15	95.09
	AA(%)	94.33	94.45	52.54	95.89
	Kappa × 100	93.13	93.29	48.28	94.70

4 Conclusion

This paper proposes an automatic feature extraction method for hyperspectral images based on MADRL. The approach aims to alleviate the burden of manual spectral index design for human experts. Our model adopts a heuristic "generation–selection" strategy that emulates the decision-making process of experts, with distinct DRL formulated for the generation and selection steps. Moreover, to expedite exploration in the high-dimensional action space characteristic of hyperspectral data, a MADRL algorithm is introduced. Comparative experiments with several feature selection and AutoFE methods demonstrate that the proposed approach outperforms others in both extraction efficiency and overall performance.

Acknowledgments. This work was supported in part by Yangtze River Delta Science and Technology Innovation Community Joint Research (Basic Research) Project (No. 2024CSJZN1300), Shanghai Municipal Education Commission Science and Technology Project(2024AI02002), National Natural Science Foundation of China (No. 42171335) and National Civil Aerospace Project of China (No. D040102), and Research Project of China Three Gorges Corporation, grant number (202103552).

References

1. Tong, Q., Zhang, B., Zhang, L.: Current progress of hyperspectral remote sensing in china. J. Remote Sens. **20**(5), 689–707 (2016)
2. Shukla, A., Kot, R.: An overview of hyperspectral remote sensing and its applications in various disciplines. IRA Int. J. Appl. Sci. **5**(2), 85–90 (2016)
3. Kruse, F.A., Boardman, J.W., Huntington, J.F.: Comparison of airborne hyperspectral data and EO-1 Hyperion for mineral mapping. IEEE Trans. Geosci. Remote Sens. **41**(6), 1388–1400 (2003)
4. Niu, C., Tan, K., Wang, X., Du, P., Pan, C.: A semi-analytical approach for estimating inland water inherent optical properties and chlorophyll a using airborne hyperspectral imagery. Int. J. Appl. Earth Obs. Geoinf. **128**, 103774 (2024)
5. Singh, P., et al.: Hyperspectral remote sensing in precision agriculture: present status, challenges, and future trends. In: Hyperspectral Remote Sensing. Elsevier, pp. 121–146 (2020)
6. Wang, Z., Wang, X., Tan, K., et al.: Hyperspectral anomaly detection based on variational background inference and generative adversarial network. Pattern Recogn. **143**, 109795 (2023)

7. Srivastava, P.K., Srivastava, S., Singh, P., et al.: Soil chemical properties estimation using hyperspectral remote sensing: a review. Earth Obs. Monit. Model. Land Use **2025**, 25–43 (2025)
8. Hughes, G.: On the mean accuracy of statistical pattern recognizers. IEEE Trans. Inf. Theory **14**(1), 55–63 (1968)
9. Hongjun, S.: Dimensionality reduction for hyperspectral remote sensing: advances, challenges, and prospects. Natl. Remote Sens. Bull. **26**(8), 1504–1529 (2022)
10. Kumar, S., Ghosh, J., Crawford, M.M.: Best-bases feature extraction algorithms for classification of hyperspectral data. IEEE Trans. Geosci. Remote Sens. **39**(7), 1368–1379 (2001)
11. Zhang, B.: Advancement of hyperspectral image processing and information extraction. J. Remote Sens. **20**(5), 1062–1090 (2016)
12. Mou, L., Saha, S., Hua, Y., et al.: Deep reinforcement learning for band selection in hyperspectral image classification. IEEE Trans. Geosci. Remote Sens. **60**, 1–14 (2021)
13. Feng, J., Li, D., Gu, J., et al.: Deep reinforcement learning for semi-supervised hyperspectral band selection. IEEE Trans. Geosci. Remote Sens. **60**, 1–19 (2021)
14. Zhao, L., Tan, K., Wang, X., et al.: Hyperspectral feature selection for SOM prediction using deep reinforcement learning and multiple subset evaluation strategies. Remote Sens. **15**(1), 127 (2022)
15. Feng, J., Gao, Q., Shang, R., et al.: Multi-agent deep reinforcement learning for hyperspectral band selection with hybrid teacher guide. Knowl. Based Syst. **2024**, 112044 (2024)
16. Chang, C.-I., Du, Q., Sun, T.-L., et al.: A joint band prioritization and band-decorrelation approach to band selection for hyperspectral image classification. IEEE Trans. Geosci. Remote Sens. **37**(6), 2631–2641 (1999)
17. Du, H., Qi, H., Wang, X., et al.: Band selection using independent component analysis for hyperspectral image processing. In: 32nd Applied Imagery Pattern Recognition Workshop (AIPR), pp. 93–98 (2003)
18. Bandos, T.V., Bruzzone, L., Camps-Valls, G.: Classification of hyperspectral images with regularized linear discriminant analysis. IEEE Trans. Geosci. Remote Sens. **47**(3), 862–873 (2009)
19. Nguyen, C.T., Chidthaisong, A., Kieu Diem, P., et al.: A modified bare soil index to identify bare land features during agricultural fallow-period in Southeast Asia using Landsat 8. Land **10**(3), 231 (2021)
20. Llorens, R., Sobrino, J.A., Fernández, C., et al.: A methodology to estimate forest fires burned areas and burn severity degrees using Sentinel-2 data. Application to the October 2017 fires in the Iberian Peninsula. Int. J. Appl. Earth Obs. Geoinf. **95**, 102243 (2021)
21. Zheng, Y., Tang, L., Wang, H.: An improved approach for monitoring urban built-up areas by combining NPP-VIIRS nighttime light, NDVI, NDWI, and NDBI. J. Clean. Prod. **328**, 129488 (2021)
22. Xiong, Y., Xu, W., Lu, N., et al.: Assessment of spatial–temporal changes of ecological environment quality based on RSEI and GEE: a case study in Erhai Lake Basin, Yunnan Province. China. Ecol. Indic. **125**, 107518 (2021)
23. Kriegler, F.J.: Preprocessing transformations and their effects on multispectral recognition. In: Proceedings of the 6th International Symposium Remote Sensing of Environment, pp. 97–131 (1969)
24. Chen, J.M., Black, T.: Defining leaf area index for non-flat leaves. In: Plant, Cell Environ. **15**(4), 421–429 (1992)
25. Xu, H.: A remote sensing urban ecological index and its application. Acta Ecol. Sin. **33**(24), 7853–7862 (2013)

26. Li, L., Wang, H., Zha, L., et al.: Learning a data-driven policy network for pre-training automated feature engineering. In: 11th International Conference on Learning Representations (ICLR) (2023)
27. Horn, F., Pack, R., Rieger, M.: The autofeat Python library for automated feature engineering and selection. In: European Conference Machine Learning and Knowledge Discovery Databases (ECML PKDD), pp. 111–120 (2019). https://doi.org/10.1007/978-3-030-43823-4_10
28. Zhu, G., Xu, Z., Yuan, C., et al.: Difer: differentiable automated feature engineering. In: International Conference on Automated Machine Learning, pp. 17/1–17 (2022)
29. Chen, X., Lin, Q., Luo, C., et al.: Neural feature search: A neural architecture for automated feature engineering. In: 2019 IEEE International Conference on Data Mining (ICDM), pp. 71–80 (2019)

Hyperspectral Image Cross-Domain Classification: A Joint Network of Masked Self-distillation and Confident Learning

Haoyu Li[1], Zhen Ye[1(✉)], Xuan Dong[1], and He Li[2]

[1] School of Electronics and Control Engineering, Chang'an University, Xi'an, China
`yezhen525@126.com`

[2] State Key Laboratory of Resources and Environmental Information System, Institute of Geographic Sciences and Natural Resources Research, Chinese Academy of Sciences, Beijing 100101, China

Abstract. In recent years, unsupervised domain adaptation methods based on deep learning have shown great potential in hyperspectral image cross-domain classification. However, existing methods often face two major challenges: domain distribution differences and data noise interference. To address these issues, this paper proposes a cross-domain classification framework combining confident learning and masked self-distillation (CL-MSD), which constructs an adversarial training network, leveraging the competition between dual classifiers and feature extractors to learn domain-invariant features, and employs a spatial-spectral dual-branch structure to enhance the joint modeling of local and global features. The framework also introduces a masked self-distillation (MSD) module to simulate missing data scenarios and a confident learning (CL) module to filter out low-confidence samples. Experiments on the Houston and Pavia datasets show that the proposed method achieves overall classification accuracies of 83.38% and 93.60%, respectively, demonstrating its effectiveness.

Keywords: hyperspectral image classification · domain adaptation · masked self-distillation · confidence learning

1 Introduction

With the continuous development of deep learning, hyperspectral image classification has gradually become one of the hot topics in the field of remote sensing, showing great potential in applications such as environmental monitoring [1], agricultural production [2], and military defense [3]. However, traditional models [4–6] are difficult to directly apply in cross-domain scenarios. Domain adaptation (DA) technology aims to use source-domain data to assist in classifying the target domain data, addressing the issue of distribution inconsistency. For example, Huang et al. [7] introduced a dual-branch attention adversarial network (TAADA) to effectively extract spatial-spectral features. Li et al. [8, 9] incorporated confidence learning into traditional pre-adaptation networks

© The Author(s), under exclusive license to Springer Nature Singapore Pte Ltd. 2026

Z. Lin et al. (Eds.): ICIG 2025, LNCS 16163, pp. 485–496, 2026.
https://doi.org/10.1007/978-981-95-3729-7_39

(CLDA, SCLUDA), which successfully mitigated noise interference and enhanced feature discriminability. However, these methods typically cannot simultaneously mitigate the dual challenges of degraded feature discriminability and noise interference. To overcome these limitations, this study integrates a masked self-Distillation (MSD) module [10] with confidence learning (CL) into an adversarial domain adaptation network, proposing a novel cross-domain hyperspectral image classification model. By improving feature discriminability while reducing interference from anomalous data, the proposed approach achieves enhanced classification performance. The main contributions are summarized as follows.

(1) A masked self-distillation (MSD) module is adopted to improve the model's feature extraction ability for low signal-to-noise ratio and spectral distorted data.
(2) By constructing a confident learning (CL) module, the proportion of high-confidence samples in the target domain is increased to enhance the quality of hyperspectral data, thereby improving the accuracy of classification.
(3) The proposed method in this paper employs a domain adaptation strategy that integrates a MSD module with a CL module to achieve cross-domain classification of hyperspectral images. By jointly optimizing feature extraction and data quality, the model significantly enhances the system's classification capability, yielding breakthrough experimental results. It also simultaneously addresses two major challenges: reduced feature discriminability and noise interference.

2 Method

As shown in Fig. 1, the proposed model integrates Confidence Learning (CL) and Masked Self-Distillation (MSD) into an adversarial domain adaptation network. The Confidence Learning module is located on the right side of Fig. 1, marked by a blue frame, while the Masked Self-Distillation module is positioned at the bottom of Fig. 1, indicated by a green frame.

The subsequent sections will elaborate on the domain adaptation strategy, MSD module, CL module, and the comprehensive training process of the proposed framework.

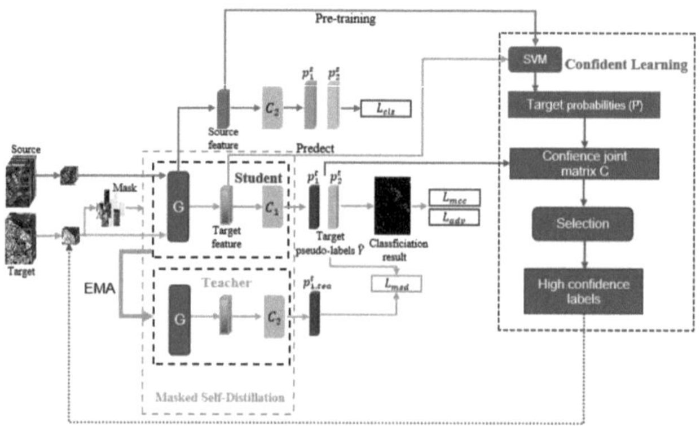

Fig. 1. The overall architecture of the proposed model.

2.1 Domain Adaptation Strategy

As shown in Fig. 2, the backbone network consists of a feature extractor G and dual classifiers. G uses a dual-channel sub-network: the spectral branch extracts features via 3D convolutions and highlights key bands, while the spatial branch captures features using 2D convolutions and identifies key regions. The concatenated features from these two branches form discriminative features that integrate spectral and spatial information for accurate classification.

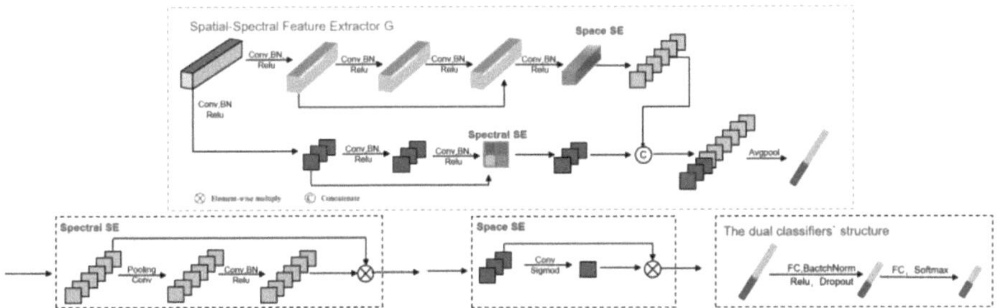

Fig. 2. Spatial-Spectral Feature Extraction Network Structure (SSFE)

As shown in Fig. 2, the dual classifiers have the same structure, stacked of a linear layer, a normalization layer, a ReLU activation layer, a dropout layer, and a linear layer sequentially. The output is passed through Softmax to produce the probability of the samples belonging to each class. The backbone network incorporates an adversarial learning mechanism. By optimizing the adversarial relationship between the feature extractor and the dual classifiers, the model is forced to learn domain-invariant features with strong generalization ability. This effectively mitigates the impact of cross-domain distribution differences on classification performance and significantly enhances the cross-domain classification performance of hyperspectral images.

To address the class confusion issue of unlabeled samples in the target domain, this paper introduces minimum class confusion loss function (MCC_Loss). First, the classifier output probabilities p_{ij} are scaled by the temperature parameter T to obtain.

$$z_{ij} = softmax(p_{ij}) = \frac{exp(p_{ij}/T)}{\sum_{j=1}^{|C|} exp(p_{ij}/T)} \tag{1}$$

Then, the class relevance matrix $R_{jj'}$ is defined to quantify the confusion between classes. The entropy function $H(z_{i.})$ is used to calculate the sample uncertainty weight W_{ii}. The operators are shown as.

$$R_{jj'} = z_{.j}^{\top} z_{.j'} \tag{2}$$

$$H(z_{i.}) = -\sum_{j=1}^{|C|} z_{ij} log z_{ij} \tag{3}$$

$$W_{ii} = \frac{B(1 + exp(-H(z_{i\cdot})))}{\sum_{i'=1}^{B}(1 + exp(-H(z_{i'\cdot})))} \tag{4}$$

Subsequently, the class relevance matrix $R_{jj'}$ is corrected and normalized using the weight matrix W_{ii} to address class imbalance. The weight W_{ii} is positively correlated with sample uncertainty, enhancing the influence between multimodal samples, where B is the batch size. Finally, the normalized class relevance matrix $R_{jj'}$ is used to define the minimized class confusion loss function.

$$L_{mcc} = \frac{1}{|C|} \sum_{j=1}^{|C|} \sum_{j' \neq j} |\overline{R}_{jj'}|. \tag{5}$$

2.2 Masked Self-distillation

The masked self-distillation module (MSD) enhances feature extraction capabilities and reduces the impact of information loss on classification performance through two core mechanisms: spatial-spectral masking and knowledge distillation. Spatial-spectral masking achieves sub-block level information masking through a random mask tensor, preserving the full spectral information of the central pixel.

$$T_m = \begin{cases} 1 \ u > \tau \\ 0 \ u < \tau \end{cases}. \tag{6}$$

where τ is the masking rate parameter and u is a randomly generated threshold. The masked image is obtained through

$$X_m = T_m \odot X_t \tag{7}$$

The core of the knowledge self-distillation module is to construct a teacher-student network. The teacher network is initialized by copying the parameters of the student network and updated via the exponential moving average (EMA) method as

$$\phi^{(t+1)} = \alpha \cdot \phi^{(t)} + (1 - \alpha) \cdot \theta^{(t)} \tag{8}$$

where ϕ represents parameters of the branch of teacher network, θ represents parameters of the branch of student network, and t denotes training step.

The teacher network predicts using complete samples X_t to generate pseudo-labels by

$$\widehat{Y}_t = \underset{c \in C}{argmax} \, C_{1,tea}(G_{tea}(x_t))_c \tag{9}$$

Subsequently, the student network predicts the class for the masked samples. The aim is to achieve high consistency between the predictions of the two networks. The discrepancy between the two predictions is quantified using the masked self-distillation loss(MSD_Loss), calculated by.

$$L_{MSD} = \sqrt[q]{2} \cdot \sqrt{L_{CE}\big(C_1(G(x_m)), \widehat{Y}_t\big)} \tag{10}$$

$L_{CE}(\cdot)$ represents cross-entropy loss function. q denotes the quality weight, which can be calculated using maximum Softmax probability by

$$q = \max_{c} p_{tea}(x_t)_c .\tag{11}$$

Throughout the training process, the student network continuously compares its predictions with the pseudo-labels generated by the teacher network, gradually enhancing its predictive accuracy. Meanwhile, the teacher network updates itself based on the historical knowledge of the student network. This mutually beneficial relationship helps to improve the performance of both teacher and student networks, ultimately enhancing the overall classification performance.

2.3 Confident Learning

Confident learning (CL) optimizes the quality of pseudo-labels in the target domain using source-domain data. First, target-domain data x_t generates pseudo-labels $\hat{y}_t$ through the backbone network, and then SVM classifiers are trained using source-domain features. These classifiers predict target-domain data, generating a prediction matrix $\widehat{P}$ as the true labels for the target domain. A joint confidence matrix $M_{\hat{y}_t,y_t}[i][j]$ is constructed by combining $\widehat{P}$ and $\hat{y}_t$. If the pseudo-label of sample x_t is i and its predicted probability for the true label j is greater than or equal to the threshold τ_j, the value in the joint confidence matrix at that position is 1, otherwise it is 0. The operation can be expressed by

$$M_{\hat{y}_t,y_t}[i][j] = \begin{cases} 1 & if\ \hat{y}_t = i \wedge \widehat{P}(y_t = j) \geq \tau_j \\ 0 & otherwise \end{cases}\tag{12}$$

where the threshold τ_j is defined as

$$\tau_j = \frac{1}{|X_t(y_t=j)|} \sum_{x_t \in X_t(y_t=j)} \widehat{P}(y_t = j)\tag{13}$$

The $M_{\hat{y}_t,y_t}[i][j]$ is normalized to obtain the normalized joint matrix $Q_{\hat{y}_t,y_t}[i][j]$. While the the class distribution can be balanced by class weights.

$$\omega_{con} = \frac{Q_{\hat{y}_t=i,}[i]}{Q_{\hat{y}_t=i,y_t=i}[i][i]} .\tag{14}$$

Then, low-confidence samples are removed, and high-confidence samples and their labels are used as additional input into the feature extractor G. Finally, the loss function is adjusted to participate in training, thereby enhancing the model's classification performance.

2.4 Training Process

Based on the algorithm design of the above four parts, this design adopts a three-stage adversarial training strategy.

In Stage 1, joint pre-training of the feature extractor and classifier is conducted, with the introduction of MSD_Loss and MCC_Loss to enhance target domain adaptability. During this process, the loss is expressed as

$$\min_{G,C_1,C_2} L_{cls}(x_s, y_s) + \lambda_1 L_{msd}(x_t, x_m) + \lambda_2 L_{mcc}(x_t) \tag{15}$$

where λ_1, λ_2 are weight coefficients used to balance the importance of different loss terms, L_{cls} is the cross-entropy loss function, defined as

$$L_{cls}(x_s, y_s) = \frac{1}{2n_s} \sum_{i=1}^{n_s} L_{ce}(C(G(x_s^i)), y_s^i) \tag{16}$$

In Stage 2, fix G and optimize C_1 and C_2. During this process, the loss is expressed as

$$\min_{C_1,C_2} L_{msd}(x_t, x_m) + L_{cls}(x_s, y_s) - L_{adv}(x_t) + \lambda_1 L_{msd}(x_t, x_m) + \lambda_2 L_{mcc}(x_t) \tag{17}$$

where L_{adv} denotes the adversarial loss between the two classifiers, defined as

$$L_{adv}(x_t) = \frac{1}{n_t} \sum_{i=1}^{n_t} \|C_1(G(x_t^i)) - C_2(G(x_t^i))\|_1 \tag{18}$$

where x_t^i represents the i-th sample in the target domain and n_t denotes the total number of target-domain samples.

When confident labels are available for the target domain, the network's discriminative power with respect to these samples is enhanced by incorporating both the cross-entropy loss and the entropy regularization loss. The operator can be formulated as

$$\min_{C_1,C_2} L_{msd}(x_t, x_m) + L_{cls}(x_s, y_s) - L_{adv}(x_t) + \lambda_1 L_{msd}(x_t, x_m) + \lambda_2 L_{mcc}(x_t)$$
$$+ \lambda_3 L_{cls}(x_t, \hat{y}_t) + \lambda_4 L_{entory}^t(x_t, \hat{y}_t)) \tag{19}$$

where the entropy regularization loss (L_{entory}^t) is defined as

$$L_{entory}^t(x_t) = L_{entory}^t(C(G(x_t))) = -\frac{1}{N} \sum_{c=1}^{C} p_c \log p_c \tag{20}$$

In stage 3, the classifier is kept fixed while focusing on optimizing the feature extractor G to achieve domain alignment. During this process, the loss is expressed as.

$$\min_{G} L_{adv}(x_t) + L_{mcc}(x_t) \tag{21}$$

The detailed steps of the final algorithm are provided in Algorithm 1 in the form of pseudo-code.

Algorithm 1 : Training Process of the Proposed CL-MSD

Input : Source domain samples x_s, source domain labels y_s , target domain samples, x_t hyperparameters P, C, r, s, T, the total epoch number epochs, and confidence learning cycle epochs number num_con

Output : The parameters θ_G of feature extractor G, and θ_{C_1} of classifier C_1 .

1. Randomly initialize the parameters θ_{C_1}, θ_{C_2} and θ_G of the dual classifier and the feature extractor G.

2. Initialize parameters φ_G , φ_{C_1} of teacher networks by copying the parameters of the student network.

3. **for** epoch in(1-epochs) **do**

4. Updating φ_G and φ_{C_1} by Eq. (8).

5. Generate x_m by Eq. (7).

6. Update θ_{C_1}, θ_{C_2} and θ_G by Eq. (11).

7. If epoch % num_con == 0:

8. Obtain the target pseudo labels Y and target predicted probabilities P.

9. Calculate confidence joint matrix $M_{\hat{y}_t,y_t}[i][j]$ by Eq.(12)

10. Remove unreliable samples to update the target domain.

11. Update θ_G by Eq. (19).

12. **else**

13. Update θ_G by Eq. (17).

14. Update θ_{C_1} and θ_{C_2} by Eq. (21).

15. **end for**

---

3   Experiments and Analysis

3.1   Dataset

To verify the effectiveness of the proposed model, experiments were conducted on two sets of publicly available hyperspectral image datasets: Houston2013 (H13) and Houston2018 (H18), as well as Pavia University (PU) and Pavia Center (PC). Specifically, H13 and PU were used as the source-domain datasets to assist in the classification of the target-domains datasets H18 and PC. For the H18 dataset, an overlapping region with a spatial size of 209 × 955 and 48 spectral bands was selected from the H13 dataset, and seven common classes were chosen as classification targets. The PU and PC datasets were preprocessed to ensure consistent spatial size and spectral band numbers, and seven common classes were selected as classification targets. Table 1 and Table 2 show the number of classes selected in the two classification tasks. Figure 3 and Fig. 4 display the false-color images and ground-truth maps of the experimental datasets.

Table 1. Land-cover classes and number of samples for Houston classification task.

No.	Class	H13	H18
1	Grass healthy	345	1353
2	Grass stressed	365	4888
3	Trees	365	2766
4	Water	285	22
5	Residential buildings	319	5347
6	Non-residential buildings	408	32459
7	Road	443	6355
Total		2530	53200

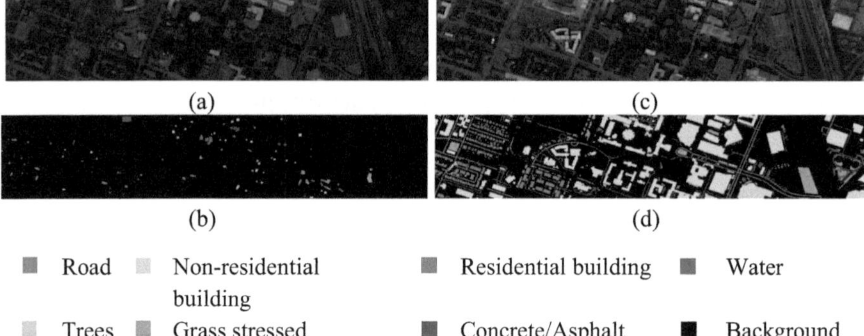

(a)

(c)

(b)

(d)

■ Road ■ Non-residential building ■ Residential building ■ Water

■ Trees ■ Grass stressed ■ Concrete/Asphalt ■ Background

Fig. 3. H13 and H18 datasets. (a) False-color image of H13. (b) Ground-truth map of H13. (c) False-color image of H18. (d) Ground-truth map of H18.

Table 2. Land-cover classes and number of samples for Pavia classification Task.

No.	Class	PU	PC
1	Tree	3064	7598
2	Asphalt	6631	9248
3	Brick	3682	2685
4	Bitumen	1330	7287
5	Shadow	947	2863
6	Meadows	18649	3090
7	Bare soil	5029	6584
Total		2530	53200

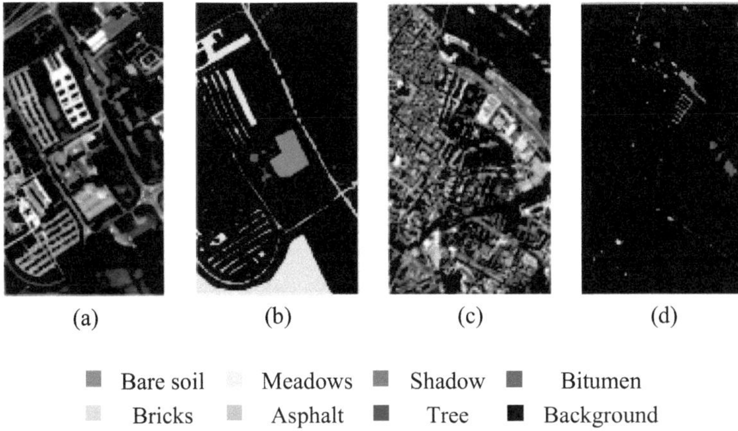

(a)   (b)   (c)   (d)

■ Bare soil   Meadows ■ Shadow ■ Bitumen
Bricks   Asphalt ■ Tree ■ Background

Fig. 4. PU and PC datasets. (a) False-color image of PU. (b) Ground-truth map of PU. (c) False-color image of PC. (d) Ground-truth map of PC.

3.2 Comparative Experiments

This study verifies the performance of the proposed CL-MSD through comparing with five advanced algorithms, with all parameters strictly following the settings from the references. For the Houston task, parameters involve learning rate of 0.1, batch size of 32, and the input with size of $7 \times 7 \times 48$, with 50 training rounds. For the Pavia task, parameters involve a learning rate of 0.1, batch size of 32, and the input with size of $9 \times 9 \times 102$, with 100 training rounds. During testing, the unmarked target samples are input into the student network, and the predictions of the classifier C_1 are used as the final labels. The classification performance of all methods was evaluated using overall accuracy (OA) and Kappa coefficient (κ).

Table 3. Classification results for Houston2018 dataset.

Class	TAADA [7]	CLDA [8]	SCLUDA [9]	MSDA [10]	MLUDA [11]	CL-MSD
1	57.35	62.10	89.07	89.62	70.51	82.20
2	57.35	86.75	69.80	53.34	77.15	70.81
3	57.35	86.75	64.09	63.29	57.29	62.37
4	78.64	79.55	98.18	79.55	90.91	80.91
5	80.43	94.16	86.30	91.07	81.00	87.16
6	73.54	54.95	78.21	79.91	81.65	**88.64**
7	80.40	75.85	69.04	75.88	56.21	72.48
OA	72.40 ± 3.88	65.04 ± 4.27	76.70 ± 1.90	77.49 ± 2.88	76.56 ± 2.67	**83.38 ± 1.49**
κ	58.56 ± 5.15	52.12 ± 4.26	64.13 ± 2.34	65.18 ± 3.36	62.50 ± 3.84	**72.85 ± 2.32**

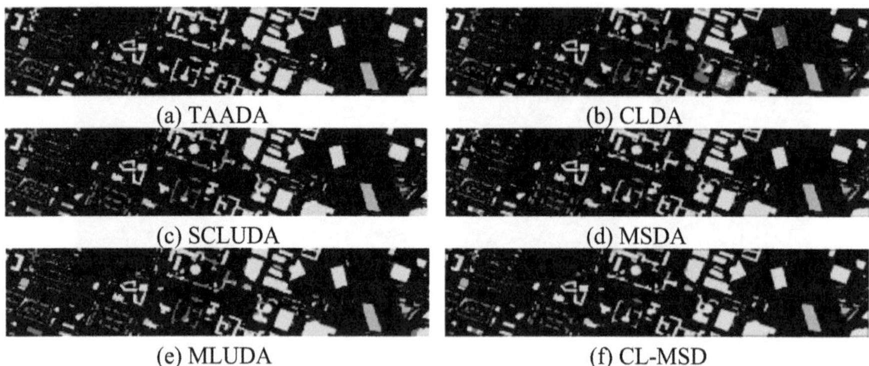

(a) TAADA

(b) CLDA

(c) SCLUDA

(d) MSDA

(e) MLUDA

(f) CL-MSD

Fig. 5. Classification maps for Houston2018 dataset.

Table 3 presents the experimental results of the proposed and comparative algorithms for the H13 → H18 classification task. In terms of overall accuracy (OA), our method leads with an OA of 83.38%, significantly outperforming CLDA and TAADA, and has more 5% gains than SCLUDA, MLUDA and MSDA. As for the Kappa coefficient (κ), our method achieves the best result of 72.84%. It can be seen in Fig. 5 that our method yields smoother classification maps than the other comparative methods with fewer erroneous outliers.

Table 4. Classification results for Pavia Center dataset.

Class	TAADA [7]	CLDA [8]	SCLUDA [9]	MSDA [10]	MLUDA [11]	CL-MSD
1	97.09	93.58	96.12	92.93	97.15	96.11
2	99.18	98.33	98.36	96.12	98.97	98.95
3	77.92	98.33	98.19	96.86	61.16	73.51
4	81.68	75.56	85.56	85.38	83.64	84.52
5	100.00	80.43	98.34	99.92	85.00	99.54
6	85.03	95.39	94.96	97.76	89.73	96.28
7	91.08	96.52	78.16	79.99	97.90	97.60
OA	91.68 ± 1.35	87.85 ± 4.44	91.90 ± 0.49	91.21 ± 0.63	91.84 ± 2.53	**93.60 ± 1.04**
κ	89.96 ± 1.62	85.37 ± 5.24	90.30 ± 0.58	89.58 ± 0.75	90.13 ± 3.12	**92.29 ± 1.25**

Table 4 presents the comparative experimental results of different algorithms for the PU → PC classification task. In terms of overall accuracy (OA), the proposed CL-MSD tops the list with an OA of 93.60%, demonstrating high classification accuracy and stability. In terms of the Kappa coefficient (κ), our method achieves the optimal classification result of 92.29%. Figure 6 shows the classification maps of different comparative algorithms, further demonstrating the advantages of the proposed CL-MSD.

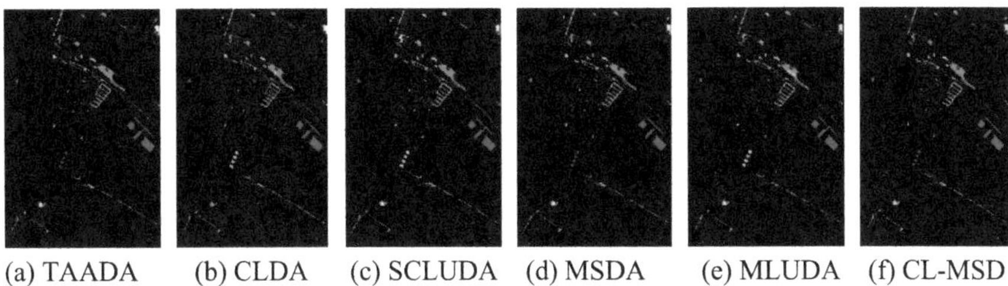

Fig. 6. Classification maps for Pavia Center dataset.

3.3   Ablation Experiments

To analyze the contributions of different components of the proposed method, ablation experiments were conducted on two classification tasks by studying various combinations. The proposed method consists of three components: domain adaptation strategy (A), masked self-distillation (B), and confidence learning (C). Table 5 presents four combinations of these three modules and analyzes the impact of different modules from the perspective of overall accuracy (OA). For the H13 $\rightarrow$ H18 classification task, the combination of ABC achieved 83.38%, significantly leading over A's 75.68%, AB's 77.49%, and AC's 82.87%. For the PU $\rightarrow$ PC classification task, the combination of ABC further outperformed with an advanced OA of 93.60%, exceeding A, AB, and AC by 7.35%, 1.53%, and 1.76%, respectively.

Table 5. Ablation analysis of three components.

	A	B	C	Houston	Pavia
Network 1	✔	×	×	75.68 ± 2.40	86.25 ± 4.39
Network 2	✔	✔	×	77.49 ± 2.88	92.07 ± 2.88
Network 3	✔	×	✔	82.87 ± 2.76	91.84 ± 2.53
Network 4	✔	✔	✔	**83.38 ± 1.49**	**93.60 ± 1.04**

4   Conclusion

In this work, the proposed CL-MSD innovatively integrates confidence learning and masked self-distillation techniques into an adversarial domain adaptation network. It optimizes parameters through adversarial training between dual classifiers and generators to achieve domain-invariant feature extraction. In terms of data processing, it periodically constructs a joint confidence matrix to dynamically remove low-confidence samples and enhance data quality. For feature extraction, it uses a spatial-spectral network combined with a masked self-distillation module to simulate data missing scenarios, complete knowledge transfer, and mine deep features. In comparative experiments on public datasets, the proposed method comprehensively outperforms five advanced comparative algorithms in terms of classification accuracy and stability. Ablation experiments further confirm the key role of confidence learning and masked self-distillation modules in model construction.

Acknowledgments. This research was supported by a grant from State Key Laboratory of Resources and Environmental Information System.

References

1. Yang, X., Yu, Y.: Estimating soil salinity under various moisture conditions: an experimental study. IEEE Trans. Geosci. Remote Sens. **55**(5), 2525–2533 (2017). https://doi.org/10.1109/TGRS.2016.2646420
2. Pascucci, S., Pignatti, S., Casa, R., Darvishzadeh, R., Huang, W.: Special issue "Hyperspectral remote sensing of agriculture and vegetation." Remote Sens. (Basel, Switzerland) **12**(21), 3665 (2020). https://doi.org/10.3390/rs12213665
3. Ma, Y., Zhang, W., Liu, D.: Characterization of hyperspectral reconnaissance technology and analysis of its threat to military targets on the ground. Shanghai Aerosp. Corp. **29**(01), 37–4059 (2012). https://doi.org/10.19328/j.cnki.1006-1630.2012.01008
4. Hu, W., Huang, Y., Wei, L., Zhang, F., Li, H.: Deep convolutional neural networks for hyperspectral image classification. J. Sensors **2015**, 258619 (2015). https://doi.org/10.1155/2015/258619
5. Song, W., Li, S., Fang, L., Lu, T.: Hyperspectral image classification with deep feature fusion network. IEEE Trans. Geosci. Remote Sens. **56**(6), 3173–3184 (2018). https://doi.org/10.1109/TGRS.2018.2794326
6. Yang, H., Yu, H., Hong, D., Xu, Z., Wang, Y., Song, M.: Hyperspectral image classification based on multi-level spectral-spatial transformer network. In: 12th Workshop on Hyperspectral Imaging and Signal Processing: Evolution in Remote Sensing (WHISPERS), pp. 1–4. IEEE, Rome, Italy (2022). https://doi.org/10.1109/WHISPERS56178.2022.9955116
7. Huang, Y., et al.: Two-branch attention adversarial domain adaptation network for hyperspectral image classification. IEEE Trans. Geosci. Remote Sens. **60**, 1 (2022). https://doi.org/10.1109/TGRS.2022.3215677
8. Fang, Z., et al.: Confident learning-based domain adaptation for hyperspectral image classification. IEEE Trans. Geosci. Remote Sens. **60**, 1–16 (2022). https://doi.org/10.1109/TGRS.2022.3166817
9. Li, Z., et al.: Supervised contrastive learning-based unsupervised domain adaptation for hyperspectral image classification. IEEE Trans. Geosci. Remote Sens. **61**, 1–17 (2023). https://doi.org/10.1109/TGRS.2023.3317301
10. Fang, Z., He, W., Li, Z., Du, Q., Chen, Q.: Masked self-distillation domain adaptation for hyperspectral image classification. IEEE Trans. Geosci. Remote Sens. **62**, 1–20 (2024). https://doi.org/10.1109/TGRS.2024.3436814
11. Cai, M., et al.: Mind the gap: Multilevel unsupervised domain adaptation for cross-scene hyperspectral image classification. IEEE Trans. Geosci. Remote Sens. **62**, 1–14 (2024). https://doi.org/10.1109/TGRS.2024.3407952

Analysis of the On-Orbit Radiation Calibration of Planetary Infrared Remote Sensing Systems Combined with Blackbody and Star

Li Xiaoman[✉], Jin Libing, Yan Xiurong, Jin Zhanlei, and Gao Huiting

Beijing Institute of Space Mechanics and Electricity, Beijing 100094, China
`lixiaoman_bisme@163.com`

Abstract. Research has shown that infrared radiation calibration technology is developing towards higher accuracy, stability, and real-time performance, providing necessary support for the widespread application of infrared technology. It is reasonable and feasible to use blackbody and infrared outer space methods for orbit all-optical path calibration of infrared space optical remote sensing cameras, with a focus on addressing issues such as blackbody working temperature uniformity, stability, and absolute radiation performance monitoring. By analyzing the factors affecting the calibration uncertainty of infrared remote sensors, we can effectively improve the radiation calibration accuracy by improving the onboard calibration scheme, providing onboard calibration blackbody temperature control accuracy, and combining infrared star calibration methods. The algorithm has been validated through ground laboratory testing. In response to the non-uniform changes caused by various factors in the in orbit space infrared remote sensor, the details of the in orbit absolute radiation calibration design scheme combining surface source blackbody calibration and stellar calibration were optimized. The temperature uniformity and stability control measures of blackbody were proposed, and the stellar extraction algorithm and data correction methods for stellar calibration and blackbody calibration were analyzed. Based on the specific development status of a certain remote sensor, we validated the algorithm based on laboratory test results and predicted the uncertainty of in orbit absolute radiation calibration. The application of infrared radiometric calibration technology in remote sensing, target recognition, and temperature measurement was also discussed, and its future development trends were discussed.

Keywords: Planetary Remote Sensing System · On-orbit Radiation Calibration · Blackbody · Star Calibration

1 Introduction

Infrared imaging can be used in planetary exploration, agricultural surveys and other civil fields. At present, the accuracy of quantitative detection of space infrared remote sensors in scientific research is increasing.

Due to the non-uniformity of the substrate material of the detector chip, inconsistency between parallel output channels, and detector readout noise, the output image of the

© The Author(s), under exclusive license to Springer Nature Singapore Pte Ltd. 2026
Z. Lin et al. (Eds.): ICIG 2025, LNCS 16163, pp. 497–509, 2026.
https://doi.org/10.1007/978-981-95-3729-7_40

focal plane array of the space infrared remote sensor exhibits non-uniformity. Moreover, the uniformity of image plane illumination of the optical system design, stray radiation of the optical system, and the variation of the optical system operating temperature will all affect the output stability. Before launching, laboratory vacuum radiometric calibration should be strictly carried out, and ground pixel-by-pixel calibration should be completed to obtain the parameter differences between pixels in order to determine the initial spectral radiometric response characteristics of the remote sensors. During the on-orbit flight of the remote sensors, space particle radiation, pollution, aging of components, etc., will cause degradation of the performance of the remote sensors, thus will change the spectral radiance response characteristics. For this reason, it is necessary to carry out on-board radiometric calibration of the remote sensors on a regular basis to satisfy the user's requirements for the application of remote sensing data in a long term and quantitative manner. Generally, external scene calibration sources (e.g., large deserts on the ground, the Sun, the Moon and the cold space background) or built-in calibration devices (e.g., lamps, silicon carbon rods, blackbodies, etc.) can be selected to reduce the uncertainty of the calibration.

The on-board surface source blackbody radiometric calibration method is a widely recognized method for high precision on-orbit radiometric absolute calibration. Using the accurate blackbody radiation model and highly stable blackbody emission performance, the uncertainty of radiation calibration can be reduced by the least transmission link, which is generally controlled within 5% in on-orbit applications, and the uncertainty of radiation calibration of international space remote sensing instruments is optimized to 2–3%, and at the same time, it is easy to achieve the absolute radiation calibration of full aperture, full optical path, and full field of view, such as the absolute radiation calibration of MODIS (MOderate-resolution Imaging Spectroradiometer) [1]. AATSR (AdvancedAlong TrackScanningRadiometer), etc. have adopted the blackbody in-orbit calibration. However, because the long-term decay of blackbody emissivity in orbit cannot be monitored, it needs to be corrected by other calibration means [2]. The Japanese infrared astronomical satellite Akari (ASTRO-F) [3], which can observe stars during the period in orbit, has carried out absolute stellar radiometric calibration by utilizing the sensitivity of the far-infrared detector and the brightness of the point source; and SPIRIT III (spatial infrared imaging telescope),which is carried on board the mid-range experimental satellite MSX, has carried out absolute stellar radiometric calibration in orbit by utilizing the sensitivity of the far-infrared detector and the brightness of the point source. Absolute stellar radiometric calibrations were carried out on board the mid-range test satellite MSX [4].

In this paper, for the non-uniformity changes caused by various factors of space infrared remote sensors in orbit we optimize the details of the on-orbit absolute radiation calibration design scheme for a surface source blackbody calibration combined with stellar calibration, put forward the temperature uniformity and stability control measures of the blackbody, and analyze the stellar extraction algorithm and the data correction method of stellar calibration and blackbody calibration; combined with the specific actuality of the research and development of a certain remote sensor, we validate the algorithm based on the laboratory test results, and predict the uncertainty of the on-orbit absolute radiation calibration, Combined with the development of a remote sensor, the algorithm is verified based on the laboratory test results, and the uncertainty of on-orbit absolute radiometric calibration is predicted.

2 Radiation Calibration Scheme Design

Laboratory calibration is the foundation of infrared radiation calibration, typically conducted under controlled environmental conditions. This method can achieve high-precision calibration but struggles to fully simulate actual application environments. Laboratory calibration mainly includes spectral calibration, radiometric calibration, and geometric calibration. Spectral calibration determines the spectral response characteristics of the detector, radiometric calibration establishes the relationship between the detector output and incident radiation, and geometric calibration determines the detector's field of view and spatial resolution [5].

On-orbit calibration is a calibration method for spaceborne infrared remote sensors, aiming to address the discrepancies between laboratory calibration and actual conditions. On-orbit calibration typically uses onboard calibrators and natural targets. Onboard calibrators include blackbodies and solar diffusers, providing stable reference radiation sources. Natural target calibration uses celestial bodies such as the Moon, deep space, or uniform terrestrial surfaces as references, suitable for long-term monitoring and correction [6].

Field calibration is conducted in actual application environments, better reflecting the true performance of the system. Field calibration typically uses portable calibration sources, such as portable blackbody furnaces or large-area uniform radiation panels. This method allows for real-time correction of system performance but is more affected by environmental factors, resulting in relatively lower calibration accuracy. In recent years, field calibration methods based on unmanned aerial vehicle platforms have gradually emerged, offering new solutions for infrared radiation calibration in complex environments.

Many factors need to be considered in the design of a radiometric calibration program, including the operating spectrum, calibration accuracy, lifetime, reliability and constraints from spacecraft and spaceborne optical remote sensors.

Typical on-star radiometric calibrations: Absolute radiometric calibrations are performed by using high and low temperature surface source blackbodies as standard sources introduced into the camera. The stability of the surface source blackbody affects the calibration accuracy. The results of the blackbody calibration could be corrected by observing the star because the radiation of the star is more stable. So it is a better way of on-star calibration for spaceborne optical remote sensors operating in the infrared spectral band.

Take the design of an astronomical detection infrared remote sensor as an example, the main technical parameters of the remote sensor are shown in Table 1, and the uncertainty of its on-orbit radiometric calibration is required to be controlled within 5%.

Due to the weak energy of the observation star reaching the pupil of the remote sensor, in order to ensure that the simulated radiation intensity of the calibration device is comparable to the radiation intensity of the observation star, if the solar diffuse reflector calibration is used, it is necessary to use the doped gray body reflections, large-angle incidence or configuration of attenuation network for energy attenuation, and there are the problems of non-uniformity increase and the large impact of stray light. The blackbody calibration method can adjust the energy reaching the pupil of the camera through the temperature of the blackbody, but it is necessary to monitor the on-orbit decay of the blackbody.

Table 1. Parameters of the remote sensing system to be tested

Technical parameters	Value
Aperture of optical system/mm	250
Focal length of optical system/mm	425
Signal to noise ratio	≥ 5
Field of view/°	0.85×0.68
Number of detector pixels	640×512
Spectral range/μm	2–3

When the camera enters the calibration mode, the camera's radiation calibration plate is moved to the camera's pupil to do the camera's on-orbit radiation calibration.

2.1 Absolute Radiation Calibration of Full Aperture, Full Optical Path, and Full Field of View Using the Blackbody

The blackbody is electrically heated to achieve precise temperature control at multiple temperature points.The blackbody is a surface source blackbody, the blackbody surface adopts a certain angle of the V-shaped groove design and anodized black surface treatment, which can ensure the black body has a good radiation uniformity and high radiation emissivity. A high-precision thermistor is installed near the radiation surface for real-time temperature monitoring, and a thin-film heating pad is installed on the bottom surface of the blackbody to accomplish heating control.

The design parameters for the blackbody on the star are shown below.

Blackbody temperature: 235–270K adjustable;

Effective size of blackbody: 270 mm × 270 mm × 20 mm (covering the pupil of the camera);

Normal emissivity: ≥ 0.97;

Temperature uniformity: ≤ 0.2K;

Temperature control precision of black body surface: ± 0.1K;

Temperature measurement accuracy: $\leq \pm 0.1$K.

Optimization of high-precision temperature control measures for blackbodies.

1) blackbody components outside the arrangement of the outer cover, through the outer cover radiation temperature control to meet the temperature requirements, the outer surface of the outer cover is arranged with active temperature control heating circuit; the inner surface of the outer cover is blackened to enhance the radiation heat transfer

between the outer cover and the black body components, the outer surface of the outer cover is coated with multi-layer heat insulation materials to reduce the radiation heat leakage, and the outermost part of the multi-layer is a black polyimide carburized film; the outer surface of the outer cover is covered with multi-layer thermal insulation materials.

2) The two ends of the blackbody are sandwich structure, the middle layer is 0.5mm thick graphite film to improve the temperature uniformity of the area in the optical path. The back of the blackbody is covered with multi-layer heat insulation material to minimize the heat leakage after cutting into the optical path.

3) Thermal insulation is installed between the black body and the supporting structure to minimize temperature interactions.

4) The black body support structure is arranged with an active temperature control heating circuit, and heat insulation is installed between the support structure and the main frame of the remote sensor.

High-temperature black body assembly mainly consists of blackbody, heating plate, heat-insulating washer and heat-insulating gasket. Selection of high thermal conductivity, light weight, high hardness of aluminum alloy 2A12 processed into a high-temperature black body, heat-insulating gaskets processed from polyimide. Titanium alloy screws with poor thermal conductivity are used to connect the high-temperature blackbody and the scanning base. Low temperature black body assembly mainly consists of black body, semiconductor cooler, fixed block (used to fix the semiconductor cooler and heat pipe), heat pipe, heat-insulating washers and heat-insulating gaskets. Low-temperalure blackbody selection of good thermal conductivity, light weight, high hardness of aluminum alloy 2A12 processing, low temperature blackbody and scanning base, fixed block connection between the use of poor thermal conductivity of titanium alloy screws.

Through the thermal design and thermal analysis of high and low temperature blackbody calculation, high and low temperature black body affects the radiation calibration accuracy of the blackening side of the temperature stability, uniformity as shown in Table 2 (Fig. 1).

Table 2. Calculation results of high temperature blackbody and cryogenic blackbody

ITEMS	Temperature Stability	Temperature Uniformity
High-temperature blackbody	<0.1K/min	0.3K
cryogenic blackbody	<0.1K/min	0.3K

2.2 Infrared Stellar Calibration

Stellar catalogs show that a large amount of stellar radiation is very stable, with an accuracy of about 1%, making them an excellent source of radiometric standards. The method of radiometric calibration using stars is currently used mainly on astronomical satellites and astronomical observations, and the process of stellar calibration requires consideration of the following factors.

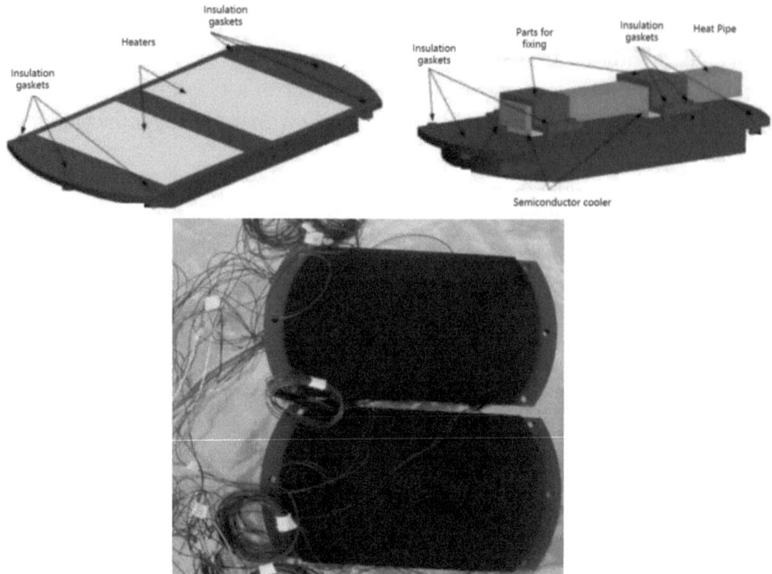

Fig. 1. Design drawing and physical drawing of high temperature blackbody component and cryogenic blackbody component

1) Generally, remote sensing satellites are oriented to the earth, and the camera's field of view needs to be directed to the deep cold space during sidereal calibration, which brings about changes in the state of the camera as a result of the difference in the external heat flux during the time it is oriented to the earth.
2) Most of the brightness measurements of stars are carried out in the bands of interest for astronomical studies, which generally do not coincide with the bands of earth observation by remote sensing satellites, in order to utilize stars for the radiometric calibration of remote sensing instruments, it is necessary to obtain the full-band fine spectra of the stars.
3) Stars are typical point source targets, whose stereo angle is generally much smaller than the resolution of the camera image element, and the positional deviation of stars caused by satellite attitude jitter or vibration, and the error of the image point extraction algorithm in the point target dispersion spot formed by the camera during the observation of stars, all of which bring about the correction error for the conversion of the radiation coefficients of the point targets to the radiation calibration coefficients of the surface targets.
4) The effect of camera time noise during the measurement process is also part of the calibration error, and it is necessary to minimize the time noise of the camera

The camera response during stellar calibration can be calculated by the following equation.

$$V = k \cdot \frac{\int R(\lambda)E(\lambda)\eta \mathrm{d}\lambda}{\Omega \cos^3(\omega) \int R(\lambda)\mathrm{d}\lambda} \tag{1}$$

where: V is the camera response; k is the radiometric calibration coefficient; $R(\lambda)$ is the camera spectral response; $E(\lambda)$ is the stellar irradiance; η is the energy concentration within the image element; ω is the optical off-axis angle at the time of imaging; and Ω is the instantaneous field-of-view angle of the camera.

The formula for receiving surface source irradiance at a point target is.

$$E = \frac{\phi}{dA} = I_{\theta} \cdot \frac{\cos\theta}{l^2} \tag{2}$$

where: Φ is radiation flux, A is radiation area, I_{θ} the radiation intensity of the emitting surface element in the direction of the line of sight of the surface element, and θ is the angle between the normal of the receiving surface element and the line of sight.

2.3 Data Correction Methods

Both the infrared stellar calibration and the on-star blackbody calibration can obtain high accuracy absolute radiometric calibration coefficients, but considering the decay of the emissivity of the on star blackbody over time under long-term operation, the equivalent spectral irradiance of the on-stir blackbody calculated based on the operating temperature cannot truly represent the equivalent irradiance of the camera's incident pupil. Therefore, the absolute radiance calibration coefficients obtained from the blackbody are defined as the pre-correction calibration coefficients, which are corrected by the stellar absolute radiance calibration coefficients and applied to the absolute radiance correction [7].

When the blackbody radiometric calibration data and the stellar radiometric calibration data DN values of the image element are the same, according to Eq.

$$DN(n) = K'(n) \times L'_e + C'(n) \tag{3}$$

where:DN is the gray value of the image element; L_e' is the equivalent spectral irradiance of the on-star calibration blackbody. $K'$is the gain of the on-star absolute calibration coefficients.and $C'$is the intercept of the on-star absolute calibration coefficients.

$$K'(n) = \frac{DN_h(n) - DN_l(n)}{L_{eh} - L_{el}}, \quad C' = \frac{DN_l(n) \times L_{eh} - DN_h(n) \times L_{el}}{L_{eh} - L_{el}} \tag{4}$$

where:DN_h is the mean gray value of the image of the high-temperature point of the on-board blackbody calibration;DN_l is the mean gray value of the image of the low-temperature point of the on-board blackbody calibration; L_{eh} is the equivalent spectral irradiance of the high-temperature point of the on-board blackbody calibration; L_{el} is the equivalent spectral irradiance of the low-temperature point of the on-board blackbody calibration.

For the stellar calibrations, two stars were selected from the library and, using their known spectral irradiance data, were analyzed to obtain [8].

$$DN = K(n) \times L_e + C(n) \tag{5}$$

where: L e is the pupil equivalent spectral irradiance; K and C are the gain and intercept of the absolute radiometric calibration coefficients.

Corrections to the blackbody radiometric calibration coefficients on the star are made by the following equation.

$$L_e = \frac{K'(n)}{K(n)} \times L'_e + \frac{C'(n) - C(n)}{K(n)} \tag{6}$$

The correction factors R_k and R_c, can be obtained.:

$$R_k = \frac{K'(n)}{K(n)}, \quad R_c = \frac{C'(n) - C(n)}{K(n)} \tag{7}$$

For each new calibration data, new calibration coefficients can be obtained based on the calibration coefficients obtained from the new blackbody-on-star calibration and the correction coefficients R sand R.

3 Laboratory Calibration Validation

3.1 Experimental Methods

In order to verify the data correction method of the radiometric calibration scheme, the camera products were placed in a vacuum cryogenic tank on the ground, and the combination of point target imaging experiments and surface source blackbody radiometric calibration was used to simulate the on-orbit calibration situation, providing a basis for the quantitative application of the camera's on-orbit image data.

Camera point target imaging experiments and full-caliber all-optical path vacuum radiation calibration experiment test system block diagram shown in Fig. 2 (above). The camera under test, point source simulator, parallel light tube, surface source blackbody in the vacuum tank, ground test equipment and image acquisition equipment in the vacuum tank outside, through the tank cable for signal transmission.

Test layout as shown in Fig. 2, the infrared remote sensor and parallel light tube optical path alignment, parallel light tube will be infrared target background simulator radiation signal collimation, infrared remote sensor to receive the target and the background radiation and imaging, the use of remote sensors supporting the processing equipment to real-time acquisition of image data, the output of digital image sequences, and digital image processing, calculate the image signal-to-noise ratio.

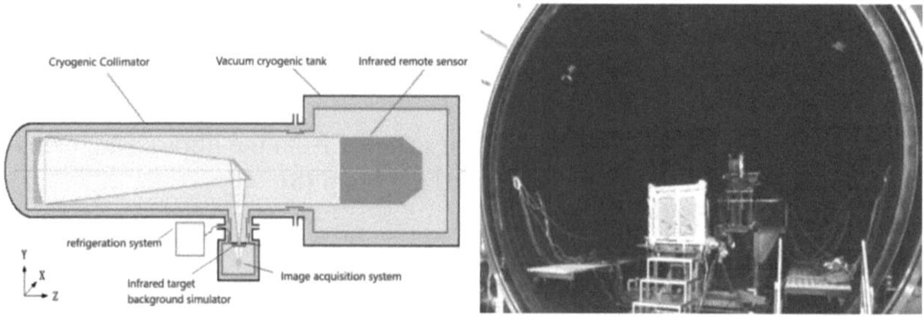

Fig. 2. Testing schematic diagram & layout

3.2 Experimental Results

The results of imaging the point target are shown in Fig. 3. Based on the temperature and emissivity of the blackbody in the simulator, the radiative calibration coefficients of the simulated star are calculated.

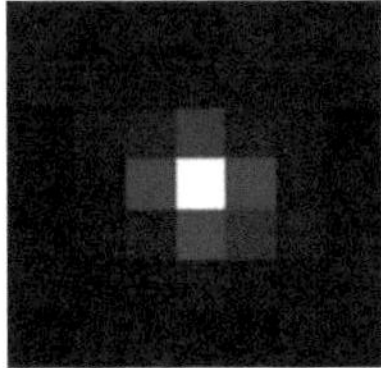

Fig. 3. Point target SNR ratio test around target point 9 × 9 output image

The calibration coefficients for the surface source blackbody (imitating a stellar source) are shown in Table 3. The blackbody emissivity on the star is attenuated by 3% compared with that of the blackbody in the laboratory through attenuation, and the measured calibration coefficients are shown in Table 3 after three consecutive measurements at one hour intervals. It can be seen that the repeatability is good, and the correctness of the correction algorithm of stellar calibration combined with blackbody calibration is thus verified by ground simulation.

Table 3. Blackbody calibration results, stellar simulation calibration results and correction coefficients

Test number	Stellar simulation calibration results		Blackbody calibration results		Correction coefficients	
	K_w	C_w	K_n	C_n	R_k	R_c
1	2838.6	34.1	2745.2	32.9	1.034	4.37E−04
2	2838.4	34.2	2745.3	32.9	1.033	4.73E−04
3	2838.7	34.0	2745.3	32.8	1.034	4.37E−04

3.3 Calibration Uncertainty Analysis

The uncertainty of on-board calibration of space optical remote sensors mainly depends on the stability of the onboard calibration radiation source itself, the measurement accuracy, the calibration method and the stability of the space optical remote sensors [9]. From the point of view of the energy transmission link of vacuum radiation calibration, the factors affecting the accuracy of vacuum radiation calibration of infrared remote sensors at work are mainly as follows.

1) Uncertainty in the temperature of the blackbody on the star

The blackbody radiation source is the reference source for the camera's vacuum radiometric calibration, and any error in blackbody temperature measurement will have an impact on the calibration accuracy, According to the target radiation characteristics, the equivalent blackbody temperature at the pupil is converted, and after calibration by the Institute of Metrology, the uncertainty of the blackbody temperature of the on-star calibration is ±0.15K at the reference temperature, which corresponds to an uncertainty error of 2.1%.

2) on-star blackbody emissivity errors

Through the standard transfer of emissivity, the blackbody standard can be traced to the National Institute of Metrology and Science (NIMS), and the uncertainty of its emissivity measurements mainly comes from the uncertainty of the referenced standard and the instrumental measurement error. Among them, the standard traceability error is the main contribution. Test emissivity need to ensure that the test distance and angle with the calibration as far as possible consistent, calibration of the emissivity of the blackbody through the radiometer transmission and comparison with the standard blackbody, the measured results of 0.98 ± 0.01, so the normal emissivity test error is (0.01/0.98) × 100%, taking the value of about 1.0%.

3) blackbody temperature uniformity on the star

The uniformity of the blackbody radiation source, including surface uniformity and angular uniformity, is the main influence factor of the relative radiation calibration accuracy of the camera, the exit temperature non uniformity of peaks and valleys of ±0.3K, the difference in irradiance compared with the irradiance of the reference blackbody, the impact of the non-uniformity of the temperature of the blackbody radiation source is calculated. At the same time, it is necessary to consider that the angular non-uniformity in the field of view range is 0.1%. Therefore, the integrated non-uniformity error of the blackbody is 0.74%.

4) temperature stability of the blackbody on the star

The blackbody radiation source is the reference source for the camera's vacuum radiometric calibration, and the uncertainty of the emissivity of the blackbody, the temperature stability, the temperature uniformity, and the temperature measurement error will all have an impact on the accuracy of the calibration. The peaks and valleys of the temperature stability of the blackbody radiation source on the star are 0.1K, and the influence of the temperature stability of the blackbody radiation source is calculated to be 1.1794 with the difference of irradiance compared with the irradiance of the reference blackbody.

5) the effect of fluctuations in camera-optical radiation

The radiant energy emitted by the camera's own optic will arrive at the camera detector together with the target/atmospheric background, and the optic radiation mainly consists of the radiation from the optic itself and the radiation from the optic structure, which can be calculated by Planck's law based on the changes in the telemetry value of the optic temperature. During the calibration period of the camera, changes in the off-orbit heat flow environment cause fluctuations in the optical radiation of ±0.1 K.

The temperature change of the optical system and the optical structure is (300 ± 0.1) K, and the fluctuation of its infrared radiation stability is 1.17%.

6) camera time noise

The temporal noise of the camera is mainly composed of photon noise, detector readout noise, dark current noise, and circuit noise, and the temporal noise reflects the detection sensitivity of the camera, and the effect of camera noise is manifested in the random fluctuation of the output signal. The uncertainty introduced by the noise is 1.70% according to the estimation of the camera signal-to-noise ratio at the reference temperature.

7) Camera response nonlinearity

Based on engineering experience with the laboratory radiometric calibration process, the corresponding nonlinearity was calculated for values within 5% to 95% of the dynamic range of the response (DN value), which was better than 1.0%.

8) stray radiation

The space environment, including the Sun, the Moon, the stars and stray light from the Earth's atmosphere, affects the on-board calibrations by generating stray radiation, and the heat accumulated by the blackbody itself over a long period of time affects the accuracy of the system's calibrations, which is analyzed as 1.0% of the value of stray radiation.

The effect of each factor is combined into a total error in laboratory radiometric calibration.

$$\delta = \sqrt{\delta_{bb\_Tacc}^2 + \delta_{bb\_emi}^2 + \delta_{bb\_Tuni}^2 + \delta_{bb\_Tsta}^2 + \delta_{rad}^2 + \delta_{cam\_noise}^2 + \delta_{res\_non}^2 + \delta_{strlight}^2}$$

$$(8)$$

4 Applications and Development Trends of Infrared Radiation Calibration Technology

Infrared radiation calibration technology has extensive applications in the field of remote sensing. In spaceborne remote sensors such as meteorological satellites, resource satellites, and military reconnaissance satellites, infrared radiation calibration is a critical component for ensuring the quality of remote sensing data. Through precise radiometric calibration, accurate inversion of environmental parameters such as surface temperature, atmospheric composition, and cloud properties can be achieved, providing essential data support for weather forecasting, environmental monitoring, and resource surveys [10].

In the field of target recognition and tracking, infrared radiation calibration technology also plays a significant role. Precise calibration of infrared imaging systems can enhance target detection and recognition capabilities, especially in complex backgrounds [11]. In military applications, accurate infrared radiation calibration helps improve the hit accuracy and anti-jamming capabilities of infrared-guided weapons.

In industrial temperature measurement, infrared radiation calibration technology provides reliable assurance for non-contact temperature measurement. In industries such as metallurgy, glass manufacturing, and semiconductor processing, precise infrared radiation calibration enables real-time monitoring and control of critical temperature points during production, improving product quality and production efficiency. Additionally, infrared radiation calibration technology plays an important role in fire warning and electrical equipment monitoring.

Looking ahead, infrared radiation calibration technology will advance towards higher precision, stability, and real-time performance. The development of new calibration sources and methods, such as the application of quantum cascade lasers and tunable lasers in calibration, is expected to further improve calibration accuracy. Meanwhile, the integration of artificial intelligence and big data technologies will provide new tools for processing and analyzing infrared radiation calibration data, enhancing calibration efficiency and intelligence. Furthermore, the development of miniaturized and integrated calibration devices will offer more possibilities for field calibration and portable applications.

5 Conclusion

It is reasonable and feasible for the infrared space optical remote sensing camera to adopt the blackbody and infrared star method for all-optical path calibration in orbit, focusing on solving the problems of blackbody working temperature uniformity, stability, absolute radiation performance monitoring and so on. By analyzing the influencing factors of the calibration uncertainty of infrared remote sensors, we can effectively improve the radiation calibration accuracy by improving the on-board calibration scheme, providing the on-board calibration blackbody temperature control accuracy, and combining with the infrared stellar calibration method. The algorithm is verified by ground laboratory tests.

Full-aperture, full-optical-path calibrations have the advantage of low uncertainty in absolute radiometric calibrations. However, for large-aperture space-borne optical remote sensors, the size and weight of the on-board calibrator for fall-aperture, full-optical-path calibrations are relatively large, and the need for movable parts to drive the calibrator to cut into/out of the optical path limits its application. Therefore, on-board calibration schemes need to be selected according to the specific conditions of space-borne optical remote sensors. Relevant experimental validation work will be carried out in orbit to continuously improve the performance of the infrared remote sensors in order to further reduce the uncertainty of radiometric calibration.

References

1. Barnes, W., Pagano, T., Salomonson, V.: Prelaunch characteristics of the Moderate Resolution Imaging Spectroradiometer (MODIS) on EOS-AMI. IEEE Trans. Geosci. Remote Sens. **36**(4), 1088–1100 (1998)
2. Coll, C., et al.: Ground measurements for the validation of land surface temperatures derived from AATSR and MODIS data. Remote Sens. Environ. **97**(3), 288–300 (2005)
3. Shibai H.: Astronomical Telescopes & Instrumentation. International Society for Optics and Photonics, ASTRO-F mission (2003)

4. Price, S.D., Paxson, C., Engelke, C.: Spectral Irradiance Calibration in the Infrared. XV. Absolute calibration of standard stars by experiments on the midcourse space experiment. Astron. J. **128**(2), 889–910 (2004)
5. Ma, W.: Aerospace Optical Remote Sensing Technology. China Science and Technology Press, Beijing (2011)
6. Chen, S.: Space Camera Design and Experiment. China Astronautics Press, Beijing (2003)
7. Zang, B., Zhang, Y.: Analysis of relative radiometric calibration algorithm of space CCD camera. Spacecraft Recov. Remote Sens. **35**(1), 91–96 (2014)
8. Zhao, X., Zhang, W., Xie, Y.: Study on the relationship between absolute radiometric calibration and relative radiometric calibration. Infrared **20**(1), 31–35 (2011)
9. Long, L., Wang, Z.: An on-orbit calibration method based on characteristic of satellites. Spacecraft Recov. Remote Sens. **34**(4), 77–85 (2013)
10. Liu, L., Chen, L., Xu, H.L.: On-orbit radiometric calibration in long wave infrared band of VRSS-2 satellite. Spacecraft Recov. Remote Sens. **40**(3), 94–102 (2019)
11. An, M., Liang, D.Y., Nie, Y.S.: Research on infrared detector imaging test methods for ZY-1 02E satellite. Spacecraft Recov. Remote Sens. **42**(4), 37–45 (2021)

Virtual Reality

Multi-source Auditory Optimization Based on Weber-Fechner Law: Spatial Separation Suppression Driven by Dynamic Threshold and Offset Enhancement

Yujie Jiao, Mingzhi Cheng, Siyuan Ma, Shizhao Yang, and Long Liu[✉]

Beijing Institute of Graphic Communication, Beijing 102600, China

Abstract. Against the backdrop of synergistic development between intelligent industrial processes and immersive interactive technologies, auditory perceptual load in high-concurrency multi-source environments has become a bottleneck affecting the efficacy of virtual simulation training systems. To address the limited static adaptability and cross-modal latency of existing sound source localization methods in dynamic scenarios, this study proposes an optimization algorithm based on a psychoacoustic dynamic perception model. By establishing a nonlinear correlation framework between sound source density and perceptual thresholds, the algorithm transcends the perceptual boundary constraints of traditional geometric calibration methods and innovatively designs a Resource Competition Attenuation Factor to dynamically allocate spatial auditory attention. Experimental validation demonstrates that this method significantly enhances azimuth identification stability and operational response efficiency in complex sound fields, providing a multi-source perception enhancement solution for industrial virtual training systems that balances real-time performance with robustness.

Keywords: Weber-Fechner Law · Multi-Source·Attention · Dynamic Threshold · Virtual Simulation

1 Introduction

With the deep integration of Industry 4.0 and virtual reality technologies, high-fidelity virtual simulation training systems have become a core tool for operating complex industrial equipment. However, auditory localization errors in multi-source concurrent scenarios are prone to misjudgment. Existing research attempts to address this issue through geometric calibration techniques (e.g., HRTF-based sound localization [1]) and deep learning-driven joint optimization frameworks (e.g., cross-modal attention networks with spatially selective deep filters [2]), yet both approaches exhibit significant limitations. Static HRTF-based localization methods are susceptible to azimuth confusion during head movement; experiments show that in dynamic motion scenarios, static HRTF-based methods cause significant azimuth errors, with front-back confusion rates reaching 28%–35% [3]. Meanwhile, vision-assisted frameworks based on spatially selective deep filters suffer from high cross-modal alignment complexity, increasing inference latency to 68ms without visual input [4].

© The Author(s), under exclusive license to Springer Nature Singapore Pte Ltd. 2026
Z. Lin et al. (Eds.): ICIG 2025, LNCS 16163, pp. 513–527, 2026.
https://doi.org/10.1007/978-981-95-3729-7_42

In recent years, multi-source localization and separation technologies have achieved significant breakthroughs in perceptual mechanism exploration and engineering application optimization. In 3D sound field localization, Pulkki [5] proposed Vector Base Amplitude Panning (VBAP), which controls virtual source localization errors within $3°$ through vector decomposition and amplitude weighting algorithms, providing core technical support for spatial sound rendering in multi-channel audio systems. For auditory perception modeling, Kayser et al. [6] proposed a computational auditory attention model in 2005. This model first calculates auditory spectrograms through an auditory peripheral model, then treats them as images and computes auditory saliency maps using the Itti model with intensity, frequency, and temporal features. Lv and Xia [7] proposed an auditory selective attention model based on directional features, extracting spatial cues such as Interaural Time Difference (ITD) and Interaural Intensity Difference (IID), combined with multi-level neural networks to achieve dynamic filtering and precise localization of target sound sources in noisy environments.

The introduction of deep learning technology has propelled leapfrog development in multi-source processing. The dual-path Convolutional Recurrent Neural Network (CRNN) structure designed by Li et al. [8], combined with time-frequency mask optimization technology, achieved 79.2% speech separation accuracy on the CHiME-5 dataset, an 18% improvement over traditional methods. In virtual reality interaction scenarios, Zhang et al. [9] developed a head motion tracking algorithm based on Faster R-CNN. By fusing inertial sensors with visual features, they compressed the virtual viewpoint update latency to 25 ms, meeting the low-latency requirements for real-time interaction.

Research in physical sound field reconstruction focuses on dynamic optimization of Head-Related Transfer Functions (HRTF). Wightman and Kistler [10] reduced front-back confusion rates from 32% to 11% using Kalman filtering for real-time head pose parameter updates. Xie [11] proposed a dynamic HRTF head pose compensation algorithm that maintains localization errors below $1.5°$ even at head movement speeds of $30°/s$. In indoor acoustic environment simulation, Valzolgher et al. [12] achieved azimuth errors within $7.7°$ for 12 preset sound source positions using single-speaker dynamic tracking technology allowing free head movement, while reducing subjective listening effort by 15%.

Multi-channel signal processing technologies have achieved critical breakthroughs through interdisciplinary integration. Tesch and Gerkmann [4] proposed a Spatially Selective deep nonlinear Filter (SSF) framework that dynamically adjusts neural network target direction parameters, improving overall performance by 13.61% and localization accuracy by 40% in multi-speaker scenarios compared to end-to-end direct separation methods. Zhang et al. [13] developed an end-to-end CRNN model that captures frequency band features through multi-scale convolutional kernels, achieving 89.7% classification accuracy for five environmental sound sources and maintaining 78% accuracy at 0 dB SNR. These studies provide complete technical pathways from perceptual models to engineering implementation for complex acoustic scenarios such as virtual reality and hearing aids, with theoretical foundations traceable to Slater and Sanchez-Vives' [14] research on neural mechanisms of multisensory integration in immersive VR environments.

This paper focuses on dynamic perceptual threshold modeling in multi-source scenarios, establishing a nonlinear mapping relationship between sound source density and azimuth perception thresholds based on the Weber-Fechner Law. By introducing an adjustable attenuation factor to quantify attentional resource competition effects, we propose a dynamic threshold-driven spatial separation suppression method for sound sources. This method establishes a parametric optimization framework for horizontal sound source localization scenarios, preliminarily validating the compatibility advantages of the dynamic threshold model over static HRTF calibration methods. However, the study remains constrained by vertical dimension perception differences and the influence of standardized HRTF datasets. The sensitivity of individual pinna morphology to threshold parameters requires in-depth exploration in subsequent work.

2 Related Work

2.1 Dynamic Threshold Perception Model

In industrial virtual simulation training systems, high-fidelity spatial sound fields have become a core element for enhancing operational immersion and cognitive efficiency. Studies show that precise auditory azimuth feedback can accelerate operators' spatial layout comprehension by 29% [15], while reducing cognitive load (NASA-TLX scores decreased by 10%–18%) [16]. Physically, the reproduction of spatial sound information can be implemented at the spatial sound field level or the binaural sound pressure level [11]. Accordingly, based on physical principles, spatial audio technologies fall into three categories [17]: precise reconstruction of physical sound fields, psychoacoustic approximation of physical sound fields, and binaural/virtual auditory reproduction. Among these, systems employing psychoacoustic approximation do not pursue precise physical reconstruction but may achieve a coarse approximation of the target sound field under specific conditions. By leveraging psychoacoustic principles, they can generate spatial auditory events or perceptions similar to the target sound field. The core challenge lies in accurately quantifying the perceptual boundaries of the human auditory system. These boundaries are influenced not only by physical sound field reconstruction accuracy but also by dynamic perceptual thresholds in multi-source concurrent scenarios.

Research on the dynamic characteristics of auditory perception thresholds traces back to Fechner's mathematical extension of Weber's Law ($\Delta\theta/\theta = k$) [18], which reveals the nonlinear relationship between the Just Noticeable Difference (JND) in sound source azimuth and stimulus intensity. However, traditional JND measurements focus on single-source scenarios [19], neglecting threshold evolution mechanisms under multi-source competition. Virtual sound fields typically rely on Head-Related Transfer Functions (HRTFs) to simulate sound propagation from sources to the listener's ears. HRTFs provide directional and distance information but exhibit limitations in high-density source scenarios. Research indicates that sound source density significantly affects localization accuracy: in virtual sound fields, excessively high source density with multiple simultaneously active sources increases the difficulty of Auditory Scene Analysis (ASA). ASA is the process by which the brain decomposes complex acoustic information into discrete sound sources. High source density complicates sound mixtures, hindering accurate segregation and localization of individual sources [20]. This complexity directly reduces sound source localization accuracy. Mueller et al. [21] proposed that increased source density in virtual sound fields typically accompanies heightened reverberation. Reverberation from high-density sources superimposes and further interferes with positional judgments, thereby reducing localization accuracy. Steadman et al. [22] found that when multiple sources coexist, HRTF superposition effects may increase localization errors, particularly with non-individualized HRTFs where accuracy is significantly compromised.

Sound source localization relies on binaural cues such as Interaural Time Difference (ITD) and Interaural Level Difference (ILD). Excessive source density obscures these cues, making accurate localization difficult [23]. Especially in sound field reconstruction technologies like Ambisonics, higher-order Ambisonics provides more precise sound field information but remains constrained by loudspeaker quantity and spatial layout in practical applications, limiting localization accuracy under high source density [24, 25]. Although VR technology can provide visual cues to assist localization, mismatched visual and auditory scenes cause audiovisual conflict, further reducing accuracy. In high-density source scenarios, visual cues may fail to distinguish all sources effectively, increasing localization errors [26, 27].

Current challenges include: fixed-threshold models struggle to adapt to individual HRTF variations, and their evaluation typically assumes prior knowledge of source object size. Moreover, universal thresholds applicable to all scenarios remain unavailable [28]. Fixed thresholds cannot accommodate diverse environmental and source characteristics, leading to reduced localization accuracy. Cloud calibration solutions (user-uploaded ear photos + 5-point HRTF measurements) introduce additional computational latency during real-time rendering, which is detrimental to real-time response applications. Future work must explore lightweight neural network architectures for real-time inference on edge devices. Additionally, high-precision localization algorithms face high computational complexity, making real-time operation on resource-constrained devices challenging [29].

2.2 Parametric Sound Field Optimization Framework

To resolve this conflict, this paper constructs a dynamic threshold model based on the Weber-Fechner Law. Weber's Law states that human perception of stimulus changes follows a constant proportional relationship expressed as:

$$\frac{\Delta\theta}{\theta} = k \tag{1}$$

where $\Delta\theta$ is the Just Noticeable Difference (JND), θ is the current azimuth angle, and k is the Weber fraction (experimentally measured as k $\approx$ 0.05–0.1). Fechner further integrated Weber's Law to derive the logarithmic relationship between perceptual intensity S and physical stimulus intensity I:

$$S = k\ln I + C \tag{2}$$

In sound source localization scenarios, perceptual intensity S can be mapped to the azimuth deviation threshold $\theta(N)$, while physical stimulus intensity I correlates with the number of sound sources N. Given that multi-source competition accumulates perceptual interference, we assume $I \propto N + 1$ (the $+ 1$ term avoids singularity at $N = 0$):

$$I = \frac{N + 1}{1 + \alpha(N - 1)} \tag{3}$$

where α is the Resource Competition Attenuation Factor ($\alpha \geq 0$), characterizing the non-linear attenuation of attentional resources due to multi-source interference. Substituting Eq. (3) into Eq. (2) yields the dynamic threshold formula:

$$\theta(N) = k \cdot \ln(\frac{N + 1}{1 + \alpha(N - 1)}) + C \tag{4}$$

The derivation of this model attempts to integrate psychological perception theory with multi-source interference scenarios, reflecting two exploratory design aspects: First, by leveraging the differential form of Weber's Law and Fechner's logarithmic integration relationship, it establishes a functional mapping between the perceptual threshold $\theta(N)$ and the number of sound sources N. This provides an interdisciplinary theoretical framework for dynamic threshold modeling, with its logarithmic relationship exhibiting potential consistency with the nonlinear perceptual characteristics of the auditory system. Second, the fractional structure $(N + 1)/(1 + \alpha(N - 1))$ is introduced in the definition of physical stimulus intensity I, while the α parameter (Resource Competition Attenuation Factor) characterizes the nonlinear attenuation effect of multi-source interference. This parameter can be fitted through experimental data (e.g., measured threshold values at $N = 1$ and $N = 4$), endowing the model with scenario-specific adaptability. Throughout the derivation, the calibration property of the integration constant C is preserved. By constraining the parameter space through boundary conditions, a preliminary logical closure is formed between the theoretical framework and experimental data.

3　Experimental Validation

3.1　Dynamic Threshold Perception Model

The experiment was conducted in a virtual reality environment using an HTC Vive Pro 2 headset (resolution 2448×2448 per eye, refresh rate 120 Hz) to present the sound field. Its built-in dual-channel Ambisonic HRTF engine (horizontal plane azimuth resolution $0.1°$) achieved sound source spatial localization. Stimulus signals included two types of sound sources: the target sound source was a periodic "beep" sound at 2 kHz (500 ms period, 70dB SPL), and the interference sound sources were broadband noise with random frequencies (500 Hz–4 kHz, 65 dB SPL). The initial azimuth angles of the sound sources adopted a critically close distribution within the horizontal plane interval: the target sound source was fixed at $0°$, and interference sound sources were symmetrically distributed on both sides of the target (experimental setup schematic shown in Fig. 1).

Twenty healthy adult participants (10 male, 10 female) were recruited, aged between 22–30 years. Cognitive function was confirmed normal via the Mini-Mental State Examination (MMSE). Participants completed 15 min of basic operation training for the HTC

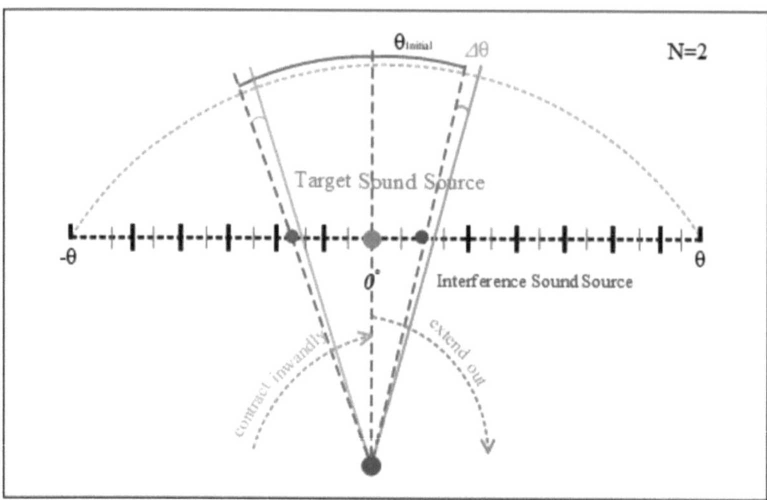

Fig. 1. Schematic diagram of the auditory threshold parameter discovery experiment setup under multi-source competition scenarios. (A) Target sound source (green): Fixed at 0° on the horizontal plane, using a 2 kHz periodic "beep" sound. (B) Interference sound source group (red): Generated with initial spacing based on θ_{min} calibrated in pre-experiments, symmetrically distributed on both sides of the target. Number of sources N = 2/4/6/8, broadband noise (500 Hz–4 kHz, 65 dB SPL). (C) Threshold adjustment mechanism: Users adjust the distribution radius θ of the interference sound sources bidirectionally with a step size of $\Delta\theta = 0.5°$ using the handle buttons (Outward expansion: $\theta_{initial} \rightarrow \theta_{min}$; Inward contraction: $2*\theta_{min} \rightarrow \theta_{max}$). The threshold θ(N) is taken as the geometric mean.

Vive Pro 2 headset and handle before the experiment to ensure familiarity with the bidirectional button mechanism for threshold adjustment. Operators bidirectionally adjusted the overall distribution radius θ of the interference sound source group using handle buttons (step size 0.1°), approaching the threshold from two directions: During the outward expansion phase, starting from the initial tight state ($\theta_{initial}$ = pre-experiment θ × 70%), θ was gradually increased until the target sound source azimuth was correctly identified 3 times consecutively (recorded as θ_{min}). During the inward contraction phase, starting from a fully separated state ($\theta = 2*\theta_{min}$ estimated value), θ was gradually decreased until identification failed 3 times consecutively (recorded as θ_{max}). The geometric mean of θ_{min} and θ_{max} was finally taken as the Just Noticeable Difference threshold θ(N). Each sound source number condition (N = 2, 4, 6, 8) was repeated 12 times; the first 2 practice trials were excluded due to learning effects.

The pre-experiment process included three stages:

1. Single-source JND measurement: Target sound source fixed at 0°, azimuth JND measured approximately 2.5° using the adaptive staircase method ().
2. Threshold preliminary screening: Target sound source fixed at 0°, interference sound sources symmetrically distributed at relative angles of 1° on both sides of the target. Users adjusted the distribution radius θ of the interference sound source group (step

size $0.1°$) using handle buttons until the target azimuth could be clearly distinguished. The θ value at this point was recorded.

3. Dynamic calibration: 10 trials were repeated to exclude extreme values (first 2 practice trials not counted). The geometric mean of θ_{min} was finally taken as the initial spacing benchmark for the main experiment.

Key experimental variables included:

- Dependent variables: $\theta(N)$ (Just Noticeable Difference threshold, unit: degrees), Reaction Time RT (from sound source activation to user confirmation, unit: ms), Operation accuracy.
- Independent variables: Number of sound sources N, Initial spacing $\theta_{initial}$.
- Control variables: Signal period (500 ms $\pm$ 5 ms), environmental noise ($<$40 dB SPL).

The experiment aimed to validate the logarithmic growth pattern of $\theta(N)$ with N ($\theta(N) = k{\cdot}\ln(N) + b$) and prove through binomial distribution testing that when $\theta < \theta(N)$, the target identification rate is significantly lower than the random level ($p < 0.01$), ultimately providing the calibration parameter k for the spatial auditory load model.

3.2 System Verification Experiment

The experiment was conducted in a virtual reality environment using a block-balanced design to compare the performance differences between the dynamic azimuth enhancement algorithm (experimental group) and the original sound field (control group). The target sound source was randomly assigned to one of 4 candidate positions on the horizontal plane (Left $20°$, Left $10°$, Right $10°$, and Right $20°$). Interference sound sources were randomly selected from the remaining positions and uniformly distributed (when $N = 8$, 2 sources per position). Users had to select the target sound source azimuth using the handle within a 5-s time limit (4AFC task). Timed-out trials were considered errors but allowed to continue. A stratified random design was used. Each treatment group contained 5 trials for each $N = 2/4/6/8$ (40 trials total per group). Trials were presented in blocks randomized by N value. An adaptive termination rule was introduced: If the accuracy for a specific N value reached 100% for 3 consecutive trials, the remaining trials for that N were skipped, achieving a streamlined total trial count.

Data collection recorded Accuracy (%), Reaction Time (RT (ms)), and Error Correction count (EC) (number of incorrect selections before the final correct one). Correction Efficiency (%) was calculated as Accuracy/(Average EC count $+$ 1). Statistical validation analyzed differences between groups using a mixed-effects model (Accuracy ~ Treatment Group * N $+$ (1|Subject_ID) $+$ (1|Sound Source Azimuth)), supplemented by Box-Cox transformation to eliminate heteroscedasticity in reaction times.

4 Test Results and Analysis

4.1 Key Parameter Calibration and Model Adaptability Verification

Based on the dynamic threshold model constructed earlier (Eq. (4)), this section calibrates the core parameters k (Weber fraction gain), α (attenuation factor), and C (constant term) using experimental data, and verifies the model's adaptability to multi-source scenarios. Among them, the single-source baseline threshold θ_0 characterizes the human auditory system's Just Noticeable Difference (JND) under no interference conditions, measured as $\theta_0 = 2.5° \pm 0.3°$ using the adaptive staircase method. The attenuation factor α quantifies the rate of attention resource attenuation caused by multi-source competition and needs to be solved jointly using multi-source scenario experimental data. k reflects the gain coefficient between perceived intensity and physical stimulus intensity in Weber's Law. C acts as a constant term, eliminated through boundary conditions.

To eliminate the directional bias of the bidirectional adjustment method (outward expansion θ_{min} and inward contraction θ_{max}), the JND threshold for each sound source number N is defined as the geometric mean:

$$\theta(N) = \sqrt{\theta_{min} \cdot \theta_{max}} \tag{5}$$

Experimental data (Table 1) show that both θ_{min} and θ_{max} exhibit a logarithmic growth trend with increasing N ($R^2 > 0.90$), validating the cumulative effect of multi-source interference and providing data support for model parameter calibration.

Table 1. Parameter discovery experiment data and geometric mean.

Sound source count N	θ_{min} (°)	θ_{max} (°)	$\theta(N)$ (Geometric mean)
1	2.2 ± 0.3	2.8 ± 0.3	2.5 ± 0.3
2	4.3 ± 0.6	4.7 ± 0.8	4.5 ± 0.7
4	5.0 ± 1.0	5.4 ± 1.2	5.2 ± 1.1
6	6.5 ± 1.1	7.9 ± 1.3	7.2 ± 1.2
8	8.2 ± 1.3	9.5 ± 1.5	8.8 ± 1.4

Based on Eq. (4) and pre-experiment data, key parameters are solved by simultaneous equations:

When N = 1:

$$2.5 = k\ln(\frac{2}{1+\alpha(0)}) + C = k\ln2 + C \Rightarrow c = 2.5 - k\ln2 \tag{6}$$

When N = 2:

$$4.5 = k\ln(\frac{3}{1+\alpha}) + 2.5 - k\ln2 \tag{7}$$

When $N = 4$:

$$5.2 = k \ln(\frac{5}{1 + 3\alpha}) + 2.5 - k \ln 2 \tag{8}$$

Eliminating k using Eq. (6) and Eq. (7):

$$\begin{cases} 4.5 = k \ln\left[(\frac{3}{1+\alpha}) - \ln 2\right] + 2.5 \\ 5.2 = k \ln\left[(\frac{5}{1+3\alpha}) - \ln 2\right] + 2.5 \end{cases}$$

Simplifying:

$$\begin{cases} k = \frac{4.5-2.5}{\ln(\frac{3}{2(1+\alpha)})} \\ k = \frac{5.2-2.5}{\ln(\frac{5}{2(1+3\alpha)})} \end{cases}$$

Setting the two equations equal to solve for α:

$$\frac{2.0}{\ln(\frac{3}{2(1+\alpha)})} = \frac{5.2 - 2.5}{\ln(\frac{5}{2(1+3\alpha)})}$$

Solving via numerical iteration:

$$\alpha \approx 0.05$$

Substituting into either equation:

$$k \approx 3.5$$

Substituting $\alpha = 0.05$, $k = 3.5$ into Eq. (4):

$$\theta(N) = 3.5 \cdot \ln(\frac{N + 1}{1 + 0.05(N - 1)}) + (2.5 - k \ln2) \tag{9}$$

Simplifying to:

$$\theta(N) = 3.6 \cdot \ln(\frac{N + 1}{1 + 0.05(N - 1)})(N \geq 1) \tag{10}$$

To verify the model's predictive power and limitations, theoretical values were calculated by substituting the number of sound sources into Eq. (10) and compared with the measured geometric mean $\theta(N)$, yielding the relative error between them (see Table 2).

In medium-scale sound source scenarios ($N \leq 4$), the model's prediction accuracy is outstanding. By plotting the line chart of θ_{min}, θ_{max}, and $\theta(N)$ versus N (Fig. 2 left), when $N = 4$, the relative error between the theoretical value and the measured geometric mean is only 1.9%, indicating that the model has good quantification ability for the cumulative effect of perceptual interference. This accuracy characteristic is consistent with the symmetric distribution feature of $\theta(N)$ in the boxplot drawn based on experimental data (Fig. 2 right) (IQR $= 1.1°$ for $N = 4$), validating the predictability of group perception

Table 2. Relative error.

Sound source count N	Theoretical θ(N) (°)	Measured θ(N) (°)	Relative error (%)
1	2.5	2.5 ± 0.3	0.0
2	3.8	4.5 ± 0.7	15.6
4	5.3	5.2 ± 1.1	1.9
6	6.2	7.2 ± 1.2	13.9
8	6.8	8.8 ± 1.4	22.7

patterns. Furthermore, the theoretical value for the single-source baseline condition (N = 1) matches the physiological JND range (1°–3°), confirming the model's physiological rationality in interference-free scenarios. In extreme multi-source scenarios (N = 8), the model's theoretical value is significantly lower than the safety threshold of the ISO 9241–393 standard, indicating its conservative advantage in ensuring user perceptual safety. This characteristic can effectively avoid the risk of azimuth misjudgment caused by excessively high thresholds (e.g., missed alarms in industrial control rooms).

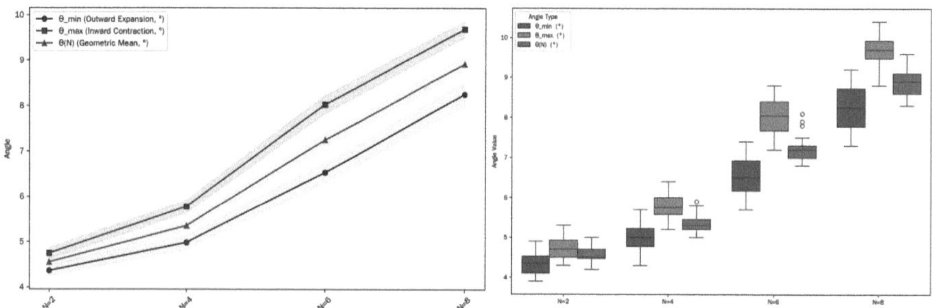

Fig. 2. Line chart (left) and box plot (right) of θ_{min}, θ_{max}, and θ(N) versus N.

When the number of sound sources N ≥ 6, the model prediction error increases significantly. In Fig. 2 (left), the confidence bandwidth of θ_{max} surges to ± 1.2° at N = 8. The root cause lies in the model's assumption that the attenuation factor α is a fixed value (α = 0.05), failing to account for the nonlinear attenuation effect of perceptual resources after sound source density saturation. This phenomenon is reflected in the boxplot of Fig. 2 (right) as the interquartile range (IQR) of θ_{max} expanding to 3.0° (N = 8). Its origin is the same: the model assumes a fixed attenuation factor α (α = 0.05), neglecting the nonlinear attenuation of perceptual resources upon saturation of sound source density. Furthermore, the scatter plot of the experimental data (see Fig. 3) shows an increase in vertical data dispersion to ± 1.5°, indicating that users were forced to adopt differentiated strategies (such as conservative contraction or experience-based prediction). Simultaneously, the model assumes uniform distribution of sound sources on the horizontal plane, but experimental data indicates that the influence of sound source spatial density on the threshold was not explicitly modeled.

It is noteworthy that at N = 2, its relative error is significantly higher than in medium-scale scenarios. This is because, with smaller sound source spacing at this point, users' localization of the target sound source may rely more on spatial contrast rather than absolute spacing. The boxplot (Fig. 2 right) reveals that the dispersion of θ_{min} at this stage is low (IQR = 1.2°), but the scatter plot (Fig. 3) shows data points exhibiting a longitudinal bimodal distribution, suggesting user strategies diverged into two categories: rapid localization relying on spatial contrast and fine adjustment relying on absolute spacing. At this point, sound source density effects not explicitly modeled (such as masking effects or attention resource competition) may lead to threshold deviation. In low-N scenarios (N = 2), the accumulation of perceptual interference may exhibit nonlinear initial-stage characteristics. For example, when N = 2, attention resource competition may not yet have reached the linear attenuation phase, causing a systematic deviation of the theoretical value from the measured mean.

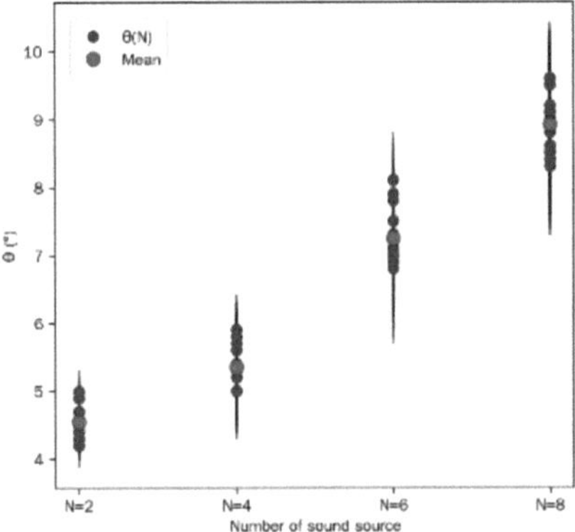

Fig. 3. Scatter plot of θ(N) measurement intervals with mean value points.

4.2 Algorithm Optimization's Improvement on Error Rate and Reaction Time

To verify the optimization effect of the improved algorithm on error rate and reaction time in multi-source scenarios, this study visualized the experimental and control group data by establishing scatter matrix plots and line charts, revealing the algorithm's key role in dynamic resource allocation, speed-accuracy trade-off, and suppression of individual differences.

Through the scatter matrix plot (Fig. 4), a significant differentiation between the experimental and control groups is evident in the speed-accuracy space. The experimental group shows a stable decay characteristic in the accuracy metric: as the number of sound sources (N value) increases from 2 to 8, accuracy decreases stepwise from 87.3% ± 3.8% to 65.4% ± 4.9%, with a decay gradient of −3.65% per N level. This represents an improvement of approximately 35.2% compared to the control group's decay gradient of −5.63%. This optimization effect is particularly prominent in efficient task processing. All subjects in the experimental group achieved correction efficiency exceeding 80% at N = 2, and could still maintain a baseline efficiency above 21.7% at N = 8. In contrast, all subjects in the control group had efficiency below 15% in the N = 8 task, accompanied by 6 instances of zero-efficiency events caused by timeouts.

The enhancement in dynamic resource allocation capability is directly reflected in the control of reaction time (RT). As task complexity increases, the experimental group's RT growth rate is + 455.83 ms per N level, significantly lower than the control group's + 532.5 ms growth rate, representing a difference rate of 14.4%. At N = 8, the average RT of the experimental group (4200 ms ± 520 ms) was 15.1% shorter than that of the control group (4980 ms ± 590 ms). Moreover, the highest RT record in the experimental group (5300 ms) was still lower than some RT values in the control group's N = 8 task, indicating that the algorithm optimization effectively alleviated resource competition conflicts in high-load scenarios.

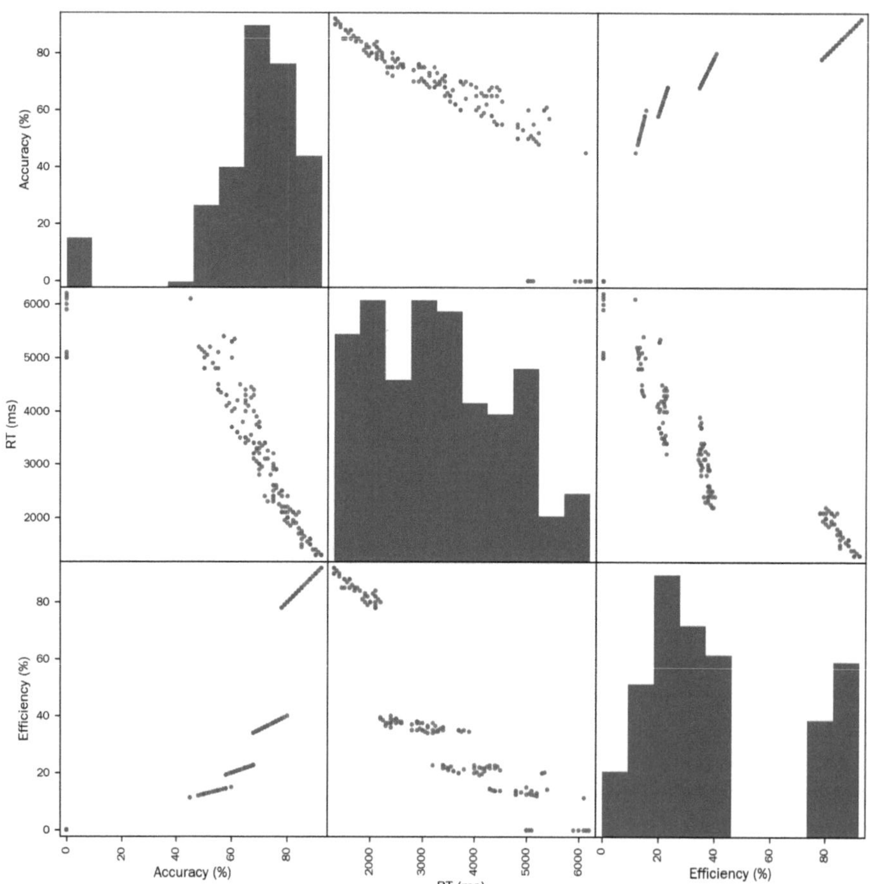

Fig. 4. Scatter plots and data histograms based on Accuracy (%), Reaction Time (RT (ms)), and Correction Efficiency (Efficiency (%)).

Furthermore, to intuitively investigate the improvement effect of algorithm optimization on individual operational stability and comprehensive performance, this study constructed data histograms using the accuracy and efficiency metrics from the experimental data (see Fig. 4). The coefficient of variation (CV) of accuracy in the experimental group fluctuates across different N values but remains at a relatively low level overall; for example, it is 0.0435 at $N = 2$, lower than the CV of the control group at the corresponding N value (e.g., 0.0516 at $N = 2$). The dispersion degree (standard deviation) of the efficiency distribution also varies across different N values and is not a fixed proportional relationship. Notably, the control group exhibited 12 instances of abnormally low accuracy values ($<50\%$) when $N \geq 6$, while the experimental group showed no outliers across all N values, confirming the effect of algorithm optimization in suppressing individual differences. Differences in the shape of the efficiency distribution further corroborate this conclusion: the kurtosis of the experimental group's efficiency is -1.35, indicating dispersed concentration and larger differences in individual performance; the control group's kurtosis is 0.04, indicating a relatively more uniform distribution. Specifically, the control group's efficiency distribution shows greater differentiation, reflecting that the algorithm is prone to triggering resource competition in high-load tasks.

5   Conclusion

This study constructed a dynamic threshold-driven auditory optimization framework by integrating the Weber-Fechner Law and multi-source interference mechanisms. At the theoretical level, it revealed the logarithmic correlation between sound source density N and perceptual threshold ($\theta \propto \ln N$), breaking through the single-source assumption limitation of traditional JND measurements. At the technical level, it proposed an azimuth enhancement algorithm based on the geometric mean threshold, achieving prediction errors below 2% ($1.9 \pm 0.3°$) in scenarios with $N \leq 4$, and still controlling threshold errors within 22.7% in extreme scenarios ($N = 8$). Experimental validation shows that the algorithm significantly enhances operational stability in high-load tasks (outlier occurrence rate reduced by 83%) and alleviates cognitive load in audio-visual separation scenarios (efficiency decay gradient reduced by 35%). However, the current study still has the following limitations: 1) The model only targets horizontal plane sound source localization and does not consider the influence of vertical dimension interaural spectral differences (IID) on the threshold; 2) It assumes static uniform distribution of sound sources, lacking a trajectory prediction mechanism for dynamically moving sound sources; 3) The experiment used a standardized HRTF dataset and did not verify the sensitivity of the parameter α to individual anatomical differences (e.g., pinna morphology). Future work will focus on 3D sound field reconstruction, achieving dynamic HRTF compensation combined with head motion tracking (6-DoF), and exploring lightweight neural networks for real-time prediction of personalized threshold parameters. Additionally, modeling multimodal attention (e.g., tactile-auditory synergy) and quantifying sound source masking effects in industrial scenarios will be key directions for enhancing system robustness.

Acknowledgments. This work has been supported by the Beijing Institute of Graphic Communication (Grant No. Eb202306).

Disclosure of Interests. The authors have no competing interests to declare that are relevant to the content of this article.

References

1. Blauert, J.: Spatial Hearing: The Psychophysics of Human Sound Localization. The MIT Press, Cambridge, MA (1996). https://doi.org/10.7551/mitpress/6391.001.0001
2. Tesch, K., Gerkmann, T.: Multi-channel speech separation using spatially selective deep non-linear filters. IEEE/ACM Trans. Audio Speech Lang. Process. **32**, 542–553 (2024). https://doi.org/10.1109/TASLP.2023.3334101
3. Rummukainen, O.S., Robotham, T., Habets, E.A.P.: Head-related transfer functions for dynamic listeners in virtual reality. Appl. Sci. **11**(14), 6646 (2021). https://doi.org/10.3390/app11146646
4. Tesch, K., Gerkmann, T.: Spatially selective deep non-linear filters for speaker extraction. In: ICASSP 2023—2023 IEEE International Conference on Acoustics, Speech and Signal Processing (ICASSP), pp. 1–5. IEEE, New York (2023). https://doi.org/10.1109/ICASSP49357.2023.10096098
5. Pulkki, V.: Virtual sound source positioning using vector base amplitude panning. J. Audio Eng. Soc. **45**(6), 456–466 (1997)
6. Kayser, C., Petkov, C.I., Lippert, M., Logothetis, N.K.: Mechanisms for allocating auditory attention: an auditory saliency map. Curr. Biol. **15**(21), 1943–1947 (2005). https://doi.org/10.1016/j.cub.2005.09.040
7. Lv, F., Xia, X.: Study on computational model of auditory selective attention with orientation feature (in Chinese). Acta Autom. Sin. **43**(4), 634–644 (2017). https://doi.org/10.16383/j.aas.2017.c160277
8. Li, Q., Ao, B., Yan, C., Chen, X., Zhang, N.: Sound event classification and localization based on convolutional recurrent neural network (in Chinese). Tech. Acoust. **44**, 1–9 (2025). https://doi.org/10.16300/j.cnki.1000-3630.22102701
9. Zhang, F., Wang, F., Xia, L.: 3D virtual sound source localization algorithm application based on head tracking (in Chinese). J. Jilin Norm. Univ. (Nat. Sci. Ed.) **45**(4), 118−123 (2024). https://doi.org/10.16862/j.cnki.issn1674-3873.2024.04.018
10. Wightman, F.L., Kistler, D.J.: Headphone simulation of free-field listening. I. Stimulus synthesis. J. Acoust. Soc. Am. **85**(2), 858−867 (1989). https://doi.org/10.1121/1.397557
11. Xie, B.: Dynamic auditory localization cue and its role on spatial sound reproduction (in Chinese). Acta Acust. **49**(6), 1131–1151 (2024). https://doi.org/10.12395/0371-0025.2024222
12. Valzolgher, C., et al.: Active listening modulates the spatial hearing experience: a multicentric study. Exp. Brain Res. **243**(1), 15 (2024). https://doi.org/10.1007/s00221-024-06955-z
13. Zhang, Z., Xu, S., Zhang, S., Qiao, T., Cao, S.: Attention based convolutional recurrent neural network for environmental sound classification. Neurocomputing **453**, 896–903 (2021). https://doi.org/10.1016/j.neucom.2020.08.069
14. Slater, M., Sanchez-Vives, M.V.: Enhancing our lives with immersive virtual reality. Front. Robot. AI **3**, 74 (2016). https://doi.org/10.3389/frobt.2016.00074
15. Bosman, I.d.V., Buruk, O.'Oz', Jørgensen, K., Hamari, J.: The effect of audio on the experience in virtual reality: a scoping review. Behav. Inf. Technol. **43**(1), 165–199 (2024). https://doi.org/10.1080/0144929X.2022.2158371
16. Kim, H., Remaggi, L., Jackson, P.J.B., Hilton, A.: Immersive spatial audio reproduction for VR/AR using room acoustic modelling from 360° images. In: 2019 IEEE Conference on Virtual Reality and 3D User Interfaces (VR), pp. 120–126. IEEE, New York (2019). https://doi.org/10.1109/VR.2019.8798247
17. Xie, B.: Spatial Sound: Principle and Applications. 1st edn. CRC Press, Boca Raton (2022). https://doi.org/10.1201/9781003081500
18. Fechner, G.T.: Elements of Psychophysics. Breitkopf & Härtel, Leipzig (1860)

19. Hacihabiboglu, H., De Sena, E., Cvetkovic, Z., Johnston, J., Smith, J.O., III.: Perceptual spatial audio recording, simulation, and rendering: an overview of spatial-audio techniques based on psychoacoustics. IEEE Signal Process. Mag. **34**(3), 36–54 (2017). https://doi.org/10.1109/MSP.2017.2666081
20. Kapralos, B., Jenkin, M.R., Milios, E.: Virtual audio systems. Presence Teleoper. Virtual Environ. **17**(6), 527–549 (2008). https://doi.org/10.1162/pres.17.6.527
21. Mueller, M.F., Kegel, A., Schimmel, S.M., Dillier, N., Hofbauer, M.: Localization of virtual sound sources with bilateral hearing aids in realistic acoustical scenes. J. Acoust. Soc. Am. **131**(6), 4732–4742 (2012). https://doi.org/10.1121/1.4705292
22. Steadman, M.A., Kim, C., Lestang, J.-H., Goodman, D.F.M., Picinali, L.: Short-term effects of sound localization training in virtual reality. Sci. Rep. **9**(1), 18284 (2019). https://doi.org/10.1038/s41598-019-54811-w
23. Strauss, H., Buchholz, J.: Comparison of virtual sound source positioning with amplitude panning and Ambisonic reproduction. J. Acoust. Soc. Am. **105**, 934 (1999). https://doi.org/10.1121/1.426307
24. Huisman, T., MacDonald, E., Ahrens, A.: Sound source localization in virtual reality with ambisonics sound reproduction. figshare. https://data.dtu.dk/articles/dataset/Sound_source_localization_in_virtual_reality_with_ambisonics_sound_reproduction_-_Dataset_csv/139 12274/1?file=26437097, Accessed 31 May 2025
25. Huisman, T., Ahrens, A., MacDonald, E.: Sound source localization with various ambisonics orders in virtual reality. J. Acoust. Soc. Am. **148**, 2786 (2020). https://doi.org/10.1121/1.514 7753
26. Ahrens, A., Lund, K.D., Marschall, M., Dau, T.: Sound source localization with varying amount of visual information in virtual reality. PLoS ONE **14**(3), e0214603 (2019). https://doi.org/10.1371/journal.pone.0214603
27. Valzolgher, C., et al.: The impact of a visual spatial frame on real sound-source localization in virtual reality. Curr. Res. Behav. Sci. **1**, 100003 (2020). https://doi.org/10.1016/j.crbeha.2020.100003
28. Juanola, X., Haro, G., Fuentes, M.: A critical assessment of visual sound source localization models including negative audio. arXiv (2025). https://doi.org/10.48550/arXiv.2410.01020
29. Yeow, J.W., Tan, E.-L., Bai, J., Peksi, S., Gan, W.-S.: Real-time sound event localization and detection: deployment challenges on edge devices. arXiv (2024). https://doi.org/10.48550/arXiv.2409.11700

Acceptance and Use of Virtual Reality in Translation of Cultural Inheritance: An Extension of TAM

Boxuan Feng, Tuhao Huang, and Han Yan[✉]

Beijing Institute of Graphic Communication, Beijing, China
Yanhan@bigc.edu.cn

Abstract. Virtual reality (VR) technology offers significant potential for cultural heritage preservation and dissemination. This study investigates VR application mechanisms for Beijing's Central Axis cultural heritage, specifically examining the presentation and interaction of its cultural elements. The current digital inheritance methods of traditional culture are confronted with problems such as insufficient depth of cultural connotation expression, complex system interaction logic, and lack of immersion in user experience, which makes it difficult to meet the public's growing demand for cultural experience. This thesis takes the cultural inheritance application of virtual reality technology as the empirical research object. Aiming at the problems existing in the current research, an innovative design strategy for empowering the cultural inheritance of the Beijing Central Axis through virtual reality technology is proposed. The intention is to break through the limitations of time and space through the rational application of virtual reality technology, explore innovative paths for the digital inheritance of traditional culture, and empower the modern expression of culture with digital technology.

Keywords: Virtual reality · Cultural inheritance · Technology acceptance model · Beijing Central Axis

1 Introduction

Virtual reality (VR) technology is a computer-based technology that provides users with an immersive, interactive three-dimensional spatial experience through computer simulation. The purpose of this study is to explore the application mechanisms of VR technology in cultural heritage preservation and to investigate innovative pathways for VR to promote the dissemination of Beijing's Central Axis cultural heritage. In this study, representative virtual reality application cases are selected to analyze the presentation methods and interaction mechanisms of Beijing's Central Axis cultural elements in virtual reality, and targeted solutions are proposed to enhance cultural dissemination effectiveness and user engagement. This paper summarizes the key factors influencing

Supported by Beijing Municipal Education Commission General Projects of Social Science Plan (NO. SM202210015002)

© The Author(s), under exclusive license to Springer Nature Singapore Pte Ltd. 2026
Z. Lin et al. (Eds.): ICIG 2025, LNCS 16163, pp. 528–539, 2026.
https://doi.org/10.1007/978-981-95-3729-7_43

the virtual reality cultural heritage experience, constructs a theoretical model for virtual reality cultural heritage products based on the technology acceptance model, proposes corresponding hypotheses based on the model factors, and analyzes the key factors influencing users' willingness to accept virtual reality cultural heritage using real data. The study identifies the current genuine needs of users for virtual reality products related to the Beijing Central Axis, conducts design research to validate the feasibility of the design, and proposes innovative design strategies for virtual reality products for the cultural heritage of the Beijing Central Axis. The ultimate goal is to provide innovative ideas and methods for the application of virtual reality technology in the field of cultural heritage of the Beijing Central Axis.

2 Literature Review

2.1 Related Research and Background

In 1965, Sutherland first proposed the theory of human-computer collaboration characterized by perceived reality and interactive reality, which provided a conceptual framework for the development of virtual reality technology (Sutherland(Sutherland 1965a) I. E.,1965). In 1968, Sutherland designed the first head-mounted display capable of connecting to a virtual reality environment, known as the Sword of Damocles. Lanier coined the term "virtual reality" in 1987, and later earned the title of "Father of Virtual Reality" for his contributions to both theory and hardware development (Lanier 1992) J.,1992). Early research and applications of virtual reality technology abroad were primarily focused on military domains. The United States began utilizing VR technology for virtual battlefield demonstrations, soldier simulation training, and joint exercises at an early stage. Japan emerged as a leader in Asia for VR technology research and application, with a primary focus on establishing large-scale VR knowledge databases (Lili Yu, 2020).

A search using the keywords "virtual reality" and "cultural heritage" reveals that virtual reality, as a cutting-edge technology, is widely applied in fields such as culture, education, news, and entertainment on the international stage. It has also spawned new research areas in other domains, demonstrating significant potential for future development. Domestic research on virtual reality technology began relatively late, but with the rapid development of the economy, science and technology, especially 5G networks, and the active response of many scholars to the national call to learn from foreign advanced industrial technologies, virtual reality technology has gained a favorable development environment. China has achieved significant breakthroughs in the research and application of virtual reality technology, with applications beginning to show a trend toward interdisciplinary development (Fig. 1).

530   B. Feng et al.

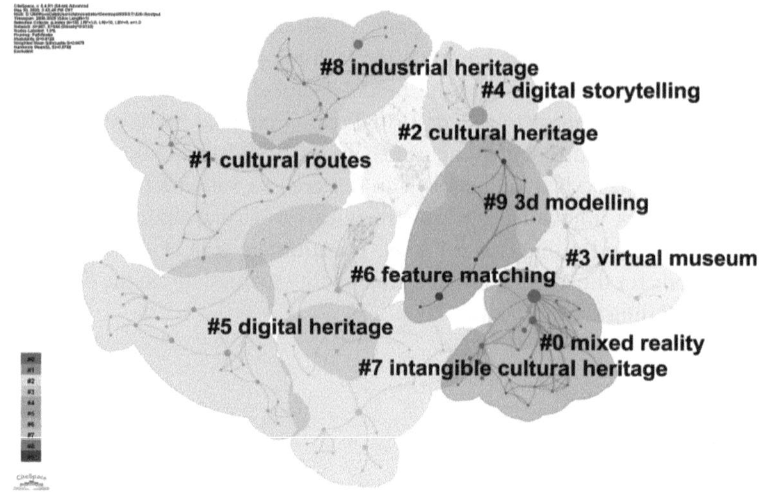

Fig. 1. Literature keyword co-occurrence map and cluster map

2.2 Theoretical Framework

The Technology Acceptance Model (TAM) is a theory of information products proposed by Fred D. Davis in 1989, which is widely used to explain and predict users' acceptance and usage behavior of new technologies. The Technology Acceptance Model is widely used in the field of information systems and is an important theory for studying technology acceptance. The technology Acceptance Model (Fig. 2) posits that users' acceptance of new technologies is primarily influenced by two key factors: perceived usefulness (PU) and perceived ease of use (PEOU). External variables are external factors that influence users' perceptions of perceived usefulness and perceived ease of use. Perceived usefulness refers to the extent to which users believe that using the technology can improve work efficiency or bring value; perceived ease of use refers to the extent to which users believe that the technology is easy to learn and use. These two factors influence users' attitudes (ATT), which in turn influence behavioral intentions (BI), ultimately determining actual usage (AU).

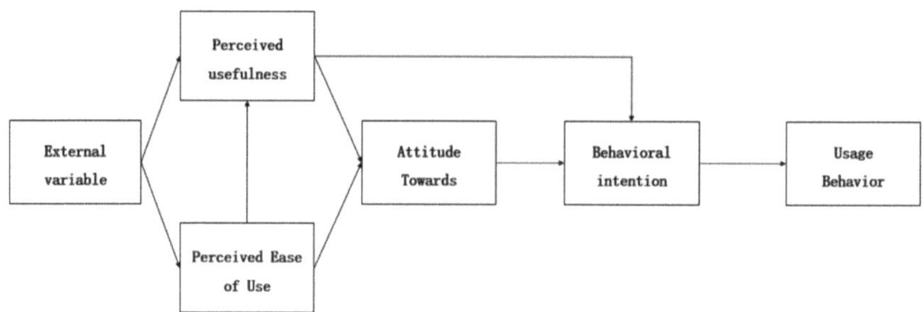

Fig. 2. Original technology acceptance model

In the technology acceptance model, external variables serve as initial antecedent variables, which can either directly and independently influence perceived usefulness and perceived ease of use, or act as intermediate variables mediating the interaction between the two. Indirectly influencing users' behavioral intentions and usage behavior; perceived ease of use can directly enhance users' attitudes toward technology use while also indirectly influencing attitudes and behavioral intentions by enhancing perceived usefulness; perceived usefulness directly and positively influences attitudes and behavioral intentions; attitudes influence the formation of behavioral intentions; and behavioral intentions drive the occurrence of usage behavior.

At present, many scholars choose to use the technology acceptance model to verify users' willingness to accept new technologies. Although previous studies have verified the effectiveness of the technology acceptance model in predicting technology usage intentions, the model still fails to fully consider individual characteristics. Therefore, it is necessary to extend the technology acceptance model to enhance its explanatory and predictive capabilities for technology acceptance behavior in different fields. This study builds upon previous extensions of the technology acceptance model, integrates three key elements of virtual reality cultural heritage experiences identified in prior research, and constructs a virtual reality technology acceptance model (Fig. 3).

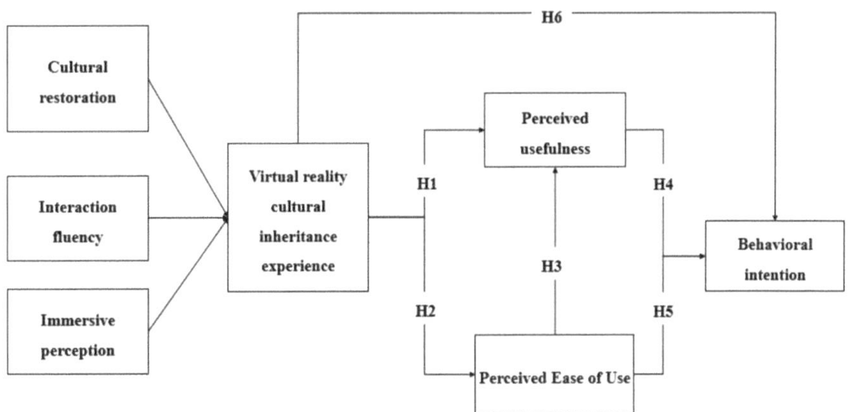

Fig. 3. Virtual Reality Technology Acceptance Model

In the theoretical model constructed in this study, external variables include cultural authenticity, interaction fluency, and immersion perception, while internal variables include perceived usefulness, perceived ease of use, and behavioral intention. According to the traditional technology acceptance model, external variables have a positive impact on perceived usefulness and perceived ease of use, and perceived ease of use, perceived usefulness, and behavioral intention are interrelated. Therefore, the following hypotheses are proposed:

H1: The experience of virtual reality cultural heritage products has a positive impact on users' perceived usefulness;

H2: The experience of virtual reality cultural heritage products has a positive impact on users' perceived ease of use;

H3: The experience of virtual reality cultural heritage products has a positive impact on users' behavioral intention;

H4: Users' perceived ease of use of virtual reality cultural heritage products has a positive impact on perceived usefulness;

H5: Users' perceived ease of use of virtual reality cultural heritage products positively influences behavioral intention;

H6: Users' perceived usefulness of virtual reality cultural heritage products positively influences behavioral intention;

3 Conceptual Framework

3.1 Immersion Perception

Immersive experiences comprise sensory, cognitive, and contextual dimensions that jointly construct cultural environments. Heightened immersion diminishes real-world awareness, focusing cognitive resources on virtual cultural contexts to enhance understanding. Immersion perception is the user's subjective assessment of environmental engagement, which can measure how effectively immersion translates to cultural cognition. It reflects emotional investment and interaction quality within the virtual space. Elevated immersion perception facilitates role embodiment, cultural content internalization, and ultimately improves cultural heritage transmission efficacy.

3.2 Interaction Fluidity

Interaction in VR cultural heritage encompasses user manipulation of cultural content through sensory, behavioral, and contextual dimensions. Sensory interaction employs multisensory channels (visual, auditory, haptic) to recreate cultural environments, while behavioral interaction enables reproduction of cultural practices. Contextual interaction establishes meaningful communication between users and historical content. Interaction fluidity measures information continuity and operational smoothness during engagement, serving as a key effectiveness metric for VR heritage applications. Its core requirement is cognitive load reduction, achieved through streamlined operations that maintain user focus. High fluidity facilitates flow states, enhancing knowledge acquisition and emotional resonance with cultural content, thereby improving learning efficiency and heritage outcomes.

3.3 Cultural Authenticity

Cultural fidelity in VR cultural heritage denotes the accurate virtual reproduction of cultural elements. It is measured through four criteria: visual (architecture, clothing), behavioral (rituals, customs), contextual (historical/spiritual settings), and interactive (authentic social exchanges via natural interfaces) restoration. These dimensions collectively determine authenticity levels, which directly enhance user identification, immersion, and emotional bonds with heritage, ultimately deepening historical comprehension.

3.4 Perceived Usefulness

Perceived usefulness refers to the extent to which users believe that using a particular technology or system can significantly improve their work performance or efficiency. This concept focuses on users' subjective judgment of the actual value of technology, i.e., whether technology can directly solve problems in their work or optimize existing processes. It is one of the core drivers of user acceptance of technology.

3.5 Perceived Ease of Use

Perceived Ease of Use refers to the extent to which users believe that a particular technology or system is simple and easy to master. This concept emphasizes the "user-friendliness" of technology, i.e., whether users can quickly get started and reduce learning costs. It represents the degree to which users perceive a specific system as easy to use and directly influences their willingness to adopt the technology.

3.6 Behavioral Intention

Behavioral intention refers to a user's willingness to use a particular technology or system, and is a direct driver of user behavior. Behavioral intention is significant in that it is an intermediary variable of user behavior. Relevant empirical studies show that behavioral intention is significantly positively correlated with actual usage behavior, and that perceived usefulness has a stronger predictive effect on behavioral intention.

4 Experimental Design Based on TAM Theory

4.1 Design Concept

In the theoretical model construction of products based on the technology acceptance model, cultural fidelity, interaction fluency, and immersion perception are the three key indicators influencing the virtual reality cultural heritage experience. This chapter will address the challenges in the contemporary expression of Beijing's Central Axis cultural symbols by analyzing them from the three-dimensional perspective of virtual reality cultural heritage experience (Table 1 and 2).

Table 1. Layered classification of existing issues with virtual reality products for the Beijing Central Axis

Three Essential Elements of Virtual Reality Cultural Heritage Experience	Existing issues with the Beijing Central Axis virtual reality product
Immersion perception	Superficial application of technology
Cultural authenticity	Fragmentation of cultural connotations
Interaction fluidity	Fragmented user experience

Table 2. Actual photographs and virtual reconstructions of heritage sites along the Beijing central axis

Panoramic view of the central axis	actual shot	virtual restoration
Tiananmen Square		
Temple of Heaven		
Yongding Gate		
Xian Nong Temple		

In the theoretical model construction of products based on the technology acceptance model, cultural fidelity, interaction fluency, and immersion perception are the three key indicators influencing the virtual reality cultural heritage experience. This chapter will address the challenges in the contemporary expression of Beijing's Central Axis cultural symbols by analyzing them from the three-dimensional perspective of virtual reality cultural heritage experience.

4.2 Design Framework

To provide users with a better interactive experience, we have designed a product framework that builds a complete experience chain from the overall product architecture to the implementation details, focusing on cultural experience, immersive exploration, and creative generation. To enhance users' understanding of the cultural knowledge of Beijing's Central Axis, this study divides the overall content of the product into three sections (Fig. 4): the Central Axis Museum section, the Central Axis Exploration section, and the Cultural Vision section.

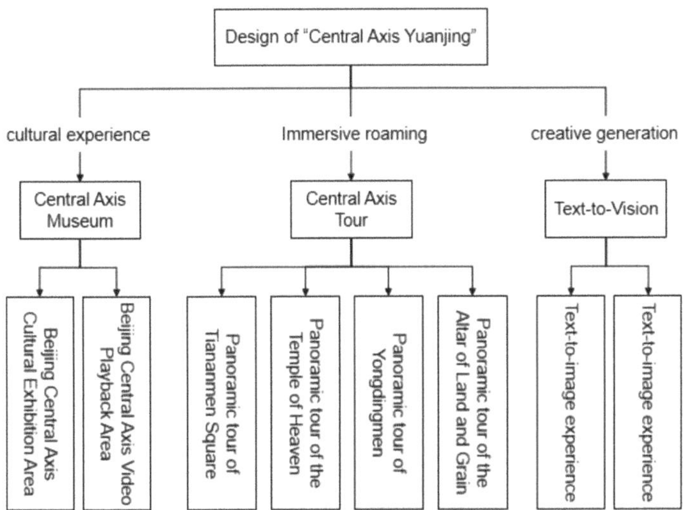

Fig. 4. Content design framework for "Central Axis Yuanjing"

The Central Axis Museum functions as a virtual science museum, eliminating spatiotemporal constraints of physical exhibitions. Users assume a "cultural ambassador" role, tasked with collecting core Beijing Central Axis cultural symbols for dissemination. A scale model provides an initial architectural layout overview, establishing foundational comprehension before exploration. Four wall-mounted photographs depict key historical sites: Tiananmen Gate, Temple of Heaven, Yongding Gate, and Xiannong Altar (Fig. 5). When users gaze at a photo's center, visual highlighting prompts interaction, seamlessly transitioning them to corresponding panoramic scenes for immersive cultural experiences (Fig. 6).

The Central Axis Exploration module facilitates panoramic navigation, enabling immersive cultural heritage exploration. Young users prioritize design detail and experiential smoothness as critical satisfaction factors. Accordingly, design optimizations focused on enhanced model accuracy and detail for refined, photorealistic visuals. Resource efficiency was achieved by substituting resource-intensive real-time rendering with pre-rendered panoramic videos, reducing computational demands. This approach strategically sacrifices minimal navigational freedom to maximize visual quality and UX improvement. Authentic scene reconstruction was executed in Unreal Engine using high-resolution reference photography of heritage sites and their surroundings, ensuring contextual precision. These technical refinements collectively elevate perceptual authenticity while preserving historical integrity (Fig. 7).

Fig. 5. Sand table of the central axis

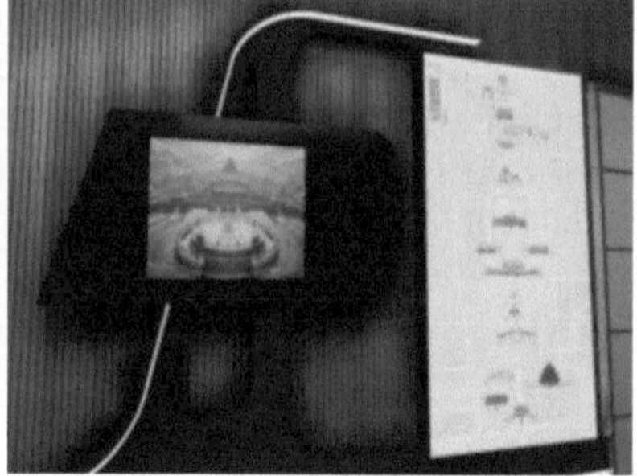

Fig. 6. Photo and experience wall

Fig. 7. Ten Thousand Nations Coming to Pay Tribute

The "Text-to-Image" module utilizes the Qing Dynasty's Ten Thousand Nations Coming to Pay Tribute (Palace Museum), a meticulous gongbi painting depicting Emperor Qianlong receiving envoys at the Hall of Supreme Harmony. This bird's-eye view exemplifies Qing imperial prestige and architectural grandeur. Through differentiated design and generative AI, the module fuses this artwork with the Beijing Central Axis, linking its spatial narrative of the Forbidden City and historical events to the Axis's landmarks. This integration deepens cultural context and enhances user engagement.

This module employs AIGC technology for personalized image generation. To achieve precise control over the meticulous brushwork style, the style model was tailored using "The Tribute of All Nations" as input, with adjustments to prompt words and ControlNet parameters. This enables generating meticulous brushwork paintings within VR. For training, the SD1.5 base model was used. "Ten Thousand Nations Paying Homage to the Emperor" was sliced into 108 images (512x512 pixels) and labeled to form the dataset. The Lora model was trained on this dataset (Fig. 8). Post-training, model stylization effects were compared to select the optimal Lora model for subsequent phases.

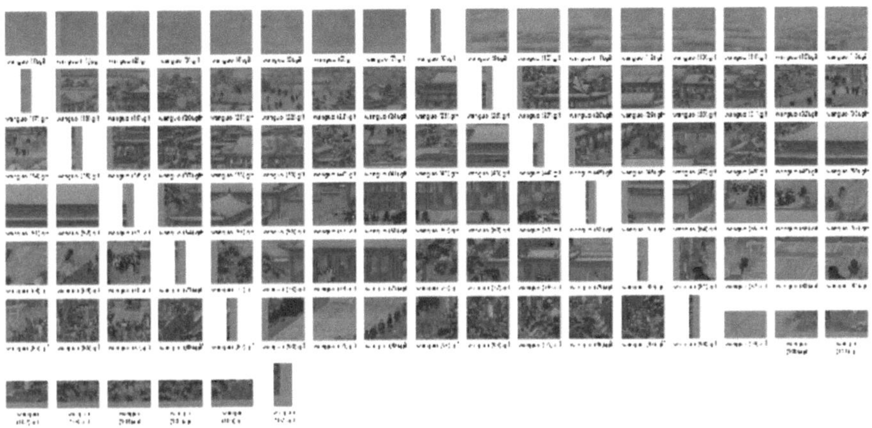

Fig. 8. Detail from "The Tribute of All Nations"

The final functionality is as follows: when the user enters the text-to-image level, they enter a prompt in the text box interface. After waiting for a period of time, a stylized image corresponding to the prompt will be generated in the image generation box (Fig. 9). In this interface, after entering the corresponding prompt in the text box, clicking the "Send" button sends the prompt information to the backend, and the image generation process begins. The progress bar advances simultaneously during the generation process, and once the progress bar is complete, the image generation is finished. Clicking the "Download" button allows the image to be downloaded locally for use in creating postcards. Clicking the "Back" button exits the interface and returns to the Central Axis Museum scene.

Fig. 9. Implementation of text-to-image function

4.3 Environment Configuration

The product design research in this study was conducted using the Unreal Engine for design and rendering. The Unreal Engine is currently widely used in various fields such as gaming, film and television, and architecture. The Unreal Engine boasts powerful rendering capabilities, enabling realistic lighting effects, material textures, and detailed texture details. The engine offers a wide range of editing tools and creative resources, covering modeling, material editing, animation production, physics simulation, and lighting rendering, among other aspects. Developers can efficiently develop projects within a visual editor. In addition to the overall project development being based on the Unreal Engine, this study utilized Photoshop 2021 for image material processing, texture mapping, and adjustments. Premiere 2023 was employed for the production of panoramic videos and educational video content. 3ds Max 2020 was used for model creation and adjustments. For AIGC creative content creation, software such as Stable Diffusion and Midjourney were utilized.

5 Conclusion

This paper focuses on the digital inheritance of traditional culture as its core content, exploring innovative pathways for leveraging virtual reality technology to enhance the dissemination of Beijing's Central Axis cultural heritage. To address the current issues in Beijing's Central Axis virtual reality products, such as superficial application of technology, fragmented cultural content, and disjointed user experiences, this study expands upon the technology acceptance model to construct a theoretical framework for the acceptance of virtual reality cultural heritage products. The theoretical model framework is applied to the study of Beijing's Central Axis virtual reality products. Through research and analysis, the study identifies the genuine needs of users of such products.

Based on user needs, the study conducts product design research, validates, and summarizes innovative design strategies for Beijing's Central Axis cultural heritage virtual reality products. Therefore, in terms of future product design and experience optimization, the scope of user research should be expanded. By optimizing interaction design, the product's usage barriers can be lowered, enabling more users to conveniently experience Beijing's Central Axis virtual reality products and expanding the audience for cultural heritage transmission.

References

Sutherland I.E. The ultimate display. In: Proceedings of the IFIP Congress, vol. 2, pp. 506–508 (1965a)

Sutherland I.E.A.: Head-mounted three dimensional display. In: Proceedings of joint Computer Conference, pp. 755–764 (1965b).

Lanier J.: Virtual Reality: The Promise of the Future[J].Interactive Learning International, 8 (1992).

Selmanović, E., Rizvic, S., Harvey, C., et al.: Improving accessibility to intangible cultural heritage preservation using virtual reality. **13**(2), 1–19 (2020)

Yi, J.H., Kim, H.S.: User experience research, experience design, and evaluation methods for museum mixed reality experience. J Comput Cult Herit. **14**(4), 1–28 (2021)

Heffer, N., Dennie, E., Ashwin, C., Petrini, K., Karl, A.: Multisensory processing of emotional cues predicts intrusive memories after virtual reality trauma. Virtual Real. **27**(3), 2043–2057 (2023)

Song, H., Lu, S.: The effect of virtual tourism experience on tourist responses: the lens from cognitive appraisal theory. Asia. Pac. J. Tour. Res. **29**(7), 885–899 (2024)

Mindful Visualization VR: A VR Gamification Design Method for Immersive Cultural Heritage Experience

Hongwei Ren[✉] and Guanda Zhu

Design College, Sichuan Fine Arts Institute, Chongqing 401331, China
Renhongwei@scfai.edu.cn

Abstract. With the development of virtual reality (VR) technology and digital heritage (DH), gamification was validated as an effective approach to improve user experience in several contexts. However, there is limited research and design guidelines on how to effectively using gamification design to convey artistic, historic and cultural knowledge of cultural heritage and present this value in an attractive and playful way to users in a virtual environment. Based on existing literature and related works, this study proposed a systematic virtual reality gamification design model VGI (Visual Aesthetic, Gamified Interaction and Immersive Narrative) for immersive cultural heritage (ICH) experience. Accordingly, taking ICH experience design of the Dazu Rock Carvings as an example, it aimed to connect users with the history of this special cultural heritage in virtual environment. In this study, we developed an interactive, gamified and narrative ICH experience design that provided users with learning and entertaining experiences, facilitating their view from appreciation to participating in the real history while engaging with ICH experience. This study demonstrated our ICH experience design motivated users interests in Dazu Rock Carvings, promoted the knowledge of cultural heritage and preservation awareness, and could be applied in gamification design for virtual reality cultural heritage.

Keywords: Virtual Reality · Gamification · Cultural Heritage · Immersive Experience

1 Introduction

Virtual reality (VR) technology has seen significant advancements in recent years. Several studies have highlighted that these improvements have made VR a practical and versatile tool across a wide range of fields. In the context of cultural heritage (CH), VR enables immersive and interactive environments that offer new possibilities for digital preservation and public engagement [1]. Museums and cultural institutions are increasingly using VR to visualize artifacts, reconstruct historical environments [2], and create virtual experience, enhancing public access and innovating cultural value dissemination [3].

© The Author(s), under exclusive license to Springer Nature Singapore Pte Ltd. 2026
Z. Lin et al. (Eds.): ICIG 2025, LNCS 16163, pp. 540–551, 2026.
https://doi.org/10.1007/978-981-95-3729-7_44

However, many existing VR heritage projects remain focused on high-fidelity visual representation and static exhibition formats. While these visual representations are informative, they often lack interactions and emotional engagement. The lack of user control and narrative integration can limit the effectiveness of VR experiences in maintaining attention and promoting meaningful cultural learning. Most applications treat users as passive observers rather than active participants, which may reduce their engagement with the heritage content.

Moreover, few studies have systematically integrated the digital representation of cultural heritage with immersive narrative and interactive gamification mechanisms within a comprehensive design framework.

Therefore, this study proposed a systematic VR gamification design method for developing immersive cultural heritage (ICH) experiences. By incorporating principles from human-computer interaction, gamification, and user experience, a three-dimensional framework was constructed that integrates visual aesthetic, gamified interaction, and immersive narrative. This approach aims to enhance presentation, dissemination, and preservation of cultural heritage. A case study involving *Yuanjue* Cave, part of the Dazu Rock Carvings, a UNESCO World Heritage site, is used to demonstrate the design method. The project reconstructs the cave environment digitally and embeds interactive and narrative elements to allow users to explore historic, cultural, and aesthetic knowledge about the cultural heritage, and to active participate in culturally meaningful interactive tasks.

This research contributes to the development of a structured and practical VR gamification design method. It provides a practical framework for designers and researchers seeking to create ICH experiences that are informative, engaging, and emotionally impactful.

2 Related Works

2.1 Virtual Reality for Cultural Heritage

In recent years, VR technology has been widely applied and continuously developed in the fields of CH presentation, education, and dissemination. With the advancement of digital, interaction, and display technologies, VR has evolved from a static and documentary medium into an experiential platform that actively engages users. The three core technological characteristics of VR, namely immersion, interactivity, and imagination [4], are critical in shaping the design of ICH experiences. These factors play a key role in shifting users from passive observers to active participants in CH VR.

Immersion is fundamental to CH VR presentations, as it fosters presence while the user is situated in the virtual environment. Presence refers to the psychological sensation of being in the virtual environment, even when users are consciously aware they are physically located elsewhere, a phenomenon mediated through technical means [5]. Immersion is the primary condition for achieving this presence [6]. A high level of immersion is capable of generating emotional connection, particularly when users are experiencing reconstructions of historical events or vanished heritage spaces.

Interactivity enables users to directly engage with virtual objects, environments, and narrative content, transforming their role from passive observers to active participants. Current interaction designs include multimodal interaction [7], gamified challenge tasks [8], and interactive narrative structures [9]. These approaches have been shown to enhance users' learning motivation and understanding of cultural content, while also deepening immersion through emotional engagement and exploratory behaviors [10]. Effective interaction design should be tightly integrated with cultural narratives and aesthetic symbolism to ensure that users can emotionally invest in and derive meaningful learning from the experience.

Imagination represents the third foundational component in VR cultural experience design. It extends beyond the pursuit of historical accuracy to emphasize users' creative participation in constructing and interpreting cultural scenarios within virtual space [11]. Users may enter reconstructed ancient ruins, interact with mythological figures, or engage in rituals that have long ceased to exist. This not only strengthens the connection to tangible cultural heritage but also facilitates the digital reinterpretation of intangible culture such as beliefs, customs, and oral traditions. By combining historical authenticity with interpretive imagination, designers can build multilayered cultural experiences in which users are not merely recipients but co-creators of cultural meaning [12].

2.2 Gamification Design in Virtual Reality for Cultural Heritage

Gamification refers to "the use of game design elements in non-game contexts", and involves applying playful strategies to design engaging experiences aimed at achieving specific goals [13]. It has been increasingly adopted in cultural heritage digital projects to improve participation and learning outcomes. Core elements such as points, badges, missions, and progression systems offer users clear objectives and a sense of accomplishment [14]. Gamification allows for flexible, goal-oriented experiences in non-entertainment contexts, making it especially suitable for cultural learning settings where attention and retention are key [13].

In VR cultural heritage contexts, gamification enhances both immersion and interaction. Through embedded tasks such as puzzle solving, artifact restoration, or role-based quests, users become active agents of cultural discovery. The use of gamification aims to improve learning and comprehension of cultural heritage knowledge, with flow experience widely recognized in educational research for its ability to enhance learner engagement, improve performance, and deepen conceptual understanding [15]. Therefore, implementing gamification designs that appropriately balance users' skill levels with task challenges can effectively induce flow experiences, thereby enhancing both engagement and the depth of cultural heritage comprehension.

Meanwhile, interactive storytelling contributes to immersive experience, as it fosters emotional and cognitive engagement, drawing users into cultural events and enhancing their connection with reconstructed historical scenes.

3 Gamification Design Method for ICH Experience

In this study, build upon the literature review, we proposed a structured VR gamification method for creating immersive and culturally meaningful ICH experiences. This approach emphasizes experience-oriented ICH experience design, aiming to utilize the features of VR technology to support the presentation, dissemination, and preservation of cultural heritage. The method based on the immersion, interactivity, and imagination of VR and focuses on enhancing user experience through three interconnected dimensions: Visual Aesthetic, Gamified Interaction, and Immersive Narrative, as shown in Fig. 1. The VGI model consists of three main dimensions and six design factors.

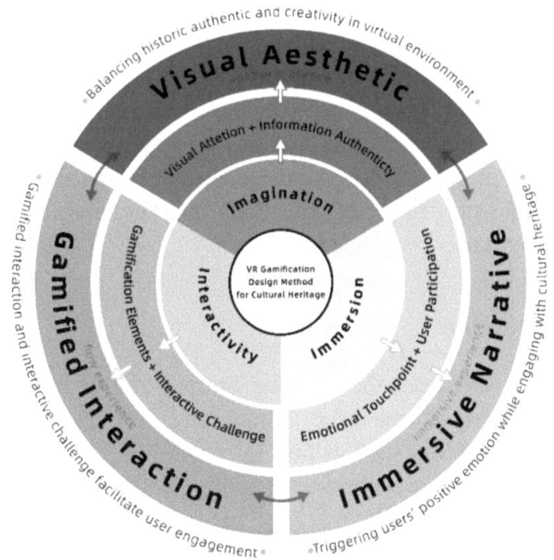

Fig. 1. VR gamification design method for ICH experience

A detailed explanation of three dimensions is as follow:

(1) Visual Aesthetic: In digital cultural heritage design, visual aesthetics ensure historical accuracy and emotional connection. Virtual environments should draw from historical records, imagery, and folklore to reduce distortion and support the reconstruction of missing elements. Clear visuals help convey cultural meaning and engage users emotionally.

(2) Gamified Interaction: This dimension enhances user engagement by promoting a state of flow through tasks, feedback, and game elements. Properly balanced gamification supports learning without turning the experience into mere entertainment. Interactive challenges should align with the user's skill level to prevent frustration and maintain interest, fostering emotional connections to the cultural content.

(3) Immersive Narrative: Storytelling is vital in communicating cultural values. Users should be fully immersed in the narrative, participating in a culturally rooted yet

creatively expanded story. Emotional engagement is key, with the experience structured around tasks and scenes that help users emotionally connect with the heritage content.

The design method constructed by these three dimensions is an iterative process in which each stage is interrelated and mutually influential within a sustainable sequence.

4 ICH Experience Design Practice

The Dazu Rock Carvings, a UNESCO World Heritage site, embody China's tradition-al culture through cliff sculptures that integrate Confucian, Buddhist, and Taoist elements. These artworks stand out for their folkloric and narrative qualities, conveying universal values in an accessible way. Inspired by the *Yuanjue* Cave, this study presents an ICH experience design Mindful Visualization VR. The project aims to digitally preserve and present these artworks, along with their cultural and aesthetic knowledge, in a VR environment. By incorporating digital representation, gamification, and interactive storytelling, the project offers an immersive experience that enables users to engage actively with history, fostering emotional connections and raising awareness about heritage preservation.

4.1 Digital Representation

The *Yuanjue* Cave, derived from the *Yuanjue* Sutra, depicts the scene where twelve bodhisattvas seek knowledge from the Buddha, conveying traditional cultural values. However, environmental factors such as humidity and lighting have caused significant damage to many details of the sculptures, resulting in the loss of valuable cultural, historical, and aesthetic information.

Through field research, we began by recording the spatial layout of the *Yuanjue* Cave, including the dimensions, proportions, and sizes of the various artworks, using both textual descriptions and imagery. We then analyzed each artwork by separating it down into its individual components, cross-referencing the descriptions in the *Yuanjue* Sutra to understand how the ancient craftsmen of Dazu designed and constructed the scenes and characters in accordance with the scriptures.

Next, we organized and analyzed textual information from ancient texts, research papers, and other sources, focusing on the depictions of the twelve Bodhisattvas and the cultural values they represent. Each Bodhisattva statue reflects unique cultural meanings through its style and form. We compiled the historical and symbolic representations of each Bodhisattva and identified the name, meaning, and value of each artwork in the *Yuanjue* Cave.

Using this methodology, we organized and summarized all relevant information about the *Yuanjue* Cave and the necessary details for presenting each artwork, as shown in Fig. 2.

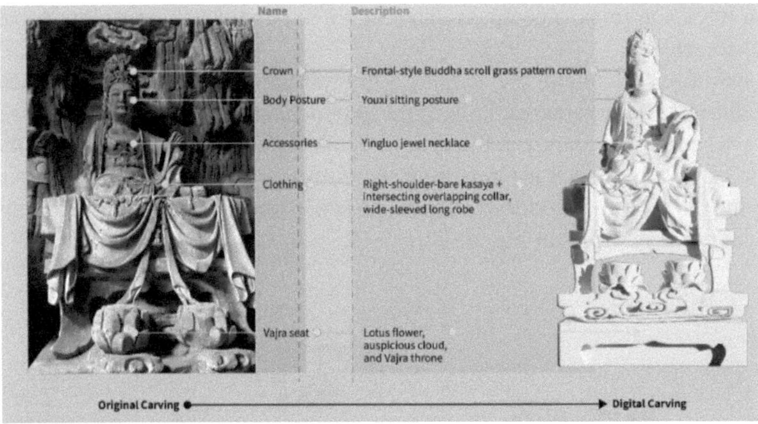

Fig. 2. Digital representation of basic digital cliff sculptures

After ensuring the authenticity of historical, cultural, and aesthetic information about the *Yuanjue* Cave, we utilize the creative potential of virtual reality to design a digital representation that captures visual attention. Based on preliminary analysis of the original sculptures and gathered information, we create digital cliff sculptures for each object in the cave, as shown in Fig. 3.

VR enables users to engage with non-existent objects and activities. After creating the basic digital sculptures, we focus on restoring missing colors and material details, referencing sculptures and murals from the same period to ensure historical accuracy. The redesigned digital sculptures also reflect cultural and aesthetic values.

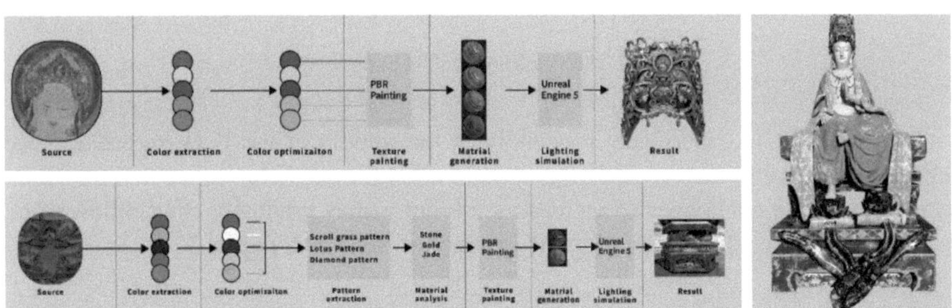

Fig. 3. Digital representation of lost details

4.2 Storytelling, Gamified Interaction in ICH Experience

In this ICH experience, gamified storytelling is based on the narrative of the *Yuanjue* Sutra, incorporating character designs and plot elements into various scenes. The story follows twelve bodhisattvas seeking the Buddha's teachings on cultivation, conveying values like kindness, peace, and mindfulness. Users assume the role of the creator of the Dazu Rock Carvings, a compassionate figure seeking ways to help the people in a turbulent society.

The narrative structure of the *Yuanjue* Sutra was adjusted, particularly the sequence of the bodhisattvas' appearances. Users, after experiencing mysterious events, are guided to a cave where a figure assigns the task of "building the cave and repairing the bodhisattvas." Challenges such as "repairing the crown, solving the pattern mystery, and painting the throne" are introduced, allowing users to reconstruct the *Yuanjue* Cave. The detailed storyline is shown in Fig. 4.

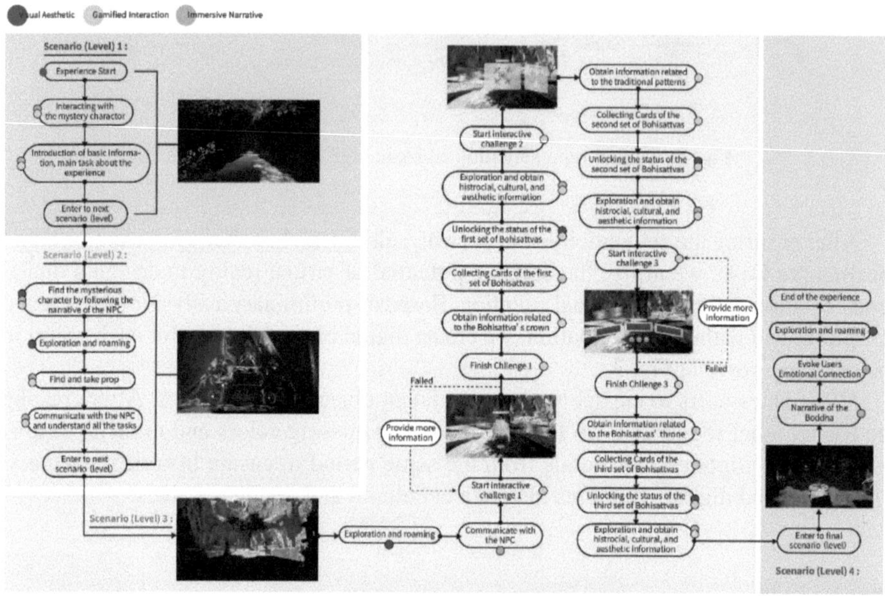

Fig. 4. Storytelling in ICH experience

During the ICH experience, especially in the middle of the ICH experience, we believe that offering interactive challenges at varying levels helps enhance immersion. As user complete challenges of increasing difficulty, they gradually enter a flow state, becoming more deeply immersed in the experience, as shown in Fig. 5.

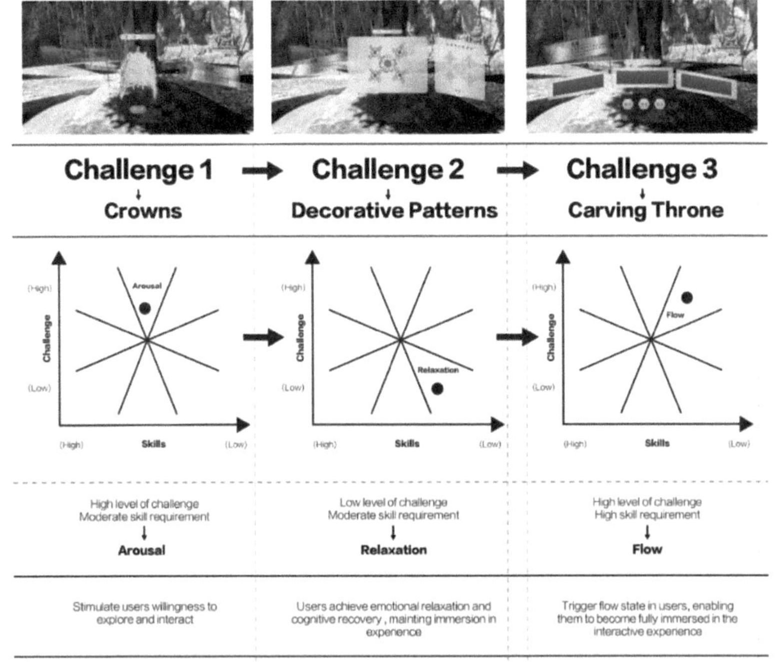

Fig. 5. Interactive challenge in ICH experience

Based on the historical, cultural, and artistic information of the *Yuanjue* Cave, three puzzle based interactive challenges are designed, each corresponding to a representative part of the bodhisattva sculptures. The first challenge involves the bodhisattva's crown, where users rotate and adjust objects to match decorative patterns, encouraging exploration with hints provided for repeated failures. The second challenge focuses on adjusting fragmented decorative patterns from the cliff sculptures, offering a lower difficulty to help users relax and maintain immersion. The third challenge builds on the previous tasks, requiring users to apply their knowledge to recreate a bodhisattva throne, reinforcing cultural and artistic understanding through a higher skill level to induce flow.

4.3 Emotional Touchpoints

Immersive narrative design played a central role in establishing an emotional connection between the user and cultural heritage in the experience. The story was embedded throughout the interaction process, using emotional touchpoints to deepen user identification. To facilitate engagement, emotional touchpoints were divided into three stages throughout the story. First, the role of user was carefully designed as a historical figure directly involved in the cave's creation, enhancing user participation. Second, after completing multiple interactive challenges, users were able to repair the Bodhisattvas themselves, fulfilling their sense of achievement. Finally, the story concluded with a symbolic moment: after completing the digital reconstruction of *Yuanjue* Cave, the user transformed into the unique, anonymous Bodhisattva within the cave. This metaphorical ending was intended to reflect the user's contribution to cultural continuity and foster a sense of heritage legacy.

4.4 Design Implementation

The ICH experience design's digital models are based on the visual aesthetic strategy and steps outlined in the design practice. After ensuring authenticity and creativity, we utilized different software to create accurate and compatible models. Following the narrative structure, we built four experience levels using Unreal Engine 5.1.1, implementing interactive challenges with Blueprint, as shown in Fig. 6.

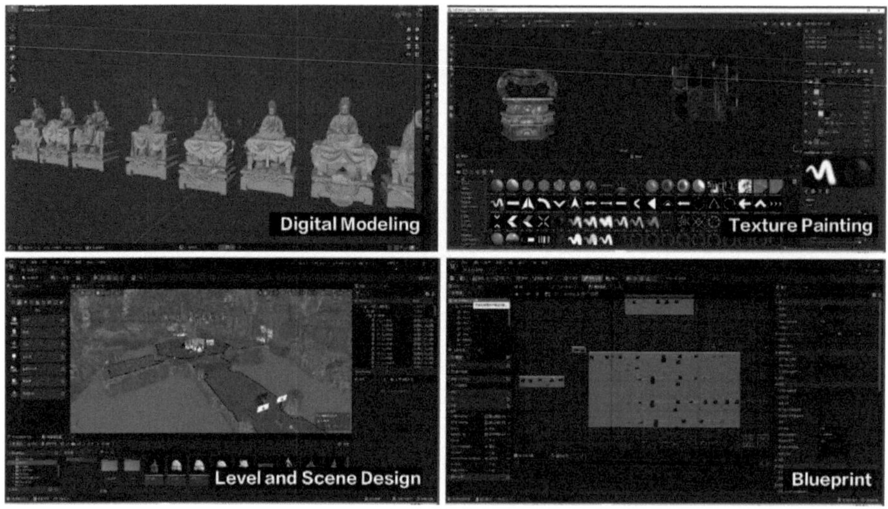

Fig. 6. Digital model and development of blueprint

Next, we created an open exhibition environment and utilized HTC VIVE PRO VR to provide the whole ICH experience. Exhibition area was divided into three areas, as shown in Fig. 7.

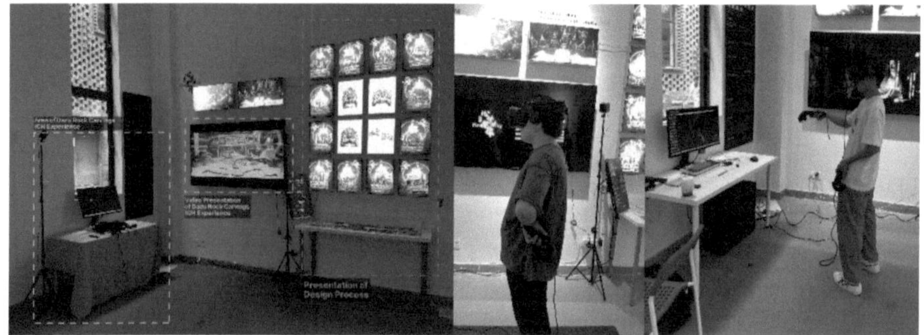

Fig. 7. Mindful Visualization VR ICH exhibition

The purpose of the exhibition environment is to test the design practice in a public setting, evaluating the effectiveness and potential of the dissemination, presentation, and preservation of the Dazu Rock Carvings at the *Yuanjue* Cave. After the experience, we selected 10 participants for qualitative interviews. The main content of the interviews is outlined in Table 1.

Table 1. Interview Questions Outline

#	Dimension	Question
Q1	Representation	Did you feel immersed in the experience? Did it feel like "being there"?
Q2		Which interactive elements did you find most realistic or engaging?
Q3		What aspects do you think could be improved to better present the cultural content?
Q4	Preservation	After the experience, did you become more concerned about the preservation of cultural heritage?
Q5		Do you think this kind of experience helps raise public support for heritage protection?
Q6	Dissemination	What new knowledge or background information about this cultural heritage did you learn during the experience?
Q7		How would you evaluate this form of dissemination? Was it easier to understand the cultural content?

5 Discussion

The ICH experience of the *Yuanjue* Cave successfully conveyed both the historical and aesthetic richness of the site. Users, particularly those unfamiliar with VR, reported a strong sense of novelty and spatial presence, with the ability to explore artifacts up close being a significant advantage over traditional site visits. The creative reconstruction of damaged sculptures, especially the restored color schemes reminiscent of Dunhuang murals, enhanced users' cultural connection. As Participant 1 described, "*...When I saw the colors on the bodhisattva statue, I immediately thought of the Dunhuang murals. It felt so familiar—like these were the colors it was always meant to have.*" This familiarity contributed to a deeper cultural identification. However, some users expressed a desire for clearer explanations of how missing details were reconstructed, suggesting that transparency could increase trust and deepen understanding.

The experience also shifted users' roles from passive observers to active contributors, promoting empathy with historical creators and increasing emotional investment in cultural preservation. As Participant 6 reflected, "*...I didn't know the Dazu Rock Carvings were built by ordinary people. After trying to make a statue myself, I realized how hard it is—and I now value the chance to see them even more.*" Users appreciated the technical difficulty and cultural responsibility involved in heritage creation, gaining a deeper understanding of the fragility and uniqueness of cultural heritage. For those who had previously visited the real site, the VR experience allowed them to revisit and reinterpret their memories, reinforcing their connection to the site's origins and cultural symbolism.

Furthermore, the narrative structure and interactive elements, such as the character driven story and gamified progression, were recognized as key to the experience's effectiveness in cultural dissemination. As Participant 9 described, "...*The story really drew me in—there was a mysterious NPC guiding me, and I kept wondering what I was working toward. The ending was a surprise: I didn't expect that the anonymous bodhisattva at the center would be me. It felt like a rewarding payoff.*" The combination of immersive environments, storytelling, and gamification made complex cultural narratives more accessible and emotionally engaging, bridging generational and educational gaps in heritage engagement. Overall, the study suggests that VR can serve not only as an educational tool but also as a means of cultural advocacy and emotional mobilization for heritage protection.

6 Conclusion

This study proposes a systematic VR gamification design method for ICH experience, structured around three interrelated dimensions: visual aesthetic, gamified interaction, and immersive narrative. Together, these form the VGI model, which integrates digital design with presentation, dissemination, and preservation. Through a case study of the *Yuanjue* Cave at the Dazu Rock Carvings, the model was implemented and evaluated via user participation and qualitative feedback.

By reconstructing visual details based on historical evidence and enhancing aesthetics, the experience preserved cultural integrity while engaging users. The integration of gamified interactions and interactive storytelling allowed active participation, fostering a more emotional connection to heritage content.

The study also demonstrates the potential of VR gamification in raising awareness and in cultural heritage protection. By positioning users as contributors, the experience enhanced empathy toward historical creators and deepened recognition of preservation challenges. Additionally, emotional touchpoints and interactive mechanics sustained attention and reinforced the cultural message's long-term impact.

The VGI model offers a practical and adaptable guideline for future cultural heritage projects. Future research may expand the application of this model to different heritage types, multiuser experiences, and AI-assisted reconstructions, while combining qualitative and quantitative analysis for deeper evaluation.

Acknowledgments. This study was supported by Chongqing Social Science Planning Project (Doctoral Project and Cultivation Project, 2024BS111), Sichuan Fine Arts Institute Doctoral Research Initiation Project (24BSQD07), Chongqing Art Science Research Planning Project (18YB09), Project of Digital Media Art Key Laboratory of Sichuan Province (21DMKL08).

References

1. Gaitatzes, A., Christopoulos, D., Roussou, M.: Reviving the past: cultural heritage meets virtual reality. In: Proceedings of the 2001 Conference on Virtual Reality, Archeology, and Cultural Heritage, pp. 103–110 (2001)
2. Bruno, F., Bruno, S., De Sensi, G., Luchi, M.-L., Mancuso, S., Muzzupappa, M.: From 3D reconstruction to virtual reality: a complete methodology for digital archaeological exhibition. J. Cult. Herit. **11**, 42–49 (2010)
3. Iacono, S., et al.: Virtual reality in cultural heritage: a setup for balzi rossi museum. Appl. Sci. **14** (2024)
4. Burdea, G.C., Coiffet, P.: Virtual Reality Technology. Wiley (2003)
5. Slater, M.: Place illusion and plausibility can lead to realistic behaviour in immersive virtual environments. Philos. Trans. Roy. Soc. London Ser. B Biol. Sci. **364**, 3549–3557 (2009)
6. Ijsselsteijn, W., Riva, G.: Being there: the experience of presence in mediated environments. Emerg. Commun. **5**, 3 (2003)
7. Chu, J.H., Mazalek, A.: Embodied engagement with narrative: a design framework for presenting cultural heritage artifacts. Multimodal Technol. Interact. **3** (2019)
8. Liu, Z., Chen, D., Zhang, C., Yao, J.: Design of a virtual reality serious game for experiencing the colors of Dunhuang frescoes. Heritage Sci. **12** (2024)
9. Yu, J., Wang, Z., Cao, Y., Cui, H., Zeng, W.: Centennial drama reimagined: an immersive experience of intangible cultural heritage through contextual storytelling in virtual reality. ACM J. Comput. Cult. Heritage **18**, Article 11 (2025)
10. Bozzelli, G., et al.: An integrated VR/AR framework for user-centric interactive experience of cultural heritage: the ArkaeVision project. Digit. Appl. Archaeol. Cult. Heritage **15**, e00124 (2019)
11. Zhang, X., Sun, L., Yan, S.: NVSHU: virtual reality design and narrative popularization for intangible cultural heritage characters. In: SIGGRAPH Asia 2023 XR, pp. Article 22. Association for Computing Machinery, Sydney, NSW, Australia (2023)
12. Selmanović, E., et al.: Improving accessibility to intangible cultural heritage preservation using virtual reality. J. Comput. Cult. Heritage **13**, Article 13 (2020)
13. Deterding, S., Dixon, D., Khaled, R., Nacke, L.: From game design elements to gamefulness: defining "gamification". In: Proceedings of the 15th International Academic MindTrek Conference: Envisioning Future Media Environments, pp. 9–15. Association for Computing Machinery, Tampere, Finland (2011)
14. O'Connor, S., Colreavy-Donnelly, S., Dunwell, I.: Fostering engagement with cultural heritage through immersive VR and gamification. In: Liarokapis, F., Voulodimos, A., Doulamis, N., Doulamis, A. (eds.) Visual Computing for Cultural Heritage, pp. 301–321. Springer, Cham (2020)
15. Guerra-Tamez, C.R.: The impact of immersion through virtual reality in the learning experiences of art and design students: the mediating effect of the flow experience. Educ. Sci. **13** (2023)

Lightweight Object Tracking and Localization for Assembly Guidance on AR Helmet

Zhiwei Ma, Youquan Liu[(✉)], and Ruizhi Wan

School of Information Engineering, Chang'an University, Xi'an, Shaanxi, China
youquan@chd.edu.cn

Abstract. To address the high cognitive demands of augmented assembly and repair for operators, this paper presents a lightweight augmented reality framework combining object tracking and registration. Specifically, we propose a new object tracking architecture named YOLOv7-TinyMRN which is improved from YOLOv7-Tiny, reducing GFLOPS by 11.45% and model size by 6%—enabling real-time performance on resource-constrained AR devices. We further propose a 3D object registration method that integrates ROI extraction with an enhanced feature-matching algorithm based on a virtual object pose dataset to achieve a more efficient solution for pose estimation. As a result, the operated target can be recognized and tracked with the corresponding virtual model precisely overlaid, which is used to provide guidance information for the on-site operators. The experiments verify our method's effectiveness and efficiency.

Keywords: Augmented assembly · Object detection · Pose estimation

1 Introduction

AR has demonstrated significant potential in assembly tasks and is increasingly applied in industrial operations and workforce training [1]. For instance, it has been used in astronaut training to accelerate adaptation to complex operational environments. In assembly and maintenance contexts, AR enhances efficiency and reduces errors [2], as reported by its successful deployment at Boeing and Airbus.

However, to alleviate users' cognitive load, AR-based guidance systems must support object recognition and tracking, which heavily rely on cloud computing, compromising the real-time responsiveness. This has created a growing demand for lightweight, on-device solutions deployable on wearable AR platforms.

This paper proposes an AR-based assembly and maintenance guidance system deployed on HoloLens 2. The system integrates object recognition, pose estimation, virtual model overlay, and real-time assembly assistance. Leveraging deep learning and feature matching, the system supports hands-free operation, reduces training costs, and mitigates cognitive load during complex tasks. The main contributions of this paper include:

© The Author(s), under exclusive license to Springer Nature Singapore Pte Ltd. 2026
Z. Lin et al. (Eds.): ICIG 2025, LNCS 16163, pp. 552–563, 2026.
https://doi.org/10.1007/978-981-95-3729-7_45

1. This paper proposes a lightweight object detection network based on YOLOv7-Tiny to address the computational constraints of mobile AR devices. By optimizing the backbone and replacing activation functions, the model reduces computational cost while maintaining accuracy and real-time performance.
2. 3D label annotation is conducted using a deep learning-based method, enabling the identification of key assembly components and the generation of corresponding AR labels for annotation purposes.
3. A method based on ROI cropping and feature matching with an image database is introduced to identify the pose that best corresponds to the current state of the object, enabling accurate pose estimation for precise virtual model placement. This approach lowers computational demands on AR devices and improves recognition and localization efficiency.

2 Related Work

Traditional assembly instructions predominantly rely on 2D text and images, often impeding task comprehension and execution efficiency [3]. Augmented reality (AR) has emerged to overcome these limitations by providing intuitive interactive guidance for assembly operations. Wang et al. [4] comprehensively reviewed AR-based assembly instructions, identifying understudied interaction cues for user cognition. Ganlin et al.'s HMD-based authoring method improved efficiency but incurred significant marker-layout overhead [5], while Eswaran et al. demonstrated AR's superior accuracy over document/VR-based methods [6]. However, most existing works focus on instructional modalities rather than integrating lightweight detection and spatial tracking suitable for wearable AR platforms, which this work addresses.

Practical validations include Cardoso et al.'s computer vision-based mobile AR for aircraft assembly [7], Mei et al.'s AR-assisted turbine rotor assembly [8], and Zhao et al.'s offline detection system [9]. Chen et al. [10] accelerated industrial AR deployment via QDARV—a toolkit combining SLAM registration and YOLOv5 detection for factory-scale visualization. Additionally, Tainaka et al. [11] proposed a systematic guideline and tool to support AR system design in complex tasks such as PC assembly and rope work, emphasizing modular design and tracking mode selection. Geng et al. [12] further addressed the challenges in small-scale, high-density industrial component (SHIC) assembly, proposing an AR-based guidance framework that integrates deep learning and rule reasoning to enhance guidance completeness and robustness. These systems validate feasibility but often rely on heavy computation or cloud services, lacking lightweight, real-time frameworks deployable on mobile AR devices.

Deep learning advances position object detection as critical for intelligent AR assembly. Zou et al. [13] and Fang et al. [14] surveyed detection methods and HMD applications respectively. Jiang et al. [15] developed YOLO-Master for wearable AR. Li et al. [16] boosted mobile AR detection accuracy by 12% through VIO-semantic fusion. Xue et al. [17] proposed an anti-occlusion AR guidance method for avionics equipment, which combines pose tracking and assembly step identification to address the challenges of narrow spaces and user overload in manual assembly. While prior studies emphasize detection or semantic guidance, they fall short of integrating efficient pose estimation using pre-rendered datasets for real-time spatial alignment.

Early feasibility studies range from Hakkarainen et al.'s 2008 client-server system [18] to Marino et al.'s tablet-based efficiency gains [19]. Siriborvornratanakul [20] proposed projector-based AR (SAR) to address visibility limitations in phone/wearable systems. Although pioneering, early AR systems lack the deep learning-based integration and deployment efficiency required for current real-time wearable applications.

To support real-time performance on resource-constrained devices, several lightweight object detection models have been proposed. Du et al. [21] introduced SODR-CNN with a dual-channel architecture, reducing detection latency by 37% while addressing the challenge of small and densely packed objects. Zhao et al. [22] presented FPN-CenterNet, which achieved 74.49% accuracy in detecting redundant components during aircraft assembly. Zaccardi et al. [23] evaluated Unity Barracuda and WinML on HoloLens 2, confirming the feasibility of deploying deep learning models locally. Wang et al. [24] further explored cognition-based multi-modal guidance with bare-hand interface, offering insights into interaction-aware guidance systems under constrained interfaces. Few of these models provide a unified pipeline for detection, pose estimation, and AR rendering optimized for wearable AR hardware, as proposed in our method.

Given the limited computing power of current AR devices, cloud–edge collaborative architectures have emerged to alleviate computational loads, though latency remains a concern [25]. Lightweight deployment and edge computing solutions [26], such as real-time YOLO implementations on HoloLens [27], offer a promising direction for real-time AR-based intelligent assembly. In contrast to these decoupled strategies, our approach offers a fully integrated, on-device AR pipeline without reliance on external computation.

3 Our Method

For an AR based guidance framework, to facilitate deployment on head-mounted AR devices, this study emphasizes lightweight, low-latency object detection and 3D object registration.

The overall system architecture is depicted in Fig. 1, comprising four core functional modules: (1) Object detection model training, (2) pose query database construction, (3) object detection, and (4) Spatial registration. The system supports hands-free operation through voice command-based initiation and termination.

Upon activation, the RGB camera captures a continuous video stream, which is segmented into frames and resized uniformly. These frames are processed by the recognition module, implemented via the optimized YOLOv7-Tiny network and Barracuda inference engine, to detect objects in real time and extract associated labels and 2D positional information. The results are passed to the registration module.

In the registration stage, 2D coordinates are projected into the camera coordinate system, and 3D spatial positions are estimated using a projection ray-based approach. The computed spatial data are stored in an object registry for downstream tasks.

Subsequently, the pose estimation module identifies the region of interest (ROI) based on detection results, performs feature matching with a pre-built database, and calculates the object's current pose. This pose is used to align and render the corresponding virtual model, which is then overlaid onto the real-world scene to achieve virtual-real fusion. During this process, assembly guidance is activated, displaying virtual components and

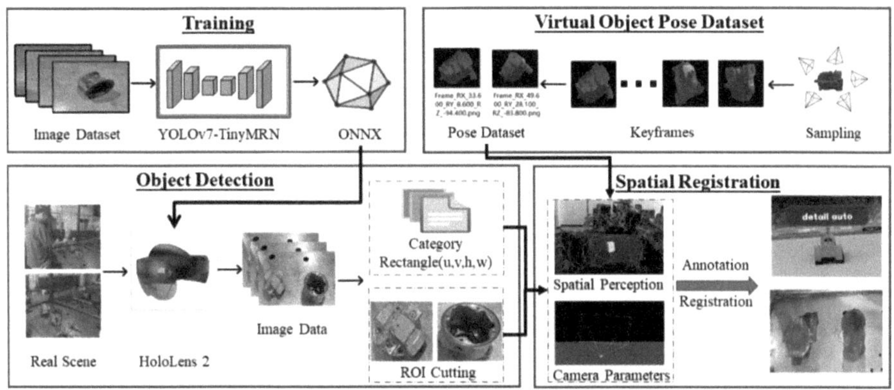

Fig. 1. The workflow of the proposed approach.

animated instructions directly over the physical object. Voice commands also enable real-time querying of part or tool locations.

Since a rough 3D scene is constructed by Hololens2, we only update the above process when the objects are moved to improve the performance further.

3.1 YOLOv7-TinyMRN for Object Detection

To enable deployment on mobile AR devices with limited onboard computational resources, the system requires a deep learning model that balances inference speed and lightweight design.

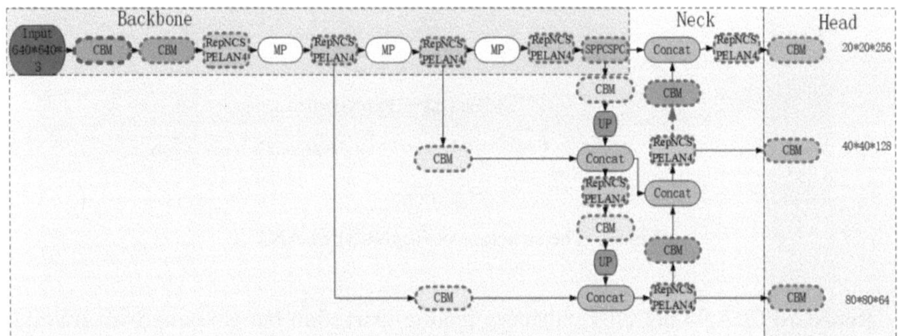

Fig. 2. The structure of Yolov7-TinyMRN.

The YOLO (You Only Look Once) [28] series is known for its real-time object detection capabilities. As an efficient lightweight variant of the YOLOv7 series [29], YOLOv7-Tiny features a backbone composed of CBL modules, multi-branch MCB modules for robust feature extraction, and MP modules for down sampling via stride-2 convolution and max pooling.

We propose an improved architecture named YOLOv7-TinyMRN (YOLOv7-Tiny with Mish & RepNcspelan4) as shown in Fig. 2, in which the original MCB modules are replaced with enhanced RepNCSPELAN4 modules. The design incorporates Cross Stage Partial (CSP) connections and an Efficient Layer Aggregation Network (ELAN) structure, enabling better local detail representation through multi-branch feature partitioning and parallel processing. To reduce inference-time complexity, structural re-parameterization is applied. Furthermore, the backbone substitutes the LeakyReLU activation with Mish, a smoother non-linear function that better preserves negative feature values, thereby mitigating gradient vanishing and improving model accuracy.

In this study, the YOLOv7-Tiny architecture was further optimized (Fig. 2). The MCB module was replaced with a CSP-ELAN-based structure to enhance local feature representation via multi-branch partitioning and parallel processing. Structural re-parameterization was applied to reduce inference complexity. Additionally, the backbone activation was changed from LeakyReLU to Mish, improving gradient flow and overall accuracy.

3.2 RepNCSPELAN4

Although the MCB module exhibits moderate parameter and FLOP demands, the RepNCSPELAN4 module—despite a higher parameter count and computational load during training due to its internal sub-modules—employs structural re-parameterization at deployment. This significantly reduces inference complexity while maintaining accuracy, thus enhancing runtime efficiency. The structural diagram of RepNCSPELAN4 is illustrated in Fig. 3.

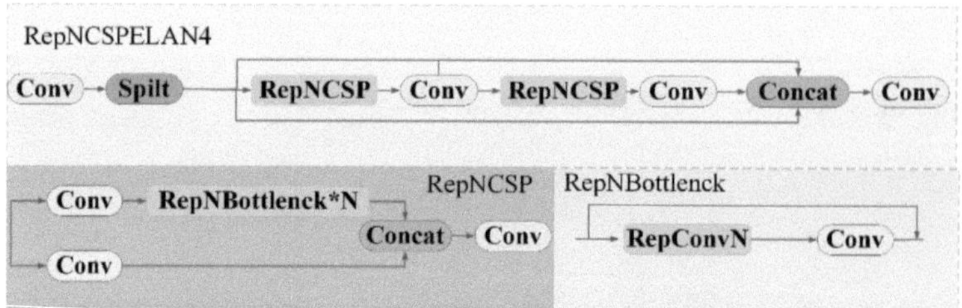

Fig. 3. The structure of RepNCSPELAN4

RepNCSPELAN4 not only enhances feature extraction but also improves training efficiency and convergence speed through optimized gradient flow, whereas the MCB module primarily targets multi-scale feature fusion. Consequently, Rep-NCSPELAN4 demonstrates superior performance when learning from large-scale datasets and in complex environments.

As shown in Table 1, the layer count increased from 200 of YOLOv7-Tiny to 462 of YOLOv7-TinyMRN, the floating-point operations (FLOPs) de-creased from 13.1 GFLOPs to 11.6 GFLOPs, representing an 11.45% reduction. This demonstrates that the modified model improves feature representation and fitting capacity while reducing computational complexity, ensuring efficient operation on AR devices.

Table 1. Performance comparison between YOLOv7-Tiny and YOLOv7-TinyRNM

Network	layers	parameters	GFLOPS	weight
YOLOv7-Tiny	200	6039010	13.1	11.7 MB
YOLOv7-TinyMRN	462	5556354	11.6	11.0 MB

3.3 Activation Function

Activation functions introduce non-linearity critical for gradient propagation and output control. In lightweight models, selecting an appropriate activation is key to balancing performance and complexity. The original YOLOv7-Tiny uses Leaky ReLU [30], which alleviates the "dying ReLU" problem but has limited non-linear expressiveness and gradient stability. This study replaces Leaky ReLU with Mish [31] in the backbone network to offset potential accuracy loss from the lightweight RepNCSPELAN4 module.

$$LeakyRelu(x) = \begin{cases} x & x > 0 \\ \alpha x & x \leq 0 \end{cases} \tag{1}$$

$$Mish(x) = x \cdot \tanh \ln(1 + x) \tag{2}$$

Mish provides stronger non-linear representation, smoother gradients, and better preservation of negative information, mitigating vanishing gradients and stabilizing training. Despite a slight increase in complexity, experimental results show a 1.47% accuracy improvement, justifying this trade-off. The mathematical formulations of Leaky ReLU and Mish are presented in Eqs. (1) and (2).

3.4 Training of Assembly Elements Dataset

To evaluate the proposed model's performance in assembly and maintenance contexts, 12 commonly used hardware components—such as hex bolts, T-bolts, round-head screws, and hexagonal steel columns (Fig. 4)—were selected. The training dataset comprised 700 images, with 200 for validation and 100 for testing. All images were resized to 640 × 640 resolution.

Experiments were conducted on a platform with AMD Ryzen 5 4600H CPU (3.00 GHz), NVIDIA GeForce GTX 1650 GPU, Windows 10 OS, and Python 3.9. Training used a batch size of 4 over 300 epochs.

Model performance was assessed using mean Average Precision at IoU thresholds from 0.5 to 0.95 (mAP@0.5:0.95), a standard metric that averages precision across IoU values with 0.05 increments, capturing detection accuracy under varying difficulty levels.

As shown in Table 2, our improved model exhibits no loss in recognition accuracy for the various hardware parts—in fact, it achieves a slight improvement over the baseline.

3.5 Rough Spatial Registration

Accurate and efficient 3D spatial registration is essential for effective AR-based assembly guidance. Mapping 2D detections from computer vision models to 3D coordinates

Fig. 4. Hardware workpiece

Table 2. Precision comparison between YOLOv7-Tiny and YOLOv7-TinyMRN.

Network	AP				mAP@.5:.95
	Hexagon screw	Hexagon nut	Key bar	Spring washer	
YOLOv7-Tiny	**0.834**	0.719	0.776	0.761	0.769
YOLOv7-TinyMRN	0.831	**0.723**	**0.783**	**0.779**	**0.774**

remains a fundamental yet challenging task in AR applications. To address this, we propose a lightweight registration method that utilizes Hololens2' spatial awareness capability combined with depth camera data to estimate the 3D coordinates of the object.

With the detection result from YOLOv7-TinyMRN, the center point (u,v) of the bounding box of the detected object is extracted in the pixel coordinate system, then is normalized and converted into image coordinates (x,y) based on the camera's intrinsic parameters. From the AR camera a ray is casted to detect the collision with the spatial mesh. The collision point will be used as the initial registration location.

3.6 Fine Pose Estimation

Assembly tasks require precise pose estimation beyond object recognition and registration. However, 2D-3D matching methods demand high computational resources, limiting their applicability on mobile AR devices. To address this, a lightweight 2D-2D pose estimation method based on processed 2D image features is proposed, reducing complexity while ensuring real-time performance.

To determine the real object's orientation, we construct a virtual object pose dataset by uniform sampling on a viewing sphere around the virtual object model, as shown in Fig. 5. The resulting images are used to construct a pose-matching image dataset. Each image is stored using a standardized naming convention, indicating the corresponding rotation angles around the X, Y, and Z axes, respectively. To eliminate redundant keyframes with over 99% similarity, we employ the Perceptual Hashing (pHash) algorithm [32], which is widely used for perceptual image similarity detection. pHash generates a compact perceptual hash by applying grayscale conversion, resizing, and Discrete Cosine Transform (DCT) to the image, and then measures the Hamming distance between hash values to determine similarity. This process effectively reduces duplicate views while preserving diverse object poses in the dataset.

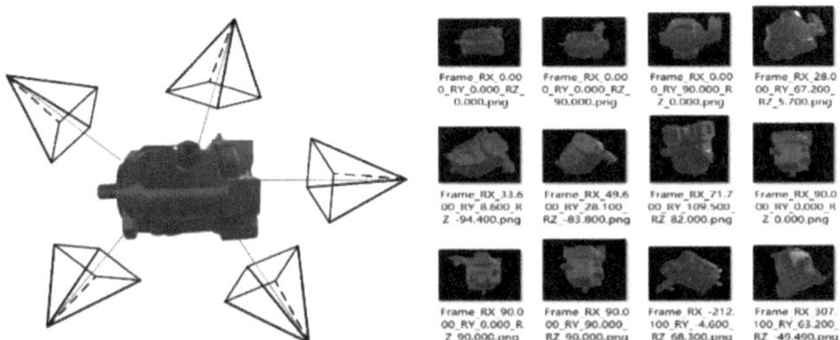

Fig. 5. Virtual object pose dataset construction

Robust feature matching is achieved using Scale-Invariant Feature Transform (SIFT), which detects scale- and rotation-invariant key points. To improve robustness under varying illumination and cluttered backgrounds, Canny edge detection is applied as a preprocessing step to extract salient contours.

Experimental results demonstrate that this approach increases correct feature matches across multiple viewpoints, achieving 80.5% pose estimation accuracy in challenging conditions. Keyframes are stored with rotation-encoded filenames, enabling pose inference by selecting the keyframe with the highest match count for virtual model alignment.

4 Experiments and Discussion

For system validation, we deployed the proposed solution on Microsoft HoloLens 2 and conducted tests on the recognition of hardware components and pose estimation of a motor.

As shown in the workflow diagram in Sect. 1, the trained model was exported in ONNX format and deployed using the Barracuda inference library. The scripting was implemented in C#, and AR components were integrated using MRTK3 (Mixed Reality Toolkit 3) in Unity3D.

During user interaction, the recognition of hardware components is illustrated in Fig. 6. Figure 6(a) shows the recognition of a single hardware component, where the user, while wearing the AR headset, is able to locate the component and view its corresponding name in real time.

Figure 6(b) presents the recognition of multiple hardware components in a complex scene. It demonstrates that even in cluttered environments with numerous parts, the system can still effectively complete the recognition process.

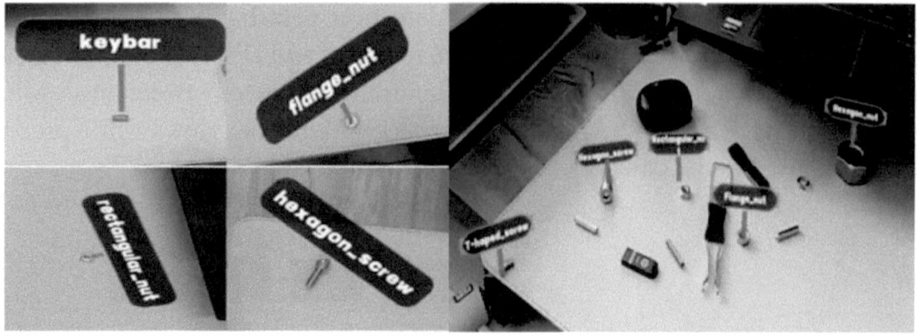

a. Single object annotation   b. Multiple object annotations

Fig. 6. Object annotation

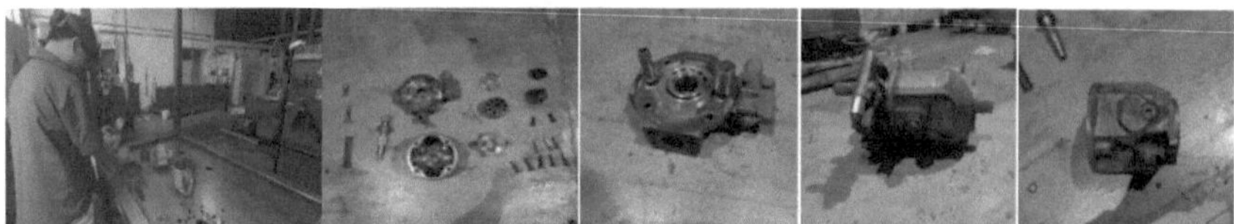

Fig. 7. Assembly workshop scene

For pose matching validation, the system was tested in a real industrial environment, specifically in a variable pump maintenance workshop. The operator wore a HoloLens 2 headset, as shown in Fig. 7.

From the first-person perspective, the system accurately identified target components, extracted ROI images based on detection results, and performed feature matching with a pre-built image database. The pose corresponding to the best-matched keyframe was assigned to the virtual model and overlaid onto the real object, achieving effective pose alignment, as illustrated in Fig. 8.

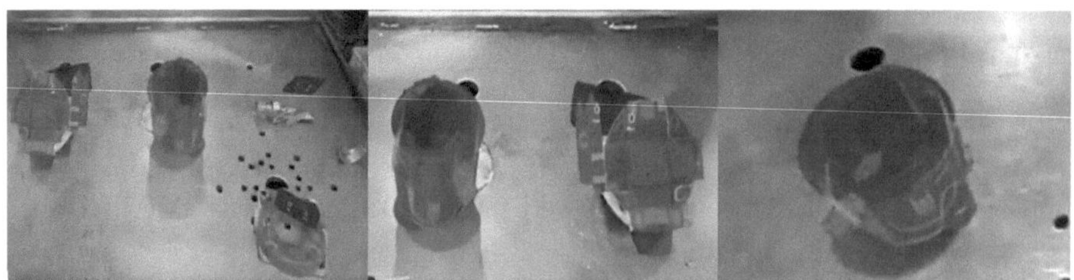

Fig. 8. Pose matching results

To assist assembly tasks, the system supports animation-based guidance for the main assembly object (the pump body in this case). Users can control the display of assembly animations via buttons or gestures.

During assembly, virtual parts animate their alignment with the main object, providing intuitive visual cues for each step, as shown in Fig. 9. A complete virtual model of

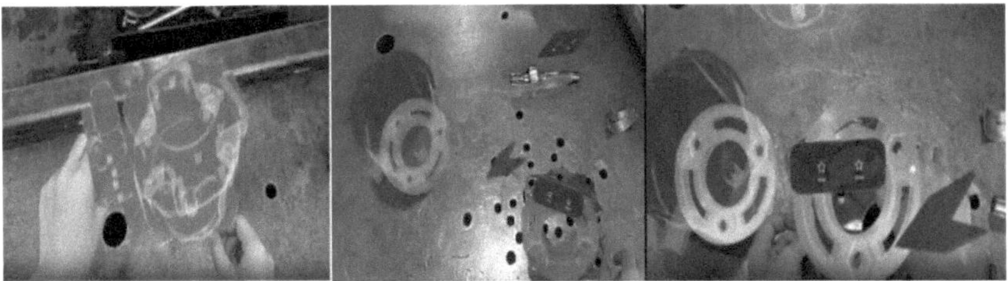

Fig. 9. Assisted assembly schematic diagram

the assembled object is also available for reference. The validation confirms the system's effectiveness in object recognition, pose estimation, and assembly assistance in practical industrial scenarios.

5 Conclusion

This paper presented a lightweight AR framework for object tracking and localization in assembly guidance. To address computational constraints on AR devices, we proposed YOLOv7-TinyMRN, an optimized detection model reducing GFLOPS by 11.45% and model size by 6% while maintaining accuracy. A streamlined spatial registration method leveraging HoloLens2's depth sensing enabled efficient 3D positioning. For pose estimation, we introduced a 2D-2D feature matching approach using a pre-rendered virtual pose dataset and SIFT with edge preprocessing, achieving real-time alignment with 80.5% accuracy.

Experimental validation on HoloLens 2 confirmed the system's effectiveness in recognizing hardware components, estimating poses, and overlaying animated assembly instructions.

Detection robustness for small, texture less, or highly complex objects requires improvement. Future work will explore multi-sensor fusion and domain adaptation for broader industrial scenarios.

Acknowledgements. This research is supported by National Natural Science Foundation of China (Key Program Grant No. 52131204).

References

1. Wang, X., Ong, S.K., Nee, A.Y.C.: A comprehensive survey of augmented reality assembly research. Adv. Manuf. **4**, 1–22 (2016)
2. Serván, J., Mas, F., Menéndez, J.L., Ríos, J.: Using augmented reality in AIRBUS A400M shop floor assembly work instructions. In: AIP Conference Proceedings. AIP, Cadiz, Spain (2012)
3. Büttner, S., et al.: The design space of augmented and virtual reality applications for assistive environments in manufacturing: a visual approach. In: Proceedings of the 10th International Conference on PErvasive Technologies Related to Assistive Environments, pp. 433–440. ACM, Island of Rhodes, Greece (2017)

4. Wang, Z., et al.: A comprehensive review of augmented reality-based instruction in manual assembly, training and repair. Robotics Comput.-Integr. Manuf. **78**, 102407 (2022)
5. Ganlin, Z., Pingfa, F., Jianfu, Z., Dingwen, Y., Zhijun, W.: Information integration and instruction authoring of augmented assembly systems. Int. J. Intell. Syst. **36**, 5028–5050 (2021)
6. Eswaran, M., Raju Bahubalendruni, M.V.A.: Augmented reality aided object mapping for worker assistance/training in an industrial assembly context: Exploration of affordance with existing guidance techniques. Comput. Ind. Eng. **185**, 109663 (2023)
7. de Souza Cardoso, L.F., Mariano, F.C.M.Q., Zorzal, E.R.: Mobile augmented reality to support fuselage assembly. Comput. Ind. Eng. **148**, 106712 (2020)
8. Mei, Y., et al.: Multi-stage rotors assembly of turbine-based combined cycle engine based on augmented reality. Adv. Eng. Inf. **58**, 102160 (2023)
9. Zhao, G., Feng, P., Zhang, J., Yu, C., Wang, J.: Rapid offline detection and 3D annotation of assembly elements in the augmented assembly. Expert Syst. Appl. **222**, 119839 (2023)
10. Chen, C., et al.: A quick development toolkit for augmented reality visualization (QDARV) of a factory. Appl. Sci. **12**, 8338 (2022)
11. Tainaka, K., Fujimoto, Y., Kanbara, M., et al.: Guideline and tool for designing an assembly task support system using augmented reality. In: Proceedings of IEEE International Symposium on Mixed and Aug-mented Reality (ISMAR), pp. 486–497. IEEE, Orlando, FL (2020)
12. Geng, J., Wang, Y., Cheng, Y., et al.: Systematic AR-based assembly guidance for small-scale, high-density industrial components. J. Manuf. Syst. **79**, 86–100 (2025)
13. Zou, Z., Chen, K., Shi, Z., Guo, Y., Ye, J.: Object detection in 20 years: a survey. Proc. IEEE **111**, 257–276 (2023)
14. Fang, W., Chen, L., Zhang, T., Chen, C., Teng, Z., Wang, L.: Head-mounted display augmented reality in manufacturing: a systematic review. Robot. Comput.-Integr. Manuf. **83**, 102567 (2023)
15. Jiang, J., Yang, Z., Wu, C., Guo, Y., Yang, M., Feng, W.: A compatible detector based on improved YOLOv5 for hydropower device detection in AR inspection system. Expert Syst. Appl. **225**, 120065 (2023)
16. Li, X., Tian, Y., Zhang, F., Quan, S., Xu, Y.: Object detection in the context of mobile augmented reality. In: 2020 IEEE International Symposium on Mixed and Augmented Reality (ISMAR), pp. 156–163 (2020)
17. Xue, Z., Yang, J., Chen, R., et al.: AR-assisted guidance for assembly and maintenance of avionics equipment. Appl. Sci. **14**(3), 1137 (2024)
18. Hakkarainen, M., Woodward, C., Billinghurst, M.: Augmented assembly using a mobile phone. In: 2008 7th IEEE/ACM International Symposium on Mixed and Augmented Reality, pp. 167–168 (2008)
19. Marino, E., Barbieri, L., Bruno, F., Muzzupappa, M.: Assessing user performance in augmented reality assembly guidance for Industry 4.0 operators. Comput. Ind. **157–158**, 104085 (2024)
20. Siriborvornratanakul, T.: Enhancing user experiences of mobile-based augmented reality via spatial augmented reality: designs and architectures of projector-camera devices (2018)
21. Du, B., Guo, J., Guo, J., Wang, L., Li, X.: A rapid oriented detection method of virtual components for augmented assembly. Expert Syst. Appl. **248**, 123357 (2024)
22. Zhao, Q., Kong, Y., Sheng, S., Zhu, J.: Redundant object detection method for civil aircraft assembly based on machine vision and smart glasses. Meas. Sci. Technol. **33**, 105011 (2022)
23. Zaccardi, S., Frantz, T., Beckwée, D., Swinnen, E., Jansen, B.: On-device execution of deep learning models on HoloLens2 for real-time augmented reality medical applications. Sensors **23**, 8698 (2023)

24. Wang, X., Ong, S.K., Nee, A.Y.C.: Multi-modal augmented-reality assembly guidance based on bare-hand interface. Adv. Eng. Inform. **30**(3), 406–421 (2016)
25. Atici-Ulusu, H., Ikiz, Y.D., Taskapilioglu, O., Gunduz, T.: Effects of augmented reality glasses on the cognitive load of assembly operators in the automotive industry. Int. J. Comput. Integr. Manuf. (2021)
26. Ahmad, H.M., Rahimi, A.: Deep learning methods for object detection in smart manufacturing: a survey. J. Manuf. Syst. **64**, 181–196 (2022)
27. Bahri, H., Krčmařík, D., Kočí, J.: Accurate object detection system on HoloLens using YOLO algorithm. In: 2019 International Conference on Control, Artificial Intelligence, Robotics & Optimization (ICCAIRO), pp. 219–224 (2019)
28. Redmon, J., Divvala, S., Girshick, R., Farhadi, A.: You only look once: unified, real-time object detection. In: Proceedings of the IEEE Conference on Computer Vision and Pattern Recognition (CVPR) (2016)
29. Wang, C.-Y., Bochkovskiy, A., Liao, H.-Y.M.: YOLOv7: Trainable bag-of-freebies sets new state-of-the-art for real-time object detectors. In: Proceedings of the IEEE/CVF Conference on Computer Vision and Pattern Recognition (CVPR) (2023)
30. Maas, A.L., Hannun, A.Y., Ng, A.Y.: Rectifier nonlinearities improve neural network acoustic models. In: Proceedings of the 30th International Conference on Machine Learning (ICML 2013), vol. 30, p. 3. JMLR.org (2013)
31. Misra, D.: Mish: a self regularized non-monotonic activation function. arXiv preprint arXiv: 1908.08681 (2019)
32. Hamming, R.W.: Error detecting and error correcting codes. Bell Syst. Tech. J. **29**(2), 147–160 (1950)

Mapping the Knowledge Landscape of Virtual Reality Interaction (1995–2024): A Bibliometric Review and Thematic Evolution Study

Lu Liu[1]([✉]) [iD], Ben Liu[2] [iD], and HouHong Huang[2]

[1] Communication University of China Nanjing, Nanjing 211172, China
liulu@cucn.edu.cn
[2] Communication University of China, Beijing 100024, China

Abstract. This study conducts a bibliometric and thematic-evolution analysis of virtual-reality interaction (VRI) research published between 1995 and 2024, addressing three research questions: first, how global and Chinese VRI output has changed over time; second, which authors, institutions, and countries form the intellectual core of the field; and third, what thematic clusters and emerging fronts define current scholarship. After retrieval and data cleaning, we obtained 1,424 valid papers from the Web of Science Core Collection database and 494 valid core journal articles from CNKI, CiteSpace 6.2 (R3) was mainly used to conduct the analysis, and author, institution, and keyword networks were generated. The study identifies that publication output follows three distinct periods internationally—an incubation phase from 1995 to 2007, an acceleration phase from 2008 to 2015, and a surge phase from 2016 to 2020—with the highest annual volume recorded in 2020; Chinese output rises sharply after 2016 and peaks in both 2018 and 2022, consistent with national policy incentives. The Chinese Academy of Sciences and University College London lead institutional productivity with eighteen papers each, while China, the United States, Germany, the United Kingdom, and Italy dominate national contributions. Applying Price's law identifies 135 core authors, with Lecuyer A. heading the most cohesive collaboration cluster. High-frequency keywords such as "virtual reality," "augmented reality," "human–computer interaction," "mixed reality," and "realism" organize eighteen thematic clusters, and burst detection reveals recent growth in topics including deep learning, brain–computer interfaces, and the metaverse, signalling a shift from device-centric studies toward intelligent, multisensory interaction and educational applications. By integrating longitudinal output metrics with rigorous network statistics, the study clarifies the VRI knowledge landscape, highlights influential contributors, and outlines future research directions that emphasise AI-enhanced interaction paradigms and cross-disciplinary collaboration.

Keywords: Virtual Reality Interaction · Knowledge Graph · Visualization Analysis · CiteSpace

---

L. Liu and B. Liu—These authors contributed equally to this work.

© The Author(s), under exclusive license to Springer Nature Singapore Pte Ltd. 2026
Z. Lin et al. (Eds.): ICIG 2025, LNCS 16163, pp. 564–586, 2026.
https://doi.org/10.1007/978-981-95-3729-7_46

1 Introduction

The term 'virtual reality' (VR) was coined by Jaron Lanier in 1987, His research and engineering contributed numerous products to the emerging virtual reality industry, integrated scattered technologies into a systematic "virtual reality" framework, and through commercialization, promoted it to become a globally recognized term. In China, Qian Xuesen translated it as 'Spiritual Realm.' Since its inception, VR technology has sparked a research boom and has seen rapid development from a laboratory concept to an industry boom over the past three decades. Its applications are extremely broad [1]. As a revolutionary innovation in human-computer interaction, VR's development is closely tied to global strategic layouts for technological innovation [2]. VR interaction has consistently taken immersion, interactivity, and presence as its core objectives, and its technological evolution and theoretical innovations have profoundly reshaped interaction paradigms in education, healthcare, industry, and entertainment. Propelled simultaneously by artificial intelligence and 5G connectivity, emerging directions such as the convergence of virtual and physical spaces and agent-based interaction are redefining the cognitive boundaries of human–computer interaction.

This study systematically reviews the literature on global virtual reality interaction from 1995 to 2024. Using CiteSpace to visualize the knowledge graph, it examines the research status, hotspots, academic frontiers, and development trends of the virtual reality interaction field across different stages and periods. It analyzes key technological breakthroughs, changes in research hotspots, and the expansion of application scenarios in the VR interaction field. The article highlights the global research progress in this field, aiming to reveal the patterns of technological development and provide theoretical references for future research directions.

2 Data Collection and Research Methods

2.1 Data Acquisition and Processing

The international literature was sourced from the Web of Science (WOS) core collection database, with 'Virtual Reality Interaction' and specific virtual reality interaction keywords used as search terms. The search query was: TS = ("virtual reality" AND interaction). After excluding invalid literatures such as conference papers, editorial materials, book articles, and retracted publications, a total of 1,424 valid literature records were obtained. To enhance the breadth and scientific rigor of the study, Chinese core journals from the Chinese CNKI database were added as a source for literature analysis. A search was conducted with the theme of "virtual reality interaction", yielding 563 retrieval records. To ensure the quality of the literature, each retrieval result was read and evaluated one by one, and editorial materials, work displays, duplicate literatures, and those unrelated to virtual reality interaction research were manually excluded, resulting in 494 valid literatures. In the Web of Science (WOS) Core Collection database and the CNKI Core Database, the earliest literatures obtained through retrieval and screening were published in 1996 and 1995, respectively. In view of the time range limitation of the study, the literature retrieval in this paper was conducted up to December 31, 2024. Therefore, the objects of analysis in this paper are the literatures published between January 1, 1995 and December 31, 2024.

2.2 Research Methods

This study employs bibliometrics and knowledge mapping, taking 1,424 international literatures from the Web of Science (WOS) Core Collection and 494 core literatures from China National Knowledge Infrastructure (CNKI) as analysis samples. By utilizing CiteSpace software and the built-in bibliometric visualization analysis tools of the databases, co-occurrence networks were constructed and visual knowledge maps were generated. The refined literatures were exported from WOS and CNKI databases as Plain text files and RefWorks text data respectively, with the files named in the format of "download-xx.txt". During the visualization analysis of research literatures using CiteSpace software, the parameters were set as follows: Time Slicing = from 1995 to 2024, Years Per Slice = 1 (consistent with the time span of the research literature); Node Types = Author/Institution/Keyword (i.e., authors, institutions, and keywords); the g-index algorithm was adopted to set the threshold with Top N = 50; Links (the association strength of network nodes); Pruning is selected as Pathfinder-Network. The selected literatures were subjected to visualization processing to analyze the research hotspots and development trends in the field of virtual reality interaction. For details regarding the specific research workflow design and methodology, please refer to Fig. 1.

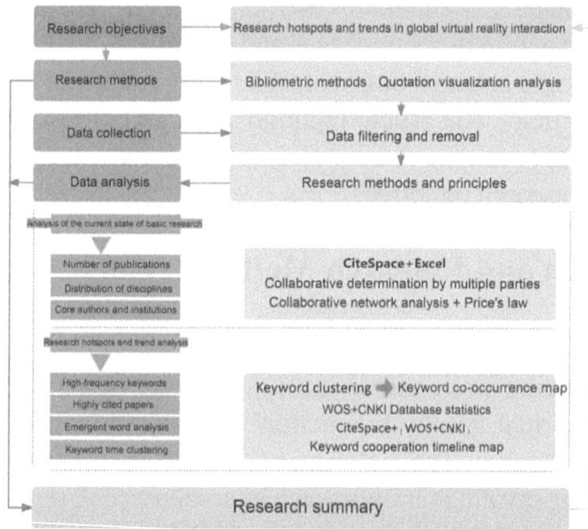

Fig. 1. Research process and methodology

3 Analysis of Current Status of Fundamental Research

3.1 Number of Published Literatures

Based on the retrieval results from the WOS database, the annual distribution map of literature quantity was generated (Fig. 2). This map macroscopically reflects the number of published literatures in the field of virtual reality interaction from 1996 to 2024. Overall, the number of international publications in this field has shown a significant upward trend over the past three decades. International research on virtual reality interaction began in 1996, with slow growth during the period 1996–2007. This stage was mainly focused on theoretical concepts and basic applications of virtual reality, representing the embryonic period of development in this field. Key milestones include: the release of Microsoft Surface touch technology in 2007, which inspired research on multimodal interaction in VR; and the public disclosure of the Oculus Rift prototype by Palmer Luckey in 2010, which drew academic attention to the development potential of consumer-grade VR. International publications entered a growth phase starting from 2008, reached a small peak in 2010, showing consistent development trends. During this period, advancements in computer graphics and sensor technologies drove the application of interaction methods (e.g., gesture recognition, force feedback).From the perspective of international publications, there was a notable acceleration in growth after 2015, reflecting a surge in research enthusiasm. The period 2016–2024 witnessed leapfrog development: the number of literatures increased sharply in 2020, experienced a slight decline between 2020 and 2022, and then surged year by year through 2024. This stage saw HTC Vive's launch of Lighthouse spatial positioning technology, which promoted research on "room-scale VR" (evidenced by a surge in "room-scale VR"-related papers in WoS). The release of Oculus Quest in 2019, with its wireless 6DOF interaction, drove growth in papers on "mobile VR". The global pandemic in 2020 spurred demand for VR-based remote collaboration, shifting the industry focus from hardware competition to optimization of interaction experiences, with wirelessization and gesture tracking emerging as key research hotspots.

An analysis of the publication status of literatures in this field from 1995 to 2024 in the CNKI database reveals that the number of publications in China fluctuated significantly within the period but showed an overall upward trend. Research on virtual reality interaction in China began to take off between 1995 and 2004, with slow growth during this period. Numerous scholars explored aspects such as perception, user interfaces, technical challenges, and theoretical research [3]. On May 19, 2015, the State Council issued the Made in China 2025 action plan, which identified promoting the in-depth integration of informatization and industrialization, and accelerating the research, development, and industrialization of products such as human-computer intelligent interaction and wearable devices as one of the strategic tasks and priorities [4]. 2016 is widely regarded as the first year of China's VR industry, which is closely related to national policy support and market environment orientation. The number of publications reached historical peaks in 2018 and 2022. An analysis of the content and themes of these literatures shows that research during this stage focused on virtual reality and human-computer interaction, interaction design, and immersive experiences.

The analysis results indicate that the global research scope and attention in this field have shown a leapfrog growth trend, suggesting that it is a research field with considerable research value and promising development prospects.

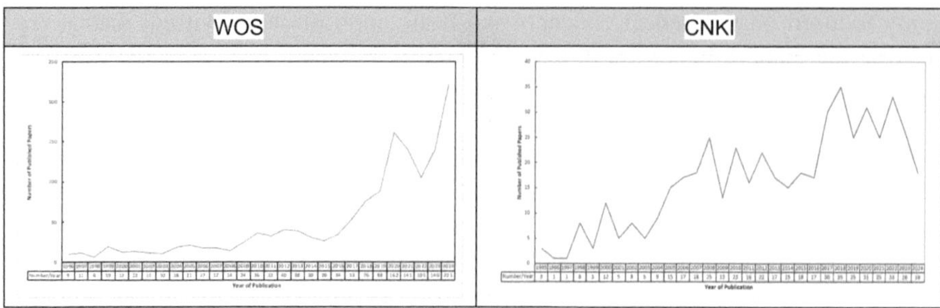

Fig. 2. Published Trend Chart

3.2 Disciplinary Distribution

The disciplinary distribution of retrieved literatures in this field within the WOS database was statistically analyzed, with the top 10 disciplines visualized (Fig. 3). The analysis reveals that international research on virtual reality interaction is closely associated with disciplines such as Computer Science Software Engineering, Computer Science Information Systems, Telecommunications, Engineering Electrical Electronic, Computer Science Cybernetics, Education Educational Research, Computer Science Artificial Intelligence, Computer Science Interdisciplinary Applications, Neuroscience, and Engineering Multidisciplinary. Among these, Computer Science Software Engineering and Computer Science Information Systems account for 21.67% and 15.48% respectively, indicating a strong connection between research in this field and computer science, which provides theoretical, algorithmic, and systematic support. Additionally, Telecommunications, Engineering Electrical Electronic, and Education Educational Research constitute 11.41%, 11.37%, and 9.57% of the disciplinary distribution, respectively.

An analysis was conducted on the literature retrieval results in the field of virtual reality interaction from the CNKI database, with the top 10 disciplines visualized. Among them, "Computer Software and Computer Applications" accounted for 67.41% of the disciplinary distribution, ranking first; "Automation Technology" ranked second with 8.02%; "Educational Theory and Educational Management" ranked third with 6.48%. Other popular disciplines included "Drama, Film and Television Arts", "Shipbuilding Industry", "General Industrial Technology and Equipment", "Mining Engineering", "Architectural Science and Engineering", "Aerospace Science and Engineering", and "Electric Power Industry".

The analysis results show that international research in this field is concentrated in computer science and its related fields, with more detailed subdivisions regarding the application of computer science in virtual reality. In contrast, Chinese research is focused on computer software and its applications, with relatively extensive penetration into other disciplines.

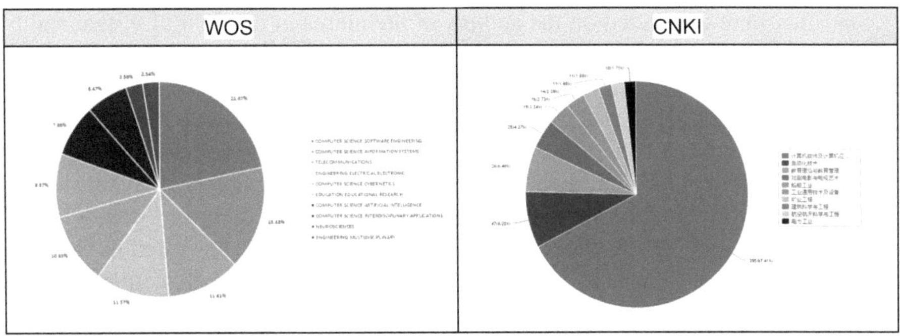

Fig. 3. Top 10 disciplines

3.3　Analysis of Core Authors and Institutions

3.3.1　Core Authors

By sorting out the researchers in this field through the WOS platform, we can identify the core authors in the field and their interrelationships, and to a certain extent, analyze the research focuses and hotspots in this field. In the citespace software, select the 'Author' node, set the time interval from January 1996 to December 2024, and set the time slice to 1, to generate an author co-occurrence graph (Fig. 4). According to Price's Law (1) [5], a paper must be published at least Mp times to be considered a core author, where Npmax represents the maximum number of publications per author in the sample data; statistical analysis shows that the maximum number of publications per author in the virtual reality interaction field is 6, and based on the formula, Mp = 1.835, meaning an author with at least 2 publications qualifies as a core author in this field. The frequency of publications by core authors is analyzed, and there are 135 authors with at least 2 publications. Due to space limitations, only the authors with more than 2 publications are listed in the table (Table 1). The graph shows that the number of author nodes (N) is 693, the number of edges (E) is 585, the density is 0.0024, and the clustering module value (Q) is 0.9825.' It is generally believed that Q > 0.3 indicates a significant clustering structure, and the closer it is to 1, the better the clustering effect' [6].

$$Mp \approx 0.749\left(\sqrt{Npmax}\right) \tag{1}$$

Nodes represent core authors, where a larger node indicates greater influence of the author in the field. The connections between nodes can reveal collaborative groups of authors. An analysis of the map shows that major core author collaborative groups have been formed, with close connections and a relatively wide scope among these groups. Among them, Lecuyer·Anatole, who has the highest number of publications, leads a group focusing on brain-computer interfaces (BCIs), enabling users to send commands to computers using only brain activity. They proposed new interaction technologies that allow users to perform complex interaction tasks and navigate in large-scale virtual environments (VEs) using only BCIs based on imagined movements (motor imagery) [7]. Subsequently, they developed an aerial haptic interface, a tool for providing haptic feedback in virtual reality applications, which eliminates the need for users to hold or wear any systems or devices [8].

Statistics were conducted on the authors of literatures in the field of virtual reality interaction from the CNKI database, and an author collaboration network map was generated. For domestic core authors, the value of Npmax is 9. Calculated by the formula, Mp = 2.247, indicating that authors with at least 3 publications are considered core authors in this field.The node size and connection density in the collaboration network map intuitively reflect the number of publications per author and the collaborative relationships among authors, presenting an overall distribution pattern of "small clusters and large dispersion" [9]. Authors with 3 or more publications are listed in the table (Table 2). There are 10 authors with more than 5 core literature publications. As can be seen from the author collaboration network map, some authors have formed stable and effective core teams. It is worth noting that most of these authors come from the same institutions or universities, and the collaborative relationships between different institutions still need to be strengthened.

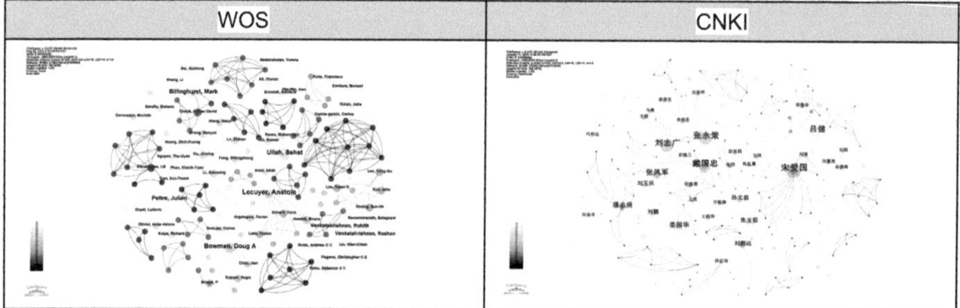

Fig. 4. Author cooperative relationship map

Table 1. List of core authors in WOS

Serial number	Frequency	Author
1	6	Lecuyer, Anatole
2	5	Bowman, Doug A
3	5	Ullah, Sehat
4	4	Billinghurst, Mark
5	4	Pan, Zhigeng
6	4	Pettre, Julien
7	4	Agus, Marco
8	3	Aristidou, Andreas
9	3	Bermudez i badia, Sergi
10	3	Cai, Yiyu
11	3	Liang, Hai-Ning
12	3	Venkatakrishnan, Rohith
13	3	Venkatakrishnan, Roshan

Table 2. List of core authors in CNKI

Serial number	Frequency	Author	Serial number	Frequency	Author
1	9	Dai Guozhong	11	4	Shen Yang
2	8	Song Aiguo	12	4	Wang Liang
3	8	Lv Jian	13	4	Jiang Guohua
4	7	Liu Zhiguang	14	4	Yong Jiu
5	7	Zhang Yongce	15	4	Zhu Xuefang
6	6	Zhang Fengjun	16	4	Wang Yangping
7	5	Zhang Yuru	17	4	Qi Binbin
8	5	Pan Zhigeng	18	3	Zeng Fenfang
9	5	Wang Dangxiao	19	3	Liu Lin
10	5	Luo Yanlin	20	3	Li Ruqin

3.3.2 Publishing Institutions

Visualization analysis was performed on the extracted literature data from the WOS database using CiteSpace software, with "institution" selected as the node type and other parameters unchanged, resulting in a collaboration map of publishing institutions (Fig. 5). Due to space constraints, this paper only presents research institutions with an occurrence frequency of ≥ 7 (Table 3). An analysis of the map reveals that there are 555 research institutions in the field of virtual reality interaction internationally, with 376 node connections and a network density of 0.0024, indicating weak collaborative relationships among institutions. Comprehensive analysis shows that among numerous international research institutions, universities are the main force in research on this field. Additionally, the top five countries with core research institutions in this field are China, the United States, Germany, the United Kingdom, and Italy, suggesting that research institutions in this field are mainly concentrated in countries with strong comprehensive national strength and advanced research environments. In the literature sample analysis, the Chinese Academy of Sciences and University College London (UCL) in the United Kingdom appeared 18 times, indicating active research in this field. Furthermore, Zhejiang University, Beihang University, and Nanyang Technological University are also relatively active in this field.

An analysis of the publishing institutions was conducted on 494 valid samples from the CNKI Core Database, resulting in a collaboration map of institutions publishing literatures (Fig. 5). Research institutions with an occurrence frequency of ≥ 3 were statistically summarized (Table 4). The analysis reveals that there are 446 institutions involved in research on virtual reality interaction, with 159 node connections. The network density is 0.0016, a value that is excessively low, indicating insufficient frequency and intensity of communication between institutions, as well as a low level of collaboration. In terms of the affiliated organizations and types of research institutions of the authors, research institutes and universities are the main contributors in this research field. The larger nodes in the network mostly represent internal collaborations within institutions, followed by significant regional divisions, indicating that inter-regional connections and collaborations need further strengthening. The Institute of Software at the Chinese Academy of Sciences conducts relatively independent research, while the State Key Laboratory of Virtual Reality Technology and Systems at Beihang University, the School of Art and Media at Beijing Normal University, and the Collaborative Innovation Center for Quality Monitoring of Basic Education at Beijing Normal University have established field cooperation. Additionally, universities, laboratories, and enterprises in southeastern China engage in industry-university-research collaboration, achieving resource sharing and leveraging the strengths of both parties.

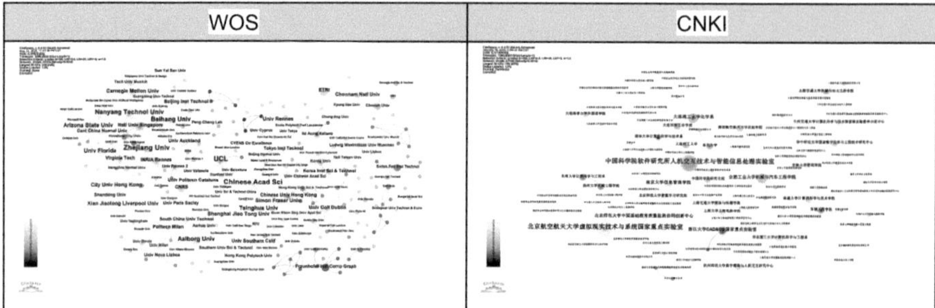

Fig. 5. Research institution cooperation map

Table 3. List of international institutions in WOS

Serial Number	Frequency	Institution
1	18	UCL
2	18	Chinese Acad Sci
3	17	Zhejiang Univ
4	13	Beihang Univ
5	13	Nanyang Technol Univ
6	11	Aalborg Univ
7	9	Arizona State Univ
8	9	Univ Florida
9	9	Tsinghua Univ
10	7	Carnegie Mellon Univ
11	7	Simon Fraser Univ
12	7	Univ Rennes
13	7	City Univ Hong Kong
14	7	Shanghai Jiao Tong Univ
15	7	Xian Jiaotong Liverpool Univ

Table 4. Research Institution List in CNKI

Serial number	Frequency	Institution
1	6	Laboratory of Human-Computer Interaction and Intelligent Information Processing, Institute of Software Chinese Academy of Sciences
2	6	State Key Laboratory Of Virtual Reality Technology And Systems,Beihang University
3	6	CAD&CG National Key Laboratory,Zhejiang University
4	4	Marine Engineering College, Dalian Maritime University
5	4	School of Arts Communication, Beijing Normal University
6	3	Dept. of Information Management,Nanjing University
7	3	School Of Instrument Science And Engineering, Southeast University
8	3	School of Information Science & Technology of BJFU
9	3	China basic education quality monitoring Collaborative Innovation Center, Beijing Normal University
10	3	College of Textiles, Donghua University
11	3	School of Mechanical Engineering, Xinjiang University
12	3	School of Chemistry Engineering, DUT
13	3	Key Laboratory of Marine Dynamic Simulation and Control for Transportation Industry, Dalian Maritime University
14	3	School of Mechanical Engineering, HeFei University

4   Research Hotspots and Trends

4.1   Analysis of Research Hotspots

4.1.1   High Frequency Keywords

Keyword co-occurrence refers to the phenomenon where two or more keywords appear simultaneously within the same text unit, which is used to analyze the relevance or thematic structure between them [10]. The frequency of keywords is positively correlated with research interest, which helps to clarify the research themes and hotspots in the field. In CiteSpace, selecting 'keywords' as nodes for high-frequency keyword clustering analysis results in the creation of a knowledge graph of international virtual reality interaction research (Figs. 6 and 7). The graph has N (nodes) = 778, E (links) = 2029, and Density (network density) = 0.0073. In the graph, the size of the keyword nodes reflects their frequency of appearance; larger nodes indicate higher frequency. By analyzing the frequency of keyword appearances, the degree centrality was calculated, and the top 20 keywords were listed (Table 5). Combining the graph and the list analysis, the top three keywords are 'virtual reality', 'augmented reality', and 'realism'. Their degree centrality values are 0.63, 0.18, and 0.06, respectively, confirming the rationality of the search term selection. It is evident that in the graph, 'virtual reality', 'augmented reality', 'human-computer interaction', 'mixed reality', and 'realism' form core nodes, radiating outwards to create a complex network structure, linking to various production factors.

In the clustering graph, the Q-clustering value (Modularity) is 0.6049, which is greater than 0.3, indicating a significant clustering structure. The S-clustering average silhouette value (Silhouette) is 0.8353, which is greater than 0.7, indicating that the clustering effect is both efficient and convincing. Keywords with clearly similar characteristics were used as clustering objects, forming a total of 18 keyword clusters from #0 to #17 within the research area [11].

Visual analysis was conducted on the literature data from the CNKI database, with the occurrence frequencies of keywords statistically counted and their betweenness centrality calculated. Keywords with an occurrence frequency of ≥ 5 are listed in the table (Table 6). Based on the analysis of the map and the list, the top three are "virtual reality," "human-computer interaction," and "interaction design," with degree centrality values of 1.37, 0.51, and 0.07, respectively. This indicates that the research hotspots in this field in China are primarily concentrated in these areas. In the graph, core nodes such as "virtual reality," "human-computer interaction," "interaction design," "interaction technology," and "augmented reality" interweave and spread, forming a new network of cooperative relationships.

The establishment and improvement of virtual reality systems are based on key core technologies. Numerous Chinese scholars have analyzed these technologies from perspectives such as the architecture of key technical systems and development essentials. Shu Jianhua [12] summarized them into five aspects: dynamic environment modeling technology, real-time 3D graphics generation and display technology, development of new interactive devices, intelligent voice virtual reality modeling, and prospects for distributed virtual reality technology. Yang Haozhong, Kong Xiaoyu, et al. [13] focused on large model technology (LM technology) in virtual reality environments, systematically sorting out and analyzing the application progress of LM technology in two aspects of VR: content generation and human-computer interaction. Their research mainly concentrated on using LM technology to create diverse virtual objects and construct virtual characters, while exploring how users can interact naturally and smoothly with intelligent agents in virtual environments. Wang Yufeng and Cao Liang [14] conducted in-depth research on the core technologies of virtual reality and their cutting-edge applications, listing key technologies including real-time 3D graphics generation, wide-angle (wide-field-of-view) stereoscopic display, user tracking, haptic and force feedback, voice and gesture recognition, dynamic environment modeling, and application system development tools. They emphasized that selecting appropriate application scenarios and objects, as well as exerting imagination and creativity, are key factors in the application of virtual reality technology. By exploring force/haptic interaction algorithms, Zhang Xiaorui, Sun Wei, et al. [15] aimed to improve the realism and practicality of these algorithms to achieve a more natural and harmonious human-computer interaction experience. Their research focused on understanding the characteristics and mechanisms of human force/haptic perception, and enhancing the stability and real-time performance of force/haptic interaction. In addition, the research intended to establish a set of standards and specifications to achieve highly realistic and high-speed interactive feedback, thereby expanding the application of this technology in multiple fields.

Core technologies serve as the link connecting the virtual and real worlds, while system functions are supported by enabling devices. Chinese scholars categorize these into software and hardware devices. Zhang Fengjun et al. [16] emphasized the interface paradigms, interaction tasks, and interaction devices of virtual reality. In terms of software, they pointed out the main issues with graphical user interfaces supported by the WIMP paradigm, and mentioned the concepts of Non-WIMP [17] and Post-WIMP [18], aiming to break through the limitations of graphical user interfaces, increase the bandwidth of human-computer interaction, and make the interaction process more natural. In terms of hardware, it includes output and input devices: output hardware such as visual displays, audio displays, and force/tactile output displays provides information to the user's sensory organs. Like output devices, input devices are also important components in virtual reality interaction, which can be divided into discrete input devices, continuous input devices, and direct human input devices. Guo Yuan, Tong Qianqian et al. [19] focused on developing a portable VR software framework integrating multi-modal haptics and immersive vision. They proposed a collision detection and response method based on the sphere-tree model, and explored how to use a three-layer VR software framework for visual-tactile fusion feedback. Combined with existing hardware devices, this framework addresses issues of spatiotemporal consistency registration and convenient accessibility, thereby achieving more efficient and realistic immersive visual and tactile experiences. In their paper Architecture and Software Development Tools for Virtual Reality Systems, Ma Xiaohu et al. [20] provided a detailed introduction to virtual reality systems, including the coordination of hardware and software, time-constrained computing in distributed environments, time-constrained graphics rendering, as well as research on 3D stereogram generation algorithms and distributed graphics applications. They emphasized the importance of technologies such as real-time systems, object-oriented programming, and graphics processing in virtual reality software development.

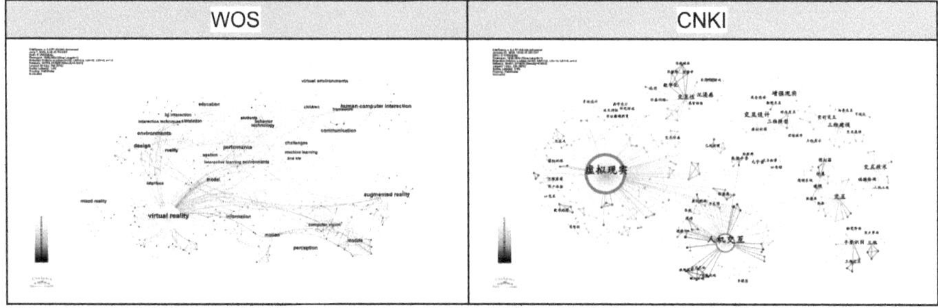

Fig. 6. Keywords co-ocurrence map

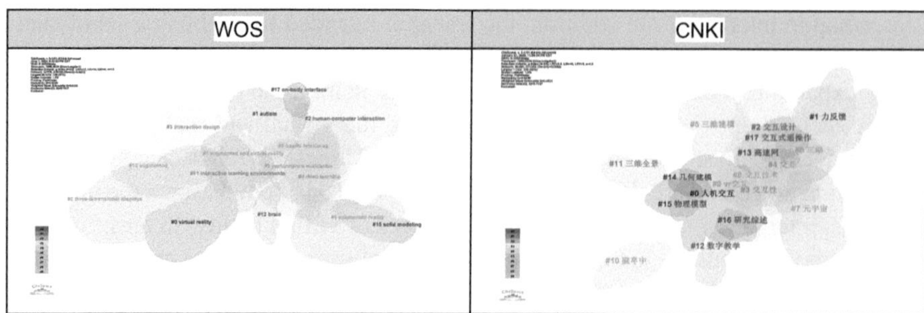

Fig. 7. Keywords clustering map

Table 5. List high-frequency key words in WOS

Serial Number	Frequency	Centrality	Years	Keywords
1	622	0.63	1996	virtual reality
2	171	0.18	1998	augmented reality
3	92	0.06	1999	reality
4	83	0.1	1999	human-computer interaction
5	80	0.12	1999	design
6	72	0.08	2010	virtual environments
7	66	0.02	2019	three-dimensional displays
8	63	0.11	1999	environments
9	58	0.05	1998	system
10	53	0.01	2020	task analysis
11	52	0.05	2004	education
12	47	0.07	2005	perception
13	46	0.01	1996	solid modeling
14	44	0.03	2012	model
15	43	0.06	2002	mixed reality
16	42	0.09	2010	performance
17	37	0.02	2012	technology
18	36	0.04	2011	human computer interaction
19	31	0.02	2020	haptic interfaces
20	30	0.02	2011	simulation

Table 6. List high-frequency key words in CNKI

Serial number	Frequency	Centrality	Years	Keywords
1	361	1.37	1995	Virtual Reality
2	118	0.51	1995	Human-Computer Interaction
3	21	0.07	2010	Interaction Design
4	20	0.04	2002	Interaction
5	17	0.08	2008	Augmented Reality
6	14	0.04	2007	3D modeling
7	13	0.04	2000	Interactivity
8	11	0.01	1995	Interactive technology
9	10	0.02	2000	Gesture recognition
10	10	0.03	2008	Immersive
11	8	0.02	2003	3D model
12	7	0.01	2008	Real-time interaction
13	7	0.01	2002	Experimental Teaching
14	6	0.02	1998	Simulation
15	6	0.01	1998	Modeling
16	5	0	1999	3D interaction
17	5	0.03	2022	Metaverse
18	5	0	2004	Force feedback
19	5	0	2000	Data glove

4.1.2 Highly Cited Literature

Analysis of highly cited literatures enables a quick understanding of core literatures, research focuses, hotspots, and other research scopes in the field. The literature data from the WOS Core Collection database were analyzed (Table 7). Among them, the article published by Rasheed, A [21] et al. in 2020 has been cited 809 times. From a modeling perspective, it reviews the development status, values, and challenges of methods and technologies related to digital twin construction. The article selects five different digital twin application scenarios such as healthcare, meteorology, manufacturing, and process technology to gain insights into the current technical level, common challenges, corresponding solutions, and future needs, with the aim of introducing more physical realism into them. The article published by Park Sang-Min [22] et al. in 2022 has been cited 745 times. It provides high-level methods for immersive experiences and proposes that the three core elements for constructing the metaverse are hardware, software, and content, while the three main approaches to realization are user interaction, application, and implementation rather than marketing or hardware methods. It focuses on relevant practices in fields such as film, games, and research. Wang Yuntao et al.

[23] summarized the social impacts, existing limitations, and open challenges of the immersive metaverse. Their research focused on the basic theories, security guarantees, and privacy protection of the metaverse, conducted in-depth discussions on an innovative distributed metaverse architecture, and detailedly analyzed its key characteristics in the interaction of the triple worlds. From a constructivist perspective, Hsiu-Mei Huang et al. [24] proposed that virtual reality learning environments (VRLEs) simulate the real world through the application of 3D models, thereby triggering interaction, immersion, and stimulating learners' imagination. They introduced the application of web-based 3D technologies in education, with special emphasis on the characteristics of VR. Then, they identified constructivist learning as the teaching engine for building VRLEs and discussed five constructivist learning methods.

The top 15 highly cited literatures in the field of virtual reality interaction from the CNKI database were statistically summarized (Table 8). The analysis reveals that these literatures span the period from 1998 to 2021, with a concentration of highly cited literatures after 2016, which is related to the development of virtual reality technology and national policy support. The most frequently co-cited literature is A Review on Human-Computer Interaction in Virtual Reality published by Zhang Fengjun et al. [16] in 2016. In this literature, the authors introduce the concept of multi-modal interaction technology, including the integration of different interaction methods such as 3D interaction, gesture interaction, and voice interaction, as well as the applications of these technologies in virtual reality. On this basis, they sort out the challenges faced by human-computer interaction in virtual reality environments, put forward suggestions for future basic research on virtual reality human-computer interaction, common key technologies, and the establishment of standards and specifications, and predict the development trend emphasizing "interaction". The literature published by Ding Nan et al. [25] in 2017 has been cited 253 times, focusing on multiple applications of virtual reality technology in education, such as providing more realistic learning experiences, enhancing students' sense of presence and flow experience, while offering personalized and gamified learning environments to stimulate students' learning motivation. Zhao Qinping et al. [26] conducted research on the development and applications of virtual reality technology, including but not limited to the user-centric design of human-computer interaction, the popularization of computer platforms, the integration of virtual and real scenarios, large-scale intelligent analysis and processing of data, etc. They also discussed the development status of virtual reality devices such as Oculus Rift, HTC Vive, and Sony Project Morpheus. In general, the study aims to provide a comprehensive perspective on the development of virtual reality technology and offer directional guidance for subsequent research and practice. In addition, an analysis of the list of highly cited literatures shows that core literatures published by Chinese scholars in this field mainly focus on human-computer interaction, technical applications, machine learning, and other directions. Among the 15 highly cited literatures, 9 were published after 2016, accounting for 60%, indicating that this field is gradually becoming a research hotspot, which is closely related to policy support, technological development, market environment, and other factors in recent years.

Table 7. List of highly cited literature in WOS

Serial Number	Article Title	Frist author	Cited Frequency	Years
1	Digital Twin: Values, Challenges and Enablers From a Modeling Perspective	Rasheed, A	809	2020
2	A Metaverse: Taxonomy, Components, Applications, and Open Challenges	Park, SM	745	2022
3	A Survey on Metaverse: Fundamentals, Security, and Privacy	Wang, YT	540	2023
4	Investigating learners' attitudes toward virtual reality learning environments: Based on a constructivist approach	Huang, HM	489	2010
5	OpenViBE: An Open-Source Software Platform to Design, Test, and Use Brain-Computer Interfaces in Real and Virtual Environments	Renard, Y	467	2010
6	Mobile Phone Sensing Systems: A Survey	Khan, WZ	395	2013
7	How does desktop virtual reality enhance learning outcomes? A structural equation modeling approach	Lee, EAL	365	2010
8	The Uncanny Valley: Effect of realism on the impression of artificial human faces	Seyama, J	364	2007
9	Deep Learning Coordinated Beamforming for Highly-Mobile Millimeter Wave Systems	Alkhateeb, A	326	2018
10	Enhancing learning and engagement through embodied interaction within a mixed reality simulation	Lindgren, R	315	2016
11	A survey of 3D object selection techniques for virtual environments	Argelaguet, F	300	2013

(continued)

Table 7. (*continued*)

Serial Number	Article Title	Frist author	Cited Frequency	Years
12	Noncontact Tactile Display Based on Radiation Pressure of Airborne Ultrasound	Hoshi, T	297	2010
13	Augmented Reality Meets Computer Vision: Efficient Data Generation for Urban Driving Scenes	Abu Alhaija, H	295	2018
14	A psychological perspective on augmented reality in the mathematics classroom	Bujak, KR	284	2013
15	EcoMOBILE: Integrating augmented reality and probeware with environmental education field trips	Kamarainen, AM	281	2013

Table 8. List of highly cited literature in CNKI

Serial Number	Article Title	First author	Cited Frequency	Years
1	A survey on human-computer interaction in virtual reality	Zhang Fengjun	598	2016
2	The Application of Virtual Reality in Education: Advantages and Challenges	Ding Nan	253	2017
3	A brief survey on virtual reality technology	Zhao Qinping	235	2016
4	Virtual Reality: A New Chapter in the Development of Educational Technology: An Interview with Professor Zhao Qinping, Academician of Chinese Academy of Engineering	Shen Yang	166	2019
5	An Interactive Environment Design Based on Digital Glove	Zeng Fenfang	132	2000
6	Reshaping Online Education by Virtual Reality: Learning Resources, Teaching Organization and System Platform	Liu Geping	128	2020

(*continued*)

Table 8. (*continued*)

Serial Number	Article Title	First author	Cited Frequency	Years
7	Application of virtual reality in motor rehabilitation	Zhou Liu	121	2007
8	Investigation of Vehicle Driving Simulator by Distributed Virtual Reality Technology	Chen Dingfang	105	2005
9	Computer Haptics: Haptic Modeling and Rendering in Virtual RealityEnvironments	Wang Dangxiao	104	2016
10	Network Culture and Education	Li Xingbao	97	2001
11	The Application of Virtual Reality Technique in Library	Wang Chenchen	95	2011
12	Virtual Museum Interaction Design Research Based on VR Technology	Li Ping	92	2017
13	Multi-mode haptic interaction technique and its application	Song Aiguo	81	2017
14	From "Blended" to "Chaotic": A Discussion on Future Teaching Mode from the Perspective of Metaverse——Taking the Cloud Exhibition Curation Course of East China Normal University as an ExampleEast China Normal University as an Example	Lu Lili	73	2021
15	The progress and trends of human-computer interaction	Gong Jiemin	72	1998

4.2 Analysis of Research Trends

4.2.1 Burst Keyword Analysis

Burst keyword analysis identifies turning points and the time periods when hotspots emerge in a research field by tracking high-frequency terms within specific periods [27]. The higher the burst intensity, the stronger the research focus on that trend during the corresponding period. Using the Burstness function in CiteSpace with the γ-value set to 1, 17 burst keywords were detected, sorted by their burst start year (Fig. 8), where the red segments indicate the time periods of their burst. Analysis of the map shows that "interactive learning environments" is the earliest emerging and longest-lasting keyword, indicating a frontier research hotspot in the field of virtual reality interaction from 2000 to 2016. "Virtual realities" is another keyword that emerged relatively early and persisted for a long duration. Three significant burst keywords appeared in 2019:

582   L. Liu et al.

"memory", "human-robot interaction", and "human computer interaction", though their burst periods were relatively short. "Task analysis" and "solid modeling" remained burst keywords until 2024, reflecting the research trends in the field in recent years.

An analysis of the burst keywords in the CNKI database reveals that "sense of presence" is the earliest emerging burst keyword. "3D modeling" ranks first with a burst intensity of 3.15. Burst keywords such as "interactivity", "3D modeling", "simulation", "data glove", "interaction", and "collision detection" concentrated in the period 2006–2008, with burst intensities of 3.15, 2.51, 1.98, 1.88, and 1.81 respectively. During this stage, China's virtual reality interaction field was in a period of rapid growth. In terms of the life cycle, the research enthusiasm for "3D interaction" lasted for 7 years; the research enthusiasm for "sense of presence" and "augmented reality" lasted for 6 years, ranking second. As mentioned above, 2016 is known as the first year of China's VR industry, and with this as a turning point, China's virtual reality interaction field entered a period of rapid development. The two burst keywords "metaverse" and "interaction design" that emerged between 2022 and 2024 have seen a rapid increase in popularity in a short period of time, indicating the current research hotspots and trends.

WOS

Top 17 Keywords with the Strongest Citation Bursts

Keywords	Year	Strength	Begin	End	1996 - 2024
interactive learning environments	2000	7.26	2000	2016	
and virtual realities	2003	4.01	2003	2015	
interaction techniques	2004	3.86	2004	2009	
human factors	2010	3.81	2010	2011	
simulation	2011	5.54	2011	2019	
design	1999	5.05	2012	2018	
visualization	1997	3.55	2015	2018	
environments	1996	3.55	2017	2019	
technology	2012	3.72	2018	2020	
memory	2019	4.27	2019	2022	
human-robot interaction	2019	3.37	2019	2021	
human computer interaction	2011	3.51	2019	2020	
three-dimensional displays	2019	4.51	2020	2021	
solid modeling	1996	3.74	2020	2024	
rendering (computer graphics)	2020	3.43	2020	2022	
task analysis	2020	7.32	2021	2024	
real-time systems	2021	3.51	2021	2022	

CNKI

Top 12 Keywords with the Strongest Citation Bursts

Keywords	Year	Strength	Begin	End	1995 - 2024
临场感	1998	1.75	1998	2004	
三维交互	1999	2.7	1999	2006	
虚拟装配	2004	1.75	2004	2006	
交互性	2000	3.03	2006	2010	
三维建模	2007	3.15	2007	2009	
仿真	1998	2.51	2007	2010	
数据手套	2000	1.98	2007	2010	
交互	2002	1.88	2008	2010	
碰撞检测	2008	1.87	2008	2013	
增强现实	2008	1.88	2016	2022	
元宇宙	2022	2.79	2022	2024	
交互设计	2010	2.72	2022	2024	

Fig. 8. List of Burst keyword

4.2.2 Temporal Clustering of Keywords

Using the Time Zone function in CiteSpace, a timeline map of keyword co-occurrence (1996–2024) was generated from the WOS Core Collection database (Fig. 9), and the phased hotspots and directions in this research field were analyzed. High-frequency keywords emerging in different periods represent the research hotspots and academic frontiers of the field at that time [28]. Each time node is highlighted in distinct colors, with a prominent purple outer ring indicating high centrality, signifying key research directions in the field [29]. Connections between nodes reveal their co-occurrence relationships and serve as a criterion for measuring research trends, among which the red node timeline represents the current focus and trajectory of research [30]. As observed in Fig. 9, the temporal visualization knowledge map of keywords from the WOS Core Collection database contains 18 clustered themes. The theme "virtual reality" is the first cluster with concentrated occurrences of keywords with intermediary centrality, dating back to 1996. Clusters #1 to #9 include "virtual reality", "autism", "human-computer interaction", "interaction design", "deep learning", "haptic interfaces", "augmented reality", "augmented and virtual reality", "three-dimensional displays", "performance evaluation", and #15 "soild modeling". These clusters, which emerged early and have persisted to the present day, indicate that they are deeply studied and remain hotspots in the field.

An analysis of the timeline map from the CNKI database reveals that 18 clustered knowledge groups emerged between 1995 and 2024. Among these, "virtual reality" and "human-computer interaction" are clustered themes that emerged in 1995 and have persisted to the present day, also being the earliest high-frequency keywords [31]. In recent years, keywords such as "augmented reality", "metaverse", and "interaction design" have gained significant traction, with some scholars focusing on exploring cutting-edge fields. Yu Guoming [32] has closely integrated technological innovation with social transformation in his exploration of frontier areas, paying particular attention to how emerging fields such as "metaverse", "virtual digital humans", "intelligent communication", and "generative AI" reshape the communication ecosystem and social structure. Cao Mingwei, Zhang Di, et al. [33] systematically analyzed the development of core technologies and application scenarios of the metaverse, conducted in-depth evaluations of existing metaverse applications, and examined the challenges faced by metaverse development. They proposed innovative approaches such as using AI to generate personalized virtual scenarios, leveraging distributed computing to ensure real-time interactive experiences, and integrating blockchain technology to enhance privacy protection.

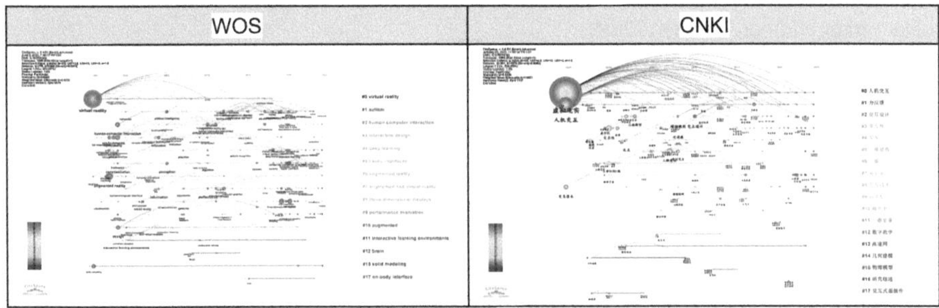

Fig. 9. Temporal Clustering Map of Keywords

5 Conclusion

This study mapped the knowledge landscape of virtual reality interaction between 1995 and 2024 by analysing 1424 records from Web of Science and 494 core journal papers from CNKI with CiteSpace and complementary bibliometric techniques. Publication output grew in three discernible periods that we identify as incubation from 1995 to 2007, acceleration from 2008 to 2015, and a surge from 2016 to 2020, followed by a levelling off that in China signals consolidation rather than retreat. The Chinese Academy of Sciences and University College London emerged as the most productive institutions, China and the United States led national contributions, and 135 core authors formed loose collaboration clusters. Keyword networks displayed strong structure with Modularity Qequal to 0.6049 and silhouette Sequal to 0.8353, revealing a thematic shift from device centred studies toward intelligent multisensory interaction, deep learning, brain computer interfaces, and metaverse oriented inquiries.

By combining English and Chinese language corpora, the work broadens the scope of previous bibliometric reviews and offers a more inclusive view of global scholarship. The results equip researchers with a historical baseline and a set of emerging themes, while practitioners and policy makers can draw on the evidence of weak inter-institutional collaboration when designing funding schemes or joint laboratories to encourage cross-regional cooperation. The thematic map also helps industry stakeholders anticipate directions in which AI enhancements and higher bandwidth networks are likely to influence interface design, training systems, and entertainment formats.

Several constraints temper these conclusions. Coverage remains limited to two databases, language and regional biases persist, and reliance on keyword co-occurrence and g-index thresholds may disguise subtle conceptual links. Future work should expand the corpus to additional multilingual sources, apply topic modelling or embedding based clustering, and complement quantitative patterns with qualitative case studies of landmark projects. Addressing these issues will sharpen our understanding of how virtual reality interaction is evolving and will support more equitable and synergistic growth across the field.

Acknowledgement. This study was funded by Communication University of China Nanjing 2025 annual university-level teaching reform research general project (grant number JG20250611) and Philosophy and Social Science Research in Higher Education of Jiangsu Province 2020 General Project (grant number 2020SJA2289).

References

1. Madden, W., Sun, L.: The review of virtual reality technology. In: The First Joint Academic Conference of the Chinese Society of Stereoscopic Vision for Image Analysis, the Simulation and Virtual Reality major of the Chinese Society of Stereoscopics, and the Signal and Information Processing of the Chinese Society of Aeronautics, pp.184–188. Wutai Mountain, Shanxi, China (2000)
2. Zeng, J.C., Xu, G.Y.: Virtual reality technology and strategy for its development. Acta Electronica Sinica (10), 57–61 (1995)
3. Zhao, Q.P., Huai, J.P., Li, B.P., et al.: A survey of activities in virtual reality. J. Comput. Res. Dev. **07**, 493–500 (1996)
4. State Council of the People's Republic of China. Notice of the State Council on Printing and Distributing "Made in China 2025" (Guo Fa [2015] No. 28) Government Information Disclosure Column (2015)
5. Zong, S.P.: Evaluation of core authors based on price law and the comprehensive index method:a case study of Chinese Journal of Scientific and Technical Periodicals. Chin. J. Sci. Technol. Perodicals **27**(12), 80–84 (2016)
6. Li, J., Chen, C.M.: CiteSpace: text mining and visualization in scientific literature, 3rd edn. Capital University of Economics and Business Publishing House, Beijing, p. 105 (2022)
7. Lotte, F., Van Langhenhove, A., Lamarche, F., et al.: Exploring large virtual environments by thoughts using a brain-computer interface based on motor imagery and high-level commands. **19**(1), 54–70 (2010). https://doi.org/10.1162/pres.19.1.54

8. Howard, T., Marchal, M., Lecuyer, A., et al.: PUMAH: Pan-Tilt Ultrasound Mid-Air Haptics for Larger Interaction Workspace in Virtual Reality. **13**(1), 38–44 (2020). https://doi.org/10.1109/TOH.2019.2963028

9. Chen, Q.: Developments and future directions: researches on the international communication of Chinese culture in the past 20 years. Chin. Cult. Stud. **126**(04), 71–84 (2024)

10. Chen, S., Fan, H.X., Jiang, M.T.: Knowledge map analysis of CiteSpace-based augmented reality in cultural heritage research. Packag. Eng. **44**(16), 329–343 (2023)

11. Yan, W.N.: Progress, hotspots and trends in research on popular science journals in China: visual analysis based on CiteSpace knowledge graph. Chin. J. Sci. Tech. Periodicals **35**(02), 25–32 (2024)

12. Shu, J.H.: The application of virtual reality technology status and future prospects. Comput. Knowl. Technol. **18**(18), 144–146 (2008)

13. Yang, H.Z., Kong, X.Z., Gu, R.K., et al.: Research progress and trends in large model technologies for virtual reality. J. Graph. **45**(06), 3–17 (2024)

14. Wang, Y.F., Cao, L.: Key technologies and cutting-edge applications of virtual reality. China Ind. Rev. **18**(08), 42–49 (2016)

15. Zhang, X.R., Sun, W., Song, A.G., et al.: Development on haptic interaction algorithm of virtual objects. J. Syst. Simul. **23**(04), 7–12 17 (2011)

16. Zhang, F.J., Dai, G.Z., Peng, X.L.: A survey on human-computer interaction in virtual reality. Sci. Sinical (Informationis) **46**(12), 23–48 (2016)

17. Green, M., Jacob, R.: SIGGRAPH '90 Workshop report: software architecturesand metaphors for non-WIMP user interfaces. ACM SIGGRAPH Computer Graphics **25**(3), 229–235 (1991)

18. van Dam A.: Post-WIMP user interface. Commun ACM **40**, 63–67 (1997)

19. Guo, Y., Tong, Q.Q., Zheng, Y.K., et al.: An adaptable VR software framework for collaborative multi-modal haptic andimmersive visual display. J. Syst. Simul. **32**(07), 189–196 (2020)

20. Ma, X.H., Pan, Z.G., Shi, J.Y.: Architecture and software development tools of virtual reality system. Comput. Eng. Appl. **08**, 38–42 (1997)

21. Rasheed, A., San, O., Kvamsdal, T.: Digital twin: values, challenges and enablers from a modeling perspective. IEEE Access **8**, 21980–22012 (2020). https://doi.org/10.1109/ACCESS.2020.2970143

22. Park, S.M., Kim, Y.G.: A metaverse: taxonomy, components, applications, and open challenges.. IEEE Access **10**, 4209–4251 (2022). https://doi.org/10.1109/ACCESS.2021.3140175

23. Wang, Y.T., Su, Z., Zhang, M., et al.: A survey on metaverse: fundamentals, security, and privacy. IEEE Commun. Surv. Tutor. **25**(1), 319–352 (2023). https://doi.org/10.1109/COMST.2022.3202047

24. Huang, H.M., Rauch, U., Liaw, S.S.: Investigating learners' attitudes toward virtual reality learning environments: based on a constructivist approach. Comput. Educ. **55**(3), 1171–1182 (2010). https://doi.org/10.1016/j.compedu.2010.05.014. ISSN 0360–1315

25. Ding, N., Wang, Y.M.: Application of virtual reality in education: advantages and challenges. Mod. Educ. Technol. **27**(02), 20–26 (2017)

26. Zhao, Q.P., Zhou, B., Li, J., et al.: A brief survey on virtual reality technology. Sci. Technol. Rev. **34**(14), 73–77 (2016)

27. Wang, T., Wei, S.P., Liao, B., et al.: The status quo, hotspots and development trends of intelligent scheduling at home and abroad —visualization contrast research based on CiteSpace. Ind. Eng. J. **23**(02), 109–119 (2020)

28. Qi, R.W., Chen, X.F.: Research progress and trend of handicraft design in china: quantitative analysis based on CiteSpace. Packag. Eng. **45**(10), 303–313 (2024)

29. Chen, Y., Chen, C.M., Hu, Z.G.: Principles and Applications of Analyzing a Citation Space. Science Press, Beijing, pp. 75–85 (2015)

30. Chen, C., Huang, Y.: Knowledge map of domestic intangible cultural heritage research based on CiteSpace. Packag. Eng. **41**(14), 239–245 (2020)
31. Dou, J.H., Zhang, B.R., Qian, X.S.: A review of AI-empowered cultural heritage:visualization analysis based on CiteSpace. Packag. Eng. **44**(14), 15–34 (2023)
32. Yu, G.M.: Metaverse, games and future media. J. Zhengzhou Univ. (Eng. Sci.) **56**(03), 115–118 (2023)
33. Cao, M.W., Zhang, D., Peng, S.J., et al.: Survey on the development and application of metaverse technology. Comput. Sci. **56**(03), 4–16 (2025)

Author Index

© The Editor(s) (if applicable) and The Author(s), under exclusive license
to Springer Nature Singapore Pte Ltd. 2026
Z. Lin et al. (Eds.): ICIG 2025, LNCS 16163, pp. 587–592, 2026.
https://doi.org/10.1007/978-981-95-3729-7

MIX
Papier aus verantwortungsvollen Quellen
Paper from responsible sources
FSC® C105338

If you have any concerns about our products,
you can contact us on
ProductSafety@springernature.com

In case Publisher is established outside the EU,
the EU authorized representative is:
Springer Nature Customer Service Center GmbH
Europaplatz 3, 69115 Heidelberg, Germany

Printed by Libri Plureos GmbH
in Hamburg, Germany